Lecture Notes in Computer Science 12751

More information about this subseries at http://www.springer.com/series/7409

Marcello La Rosa · Shazia Sadiq ·
Ernest Teniente (Eds.)

Advanced Information Systems Engineering

33rd International Conference, CAiSE 2021
Melbourne, VIC, Australia, June 28 – July 2, 2021
Proceedings

 Springer

Editors
Marcello La Rosa ⓘ
The University of Melbourne
Melbourne, VIC, Australia

Shazia Sadiq ⓘ
The University of Queensland
St Lucia, QLD, Australia

Ernest Teniente ⓘ
Universitat Politècnica de Catalunya
Barcelona, Spain

ISSN 0302-9743   ISSN 1611-3349   (electronic)
Lecture Notes in Computer Science
ISBN 978-3-030-79381-4   ISBN 978-3-030-79382-1   (eBook)
https://doi.org/10.1007/978-3-030-79382-1

LNCS Sublibrary: SL3 – Information Systems and Applications, incl. Internet/Web, and HCI

This Springer imprint is published by the registered company Springer Nature Switzerland AG
The registered company address is: Gewerbestrasse 11, 6330 Cham, Switzerland

Preface

The 33rd International Conference on Advanced Information Systems Engineering (CAiSE'21) was organized to be held in Melbourne, Australia, during June 28 – July 2, 2021. Due to the COVID-19 global pandemic, the conference was moved online and held virtually over the same time period.

The CAiSE conference continues its tradition as the premiere venue for innovative and rigorous research across the whole spectrum of information systems (IS) engineering. This year, the conference focussed on the theme of Intelligent Information Systems, acknowledging the high level of uncertainty that organizations have to deal with, and the increasing need to respond through Intelligent Information Systems that provide trusted, adaptive, agile, and autonomous solutions. In the backdrop of recent advancements in IoT, big data analytics, artificial intelligence, machine learning, and blockchain, the Information Systems Engineering research community is ideally positioned to bring together the technical and empirical aspects of Information Systems and contribute to progress in the field.

The CAiSE'21 program included three invited keynotes by Professor Michael Rosemann (Queensland Institute of Technology, Australia), Professor Felix Naumann (HPI, University of Potsdam, Germany), and Professor Sudha Ram (University of Arizona, USA). The call for papers solicited research papers in the categories of Technical, Empirical and Exploratory papers, in all areas of IS engineering, including novel approaches to IS engineering; models, methods, and techniques in IS engineering; architectures and platforms for IS engineering; and domain-specific and multi-aspect IS engineering. 172 full paper submissions were received. We followed the selection process consolidated in the previous years, where each paper was initially reviewed by at least two Program Committee (PC) members; papers with only negative evaluations were rejected; all papers with at least one positive evaluation were reviewed by a member of the Program Board (PB); all reviewers then engaged in an online discussion led by another PB member; finally, during an all-hands meeting of the PB held virtually over-two days in February 2021, the final decision was made about the acceptance or rejection of each paper. The overall evaluation process of the papers resulted in the selection of 33 high-quality papers, which amounted to an acceptance rate of 19%. The final program of CAiSE'21 was complemented by the CAiSE Forum, workshops, co-located working conferences, tutorials and panels, and a PhD consortium. For each of these events, separate proceedings were published.

We would like to thank the general chair, Professor Marcello La Rosa, the organization chair, Laura Juliff, and the whole organization team at The University of Melbourne for their support and incredible work. We thank also the Forum chairs, Axel Korthaus and Selmin Nurcan, the Workshop chairs, Artem Polyvyanyy and Stefanie Rinderle-Ma, the Tutorial/Panel chairs, Pierluigi Plebani and Arthur ter Hofstede, the Doctoral Consortium chairs, Chun Ouyang, John Krogstie and Jolita Ralyté, and the publicity chairs, Abel Armas-Cervantes, Fabrizio Maggi, Kate Revoredo Lin Liu, and

Pnina Soffer, for their extraordinary and professional work. We thank all PC and PB members, who played a fundamental role in the selection process. Finally, we would like to express our deepest gratitude to all those who served as organizers, session chairs, and hosts, and went above and beyond to ensure that CAiSE continues to provide an engaging and high value forum for scientific exchange and networking within the Information Systems engineering community, in spite of challenges posed by the online setting.

CAiSE'21 was organized with the support of the School of Computing and Information Systems at The University of Melbourne, the Melbourne Convention Bureau, and Springer.

May 2021   Shazia Sadiq
                                                                                              Ernest Teniente

Organization

Program Chairs

Shazia Sadiq   The University of Queensland, Australia
Ernest Teniente   Universitat Politècnica de Catalunya, Spain

General Chair

Marcello La Rosa   The University of Melbourne, Australia

Workshop Chairs

Artem Polyvyanyy   The University of Melbourne, Australia
Stefanie Rinderle-Ma   University of Vienna, Austria

Forum Chairs

Axel Korthaus   Swinburne University of Technology, Australia
Selmin Nurcan   Université Paris 1 Panthéon-Sorbonne, France

Tutorial/Panel Chairs

Pierluigi Plebani   Politecnico di Milano, Italy
Arthur ter Hofstede   Queensland University of Technology, Australia

Doctoral Consortium Chairs

Chun Ouyang   Queensland University of Technology, Australia
John Krogstie   Norwegian University of Science and Technology, Norway
Jolita Ralyté   University of Geneva, Switzerland

PhD Award Chair

Eric Dubois   LIST, Luxembourg

Publicity Chairs

Abel Armas-Cervantes (Coordinator)   The University of Melbourne, Australia
Fabrizio Maggi   Free University of Bozen-Bolzano, Italy
Kate Revoredo   Vienna University of Economics and Business, Austria

| Lin Liu | Tsinghua University, China |
| Pnina Soffer | University of Haifa, Israel |

Organization Chair

| Laura Juliff | The University of Melbourne, Australia |

Conference Steering Committee Chairs

Johann Eder	Alpen Adria Universität Klagenfurt, Austria
John Krogstie	Norwegian University of Science and Technology, Norway
Eric Dubois	LIST, Luxembourg

Conference Advisory Board

Janis Bubenko	KTH Stockholm, Sweden
Oscar Pastor	Universidad Politécnica de Valencia, Spain
Barbara Pernici	Politecnico di Milano, Italy
Colette Rolland	Université Paris 1 Pantheon-Sorbonne, France
Arne Solvberg	Norwegian University of Science and Technology, Norway

Program Board

Valeria De Antonellis	University of Brescia, Italy
Eric Dubois	Luxembourg Institute of Science and Technology. Luxembourg
Johann Eder	Alpen Adria Universität Klagenfurt, Austria
Xavier Franch	Universitat Politècnica de Catalunya, Spain
Matthias Jarke	RWTH Aachen University, Germany
John Krogstie	Norwegian University of Science and Technology, Norway
Massimo Mecella	Sapienza University of Rome, Italy
Jan Mendling	Wirtschaftsuniversität Wien, Austria
Selmin Nurcan	Université Paris 1 Panthéon-Sorbonne, France
Oscar Pastor Lopez	Universitat Politècnica de València, Spain
Barbara Pernici	Politecnico di Milano, Italy
Geert Poels	Ghent University, Belgium
Jolita Ralyté	University of Geneva, Switzerland
Manfred Reichert	University of Ulm, Germany
Hajo A. Reijers	Utrecht University, the Netherlands
Stefanie Rinderle-Ma	University of Vienna, Austria
Antonio Ruiz-Cortés	University of Seville, Spain
Camille Salinesi	Université de Paris 1 Panthéon-Sorbonne, France
Pnina Soffer	University of Haifa, Israel

Barbara Weber   University of St. Gallen, Switzerland
Matthias Weidlich   Humboldt-Universität zu Berlin, Germany
Jelena Zdravkovic   Stockholm University, Sweden

Program Committee

Raian Ali   Hamad Bin Khalifa University, Qatar
Joao Araujo   Universidade NOVA de Lisboa, Portugal
Marko Bajec   University of Ljubljana, Slovenia
Alistair Barros   Queensland University of Technology, Australia
Boualem Benatallah   The University of New South Wales, Australia
Alex Borgida   Rutgers University, USA
Sjaak Brinkkemper   Utrecht University, the Netherlands
Andrea Burattin   Technical University of Denmark, Denmark
Cristina Cabanillas   University of Seville, Spain
Cinzia Cappiello   Politecnico di Milano, Italy
Josep Carmona   Universitat Politècnica de Catalunya, Spain
Fabiano Dalpiaz   Utrecht University, the Netherlands
Ernesto Damiani   University of Milan, Italy
Maya Daneva   University of Twente, the Netherlands
Adela Del Río Ortega   University of Seville, Spain
Claudio Di Ciccio   Sapienza University of Rome, Italy
Oscar Diaz   University of the Basque Country, Spain
João Falcão E. Cunha   University of Porto, Portugal
Pablo Fernández   University of Seville, Spain
Agnès Front   Grenoble Alpes University, France
Giancarlo Guizzardi   Federal University of Espirito Santo, Brazil
Jennifer Horkoff   Chalmers University of Technology and the University
                                of Gothenburg, Sweden
Jan Jürjens   Fraunhofer Institute for Software and Systems
                                Engineering ISST and University
                                of Koblenz-Landau, Germany
Marite Kirikova   Riga Technical University, Latvia
Agnes Koschmider   Kiel University, Germany
Sander J. J. Leemans   Queensland University of Technology, Australia
Henrik Leopold   Kühne Logistics University, Germany
Fabrizio Maria Maggi   Free University of Bozen-Bolzano, Italy
Andrea Marrella   Sapienza University of Rome, Italy
Florian Matthes   Technical University of Munich, Germany
Raimundas Matulevicius   University of Tartu, Estonia
Patrick Mikalef   Norwegian University of Science and Technology,
                                Norway
Marco Montali   Free University of Bozen-Bolzano, Italy
Haralambos Mouratidis   University of Brighton, UK
John Mylopoulos   University of Toronto, Canada
Andreas L. Opdahl   University of Bergen, Norway

Xavier Oriol	Universitat Politècnica de Catalunya, Spain
Jeffrey Parsons	Memorial University of Newfoundland, Canada
Anna Perini	Fondazione Bruno Kessler, Italy
Pierluigi Plebani	Politecnico di Milano, Italy, Italy
Klaus Pohl	University of Duisburg-Essen, Germany
Artem Polyvyanyy	The University of Melbourne, Australia
Henderik A. Proper	Luxembourg Institute of Science and Technology, Luxembourg
Gil Regev	Ecole Polytechnique Fédérale de Lausanne, Switzerland
Iris Reinhartz-Berger	University of Haifa, Israel
Manuel Resinas	University of Seville, Spain
Marcela Ruiz	Zurich University of Applied Sciences, Switzerland
Flavia Santoro	Universidade do Estado do Rio de Janeiro, Brazil
Samira Si-Said Cherfi	Conservatoire National des Arts et Métiers, France
Kari Smolander	Lappeenranta University of Technology, Finland
Monique Snoeck	Katholieke Universiteit Leuven, Belgium
Janis Stirna	Stockholm University, Sweden
Arnon Sturm	Ben-Gurion University, Israel
Boudewijn Van Dongen	Eindhoven University of Technology, the Netherlands
Panos Vassiliadis	University of Ioannina, Greece
Ingo Weber	TU Berlin, Germany
Hans Weigand	Tilburg University, the Netherlands
Lijie Wen	Tsinghua University, China
Mathias Weske	University of Potsdam, Germany
Jian Yang	Macquarie University, Australia

Additional Reviewers

Affia, Abasi-Amefon
Ahmadian, Amir Shayan
Bondel, Gloria
Burke, Adam
Ehl, Marco
Ehrendorfer, Matthias
Elnaggar, Ahmed
Estrada Torres, Irene Bedilia
Farshidi, Siamak
Flake, Julian
Fumagalli, Mattia
Gianola, Alessandro

Haarmann, Stephan
Heindel, Tobias
Hobeck, Richard
Hyrynsalmi, Sonja
Iqbal, Mubashar
Jansen, Slinger
Kalenkova, Anna
Kostova, Blagovesta
Ladleif, Jan
Lux, Marian
Lāce, Ksenija
Mamudu, Azumah

Mangat, Amolkirat Singh
Nägele, Sascha
Padró, Lluís
Peldszus, Sven
Penicina, Ludmila
Ramadan, Qusai
Rivkin, Andrey

Scheibel, Beate
Spijkman, Tjerk
Sànchez-Ferreres, Josep
Turki, Slim
Vuolasto, Jakko
Wang, Qi

Extended Abstracts of Invited Keynote Talks

Designing Intelligent Systems: The Role of Affordances and Trust

Michael Rosemann ⓘ

Queensland University of Technology, Centre for Future Enterprise, 2
George Street,
Brisbane, 4000, Qld, Australia
m.rosemann@qut.edu.au

Abstract. In a world in which the capabilities of systems grow faster than our
ability to comprehend these, we need revised approaches for the design of such
increasingly intelligent systems. No longer is a requirements-driven approach the
only paradigm. Instead, the affordances of systems provide a rich design space
that needs to be explored. Such an affordances-driven approach, however, is still
in its infancy. The incomprehensibility of systems also leads to new challenges
for system use. Though trust is now a key factor determining the user acceptance
of systems, we are still at the beginning of a trusted-by-design discipline. Thus,
we need to invest our research efforts into deriving a better understanding of the
role and the integration of affordances and trust in contemporary system design.

Keywords: Intelligent systems · System design · Affordances · Trust

1 The Growing Gap

The capabilities of technology in general, and intelligent information systems in particular, are developing rapidly and often exponentially. However, our capability to
comprehend this rapid change, i.e. our digital intelligence, is not developing in the
same speed [1]. As a result, the gap between what intelligent systems can do and what
humans comprehend is growing (Fig. 1).

This growing gap between the capabilities of intelligent systems and our digital
intelligence leads to the *problem of incomprehensibly* with two significant design
implications.

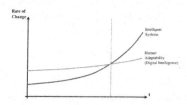

Fig. 1. The growing gap between intelligent systems and digital intelligence (inspired [1]).

First, there is the danger of under-capitalization when it comes to the design of systems. The dominating paradigm of design-follows-requirements ignores that unconscious incompetence prevents us from articulating entirely new design options. As a consequence, a shift needs to occur from a focus on specifying requirements (to the left of the dotted line in Fig. 1) to an exploration of affordances (what is possible?). Affordances-driven approaches to system design, however, are far less understood than the domain of requirements engineering.

Second, if systems have a level of intelligence that is beyond the comprehension of the system's users, trust concerns might emerge as a barrier to the acceptance of such systems. As a result, we need to go beyond a focus on ease-of-use and usefulness, and add trust-building design principles and mechanisms into our design methodologies.

2 Affordances-Driven Design

Affordances are action possibilities arising from the relation between the features of a technology and goal-oriented actors determining how the technology can be used in a value-creating way [2]. Such a definition assumes an actor capable of assessing technological' capabilities. As technology develops rapidly, however, actors will be challenged to identify and capitalise from relevant affordances meaning they remain hidden affordances [3].

One approach to overcome the incomprehensibly of technology is to systematically identify tiered layers of affordances in order to derive higher-order affordances [4, 5]. In particular, we differentiate here the three layers of technical, design and business affordances.

For example, for blockchain we identified via an empirical study of the practices of the 30 largest financial institutions globally, the immediate *technical affordances* tokenization, tracing and triggering [6]. Technical affordances are explicit as they can be perceived directly by a technology-aware user. *Design affordances* are action possibilities an organization can embed when designing with blockchain in mind. These include in the context of blockchain integrity, validity and compatibility. Design affordances are implicit and on a higher order of abstraction. Finally, *business affordances* are possibilities to create new value for customers using technical and design affordances. For example, blockchain's business affordances are micro-fulfilment, synergistic delivery and sovereignty.

Affordances-driven design requires embedding such affordances into the specification of requirements. Such requirements would be proactive requirements as they do not (reactively) emerge from an organization's demands, but are inspired by new design opportunities made available by external enablers.

3 Trusted-by-Design

The interactions of users with contemporary systems are becoming more trust-intensive. There are three reasons why trust increasingly matters for systems' acceptance.

First, the move from offline to online transactions is reducing *tangibility* (e.g., online grocery shopping) and as a result leads to new trust concerns. Second, there is limited *visibility* of the implications in those cases where a user contributes, directly or indirectly, personal data to the interactions with a system. Third, the sophistication of the intelligence embedded in contemporary systems (e.g., Amazon Go) does not only lead to new levels of convenience and experience, but also raises the issue of *explainability*. However, despite this increasing relevance of trust as a design goal, the overall trust literacy is still low.

Like affordances, trust is a relational concept. It describes the willingness of a trustor (e.g., a customer) to rely on a trustee (e.g., an organization, a business process, a system) in light of uncertainty. However, the notion of trust in organizations (e.g., ability, integrity, benevolence [7]) and trust in systems (trustworthiness) varies.

Therefore, it is suggested to decompose trust design more broadly into reducing uncertainty and increasing confidence [8]. A system that is trusted-by-design is low in uncertainty. Uncertainty an be further broken down into the elements of systemic uncsertainty, behavioral uncertainty, perceived uncertainty and vulnerability. While a design targeting uncertainty directly changes the system, confidence is about the perception of the system. Various confidence mechanisms need to be differentiated (e.g., confidence derived from peers, experts or previous experiences) and context-specifically be activated.

Therefore, trust designers, a new species, will need to develop skills to manage the uncertainty of and the confidence in a system. Advanced trust design will not only be needed to ensure that systems perform according to expectations (*core trust*), but, and especially in the context of intelligent systems, to facilitate entirely new forms of extreme trust. *Extreme trust* is the situation in which a system makes decisions on behalf of the user, and the user expects and accepts that this is the case. Examples for such systems can already be found in the domain of personalized healthcare and entertainment (e.g., music streaming), but are also emerging in areas such as banking, insurance, transportation and retail. Extremely trusted systems are a design option for intelligent systems. They are grounded in the business affordance proactivity; organizations increasingly have more data and higher algorithmic capabilities than their customers which provides them with the action possibility to ultimately make better and faster decisions than their customers.

References

1. Friedman, Th.L.: Thank You for Being Late. An Optimist's Guide to Thriving in the Age of Accelerations. Farrar, Strauss and Giroux. New York (2016)
2. Volkoff, O., Strong, D. M. Critical realism and affordances: theorizing IT-associated organizational change processes. MIS Q. **37**(3), pp. 819–834 (2013)
3. Gaver, W.W.: Technology affordances. In: Robertson, S.P., et al. (eds.) Proceedings of the SIGCHI Conference on Human Factors in Computing Systems, New Orleans, pp. 79–84, ACM: New York (1991)

4. Bygstad, B., Munkvold, B.E.: In search of mechanisms: conducting a critical realist data analysis. In: Beath, C., et al. (eds.) Proceedings of the 32nd International Conference on Information Systems (ICIS 2011), Shanghai, 4–7 December 2011
5. Ostern, N., Rosemann, M.: A framework for digital affordances. In: Matook, S., et al. (eds.) Proceedings of the 29th European Conference on Information Systems (ECIS 2021), Marrakech, 14–16 June 2021
6. Ostern, N., Rosemann, M., Moormann, J.: Determining the idiosyncrasy of blockchain: an affordances perspective. In: Proceedings of the 41st international Conference on Information Systems (ICIS 2020). Hyderabad, 13–16 December 2020
7. Mayer, R.C., Davis, J.H., Schoorman, F.D.: An integrative model of organizational trust. Acad. Manage. Rev. **20**(3), 707–734 (1995)
8. Rosemann M.: Trust-aware process design. In: Hildebrandt T., van Dongen B., Röglinger M., Mendling J. (eds.) Business Process Management. BPM 2019. LNCS, vol. 11675, pp. 305–321. Springer, Cham (2019). https://doi.org/10.1007/978-3-030-26619-6_20

Leveraging Artificial Intelligence and Big Data to Address Grand Challenges

Sudha Ram

Anheuser-Busch Professor of MIS, Entrepreneurship & Innovation, Director, INSITE Center for Business Intelligence and Analytics, Eller College of Management University of Arizona, Tucson, AZ 85721
ram@eller.arizona.edu

Abstract. The phenomenal growth of social media, mobile applications, sensor-based technologies and the Internet of Things is generating a flood of "Big Data" and disrupting our world in many ways. Simultaneously, we are seeing many interesting developments in machine learning and Artificial Intelligence (AI) technologies. In this keynote I will examine the paradigm shift caused by recent our society. Using examples from health care, smart cities, education, and businesses in general, this talk will highlight challenges and research opportunities to address problems that have social implications.

Keyword: Big data · Machine learning · Artificial intelligence · Prediction models · Social good

Introduction

We live in an exciting world of the Fourth Industrial Revolution where we are witnessing a convergence of technological advances and a data deluge. These advances are merging the physical and worlds in ways developments in AI and Big Data and ways to harness their power to address grand challenges facing that create a paradigm shift and hold great promise for the future. The phenomenal growth of social media, mobile applications, sensor based and wearable devices, and the Internet of Things, is generating a flood of "Big Data" and disrupting our world in many ways. Simultaneously, we are seeing many interesting developments in machine learning and Artificial Intelligence (AI) technologies and methods. Organizations and individuals as well as societies are in a position to harness these advancements in AI and Big data analytics to identify grand challenges facing us and to solve them in new ways.

Paradigm Shift in Big Data and AI

The term "Big Data" is often understood to reflect characteristics such as volume, velocity, and variety. While these may appear to be terms that describe big data, we need to dig deeper to truly appreciate its potential. These characteristics do not do justice to explain how big data can be harnessed. I will go beyond these terms to reflect on why big data is changing our world to create a paradigm shift. Specifically, I will focus on three specific properties of big data related to the "datafication" of the world, dissolution of the line between the physical and digital world, and the temporal and spatial characteristics of granular big data. These three characteristics are fundamental to big data and can be harnessed in multiple ways to creatively solve problem.

Simultaneously there has been a paradigm shift in machine learning and artificial intelligence (AI). The founding fathers of AI coined the term Artificial Intelligence in 1956 and predicted great optimism for the field. Two distinct approaches were proposed for AI – one mathematical using deductive reasoning or statistical using inductive reasoning and the other biological or psychological to create reasoning akin to the human brain.

One paradigm started dominating in AI soon after, with its focus on using symbolic logic where computers were taught given symbols and operators. This approach has been now supplanted by another paradigm i.e., sub symbolic approach, inspired by psychologists such as Rosenblatt. This approach proposed the idea of "perceptrons" which were inspired by the functioning of the human brain and which needed to fire neurons based on weights and thresholds. The symbolic approach was transparent and interpretable, while the sub symbolic approach is not. Development of large-scale computational power and availability of large amounts of data with the advent of the WWW have spurred the sub symbolic approach and consequent AI advancements. Today we have multilayer neural networks (deep learning methods) such as Convolutional neural nets or Recurrent neural nets. While these types of neural nets started as black boxes, we have "attention mechanisms" that can now open up these neural nets to some extent. However, these are all still supervised techniques in that they need data and examples to learn. Emerging areas now include unsupervised methods such as reinforcement learning which start with a goal and learning to progress toward that goal.

Interdisciplinary Approaches to Address Grand Challenges

Given these developments in AI and Big data, we are perfectly positioned to make contributions to solving grand challenges particularly to address problems that have social implications [1].

The Information Systems and Computer Science fields have a unique opportunity to lead by embracing a new research approach for identifying and solving interesting problems [2]. Many opportunities abound for data science based research that exploits the temporal and spatial characteristics of big data, the datafication phenomenon and the dissolving line between the physical and digital world. These research methods can also exploit the developments in deep learning methods particularly to identify and remove bias in results of predictions from machine learning. Research that is able to open up the "black boxes" of deep learning to explain the results is also very important. Finally this is an opportunity to develop interdisciplinary collaborations to solve grand challenges in areas that include health care, environmental, and social justice challenges.

References

1. Ram, S., Goes, P.: Focusing on programmatic high impact information systems research, not theory, to address grand challenges, MIS Q. **45**(1) 479-483 (2021)
2. Zhang, W., Ram, S.: A comprehensive analysis of risk factors for asthma: based on machine learning and large heterogeneous data sources. MIS Q. **44**(1), 305–349 (2020). Special Issue on the Role of Information Systems in Chronic Disease Prevention and Management

Bad Files, Bad Data, Bad Results: Data Quality and Data Preparation

Felix Naumann

Hasso Plattner Institute, University of Potsdam, Germany
felix.naumann@hpi.de

Abstract. A significant obstacle when developing and deploying data science solutions is the poor state of data: *files* will not load, schemata are outdated, *data* are ill-formatted, incorrect, or simply missing. Data stewards, data scientists, and developers spend too much time finding, wrangling, and cleaning their training and test data to ensure reliable *results*. Only recently has our community begun to recognize such shortcomings as a research (and tooling) opportunity. We examine data quality problems through all stages of the data science pipeline – from the mundane, such as unexpected field delimiters, to the complex, such as violations of data dependencies. We explore methods to discover and repair such problems and point to the still many open research challenges in the field of data quality and data preparation.

1 Bad Files and Bad Data

Raw data come in many shapes and forms, most of which are not what a data engineer, data scientist, or an analytics tool expects. And more often than not, even after massaging the data into an amenable format, the data themselves might contain errors, have missing values, or are outdated. Incorrectly read files and poorly cleaned data lead to incorrect or poor decisions – by humans analyzing the data or by machines building models based on that data, following the well-known garbage-in-garbage-out principle.

Information systems research has developed a rich foundation on the topic of *information quality*, encompassing a wide range of quality dimensions [15] to be assessed [12] and potentially improved through organizational and technical measures. Database research has traditionally focused on the data quality dimension of *accuracy*, essentially devising methods to identify erroneous data, such as duplicates [1] or violations of data dependencies [8].

Raw data are rarely in a shape that can be directly consumed by down-stream applications. Rather, they need to be prepared. In fact, Trifacta's data preparation study shows that 72% of respondents indicated that data preparation by data users is critical [14]. Data scientists spend approximately 80% of the time on collecting and preparing data and about 20% on actual model implementation and deployment [4, 9, 13].

Yet beyond "bad data", a new dimension of information quality has only recently been identified and is only beginning to be systematically addressed: "bad files". Typical problems in csv-files include multiple tables in a single file, titles, footnotes and other metadata mingling among the data [6], aggregate rows, uncaught reserved characters, heterogeneous delimiters, empty rows, and many other issues that deviate from the (rather loose) standard for csv-files [11]. For instance, among 23k open data files a study identified 14 different encodings, five different delimiters, and up to 226 tables in a single file [2]. Such files typically cannot even be loaded into the target system. Further, even when data can be loaded from raw files, many data preparation tasks along the data-engineering pipeline remain, such as standardizing formats [7], splitting columns, or detecting disguised missing values [10].

2 Data Preparation and Data Cleaning

To achieve high quality results and insights from data, they must usually undergo many syntactic and semantic transformations: data preparation and data cleaning. Data preparation is the set of operations performed in early stages of a data processing pipeline, i.e., transformations at the structural and syntactical levels, which are independent of the data content. In contrast, data cleaning concerns subsequent data transformations and corrections at the semantic level, i.e., correcting erroneous data. Figure 1 shows this spectrum.

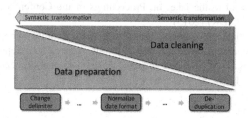

Fig. 1. Data preparation vs. data cleaning from [3].

While there is a rich literature in the field of data cleaning [5] and commercial products abound, the field of data preparation is only budding [3], despite its great potential both in automation opportunities and in time-savings for data engineers and data scientists [4]. Open or yet unsatisfyingly solved challenges include the automatic extraction of data from human-readable files, the standardization of data values and row formats, the automatic suggestion of preparation steps, and finally the ability to properly load any relevant data file into a system without human intervention.

References

1. Christen, P.: Data Matching. Springer Verlag, Heidelberg (2012). https://doi.org/10.1007/978-3-642-31164-2
2. Christodoulakis, C., Munson, E., Gabel, M., Brown, A.D., Miller, R.J.: Pytheas: pattern-based table discovery in CSV files. PVLDB **13**(11), 2075–2089 (2020)

3. Hameed, M., Naumann, F.: Data preparation: a survey of commercial tools. SIGMOD Record **49**(3), 18–29 (2020)
4. Hellerstein, J.M., Heer, J., Kandel, S.: Self-service data preparation: research to practice. IEEE Data Eng. Bull. **41**(2), 23–34 (2018)
5. Ilyas, I.F., Chu, X.: Data cleaning. ACM (2019)
6. Jiang, L., Vitagliano, G., Naumann, F.: Structure detection in verbose CSV files. In: Proceedings of the International Conference on Extending Database Technology (EDBT), pp. 193–204 (2021)
7. Jin, Z., Anderson, M.R., Cafarella, M.J., Jagadish, H.V.: Foofah: transforming data by example. In: Proceedings of the International Conference on Management of Data (SIGMOD), pp. 683–698 (2017)
8. Pena, E.H.M., Filho, E.R.L., de Almeida, E.C., Naumann, F.: Efficient detection of data dependency violations. In: Proceedings of the International Conference on Information and Knowledge Management (CIKM), pp. 1235–1244 (2020)
9. Press, G.: Cleaning data: most time-consuming, least enjoyable data science task. Forbes, March 2016
10. Qahtan, A.A., Elmagarmid, A., Castro Fernandez, R., Ouzzani, M., Tang, N.: FAHES: a robust disguised missing values detector. In: Proceedings of the International Conference on Knowledge discovery and data mining (SIGKDD), pp. 2100–2109 (2018)
11. RFC 4180. https://tools.ietf.org/html/rfc4180. Accessed 12 Mar 2021
12. Sadiq, S., et al.: Data quality – the role of empiricism. SIGMOD Record **46**(4), 35–43 (2018)
13. Terrizzano, I.G., Schwarz, P.M., Roth, M., Colino, J.E.: Data wrangling: The challenging journey from the wild to the lake. In: Proceedings of the Conference on Innovative Data Systems Research (CIDR) (2015)
14. Trifacta end user data preparation. https://www.trifacta.com/wp-content/uploads/2018/02/End-User-Data-Preparation-Market-Study-2018.pdf. Accessed 19 Sept 2019
15. Wang, R.Y., Strong, D.M.: Beyond accuracy: What data quality means to data consumers. Manage. Inf. Syst. **12**(4), 5–34 (1996)

Contents

Novel Applications

Privacy and Security

Towards an Ecosystem of Domain Specific Languages for Threat Modeling

Simon Hacks[(✉)] and Sotirios Katsikeas

Division of Network and Systems Engineering, KTH Royal Institute of Technology,
Stockholm, Sweden
{shacks,sotkat}@kth.se

Abstract. Today, many of our activities depend on the normal operation of the IT infrastructures that supports them. However, cyber-attacks on these infrastructures can lead to disastrous consequences. Therefore, efforts towards assessing the cyber-security are being done, such as attack graph simulations based on system architecture models. The Meta Attack Language (MAL) was previously proposed as a framework for developing Domain Specific Languages (DSLs) that can be used for the aforementioned purpose. Since many common components exist among different domains, a way to prevent repeating work had to be defined. To facilitate this goal, we adapt taxonomy building by Nickerson and propose an ecosystem of MAL-based DSLs that describes a systematic approach for not only developing, but also maintaining them over time. This can foster the usage of MAL for modeling new domains.

Keywords: Ecosystem · Domain specific language · Cyber-security modeling · Cyber-security simulations

1 Introduction

Today, our society is heavily dependent on IT infrastructures and cyber-attacks on them can have disastrous consequences for individuals, regions, and whole nations [28, 29, 35]. Therefore, it is necessary to keep such critical IT infrastructures secure. One approach is the assessment of their cyber-security, which can foster a higher degree of security and resilience. However, such an assessment is difficult as the security-relevant parts of the system must be understood, and all potential attacks must be identified [24]. We can determine three core challenges related to these needs: identification of all relevant security properties of a system; collection of further information on these properties; processing of the information needs to uncover all weaknesses that can be exploited.

Hitherto, we used attack graph simulations based on system architecture models [9] to support these tasks. Our attack simulation tool enables the security assessor to focus on the collection of the information about the system, as the simulation addresses the first and the third challenges. As the previous approach relies on a static implementation, we developed MAL (the Meta Attack

© Springer Nature Switzerland AG 2021
M. La Rosa et al. (Eds.): CAiSE 2021, LNCS 12751, pp. 3–18, 2021.
https://doi.org/10.1007/978-3-030-79382-1_1

Language) [16]. MAL is a framework for domain-specific languages (DSLs) and used to define which information about a system is required. Moreover, it specifies the generic attack logic. Then, MAL automatically generates attack graphs involving the modeled system. Since MAL is a meta language (i.e., the set of rules that should be used to create a new DSL), no particular domain of interest is represented.

Over the last three years, after MAL was originally proposed on 2018 [16], a number of MAL-based DSLs started being developed. Over the past three years, we can notice that in the first two years the rate of new languages starting to be developed was steady (four new languages per year) but in the last year, that rate was significantly increased (nine new languages in 2020). This increasing trend can be explained by the fact that MAL has gained more recognition through conference paper presentations as well as journal article publications.

We noticed that the developers were reasoning on similar parts among different languages. Thus, we started the initiative to develop a multi-purpose language covering these repeating parts: coreLang [18]. coreLang includes the common concepts that are needed to model IT related networks, but on an abstract level. While specifying coreLang into more concrete languages, we recognized that we were still repeating work in certain domains. Thus, a more systematic approach for developing MAL-based languages is needed, leading to our research question: *RQ1: What are the properties of a MAL-based languages' ecosystem of that reduces redundant work?* Simultaneously, a method is needed how such an ecosystem can be maintained. Accordingly, we formulate our second research question: *RQ2: How can MAL-based languages be developed and maintained to preserve the ecosystem's characteristics?* The resulting ecosystem's purpose is to support the end-user in finding suitable languages for their demands and to reduce the effort for language developers by avoiding redundancy.

The rest of the paper is structured as follows: Next, we present the related work, which is on threat modeling in general and the systematic development of DSLs. To ease the understanding of MAL, we present the idea behind MAL, before we explain the fundamental properties of the ecosystem. This is followed by our vision for the future ecosystem as well as the explanation how single languages should be developed and maintained to fit into the ecosystem. Before we conclude our work, we discuss different insights regarding the ecosystem and possible changes to MAL to improve the ecosystem development.

2   Related Work

MAL languages count towards the domain of model-driven security engineering, in which many domain-specific languages exist [17,27]. These languages usually facilitate a model of a system, which incorporates its components, the interaction among these, and security properties such as constraints, requirements, or threats. One common formalism for model checking and searching for constraint violations are attack trees [21,33]. Apart from MAL, which is using this concept, there are several other approaches elaborating on attack graphs [22,38].

Hitherto, we have united the approaches of attack graphs and system modeling in our previous work [9] by automatically generating probabilistic attack graphs based on a existing system specification. However, the used languages to create the attack graphs were hard-coded. Therefore, we have proposed MAL [16] that allows to create domain specific languages. So far, several languages have been built in MAL like vehicleLang [19], which allows modeling cyber-attacks on modern vehicles, or coreLang [18], which contains the most common IT entities and attack steps. Another approach is the automated creation of MAL languages by translating existing concepts to MAL [11].

As already indicated, the languages created with MAL are DSLs and we aim to develop an ecosystem around these languages. Hence, other related work elaborates on the development of DSLs and hierarchies of DSLs. do Nascimento et al. [25] performed a systematic mapping study on DSLs. Besides an increasing interest in DSLs, do Nascimento et al. notice that security related DSLs receive a lower attention than other DSLs e.g., related to software engineering purposes. Developing DSL for special purposes is a common endeavor in software engineering research. Accordingly, a broad range of DSLs has been developed [25]. Hence, researchers [20,34] took a closer look at the different DSLs and distilled different reoccurring patterns.

In our work, we create hierarchies between DSLs, which is scarce in existing research. Nonetheless, different authors [15,32] combine different DSLs in a hierarchical fashion, similar to our idea. In their approaches, each layer is used by different kinds of experts and the upper layer consumes the outputs of the lower layers. Thus, the developers on the lower layers do not need to have the overarching knowledge of the higher layers, while the developers of the higher layers do not need the detailed knowledge of the lower levels. Preschern et al. [30,31] propose a meta-DSL which is similar to MAL as it provides a framework to develop other DSLs. However, while MAL's purpose is situated in the threat modeling domain, their meta-DSL is used for physical automation. In contrast to our work, they do not consider further dependencies between languages developed with their meta-DSL.

Cleenewerck [8] suggests defining so called "key words" to create components in DSLs that can be reused among other DSLs. This is similar to our idea of creating abstract DSLs that then are reused to create more specific languages. However, his approach is different in the sense that he proposes single fragments that are then reused, while we reuse the entire language. His approach has the advantage that the language designer can explicitly choose what to reuse, while our approach can cover concepts that the designer might have not considered.

3   The Meta Attack Language

Next, we give a short presentation of the MAL. For a detailed overview of the MAL, we refer readers to the original paper [16]. First, a MAL-based DSL contains the main elements that are encountered on the domain under study, those are called **assets** in MAL. The assets contain **attack steps**, which represent the actual attacks/threats that can happen on them.

An attack step can be connected with one or more following attack steps so that an attack path is created. Those attack paths are then used to create attack graphs which are facilitated when the attack simulation is run. Attack steps can be either of the type OR or of the type AND, respectively indicating that performing any individual parental attack step is required (OR) or performing all parental attack steps is required (AND) for the current step to be performed.

Assets should also have relations between them in order for a model to be constructed, those relations are called `associations` in MAL. Inheritance between `assets` is also possible and each child asset inherits all the attack steps of the parent asset. It should be, nevertheless, mentioned that multiple inheritance is not currently supported in MAL. Additionally, the assets can be organized into categories for purely organization reasons.

In Listing 1, a short example of how a MAL-based DSL is presented. In this example, four modeled assets can be seen together with the connections of attack steps from one asset to another. In the `Host` asset, the *connect* attack step is an OR attack step while *access* is an AND attack step. Then, the -> symbol denotes the connected next attack step. For example, if an attacker performs *phish* on the `User`, it is possible to reach *obtain* on the associated `Password` and as a result finally perform *authenticate* on the associated `Host`. In the last lines of the example the `associations` between the assets are defined.

```
1    category System {                      23              -> passwords.obtain
2      asset Network {                       24    }
3      | access                              25
4        -> hosts.connect                    26    asset Password extends Data {
5      }                                      27    | obtain
6                                             28        -> host.authenticate
7      asset Host {                           29    }
8      | connect                             30  }
9        -> access                           31
10     | authenticate                        32  associations {
11       -> access                           33    Network [networks] *
12     | guessPwd                            34      <-- NetworkAccess -->
13       -> guessedPwd                       35    * [hosts] Host
14     | guessedPwd [Exp(0.02)]              36    Host [host] 1
15       -> authenticate                     37      <-- Credentials -->
16     & access                              38    * [passwords] Password
17     }                                      39    User [user] 1
18                                            40      <-- Credentials -->
19     asset User {                          41    * [passwords] Password
20     | attemptPhishing                     42  }
21       -> phish
22     | phish [Exp(0.1)]
```

Listing 1: Exemplary MAL Code

4   Properties of Ecosystems

Jacobidis et al. [14] identified three streams of strategy research elaborating on ecosystems: the first stream focuses on a company and its environment [36]; the second stream concentrates on a particular innovation and the related actors [1];

the third stream centers around technological platforms and the actors interacting around them [6]. MAL and the languages created with it, can be understand as a technological platform and, thus, count towards the third stream.

For ecosystems in the third stream, Jacobidis et al. [14] identified three different types of stakeholders as a common property (P1): the platform sponsors, the complementors, and the consumers. For our envisioned ecosystem, the platform sponsor is the developer team of the MAL compiler, as their decisions on MAL's feature frame the opportunities that the MAL language developers (i.e., the complementors) can work with. Both together provide the final value to the users of the language respectively the consumers. From a complementor perspective, a property of ecosystems (P2) is the ability to reuse existing components and sometimes also combine them [14]. In our ecosystem, the complementor will choose from the different languages those, which are closest to their demands, and even combine different languages to address overarching demands (cf. Sect. 6). Moreover, this property is mirrored to the consumers (P3), that are free to choose from the ecosystem and combine different components [14].

Another important property of ecosystems (P4) is to provide an alignment structure for the different stakeholders creating the single parts of it [2], while preserving stakeholders' autonomy [14]. This is achieved by a modular architecture [4] and related design parameters can be set by the platform sponsor. Thus, an ecosystem provides processes and rules to solve coordination issues arising along the ecosystem evolution [14].

A fundamental rule of our ecosystem is that at the top, there are languages that cover criteria of a broad range of demands, while the deeper in the hierarchy the more specific the languages are. This reminds of the characteristics of a taxonomy [26], which is comprised by a set of n dimensions that consist of k characteristics. These characteristics are mutual exclusive in each dimension for the object that is classified. From a language development perspective, the mutual exclusivity still holds as the languages should be differentiable from each other. However, we relax the demand for one layer of characteristics to have several levels of concretization. As the relaxation is the only difference, the approach of Nickerson et al. [26] is still applicable to create an ecosystem of MAL-based languages. Thus, we present following our adoption of Nickerson et al.

First, the meta-characteristic of the taxonomy –or rather of the DSL ecosystem in our case– needs to be determined. Nickerson et al. [26] point out that "The meta-characteristic is the most comprehensive characteristic that will serve as the basis for the choice of characteristics in the taxonomy." Thus, the meta-characteristic guides the development of the ecosystem and should be related to its purpose. On the one hand, it should support the developer of new MAL-based languages to situate their language properly with respect to existing languages. On the other hand, it should serve as aid for the language users to choose the best suiting language. However, future development of the ecosystem might lead to changes of the purpose, as also mentioned by Nickerson et al. [26].

Second, the ending conditions need to be determined. The development of the ecosystem is a continuous effort. Consequently, there is no general ending

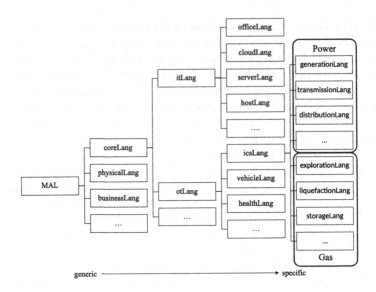

Fig. 1. Vision of an ecosystem for MAL-based languages

condition. If a new language is added to the ecosystem, the ending condition is its successful situation within the ecosystem. However, the addition of a new language may also lead to changes in the ecosystem's structure. Within this work, we temporally extend these ending conditions to make sure that all existing MAL-based languages are included and to include imaginary examples to illustrate the application of the ecosystem.

Next, we develop the ecosystem itself. For the first version of the ecosystem, we follow a conceptual-to-empirical approach [26]. Therefore, we envision a structure that is detailed in Sect. 5 and incorporate the existing MAL-based languages into it. Following the conceptual-to-empirical approach is motivated by the facts that the number of MAL-based languages is yet not large enough to follow the empirical-to-conceptual approach and that the ecosystem structure shall inspire future language development. However, future alterations of the ecosystem's structure will obviously follow the empirical-to-conceptual approach, as a new object will join, which causes a revision of the structure.

5   A Vision for the Structure of an Ecosystem

Before, we have developed the characteristics that lead to the structure for the ecosystem. Next, we will present the outcome of the application of processes constituted in P4 (cf. Fig. 1). We like to note, that this is just a vision and a future structure might look different. However, this vision should serve as an inspiration for the future development of MAL-based languages.

Before diving into the details of Fig. 1, we like to discuss shortly the founding ideas. First, the structure follows the principle from general to specific. In other words, we situate languages that cover general domains on the top of the hierarchy and specify the languages to specific domains. This is thought to reduce the effort for creating languages. Second, we indicate cluster of languages. These cluster represent languages that belong to a certain domain. They are thought as help for the end-user to select the best suited language(s). This leads also to aspect three: each language is not planned as a silver bullet. Instead, the end-user chooses several languages that satisfy together the overall demand.

As indicated, we envision the future structure of MAL-based languages in a hierarchical structure. By definition, the origin of all MAL-based languages are the concepts of MAL (cf. Sect. 3). The second layer defines languages that cover certain overall concepts, like coreLang [18] representing common aspects of IT related networks. So far, coreLang depicts the only existing language on this layer. Another possible direction for future languages is to include business aspects into the threat modelling [3,10].

The next layer concretizes the general-purpose languages. As a first step of concretization, we envision a differentiation between languages that cover the specifics related to IT and OT. The languages of the IT branch cover aspects related to classical IT. The OT branch is characterized by a much broader diversification of languages as the spectrum of languages will need to represent very different domains with different terminologies. So far, we have a language that is used to model the internals of vehicles (vehicleLang [19]) and a language that satisfies the need to simulate attackers in industrial environments (icsLang).

We assume that there will not be much need to specify the aforementioned layer of languages further. For example, to provide the power domain with necessary and to their terminology tailored assets, icsLang can be refined into certain languages, inspired by the facets included in the Smart Grid Architecture Model (SGAM) [7]. Similarly, this can be done for the gas domain, inspired by its value chain [37]. These most concrete languages will mainly rename already existing concepts to meet the domain specific terminology.

Hitherto, we have described languages that can be arranged into an inheritance hierarchy. However, we recognized possible languages that do not fit into this hierarchy as they cover orthogonal aspects that might or might not be of relevance for certain languages in the hierarchy. For example, enterpriseLang [39] codifies the techniques of MITRE ATT&CK[1] into MAL.

6   Single Language Development

So far, we have discussed the overall structure of the DSL ecosystem. However, the ecosystem is constituted by its languages. Therefore, we will discuss following how new languages can be integrated into the existing ecosystem and how existing languages should be maintained to keep the spirit of the ecosystem alive.

---

[1] https://attack.mitre.org/.

6.1   Developing a New Language

Before developing a new language, the developer needs to determine the requirements towards the language. In other words, which certain domain(s) should be covered by the language. Here, the techniques of domain analysis (e.g., [13]) might be of support for the developer. Based on this recognition, the developer needs to decide if an existing language or a combination of languages within the ecosystem are already (partly) satisfying the requirements.

If the requirements are already fulfilled, there is no need for an additional language. However, it might be the case that a language satisfies the requirements functionally, but the desired domain demands another terminology. In this case, we recommend an inherited language from the existing language, that simply introduces the common terminology of the domain. If the requirements are already fulfilled by a set of different languages, then a new language should be comprised of these languages (see Sect. 6.3).

Finally, if the requirements are not met, there is a need for a new language. To situate the language properly within the ecosystem, the developer should determine the language that covers the requirements best. Therefore, the developer should traverse the ecosystem's structure from its root by choosing always the best suiting domain. The traversing ends when the developer reaches a language that is too specific and, thus, does not satisfies the requirements anymore. Accordingly, the new language should be placed on the same level as the first language that is not satisfactory. If a further reorganization (cf. Sect. 4) of the following hierarchies is necessary, needs to be decided case by case. If several languages are identified as suitable for an extension. Then these languages need to be extended by several different new languages that are combined by the mechanisms described in Sect. 6.3.

6.2   Language Maintenance

Hitherto, we have discussed how developers should situate new languages within the ecosystem. However, it might be the case that an already existing language is covering the domain. In these cases, the reuse of existing languages should be prioritized. Nonetheless, it might be possible that the language does not contain all needed concepts. For example, a certain asset could be missing. Then, the language needs to be maintained.

To minimize site effects on other languages, we recommend adding new assets to languages that are at the lowest level of the ecosystem's structure. If the asset is shared among different languages on the same level of abstraction, then the asset should be moved up to the language of which these languages inherit from. However, if the there are other languages sharing the same parenting language and these languages do not contain the same asset, an additional abstract language could be necessary. This additional language would be then introduced as parent language for the languages sharing the certain asset. Those two cases are depicted in Fig. 2.

Following this pattern will ensure the downward compatibility of the languages and, thus, create a more robust ecosystem. Drawbacks of this application are an increasing number of languages and deep inheritance hierarchies. Additionally, in such a deep inheritance chain, many unnecessary assets can be inherited when creating a new language. A possible solution for these drawbacks is the introduction of multiple inheritance and partial inheritance, respectively.

The deletion or the change of assets on the lowest level is without danger to the integrity of the ecosystem, as this will have no influence on other languages. However, adding, deleting, and changing on higher levels will have direct influence on all related lower languages. Therefore, these actions should be avoided on higher levels to impede undesired site effects. If such changes are necessary, a thorough analysis on the effects will be necessary and even a restructuring of ecosystem parts might be needed. Thus, we highly recommend to perform changes just on the lowest levels.

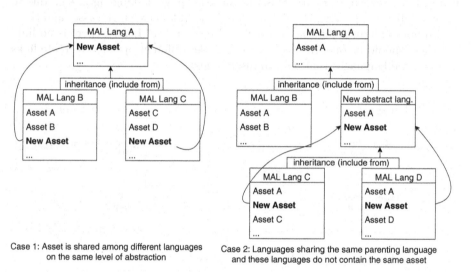

Case 1: Asset is shared among different languages on the same level of abstraction

Case 2: Languages sharing the same parenting language and these languages do not contain the same asset

Fig. 2. Two cases of adding new assets in the ecosystem

6.3 Combining Languages

As indicated before, the combination of different languages can satisfy the needs of the end-user. Usually, this will be the case if the end-user wants to model entire organizations that cover different domains. For example, for manufacturing organizations there will be the computing systems that are necessary for the manufacturing parts. Further, there will be other systems that support the administrative parts within the organization, like accounting or human resources. To perform simulations for such kind of organizations, the two languages covering these different aspects are needed. The ecosystem behaves in such cases similar to the product line pattern [23], as the developer combines the languages from the ecosystem like the features for product lines.

The determination of the best suiting languages follows basically the same process as described in Sect. 6.1, except that the domain analysis [13] will result in several domains. Thus, the process needs to be performed for each of the domains to identify the best suiting language.

Next, the languages need to be linked to each other. First, the developer needs to identify the desired connection points between the languages. Connection points refer here to certain assets that are on the border (or close to) between two domains. These assets serve as transition for the attacker from one language to the other. Afterwards, it should be checked if there already exist links between the languages due to shared associations inherited from a parent language.

This examination can lead to four kinds of possible findings: First, the existing link is in line and no further actions are needed. Second, the found link is contradictory to our intentions and it needs to be removed. Actually, the languages need to be redesigned to achieve this. However, in future versions of MAL it might be possible to realize this without changing the languages, e.g., due to the specialization patter [34]. Third, there is no link between the asset and there is also non desired. Again, no actions need to be taken. Lastly, there is no link, but there should be one. In this last case, we see different options to create links between the languages that we will discuss next.

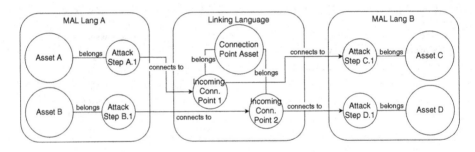

Fig. 3. Combining languages using an intermediate language

The first option is using inheritance between assets of the different languages as we did in powerLang [12]. The advantage is that the changes to the language are minimal, as just an extension between two assets has to be added. However, this is still a change on one language. Additionally, this works only if the asset does not already have an extension, as MAL does not support multiple inheritance (now). Another drawback is that the inheritance might cause unintended behavior if attack steps get overwritten. To sum up, the disadvantages prevail the advantages and, thus, inheritance should not be used to link languages.

The second option is to add a dedicated attack step that leads to another attack step in the other language. This gives a better control on how an attacker moves between languages and no unwanted side-effects arise. But changes to at least one language are needed. Further, a deeper understanding of both languages is needed to determine suitable attack steps for the transition. To sum up, this approach seems better, due to less unwanted side effects, but should also not be preferred as changes to the languages are necessary.

For the last option, the languages of the ecosystem need to be prepared first. Basically, the designer of the language foresees certain attack steps, preferably encapsulated in a designated asset, that serve as incoming and outgoing connection points. As these attack steps are of technical nature, they might be hidden to the end-users. A third language can be created in which the outgoing connection points are linked to the incoming connection points, similar to the adapter pattern [20]. Thus, no changes to the languages of the ecosystem would be necessary (cf. Fig. 3). Alternatively, outgoing connection points can automatically be linked to incoming connection points, but we think that a human evaluation of which concrete points are connected to each other is necessary. A disadvantage of this technique is the additional effort for the language designers to consider and model the connections points. However, the effort will be worth it, as no changes to the languages will be necessary.

When combining languages, the question of responsibility for the maintenance of the linked languages needs to be answered and what happens if changes are introduced on those languages. The main responsibility for the maintenance of the languages falls to the developer but if proper versioning is used on them, then, changes on those languages should not adversely affect the linking languages.

6.4   First Experimentation Insights

As a first evaluation of our proposed approach, we developed icsLang. icsLang's purpose is to provide a set of assets that can be used to model industrial control systems (ICS) such as substations in power grids. Therefore, we considered existing MAL-based languages as starting point. The only feasible language was coreLang [18], as all other languages were in domains that did not fit.

The next step was to determine the needed assets within icsLang. Hence, we used ATT&CK for Industrial Control Systems[2] as inspiration and created for each of the mentioned assets a representation in icsLang. Next, we defined which icsLang assets inherit from which coreLang assets based on their description, where possible. Afterwards, we ensured that behavior, that was not already covered by the inheritance, was implemented in icsLang. We did not recognize the need to move new assets up to coreLang as all assets were specific for the ICS domain (such as physical processes), but we identified several bugs in coreLang that were corrected afterwards.

To check the applicability of icsLang, we tried to model a substation with it, which was no challenge. However, we recognized that the used terminology was slightly different. Therefore, we decided to create substationLang that inherits the concepts of icsLang and renames to the terminology used in substation. Moreover, we came along the concept of signaling that was not implemented in

---

[2] https://collaborate.mitre.org/attackics.

icsLang. As this concept is not mutual exclusive to substation, but also exists in other ICS domains such as power generation, we moved the asset up to icsLang.

Using coreLang, icsLang, and substationLang in combination to model both IT and OT environments that interact with each other, caused no issues due to the inheritance structure. Consequently, we are not able to provide any deeper insights on the means for linking substantial different languages to each other.

7   Discussion

Before, we have presented the properties of the ecosystem, a vision for the future structure of the ecosystem, and the guidelines language developers should follow to create a sustainable ecosystem. Next, we discuss how our ecosystem meets the identified properties (cf. Sect. 4):

The first property, P1, is related to the stakeholders of the ecosystem. In our case, we have three different groups: the developer team of the compiler (platform sponsor), the language developers (complementors), and the users of the ecosystem (consumers). One might argue that security experts that provide knowledge to the language developers might be also stakeholders. We do not agree directly, since their role as experts does not create an interest in the ecosystem per se. But they might use the ecosystem for their analysis and, accordingly, they belong to the consumer group.

To guarantee the ability to reuse and combine the single components of the ecosystem (P2), we have described a certain set of rules that are thought to ensure these capabilities (cf. Sect. 6). However, these guidelines may foster a deep hierarchy of inheritance. Even if our first experiences with icsLang have shown that approximately three layers of inheritance might be sufficient, there are means to cope with deep hierarchies. On the one hand, one could introduce the concept of multiple inheritance to MAL. In that case, it would be possible to design language more finely structured and, thus, avoid several levels of inheritance. In contrast, this would lead to a bigger number of different languages, which need to be considered. On the other hand, MAL could be extended so that is possible to deactivate certain relations between assets or attacks, similar to the "language specialization patter" [34]. This would not reduce the inheritance depth but would enable the language developer to reduce the complexity of the language and opt out undesired behavior.

The latter would not only be useful in the context of inheritance, but also by combining languages that have a common parent language. It might be the case that in such settings, relations are inherited that are unintentional. Thus, removing them from the language would improve the language design.

The free choice and combination of the end-user (P3) is realized, due to the fact that each language of the ecosystem works standalone, at least for a certain demand. Moreover, if the languages of the ecosystem follow the guidelines described in Sect. 6.3, then the user will be easily able to combine different languages with each other. However, this interoperability is restricted by the effort the language developers spend to allow it. One option could be to demand that every language needs to provide the features that are needed to achieve interoperability.

The last property, P4, is linked to means that achieve an alignment structure. Therefore, we present a process to develop a structure for an ecosystem of DSLs (cf. Sect. 4). The process is inspired by Nickerson et al. [26], thus the process itself can be considered as quality ensured. However, we cannot state the same for the resulting vision of the ecosystem. A solution to evaluate this, would be to split the existing MAL-based languages into two sets and use one for evaluation of the result [5]. Unfortunately, the number of existing MAL-based languages is too small so far. Thus, the structure of the ecosystem cannot be evaluated, which should be tackled in future work.

Finally, to ensure that future MAL-based languages will be added to our envisioned ecosystem and do not alter its properties, an appropriate tool support is vital to reduce the effort for developers. This includes classical coding features such as automatic code completion or refactoring capabilities. But also, more advanced features are needed, such as a central repository and automated provision of existing languages, similar to the mechanisms of maven.

8   Conclusion

It is very clear today that protecting our IT infrastructures is of great importance. One way of achieving this is by defensive protections but another one is through offensive security. A characteristic example is cyber-attack modeling and simulations and a framework that allows this is the MAL. MAL has been proposed in 2018 but since then it has noted an increase in usage and the number of MAL-based DSLs is constantly increasing year by year.

Because of that and because how closely, in terms of similarity, the different IT infrastructures of different domains are, a systematic way of developing such DSLs and maintaining them needed to be defined. In this paper, we have proposed our vision towards the ecosystem of DSL for threat modeling. This ecosystem, whose properties are the answer to our first research question, contains guidelines, best practices and lessons learned for the process of developing such languages, combining them, but also for the maintenance of them after the development phase has concluded. All those constitute the answers to our second research question, which was how MAL-based languages can be developed and maintained in order to preserve the ecosystem's properties. Then, in the last parts of this paper, a thorough discussion on what the plan for the future of this proposed ecosystem is, was done.

Regarding future work, an evaluation of our proposed ecosystem is on our plans and from the feedback we will get out of it more concrete advises for the development of languages inside the ecosystem could be made. Hitherto, we solely had a look at work contributing to reuse from the DSL domain. However, other possible inputs might be found in using components, method chunks, or in research related to product lines. Another point of future work is improvements to MAL itself, such as the addition of multiple inheritance as mentioned before.

Acknowledgement. This project has received funding from the European Union's H2020 research and innovation programme under the Grant Agreement No. 832907, and the Swedish Centre for Smart Grids and Energy Storage (SweGRIDS).

References

1. Adner, R.: Match your innovation strategy to your innovation ecosystem. Harvard Bus. Rev. **84**(4), 98–107 (2006)
2. Adner, R.: Ecosystem as structure: an actionable construct for strategy. J. Manage. **43**(1), 39–58 (2017)
3. Aldea, A., Vaicekauskaite, E., Daneva, M., Piest, J.S.: Assessing resilience in enterprise architecture: a systematic review. In: 24th International EDOC Conference, pp. 1–10. IEEE CS, Los Alamitos (2020)
4. Baldwin, C.Y., Clark, K.B.: Design rules: the power of modularity, vol. 1. MIT press (2000)
5. Barbosa, A., Santana, A., Hacks, S., Stein, N.v.: A taxonomy for enterprise architecture analysis research. In: 21st ICEIS, vol. 2, pp. 493–504. SciTePress (2019)
6. Ceccagnoli, M., Forman, C., Huang, P., Wu, D.J.: Cocreation of value in a platform ecosystem! the case of enterprise software. MIS Q. **36**(1), 263–290 (2012)
7. CEN-CENELEC-ETSI, Smart Grid Coordination Group: Smart grid reference architecture (2012)
8. Cleenewerck, T.: Component-based DSL development. In: Pfenning, F., Smaragdakis, Y. (eds.) GPCE 2003. LNCS, vol. 2830, pp. 245–264. Springer, Heidelberg (2003). https://doi.org/10.1007/978-3-540-39815-8_15
9. Ekstedt, M., Johnson, P., Lagerström, R., Gorton, D., Nydrén, J., Shahzad, K.: securiCAD by foreseeti: a CAD tool for enterprise cyber security management. In: 19th International EDOC Workshop, pp. 152–155. IEEE (2015)
10. Goluch, G., Ekelhart, A., Fenz, S., Jakoubi, S., Tjoa, S., Muck, T.: Integration of an ontological information security concept in risk aware business process management. In: 41st HICSS 2008, pp. 377–386 (2008)
11. Hacks, S., Hacks, A., Katsikeas, S., Klaer, B., Lagerström, R.: Creating meta attack language instances using archimate: applied to electric power and energy system cases. In: 23rd International EDOC, pp. 88–97 (2019)
12. Hacks, S., Katsikeas, S., Ling, E., Lagerström, R., Ekstedt, M.: powerLang: a probabilistic attack simulation language for the power domain. Energy Inform. **3**(1), 1–17 (2020). https://doi.org/10.1186/s42162-020-00134-4
13. Hjørland, B.: Domain analysis in information science. J. Documentation **58**(4), 422–462 (2002)
14. Jacobides, M.G., Cennamo, C., Gawer, A.: Towards a theory of ecosystems. Strateg. Manage. J. **39**(8), 2255–2276 (2018)
15. Johanson, A.N., Hasselbring, W.: Hierarchical combination of internal and external domain-specific languages for scientific computing. In: ECSAW. ACM (2014)
16. Johnson, P., Lagerström, R., Ekstedt, M.: A meta language for threat modeling and attack simulations. In: Proceedings of the 13th International Conference on Availability, Reliability and Security, p. 38. ACM (2018)
17. Jürjens, J.: Secure Systems Development with UML. Springer, Heidelberg (2005). https://doi.org/10.1007/b137706
18. Katsikeas, S., et al.: An attack simulation language for the IT domain. In: Eades III, H., Gadyatskaya, O. (eds.) GraMSec 2020. LNCS, vol. 12419, pp. 67–86. Springer, Cham (2020). https://doi.org/10.1007/978-3-030-62230-5_4

19. Katsikeas, S., Johnson, P., Hacks, S., Lagerström, R.: Probabilistic modeling and simulation of vehicular cyber attacks: an application of the meta attack language. In: 5th ICISSP (2019)
20. Keepence, B., Mannion, M.: Using patterns to model variability in product families. IEEE Softw. **16**(4), 102–108 (1999)
21. Kordy, B., Mauw, S., Radomirović, S., Schweitzer, P.: Foundations of attack–defense trees. In: Degano, P., Etalle, S., Guttman, J. (eds.) FAST 2010. LNCS, vol. 6561, pp. 80–95. Springer, Heidelberg (2011). https://doi.org/10.1007/978-3-642-19751-2_6
22. Kordy, B., Piètre-Cambacédès, L., Schweitzer, P.: Dag-based attack and defense modeling: don't miss the forest for the attack trees. Comput. Sci. Rev. **13**, 1–38 (2014)
23. Mernik, M., Heering, J., Sloane, A.M.: When and how to develop domain-specific languages. ACM Comput. Surv. **37**(4), 316–344 (2005)
24. Morikawa, I., Yamaoka, Y.: Threat tree templates to ease difficulties in threat modeling. In: 14th NBiS, pp. 673–678 (2011)
25. do Nascimento, L.M., Viana, D.L., Neto, P., Martins, D., Garcia, V.C., Meira, S.: A systematic mapping study on domain-specific languages. In: The Seventh ICSEA, pp. 179–187 (2012)
26. Nickerson, R.C., Varshney, U., Muntermann, J.: A method for taxonomy development and its application in information systems. EJIS **22**(3), 336–359 (2013)
27. Paja, E., Dalpiaz, F., Giorgini, P.: Modelling and reasoning about security requirements in socio-technical systems. Data Knowl. Eng. **98**, 123–143 (2015)
28. Petermann, T., Bradke, H., Lüllmann, A., Poetzsch, M., Riehm, U.: Was bei einem Blackout geschieht: Folgen eines langandauernden und großflächigen Stromausfalls, vol. 662. Büro für Technikfolgen-Abschätzung (2011)
29. Petit, J., Shladover, S.E.: Potential cyberattacks on automated vehicles. IEEE Trans. Intell. Transp. Syst. **16**(2), 546–556 (2015)
30. Preschern, C., Kajtazovic, N., Kreiner, C.: Efficient development and reuse of domain-specific languages for automation systems. Int. J. Metadata Semant. Ontol. **9**(3), 215–226 (2014)
31. Preschern, C., Leitner, A., Kreiner, C.: Domain specific language architecture for automation systems: an industrial case study. In: 8th ECMFA, pp. 1–12 (2012)
32. Prähofer, H., Hurnaus, D.: Monaco - a domain-specific language supporting hierarchical abstraction and verification of reactive control programs. In: 2010 8th IEEE International Conference on Industrial Informatics, pp. 908–914 (2010)
33. Schneier, B.: Attack trees. Dr. Dobb's J. **24**(12), 21–29 (1999)
34. Spinellis, D.: Notable design patterns for domain-specific languages. J. Syst. Softw. **56**(1), 91–99 (2001)
35. Stellios, I., Kotzanikolaou, P., Psarakis, M., Alcaraz, C., Lopez, J.: A survey of IOT-enabled cyberattacks: assessing attack paths to critical infrastructures and services. IEEE Commun. Surv. Tutorials **20**(4), 3453–3495 (2018)
36. Teece, D.J.: Explicating dynamic capabilities: the nature and microfoundations of (sustainable) enterprise performance. Strateg. Manage. J. **28**(13), 1319–1350 (2007)

37. Weijermars, R.: Value chain analysis of the natural gas industry: lessons from the us regulatory success and opportunities for Europe. J. Nat. Gas. Sci. Eng. **2**(2), 86–104 (2010)
38. Williams, L., Lippmann, R., Ingols, K.: GARNET: a graphical attack graph and reachability network evaluation tool. In: Goodall, J.R., Conti, G., Ma, K.-L. (eds.) VizSec 2008. LNCS, vol. 5210, pp. 44–59. Springer, Heidelberg (2008). https://doi.org/10.1007/978-3-540-85933-8_5
39. Xiong, W., Legrand, E., Åberg, O., Lagerström, R.: Cyber security threat modeling based on the mitre enterprise att&ck matrix. submitted to SoSyM Journal (2020)

Privacy-Aware Process Performance Indicators: Framework and Release Mechanisms

Martin Kabierski$^{(\boxtimes)}$, Stephan A. Fahrenkrog-Petersen, and Matthias Weidlich

Humboldt-Universität zu Berlin, Berlin, Germany
{martin.bauer,stephan.fahrenkrog-petersen,matthias.weidlich}@hu-berlin.de

Abstract. Process performance indicators (PPIs) are metrics to quantify the degree with which organizational goals defined based on business processes are fulfilled. They exploit the event logs recorded by information systems during the execution of business processes, thereby providing a basis for process monitoring and subsequent optimization. However, PPIs are often evaluated on processes that involve individuals, which implies an inevitable risk of privacy intrusion. In this paper, we address the demand for privacy protection in the computation of PPIs. We first present a framework that enforces control over the data exploited for process monitoring. We then show how PPIs defined based on the established PPINOT meta-model are instantiated in this framework through a set of data release mechanisms. These mechanisms are designed to provide provable guarantees in terms of differential privacy. We evaluate our framework and the release mechanisms in a series of controlled experiments. We further use a public event log to compare our framework with approaches based on privatization of event logs. The results demonstrate feasibility and shed light on the trade-offs between data utility and privacy guarantees in the computation of PPIs.

Keywords: Performance indicators · Process monitoring · Differential privacy

1 Introduction

Many companies improve their operation by applying process-oriented methodologies. In this context, Business Process Management (BPM) provides methods and techniques to aid in the monitoring, analysis, and optimization of business processes [4]. Important means to enable the continuous optimization of processes are *process performance indicators* (PPIs), i.e. numerical measures computed based on data recorded during process execution [3]. PPIs assess whether predefined goals set by the process owner are fulfilled, e.g., related to the mean sojourn time of a business process. Figure 1 illustrates a simple insurance claim handling process and respective PPIs. Each indicator comprises a definition of a measure, a target value, and an observation period, called scope.

© Springer Nature Switzerland AG 2021
M. La Rosa et al. (Eds.): CAiSE 2021, LNCS 12751, pp. 19–36, 2021.
https://doi.org/10.1007/978-3-030-79382-1_2

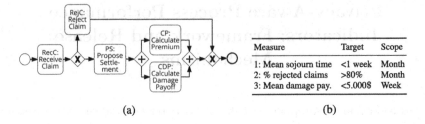

Measure	Target	Scope
1: Mean sojourn time	<1 week	Month
2: % rejected claims	>80%	Month
3: Mean damage pay.	<5.000$	Week

(a)   (b)

Fig. 1. (a) Model of a claim handling process; (b) PPIs defined on the model.

The data used to calculate PPIs often includes personal data. In Fig. 1, such data relates to the knowledge workers handling the claims or the customers who submitted them. Processing of personal data is strictly regulated. The GDPR [7], as an example, prohibits the use of personal data without explicit consent and especially restricts their *secondary use*, i.e., the processing of data beyond the purpose for which they were originally recorded. Process optimization typically represents such a secondary use of process execution data [14]. To motivate, why unregulated access to process execution data may be problematic, we turn back to the example model and PPI in Fig. 1b. Assume that data is recorded about three claims handled by Alice with sojourn times of 4, 4, and 5 d; three claims handled by Bob within 2, 6, and 6 d; and three claims handled by Sue lasting for 7, 8, and 8 d. Here, the mean sojourn time of these nine process instances is ~5.5 d and thus fulfils PPI 1 set by management. Yet, considering this data directly would reveal Sue's generally slower processing times, which may be prohibited by privacy regulations. Here, privacy-protected PPI schemes, i.e., techniques that incorporate data anonymization in the computation of PPIs, would allow for the evaluation of PPIs, while protecting the privacy of the recorded individuals in the log file, thus lifting these privacy regulations. Yet, data anonymization commonly leads to a trade-off between the strength of a privacy guarantee and a loss in data utility, thus a privacy-protected PPI scheme needs to minimize the accuracy loss introduced.

Models for privacy-aware computation of traditional aggregates [16,20] have limited applicability for PPIs, though. Since these models do not take into account the highly structured nature of data generated by processes and PPIs defined on them, these methods are not suitable for privatizing PPIs. Approaches for privacy-aware publishing and querying of process execution data [8,13], in turn, are too coarse-grained. Handling comprehensive execution data, these techniques cannot be tailored to minimize the loss in data utility for a given set of PPIs. Against this background, we identify the research question of *how to design a framework for the evaluation of privacy-protected PPIs.*

In this paper, we address the above question, by proposing PaPPI, a first framework for privacy-aware evaluation of **PPIs**. It separates trusted and untrusted environments to handle process execution data. They are connected by a dedicated interface that serves as a privacy checkpoint, ensuring ϵ-differential privacy [5]. We then instantiate this framework with data release mechanisms for PPIs that are defined based on the established PPINOT meta-model [3]. This way, we enable organizations to compute expressive PPIs without risking privacy violations. Finally, we explore the impact of privacy-aware evaluation of PPIs on their quality. We report on controlled experiments using synthetic data and a case study with a publicly available event log. Our results demonstrate the feasibility of the framework and its instantiation through specific release mechanisms, given that a reasonable amount of process execution data has been recorded.

In the remainder, Sect. 2 provides background on PPIs and privacy guarantees. Section 3 introduces our framework for privacy-aware evaluation of PPIs, which is instantiated with specific release mechanisms in Sect. 4 and evaluated in Sect. 5. Finally, we review related work in Sect. 6, before we conclude in Sect. 7.

2   Background

We introduce a basic model for event logs (Sect. 2.1) and process performance indicators (Sect. 2.2). Finally, we review the concept of differential privacy (Sect. 2.3).

2.1   Notions and Notations for Event Logs

We consider ordered, finite datasets, each being a set of elements $X = \{x_1, \ldots, x_n\}$ that carry a numeric value and are partially ordered by $\leq$.[1] The cardinality of the dataset is denoted as $|X| = n$. For one of the (potentially many) elements of X that are minimal and maximal according to $\leq$, we write $\underline{X}$ and $\overline{X}$, respectively. An interval of the dataset is defined by $I = (x_{lower}, x_{upper})$ with $x_{lower}, x_{upper} \in X$ and $x_{lower} \leq x_{upper}$. Lifting the notation for minima and maxima to I, we define $\underline{I} = x_{lower}$ and $\overline{I} = x_{upper}$.

Our notion of an event log is based on a relational event model [1]. That is, an *event schema* is defined by a tuple of attributes $A = (A_1, \ldots, A_n)$, so that an *event* is an instance of the schema, i.e., a tuple of attribute values $e = (a_1, \ldots, a_n)$. An event schema consists of at least three attributes, the *case* that identifies the process instance to which an event belongs, the *timestamp* for the point in time an event has been recorded, and the *activity*, for which the execution is signalled by an event. The *timestamp*-ordered list of events corresponding to a single *case* is called a *trace*. Such a trace represents the execution of a single process instance. An *event log* is a set of traces.

2.2   Process Performance Indicators

A *key performance indicator (KPI)* is a metric that quantifies, to which extent the goals set for an organisation are fulfilled. A *process performance indicator*

---

[1] For ease of presentation, we exemplify datasets as sets of integers or real numbers, even though in practice, a dataset may contain multiple elements referring to the same numeric value.

(PPI) is a KPI, which is related to a single business process and which is evaluated solely based on the traces recorded during process execution. The *Process Performance Indicator Notation (PPINOT)* [3] is a meta-model for the definition and evaluation of PPIs. At its core, the PPINOT model relies on the composition of measures, i.e., simple, well-defined functions that enable the definition and automated evaluation of more complex PPIs:

> *Base measures* concern a single instance of a process and include event counts (e.g., to count activity executions), timestamp differences between events, the satisfaction of conditions, or aggregations over the events' attribute values.
> *Aggregation measures* are multi-instance measures that combine values from multiple process instances into a single value. PPINOT includes aggregation measures to calculate the minimum, maximum, mean, and sum of a set of input values.
> *Derived measures* are user-defined functions of arbitrary form, applied to a single process instance, or a set thereof.

A PPI defined using the PPI meta-model is represented as a function composition tree. Figure 2 exemplifies such a tree for the PPI 2 of our example from Fig. 1b. It calculates the fraction of rejected insurance claims and received claims. Here, *count* is a base measure; *sum* is an aggregation measure; and the fraction $r(x, y)$ is a derived measure.

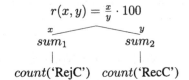

Fig. 2. The function composition tree of PPI 2 in Fig. 1b.

2.3 Differential Privacy

Differential privacy [5] is a privacy guarantee that limits the impact a single element may have on the output of a function f that is computed over a set of elements. Therefore, it limits an adversary to conclude on the set of used input elements (or the presence of a certain input element) from the result of the function. This obfuscation is usually achieved by adding noise, for which the magnitude depends on the sensitivity Δf of function f, i.e., the maximal impact any element $x \in X$ may have on $f(X)$.

A randomized mechanism K is a randomized function that can be applied to a dataset, with $range(K)$ as the set of possible results. Let D_1, D_2 be two neighbouring datasets, i.e., they differ in exactly one element. The randomized mechanism K provides (ϵ, δ)-differential privacy, if the following inequality holds for the probabilities of the function result falling into a sub-range of all possible results:

$$\forall\, S \subseteq range(K): \ P(K(D_1) \in S) \ \leq \ e^\epsilon P(K(D_2) \in S) + \delta$$

Differential privacy enforces an upper bound on the difference in result probabilities of neighbouring datasets. If $\delta = 0$, K is ϵ-differentially private (or ϵ is omitted altogether). Larger ϵ values imply weaker privacy, while the contrary holds true for smaller values.

A specific mechanism to achieve differential privacy is the Laplace mechanism [5]. It adds noise sampled from a Laplace distribution with parameters $\mu = 0$ and $b = \Delta f/\epsilon$ onto $f(X)$. Due to the symmetric nature of the Laplacian and the exponential falloff, results are expected to lie close to $f(X)$.

The symmetrical monotonous falloff of the Laplace mechanism may yield undesirable results, e.g., if values close to the true result have a disproportionally negative effect on the utility. The *exponential mechanism* [15] avoids this problem, by constructing a probability space based on a function $q(D, r)$, which assigns a score to all results $r \in range(K)$ based on the input dataset D. Here, a higher score is assigned to more desirable results. The mechanism then chooses a result $r \in range(K)$ with a probability proportional to $e^{(\epsilon q(D,r))/(2\Delta q)}$, where Δq is the sensitivity of the scoring function, i.e., the maximum change in assigned scores possible for two neighbouring datasets.

Both above mechanisms assume that Δf and Δq are known beforehand. The *sample-and-aggregate framework* [17] drops this assumption by sampling subsets of the input set and evaluating the given function per sample. The obtained results are then combined using a known differentially private aggregator. If function f can be approximated well on small sub-samples, then the results per sample are close to $f(X)$. By aggregating these approximated results using a differentially private mean, i.e., by computing the mean and adding noise drawn from a Laplacian calibrated with $\Delta(mean)$, one achieves a differentially private result for $f(X)$.

3   A Framework for Privacy-Aware PPIs

In this section, we introduce a generic framework for the evaluation of privacy-protected PPIs, thereby addressing the research question raised above. Specifically, we discuss design decisions, as well as the underlying assumptions and limitations of the framework.

Fig. 3. Overview of the framework for privacy-aware PPIs.

The evaluation of PPIs is usually conducted on event data recorded and administered by the process owner. As such, we consider a centralized model and assume that the entity collecting and persistently storing the event data is trustworthy. However, as illustrated in Fig. 3, the actual information demand regarding the PPIs is external to this environment. Following existing models for the flow of data in the analysis of information systems, the evaluation of PPIs is conducted in an untrusted environment [2,14].

Considering the handling of event data in the trusted environment in more detail, the following phases are distinguished. First, the *Data Capture* phase concerns the collection of process-related event data, i.e., whenever an activity has been executed, a respective event is created. Subsequently, the phase of *Primary Use* represents that the captured event data is exploited for the purposes for which it was recorded, which is commonly the proper execution of an individual instance of the process. For example, the recorded events may be used to invoke services, trigger notifications, or schedule tasks for knowledge workers. At the same time, the event data is made persistent, which is modelled as a *Data Storage* phase. The persisted event data may then be used for *Secondary Use*, such as process improvement initiatives conducted by process analysts. Eventually, the event data may be deleted from the persistent storage, in a *Data Deletion* phase. All phases, except the *Secondary Use*, are conducted within the realms of the trusted environment. The *Secondary Use* is part of the untrusted environment, since the data was recorded without having any consent on their use for these applications.

Unlike common primary use of process-related event data, process improvement in general, and the computation of PPIs in particular, aim at generalizing the observations made for individual process instances in some aggregated measures. Thus, in these contexts, the privacy of an involved individual would be compromised, if their contribution to the published aggregate would be revealed to the process analyst. To enable such secondary use without compromising an individual's privacy, we need to prevent a process analyst to assess the impact of a single process instance on the aggregated result. Hence, we consider each trace and the information inferred from it as sensitive information. For example, when a PPI is based on the mean sojourn time of all process instances, we aim to protect the specific sojourn time of each instance.

To achieve this protection, any access to the event data from the untrusted environment must be restricted. Therefore, we propose to design an interface for the evaluation of PPIs, thereby realizing an explicit privacy checkpoint. The interface receives PPI queries stated in PPINOT syntax and answers them while ensuring differential privacy. To this end, the interface fetches relevant event data from the persistent storage based on the scope of the PPI query, calculates the result, and adds noise to the result, before releasing the result to the process analyst. Any such release reduces a privacy budget, which is chosen based on the desired strength of the privacy guarantee to implement. Since the noise added to the result is calibrated based on the specifics of a PPINOT query and the event data retrieved for evaluating it, we ensure ϵ-differential privacy.

By the above, we achieve *plausible deniability*: An analyst cannot distinguish between query results that contain a particular process instance and those that do not.

While access to the event data is restricted, our framework assumes that an analyst has access to models of the respective processes in order to specify the PPIs. Another assumption of our framework is that, for a given time scope, an upper bound for the appearances of an individual in the recorded process instances is known. An individual appearing in n process instances dilutes ϵ-differential privacy by at most $e^{\epsilon n}$. Knowing an upper bound for n, however, enables mitigation of this effect by changing the privacy parameter ϵ accordingly. For our example in Fig. 1, we would need to know the maximal number of claims that can be handled by a knowledge worker within a single month. Lastly, we acknowledge that, while we focus on the evaluation of PPIs, further privacy threats in the trusted environment require additional protection mechanisms [2].

4 Release Mechanisms for Privacy-Aware PPIs

In this section, we instantiate the above framework and introduce a specific realization of the interface for the evaluation of PPIs. We first show how the interface leverages the compositional structure of PPIs defined based on the PPINOT meta-model in Sect. 4.1. We then provide a set of ϵ-differentially private release mechanisms in Sect. 4.2.

4.1 Using Function Composition Trees for Privacy Protection

Our idea is to exploit the compositional nature of PPIs defined in the PPINOT meta-model for privacy protection. Instead of adding noise to the final query result, we introduce noise, with smaller magnitude, at the inner functions of a PPI. Such a compositional approach still guarantees ϵ-differential privacy of the result. At the same time, it enables us to minimize the overall introduced error. Hence, data utility is preserved to a higher degree, which leads to more useful process analysis, under the same privacy guarantees.

We aim to protect the privacy of individuals, of whom personal data is materialized in a trace. Hence, the results of single-instance measures (base or derived measures) shall be protected. However, common PPIs assess the general performance of process execution by aggregating these results in multi-instance measures (aggregation or derived measures), so that guarantees in terms of differential privacy may be given for these measures. This raises the question of selecting a subset of the multi-instance measures for privatization. On the one hand, this selection shall ensure that the results of *all* aforementioned single-instance measures are protected. On the other hand, the selection shall be *minimal* to keep the introduced noise to the absolutely necessary magnitude.

We capture the above intuition with the notion of an admissible set of measures of a PPI. Let (F, ρ) be the function composition tree of a PPI, with F as the set of measures and $\rho : F \rightarrow 2^F$ as the function assigning child measures to measures. With ρ^* as the transitive closure of ρ, a set of measures $F' \subseteq F$ is admissible, if it:

- contains only multi-instance measures: $f \in F'$ implies that $f \in \mathrm{dom}(\rho)$;

- covers all trace-based measures: $\forall\ f \in (F \setminus \mathrm{dom}(\rho)) : \exists\ \mathrm{f}' \in \mathrm{F}' : \mathrm{f} \in \rho^*(\mathrm{f}')$;
- is minimal: $\forall\ F'' \subset F' : \exists\ f \in (F \setminus \mathrm{dom}(\rho)) : \forall\ \mathrm{f}'' \in \mathrm{F}'' : \mathrm{f} \notin \rho^*(\mathrm{f}'')$.

The first condition of an admissable set applies, as differential privacy may only be used for the aggregation of multiple inputs, thus single-instance measures cannot be privatized with the given privacy framework. The second condition ensures, that the selected set of functions privatizes all single-instance derived or base measures, that directly access trace information. Finally, the third condition ensures, that only the minimum amount of noise to achieve ϵ-differential privacy is added onto the intermediate results.

The function composition tree in Fig. 2 has two sets of admissible measures, $\{r\}$ and $\{sum_1, sum_2\}$, which both cover the single-instance measures $count$ ('RejC') and $count$ ('RecC'). In contrast, the set $\{sum_1\}$ is not admissible, as $count$ ('RecC') is not covered (second constraint). Likewise, selecting both base measures or $\{r, sum_1, sum_2\}$ is not admissible, as this would violate the first and third constraint, respectively.

Once a set of admissible measures is selected, the evaluation of the PPI is adapted by incorporating a release mechanism, as defined next, for the chosen measures.

4.2 Release Mechanisms for Multi-Instance Measures

The design of a release mechanism for a specific multi-instance measure is influenced by (i) the ability to assess the domain of input values over which the measure is evaluated, and (ii) the ability to assess the sensitivity of the measure. As for the first aspect, the PPI interface of our framework, see Sect. 3, can rely on an estimation of the respective domain. Here, a simple estimation is based on the minimal and maximal values, $\underline{X}$ and $\overline{X}$, of the dataset X used as input for the measure (i.e., the result of the child measures). The bounds may be extended by constant offsets to account for the fact that the dataset X is merely a sample of an unknown domain. The sensitivity of the measure, in turn, depends on the semantics of the measure. While for the aggregation functions of PPINOT, this sensitivity may be estimated, it is unknown in the general case of derived measures.

Against this background, this section first introduces three release mechanisms for aggregation measures: an instantiation of the Laplace mechanism; an interval-based mechanism based on the traditional exponential mechanism; and a threshold-sensitive mechanism that extends the interval-based one to preserve the significance of a measure related to a threshold. Finally, we discuss how derived measures, in the absence of an estimate of their sensitivity, can be privatized using a sample-and-aggregate strategy.

Laplace Mechanism for Aggregation Measures. Privatization of an aggregation measure can be based on the addition of Laplace noise to the actual result. As mentioned, this requires to estimate the sensitivity Δf of the given aggregation function, i.e., the maximal impact any element $x \in X$ may have on $f(X)$.

For the aggregation functions of the PPINOT meta-model, the sensitivity is derived as $\Delta(min) = \Delta(max) = |\overline{X} - \underline{X}|$, $\Delta(sum) = \overline{X}$ and $\Delta(mean) = |\overline{X} - \underline{X}|/|X|$. Based thereon, noise from a Laplacian (with parameters $\mu = 0$ and $b = \Delta f/\epsilon$, see Sect. 2.3) is added to $f(X)$.

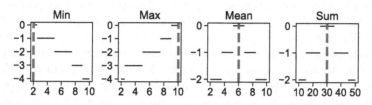

Fig. 4. Intervals and scores for the aggregation functions for dataset $X = \{2, 3, 7, 8, 10\}$.

Since the sensitivity Δf directly influences the magnitude of added noise, for *mean* measures, this mechanism potentially leaks information about the number $|X|$ of process instances (and hence, individuals) within the given scope. An adversary may conclude on the difference $|\overline{X} - \underline{X}|$ based on the magnitude of noise from another PPI incorporating a *min* or *max* measure and, based thereon, derive $|X|$ from the magnitude of noise in a PPI with a *mean* measure. However, in practice, $|X|$ may be revealed explicitly to enable a process analyst to assess the statistical reliability of the PPI result.

Interval-based Mechanism for Aggregation Measures. The drawback of the Laplace mechanism to privatize aggregation measures is the inherently high sensitivity, which scales linearly with the domain of input values. Our idea, therefore, is to group similar result values into intervals and score them using the exponential mechanism. This way, we obtain a release mechanism with a score function sensitivity $\Delta q = 1$, which ultimately leads to a smaller magnitude of noise for large domains of input values.

To realize this idea, our interval-based release mechanisms consists of three phases:

(1) *Interval creation:* We partition the domain and the range of the aggregation function into a set of intervals.
(2) *Interval probability construction:* Scores are assigned to these intervals, which are then converted to result probabilities.
(3) *Result sampling:* Using these probabilities, an interval is chosen as the output interval, from which the result value is sampled.

The *interval creation* is based on the range of the aggregation function, given as $range(f(X)) = (\underline{X}, \overline{X})$ for $f \in \{min, max, mean\}$ and $range(f(X)) = (\underline{X} \cdot |X|, \overline{X} \cdot |X|)$ for $f = sum$. This range is split into non-overlapping intervals $I = \{I_0, \ldots, I_n\}$, with $I_0 \cap \ldots \cap I_n = \emptyset$ and $I_0 \cup \ldots \cup I_n = range(f(X))$. Let $\tau(x_i, x_j) = (x_i + x_j)/2$ be the mean of x_i, x_j and let I_f be the interval containing the result value, i.e. $f(X) \in I_f$. For *mean* and *sum*, the range of $f(X)$ is divided into evenly spaced intervals of size Δf, so that $f(X) = \tau(\underline{I_f}, \overline{I_f})$ is the mean of its containing interval. For *min* and *max*, the range of $f(X)$ is divided into n intervals of different size, for which the boundaries are the means of neighbouring values $\tau(x_i, x_{i+1})$ with $x_i, x_{i+1} \in X$.

Figure 4 exemplifies the intervals for a dataset $X = \{2, 3, 7, 8, 10\}$. For *min* and *max*, the interval boundaries are 2.5, 5, 7.5, and 9. For *mean* and *sum*, the intervals have size $\Delta f = 1.6$ and $\Delta f = 10$, and are centred around $mean(X) = 6$ and $sum(X) = 30$.

The *interval probability construction* relies on a scoring function that assigns higher scores to intervals that are closer to the interval containing $f(X)$. Let $I_1, \ldots, I_n$ be the intervals in the order induced by $\leq$ over their boundaries, and let $1 \leq k \leq n$ be the index of interval I_f containing the result value. Then, the score for each interval I_i is defined as $q(i) = -|k - i|$, as illustrated in Fig. 4 for the example. Here, intervals, that lie closer to $f(X)$, denoted by the blue dashed lines, are scored higher, than those further away. Since each interval I_i corresponds to a set of potential result values, we incorporate the size of this set in the probability computation. Hence, the probability for I_i is defined as:

$$P(I_i) = \frac{|I_i| \cdot e^{(\epsilon \cdot q(i)/2 \cdot \Delta q)}}{\Sigma_{1 \leq j \leq n} |I_j| \cdot e^{(\epsilon \cdot q(j)/2 \cdot \Delta q)}}$$

Result sampling chooses one interval based on their probabilities. From this interval one specific value is drawn based on a uniform distribution over all interval values.

Threshold-Sensitive Mechanism for Aggregation Measures. The interval-based mechanism is problematic, if a PPI is tested against a threshold, as often done in practice. Consider the dataset X and assume that the *sum* function is the root of a PPI's function composition tree, i.e., $f(X) = 30$ as shown in Fig. 4. Assume that it is important whether the PPI is less or equal than 30. Then, adding noise may change the actual interpretation of the PPI, since the release mechanism will sometimes publish values larger than 30.

To mitigate this effect, we present a threshold-sensitive release mechanism that extends the previous mechanism in terms of *interval creation* and *interval probability construction*. Let χ be a Boolean function formalizing a threshold, e.g., $\chi(x) = x \leq 30$. Then, the Boolean predicate $\phi(x, f(X), \chi) \Leftrightarrow \chi(x) \equiv \chi(f(X))$ describes, whether the possible result value $x \in range(f(X))$ leads to the same outcome of χ as the true result $f(X)$. For our example, $\phi(20, 30, \chi)$ holds true ($20 \leq 30$ and $30 \leq 30$), whereas $\phi(40, 30, \chi)$ is false ($40 \not\leq 30$, but $30 \leq 30$).

Using this predicate, we adapt the intervals $I = I_1, \ldots, I_n$ obtained during *interval creation*, so that interval boundaries coincide with changes in ϕ. Let $B(\phi)$ be the boundary values of ϕ, i.e., the values $x \in range(f(X))$ with $\lim_{y<x,y \to x} \phi(y, f(X), \chi) \neq \lim_{y>x,y \to x} \phi(y, f(X), \chi)$. For our example, we arrive at $B(\phi) = \{30\}$. Based thereon, we split each interval I_i containing a boundary value $b \in B(\phi)$ into two new intervals $(\underline{I_i}, b), (b, \overline{I_i})$. Hence, each interval contains only values that share the outcome of the Boolean function χ. In our example, the interval $(25, 35)$ is split into $(25, 30)$ and $(30, 35)$, as shown in Fig. 5.

Finally, the scoring function used for *interval probability construction* is adapted. Let $d(i)$ be the minimal inter-interval-distance of interval I_i to any other interval I_j with $\phi(x, f(X), \chi) \neq \phi(y, f(X), \chi)$ for all $\underline{I_i} \leq x \leq \overline{I_i}$ and $I_j \leq y \leq \overline{I_j}$. As before, let k be the index of interval I_f containing the result value. Then, scores assigned to intervals that preserve the outcome of the Boolean function χ remain unchanged. For all other intervals I_i, the score is reduced by $\xi \cdot d(i)$, i.e., by the distance to the closest interval preserving the outcome multiplied by a falloff factor $\xi \in \mathbb{N}$. The adapted scoring function is defined as:

$$q(i) = \begin{cases} -|k - i| & \text{if } \phi(x, f(X), \chi) \text{ for all } \underline{I_i} \leq x \leq \overline{I_i}, \\ -|k - i| - \xi \cdot d(i) & \text{otherwise.} \end{cases}$$

Figure 5 Illustrates the adapted scores for our running example, using $\xi = 3$. The scores of the right-most three intervals are reduced, as all of their values lead to a different outcome compared to the true result, $f(X) = 30$, when testing against $\chi(x) = x \leq 30$.

We obtain $d(4) = 1, d(5) = 2$, and $d(6) = 3$ for those intervals, given that the third interval $(25, 30)$ is the closest one retaining ϕ to any of those three. Thus, we arrive at $q(4) = -4, q(5) = -8$, and $q(6) = -12$. As the largest possible change in scores assigned to a possible result value in neighbouring input sets is never larger than ξ and as the interval sizes are determined based on Δf, we conclude that $\Delta q = \xi$.

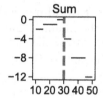

Fig. 5. Adapted intervals and scores.

Sample-and-aggregate Mechanism for Derived Measures. Since the sensitivity of a derived multi-instance measures is unknown in the general case, the above mechanisms are not applicable. However, many derived measures may be approximated using small samples, since their range is often independent of the domain of their input values. Functions that compute a normalized result are an example of this class of measures. For instance, the derived measure that denotes the root of the function composition tree of the example in Fig. 2 yields a percentage, i.e., it is normalized to 0% to 100%. For such measures, the sample-and-aggregate-framework mentioned in Sect. 2.3 may be instantiated. That is, the actual result $f(X)$ is computed on n partitions of X. The obtained results per sample are then aggregated using a differentially private mean function to achieve privatization of the derived measure.

5   Experimental Evaluation

To assess the feasability and utility of the proposed approach, we realized the PPI interface on top of an existing PPINOT implementation.[2] We conducted controlled experiments using synthetic data (Sect. 5.1) and a case study with the

---

[2] https://mvnrepository.com/artifact/es.us.isa.ppinot/ppinot-model.

Sepsis Cases log (Sect. 5.2). The latter compares the proposed tree-based privatization with the direct evaluation of PPIs on logs that have been anonymized with the PRIPEL framework [10] beforehand. Our implementation and evaluation scripts are publicly available.[3]

5.1 Controlled Experiments

In a first series of experiments, we assessed the impact of different properties of the dataset X used as input. Specifically, we consider the impact of the estimation of the domain of input values, its size and underlying value distribution, and the privacy parameter ϵ. We sampled sets of 10, 50, 100, and 200 random values from a Gaussian distribution, a Pareto distribution, and a Poisson distribution. We chose these distributions, as they are often observed in event data recorded by business processes. We performed 200 runs per experiment. Unless noted otherwise, the input domain is estimated using the minimal and maximal element of X, the dataset comprises 200 values drawn from a Gaussian distribution, and the privacy parameter is set as $\epsilon = 0.1$.

Input Boundary Estimation. First, we compare the boundary estimation using the minimal and maximal elements in X with extensions of these boundaries by 15% and 30% at either boundary. The results for the interval-based mechanism, see Fig. 6, show that an extension of the domain increases the introduced magnitude of noise for all functions due to an increase in sensitivity. These observations are confirmed for the Laplace mechanism. Yet, for *min* and *max*, there is a shift of the expected result towards the true result $f(X)$ (denoted by the blue line). The reason is that, without the extension, $f(X)$ coincides with boundary values of X. The extension increases the size of the interval containing $f(X)$, which increases the probability of this interval to be chosen.

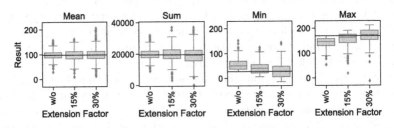

Fig. 6. Impact of the input boundary estimation on the results.

Input Size and Distribution. For the Laplace and interval-based mechanisms, we identify a dependency of Δf on the input size for *mean* functions. This dependency coincides with smaller noise magnitudes for larger input sizes, as illustrated in Fig. 7.

---

[3] https://github.com/Martin-Bauer/privacy-aware-ppinot.

These trends were confirmed for the interval-based mechanism for *min* and *max*. Here, the increased number of intervals and a more fine-grained differentiation between result values leads to higher utility, i.e., the expected result is close to the actual one. Yet, the trends are only visible for distributions with small inter-value distances, such as the Gaussian. For the Pareto- and Poisson-distributions,

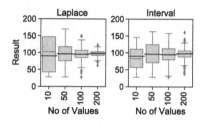

Fig. 7. Impact of the cardinality of the dataset X on the results for *mean*.

there was a significant reduction in utility for larger inputs using *max*. These distributions preserve most of their probability mass on the smaller values, This inadvertently results in the creation of disproportionally large intervals and the same output probability for large portions of the output space.

Epsilon. The results obtained when changing the privacy parameter ϵ are shown in Fig. 8a for *mean*. Both the Laplace and interval-based mechanism show a similar increase in the introduced noise. The Laplace mechanism yields better results for larger ϵ.

For *min* and *max*, however, the interval-based mechanism clearly outperforms the Laplace mechanism for all values of ϵ, see Fig. 8b for the maximum function. Here, the large sensitivity for the Laplace mechanism completely obfuscates the actual result $f(X)$, rendering the mechanism inappropriate for these functions.

Threshold-sensitive Mechanism. For the extension of the interval-based mechanism that aims to preserve the significance for thresholds, the general trends remain unaffected. However, the threshold-sensitive mechanism shifts large portions of the probability mass of the output space, as shown in Fig. 9. Here, the threshold to preserve is $\phi(x) : x < f(X) \pm y$, with y being 100 for *sum* and 10 for the other aggregation functions. For comparison, the results for the interval-based mechanism without threshold preservation are also given. There is a clear shift in output probabilities, depending on which values preserve the same properties as $f(X)$. Note that the results should not be interpreted in absolute terms, but serve as a binary indicator regarding the threshold.

Derived Measures. The sample-and-aggregate mechanism for derived measures mirrored the trends of the Laplace mechanism for *mean*. This is expected since the mechanism is based on the privatized mean. Yet, due to the use of m buckets of size n, the magnitude of noise is larger. The mechanism requires m times as many values in X to achieve the same sensitivity as the mechanism for the *mean*. Since the mean is computed using n values per bucket, the result estimation is accurate only for large datasets.

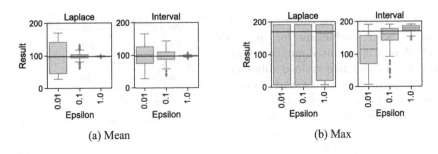

(a) Mean   (b) Max

Fig. 8. Sensitivity of mean and maximum function towards ϵ.

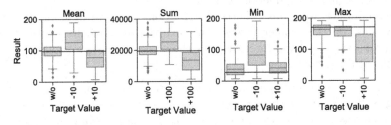

Fig. 9. Results for the threshold-sensitive mechanism using differing result thresholds.

5.2   Case Study: Process for Sepsis Cases

To explore how the presented mechanisms perform in a real-world application, we conducted a study using the Sepsis Cases log. As part of that, we compare our approach to a state-of-the-art privatization approach for event logs. That is, we evaluated the same PPIs non-anonymously using logs that have been anonymized with PRIPEL [10]. The PPIs used in our case study were created based on criteria and guidelines presented in [12,21] and are listed in Table 1, together with the employed mechanism used for privatization. Some concern the lengths of stays and treatments for patients (PPI 1–4), wile others target the adherence to treatment guidelines (PPI 5–6). To illustrate the behaviour of our release mechanism, we calculated each PPI 10 times using $\epsilon = 0.1$ and report aggregate values. While results for all PPIs are available online, due to space constraints, we here focus on PPI 1 and PPI 6, see Fig. 10 and Fig. 11, respectively.

For PPIs 1 to 3, we were able to reconstruct the general trends of the non-privatized analysis (exemplified for PPI 1 in Fig. 10). Yet, we also observed specific months with high result variances. For PPI 1 and 2 (*mean* functions), the variance stems from the large domain of input values, resulting in higher sensitivities. For PPI 3 (*max* function), variances were relatively small, except for one month, which represents a notable outlier.

The results obtained with our framework are in sharp contrast to those achieved when privatizing the event log with PRIPEL before computing the PPIs in a regular manner. As shown in Fig. 10 (right), the latter approach

Table 1. PPIs defined for the Sepsis Cases log.

ID	Measure	Target values	Scope	Mechanism
1:	Avg waiting time until admission	<24 h	Monthly	Mean - Interval
2:	Avg length of stay	<30 days	Monthly	Mean - Interval
3:	Max length of stay	<35 days	Monthly	Max - Interval
4:	Returning patient within 28 days	<5%	Monthly	Sum - Laplace
5:	Antibiotics within one hour	>95%	Monthly	Sum - Laplace
6:	Lactic acid test within three hours	>95%	Monthly	Sum - Laplace

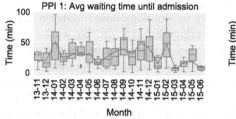 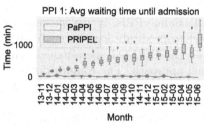

Fig. 10. Evaluation results for PPI1, only PaPPI (left), and PaPPI and PRIPEL (right).

accumulates an error over the recorded time period. The steadily increasing deviation from the true value is caused by traces that represent outlier behaviour, which was artificially created by PRIPEL.

PPIs 4 to 6 were calculated using privatized *sum* functions. Due to the relatively low number of traces recorded per month, the application of the sample-and-aggregate-framework for the calculation of the final percentage value led to worse results. Here, the buckets contained not enough values to approximate the true result well. However, using privatized *sum* functions, the results for PPIs 4 to 6 follow the general trends of

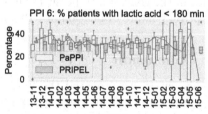

Fig. 11. Evaluation Results of PPI6

the true values, see Fig. 11 for PPI 6. Similarly, also the computation based on logs privatized with PRIPEL yields comparable results. In months, in which few traces are selected for a PPI, e.g., at the beginning and end of the covered time period, the variance is notably larger for our proposed framework, an effect that is avoided by the approach based on event log privatization.

Turning to research question *RQ3*, our results provide evidence that the proposed framework enables the computation of privacy-aware PPIs that mirror the general trends of their true values. Only for time periods, in which the PPI computation is based solely on a few traces, our framework does not yield sensible results. Thus, given a sufficiently large number of traces as the basis for the evaluation of PPIs, we can expect our framework to retain the trends.

6 Related Work

For a general overview of privacy-preserving data mining, as mentioned in Sect. 1, we refer to [16] and [20]. However, data anonymization commonly leads to a trade-off between the strength of a privacy guarantee and a loss in data utility. This calls for anonymization schemes that minimize the accuracy loss of PPI queries, so that management may still assess the fulfilment of operational goals, while the privacy of involved individuals is protected.

To define PPIs, it was suggested to rely on ontology-based systems [24] or resort to predicate logic to enable formal verification [18]. In this work, we followed the PPINOT meta-model, which is very expressive due to its compositional approach. The compositionality is also the reason why we opted for the adoption of differential privacy in our approach. Other privacy models include k-anonymity [22] and its derivatives [9,11], which statically mask recorded data points. Yet, since the evaluation of PPIs is driven by queries and processes continuously record data, these techniques are not suitable.

In the context of data-driven business process analysis, the re-identification risk related to event data was highlighted empirically in [23]. To mitigate this risk, various directions have been followed, including the addition of noise to occurrence frequencies of activities in event logs [13], transformations of logs to ensure k-anonymity or t-closeness before publishing them [8,19], and the adoption of secure multi-party computation [6]. However, since these approaches focus on the control-flow perspective of processes, they cannot be employed for the privacy-aware evaluation of PPIs in the general case.

7 Conclusion

In this paper, we proposed the first approach to privacy-aware evaluation of process performance indicators based on event logs recorded during the execution of business processes. We presented a generic framework that includes an explicit interface to serve as the single point of access for PPI evaluation. In addition, for PPIs that are defined following the PPINOT meta-model, we showed how to design release mechanisms that ensure ϵ-differential privacy. We evaluated our mechanisms on both synthetic data and in a case study using the Sepsis Cases log. The results highlight the feasibility of our approach, given that a sufficiently large number of process executions is available.

In future work, we aim to extend the evaluation of the mechanisms, in order to recommend which functions to privatize, for a given function tree. This would aid process analysts in receiving PPI results, with minimal quality loss.

References

1. Arasu, A., et al.: STREAM: the Stanford data stream management system. Data Stream Management. DSA, pp. 317–336. Springer, Heidelberg (2016). https://doi.org/10.1007/978-3-540-28608-0_16
2. D'Acquisto, G., Domingo-Ferrer, J., Kikiras, P., Torra, V., de Montjoye, Y., Bourka, A.: Privacy by design in big data: an overview of privacy enhancing technologies in the era of big data analytics. CoRR abs/1512.06000 (2015). http://arxiv.org/abs/1512.06000
3. del-Río-Ortega, A., Resinas, M., Cabanillas, C., Cortés, A.R.: On the definition and design-time analysis of process performance indicators. Inf. Syst. 38(4), 470–490 (2013)
4. Dumas, M., Rosa, M.L., Mendling, J., Reijers, H.A.: Fundamentals of Business Process Management, 2nd edn. Springer, Berlin (2018). https://doi.org/10.1007/978-3-662-56509-4
5. Dwork, C.: Differential privacy. In: Automata, Languages and Programming, pp. 1–12 (2006)
6. Elkoumy, G., Fahrenkrog-Petersen, S.A., Dumas, M., Laud, P., Pankova, A., Weidlich, M.: Secure multi-party computation for inter-organizational process mining. In: Nurcan, S., Reinhartz-Berger, I., Soffer, P., Zdravkovic, J. (eds.) BPMDS/EMMSAD -2020. LNBIP, vol. 387, pp. 166–181. Springer, Cham (2020). https://doi.org/10.1007/978-3-030-49418-6_11
7. European Commission: A new era for data protection in the EU. https://ec.europa.eu/commission/sites/beta-political/files/data-protection-factsheet-changes_en.pdf. Accessed 1 Dec 2020
8. Fahrenkrog-Petersen, S.A., van der Aa, H., Weidlich, M.: PRETSA: event log sanitization for privacy-aware process discovery. In: ICPM, pp. 1–8. IEEE (2019)
9. Li, N., Li, T., Venkatasubramanian, S.: T-closeness: Privacy beyond k-anonymity and l-diversity. In: ICDE. IEEE (2007)
10. Fahrenkrog-Petersen, S.A., van der Aa, H., Weidlich, M.: PRIPEL: privacy-preserving event log publishing including contextual information. In: Fahland, D., Ghidini, C., Becker, J., Dumas, M. (eds.) BPM 2020. LNCS, vol. 12168, pp. 111–128. Springer, Cham (2020). https://doi.org/10.1007/978-3-030-58666-9_7
11. Machanavajjhala, A., Kifer, D., Gehrke, J., Venkitasubramaniam, M.: L-diversity: privacy beyond k-anonymity. ACM Trans. Knowl. Discov. Data 1(1), 3 (2007)
12. Mannhardt, F., Blinde, D.: Analyzing the trajectories of patients with sepsis using process mining. In: BPMDS/EMMSAD/EMISA. CEUR Workshop Proceedings, vol. 1859, pp. 72–80. CEUR-WS.org (2017)
13. Mannhardt, F., Koschmider, A., Baracaldo, N., Weidlich, M., Michael, J.: Privacy-preserving process mining - differential privacy for event logs. Bus. Inf. Syst. Eng. 61(5), 595–614 (2019)
14. Mannhardt, F., Petersen, S.A., Oliveira, M.F.: Privacy challenges for process mining in human-centered industrial environments. In: 14th International Conference on Intelligent Environments, IE, pp. 64–71 (2018)
15. McSherry, F., Talwar, K.: Mechanism design via differential privacy. In: FOCS, pp. 94–103. IEEE (2007)
16. Mendes, R., Vilela, J.: Privacy-preserving data mining: methods, metrics and applications. IEEE Access, p. 1 (2017)
17. Nissim, K., Raskhodnikova, S., Smith, A.: Smooth sensitivity and sampling in private data analysis. In: STOC. ACM (2007)

18. Popova, V., Sharpanskykh, A.: Modeling organizational performance indicators. Inf. Syst. **35**(4), 505–527 (2010)

19. Rafiei, M., Wagner, M., van der Aalst, W.M.P.: TLKC-privacy model for process mining. In: RCIS, pp. 398–416 (2020)

20. Aldeen, Y.A.A.S., Salleh, M., Razzaque, M.A.: A comprehensive review on privacy preserving data mining. SpringerPlus **4**(1), 1–36 (2015). https://doi.org/10.1186/s40064-015-1481-x

21. Stefanini, A., Aloini, D., Benevento, E., Dulmin, R., Mininno, V.: Performance analysis in emergency departments: a data-driven approach. Measuring Bus. Excellence **22**(2), 130–145 (2018)

22. Sweeney, L.: k-anonymity: a model for protecting privacy. IEEE Secur. Priv. **10**, 1–14 (2002)

23. von Voigt, S.N., et al.: Quantifying the re-identification risk of event logs for process mining. In: Dustdar, S., Yu, E., Salinesi, C., Rieu, D., Pant, V. (eds.) CAiSE 2020. LNCS, vol. 12127, pp. 252–267. Springer, Cham (2020). https://doi.org/10.1007/978-3-030-49435-3_16

24. Wetzstein, B., Ma, Z., Leymann, F.: Towards measuring key performance indicators of semantic business processes. In: Abramowicz, W., Fensel, D. (eds.) BIS 2008. LNBIP, vol. 7, pp. 227–238. Springer, Heidelberg (2008). https://doi.org/10.1007/978-3-540-79396-0_20

P-SGD: A Stochastic Gradient Descent Solution for Privacy-Preserving During Protection Transitions

Karam Bou-Chaaya[1]([✉]), Richard Chbeir[1], Mahmoud Barhamgi[2],
Philippe Arnould[3], and Djamal Benslimane[2]

[1] Universite de Pau et des Pays de l'Adour, E2S UPPA, LIUPPA, Anglet, France
{karam.bou-chaaya,richard.chbeir}@univ-pau.fr
[2] LIRIS Laboratory, Claude Bernard Lyon1 University, Lyon, France
{mahmoud.barhamgi,djamal.benslimane}@univ-lyon1.fr
[3] Universite de Pau et des Pays de l'Adour, E2S UPPA, LIUPPA,
Mont-de-Marsan, France
philippe.arnould@univ-pau.fr

Abstract. Advances in privacy-enhancing technologies, such as context-aware and personalized privacy models, have paved the way for successful management of the data utility-privacy trade-off. However, significantly lowering the level of data protection when balancing utility-privacy to meet the individual's needs makes subsequent protected data more precise. This increases the adversary's ability to reveal the real values of the previous correlated data that needed more protection, making existing privacy models vulnerable to inference attacks. To overcome this problem, we propose in this paper a stochastic gradient descent solution for privacy-preserving during protection transitions, denoted P-SGD. The goal of this solution is to minimize the precision gap between sequential data when downshifting the protection by the privacy model. P-SGD intervenes at the protection descent phase and performs an iterative process that measures data dependencies, and gradually reduces protection accordingly until the desired protection level is reached. It considers also possible changes in protection functions and studies their impact on the protection descent rate. We validated our proposal and evaluated its performance. The results show that P-SGD is fast, scalable, and maintains low computational and storage complexity.

Keywords: Data privacy · Data protection transitions · Stochastic gradient descent methods · Context-awareness · Internet of Things

1 Introduction

The rapid expansion of cyber-physical systems and the technological advances in sensing technologies and data mining techniques have contributed to the tremendous development of smart people-driven applications. These applications tend

© Springer Nature Switzerland AG 2021
M. La Rosa et al. (Eds.): CAiSE 2021, LNCS 12751, pp. 37–53, 2021.
https://doi.org/10.1007/978-3-030-79382-1_3

to reshape the lives of people in many domains by providing them with advanced services (e.g., increasing comfort, monitoring patients and elderlies). Delivering such services requires collecting and processing massive amounts of data (e.g., location data, health data) to discover underlying patterns and trends. However, privacy concerns hinder the wider use of these data especially as data processing may give rise to serious privacy risks for individuals, such as disclosing their health conditions, habits and daily activities [4]. Consequently, balancing the trade-off between data utility and privacy protection has been subject to intense study in recent years [2,5,6,15,16]. Current context-aware privacy solutions [2,13,16,20] and personalized privacy solutions [6,17,24] aim to maximize the usefulness of data by optimizing the level of protection according to data sensitivity in the current context or/and user preferences. However, these solutions do not consider the effect of temporal correlations between sequential data values on privacy loss. They assign the appropriate level of protection to the data according to the user's context (e.g., privacy risks involved) or/and preferences. Nonetheless, continuously balancing the protection levels without considering previous protection patterns may entail temporal privacy leakage. In particular, this leakage occurs when the protection level significantly decreases, which widens the precision gap between prior/subsequent correlated data and makes subsequent data more precise. The large gap in precision improves the capabilities of an adversary, when using advanced mining techniques, to reveal the real values of prior data pieces that required more protection. This makes existing privacy-preserving solutions vulnerable to data inference attacks. A data inference attack is a data mining attack in which adversaries are capable of estimating/inferring real values of protected data with high confidence. One of the possible solutions to address this vulnerability is to integrate a gradient descent mechanism at the protection descent phase. This helps to reduce the precision gap between sequential protected data when downshifting the protection level. Gradient descent is a general paradigm that underlies algorithms for solving optimization problems [8]. It has been widely applied to many fields such as location-based applications for predicting moving destination [23], differential privacy [18], and personalized privacy [14]. Nonetheless, to the best of our knowledge, there has not been any work on securing data protection transitions using gradient descent.

The implementation of a gradual descent process for the protection level is challenging, as the corresponding deviation rate depends on several dynamic factors. First, the temporal correlations between sequential data values, which may vary from sequence to sequence as the data can be generated in regular or irregular time series. Second, the dynamicity of the protection function chosen by the system to be executed on data values. In fact, the system can change the data protection function at the protection transition phases with a view to improving protection, reducing the cost of protection (i.e., computational costs), or due to errors in function operations. However, the protection functions can share similarities in their operations (e.g., generalization and random-noise functions add noise to the real value of data), making it important to consider their dependence and its impact on the protection deviation rate. What makes it more challenging is the need for a fast and low complex solution, which makes it re-usable by various privacy models, including those offering real-time protection, and operational even for resource-constrained devices. Finally, the solution should follow a non-deterministic descent to avoid revealing the deviation rate by adversaries in case of repeated descent patterns.

To answer these challenges, this paper introduces P-SGD, a stochastic gradient descent solution for privacy-preserving during protection transitions. P-SGD empowers existing privacy models against data inference attacks, by minimizing the precision gaps of sequential protected data values during the protection descent phase. It follows an iterative process to identify the appropriate protection level to be assigned to each transitional data until the targeted level is reached. Computed protection levels consider the temporal dependencies between data values and the dependencies between protection functions (in case of change). Our solution is generic (i.e., it handles attributes with different data types and formats), and supports simultaneous reasoning over multiple attributes. We validated our proposal and evaluated its performance. Results show that P-SGD is fast, scalable, and maintains low computational and storage complexity.

The rest of the paper is organized as follows. Section 2 presents the motivating scenario. Section 3 details our proposal and provides formal definitions of the key terms used. Section 4 outlines the experiments and results. Section 5 discusses existing privacy models and data protection functions. Finally, Sect. 6 concludes the paper and discusses future research directions.

2 Motivating Scenario

To motivate our proposal, we investigate a real-life scenario of Alice, a cancer patient who shares her location data with a remote monitoring platform for cancer care. Alice shares also her location data with several other service providers through applications and social media platforms to benefit from their services (e.g., Facebook, Google Maps). The trust relationship between Alice and the providers may vary greatly due to many factors, such as the privacy risks associated with the sharing of data, the sensitivity of her context (e.g., private meeting), or the third parties with whom her data is communicated. Alice may therefore want to protect her privacy in some situations but without completely losing associated services. To do so, she uses a context-aware privacy-preserving system that optimizes the data protection according to her contexts and preferences. Consider that Alice has a medical appointment at the Belharra-Ramsay center for her cancer treatment. She takes the road from her home to the treatment center. However, locating Alice in the cancer center can entail the disclosure of her health conditions, which involves privacy concerns for her. Accordingly, assume that the privacy system increases data protection to 80% when Alice arrives at the center, and then shifts the level of protection to 20% when she leaves. The system protects sensed data using a generalization-based protection function. In the following, three cases are considered to highlight the impact of the second protection transition phase (from 80% to 20%) on privacy loss.

In case-1, represented in Fig. 1, the system shifts the level of protection to 20% and continues to perform the same protection function on generated data (i.e., the generalization function). The location data are generated at a regular time interval. When processing and analyzing protected data values, an adversary can notice a significant gap in the level of precision between transitional/correlated data (see in Fig. 1). The precision gap limits the range for estimating previous user locations where protection was critical (e.g., Alice's presence in the medical center), which entails privacy problems. This consequently underlines the need for a gradual descent in the protection level in order to overcome vulnerabilities that may arise during protection transitions.

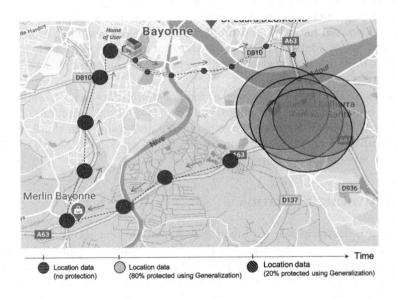

Fig. 1. Case-1

As previously mentioned in Sect. 1, the system can change the protection function to be executed on data at the protection transition phase. In case-2, illustrated in Fig. 2, the system changes the function when the protection level shifts to 20%, and adopts a randomization-based function that adds random noise to the real location positions. However, the generalization and randomization functions share similarities. They both add noise to the data, which makes them dependent, and the privacy issues related to lowering the protection level persist. This highlights the need to examine dependencies between protection functions and their impact on the protection deviation rate.

In the previous two cases we considered regular time series data. However, data can be also collected in irregular time series, i.e., the data

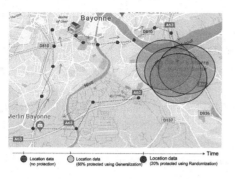

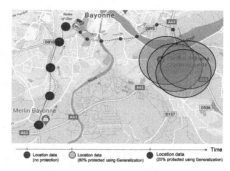

Fig. 2. Case-2   Fig. 3. Case-3

collected follow a temporal sequence, but the measurements may not occur at regular time intervals. For instance, case-3 assumes that after leaving the medical center, the system has stopped sharing (protected) location data only for a specific time interval due to loss of connectivity with the GPS sensor (cf. Fig. 3). When data sharing started again, the temporal distance between the last data shared and the current one has already exceeded the temporal granularity of the attribute (i.e., location). The two data pieces are thus independent and the adversary will not be able to link previous and subsequent location patterns. It is thereby important to measure the temporal correlations between sequential data and study its impact on data protection. Consequently, building up the gradient descent solution requires addressing the following challenges:

- **Challenge 1.** *Data Dependency:* How to track and measure the temporal dependencies of sequential data values and study their impact on the protection descent rate?
- **Challenge 2.** *Protection Function Dependency:* How to compute the similarity between transitional protection functions (in case of change) and adjust the downshifting mechanism accordingly?
- **Challenge 3.** *Non-deterministic Solution:* The protection level can fluctuate between two same values for several transitions. This may entail the disclosure of the deviation rate by adversaries if the executed process is deterministic (cf. Fig. 4). The solution should therefore be non-deterministic to overcome the vulnerabilities arising from repeated transition patterns.
- **Challenge 4.** *Scalability & Efficiency:* The solution must be scalable, i.e., handles simultaneous reasoning over an increasing number of attributes. Moreover, it should maintain computational and storage efficiency, which increases its re-usability to also include privacy models subject to real-time constraints, and makes it operational on a variety of devices, including those with limited resources.

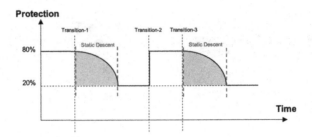

Fig. 4. Repeated protection transition patterns

3   P-SGD Proposal

Current privacy-preserving models, such as context-aware and personalized privacy models, enable data protection variation according to the individual's needs or/and situations (e.g., privacy risks involved in the data sharing, preferences) in order to optimize the balancing of data utility-privacy. However, these models perform direct shifting of the data protection level, which may lead in certain cases to temporal privacy leakage due to data correlations. In particular, the data privacy leakage occurs when significantly decreasing the level of protection, creating a significant gap in the level of precision between previous and subsequent data. This increases the ability of an adversary to reveal the real values of previous correlated data that needed more protection, entailing privacy concerns for the individual. To overcome this vulnerability, we propose P-SGD, a privacy-based stochastic gradient descent solution that operates during protection descent phases to minimize precision gaps between sequential protected data values. P-SGD addresses the challenges mentioned in Sect. 2. It features an iterative protection descent process that identifies the appropriate level of protection to be assigned to each data prior to its release until the final level is reached (i.e., the lowest desired level). The proposed solution supports attribute diversity, i.e., it handles attributes with different data types and formats (e.g., scalar data such as location and temperature data, as well as multimedia data such as camera recordings). This makes it therefore generic and compatible with numerous existing privacy models in different application domains. The P-SGD process can be plugged into the privacy model, as shown in Fig. 5, to provide an additional layer of protection against inference attacks. Let u denotes the user (or data subject as defined by the General Data Protection Regulation [21]). In what follows, we formally define an *attribute* and a *data node*.

Definition 1. (Attribute). Let A be the **set of spatio-temporal attributes** $\{a_1, a_2, ..., a_n\}$ shared by u with data consumers. $a \in A$ is defined as follows:

$$a : \langle\ desc\ ;\ access\ ;\ source\ ;\ D_{consumer}\ ;\ \tau\ ;\ Log\ \rangle\ , \text{ where:}$$

- *desc* is the textual description of a (e.g., location, heart-rate, temperature)
- *access* $\in \{r; r/w\}$ denotes the access rights of the privacy model to the data values of a, which can be read or read/write
- *source* $\in DN$ is a *data node* (cf. Definition 2) expressing the data source from which the data of a is collected (e.g., GPS sensor)

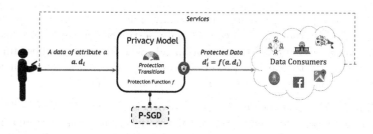

Fig. 5. Integration of P-SGD

- $D_{consumer}$ is the set of data consumers (i.e., service providers and third parties) with whom a is shared, such that:

$$D_{consumer} = \{ dc_1 ; dc_2 ; ... ; dc_n \} \cup \{\bot\}, \text{ where:}$$

- $dc_i \in DN$ is a *data node* expressing a data consumer
- $D_{consumer} = \varnothing$ indicates that data consumers are unknown
- $D_{consumer} = \{\bot\}$ denotes that a is a public attribute
- τ denotes the standard time period during which two data values of a are said to be time-dependent
- $Log = \{\langle d ; M \rangle\}$ is the set of data values of a where:
  - d denotes the data value
  - M is the set of metadata characterizing d (e.g., time/location of capture, data-type, format)   ∎

Definition 2. (Data Node). Let DN be the set of source/destination *data nodes* $\{n_1, ..., n_n\}$. Source nodes are data sources from which the data is collected. Destination nodes are data consumers with whom the data is shared.

$$\forall n \in DN, n : \langle desc ; id \rangle, \text{ where:}$$

- $desc$ is the textual description of n (e.g., gps-sensor, health-provider)
- id is the identity of n, expressed as a uniform resource identifier (URI)   ∎

Example 1. The location attribute shared by Alice can be represented as follows:

- a_1 : $\langle desc$: Location ; $access$: r/w ; $source$: sensor-1 ; $D_{consumer} = \{prov\text{-}1\}$; t_{gran} : 86400 ; t_{gen} : 1 ; $Log = \{\langle$ (-33.0534, 16.3103) ; $M_1\rangle\}\rangle$
- *sensor-1:* $\langle desc$: GPS-sensor ; id : 46.89.1.47$\rangle$
- *prov-1:* $\langle desc$: Healthcare-provider ; id : 58.17.37.23$\rangle$
- M_1 : $\{t_{capture}$: 15:17:00 ; d_{type} : float ; d_{format} : (longitude, latitude)$\}$

We consider here that t_{gran} is provided as an input parameter. The challenges of identifying the temporal granularity of attributes will be explored in future work.

P-SGD also supports protection function diversity. In fact, existing protection functions vary from data anonymization, data perturbation using noise addition, privacy-aware access control to encryption (cf. Sect. 5). Each of these functions achieves differently the desired protection level. We provide in what follows formal definitions of a *protection function* and *protection level*.

Definition 3. (Protection Function). A *protection function*, $f \in PF$, is a protection method performed by the privacy model on data values of an attribute $a \in A$ prior to their release to consumers. $f \in PF$ is formalized as follows:

$$f : \langle\ name\ ;\ class\ ;\ Feature\ ;\ Param\ \rangle, \text{ where:}$$

- *name* denotes the textual name of f (e.g., generalization, random-noise)
- *class* represents the class to which f belongs, such that:

    $class \in \{\text{noiseAddition ; anonymization ; accessControl ; encryption}\}$

- *Feature* is the set of features characterizing f, including at least: *cost*, the computational cost of f in terms of processing time and memory overhead
- *Param* represents the set of input parameters of f, including at least:
    - $A' \sqsubseteq A$ is the set of attributes on which f is performed
    - P is the set of protection levels to reach for all $a \in A'$ ∎

Definition 4. (Protection Level). A *protection level*, p, expresses the amount of protection to be achieved for the data values of an attribute $a \in A$. p is probabilistic with a value between $[0, 1]$, where 0 means that data is shared without any protection, and 1 means that data is not shared. A value between 0 and 1 indicates the level of protection that should be reached when executing a *protection function* $f \in PF$ on the data of a. Knowing that the way to achieve p depends on the selected *protection function*.   ∎

A stochastic gradient descent method is generally defined as an iterative method for optimizing an objective function with suitable smoothness properties [1]. It has been widely adopted mainly for high-dimensional optimization problems as it reduces the computational burden, achieving faster iterations in trade for a lower convergence rate. This agrees with our needs listed in Challenge 4. Consequently, we detail in the following our proposed P-SGD method. According to Fig. 6, let:

- p_i^{target} refers to the *targeted protection level*, i.e., the next protection level specified by the privacy model for data of attribute $a_i \in A$. This level indicates the target level that must be reached in order to complete the P-SGD process
- p_i^{old} denotes the level of protection of the previous data value of attribute $a_i \in A$
- $p_i^{current}$ expresses the protection level to be assigned to the current data value of attribute $a_i \in A$, such that $p_i^{current} \in [p_i^{target}; p_i^{old}]$

The iterative process followed by P-SGD is thus defined by the following formula:

$$p^{current} = p^{old} - \eta \nabla \quad \text{, where:} \tag{1}$$

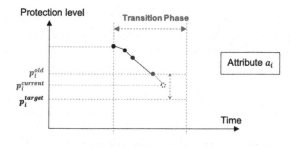

Fig. 6. P-SGD process

- η represents the deviation rate of the protection level (the quantification of η is provided in the following subsection)
- $\nabla \in [0; 1]$ expresses the random noise added to η

We consider in this study that attributes are independent. The P-SGD process is thus performed on the data values of each attribute separately. In order to track and measure the correlations in sequential data and the dependencies between their associated protection functions (cf. Challenges 1 and 2), we define a **transition matrix**, **Trans**, that contains only the properties of the last data value (d_i^{old}) of each shared attribute $a_i \in A$. We store only the properties of the last data values since the process operates iteratively. This helps reduce storage overhead and allows for scalability in attribute number (cf. Challenge 4). **Trans** denotes therefore the cache, and can be represented as follows:

$$Trans = \begin{bmatrix} t_1^{old} & p_1^{old} & f_1^{old} \\ t_2^{old} & p_2^{old} & f_2^{old} \\ \vdots & \vdots & \vdots \\ t_n^{old} & p_n^{old} & f_n^{old} \end{bmatrix} \text{, where:} \tag{2}$$

- t_i^{old} denotes the time of capture of d_i^{old} of attribute a_i
- f_i^{old} is the protection function associated to d_i^{old} of attribute a_i

3.1 Deviation Rate Quantification

η depends on (1) the temporal dependency of previous and current data values of a_i, i.e., d_i^{old} and $d_i^{current}$; and (2) the level of dependency of their related protection functions, i.e., f_i^{old} and $f_i^{current}$.

Definition 5. (Time Dependency of Data). Let $depend_t$ denotes the temporal dependency score of two data values, d_i^{old} and $d_i^{current}$, of an attribute $a_i \in A$. $depend_t$ has a value between 0 and 1, where 0 means that the data are time-independent, and 1 means that the data are fully dependent (time-wise), which typically occurs only when t_i^{old} and $t_i^{current}$ are similar. The higher the temporal distance between the two data values is, the lower their time dependency is. The two data values are said to be time-dependent only if their temporal distance is less than the *standard time period* of their attribute a_i (i.e., $a_i.\tau$). $depend_t$ is therefore computed as follows:

$$depend_t(d_i^{old}, d_i^{current}) = \begin{cases} 1 - \frac{t_i^{current} - t_i^{old}}{a_i.\tau} & \text{if } (t_i^{current} - t_i^{old}) \leqslant a_i.\tau \\ 0 & \text{otherwise} \end{cases} \blacksquare$$

Definition 6. (Protection Function Dependency). Let $\boldsymbol{f_i^{old}}$ and $\boldsymbol{f_i^{current}}$ denotes two protection functions. $\boldsymbol{f_i^{old}}$ and $\boldsymbol{f_i^{current}}$ are said to be dependent only if their similarity score is above or equal 0.

$$sim(\boldsymbol{f_i^{old}}, \boldsymbol{f_i^{current}}) \rightarrow [0; 1], \text{ where:}$$

- $\boldsymbol{sim}$ is a unit similarity function that checks the exact matching between the classes and the lists of features of the two protection functions, and returns a value between 0 and 1, such that:

$$sim(f_i^{old}, f_i^{current}) = 1 \text{ only if:}$$

$$f_i^{old}.class = f_i^{current}.class \text{ and } f_i^{old}.Feature = f_i^{current}.Feature \qquad \blacksquare$$

The P-SGD process will be therefore executed only if the sequential data values are dependent and their associated protection functions are also dependent (i.e., $depend \neq 0$ and $sim \neq 0$). The higher the temporal distance between previous/current data is, the lower is their time dependency, and the higher is η (i.e., the larger can be the protection gap between the two data). As well, the higher is the similarity between protection functions, the lower is η. Accordingly, η is quantified as follows:

$$\eta = c_i \times sim(f_i^{old}, f_i^{current}) \times depend_t(d_i^{old}, d_i^{current}) \qquad (3)$$

- $\boldsymbol{c_i} \in \boldsymbol{C}$ is a system parameter that expresses the maximum deviation value of data protection for attribute $\boldsymbol{a_i} \in \boldsymbol{A}$. It therefore controls the convergence speed of the protection level towards $\boldsymbol{p_i^{target}}$
- $\boldsymbol{sim(f_i^{old}, f_i^{current})} \rightarrow]0; 1]$ is the similarity score
- $depend_t(d_i^{old}, d_i^{current}) \in \,]0; 1]$ is the temporal dependency score

3.2   P-SGD Algorithm

We present here the reasoning algorithm of our solution.

Algorithm 1. Presents the algorithm of our P-SGD solution that takes as input the concerned attribute a, the properties of the current data value (i.e., $t^{current}$ and $f^{current}$), and the targeted protection level p^{target}. It outputs the calculated protection level to be assigned to the current data value, i.e. $p^{current}$. The process starts by computing the dependency score of previous/current data values and the similarity score of associated protection functions (lines 3–4). If data or/and associated functions are independent (line 12), the gradual descent process is not executed, and the protection level is downshifted directly to p^{target} (line 13). Else, this means that data and associated functions are dependent (line 5). The process calculates the random noise $\bigtriangledown$ to be appended to η, the value of η, and then the value of $p^{current}$ (lines 7–9). It checks after the validity of the $p^{current}$ value (lines 10–11). Finally, the properties of the relevant attribute are updated in the transition matrix $Trans[][]$ (line 14) and the process is ended.

Algorithm 1: P-SGD Process

Input: a, c, $t^{current}$, $f^{current}$, p^{target}; // attribute, default deviation value, time of capture and protection function of $d^{current}$, and the targeted protection level;
Output: $p^{current}$; // the protection level to be assigned to $d^{current}$;

1 **Variables:** $Trans[][]$, $depend_t$, $simScore$, $\bigtriangledown$, η; // transition matrix, dependency score of data, similarity score of prot-functions, random noise and deviation rate;

2 **begin**

3    $depend_t := 1 - \frac{t^{current} - Trans[a][0]}{a.\tau}$; // Trans[][0] is the t^{old} column of d^{old} values;

4    $simScore \leftarrow sim(f^{current}, Trans[a][2])$; // Trans[][2] is the f^{old} column associated to d^{old} values;

5   **if** *(depend_t $\neq 0$ AND simScore $\neq 0$)* **then**

6 | // dependent data values and dependent protection functions;

7 | $\bigtriangledown \leftarrow randomNumber(0,1)$; // returns a random value between 0 and 1;

8 | $\eta := c \times simScore \times depend_t$;;

9 | $p^{current} := p^{old} - \eta\bigtriangledown$;

10 | **if** *(p^{current} $\leq p^{target}$)* **then**

11 | $\lfloor$ $p^{current} := p^{target}$; // check the validity of the calculated $p^{current}$ value ;

12   **else**

13       $\lfloor$ $p^{current} := p^{target}$; // data values or/and protection functions are independent;

14    $\lfloor$ $Trans \leftarrow updateTransMatrix(a, t^{current}, p^{current}, f^{current})$;

15 **return** $p^{current}$

This paper presents only the pseudo-code of the main P-SGD process due to space limitations. The pseudo-codes of the aforementioned functions are detailed in the prototype source code provided in Sect. 4.

4 Experimental Validation and Evaluation

In order to implement and validate our approach, we developed a Java-based prototype (the source code is available online through this link[1]). We illustrate in the following the prototype operation by considering the scenario of Alice

---

[1] https://spider.sigappfr.org/research-projects/psgd/ (P-SGD Prototype).

described in Sect. 2. We focus on the second protection transition (i.e., from 80% to 20%), and assume that the protection function remains unchanged. We repeated the descent process three times to emphasize the non-deterministic nature of the solution in the case of repeated transition patterns (cf. Challenge 3). We consider here regular time series data with a data generation time of 1s, and we fix c at 0.5 (i.e., the maximum protection deviation is 50%). As shown in Fig. 7, the proposed P-SGD process is able to iteratively and gradually decrease the protection level until reaching the targeted one (i.e., 20%), with an average of 35 ms per iteration. The deviation pattern varied between the three similar transition cases, as well as the number of data values required to achieve protection convergence (7 for transitions 1–2 and 8 for transition 3). This is due to the noise value associated with the deviation rate (i.e., ∇), which varies randomly with each iteration.

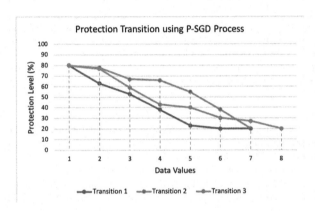

Fig. 7. Securing protection transitions using the P-SGD process

4.1 Performance Evaluation

The objective here is to evaluate the approach's effectiveness, in terms of performance, to operate in different scenarios. The approach is said to be effective if it meets the needs outlined in Challenge 4: (1) fast; (2) scalable (i.e., supports multi-attribute handling); and (3) low-complex in time and space (i.e., in terms of memory overhead and storage). To do so, we start by considering two cases to study the impact of the following two metrics on performance: (i) the complexity of the protection functions dependency; and (ii) the number of attributes handled simultaneously. Then, we formally study the storage complexity of the proposal. The performance is evaluated based on two criteria: the total execution time of one iteration and the memory overhead. The tests were conducted on a machine equipped with an Intel i7 2.80 GHz processor and 16 GB of RAM. The chosen execution value for each scenario is an average of 10 sequenced values.

Case 1: We consider two dimensions to study the complexity of the functions dependency: the first increases the number of features and the second increases the diversity in features between the two functions. We execute the P-SGD process 13 times, taking into account the following number of features for each iteration: 1, 5, 10, 15, 20, 30, 40, 50, 60, 70, 80, 90 and 100. For each of these scenarios, we consider three sub-scenarios where we vary respectively the percentage of diverse features from 0%, 50% to 100%. As shown in Fig. 8 and 9, the number and diversity of the features have no impact on the function dependency procedure, and thus on performance. This is due to the fact that the procedure verifies only the exact matching of the features' names and values. The process is executed in all scenarios with an average time of 35 ms and 10 MB of RAM usage.

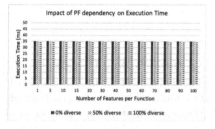

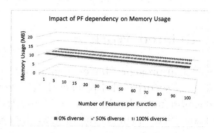

Fig. 8. Case-1: execution time   **Fig. 9.** Case-1: memory usage

Case 2: To study the impact of multi-attribute handling, we incorporate multithreading features in order to perform parallel execution of the process on an increasing number of attributes. We consider the following number for each iteration: 1, 5, 10, 20, 30, 40, 50, 60, 70, 80, 90, and 100. Figure 10 shows that increasing the number of attributes has a quasi-linear impact on the total execution time, with an average time of 35 ms for 5 attributes and up to 100 ms for 100 attributes. The RAM usage remains constant with an average of 10 MB (cf. Fig. 11). This highlights the importance of integrating a low-cost transition matrix.

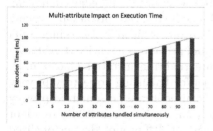

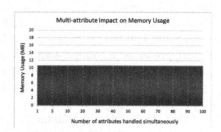

Fig. 10. Case-2: execution time   **Fig. 11.** Case-2: memory usage

Theorem 1. The P-SGD process maintains low storage complexity.

PROOF. Let n denotes the maximum number of *attributes* that could be shared by the user with data consumers. As previously mentioned in Sect. 3, the solution stores only the three properties of the last data value for each attribute in *Trans*, and the values of $c_i \in C$, resulting in a linear storage complexity of $O(4n)$. However, the number of *attributes* shared by the user will not practically exceed 100, which makes the storage complexity low.   □

Discussion. The experiments conducted show that P-SGD is scalable and efficient in time and space (cf. Challenge 4). The solution is able to maintain effective performance in different scenarios, including worst-case ones. This increases its re-usability to also include privacy models that require real-time reasoning, and allows it to operate on a variety of devices, including resource-constrained ones.

5   Related Work

Several approaches have been proposed in the literature to address the challenges of security and privacy in the fields of pervasive Internet of Things (IoT) environments, also known as connected environments. However, to the best of our knowledge, this is the first work to tackle the problem of preserving user privacy against data inference attacks during protection transitions. Therefore, we discuss in this section existing privacy-preserving models to which our solution could be connected. Then, we introduce a classification of existing protection functions that could be used by these models.

5.1   Context-Aware and Personalized Privacy Models

Balancing data utility-privacy has received extensive attention in the last decade. Existing approaches vary from context-aware to personalized privacy-preserving. Bou-Chaaya et al. [2] introduced CaPMan, a user-centric context-aware model for privacy management in connected environments that meets current privacy standards (i.e., Privacy by Design and ISO/IEC 27701 standards). Matos et al. [13] proposed a context-aware security approach, that provides authentication, authorization, access control, and privacy-preserving to fog and edge computing environments. Gheisari et al. [7] introduced a context-aware privacy-preserving approach for IoT-based smart city using Software Defined Networking. Sylla et al. [20] presented a context-aware security and privacy as a service (CASPaaS) architecture to inform the user about the contextual risks involved. Gao et al. [6] proposed a personalized anonymization model for balancing trajectory privacy and data utility. Qiu et el. [17] provided a semantic-aware personalized privacy model that studies user requirements and location's privacy sensitivity to adapt the trajectory construction accordingly. Xiong et al. [24] proposed a personalized privacy protection model based on game theory and data encryption.

5.2 Privacy Protection Functions

Existing functions for data protection vary from data perturbation (anonymization and noise-addition), to data restriction (access control and encryption). On this basis, we introduce a new classification of these functions based on their perspective for data protection. The first category consists of data perturbation functions, which comprises two sub-categories: anonymization and noise-addition. Anonymization functions focus on masking user's identity from generated data by removing explicit identifiers, and decreasing the granularity of quasi-identifiers using operations such as generalization and suppression (e.g., k-Anonymity [19], l-Diversity [12], CASTLE [3]). Noise-addition functions focus on perturbating original data values instead of protecting the owner identity, and that by injecting additive noise (e.g., Generalization [10], Random-noise [9]). The second category regroups data restriction functions that aim at limiting data use by blocking access or encrypting inputs. This category is composed of two sub-categories: access control and encryption. Access control functions (e.g., [11]) achieves privacy protection through authorization models and access control policy operations. Encryption functions applies encryption mechanisms on data values (e.g., Secure Multi-party Computation [22]).

6 Conclusion and Future Work

This paper introduces a privacy-based stochastic gradient descent solution (P-SGD) that can be integrated into numerous existing privacy models in order to provide an additional layer of protection against data inference attacks during protection transitions. P-SGD features an iterative non-deterministic process that gradually decreases the data protection level during the protection descent phases. This allows preserving an appropriate precision gap between sequential protected data values to avoid potential data leakages. However, several improvements still need to be considered for this solution and addressed in future work. First, sensor data are spatio-temporal in nature, which means they also hold spatial dependencies that must be considered when measuring data dependency. In addition, the spatial and temporal distances between sequential data vary according to the user's context. For example, distances between location data vary whether the user is driving a vehicle, running, or walking. Consequently, we aim to improve the data dependency measurement by introducing a three-dimensional dependency graph that considers temporal, spatial, and contextual dimensions. Second, we want to improve the protection function dependency procedure to further consider the semantic similarity of the features. Finally, we aim to connect P-SGD to an existing privacy model in order to test its applicability in real-life scenarios.

References

1. Bottou, L., Bousquet, O.: The tradeoffs of large scale learning. Adv. Neural Inf. Process. Syst. **20**, 161–168 (2007)

2. Bou-Chaaya, K., et al.: δ-Risk: Toward Context-aware Multi-objective Privacy Management in Connected Environments. ACM Trans. Internet Technol. **21**(2), 1–31 (2021)
3. Cao, J., et al.: Castle: continuously anonymizing data streams. IEEE Trans. Dependable Secure Comput. **8**, 337–352 (2010)
4. Chaaya, K.B., Barhamgi, M., Chbeir, R., Arnould, P., Benslimane, D.: Context-aware system for dynamic privacy risk inference: application to smart IoT environments. Future Gener. Comput. Syst. **101**, 1096–1111 (2019)
5. Chamikara, M., et al.: An efficient and scalable privacy preserving algorithm for big data and data streams. Comput. Secur. **87**, 101570 (2019)
6. Gao, S., Ma, J., Sun, C., Li, X.: Balancing trajectory privacy and data utility using a personalized anonymization model. J. Netw. Comput. Appl. **38**, 125–134 (2014)
7. Gheisari, M., et al.: A context-aware privacy-preserving method for IoT-based smart city using software defined networking. Comput. Secur. **87**, 101470 (2019)
8. Han, S., et al.: Privacy-preserving gradient-descent methods. IEEE Trans. Knowl. Data Eng. **22**, 884–899 (2010)
9. Islam, M.Z., Brankovic, L.: Privacy preserving data mining: a noise addition framework using a novel clustering technique. Knowl.-Based Syst. **24**, 1214–1223 (2011)
10. Komishani, E.G., Abadi, M., Deldar, F.: PPTD: preserving personalized privacy in trajectory data publishing by sensitive attribute generalization and trajectory local suppression. Knowl.-Based Syst. **94**, 43–59 (2016)
11. Li, M., Sun, X., Wang, H., Zhang, Y., Zhang, J.: Privacy-aware access control with trust management in web service. World Wide Web **14**, 407–430 (2011). https://doi.org/10.1007/s11280-011-0114-8
12. Machanavajjhala, A., Kifer, D., Gehrke, J., Venkitasubramaniam, M.: l-diversity: privacy beyond k-anonymity. ACM Trans. Knowl. Discov. Data (TKDD) **1**(1), 3-es (2007)
13. de Matos, E., et al.: Providing context-aware security for IoT environments through context sharing feature. In: TrustCom/BigDataSE, pp. 1711–1715. IEEE (2018)
14. Meng, X., et al.: Towards privacy preserving social recommendation under personalized privacy settings. World Wide Web **22**(6), 2853–2881 (2018). https://doi.org/10.1007/s11280-018-0620-z
15. Michael, J., Koschmider, A., Mannhardt, F., Baracaldo, N., Rumpe, B.: User-centered and privacy-driven process mining system design for IoT. In: Cappiello, C., Ruiz, M. (eds.) CAiSE 2019. LNBIP, vol. 350, pp. 194–206. Springer, Cham (2019). https://doi.org/10.1007/978-3-030-21297-1_17
16. Pingley, A., Yu, W., Zhang, N., Fu, X., Zhao, W.: Cap: a context-aware privacy protection system for location-based services. In: 2009 29th IEEE International Conference on Distributed Computing Systems, pp. 49–57. IEEE (2009)
17. Qiu, G., et al.: Mobile semantic-aware trajectory for personalized location privacy preservation. IEEE IoT J. (2020). https://doi.org/10.1109/JIOT.2020.3016466
18. Shin, H., Kim, S., Shin, J., Xiao, X.: Privacy enhanced matrix factorization for recommendation with local differential privacy. IEEE Trans. Knowl. Data Eng. **30**(9), 1770–1782 (2018)
19. Sweeney, L.: k-anonymity: a model for protecting privacy. Int. J. Uncertainty, Fuzziness Knowl.-Based Syst. **10**, 557–570 (2002)
20. Sylla, T., Chalouf, M.A., Krief, F., Samaké, K.: Towards a context-aware security and privacy as a service in the internet of things. In: Laurent, M., Giannetsos, T. (eds.) WISTP 2019. LNCS, vol. 12024, pp. 240–252. Springer, Cham (2020). https://doi.org/10.1007/978-3-030-41702-4_15

21. Vollmer, N.: Table of contents EU General Data Protection Regulation (2018)
22. Vu, D.H., et al.: An efficient approach for secure multi-party computation without authenticated channel. Inf. Sci. **527**, 356–368 (2020)
23. Wang, L., Yu, Z., Guo, B., Ku, T., Yi, F.: Moving destination prediction using sparse dataset: a mobility gradient descent approach. ACM Trans. Knowl. Discov. Data (TKDD) **11**(3), 1–33 (2017)
24. Xiong, J., et al.: A personalized privacy protection framework for mobile crowd sensing in IoT. IEEE Trans. Industr. Inf. **16**, 4231–4241 (2019)

Natural Language Processing and Text

Extracting Semantic Process Information from the Natural Language in Event Logs

Adrian Rebmann$^{(\boxtimes)}$ and Han van der Aa

Data and Web Science Group, University of Mannheim, Mannheim, Germany
{rebmann,han}@informatik.uni-mannheim.de

Abstract. Process mining focuses on the analysis of recorded event data in order to gain insights about the true execution of business processes. While foundational process mining techniques treat such data as sequences of abstract events, more advanced techniques depend on the availability of specific kinds of information, such as resources in organizational mining and business objects in artifact-centric analysis. However, this information is generally not readily available, but rather associated with events in an ad hoc manner, often even as part of unstructured textual attributes. Given the size and complexity of event logs, this calls for automated support to extract such process information and, thereby, enable advanced process mining techniques. In this paper, we present an approach that achieves this through so-called semantic role labeling of event data. We combine the analysis of textual attribute values, based on a state-of-the-art language model, with a novel attribute classification technique. In this manner, our approach extracts information about up to eight semantic roles per event. We demonstrate the approach's efficacy through a quantitative evaluation using a broad range of event logs and demonstrate the usefulness of the extracted information in a case study.

Keywords: Process mining · Natural language processing · Semantic labeling

1 Introduction

Process mining [1] enables the analysis of business processes based on event logs that are recorded by information systems in order to gain insights into how processes are truly executed. Process mining techniques obtain these insights by analyzing sequences of recorded events, also referred to as *traces*, that jointly comprise an *event log*. Most foundational process mining techniques treat traces as sequences of abstract symbols, e.g., $\langle a, b, c, d \rangle$. However, more advanced techniques, such as social network analysis [3] and object-centric process discovery [2] go beyond this abstract view and consider specific kinds of information contained in the events' labels or attributes, such as *actors*, *business objects*, and *actions*.

A key inhibitor of such advanced process mining techniques is that the required pieces of information, which we shall refer to as *semantic components*,

© Springer Nature Switzerland AG 2021
M. La Rosa et al. (Eds.): CAiSE 2021, LNCS 12751, pp. 57–74, 2021.
https://doi.org/10.1007/978-3-030-79382-1_4

are not readily available in most event logs. A prime cause for this is the lack of standardization of attributes in event logs. While the XES standard [4] defines certain standard extensions for attributes (e.g., `org:resource`), the use of these conventions is not enforced and, thus, not necessarily followed by real-life logs (cf., [9]). Furthermore, the standard only covers a limited set of attributes, which means that information on components such as *actions* and *business objects*, are not covered by the standard at all and, therefore, often not explicitly represented in event logs.

Rather, relevant information is often captured as part of unstructured, textual data attributes associated with events, most commonly in the form of an event's label. For example, the "*Declaration submitted by supervisor*" label from the most recent BPI Challenge [10] captures information on the business object (*declaration*), the action (*submitted*), and the actor (*supervisor*). Since these components are all encompassed within a single, unstructured text, the information from the label cannot be exploited by process mining techniques. Enabling this use, thus, requires the processing of each individual attribute value in order to extract the included semantic information. Clearly, this is an extremely tedious and time-consuming task when considered in light of the complexity of real-life logs, with hundreds of event classes, dozens of attributes, and thousands of instances. Therefore, this calls for automated support to extract semantic components from event data and make them available to process mining techniques.

To achieve this, we propose an approach that automatically extracts semantic information from events while imposing no assumptions on a log's attributes. In particular, it aims to extract information on eight *semantic roles*, covering various kinds of information related to business objects, actions, actors, and other resources. The choice for these specific roles is based on their relevance to existing process mining techniques and presence in available real-life event logs. To achieve its goal, our approach combines state-of-the-art natural language processing (NLP) techniques, tailored to the task of semantic role labeling, with a novel technique for semantic attribute classification.

Following an illustration of the addressed problem (Sect. 2) and presentation of our approach itself (Sect. 3), the quantitative evaluation presented in Sect. 4 demonstrates that our approach achieves accurate results on real-life event logs, spanning various domains and varying considerably in terms of their informational structure. Afterwards, Sect. 5 highlights the usefulness of our approach by using it to analyze an event log from the 2020 BPI Challenge (BPI20). Finally, Sect. 6 discusses streams of related work, before concluding in Sect. 7.

2   Motivation

This section motivates the goal of semantic role labeling of event data (Sect. 2.1) and discusses the primary challenges associated with this task (Sect. 2.2).

2.1 Semantic Roles in Event Data

Given an event log, our work sets out to label pieces of information associated with events that correspond to particular *semantic roles*. In this work, we focus on various roles that support a detailed analysis of business process execution from a behavioral perspective, i.e., we target semantic roles that are commonly observed in event logs and that are relevant for an order-based analysis of event data. Therefore, we consider information related to four main categories: *business objects*, *actions*, as well as *active* and *passive* resources involved in a process' execution. For each category, we define multiple semantic roles, which we jointly capture in a set $\mathcal{R}$:

Business Objects. In line with convention [19], we use the term *business object* to broadly refer to the main object(s) relevant to an event. Particularly, we define (1) obj as the type of business object to which an event relates, e.g., a *purchase order*, an *applicant*, or a *request* and (2) obj_{status} as an object's status, e.g., *open* or *completed*.

Actions. We define two roles to capture information on the actions that are applied to business objects : (1) action, as the kind of action, e.g., *create*, *analyze*, or *send*, and (2) $action_{status}$, as further information on its status, e.g., *started* or *paused*.

Actors. Information regarding the active resource in the event is captured in the following two roles: (1) actor as the type of active resource in the event, e.g., a *"supervisor"* or a *"system"*, and (2) $actor_{instance}$ for information indicating the specific actor instance, e.g., an employee identifier.

Passive Resources. Aside from the actor, events may also store information on *passive* resources involved in an event, primarily in the form of *recipients*. For this, we again define two roles: (1) passive as the type of passive resource related to the event, e.g., the role of an employee receiving a document or a system on which a file is stored or transferred through, and (2) $passive_{instance}$ for information indicating the specific resource, e.g., an employee or system identifier.

The considered semantic roles enable a broad range of fine-granular insights into the execution of a process. For example, the *business object* and *action* categories allow one to obtain detailed insights into the business objects moving through a process, their inter-relations, and their life-cycles. Furthermore, by also considering the resource-related roles, one can, for instance, gain detailed insights into the resource behavior associated with a particular business object, e.g., how resources jointly collaborate on the processing of a specific document. While the covered roles, thus, support a wide range of analyses and are purposefully selected based on their relevance in real-life event logs, our approach is by no means limited to these specific roles. Given that we employ state-of-the-art NLP technology that generalizes well, the availability of appropriate event data allows our approach to be easily extended to cover additional semantic roles, both within and outside the informational categories considered here.

2.2 The Semantic Role Labeling Task

To ensure that all relevant information is extracted from an event log, our work considers two aspects of the *semantic role labeling* task, concerned with two kinds of event attributes: *attribute-level classification* for attributes dedicated to a single semantic role and *instance-level labeling* for textual attributes covering various roles:

Attribute-Level Classification. Attribute-level classification sets out to determine the role of attributes that correspond to the same, dedicated semantic role throughout an event log, e.g., a `doctype` attribute indicating a business object. Although the XES standard [4] specifies several standard event attributes, such as `org:resource` and `org:role`, these only cover a subset of the semantic roles we aim to identify. They omit roles related to business objects, actions, and passive resources. These other semantic roles may, thus, be captured in attributes with diverse names, e.g., the obj_{status} role corresponds to event attributes such as `isClosed` or `isCancelled` in the Hospital log[1]. Furthermore, even for roles covered by standard attributes, there is no guarantee that event logs adhere to the conventions, e.g., rather than using `org:group`, the BPI14 log captures information on actors in an `Assignment_Group` attribute.

Instance-Level Labeling. Instance-level labeling, instead, sets out to derive semantic information from attributes with unstructured, textual values that encompass various semantic roles, differing per event instance. This task is most relevant for so-called event labels, often stored in a `concept:name` attribute. These labels contain highly valuable semantic information, yet also present considerable challenges to their proper handling, as illustrated through the real-life event labels in Table 1. The examples highlight the diversity of textual labels, in terms of their structure and the semantic roles that they cover. It is worth mentioning that such differences may even exist for labels within the same event log, e.g., labels l_5 and l_6 differ considerably in their textual structure and the information they cover, yet they both stem from the BPI19 log. Another characteristic to point out is the possibility of recurring roles within a label, such as seen for label l_1, which contains two **action** components: *draft* and *send*. Hence, an approach for instance-level labeling needs to be able to deal with textual attribute values that are highly variable in terms of the information they convey, as well as their structure.

---

[1] We kindly refer to Sect. 4.1 for further information on the event logs referenced here.

Table 1. Exemplary event labels from real-life event logs.

Log	ID	Event label	Contained semantic roles
WABO	l_1	Draft and send request for advice	action ($\times$2), obj
BPI15	l_2	Send design decision to stakeholders	action, obj, passive
BPI15	l_3	Send letter in progress	action, obj, action$_{status}$
RTFM	l_4	Insert date appeal to prefecture	action, obj, passive
BPI19	l_5	Vendor creates invoice	actor, action, obj
BPI19	l_6	SRM: In Transfer to Execution Syst.	action, passive
BPI20	l_7	Declaration final_approved by supervisor	obj, action$_{status}$, action, actor

3   Semantic Event Log Parsing

This section presents our approach for the semantic labeling of event data. Its input and main steps are as follows:

Approach Input. Our approach takes as input an event log L that consists of events recorded by an information system. We denote the universe of all events as $\mathcal{E}$, where each event $e \in \mathcal{E}$ carries information in its payload. This payload is defined by a set of (data) *attributes* $\mathcal{D} = \{D_1, \ldots, D_p\}$ with dom(D_i) as the domain of attribute D_i, $1 \leq i \leq p$ and name(D_i), its name. We write $e.D$ for the value of D for an event e.

Note that we do not impose any assumptions on the attributes contained in an event log L, meaning that we do not assume that attributes such as concept:name and org:role are included in $\mathcal{D}$.

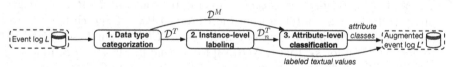

Fig. 1. Overview of the approach.

Approach Steps. The goal of our approach is to label the values of event attributes with their semantic roles. To achieve this, our approach consists of three main steps, as visualized in Fig. 1. Given a log L and its set of event attributes $\mathcal{D}$, Step 1 first identifies sets of *textual attributes* $\mathcal{D}^T \subseteq \mathcal{D}$ and of *miscellaneous attributes* $\mathcal{D}^M \subseteq \mathcal{D}$. Afterwards, Step 2 labels the values of textual attributes in $\mathcal{D}^T$ to extract the parts that correspond to semantic roles, e.g., recognizing that a "*document received*" event label contains the business object "*document*" and the action "*received*". Step 3 focuses on the attribute-level classification of miscellaneous attributes in $\mathcal{D}^M$, as well as some textual attributes $\mathcal{D}_n^T \subseteq \mathcal{D}^T$ that were deemed unsuitable for instance-level labeling during the previous step. This classification step aims to determine the semantic role that corresponds to all values of a certain attribute in $\mathcal{D}^M \cup \mathcal{D}_n^T$, e.g., recognizing that all values of a doctype attribute correspond to the obj role.

In the remainder, Sects. 3.1 through 3.3 describe the steps of our approach in detail, whereas Sect. 3.4 discusses how their outcomes are combined in order to obtain an event log L' augmented with the extracted semantic information.

3.1 Step 1: Data Type Categorization

In this step, our approach sets out to identify the sets of textual attributes $\mathcal{D}^T$ and miscellaneous attributes $\mathcal{D}^M$. As a preprocessing step, we first identify string, timestamp, and numeric attributes using standard libraries, e.g., *Pandas* in Python[2].

Identifying Textual Attributes. To identify the set of textual attributes $\mathcal{D}^T$, we need to differentiate between string attributes with true natural language values, e.g., "*document received*" or "*Create_PurchaseOrder*", and other kinds of alphanumeric attributes, with values such as "*A*", "*USER_123*", and "*R_45_2A*". Only the former kind of attributes will be assigned to $\mathcal{D}^T$ and, thus, analyzed on an instance-level in the remainder of the approach. We identify such true textual attributes as follows:

1. Given a string attribute, we first apply a tokenization function *tok*, which splits an attribute value into lowercase tokens (based on whitespace, camel-case, underscores, etc.) and omits any numeric ones. E.g., given $s_1 =$ "*Create_PurchaseOrder*", $s_2 =$ "*USER_123*", and $s_3 =$ "*08_AWB45_005*", we obtain: $tok(s_1) = [create, purchase, order]$, $tok(s_2) = [user]$ and $tok(s_3) = [awb]$.
2. We apply a *part-of-speech tagger*, provided by standard NLP tools (e.g., Spacy [14]), to assign a token from the Universal Part of Speech tag set[3] to each token. In this manner, we obtain $[(create, VERB)\ (purchase, NOUN)$, $(order, NOUN)]$ for s_1, $[(user, NOUN)]$ for s_2, and $[(awb, PROPN)]$ for s_3.
3. Finally, we exclude any attribute from $\mathcal{D}^T$ that only has values with the same token in $tok(s)$ or do not contain any NOUN, VERB, ADV, or ADJ tokens. In this way, we omit attributes with values such as $s_2 =$ "*USER_123*" and $s_3 =$ "*08_AWB45_005*", which are identifiers, rather than textual attributes. The other attributes, which have diverse, textual values, e.g., $s_1 =$ "Create_PurchaseOrder", are assigned to $\mathcal{D}^T$.

Selecting Miscellaneous Attributes. We also identify a set of non-textual attributes that are candidates for semantic labeling, referred to as the set of miscellaneous attributes, $\mathcal{D}^M \subseteq \mathcal{D} \setminus \mathcal{D}^T$. This set contains attributes that are not included in $\mathcal{D}^T$, yet have a data type that may still correspond to a semantic role in $\mathcal{R}$.

---

[2] https://pandas.pydata.org.
[3] https://universaldependencies.org/docs/u/pos/.

To achieve this, we discard those attributes in $\mathcal{D}\backslash\mathcal{D}^T$ categorized as `timestamp` attributes, as well as `numeric` attributes that include *real* or *negative* values. We exclude these because they are not used to capture semantic information. By contrast, the remaining attributes have data types that may correspond to roles in $\mathcal{R}$, such as `boolean` attributes that can be used to indicate specific states, e.g., `isClosed`, whereas non-negative integers are commonly used as identifiers. Together with the `string` attributes not selected for $\mathcal{D}^T$, the retained attributes are assigned to $\mathcal{D}^M$.

3.2 Step 2: Instance-Level Labeling of Textual Attributes

In this step, our approach sets out to label the values of textual attributes in order to extract the parts that correspond to certain semantic roles, e.g., recognizing that a *"create purchase order"* event label contains *"purchase order"* as the `obj` and *"create"* as the `action`. As discussed in Sect. 2.2, this comes with considerable challenges, given the high diversity of textual attribute values in terms of their linguistic structure and informational content. To be able to deal with these challenges, we therefore build on state-of-the-art developments in the area of natural language processing.

Tagging Task. We approach the labeling of textual attribute values with semantic roles as a text tagging task. Therefore, we instantiate a function that assigns a semantic role to chunks (i.e., groups) of consecutive tokens from a tokenized textual attribute value. Formally, given the tokenization of an attribute value, $tok(e.D) = \langle t_1, \ldots, t_n \rangle$, for an attribute $D \in \mathcal{D}^T$, we define a function $tag(\langle t_1, \ldots, t_n \rangle) \rightarrow \langle c_1 \backslash r_1, \ldots, c_m \backslash r_m \rangle$, where c_i for $1 \leq i \leq m$ is a chunk consisting of one or more consecutive tokens from $\langle t_1, \ldots, t_n \rangle$, with $r_i \in \mathcal{R} \cup \{\texttt{other}\}$ its associated semantic role. For instance, $tag(\langle create, purchase, order \rangle)$ yields: $\langle create \backslash \texttt{action}, purchase\ order \backslash \texttt{obj} \rangle$.

BERT. To instantiate the *tag* function, we employ BERT [8], a language model that is capable of dealing with highly diverse textual input and achieves state-of-the-art results on a wide range of NLP tasks. BERT has been pre-trained on huge text corpora in order to develop a general understanding of a language. This model can then be *fine-tuned* by training it on an additional, smaller training data collection to target a particular task. In this manner, the trained model combines its general language understanding with aspects that are specific to the task at hand. In our case, we thus fine-tune BERT in order to tag chunks of textual attribute values that correspond to semantic roles.

Fine-Tuning. For the fine-tuning procedure, we manually labeled a collection of 13,231 unique textual values stemming from existing collections of process models [15], textual process descriptions [16], and event logs (see Sect. 4.1). As expected, the collected samples do not capture information on resource instances, and rather contain information on the type level (i.e., `actor` and `passive`). For those semantic roles that are included in the samples, we observe a considerable imbalance in their commonality, as depicted in Table 2. In particular, while roles such as obj (14,629 times), action (12,573), and even passive (1,191) are relatively common, we only found few occurrences of actor (135), obj_{status} (92), and $action_{status}$ (30) roles.

Table 2. Training data used to fine-tune the language model, with $s = status$

Source	Count	obj	obj_s	action	$action_s$	actor	passive	other
Process models	11,658	13,543	50	11,445	3	58	1,058	4,966
Textual desc.	498	503	11	498	0	8	114	206
Event logs	625	583	31	630	27	69	19	291
Augmentation	450	350	100	350	150	200	0	150
Total	13,231	14,979	192	12,923	180	335	1,191	5,613

To counter this imbalance, we created additional training samples with obj_{status}, $action_{status}$, and actor roles through established data augmentation strategies. In particular, we created samples by complementing randomly selected textual values with (1) known actor descriptions, e.g., "*purchase order created*" is extended to "*purchase order created by supervisor*", and (2) common life-cycle transitions from [1, p.131] to create samples containing obj_{status} and $action_{status}$ roles, e.g., "*check invoice*" is extended to "*check invoice completed*". However, as shown in Table 2, we limited the number of extra samples to avoid overemphasizing the importance of these roles.

Given this training data, we operationalize the *tag* function using the *BERT base uncased pre-trained language model*[4] with 12 transformer layers, a hidden state size of 768 and 12 self-attention heads. As suggested by its developers [8], we trained 2 epochs using a batch size of 16 and a learning rate of $5e - 5$.

Reassigning Noun-Only Attributes. After applying the *tag* function to the values of an attribute $D \in \mathcal{D}^T$, we check whether the tagging is likely to have been successful. In particular, we recognize that it is hard for an automated technique to distinguish among the obj, actor, and passive roles, when there is no contextual information, since their values all correspond to nouns. For instance, a "*user*" may be tagged as obj rather than actor, given that business objects are much more common in the training data and there is no context that indicates the correct role. Therefore, we establish a set $\mathcal{D}_n^T \subseteq \mathcal{D}^T$ that contains all such *noun-only* attributes, i.e. attributes of which all values correspond solely to the obj role. This set is then forwarded to Step 3, whereas the tagged values of the other attributes directly become part of our approach's output.

3.3   Step 3: Attribute-Level Classification

In this step, the approach determines the semantic role of miscellaneous attributes, $\mathcal{D}^M$ identified in Step 1, and the noun-only textual attributes, $\mathcal{D}_n^T$,

---

[4] https://github.com/google-research/bert.

identified in Step 2. We target this at the attribute level, i.e., we determine a single semantic role for each $D \in \mathcal{D}^M \cup \mathcal{D}_n^T$ and assign that role to each occurrence of D in the event log. For attributes in $\mathcal{D}^M$, the approach determines the appropriate role (if any) based on an attribute's name, whereas for attributes in $\mathcal{D}_n^T$, it considers the name as well as its values. Note that we initially assign each attribute a role $r \in \mathcal{R}'$, where $\mathcal{R}'$ excludes the *instance* resource roles, i.e. $\mathrm{actor}_{instance}$ and $\mathrm{passive}_{instance}$, and later distinguish between type-level and instance-level based on the attribute's domain.

Classifying Miscellaneous Attributes. To determine the role of miscellaneous attributes, we recognize that their values, typically alphanumeric identifiers, integers or Booleans, are mostly uninformative. Therefore, we determine the role of an attribute $D \in \mathcal{D}^M$ based on its name. In particular, we build a classifier that compares a $name(D)$ to a set of manually labeled attributes $\mathcal{D}^{\mathcal{L}}$, derived from real-life event logs $\mathcal{L}$ (with $L \notin \mathcal{L}$).

Using $\mathcal{D}^{\mathcal{L}}$, we built a multi-class text classifier function $classify(D)$ that, given an attribute D, returns $r_D \in \mathcal{R}' \cup \{\mathrm{other}\}$ as the semantic role closest to $name(D)$, with $conf(r_D) \in [0,1]$ as the confidence. To this end, we encode the names from $\mathcal{D}^{\mathcal{L}}$ using the GloVe [20] vector representation for words. Subsequently, we train a logistic regression classifier on the obtained vectors, which can then be used to classify unseen attribute names. Since GloVe provides a state-of-the-art representation to detect *semantic similarity* between words, the classifier can recognize that, e.g., an `item` attribute is more similar to `obj` attributes like `product` than to `actor` attributes in $\mathcal{D}^{\mathcal{L}}$.

Classifying Noun-Only Attributes. Given an attribute in $D \in \mathcal{D}_n^T$, we first apply the same classifier as used for miscellaneous attributes. If $classify(D)$ provides a classification with a high confidence value, i.e., $conf(r_D) \geq \tau$ for a threshold τ, our approach uses r_D as the role for D. In this way, we directly recognize cases where $name(D)$ is equal or highly similar to some of the known attributes in $\mathcal{D}^{\mathcal{L}}$. However, if the classifier does not yield a confident result, we instead analyze the textual values in $\mathrm{dom}(D)$.

Since noun-only attributes were previously re-assigned due to their lack of context, we here analyze them by artificially placing each attribute value into contexts that correspond to different semantic roles. In particular, as shown in Fig. 2, we insert a candidate value (e.g., *"vendor"*) into different positions of a set T of highly expressive textual attribute values (i.e., ones with at least 3 semantic roles). The resulting texts are then fed into the language model employed in Step 2, allowing our approach to recognize which context and, therefore, which semantic role, best suits the candidate value (i.e., `passive` in Fig. 2). Finally, we assign $r_D \in \mathcal{R}' \cup \{\mathrm{other}\}$ as the role that received the most votes across the different texts in T and values in $\mathrm{dom}(D)$.

Recognizing Instance-Level Attributes. Since we only focused on the type-level roles $\mathcal{R}'$ in the above, we lastly check for every resource-related attribute $D \in \mathcal{D}^M$, with $r_D \in \{\mathrm{actor}, \mathrm{passive}\}$, if it actually corresponds to an instance-level role instead. Particularly, we change r_D to the corresponding instance-level

Original sentence	confirm to customer that paperwork is ok
Replacing "confirm"	*vendor* to customer that paperwork is ok ⟶ prob(action) = 0.03
Replacing "customer"	confirm to *vendor* that paperwork is ok ⟶ prob(passive) = 0.90

Fig. 2. Exemplary insertion of a value from an attribute in $\mathcal{D}_n^T$ into an existing context.

role if $\mathrm{dom}(D)$ has values that contain a numeric part or only consist of named-entities (e.g., "*Pete*"). For instance, an attribute D_1 with values like *user_019* and *batch_06*, contains numeric parts and is, thus reassigned to $\mathrm{actor}_{instance}$, while an attribute D_2 with $\mathrm{dom}(D_2) = \{staff\ member,\ system\}$ will retain its actor role.

3.4 Output

Given an event e, our approach returns a collection of tuples (r, v) with $r \in \mathcal{R}$ a semantic role and v a value, where v either corresponds to an entire attribute value $e.D$ (for attribute-level classification applied to attributes in $\mathcal{D}^M \cup \mathcal{D}_n^T$) or to a part thereof (stemming from the instance-level labeling applied to $\mathcal{D}^T \setminus \mathcal{D}_n^T$).

To enable the subsequent application of process mining techniques, the approach returns an XES event log L' that contains these labels as additional event attributes, i.e., it does not override the names or values of existing ones. Note that we support different ways to handle cases where an event has multiple tuples with the same semantic role, e.g., the "*draft*" and "*send*" actions stemming from a "*draft and send request*" label: the values are either collected into one attribute, i.e., $\mathrm{action} = [draft,\ send]$, or into multiple, uniquely-labeled attributes, i.e., $\mathrm{action:0} = draft$, $\mathrm{action:1} = send$. Furthermore, if multiple obj_{status} (or action_{status}) attributes exist that each have Boolean values, e.g., isCancelled and isClosed for the Hospital log, these are consolidated into a single attribute, for which events are assigned a value based on their original Boolean attributes, e.g., $\{\bot, isCancelled, isClosed\}$.

4 Evaluation

We implemented our approach as a Python prototype[5], using the PM4Py library [5] for event log handling. Based on this prototype, we evaluated the accuracy of our approach and individual steps on a collection of 14 real-life event logs.

---

[5] https://gitlab.uni-mannheim.de/processanalytics/extracting-semantic-process-information.

4.1 Evaluation Data

To conduct our evaluation, we selected all real-life event logs publicly available in the common 4TU repository[6], except from those capturing data on software interactions or sensor readings, given their lack of natural language content. For collections that included multiple event logs with highly similar attributes, i.e., BPI13, BPI14, BPI15 and BPI20, we only selected one log per collection, to maintain objectivity of the obtained results. Table 3 depicts the details on the resulting collection of 14 event logs. They cover processes of different domains, for instance financial services, public administration and healthcare. Moreover, they vary significantly in their number of event classes, textual attributes, and miscellaneous attributes.

Table 3. Characteristics of the considered event logs, with $\mathcal{C}$ as the set of event classes

ID	Log name	$|\mathcal{C}|$	$|\mathcal{D}|$	$|\mathcal{D^T}|$	ID	Log name	$|\mathcal{C}|$	$|\mathcal{D}|$	$|\mathcal{D^T}|$
L1	BPI12	24	4	2	L8	BPI20	51	5	4
L2	BPI13	4	11	4	L9	CCC19	29	11	4
L3	BPI14	39	5	2	L10	Credit Req.	8	4	3
L4	BPI15	289	13	3	L11	Hospital	18	22	2
L5	BPI17	26	13	4	L12	RTFM	11	15	2
L6	BPI18	41	13	5	L13	Sepsis	16	31	1
L7	BPI19	42	4	2	L14	WABO	27	6	2

4.2 Setup

As a basis for our evaluation, we jointly established a *gold standard* in which we manually annotated all unique textual values (for instance-level labeling) and attributes (for attribute-level classification) with their proper semantic roles[7]. Since our approach requires training for the language model used in the instance-level labeling (Sect. 3.2) and for the attribute-name classifier (Sect. 3.3), we perform our evaluation experiments using *leave-one-out* cross-validation, in which we repeatedly train our approach on 13 event logs and evaluate it on the 14th. This procedure is repeated such that each log in the collection is considered as the test log once.

To assess the performance of our approach, we compare the annotations obtained using our approach against the manually created ones from the gold standard. Specifically, we report on the standard *precision, recall*, and the F_1-*score*. Note that for instance-level labeling, we evaluate correctness per chunk, e.g., if a chunk (*purchase order*, obj) is included in the gold standard, both *"purchase"* and *"order"* need to be associated with the obj role in the result, otherwise, neither is considered correct.

---

[6] https://data.4tu.nl/search?q=:keyword:%20%22real%20life%20event%20logs%22.
[7] For reproducibility, the gold standard is published alongside the implementation.

4.3 Results

Table 4 provides an overview of the main results of our evaluation experiments. In the following, we first consider the performance of the instance-level labeling and attribute-level classification steps separately, before discussing the overall performance.

Table 4. Results of the evaluation experiments

Semantic role	Instance-level				Attribute-level				Overall			
	Count	Prec.	Rec.	F_1	Count	Prec.	Rec.	F_1	Count	Prec.	Rec.	F_1
obj	583	0.89	0.88	0.88	2	0.50	0.50	0.50	585	0.89	0.88	0.88
obj$_{status}$	31	0.85	0.77	0.78	6	0.50	0.33	0.40	37	0.79	0.70	0.72
action	630	0.94	0.95	0.94	0	-	-	-	630	0.94	0.95	0.94
action$_{status}$	27	0.85	0.81	0.82	6	1.00	1.00	1.00	33	0.88	0.84	0.85
actor	69	0.93	0.84	0.88	0	-	-	-	69	0.93	0.84	0.88
actor$_{instance}$	0	-	-	-	16	1.00	0.94	0.97	16	1.00	0.94	0.97
passive	19	0.84	1.00	0.91	0	-	-	-	19	0.84	1.00	0.91
Overall	1,359	0.91	0.91	0.91	30	0.87	0.79	0.83	1,389	0.91	0.90	0.90

Instance-Level Labeling Results. The table reveals that our instance-level labeling approach is able to detect semantic roles in textual attributes with high accuracy, achieving an overall F_1-score of 0.91. The comparable precision and recall scores, e.g. 0.94 and 0.95 for action or 0.89 and 0.88 for obj, each suggest that the approach can accurately label roles while avoiding false positives. This is particularly relevant, given that nearly half of the textual attribute values also contain information beyond the scope of the semantic roles considered here (see also Table 2). An in-depth look reveals that the approach even performs well on complex values, such as *"t13 adjust document x request unlicensed"*. It correctly recognized the business objects (*document* and *request*), the action (*adjust*) and status (*unlicensed*), omitting the superfluous content (*t13* and *x*).

Challenges. We observe that the primary challenge for our approach relates to the differentiation between relatively similar semantic roles, namely between the two kinds of statuses, obj$_{status}$ and action$_{status}$, as well as the two kinds of resources, actor and passive. Making this distinction is particularly difficult in cases that lack sufficient contextual information or proper grammar. For example, an attribute value like *"denied"* can refer to either type of status, whereas it is even hard for a human to determine whether the *"create suspension competent authority"* label describes *competent authority* as a primary actor or a passive resource.

Baseline Comparison. To put the performance of our approach into context, we also compared its instance-level labeling step to a baseline: a state-of-the-art technique for the parsing of process model activity labels by Leopold et al. [15]. For a fair comparison, we retrained our approach on the same training data as used to train the baseline (corresponding to the collection of process models in Table 2) and only assess the performance with respect to the recognition of *business objects* and *actions*, since the baseline only targets these. Table 5 presents the results obtained in this manner for the event labels from all 14 considered event logs.

The table shows that our approach greatly outperforms the baseline, achieving an overall F_1-score of 0.75 versus the baseline's 0.47. Post-hoc analysis reveals that this improved performance primarily stems from event labels that are more complex (e.g., multiple actions, various semantic roles or compound nouns spanning multiple words) or lack a proper grammatical structure. This is in line with expectations, given that the baseline approach has been developed to recognize several established labeling styles, whereas we observe that event data often does not follow such expectations. Finally, it is worth observing that the performance of our approach in this scenario is considerably lower than when trained on the full data collection (e.g., an F_1 of 0.66 versus 0.88 for the obj role), which highlights the benefits of our data augmentation strategies.

Table 5. Comparison of our instance-level labeling approach against a state-of-the-art label parser; both trained on process model activity labels and evaluated on event labels.

Semantic role	Count	Our approach			Baseline [15]		
		Prec.	Rec.	F_1	Prec.	Rec.	F_1
obj	562	0.65	0.68	0.66	0.40	0.40	0.40
action	618	0.86	0.81	0.83	0.59	0.48	0.53
Overall	1,180	0.76	0.75	0.75	0.50	0.44	0.47

Attribute-Level Classification Results. As shown in Table 4, our also approach achieves good results on the attribute-level classification of attributes, with an overall precision of 0.87, recall of 0.79, and an F_1 of 0.83. We remark that the outstanding performance of our approach with respect to the $action_{status}$ and $actor_{instance}$ roles is partially due to the usage of standardized XES names for some of these attributes, enabling easy recognition. Yet this is not always the case. For instance, 7 out of 16 $actor_{instance}$ attributes handled by this step use alternatives to the XES standard, such as User or Assingment_Group. Our approach maintains a high accuracy for these cases, correctly recognizing 6 out of 7 of such attributes. Notably, the overall precision of our attribute-classification technique reveals that it is able to avoid false positives well, even though a substantial amount of event attributes are beyond the scope of our semantic roles, such as monetary amounts or timestamps. This achievement can largely be attributed to the domain analysis employed in our approach's first step.

Nevertheless, it is important to consider that these results were obtained for a relatively small set of 30 non-textual attributes. Therefore, the lower results for certain uncommon semantic roles (e.g., obj), as well as the overall high accuracy for this step should be considered with care. This caveat also highlights the need additional training data, in order to expand the generalization of this part of our approach.

Overall Results. The overall performance of the approach can be considered as the average over the instance-level and attribute-level results, weighted against the number of entities that were annotated (cf., *count* in Table 4), i.e., a unique textual attribute value (instance-level) or an entire attribute (attribute-level).

We observe that the approach achieves highly accurate overall results, with a micro-average precision of 0.91, and a recall and F_1-score of 0.90. Still, when considering the results per semantic role, we observe that there exist considerable differences. These differences are largely due to the lower scores obtained for the underrepresented roles in the data set, since it is clear that our approach is highly accurate on more common roles, such as the F_1 score of 0.94 for the recognition of actions.

5   Case Study

This section demonstrates some of the benefits to be obtained by using the semantic information extracted by our proposed approach. To this end, we applied our approach to the *Permit Log* published as part of the BPI20 collection [10], which contains 7,065 cases and 86,581 events, divided over 51 event classes (according to the event label, i.e., the concept:name attribute). By applying our approach on the log, we identify information on five semantic roles. Most prominently, our approach is able to extract information about the action, action$_{status}$, obj, and actor roles from the log's unstructured, textual event labels. The availability of these semantic roles as attributes in the augmented event log, created by our approach, enables novel analyses, such as:

Event Class Refinement. The event log contains event labels that are polluted with superfluous information, e.g., by including resource information such as '*by budget owner*', resulting in a total of 51 event classes. Any process model derived on the basis of these classes, therefore, automatically exceeds the recommended maximum of 50 nodes in a process model [18], which impedes its understandability. To alleviate this, we can use the output of our approach to refine the event classes by grouping together events that involve the same action and obj. For instance, we group events with labels like "*declaration approved by budget owner*" and "*declaration approved by administration*", while deferring the actor information to a dedicated actor attribute. In this manner, we reduce the number of event classes from 51 to 21, which yields smaller and hence more understandable process models through process discovery techniques.

Object-Centric Analysis. The extracted semantic information also enables us to investigate the behavior associated with specific business objects. Through the analysis of event labels, our approach recognizes that the log contains six of these: *permit, trip, request for payment, payment, reminder,* and *declaration.* In Fig. 3 we show the directly-follows graph computed for the latter, obtained by selecting all events with $e.obj = $ '*declaration*', and using the identified actions to establish the event class. The figure clearly reveals how declarations are handled the process. Mostly, declarations are *submitted, approved,* and then *final approved.* Interestingly, though, we also see 112 cases in which a declaration was definitely approved, yet rejected afterwards.

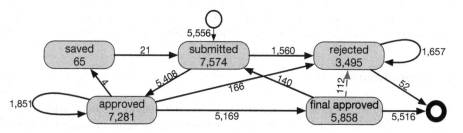

Fig. 3. Example for object-centric analysis. The directly-follows graph shows the actions applied to the object *declaration* in the log (includes 100% activities, 50% paths).

It is important to stress that both the *event class refinement* and *object-centric analysis* are based on information extracted from the unstructured, textual labels of the `concept:name` attribute in the original log. Therefore, the presented insights cannot be obtained by manually categorizing the attributes of the event log, but rather require the thorough, instance-level event analysis provided by our approach.

6 Related Work

Our work primarily relates to streams of research focused on the analysis of event and process model activity labels, as well as to the semantic role labeling task in NLP.

Various approaches strive to either disambiguate or consolidate labels in event logs. Lu et al. [17] propose an approach to detect duplicate event labels, i.e., labels that are associated with events that occur in different contexts. By refining such duplicates, the quality of subsequently applied process discovery algorithms can be improved. Work by Sadeghianasl et al. [22] aim to detect the opposite case, i.e., situations in which different labels are used to refer to behaviorally equivalent events. Other approaches strive for the semantic analysis of labels, such as work by Deokar and Tao [7], which group together event classes with semantically similar labels, as well as the label parsing approach by Leopold et al. [15] against which we compared our work in the evaluation. Finally, complementary to our approach, work by Tsoury et al. [23] strives to augment logs with additional information derived from database records and transaction logs.

Beyond the scope of process mining, our work also relates to semantic annotation applied in various other contexts. Most prominently, semantic role labeling is a widely recognized task in NLP [6,12], which labels spans of words in sentences that correspond to semantic roles. The tasks' goal is to answer questions like *Who is doing what, where and to whom?* While early work in this area mostly applied feature engineering methods [21], recently deep learning-based techniques have been successfully applied, e.g., [13,24]. In the context of web mining, semantic annotation focuses on assigning semantic concepts to columns of web tables [25], while in the medical domain it is e.g. used to extract the symptoms and their status from clinical conversations [11].

7   Conclusion

In this paper, we proposed an approach to extract semantic information from events recorded in event logs. Namely, it extracts up to eight semantic roles per event, covering business objects, actions, actors, and other resources, without imposing any assumptions on the structure of an event log's attributes. We demonstrated our approach's efficacy through evaluation experiments using a wide range of real-life event logs. The results show that our approach accurately extracts the targeted semantic roles from textual attributes, while considerably outperforming a state-of-the-art activity label parser in terms of both scope and accuracy, whereas our attribute classification techniques were also shown to yield satisfactory results when dealing with the information contained in non-textual attributes. Finally, we highlighted the potential of our work by illustrating some of its benefits in an application scenario based on real-life data. Particularly, we showed how our approach can be used to refine and consolidate event classes in the presence of polluted labels, as well as to obtain object-centric insights about a process.

In the future, we aim to expand our work in various directions. To improve its accuracy, we aim to include data from external resources such as common sense knowledge graphs or dictionaries of domain-specific vocabulary into the approach. Furthermore, we intend to broaden its scope by introducing additional kinds of semantic roles, such as roles that disambiguate between human actors and systems. However, most importantly, through its identification of semantic information, our work provides a foundation for the development of wholly novel, semantics-aware process mining techniques.

Reproducibility: The implementation, dataset, and gold standard employed in our work are all available through the repository linked in Sect. 4.

References

1. van der Aalst, W.M.P.: Process Mining: Data Science in Action. Springer, Heidelberg (2016). https://doi.org/10.1007/978-3-662-49851-4
2. Aalst, W.M.P.: Object-centric process mining: dealing with divergence and convergence in event data. In: Ölveczky, P.C., Salaün, G. (eds.) SEFM 2019. LNCS, vol. 11724, pp. 3–25. Springer, Cham (2019). https://doi.org/10.1007/978-3-030-30446-1_1
3. van der Aalst, W.M.P., Reijers, H.A., Song, M.: Discovering social networks from event logs. Comput. Support. Coop. Work (CSCW) 14(6), 549–593 (2005). https://doi.org/10.1007/s10606-005-9005-9
4. Acampora, G., Vitiello, A., Di Stefano, B., van der Aalst, W., Günther, C., Verbeek, E.: IEEE 1849tm: The XES standard. IEEE Comput. Intell. Mag. 12(2), 4–8 (2017). https://ieeexplore.ieee.org/document/7895272
5. Berti, A., van Zelst, S.J., van der Aalst, W.: Process mining for python (PM4Py): bridging the gap between process-and data science. ICPM Demo Track 2019, 13–16 (2019)
6. Carreras, X., Màrquez, L.: Introduction to the CoNLL-2005 shared task: semantic role labeling. CoNLL 2005, 152–164 (2005)
7. Deokar, A.V., Tao, J.: Semantics-based event log aggregation for process mining and analytics. Inf. Syst. Front. 17(6), 1209–1226 (2015). https://doi.org/10.1007/s10796-015-9563-4
8. Devlin, J., Chang, M.W., Lee, K., Toutanova, K.: BERT: pre-training of deep bidirectional transformers for language understanding. In: NAACL, pp. 4171–4186. ACL (2019)
9. van Dongen, B.F.: BPI challenge (2014). https://doi.org/10.4121/uuid:c3e5d162-0cfd-4bb0-bd82-af5268819c35
10. van Dongen, B.F.: BPI challenge (2020). https://doi.org/10.4121/uuid:52fb97d4-4588-43c9-9d04-3604d4613b51
11. Du, N., Chen, K., Kannan, A., Tran, L., Chen, Y., Shafran, I.: Extracting symptoms and their status from clinical conversations. In: ACL. pp. 915–925 (2019)
12. Gildea, D., Jurafsky, D.: Automatic labeling of semantic roles. Comput. Linguist. 28(3), 245–288 (2002)
13. He, L., Lee, K., Lewis, M., Zettlemoyer, L.: Deep semantic role labeling: what works and what's next. In: ACL, pp. 473–483 (2017)
14. Honnibal, M., Montani, I.: spacy 2: Natural language understanding with bloom embeddings, convolutional neural networks and incremental parsing (2017, To appear)
15. Leopold, H., van der Aa, H., Offenberg, J., Reijers, H.A.: Using hidden Markov models for the accurate linguistic analysis of process model activity labels. Inf. Syst. 83, 30–39 (2019)
16. Leopold, H., van der Aa, H., Reijers, H.A.: Identifying candidate tasks for robotic process automation in textual process descriptions. In: Gulden, J., Reinhartz-Berger, I., Schmidt, R., Guerreiro, S., Guédria, W., Bera, P. (eds.) BPMDS/EMMSAD -2018. LNBIP, vol. 318, pp. 67–81. Springer, Cham (2018). https://doi.org/10.1007/978-3-319-91704-7_5
17. Lu, X., Fahland, D., van den Biggelaar, F.J.H.M., van der Aalst, W.M.P.: Handling duplicated tasks in process discovery by refining event labels. In: La Rosa, M., Loos, P., Pastor, O. (eds.) BPM 2016. LNCS, vol. 9850, pp. 90–107. Springer, Cham (2016). https://doi.org/10.1007/978-3-319-45348-4_6

18. Mendling, J., Reijers, H.A., van der Aalst, W.M.: Seven process modeling guidelines (7PMG). Inf. Softw. Technol. **52**(2), 127–136 (2010)
19. Mendling, J., Reijers, H.A., Recker, J.: Activity labeling in process modeling: empirical insights and recommendations. Inf. Syst. **35**(4), 467–482 (2010)
20. Pennington, J., Socher, R., Manning, C.D.: GloVe: global vectors for word representation. In: EMNLP, pp. 1532–1543 (2014)
21. Pradhan, S., Ward, W., Hacioglu, K., Martin, J.H., Jurafsky, D.: Semantic role labeling using different syntactic views. In: ACL, pp. 581–588 (2005)
22. Sadeghianasl, S., ter Hofstede, A., Suriadi, S., Turkay, S.: Collaborative and Interactive Detection and Repair of Activity Labels in Process Event Logs. In: ICPM, pp. 41–48 (2020)
23. Tsoury, A., Soffer, P., Reinhartz-Berger, I.: A conceptual framework for supporting deep exploration of business process behavior. In: Trujillo, J.C., et al. (eds.) ER 2018. LNCS, vol. 11157, pp. 58–71. Springer, Cham (2018). https://doi.org/10.1007/978-3-030-00847-5_6
24. Zhang, Z., et al..: Semantics-aware BERT for language understanding. In: AAAI, vol. 34, issue number 05, pp. 9628–9635 (2020)
25. Zhang, Z.: Effective and efficient semantic table interpretation using tableminer+. Seman. Web **8**(6), 921–957 (2017)

Data-Driven Annotation of Textual Process Descriptions Based on Formal Meaning Representations

Lars Ackermann(✉), Julian Neuberger(✉), and Stefan Jablonski

University of Bayreuth, Bayreuth, Germany
{lars.ackermann,julian.neuberger,stefan.jablonski}@uni-bayreuth.de

Abstract. Business process management encompasses a variety of tasks that can be solved system-aided but usually require formal process representations, i.e. process models. However, it requires a significant effort to learn a formal process modeling language like, for instance, BPMN. Among others, this is one reason why companies often still stick to informal textual process descriptions. However, in contrast to formal models, information from natural language text usually cannot be automatically processed by algorithms. Hence, recent research also focuses on annotated textual process descriptions to make text machine processable.

While still human-readable, they additionally contain annotations following a formal scheme. Thus, they also enable automated processing by, for instance, formal reasoning and simulation. State-of-the-art techniques for automatically annotating textual process descriptions are either based on hand-crafted rule sets or artificial neural networks. Maintaining complex rule sets requires a significant manual effort and the approaches using neural networks suffer from rather low result quality. In this paper we present an approach based on Semantic Parsing and Graph Convolutional Networks that avoids manually defined rules and provides significantly better results than existing techniques based on neural networks. A comprehensive evaluation using multiple data sets from both academia and industry shows encouraging results and differentiates between several applied text features.

Keywords: Process modeling · Text annotation · Semantic parsing · Graph convolutional networks

1 Introduction

Business process models are a valuable means serving various purposes in Business Process Management (BPM). Due to their formal foundation they can be formally analyzed and used to configure workflow systems for process execution. Though they are intended to serve as a means of communication between domain experts and software specialists, too, they have to be specified in a predefined Process Modeling Language the stakeholders might not be familiar with.

© Springer Nature Switzerland AG 2021
M. La Rosa et al. (Eds.): CAiSE 2021, LNCS 12751, pp. 75–90, 2021.
https://doi.org/10.1007/978-3-030-79382-1_5

Thus, the formal and, therefore, unfamiliar foundation of process models hinders their utilization, which among other reasons causes companies to rather rely on *textual process descriptions* in natural language, which can be observed [1–3,14,15,26,27], for instance, in terms of procedure instructions and process manuals. However, textual process descriptions impede the application of tools that operate on process models. Since studies have shown that hand-crafting process models consumes up to 60% of the overall time spent in business process management projects [15], research in the BPM discipline meanwhile considers techniques for transforming textual process descriptions into formal or semi-formal representations [1,2,15,26,27]. One representation type is *annotated textual process description* [23,26,27,31], which is still natural-language text but enriched with schematic information (*annotations*), which foster the derivation of formal process models [1,2,15,26], validate existing models against their descriptions in natural language [3] or against queries for formal reasoning [27,31] and also assist unfamiliar users in the creation of event logs [4,27]. There are only few approaches that automate this task [26,27], avoiding a labor-intensive manual annotation and all of them have drawbacks (see Sect. 3).

In this paper, we propose a technique for automatically annotating textual process descriptions based on semantic parsing [16], which formally describes the semantics of a natural language text, and linguistic features like, for instance, word embeddings [24,25]. Our approach utilizes established techniques but combines them in a novel way to contribute a step towards automated text annotation. We evaluate our approach on datasets from academia and industry [2,15,26,27] as well as a newly created dataset. The evaluation includes a comparison with results from two state-of-the-art approaches [26,27] and is two-fold: *(i)* we calculate metrics widely used in BPM research and *(ii)* we suggest metrics common in text annotation research [11,32] but that are not yet established in the BPM community. Regarding the state-of-the-art solutions our approach contributes to the research field by achieving the following objectives:

O1 It applies to different annotation tasks on textual process descriptions,
O2 It abstracts from plain syntactic variations and, therefore, reduces the number of linguistic patterns that express the same meaning,
O3 It is data-driven, which avoids the effort of manual rule definition but with similar result quality like a recent rule-based approach,
O4 It is less data-intensive than currently leading data-driven approaches,
O5 while showing a higher quality of the annotation results, and
O6 It is open for additional features it uses for solving the annotation tasks.

The achievement of the objectives is discussed in Sect. 6.

2   Preliminaries

2.1   Natural Language Processing

Subsequently, a selection of Natural language processing (NLP) techniques is introduced that is used in the proposed approach or in related approaches.

Sentence splitting and Tokenization. Splits a text into sequences of basic units (e.g. words and punctuation marks), which are then grouped into sentences.

Part-of-Speech (POS) Tagging. Assigns each token a lexical item category (e.g. VERB and NOUN) that indicates its syntactic properties and functions.

Dependency Parsing. Analyzes the syntactical structure of a sentence by means of a specific syntax tree that describes dependencies between the words of a sentence (*dependency tree*). They are, by nature, sensitive to plain syntactic variations, which is discussed in detail in Sect. 2.2.

Formal Meaning Representation. In contrast to dependency trees a formal meaning representation covers semantic relations between words (see Sect. 2.2).

Word embedding techniques. Map words (or their meanings) from a vocabulary to vectors of real numbers. In our experiments (see Sect. 5), we vary between pre-trained models for word embedding techniques Word2Vec [24] and Glove [25].

Text annotation. Means enriching sentences and tokens with schematic information. For the current paper these are information relevant for process modeling. The text annotation schemes relevant for this paper are explained in Sect. 2.4.

2.2 Semantic Parsing, Formal Meaning Representation and UCCA

Semantic parsing precisely transforms natural language utterances into formal meaning representations [17]. In contrast to syntactic representations, formal meaning representations describe the meaning of natural language texts [7] instead of providing insights in the formal constructions used for expressing this meaning [6]. This has three advantages:

1. *Abstraction from plain syntactical variations* in natural language utterances,
2. *Reflection of differences in their meanings*, at the same time, and,
3. *Reduction of their complexity*, and *Disambiguation of their meanings*.

Consequently, semantic parsing can be used as an intermediate step for easing language understanding tasks like the annotation task discussed in this paper. The benefit is illustrated in Fig. 1, which basically describes two situations by means of syntactic dependency trees: authors that took some book (a) and authors that showered (b and c). The phrases "took a book" and "took a shower" are described by exactly the same syntactic structure. Hence, approaches that aim at extracting information like actors, actions and business objects from

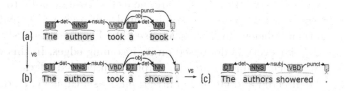

Fig. 1. Limitations of syntactical dependency trees

natural language text have to disambiguate whether "shower" and "book" are objects that can be taken in terms of "grasping" them. In formal meaning representations this disambiguation is already covered.

Because of the drawbacks of syntactic representations described above, our approach is based on formal meaning representations. Though there are multiple formal meaning representation schemes available, our approach is based on the graph-based *Unified Conceptual Cognitive Annotation (UCCA)* for the following reasons [6]: *(i)* It forms a cross-linguistically applicable scheme, *(ii)* it is able to describe the semantics of whole paragraphs and not only sentences, and *(iii)* it is based on cognitive categories that bear information, which is also relevant in the domain of business processes. For this paper, we focus on the latter advantage, which is depicted by the UCCA graphs shown in Fig. 2. The shown UCCA graphs differentiate between a procedure of doing something (a) and a procedure of doing something with a particular object (b). In contrast to "shower", "book" is located in a different sub-graph with a different meaning, which directly solves the issue shown in Fig. 1. The meaning of the different sub-graphs are defined by their nodes, which are, in turn, related to each other with cognitive categories defined in [6]. *(P)rocess* describes that something evolves over time (e.g. actions or movements). *(S)tate* is the opposite since it marks something that does not evolve over time and a *P(A)rticipant* is anything that participates in a process or state (e.g. locations or entities). An in-depth discussion of all available cognitive categories can be considered out-of-scope for this paper. We, therefore, refer to [6] for further reading.

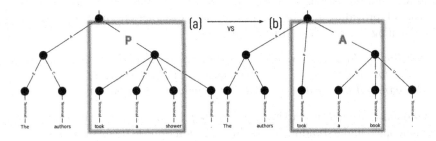

Fig. 2. Two UCCA graphs disambiguating a syntactically ambiguous utterance

2.3   Artificial Neural Networks for Graphs

Graph convolutional networks (*GCN*) are neural networks able to process graphs. Their core idea is based in graph signal processing [29] and recent advances made them efficient in large scale use [20]. They continuously update a hidden state $h^{(l)}$ for every node, based on its incoming edges. In this work we use *R-GCN* [28], which is able to process graphs with labeled edges.

We define the directed and labeled multi-graph G as a tuple (V, E, R), where V is a set of nodes $v_i \in V$; E a set of labeled and directed edges $(v_i, r, v_j) \in E$

and R a set of edge types, so that $r \in R$. The function for updating hidden state $h_i^{(l)}$ for node v_i at iteration l, also called propagation rule is then

$$h_i^{(l+1)} = \sigma(\sum_{r \in R} \sum_{j \in N_i^r} \frac{1}{c_{i,r}} W_r^{(l)} h_j^{(l)} + W_0^{(l)} h_i^{(l)})$$

N_i^r is the set of indices for nodes connected to node v_i by an edge of type r. $W^{(l)}$ is a matrix of learnable weights, σ is an element-wise activation function such as the rectified linear unit $ReLU(x) = max(0, x)$ or $softmax(x_i) = \frac{exp(x_i)}{\sum_j exp(x_j)}$. $c_{i,r}$ is a normalization constant, which is usually set to $|N_i^r|$. The output of this propagation rule is then either used as input for the next graph convolutional layer or as the net's final output, see Sect. 4.

2.4   Annotation Schemes and Tasks for Textual Process Descriptions

There are several formalisms how textual process descriptions can be annotated with schematic information. In order to evaluate the applicability of our approach, we discuss experiments that are based on two different annotation schemes: *(i)* An important subset of the *Annotated Textual Descriptions of Processes (ATDP)* [27] scheme that has proven to enable formal reasoning [31] and *(ii)* the *multi-grained text-classification (MGTC)* scheme used in [26] to automatically derive procedural business process models from annotated texts.

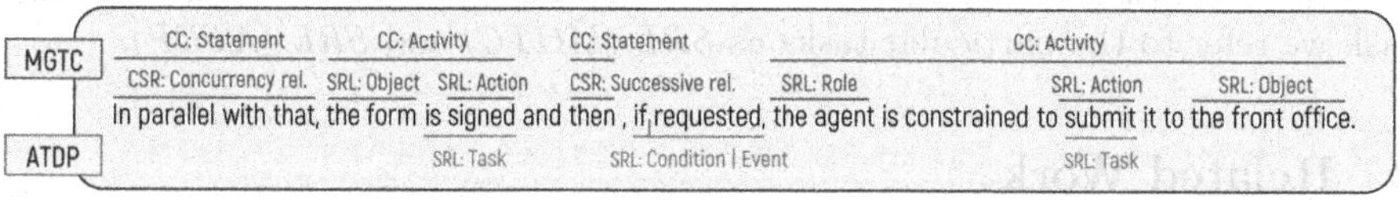

Fig. 3. Example of an annotated textual process description

The MGTC scheme defines three annotation tasks[1] on two different levels (clause and token level) and with different annotation types (see Fig. 3).

- *Clause Classification (CC):* Annotate a clause as an *activity* or a *statement*.
- *Clause Semantics Recognition (CSR):* Determines the semantics of a statement clause, i.e. extracts the concrete control flow pattern.
- *Semantic Role Labeling (SRL):* Classifies the tokens of each activity clause.

Activity clauses describe, which *Roles* perform which *Actions* on what *Objects*, which determined by the SRL task. From statement clauses concrete control-flow relations are extracted. These refer to the beginning of a block of

---

[1] Literature refers to Clause Classification and Clause Semantics Recognition as Sentence Classification and Sentence Semantics Recognition, which suggests processing of whole sentences, though the discussed approach operates on clauses instead.

actions *(block begin)*, the ending of such a block *(block ends)*, a relation organizing activities as a sequence *(successive relation)*, a decision point *(optional relation)* and a parallelization of the control flow *(concurrency relation)*.

In contrast to MGTC, the ATDP scheme does not include annotation tasks like CC or CSR (see Fig. 3). Instead, in an SRL task similar to that in MGTC, it provides annotation types for distinguishing between *activity fragments*:

- *Task* represents the atomic units of work in business processes,
- *Event* is usually part of the process flow but are out-of-scope for the organization responsible for executing the process,
- *Condition* describes circumstances under which other information pertain.

Though the ATDP scheme is far more expressive, we limit the description to the mentioned fragments for two reasons: *(i)* This paper focuses upon the SRL tasks, which means that, for instance, relation extraction is out of scope and *(ii)* several other ATDP classes are not evaluated in [27] making annotation results incomparable. Besides that we consider the CC and CSR tasks according to the MGTC scheme because they are rather similar to the SRL task, except that whole clauses are annotated instead of tokens. Furthermore, the approach that builds upon MGTC [26] and our approach are, in contrast to the approach that uses ATDP [27], both data-driven and, consequently, more comparable.

In addition to the annotation types described above, we introduce a *None* type for the SRL task. This is necessary since our approach treats this task as a token classification problem and, thus, has to reflect tokens that are irrelevant for the SRL task (see Sect. 4). Since both MGTC and ATDP contain an SRL task we refer to the particular tasks as *SRL (MGTC)* and *SRL (ATDP)*.

3   Related Work

To clarify the focus of this paper, we concentrate on a discussion of related approaches that explicitly involve or focus on annotating textual process descriptions following a specified scheme and that are state of the art [15,26,27]. Here we distinguish between *rule-based* and *machine-learning-based* techniques. While the former rely on sets of hand-crafted rules to extract annotations, the latter build upon machine-learning techniques like artificial neural networks. We also briefly discuss experiences and similarities with approaches related to information modeling tasks like object-oriented modeling and database modelling.

Rule-based Approaches. Friedrich et al. [15] build upon standard NLP tools that, for instance, extract language features like syntax trees from sentences in order to analyze them using an extensive set of rules. Some of the extracted information are annotations, which are finally processed to generate a BPMN model. Quishpi et al. [27] extract annotations that conform to the ATDP scheme (see Sect. 2.4) and define tree-based rules that analyze dependency trees in order to generate candidates that fit this scheme. Both approaches rely on rule sets that are defined upon syntax trees, which are inherently sensitive to syntactical changes of the underlying natural language utterance. Consequently, this significantly raises the number of required rules to cover all interesting syntactic patterns. This means that experts for the particular approach have to be mindful of for missing rules and, at the same time, have to avoid ambiguities due to overlaps. Eventually, this usually lowers the portability of rule-based approaches to unseen data (see Sect. 5.2). Furthermore, two natural language utterances might have the same syntactic structure but can likewise have distinct meanings (see Sect. 2.2), which lowers the information content of syntax trees. Another drawback is the limitation to human-interpretable features, i.e. it is hard to hand-craft rules on, for instance, high-dimensional word embedding vectors.

Machine-learning-based Approaches. The approach proposed by Qian et al. [26] extracts annotations conforming to the MGTC scheme (see Sect. 2.4) and, thus, builds upon a multi-grained analysis of textual process descriptions, which consists of three annotation tasks (see Sect. 2.4). For each of the three tasks the approach builds upon a separate artificial-neural-network architecture. Since all of these architectures rely on word embeddings of several hundreds of dimensions (e.g. Word2Vec) the approach depends on the availability of rather huge amounts of data (see Sect. 5.2). Another drawback of the approach discussed in [26] is that it omits the issue of *finding* the correct span of tokens that forms a clause, which can be classified. Instead it requires a manual pre-processing of all input data, which segments natural language utterances. The approach described in [22] extracts and classifies candidate tasks for robotic process automation from textual process descriptions. However, since it focuses on distinguishing between activity types its comparability to our approach is rather low.

Distantly Related Approaches. In [12] 13 approaches are compared, which are tailored to transform textual requirements specifications into UML models and an included study emphasizes the need for automated transformation tools. Several approaches involve text annotation as an intermediate step making them comparable to our proposed approach (e.g. [21]). Other approaches aim at extracting *database models* from requirements specifications [9]. Most of the approaches rely on syntactic features, hand-crafted rules and external knowledge sources (e.g. ontologies). Hence, they suffer from the same drawbacks discussed above and that are in the focus of our research. However, most of them use token-level features like POS tags to disambiguate word senses. Finally, another interesting approach extracts process activities from email logs [18]. While it focuses on issues caused by specific characteristics of emails, it uses word embeddings to derive the semantics of words and sentences. We conclude from this observation that widely used token-level features like POS tags and word embeddings can be valuable for our approach (see Sect. 4), too. Though some approaches overlap with our proposed approach, they cannot be applied directly since they do not achieve the defined objectives: *(i)* According to objective O1 the approach has to solve very different annotation tasks (see Sect. 2.4), *(ii)* according to objective O3 it should be data-driven, and *(iii)* objective O6 requires feature extension to be part of the concept. Finally, the annotation schemes are specific for the process domain and, in contrast to standardized languages like UML in object-oriented modeling, they are highly variable and bear process-specific challenges (see Sect. 2.4). Other approaches process alternative input types (e.g. controlled natural language), which are easier to be interpreted automatically. But since we focus on already existing textual process descriptions, they are out of scope.

4 Approach

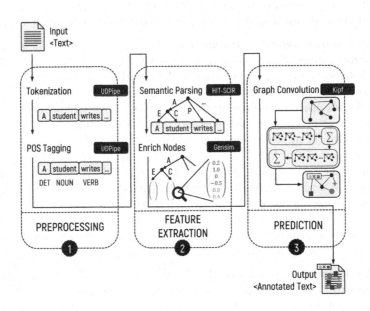

Fig. 4. Approach overview (depiction of graph convolution based on [34])

The input for our approach is a textual process description, which is tokenized and segmented into sentences. Each token is associated with its part of speech (POS tagging). We denote this phase as *PREPROCESSING (1)*.

Sequences of tokens prepared in this manner are passed on to the second phase, *FEATURE EXTRACTION (2)*. Here, a semantic parser generates a formal meaning graph, which describes the semantic structure of a sentence. Graph nodes corresponding to tokens are called terminal nodes. These contain features obtained in the previous step, namely POS-tags and token text.

Every node in the graph is then transformed into a numerical representation. Transformations include one of the following:

1. *No Features:* We evaluate the discriminative power of formal meaning representations in isolation, by encoding each node's index to a one-hot-vector. This way subsequent steps have no detailed information about tokens.

2. *Word embedding:* The numerical vector representation for each word from a pre-trained embedding model. Since we use techniques that generate meaningful vector representations, we call this whole step *node enrichment.* Non-terminal nodes, not containing text information are assigned the zero-vector.
3. *POS tag encoding:* POS tags are one-hot-vector encoded. Non-terminal nodes, not containing text information are assigned the zero-vector.

Eventually, terminal nodes are then transformed into class predictions during the *PREDICTION (3)* phase. Here we extract adjacency matrices A_r from the formal meaning graphs. We then generate a node feature matrix X by stacking all node feature vectors obtained in (2). The choice of features influences final accuracy significantly, which is why we analyse different node features in detail in Sect. 5.2. Terminal nodes in UCCA graphs can correspond to several tokens, in which case their feature vectors must be combined, to form a single one. We use averaging in case of word embeddings and addition in case of part-of-speech tags.

Building the adjacency matrices A_r requires some additional steps to fulfill several assumptions made by [20] and [28]:

1. Graph convolutions as proposed by [20] rely on self loop edges to incorporate a node's current information $h^{(l)}$ into its next state $h^{(l+1)}$. Without self loops a node's new state solely relies on its neighbours' information (see Sect. 2.3). Therefore, we extend the set of edges with $\{(v, r_s, v)|\forall v \in V\}$, where r_s is a special self loop relation type added to R, so that $r_s \in R$.
2. UCCA graphs are defined as directed acyclic and labeled graphs. To be able to process UCCA graphs, we transform the graph into an undirected and labeled one by extending the set of edges E with $\{(v, r, u)|\forall(u, r, v) \in E\}$.
3. GCNs as proposed by [20] and [28] do not allow for classifying graphs globally, something we need for the CC task. This can be implemented via Global Pooling Layers, Attention Sum or a Global Readout Node [34]. We chose the latter. Therefore, to classify graphs globally we add a new node v_g and edges $\{(v, r_g, v_g)|\forall v \in V\}$, where r_g is a special global relation type added to R.

Evaluating the propagation rule for given number of hidden layers l, adjacency and node feature matrices, we are left with final node state vectors $h_i^{(l)}$, which represents our model's output. Node classes can now be predicted by masking non-terminal nodes and applying a softmax. Graph-level classes can be predicted by the same process, but instead of masking all non-terminal nodes of the original graph, all nodes except the global node are masked.

5   Evaluation

5.1   Dataset Description and Experimental Setup

The subsequent quantitative analysis of the proposed approach is based on the datasets shown in Table 1. The datasets COR and MAM stem from [26] and contain textual cooking recipes and maintenance manuals. Though, the two datasets are of considerable size, they vary comparably little regarding their vocabulary and linguistic structures. We show in Table 2 that our approach achieves a saliently high performance, which causes us to validate it on a dataset of smaller size and higher linguistic variability. Hence, we also evaluate the approach on the dataset stemming from [27] (QCD) and another dataset newly created by us (VBP). Covered domains are, for instance, document management and quality management. For the VBP dataset we intentionally omitted any data curation since we also measure how the approach reacts to noisy data in terms of inconsistent labeling. We consider this, because a common issue in text annotation are ambiguous gold standard labels [11,32] (e.g. including determiners or not).

Table 1. Statistics of the datasets used for evaluation

Domain	COR	MAM	QCD	VBP
	Recipe	Maintenance	Mixed	Mixed
# Labeled sentences	17,562	14,370	203	250
# Labeled tokens	34,439	28,174	3,581	6,600
# Sentence-level categories	8	8	-	5
# Word-level categories	4	4	5	6

We implemented our approach using Python 3.6.11 and it consists of R-GC layers proposed by [28]. It is implemented in the Deep Graph Library [33] at version 0.5.2, which allows for different backends, i.e. Tensorflow [5], which we use at version 2.3.1. We build our approach with 2 hidden graph convolutional layers, each consisting of 64 hidden units and train it using the categorical cross-entropy loss [35] and Adam [19] optimizer with learning rate set to 5e−5. For converting text to UCCA graphs we first tokenize and tag them using spaCy (https://spacy.io/. Accessed 5 Dec 2020) and UDPipe [30]. The HIT-SCIR parser [10] creates the graphs, which are then processed as described in Sect. 4.[2]

For each experiment we employ a 5-fold stratified cross validation. Using a stratified cross validation we ensure the same distribution of target classes is present in training and test sets. We remove samples with targets that do not have at least 5 instances across all data sets to guarantee test splits with at least one instance of every class. We report the mean over five folds, with exception of approach by [27], where values are obtained without cross validation, since rule-based methods do not profit from splitting the data into train and test sets.

We intend to capture the ambiguity [32] during labeling with varying degrees of fuzziness. As such, metrics reported are F1 score variants. The *Exact* F1-score is a valid goal but fails to recognize the inherent uncertainty described in Sect. 5.1. F1 is defined as harmonic mean $F1 = 2PR/(P + R)$ of Precision $P = \#ok/\#pred$ and Recall $R = \#ok/\#gold$. $\#pred$ is the number of predicted spans, $\#gold$ is the number of expected spans. Calculation of $\#ok$ follows [11,32].

---

[2] Our code can be accessed at https://github.com/JulianNeuberger/UCCA4BPM.

Exact. #*ok* is increased by 1, if the predicted annotations for a span and its boundaries match those of the gold standard.

Partial. #*ok* is increased by 1, if requirements for *Exact* hold; if at least one predicted token annotation matches the gold standard, #*ok* is increased by 0.5.

Fragment. works on token-level instead of span-level. All spans are fragmented and then handled like in *Exact* while adjusting #*pred* and #*gold*.

5.2 Overall Results and Further Analysis

We compare our approach to a state-of-the-art machine learning approach that outperforms several traditional methods [26]. To address the problems described in Sect. 3, we additionally chose a recent rule-based approach with a much smaller data set [27] as a second baseline. Our approach outperforms [26] on their data sets COR and MAM as well as our smaller and noisier data set. When comparing our approach to the rule-based approach by [27] we perform worse on their data set, while outperforming them on ours, as shown in Table 2. For our dataset MGTC seems to be unable to learn the SRL task and consistently predicts the *None* class, resulting in no exact span matches. Values reported under *Our approach* are for the optimal configuration (see Sect. 5.1). Results marked with "–" are not reported, since they correspond to tasks with a single readout node (see Sect. 4). In the following, we discuss the main aspects impacting our approach's performance.

Table 2. Results on datasets by related work and ours.

Dataset	Public code by [26]			Our approach		
	F1 exact	F1 partial	F1 fragment	F1 exact	F1 partial	F1 fragment
COR (CC)	–	–	66.11	–	–	**99.94**
COR (CSR)	–	–	60.95	–	–	**96.77**
COR (SRL)	43.45	59.90	64.97	97.03	97.86	**98.26**
MAM (CC)	–	–	67.57	–	–	**99.89**
MAM (CSR)	–	–	60.50	–	–	**97.46**
MAM (SRL)	41.78	59.09	63.86	96.08	97.20	**97.78**
Our data set (CC)	–	–	69.13	–	–	**87.89**
Our data set (CSR)	–	–	69.24	–	–	**77.19**
Our data set (SRL)	0.0	39.19	61.28	36.09	53.45	**65.05**
	Public code by [27]			Our approach		
Dataset from [27]	54.61	68.22	**91.59**	45.21	63.52	88.15
Our dataset (SRL)	24.07	49.54	88.40	39.35	61.98	**90.66**

Node Features. Rich features allow the approach to distinguish in harder annotation cases, where the UCCA graph alone is not enough. Highly dimensional feature vectors introduce many new learnable parameters however, which in turn can not be trained with small datasets [8]. The trend in Fig. 5 suggests using no node features, the UCCA graph itself contains enough information to reach performance comparable to or better than other state-of-the-art approaches. The usefulness of word embeddings depends on the corpus they were trained on. Certain stop words (i.e. "if", "before"), are useful in deciding whether a clause contains Conditions or Tasks. If the word embedding model was trained without those tokens the additional model complexity does not pay off. Fine POS tags seem to strike a good balance between additional information, while condensing it into a fairly small one-hot encoded vector of up to 17 elements[3].

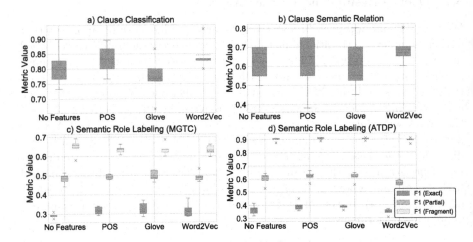

Fig. 5. Comparing node features for tasks CC, CSR, SRL(MGTC) and SRL(ATDP)

Learning Rate. A high learning rate will cause the optimizer to change weights by a large delta, therefore, resulting in faster but more unstable training. On the other hand a smaller learning rate will result in more stable training at the cost of longer training times. We trained the network in its optimal configuration only changing learning rate and determined a learning rate of 5e−5 as optimal.

Size of Hidden Node State. Larger hidden node states allow for more complex aggregation of neighbouring node states so the model is able to represent more variance in the data. This comes with the cost of having more parameters, which need fitting, though – unlike with e.g. the number of relations [28] – increasing the number of hidden units in a given layer increases the number of weights linearly [20]. Our experiments indicate an optimal number of hidden units of 64.

Number of Graph Convolutional Layers. Intuitively the number of hidden graph convolutional layers affects the distance one node can collect neighbourhood information from. Initially we suspected a relatively high number of edges need to be traversed to gain the information needed for the text annotation

---

[3] see https://universaldependencies.org/u/pos/, accessed 2020/12/5.

tasks. But, like Fig. 6 shows, proper node features and the incoming edge[4] alone is enough. We suspect that a model trained on a larger dataset for solving a more complex task would make use of more neighbourhood information.

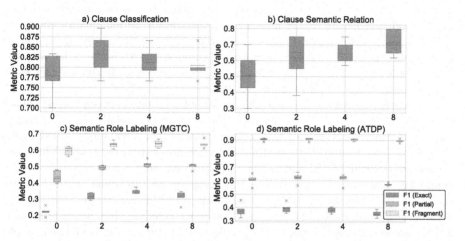

Fig. 6. Importance of choosing the right number of hidden layers in our model.

Assumptions. From a conceptual perspective our approach assumes plain text (i.e. no markup language) as input or requires an additional pre-processing step (see Fig. 4). The implementation has a modular structure and further assumptions might arise when adding new or replacing existing features and implementations, like the word-embedding model and the semantic parser. Our implementation involves a semantic parser trained on a mixture of web reviews and Wikipedia articles, while our word embedding models are either trained on Google's news aggregations (Word2Vec) or Twitter tweets (Glove). Hence, the quality of our implementation is to some extent dependent on the differences regarding linguistic structures and vocabularies between the input and the data used for pre-training. The current implementation is language-independent. However, if using the pre-trained Glove model input documents in English are required or one has to retrofit Glove to the intended input language.

6 Conclusion and Future Work

In this paper, we propose an annotation approach for textual process descriptions and qualitatively measure its contribution based on a set of objectives (see Sect.

---

[4] Using token based node features, inner nodes use the zero vector as feature, since they do not have a corresponding token. Therefore, two edges need to be traversed before the incoming edge information is aggregated in a terminal node: The artificial inverse edge "up" the UCCA structure and only then the edge in question, see Sect. 4.

1). It is data-driven, relies on artificial neural networks (O3), and outperforms the currently best-performing data-driven approach (see Sect. 5) (O5) in all defined annotation tasks (see Sect. 2.4) (O1). At the same time we use lower-dimensional word-embedding features, which makes the approach less data-intensive (O4). Though, the state-of-the-art rule-based approach shows better results on one dataset, we outperform it on another dataset with a similar quality showing that our approach is more stable on unseen data. Since the approach proposed in this paper is based on formal meaning representations it abstracts, by nature, from syntactic variations (O2). Finally, we describe how different features can be incorporated in the annotation task (O6).

Currently the approach is not able to model relations between tokens. This drawback presents an exciting avenue of future work, especially since our technical backbone, GCN, is able to perform this task via a technique called *Link Prediction* [28]. Similarly, we are limited to one annotation per token. This can be solved by using a different activation function in the last graph convolutional layer, but it stands to show that training on our small, inter-domain dataset yields comparable results. Finally we would like to advance our experiments with regards to different node features, including, but not limited to, knowledge-graphs like WordNet [13], Universal Features[5] and combinations of different features, e.g. part-of-speech tags and word embeddings.

Acknowledgements. We thank Omri Abend (HUJI) and Daniel Hershcovich (UCPH) for their assistance with UCCA, Lluís Padró, Luis Quishpi and Josep Carmona (UPC) for valuable advice regarding their approach, and the DBIS Chair (UBT) for assistance creating the new dataset.

References

1. van der Aa, H., Carmona, J., Leopold, H., Mendling, J., Padró, L.: Challenges and opportunities of applying natural language processing in business process management. In: Proceedings of COLING. ACL (2018)
2. van der Aa, H., Di Ciccio, C., Leopold, H., Reijers, H.A.: Extracting declarative process models from natural language. In: Giorgini, P., Weber, B. (eds.) CAiSE 2019. LNCS, vol. 11483, pp. 365–382. Springer, Cham (2019). https://doi.org/10.1007/978-3-030-21290-2_23
3. van der Aa, H., Leopold, H., Reijers, H.A.: Detecting inconsistencies between process models and textual descriptions. In: Motahari-Nezhad, H.R., Recker, J., Weidlich, M. (eds.) BPM 2015. LNCS, vol. 9253, pp. 90–105. Springer, Cham (2015). https://doi.org/10.1007/978-3-319-23063-4_6
4. Aalst, W.: Data science in action. Process Mining, pp. 3–23. Springer, Heidelberg (2016). https://doi.org/10.1007/978-3-662-49851-4_1
5. Abadi, M., et al.: Tensorflow: a system for large-scale machine learning. In: Proceedings of OSDI (2016)
6. Abend, O., Rappoport, A.: Universal conceptual cognitive annotation (UCCA). In: Proceedings of the ACL. ACL (2013)

---

[5] https://universaldependencies.org/u/feat/index.html, accessed 2020/12/5.

7. Abend, O., Rappoport, A.: The state of the art in semantic representation. In: Proceedings of the ACL. ACL (2017)
8. Allen-Zhu, Z., Li, Y., Liang, Y.: Learning and generalization in overparameterized neural networks, going beyond two layers. In: Proceedings of NeurIPS (2019)
9. Btoush, E.S., Hammad, M.M.: Generating ER diagrams from requirement specifications based on natural language processing. In: IJDTA (2015)
10. Che, W., Dou, L., Xu, Y., Wang, Y., Liu, Y., Liu, T.: HIT-SCIR at MRP 2019: a unified pipeline for meaning representation parsing via efficient training and effective encoding. In: Proceedings of the Shared Task on Cross-Framework Meaning Representation Parsing at the 2019 CoNLL (2019)
11. Chinchor, N., Sundheim, B.: Muc-5 evaluation metrics. In: Proceedings of MUC. ACL (1993)
12. Dawood, O.S., et al.: From requirements engineering to UML using natural language processing-survey study. In: EJERS (2017)
13. Fellbaum, C. (ed.): WordNet: An Electronic Lexical Database. Language, Speech, and Communication. MIT Press (1998)
14. Figl, K., Recker, J.: Exploring cognitive style and task-specific preferences for process representations. Requirements Eng. **21**(1), 63–85 (2014). https://doi.org/10.1007/s00766-014-0210-2
15. Friedrich, F., Mendling, J., Puhlmann, F.: Process model generation from natural language text. In: Mouratidis, H., Rolland, C. (eds.) CAiSE 2011. LNCS, vol. 6741, pp. 482–496. Springer, Heidelberg (2011). https://doi.org/10.1007/978-3-642-21640-4_36
16. Hershcovich, D., Abend, O., Rappoport, A.: A transition-based directed acyclic graph parser for UCCA. In: Proceedings of the ACL. ACL (2017)
17. Jia, R., Liang, P.: Data recombination for neural semantic parsing. In: Proceedings of ACL. ACL (2016)
18. Jlailaty, D., Grigori, D., Belhajjame, K.: Email business activities extraction and annotation. In: Kotzinos, D., Laurent, D., Spyratos, N., Tanaka, Y., Taniguchi, R. (eds.) ISIP 2018. CCIS, vol. 1040, pp. 69–86. Springer, Cham (2019). https://doi.org/10.1007/978-3-030-30284-9_5
19. Kingma, D.P., Ba, J.: Adam: a method for stochastic optimization. In: ICLR (2015)
20. Kipf, T.N., Welling, M.: Semi-supervised classification with graph convolutional networks. In: Proceedings of ICLR (2017)
21. Körner, S.J., Landhäußer, M.: Semantic enriching of natural language texts with automatic thematic role annotation. In: Hopfe, C.J., Rezgui, Y., Métais, E., Preece, A., Li, H. (eds.) NLDB 2010. LNCS, vol. 6177, pp. 92–99. Springer, Heidelberg (2010). https://doi.org/10.1007/978-3-642-13881-2_9
22. Leopold, H., van der Aa, H., Reijers, H.A.: Identifying candidate tasks for robotic process automation in textual process descriptions. In: Gulden, J., Reinhartz-Berger, I., Schmidt, R., Guerreiro, S., Guédria, W., Bera, P. (eds.) BPMDS/EMMSAD -2018. LNBIP, vol. 318, pp. 67–81. Springer, Cham (2018). https://doi.org/10.1007/978-3-319-91704-7_5
23. López, H.A., Debois, S., Hildebrandt, T.T., Marquard, M.: The process highlighter: from texts to declarative processes and back. In: CEUR Workshop Proceedings (2018)
24. Mikolov, T., Chen, K., Corrado, G., Dean, J.: Efficient estimation of word representations in vector space. In: ICLR, Workshop Track Proceedings (2013)
25. Pennington, J., Socher, R., Manning, C.D.: Glove: global vectors for word representation. In: Proceedings of the Conference on EMNLP (2014)

26. Qian, C., et al.: An approach for process model extraction by multi-grained text classification. In: Dustdar, S., Yu, E., Salinesi, C., Rieu, D., Pant, V. (eds.) CAiSE 2020. LNCS, vol. 12127, pp. 268–282. Springer, Cham (2020). https://doi.org/10.1007/978-3-030-49435-3_17

27. Quishpi, L., Carmona, J., Padró, L.: Extracting annotations from textual descriptions of processes. In: Fahland, D., Ghidini, C., Becker, J., Dumas, M. (eds.) BPM 2020. LNCS, vol. 12168, pp. 184–201. Springer, Cham (2020). https://doi.org/10.1007/978-3-030-58666-9_11

28. Schlichtkrull, M., Kipf, T.N., Bloem, P., van den Berg, R., Titov, I., Welling, M.: Modeling relational data with graph convolutional networks. In: Gangemi, A., et al. (eds.) Modeling relational data with graph convolutional networks. In: Proc. of ESWC. Springer (2018). LNCS, vol. 10843, pp. 593–607. Springer, Cham (2018). https://doi.org/10.1007/978-3-319-93417-4_38

29. Shuman, D.I., Narang, S.K., Frossard, P., Ortega, A., Vandergheynst, P.: The emerging field of signal processing on graphs: extending high-dimensional data analysis to networks and other irregular domains. In: IEEE SPM (2013)

30. Straka, M., Straková, J.: Tokenizing, POS tagging, lemmatizing and parsing UD 2.0 with UDPipe. In: Proceedings of the CoNLL 2017 Shared Task: Multilingual Parsing from Raw Text to Universal Dependencies (2017)

31. Sànchez-Ferreres, J., Burattin, A., Carmona, J., Montali, M., Padró, L.: Formal reasoning on natural language descriptions of processes. In: Hildebrandt, T., van Dongen, B.F., Röglinger, M., Mendling, J. (eds.) BPM 2019. LNCS, vol. 11675, pp. 86–101. Springer, Cham (2019). https://doi.org/10.1007/978-3-030-26619-6_8

32. Tsai, R.T.H., et al.: Various criteria in the evaluation of biomedical named entity recognition. BMC Bioinform. 7, 92 (2006)

33. Wang, M., et al.: Deep graph library: a graph-centric, highly-performant package for graph neural networks. arXiv: Learning (2019)

34. Wu, Z., Pan, S., Chen, F., Long, G., Zhang, C., Yu, P.S.: A comprehensive survey on graph neural networks. In: IEEE Transactions on NNLS (2020)

35. Zhang, Z., Sabuncu, M.: Generalized cross entropy loss for training deep neural networks with noisy labels. In: NeurIPS (2018)

An NLP-Based Architecture
for the Autocompletion of Partial
Domain Models

Loli Burgueño[1,2]($\boxtimes$) (ID), Robert Clarisó[1] (ID), Sébastien Gérard[2], Shuai Li[2],
and Jordi Cabot[3] (ID)

[1] Open University of Catalonia, Av. Tibidabo, 39-43, Barcelona, Spain
{lburguenoc,rclariso}@uoc.edu
[2] Institut LIST, CEA, Université Paris-Saclay, Avenue de la Vauve, Palaiseau, France
{Sebastien.GERARD,Shuai.LI}@cea.fr
[3] ICREA, Barcelona, Spain
jordi.cabot@icrea.cat

Abstract. Domain models capture the key concepts and relationships of a business domain. Typically, domain models are manually defined by software designers in the initial phases of a software development cycle, based on their interactions with the client and their own domain expertise. Given the key role of domain models in the quality of the final system, it is important that they properly reflect the reality of the business.

To facilitate the definition of domain models and improve their quality, we propose to move towards a more assisted domain modeling building process where an NLP-based assistant will provide autocomplete suggestions for the partial model under construction based on the automatic analysis of the textual information available for the project (contextual knowledge) and/or its related business domain (general knowledge). The process will also take into account the feedback collected from the designer's interaction with the assistant. We have developed a proof-of-concept tool and have performed a preliminary evaluation that shows promising results.

Keywords: Domain model · Autocomplete · Modeling recommendations · Assistant · Natural language processing

1 Introduction

Domain modeling is the activity in which informal descriptions of a (business) domain are translated into a structured and unambiguous representation using a concrete (formal) notation. Domain models, also known as conceptual schemas [29], are built as part of a software development project to abstract the key concepts of the domain relevant for the project, leaving out superfluous details.

Supported by Spanish project TIN2016-75944-R and CEA's initiative Modelia.

M. La Rosa et al. (Eds.): CAiSE 2021, LNCS 12751, pp. 91–106, 2021.
https://doi.org/10.1007/978-3-030-79382-1_6

The use of domain models is widely extended and there is a broad variety of languages (UML, DSLs, ER, etc.), tools and methods [12] that promote and facilitate their creation and manipulation. Nevertheless, they are typically created by hand during the analysis and design phases of software development, making their definition a crucial (but also time-consuming) task in the development life-cycle. On the other hand, the knowledge to be used as input to define such domain models is already (partially) captured in textual format in manuals, requirement documents, technical reports, transcripts of interviews, etc. provided by the different stakeholders in the project.

We believe we could exploit this information to assist designers defining domain models. In software development, autocompletion has been heavily studied for years. Mature features such as code autocompletion are integrated by default in IDEs and numerous benefits like faster coding, error prevention and the discovery of new language elements have been proven. Similarly, we propose model completion as a new feature for a future generation of modeling/design tools (i.e., intelligent modeling assistants [28]) that could significantly improve the domain modeling task.

A couple of commercial low-code platforms [26,30] and research efforts [15,37] are exploring model autocompletion but using other knowledge sources or techniques, e.g., the analysis of a collection of previously developed models from where patterns are extracted or ontologies [8]. However, most companies do not have enough models to obtain meaningful results from the former, while the latter limits its suggestions to general knowledge sources. We believe that we can complement these approaches with autocompletions derived from contextual information in natural language documents. Other approaches [1] have leveraged textual information in general data sources like Wikipedia to provide model suggestions. In contrast, in this paper, we propose combining information from different textual sources: documents generated around the project and general data sources (which include basic information that is omitted from the previous ones as it is supposed to be common knowledge in that community). Moreover, we also consider historic information about previously accepted or rejected suggestions.

More specifically, our goal is to assist the software designer by generating potential new model elements to add to the partial model she is already authoring. We believe this is more realistic than trying to generate full models out of the requirements documents in a fully automated way. In this paper, we propose a configurable framework that follows an iterative approach to help in the modeling process. It uses Natural Language Processing (NLP) techniques for the creation of word embeddings from text documents together with additional NLP tools for the morphological analysis and lemmatization of words. With this NLP support, we have designed a model recommendation engine that queries the NLP models and historical data about previous suggestions accepted or rejected by the designer and builds and suggests potential new domain model elements to add to the ongoing working domain model. Our first experiments show the potential of this line of work.

The rest of the paper is structured as follows. Section 2 describes our NLP-based architecture for model autocompletion. Section 3 describes the implementation details and Sect. 4 assesses the feasibility of the approach over an industrial case study. Section 5 presents the related work and Sect. 6, we conclude our work.

2   Approach

Our proposal aims to assist designers while they build their domain models. Given a partial domain model, our system is able to propose new model elements that seem relevant to the model-under-construction but are still missing. To provide meaningful suggestions, it relies on knowledge extracted out of textual documents. Two kinds of knowledge/sources are considered: *general*[1] documents and *contextual* (all the specific information that we collect about the project) documents. We do not require these documents to follow any specific template.

General and contextual knowledge complement each other. The need for contextual knowledge is obvious and intuitive: designers appreciate suggestions coming from documents directly related to the project they are modeling. General knowledge is needed when there is no contextual knowledge or this is not enough to provide all meaningful suggestions (i.e., it may not cover all the aspects that have to be described in the domain model as some textual specifications omit aspects considered to be commonly understood by all parties). For instance, project documents may never explicitly state that users have a name since it is common sense and both concepts go hand-by-hand. Thus, general sources of knowledge fill the gaps in contextual knowledge and make this implicit knowledge explicit. Leveraging both types of knowledge to provide model autocomplete suggestions to the designer would significantly improve the quality and completeness of the specified domain models. As most common knowledge sources are available as some type of text documents (this is specially true for the contextual knowledge, embedded in the myriad of documents created during the initial discussions on the scope and features of any software project), we propose to use state-of-the-art NLP techniques to leverage this textual-based knowledge sources.

Methods such as GloVE [31], word2vec [27], FastText [17], BERT [10] and GPT-3 [4] create *word embeddings* (i.e., vectorial representations of words) that preserve certain semantic relationships among the words and about the context in which they usually appear. For instance, a NLP model[2] trained with a general knowledge corpus is able to tell us that the concepts *plane* and *airport* are more closely related than *plane* and *cat* because they appear more frequently together. For example, the Stanford NLP Group's pretrained GloVe model with

---

[1] According to the Cambridge dictionary: "information on many different subjects that you collect gradually, from reading, television, etc., rather than detailed information on subjects that you have studied formally".

[2] Note that "NLP model" and "domain model" do not refer to the same type of model at all. In the NLP field, a model is the result of analyzing the textual corpus of data (it could be a trained neural network, a statistical model,...). To avoid confusion, in this work, each time we refer to a NLP model, we always refer to it as "NLP model" and never as "model" alone.

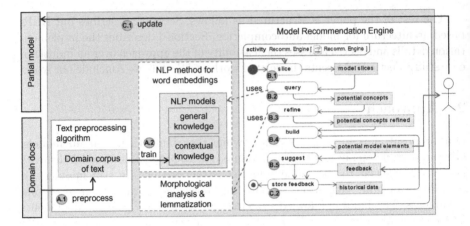

Fig. 1. Autocompletion Framework and Process. *Legend:* Green boxes are data. White boxes are software artifacts. Dotted lines denote already implemented software that we reuse. Solid lines are our contribution/implementation. (Color figure online)

the Wikipedia corpus estimates that the relatedness (measured as the euclidean distance between vectors) between *plane* and *airport* is 6.94, while the distance between *plane* and *cat* is 9.04. Relatedness is measured by the frequency in which words appear closely together in a corpus of text. Apart from giving a quantifiable measure of relatedness between words, once an NLP model is trained, it enables us to make queries to obtain an ordered list with the closest words to a given word or set of words. This latter functionality is the one we use in our approach. Another advantage of these techniques is that they are able to deal with text documents regardless of whether they contain structured or unstructured data.

Our framework uses the lexical and semantic information provided by NLP learning algorithms and tools, together with the current state of the partial model and the historical data stored about the designer's interaction with the framework. As output, it provides recommendations for new model elements (classes, attributes and relationships). The main components of our configurable architecture as well as the process that it follows to generate autocompletion suggestions are depicted in Fig. 1. The logic of the algorithm implemented for the recommendation engine is depicted using an UML Activity Diagram. We describe our framework architecture as well as all its steps in detail in the following, while Sect. 3 on tool support provides further technical details.

2.1   Step A: Initialization

Our process starts by preprocessing all the available documentation about the project to use it as input for the NLP training process. This step provides a corpus of text that satisfies the requirements imposed by the NLP algorithm chosen to create the NLP models, e.g., a single text file that contains words separated by spaces. For most NLP algorithms, this step consists of the basic NLP pipeline: tokenization, splitting, and stop-word removal.

Once all the natural language text has been preprocessed (i.e., the domain corpus is available), the NLP contextual model is trained. Note that we could use any of the NLP language encoding/embeddings alternatives mentioned before. Instead, we do not train a NLP model for the general knowledge every time. Due to the availability of NLP models trained on very large text corpora of general knowledge data (such as Twitter, Wikipedia or Google News[3]), we propose to reuse them. Therefore, neither *Step A.1* nor *A.2* apply to the general knowledge. Nevertheless, if desired, the use of a pretrained model could be easily replaced by collecting general knowledge documents and executing *Steps A.1* and *A.2* with them.

2.2   Step B: Suggestion Generation

Step B.1. Model Slicing. The input to this step is a partial domain model (e.g., a UML model). To optimize the results, we do not generate autocomplete suggestions using the full working model as input. Instead, we slice the model according to multiple (potentially overlapping) dimensions and generate suggestions for each slice. This generates a more varied style and a higher number of suggestions and enables the designer to also focus on the types of suggestions she is more interested in (e.g. attribute suggestions vs class suggestions).

The slicing patterns have been thoroughly designed taking into account the information and encoding of the NLP models to take full advantage of them. Each type of slice focuses on a specific type of suggestion. For instance, if we want to generate attribute suggestions, it is better to slice the model isolating the class for which we want to generate the attribute suggestions so that the NLP recommendations are more focused around the semantics of that class and avoid noise coming from other not-so-close classes in the model. There is clearly a trade-off of how much content should be included in each slice depending on the goal. We have refined our current patterns based on our experimental tests.

In short, in each iteration (steps B.1–C.2), we slice the model according to these patterns[4]:

- one slice that contains all the classes in the model after removing their features (attributes and relationships);
- one slice for each class C in the model (keeping its attributes and dangling relationships); and
- one slice for each pair of classes (keeping its attributes and dangling relationships). These slices aim to suggest new classes, attributes and relationships, respectively, as we explain in Sect. 2.2.

Step B.2. Querying the NLP Models and Historical Data to Obtain Word Suggestions. Given a slice, we start by extracting the element names. They become the list of positive words employed to query the two NLP models

---

[3] https://nlp.stanford.edu/projects/glove/,   https://wikipedia2vec.github.io/wikipedia2vec/pretrained/, https://code.google.com/archive/p/word2vec/.
[4] Note that, for each model, there is a finite number of slices.

(i.e., general knowledge and contextual knowledge). The historical data is used to provide negative words when querying the NLP models. Indeed, if the same list of possible words was used in the past to query the NLP models and the designer rejected a suggestion, that suggestion is stored in the historical data (as explained next in Step C.2), and used as a negative case here.

Each query returns a list of new word suggestions sorted by the partial ordering relation (e.g., euclidean distance) between the embeddings of the initial list of words (i.e., the element names extracted from the model slice) and each suggestion. Therefore, the result after querying the two NLP models for each model slice returns two different lists of related concepts, sorted by shorter to longer distance between embeddings (i.e., sorted by relatedness) that we use to prioritize our suggestions. By default, we merge the two lists (the one coming from the contextual knowledge and the one from the general NLP models) into a single sorted list. If a word appears in both lists, the position in which the word appears in the merged list is that whose distance to the slice is smaller (i.e., the relatedness to the slice is higher).

This process can be customized. Our framework is parametrizable in two ways: (i) you can select the number of suggestions to receive at once, and (ii) customize how the two lists should be prioritized by defining a weight parameter. Regarding the latter, as previously said, by default, our engine mixes the recommendations coming from both sources into only one sorted list. Nevertheless, we provide a parameter to assign different weights to the two sources of knowledge, gn, a value in the range $[0..1]$, where $gn=0$ means that the user does not want general knowledge suggestions at all, and $gn=1$ that she only wants general knowledge suggestions. The weight assigned to the contextual knowledge will be $1 - gn$. This prioritization can be used to only get contextual information suggestions, general ones, give different weights to each of them (so that they appear higher in the list) or even to ask for two different lists, which helps trace where the suggestions come from, improving the explainability.

Step B.3. Morphological Analysis. Before building the potential model elements that will be presented to the designer, we perform some final processing of the lists to remove/refactor some candidate suggestions.

In particular, we use auxiliary NLP libraries [7,13] to perform a morphological analysis of each word (Part-of-Speech (POS) tagging) followed by a lemmatization[5] process, paying especial attention to inflected forms. For instance, if one of the terms returned by a query to an NLP model returns the word *flyers*, our engine lemmatizes it as a verb, resulting in the word *fly*; and as a noun, resulting in the word *flyer*. Therefore, it considers the three words as possible candidates to be the name of a new model element. We also use the POS tag to discard words when they do not apply (for instance, verbs as class names).

---

[5] In linguistics, lemmatization is the process of grouping together the inflected forms of a word so they can be analysed as a single item, identified by the word's lemma, or dictionary form.

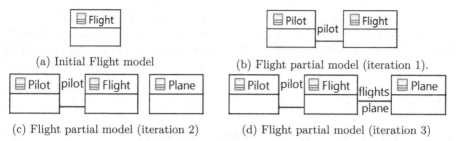

(a) Initial Flight model   (b) Flight partial model (iteration 1).

(c) Flight partial model (iteration 2)   (d) Flight partial model (iteration 3)

Fig. 2. Flight model evolution

Step B.4. Building Potential Model Elements to Add. As a final step, we transform the refined lists of words into potential new model elements. The interpretation of the right type of model element to suggest depends on the type of slice we are processing.

For slices aiming at new class suggestions, the list of potential concepts refined returned by the NLP morphological analysis refinement step (B.3) is filtered to remove verbs, adjectives and plural nouns. After the filtering process, each of the remaining words, w, is a candidate to become a new class named w. For instance, let us assume that we are going to build a model in the domain of flights. Consider that we start from a partial model with a single class named *Flight* and no attributes as Fig. 2a shows. After the slicing, querying and lemmatization, we obtain the list of potential concepts refined *[flights, plane, pilots, pilot, flying, fly, airline, airlines, airplane, jet]*. We use the POS tag to filter the list by discarding verbs, adjectives and plural nouns. The list of remaining words is *[plane, pilot, flying, fly, airline, airplane, jet]*. For each word in this list, our algorithm suggests to add a new class with the same name.

For slices aimed at suggesting new features for a class C, for each output word, w, we offer the user three options: (a) add a new attribute named w to C (the user is in charge of selecting the right datatype); (b) add a new class called w and a new relationship between C and w; (c) if there is already a class called w in the partial model, our engine suggests the addition of a relationship between C and w. Continuing with the example, for a slice containing the class *Flight* with no features (Fig. 2a), the list of potential concepts refined is: *[flights, plane, pilots, pilot, flying, fly, airline, airlines, airplane, jet]*. For example, when the designer picks the word *pilot*, she will receive the three options above, and she could select, for instance, to add it to the model as a new class and relationship (option b) and obtain the model in Fig. 2b.

For slices aimed at discovering new associations, each word, w, is suggested as a new association between the two classes in the slice. For instance, let us assume that we kept building the model and added a new class called *Plane* with no association with the other two (Fig. 2c). In this partial model, for the pair of classes *Flight* and *Plane*, our engine suggests the engineer to add associations with names: *flights, pilots, pilot, flying, fly, jet, airplane*. Our designer could select to add two relationships *flights* and *plane* to obtain the model in Fig. 2d.

Step B.5. Suggestions Provided to User. In this step, the generated suggestions are provided to the designer. She can accept, discard or ignore each of them. While the two first options are processed (either by integrating them into the partial model or by marking them as negative test cases), when suggestions are ignored, we do not handle them and they can be presented to the designer in the future again.

2.3 Step C: Update Model and Historical Data

Step C.1. Partial Model Update. In this step, the suggestion(s) accepted by the designer are integrated into the partial model.

Step C.2. Feedback and Historical Data. Every time the designer discards a recommendation, we store and annotate it as a negative example in order to avoid recommending it again and to guide the NLP model in an opposite direction (i.e., providing the concept as a negative case). See Sect. 3 (Historical Data) for more details.

Note that the more complete the partial model is and the more feedback we have, the more accurate our suggestions will be.

3 Tool Support

We present the implementation of our architecture in Fig. 1. The source code and pretrained NLP models to reproduce the experiments are available in our Git repository[6].

The text preprocessing algorithm that generates the **domain corpus of text** is implemented as a Java program that reads the input text documents, removes all special characters and merges them into a single textual file. The resulting file only contains words, line breaks and spaces.

To build the **NLP models** we use GloVe [31], which is an unsupervised learning method that creates word embeddings via an statistical data analysis. It is trained on the entries of a global word-word co-occurrence matrix, which tabulates how frequently words co-occur with one another in a given corpus. Populating this matrix requires a single pass through the entire corpus to collect the statistics, which makes it an efficient method. Note that, while different methods for the computation of word embeddings (e.g., GloVe, word2vec and FastText) differ in its implementation, they can be used equally for the purposes of this work. We have used the Stanford's implementation of GloVe written in Python.

Our NLP component encapsulates two GloVe models, one trained with general data and one with contextual project one (when available). We have created a simple Java library with the necessary methods to create, train, load and query these two NLP models. This library provides functions such

---

[6] https://github.com/modelia/model-autocompletion.

as `get_suggestions(nlp_model, positive_concepts, negative_concepts, num_suggestions)`.

As auxiliary **NLP tools** for morphological analysis and lemmatization, we use WordNet [13], which is part of the Python NLTK (Natural Language Toolkit). We query WordNet to obtain the parts of speech of words (i.e., noun, verb, adjective, etc.) and use its lemmatization tool.

Our implementation supports models in EMF (Eclipse Modeling Framework)[7] [39] format. Since this framework is implemented in Java and our engine needs to heavily interact with it, the **Model Recommendation Engine** is implemented in Java, too. For example, our engine uses the EMF API to read the input domain model, represented as a UML class model and slices it. The engine is in charge of orchestrating also the previous Python components and implements the suggestion algorithm described in Sect. 2.

Finally, the **Historical Data** component stores feedback from the designer. This feedback is stored for each user and model, i.e., it keeps track of the suggestions that the designer has discarded for each model. The discarded suggestions are used to both avoid suggesting them again and use them as negative cases from which we also learn. Given the way in which GloVe word embeddings are encoded, it enables the search of words that are both as close as possible to a set of words (positive cases) and as far as possible to other set of words (negative cases). The recommendation engine uses this feature when querying the NLP models.

4 Validation

4.1 Experiment and Setup

Let us consider an example of an industrial project: the introduction of a notice management system for incidents in the municipal water supply and sewage in the city of Malaga, Spain. In 2015, the Malaga city hall and the municipal water and sewage company (EMASA) started a project to manage the incidents that clients and citizens notify to have occurred either in private properties or public locations. This project replaced the previous process that was handled via phone calls and paper forms. In this project, contextual knowledge can be derived from the project documentation (e.g. requirements specification). Meanwhile, general knowledge can be extracted from texts in Wikipedia entries, Google News, or similar sources covering general water supply and sewage issues. The project developers produced manually the domain model of this system shown in Fig. 3a. The goal of this section is to evaluate how well our approach can regenerate this manual model by means of autocompleting partially seeded models to show the quality and benefits of our proposal.

For this experiment, the contextual model was trained with the project documentation provided by the client: a presentation (21 slides), forms and the software requirement specification document (78 PDF pages) that after being

---

[7] https://www.eclipse.org/modeling/emf/.

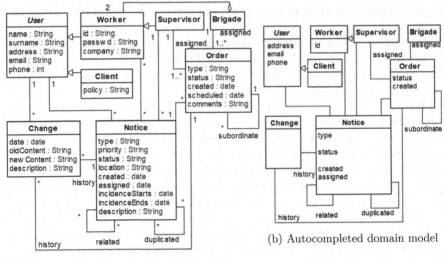

(a) Manually Created Domain Model

(b) Autocompleted domain model

Fig. 3. Emasa domain models

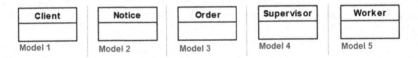

Client	Notice	Order	Supervisor	Worker
Model 1	Model 2	Model 3	Model 4	Model 5

Fig. 4. Initial models.

preprocessed turned into a 48 KB text file with 7,675 words[8]. For the general knowledge model, we have reused the pretrained word embeddings available at https://nlp.stanford.edu/projects/glove/, which has been trained with the corpus of text from Wikipedia.

As a preliminary evaluation, we have taken 5 different sub-models from Fig. 3a, each simulating a potential partial model with a single class and no attributes/relationships. Figure 4 shows our five initial models. The goal is to reconstruct the model shown in Fig. 3a from each partial model. We have parameterized our engine to provide 20 suggestions per round and opted to receive contextual and general knowledge separately.

We have automated the reconstruction process by automatically simulating the behaviour of a designer using our framework. As we know the final target (the full model) we can automatically accept/reject the suggestions based on whether they do appear in the full model or not. Accepted ones are integrated in the (now extended) partial model. New rounds of suggestions are requested until no more acceptable suggestions are received. Note that this evaluation can

---

[8] These documents are not publicly available due to industrial property right. Nevertheless, the software artifacts derived from them are available in our Git repository.

be regarded as a worst case scenario as the evaluation criteria is very strict: in a real-case scenario, a designer could consider as good suggestions a broader set of scenarios as there is no single and unique correct model for any domain. And, obviously, real designers can completely stop the suggestions at any time, edit the model manually and then resume the suggestions again.

As part of this evaluation, we consider the answer to the following research questions for our experiment:

- **RQ1.** Recall: what percentage of the elements of the final model are we able to reconstruct?
- **RQ2.** Precision: what percentage of suggestions are accepted and integrated into the domain model?
- **RQ3.** Source of accepted suggestions: what percentage of accepted suggestions are coming from general knowledge and contextual knowledge?
- **RQ4.** Performance: how does our prototypical implementation perform?

4.2 Recall (RQ1)

Our experiments show that, in all cases, our simulation has been able to reconstruct all classes; for the attributes it has identified an average of 9.67 out of the 27 that the complete model has with a standard deviation of 0.58 (i.e. 9.67 ± 0.58), 9.67 ± 0.58 out of the 13 relationships; and 6.67 ± 0.6 out of the 7 association names. In total, it has identified an average of 34 ± 1.73 out of the 55 model elements, which is approximately a 62% of the model. As an example, Fig. 3b shows the autocompletion produced starting from an empty class *Notice*.

4.3 Precision (RQ2)

On average, our framework has been queried 15.67 times (each query returning 20 possible suggestions for each source of knowledge), with a standard deviation of 5.69 (15.7 ± 5.69). This means that our designer bot has received, on average, a total of 626.7 ± 227.4 suggestions. It has accepted an average of 25.67 ± 0.58 suggestions, resulting on 34 ± 1.73 model elements added to the domain model. Thus, the precision of our approach is 4.46%. Although in absolute terms it seems low, note that the average number of suggestions accepted per set of suggestions is 1.79 ± 0.62 suggestions and that our partial model includes very limited knowledge (a single class name). Furthermore, our automatic acceptance criteria is very strict, i.e., it considers a single target domain model as the ground truth. In reality, several alternatives models are feasible so a human designer might have accepted suggestions rejected by the bot.

4.4 Source of Accepted Suggestions (RQ3)

On average, an 85.7% of accepted suggestions came from the contextual knowledge. This is expected as this is a very particular domain for which it is difficult to assume there is a rich-enough description in a general knowledge source. Nevertheless, the general knowledge has complemented the contextual one and has helped discovering implicit knowledge in the contextual descriptions.

4.5   Performance (RQ4)

We have measured independently the execution time that each component of our framework and its main steps takes. The experiments have been executed in a machine with Windows 10, an Intel i7 8th generation processor at 1.80 GHz, 16Gb of RAM memory and 4 cores with 8 logical processors.

We have observed that, for our experiment, all the times are under one second. For instance, the model slicing takes on average 19 milliseconds (ms), the build of the potential model suggestions takes on average 1 ms, etc. The only step that heavily affects the overall performance of our framework is the querying of the NLP models. Thus, we have paid special attention to that.

On the one hand, the training of the contextual knowledge model using the project documents only took several ms. It resulted in a file that contains the word embeddings with a size of 121 KB. After training, the time to load the word embeddings—this is done only when the system is initialized—as well as the time to query the model are negligible. This is due to the small size of the contextual data (text documents, the derived word embeddings).

On the other hand, for the general knowledge model, the file with the pre-trained embeddings has a size of 989 MB and it takes around 32 s to be loaded. Once loaded, a query takes several seconds. For this reason, we plan in the future to replace the Python implementation of GloVe with a pure C implementation that will improve the performance considerably.

5   Related Work

Our work is related to works on autocompletion in software development, extraction of models from text and modeling assistants. In the following we give an overview of the state of the art in each group and discuss the differences with our own proposal.

Autocompletion in software development. Development tools can offer different types of recommendations to software developers [16,18,33]. Among them, *code completion* [5,25] is a standard feature of IDEs. A similar notion is *query (auto)completion* in information retrieval [38], *e.g.*, search engines. Both approaches propose textual completions and use a combination of frequent patterns, information about the context and historic data to provide useful suggestions.

In this paper, we target model completion rather than source code or query completion. While some of the techniques employed in these problems are related, there are fundamental differences among them:

- Code and query completion place a very strong emphasis the analysis of historic data. This requires a large repository of examples, which is usually not available at such a large scale in the case of modeling. For this reason, similarity and relatedness, which play a complementary role in code and query completion, are the key components of model completion.

- Some coding activities are predictable and repetitive (e.g., define a constructor to initialize all attributes of an object) so code completion can provide useful suggestions simply by considering frequent patterns. On the other hand, models tend to be one-of-a-kind: even when considering a ubiquitous domain (e.g., the structure of an organization), the vocabulary, constraints and level of detail may vary from one model to another.
- Code and query completion is typically *local*: completions are proposed for the current method or query. Meanwhile, model completion can be local or *global*, i.e., identify missing elements in the entire model.
- In addition to proposing relevant missing elements, model completion needs to assign a category/type to these proposed elements (attribute, class, relationship) and establish how it relates to the existing model, e.g. a relationship between classes X and Y.

Model extraction from textual requirements. Several approaches aim to generate software models from textual specifications. Among them, some works extract structural information such as UML class diagrams [2,19,20,22,34–36], or domain ontologies [6,9,24,40]. Others focus on other type of information, like variability [3,32] (commonalities and differences among the products in a software product line) or behavior [14] (such as the workflow in a business process). Their goal is not the completion of a partial model, but the construction of a new model from scratch.

Even though the type of models varies, all these approaches rely on NLP techniques and tools and share similar subtasks as ours. Nevertheless, they do not take into account the partial model, as we do in the context of this paper. This means that their approach cannot be guided by the designer nor can they integrate any type of feedback during the model creation process. As a consequence, their predictions will be less accurate. An exception is DoMoBOT [35], that allows designers to correct the extracted model and learns from those updates. In any case, DoMoBOT targets full model construction rather than model completion, *i.e.*, it does not support or take advantage of partial models.

Modeling assistants. Several tools apply model autocompletion with different goals. For instance, [23] analyzes designer actions in the GUI of a model editor to detect ongoing high-level activities from a predefined catalog (*e.g.*, a refactoring) and propose actions to auto-complete the activity. [21] suggests meaningful names for methods and UML model elements. Meanwhile, [37] suggests completions of a domain-specific model in order to satisfy well-formedness rules. These completions are proposed by used either a relational model finder (Alloy) or a constraint solver. Another approach, [11], clusters classes in a metamodel repository according to a similarity metric to identify related classes. Then, it recommends related classes to those in the partial model. None of them leverage any project textual documents to improve the recommendations. Moreover, two commercial software development tools provide AI-powered assistants: ServiceStudio from OutSystems [30] and Mendix Assist [26], based on existing models in their private repositories. As before, they do not use any type of project document as additional input. Finally, [1] recommends related models based on knowledge from Google Books, but it does not consider feedback nor contextual knowledge as we do.

6   Conclusions

This paper has proposed a model recommendation engine that, once fed with textual descriptions of a domain, generates autocompletions for domain models under development. This is a first step towards a more general modeling assistant that effectively helps modelers specify better models faster.

As further work, we plan to integrate in our framework other types of information (such as past models created by the same company in the same or similar domains and general ontologies, e.g., SUMO) to provide richer suggestions. This will imply dealing with prioritization/inconsistencies among the different sources.

Usability will be a key point to ensure the framework is well accepted by software designers. We will explore the optimal parameters for our system such as the number of suggestions, the confidence threshold to suggest a new model element, the timeliness (i.e., when to trigger the suggestions) and the level of automation (i.e., they are automatically sent to the user versus they are provided only on-demand). We will ensure that our approach can be effectively used by carrying out an empirical evaluation with a group of experienced designers.

We will keep refining the techniques presented in this paper, e.g., accounting for aggregation, composition, and generalization relations and suggesting also data types and potentially missing constraints beyond just new elements. We will also like to extend the type of suggestions we offer to include the replacement and removal of elements. Finally, we will study the application of our approach on other types of models and modeling languages (e.g., behavioral languages) and the exploitation of other types of NLP models in software modeling.

References

1. Agt-Rickauer, H., Kutsche, R., Sack, H.: Automated recommendation of related model elements for domain models. In: MODELSWARD 2018, vol. 991, pp. 134–158 (2018)
2. Arora, C., Sabetzadeh, M., Briand, L.C., Zimmer, F.: Extracting domain models from natural-language requirements: approach and industrial evaluation. In: MODELS 2016, pp. 250–260 (2016)
3. Bakar, N.H., Kasirun, Z.M., Salleh, N.: Feature extraction approaches from natural language requirements for reuse in software product lines: a systematic literature review. J. Syst. Softw. **106**, 132–149 (2015)
4. Brown, T.B., Mann, B., Ryder, N., Subbiah, M., Kaplan, J., et al.: Language models are few-shot learners (2020). https://arxiv.org/abs/2005.14165
5. Bruch, M., Monperrus, M., Mezini, M.: Learning from examples to improve code completion systems. In: ESEC-FSE 2009, pp. 213–222 (2009)
6. Buitelaar, P., Cimiano, P., Magnini, B.: Ontology learning from text: methods, evaluation and applications, vol. 123. IOS press (2005)

7. CEA NLP tech: LIMA: LIbre Multilingual Analyzer. https://github.com/aymara/lima/wiki/DeepLima-beta#the-lima-multilingual-nlp-tool (2020)
8. Conesa, J., Olivé, A.: A method for pruning ontologies in the development of conceptual schemas of information systems. In: JoDS V, pp. 64–90 (2006)
9. Dahab, M.Y., Hassan, H.A., Rafea, A.: TextOntoEx: automatic ontology construction from natural English text. Expert Syst. Appl. **34**(2), 1474–1480 (2008)
10. Devlin, J., Chang, M., Lee, K., Toutanova, K.: BERT: pre-training of deep bidirectional transformers for language understanding (2018). http://arxiv.org/abs/1810.04805
11. Elkamel, A., Gzara, M., Ben-Abdallah, H.: An UML class recommender system for software design. In: AICCSA 2016, pp. 1–8 (2016)
12. Evans, E.: Domain-driven design: tackling complexity in the heart of software. Addison-Wesley Professional (2004)
13. Fellbaum, C.: WordNet: an electronic lexical database. Bradford Books (1998). https://wordnet.princeton.edu/
14. Friedrich, F., Mendling, J., Puhlmann, F.: Process model generation from natural language text. In: CAISE 2011, pp. 482–496 (2011)
15. Ganser, A., Lichter, H.: Engineering model recommender foundations. In: MODELSWARD 2013, vol. 19, pp. 135–142 (2013)
16. Gasparic, M., Janes, A.: What recommendation systems for software engineering recommend. J. Syst. Softw. **113**, 101–113 (2016)
17. Grave, E., Bojanowski, P., Gupta, P., Joulin, A., Mikolov, T.: Learning word vectors for 157 languages. In: LREC 2018 (2018)
18. Harel, D., Katz, G., Marelly, R., Marron, A.: Wise computing: toward endowing system development with proactive wisdom. Computer **51**(2), 14–26 (2018)
19. Harmain, H.M., Gaizauskas, R.J.: Cm-builder: a natural language-based case tool for object-oriented analysis. Autom. Softw. Eng. **10**, 157–181 (2003)
20. Ibrahim, M., Ahmad, R.: Class diagram extraction from textual requirements using natural language processing (NLP) techniques. In: ICCRD 2010, pp. 200–204 (2010)
21. Kuhn, A.: On recommending meaningful names in source and UML. In: RSSE 2010, pp. 50–51 (2010)
22. Kumar, D.D., Sanyal, R.: Static UML model generator from analysis of requirements (SUGAR). In: ASEA 2008, pp. 77–84 (2008)
23. Kuschke, T., Mäder, P.: Pattern-based auto-completion of UML modeling activities. In: ASE 2014, pp. 551–556 (2014)
24. Lee, C.S., Kao, Y.F., Kuo, Y.H., Wang, M.H.: Automated ontology construction for unstructured text documents. Data Knowl. Eng. **60**(3), 547–566 (2007)
25. Marasoiu, M., Church, L., Blackwell, A.F.: An empirical investigation of code completion usage by professional software developers. In: PPIG 2015, p. 14 (2015)
26. Mendix: Mendix assist (2020). https://www.mendix.com/platform/#assist
27. Mikolov, T., Sutskever, I., Chen, K., Corrado, G., Dean, J.: Distributed representations of words and phrases and their compositionality. In: NIPS 2013, vol. 2 (2013)
28. Mussbacher, G., Combemale, B., Kienzle, J., et al.: Opportunities in intelligent modeling assistance. Softw. Syst. Model. **19**(5), 1045–1053 (2020)
29. Olivé, A.: Conceptual Modeling of Information Systems. Springer, Berlin (2007). https://doi.org/10.1007/978-3-540-39390-0
30. OutSystems: (2020). https://www.outsystems.com/p/low-code-platform/
31. Pennington, J., Socher, R., Manning, C.D.: GloVe: global vectors for word representation. In: EMNLP 2014, pp. 1532–1543 (2014)

32. Reinhartz-Berger, I., Kemelman, M.: Extracting core requirements for software product lines. Requirements Eng. **25**(1), 47–65 (2020)
33. Robillard, M., Walker, R., Zimmermann, T.: Recommendation systems for software engineering. IEEE Softw. **27**(4), 80–86 (2009)
34. Sagar, V.B.R.V., Abirami, S.: Conceptual modeling of natural language functional requirements. J. Syst. Softw. **88**, 25–41 (2014)
35. Saini, R., Mussbacher, G., Guo, J.L., Kienzle, J.: DoMoBOT: a bot for automated and interactive domain modelling. In: MDE Intelligence 2020, pp. 1–10 (2020)
36. Saini, R., Mussbacher, G., Guo, J.L., Kienzle, J.: Towards queryable and traceable domain models. In: RE 2020, pp. 334–339. IEEE (2020)
37. Sen, S., Baudry, B., Vangheluwe, H.: Towards domain-specific model editors with automatic model completion. Simulation **86**(2), 109–126 (2010)
38. Shao, T., Chen, H., Chen, W.: Query auto-completion based on word2vec semantic similarity. J. Phys. Conf. Ser. **1004**(1), 12–18 (2018)
39. Steinberg, D., Budinsky, F., Paternostro, M., Merks, E.: EMF: Eclipse Modeling Framework 2.0., 2nd edn. Addison-Wesley Professional, Boston (2009)
40. Wong, W., Liu, W., Bennamoun, M.: Ontology learning from text: a look back and into the future. ACM Comput. Surv. (CSUR) **44**(4), 1–36 (2012)

Process Discovery

Learning of Process Representations Using Recurrent Neural Networks

Alexander Seeliger[✉] [iD], Stefan Luettgen[iD], Timo Nolle[iD],
and Max Mühlhäuser[iD]

Telecooperation Lab, Technical University of Darmstadt, Darmstadt, Germany
{seeliger,luettgen,nolle,max}@tk.tu-darmstadt.de

Abstract. In process mining, many tasks use a simplified representation
of a single case to perform tasks like trace clustering, anomaly detection,
or subset identification. These representations may capture the control
flow of the process as well as the context a case is executed in. However, most of these representations are hand-crafted, which is very time-
consuming for practical use, and the incorporation of event and case
attributes as contextual factors is challenging. In this paper, we propose
a neural network architecture for representation learning to automate
the generation. Our network is trained in a supervised fashion to learn
the most meaningful features to obtain highly dense and accurate vector representations of cases of an event log. We implemented our approach and conducted experiments in the context of trace clustering with
publicly available event logs to show its applicability. The results show
improvements regarding the separation of cases, and that process models
discovered from identified subsets are of high quality.

Keywords: Process mining · Recurrent neural network ·
Representation learning · Clustering

1 Introduction

In recent years, process mining has become an important technology for organizations analyzing their business processes. Instead of conducting interviews
to collect information about a business process, event data from process-aware
information systems provides more accurate and objective knowledge about how
a process is executed in reality. For instance, process discovery allows analysts
to reconstruct a process model solely from an event log. Although the control
flow of the process is the central aspect in process mining for representing a
case, more and more techniques also consider the context a process is executed
in. The context may be the department, supplier, or any other additional information that is related to the case and provides an extended view onto a case.
Including the contextual factors of a case into the corresponding representation
allows analysts to obtain further insights.

However, it is not trivial to incorporate context into a single representation
used by other process mining techniques. In fact, many approaches propose the

© Springer Nature Switzerland AG 2021
M. La Rosa et al. (Eds.): CAiSE 2021, LNCS 12751, pp. 109–124, 2021.
https://doi.org/10.1007/978-3-030-79382-1_7

use of a manually created representation where the included information must be selected and transformed manually. Additionally, this manual process may need to be performed individually for each event log and process because different attributes, i.e., the event and case attributes, may be of different importance. A major challenge here is that the importance of a single attribute is not directly apparent, so manual exploration is necessary which is complex and time-consuming. Often extensive domain knowledge is needed to obtain case representations of high quality.

In this paper, we introduce a neural network architecture based on *recurrent neural networks* (RNNs) to automatically learn highly condensed vector representations for process mining. Our approach is to transform this unsupervised task into a supervised learning task by training a neural network and incorporating the sequence of activities as well as the event and case attributes. Instead of predicting the next activity [10,24], our neural network architecture uses the predictive power of RNNs to predict the case attributes of a case. This technique forces the network to learn the control flow of the case as well as the corresponding contextual factors. As a result, we can obtain a very dense and compact vector for each case from the neural network's internal state as the representation. These representation vectors can then be used for other process mining tasks. We evaluate our approach in the context of trace clustering to demonstrate that the resulting representation vectors can generate clusters with very similar cases. Furthermore, we evaluate if the resulting process models from these clusters are of high quality regarding fitness, precision, and simplicity.

The rest of the paper is organized as follows: First, we discuss the related work (Sect. 2). Second, we present our representation learning technique to learn highly dense vector representations automatically (Sect. 3). Then, we describe our evaluation method and present the results using synthetic and real-life event logs (Sect. 4). Finally, we discuss the results (Sect. 5) and conclude (Sect. 6).

2   Related Work

In process mining, different vector representations are used for various application scenarios such as clustering, anomaly detection, and subset identification.

Trace Clustering. Trace clustering is a major research field where different representations [26,27] are used to improve process model quality. Early approaches use frequent sequences [12] or sequence patterns [2,3,16]. Song et al. [23] propose the use of profiles (e.g., activities, duration, or case attributes), which are customized feature vectors, to also consider contextual factors. An approach to combine multiple profiles is introduced by Appice et al. [1]. The authors propose a co-training approach which is a machine learning algorithm that iteratively adjusts the representations to improve the quality. De Koninck et al. [7] transfer the idea of word2vec to the process mining domain, in which sequence activities are mapped to a vector space to capture semantic relationships. Case2vec by Luettgen et al. [17] enhances this approach by including event and case attributes. Jablonski et al. [14] introduce a customized distance metric that combines multiple vector representations of different process perspectives. Seeliger et al. [22] introduce a hybrid approach that includes multiple process perspectives to form a vector space. The weighting of the perspectives is optimized automatically by evaluating the quality of reconstructed candidate process models. A scalable mixed-paradigm trace clustering approach using super-instances is introduced by De Koninck et al. [6], which first learns super-instances using a simple distance-based approach and then subsequently applies a model-based approach to cluster the instances. An RNN-based approach is introduced by Bui et al. [4] which uses the sequence of activities to learn vector representations. Different from our approach that aims to predict case attributes, the authors train the network to predict the trace context, i.e., common sequence of activities.

Anomaly Detection, Conformance Checking, and Event Abstraction. Besides the use in trace clustering, some of the same techniques were also used for anomaly detection, conformance checking, and event abstraction. Anomaly detection using word2vec embeddings and one-class classification to detect anomalies by relying on normal behavior is introduced by Junior et al. [15]. Peeperkorn et al. [20] introduce a fully data-driven conformance checking approach based on word embeddings. Another application scenario of word embeddings is demonstrated by Sánchez-Charles et al. [21] who improve process discovery by reducing event variability.

Different from the related work, our approach includes the control flow as well as contextual factors and works entirely automatic. It adapts to the given event log and includes the contextual factors based on the predictive power.

3   Representation Learning

In process mining, various forms of case representations are used for different analysis techniques. Many of these approaches use case representations that mainly focus on the control flow of a case. However, a case is often executed within a specific context, captured by additional information attached to each case in form of event and case attributes in an event log. Event level attributes are attributes that can change during the lifetime of a case, e.g., the executor of the activities within a trace. Case level attributes are attributes which are consistent over the whole case, e.g., the desired item to acquire in a purchase-to-pay process. Incorporating these additional attributes into the case representation is often very challenging and time-consuming. The major challenge here is that such representations are often hand-crafted and need to be adjusted for each event log individually. Furthermore, identifying the most valuable contextual factors for inclusion is not trivial without a deep understanding of the process.

In machine learning, neural networks have shown that they can learn dense data representations of high quality automatically. The use of such neural networks helps to overcome both issues, namely the manual definition of the representations as well as the individual adaptation to the given event log. Different from the related work in the field of process mining, where neural networks are used for classification, prediction, or anomaly detection, we use the internal state of the neural network to obtain case representations. The internal state of a neural network represents the observed input in a compact form to predict the output. Also, we do not train our network to predict the next activity, but the contextual factors. Our work focuses on creating good internal representations of a single case but also needs to be capable of producing good prediction results.

3.1   Recurrent Neural Networks (RNNs)

We use a recurrent neural network (RNN) architecture because RNNs are specifically designed to learn sequential data such as sentences in natural language or sequences of activities in process event data. In order to retain information about past events, an RNN uses an internal state, also called memory, that is updated for each event. This internal state resembles a representation of the event sequence up until that point. The memory update is again controlled by a separate set of weights which are also optimized as part of the training procedure.

A drawback of the design of a classic RNN is that it is forced to update its memory with each new event, thereby potentially overwriting previous information. As a consequence, older events are not as strongly remembered as more recent ones. The RNN quickly forgets about the distant past due to numerical issues when computing derivatives during weight updates when training the network. Hochreiter and Schmidhuber have addressed this problem with their design of the long short-term memory (LSTM) [13].

A similar technique to an LSTM is the gated recurrent unit (GRU) [5]. It has better performance on small data sets, but less strong prediction on data which needs stronger modeling potential. However, we can still use GRUs as process data is naturally sparse, because even with a high number of cases, the set of activities usually does not increase, activities within the traces are highly repetitive and mainly change in order.

3.2   Our Neural Network Architecture

As motivated in the previous sections, RNNs have shown to provide solid results for predictive tasks [11,19,24], thus making use of their structure may also be beneficial for representation learning. Therefore, we transformed the task of representation learning into an supervised learning task, i.e., use the predictive capability of RNNs. Our main goal is to force the network to learn the characteristics of a case, including the contextual factors in the most compact form.

We propose a neural network architecture akin to the BINet architecture presented in [19]. The BINet architecture is used to predict the next event in an ongoing case based on the information in the preceding events. Instead of predicting the next event, we first read the complete case, transforming it into an internal representation, and then predict the case attributes (see Fig. 1). The main idea is that contextual factors may influence the way a process is executed. Related work [25] investigated the dependency between the different execution sequences and the contextual factors. Many processes are highly dependent on the context such as procure to pay, order to cash, or production processes. For example, ordering a high price product may require additional approval steps, or specific resources need to be involved in the process.

Our architecture first reads the entire sequence of activities and then searches for relationships to the contextual factors. The network architecture consists of as many inputs as there are event attributes in the event log, including the activities (see Fig. 1). Each activity in the sequence is one-hot encoded one after another and then fed into a separate embedding layer. Similarly, attributes attached to each activity are encoded and embedded in the same way. Each event attribute is represented as a separate embedding layer in the architecture. All embedding layers are then concatenated to form a single vector which is fed into the GRU/LSTM layer. The output of the GRU/LSTM layer is then linked to the fully connected softmax layers, each referring to the case attributes of the corresponding case. It is important to notice that the size of the embedding and GRU/LSTM layer is much smaller as the input layer, so we force the network to actually learn a more compact representation of the entire case.

The size of the LSTM/GRU layer determines how much the network needs to compress the input for accurate prediction. Since we are interested in the internal state of the network for the case representation, the size of the LSTM/GRU layer also controls how generic or specific the representation vector may be. If the vector size is low, the network may only learn very generic relationships, e.g., the department, whereas a larger vector may also incorporate specific details, e.g., the executing resource. The internal state of the LSTM/GRU is then obtained for clustering and acts as the vector representation.

3.3 Limitations

Our approach has some limitations that should be noted and discussed. First, we have made the assumption that contextual factors in form of case and event attributes exist in the event log. We argue that a large number of processes are executed within a certain context or at least have some contextual information that is attached to each case. If there is no contextual information (e.g., constant values for the entire process or random values) available, a representation of this kind would yield little to no advantage over control-flow only approaches.

Another limitation of our approach is that a neural network is a black-box model and it is unclear what exactly the network has learned. This issue is specifically relevant for neural networks used for prediction tasks. But in our case this may not be as critical because the output of our approach, i.e., the vector representation, can be analyzed and investigated. Also, we don't use unknown cases as input for the network, thus, we know the exact output of the network for the given input when obtaining the vector representation. However, an arguable limitation may be that the contextual factors cannot be directly linked to the components of the resulting representation vector.

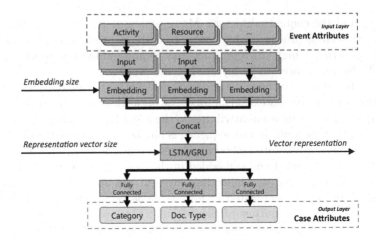

Fig. 1. Architectural overview of the RNN architecture. Each activity and their corresponding event attributes are fed into the network one by one with the goal to predict case attributes.

4   Evaluation

We implemented the described representation learning technique using *tensorflow*, *scikit-learn*, *fastcluster* and *pm4py* in Python to evaluate the performance in the context of clustering. The implementation of our approach is publicly available including the used data sets[1]. We use the vector representation of each case to cluster similar process instances with the goal to improve process discovery. We evaluate the quality of the representations regarding their discrimination and their quality regarding the process models discovered.

4.1   Datasets

We use two synthetic datasets *TC-DS2018*[2] and *TC-DS2020*[3] to measure the quality of the subset separation as well as the quality of the resulting process models discovered from each subset (see Table 1). Both datasets contain event logs generated from five artificial process models which were introduced in [18]. The models are of different complexity regarding the number of activities and transitions. Generated event logs contain event and case attributes that share certain relationships such that the combination of control flow and attributes form five clusters.

For each attribute, a set of 20 values is generated. In *TC-DS2018* attribute dependencies are generated by randomly assigning each process variant a fixed set of attribute values such that certain value combinations occur more frequently than others. Hence, each unique sequence has certain attribute values

---

[1] https://github.com/alexsee/deep-trace-clustering.

[2] https://tudatalib.ulb.tu-darmstadt.de/handle/tudatalib/2338.

[3] https://tudatalib.ulb.tu-darmstadt.de/handle/tudatalib/2415.

Table 1. Overview of the two synthetic event log datasets.

Dataset	Logs	Parameter	Values
TC-DS2018 [22]	288	Noise	0.0, 0.1, 0.2
		Attributes	5, 10, 15, 20
		Size	1000, 2000, 5000, 10000
TC-DS2020	792	Noise	0.0, 0.1, ... 1.0
		Attributes	10 with 20 values
		Dependencies	1, 2, 3
		Size	500, 1000, 5000, 10000

that represent causalities. Due to the random assignment, overlaps between the generated values are possible. In *TC-DS2020* the set of attribute values is split into distinct sets and each resulting set is assigned to a process variant. Assignment is not random but based on the order of a breadth-first search to obtain the variants from the process model. Both datasets contain the *org:resource* event attribute that corresponds to the executing user and also corresponds to the dependent sequence. In total, 1080 different synthetic event logs were generated.

Besides the synthetic event logs, we use two real-life event logs (*BPIC 2015* [8] and *BPIC 2019* [9]). We selected a case attribute for both event logs that can be considered as the ground truth label for clustering. For *BPIC 2015*, event logs are already split into five different municipalities which we use as our ground truth. In *BPIC 2019*, the case attribute *Item Type* is used without the *Standard* cases to obtain evenly distributed clusters. Even if this selection of ground truth may not be exact, we can at least see if the identified subsets are adequately distinguishable.

4.2 Experimental Setup

We compare our approach, LSTMClust and GRUClust, with an autoencoder [18], Trace2vec [7], Case2vec [17], HybridClusterer [22] (HC), bag-of-activities (BOA), and Levenshtein distance (LED). The detailed procedure of our evaluation is illustrated in Fig. 2.

For training the networks, all available activities and attributes (excluding the ground truth label) are used. Further, we used the standard methodologies to prevent the network from overfitting, i.e., reduced number of hidden units, early stopping. Afterwards, we obtain the internal representation of each case and use the feature vectors as input for the cluster algorithm. We vary the vector size of the hidden and the embedding layer (2, 3, 4, 8, 16, 32, 64, 128), and the number of epochs (10, 25). The learning rate is set to be constant (autoencoder $lr = 0.0001$, GRUClust and LSTMClust $lr = 0.01$, Trace2vec and Case2vec $lr = 0.025$) and the batch size is set to 64. For Trace2vec and Case2vec, the window size is 5, the minimum count is 0, and the number of inference epochs

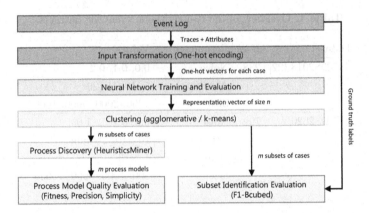

Fig. 2. Overview of our evaluation setup, showing the flow diagram of the event log data. It also illustrates our training and validation approach for the synthetic and real-life event logs.

is set to 50. For the autoencoder, LSTMClust, and GRUClust we use the Adam optimizer. We use agglomerative and k-means clustering.

4.3   Evaluation Metrics

We evaluate our approach with respect to two aspects:

(1) The quality of the subset separation of the clustering using the obtained representation vectors of the RNN compared with the ground-truth clusters (i.e., *F1-BCubed*), and

(2) the quality of the process models discovered from each subset (i.e., *fitness, precision,* and *simplicity*).

We analyzed the results using the non-parametric Friedman test. When the Friedman test indicated significance, we used the Bonferroni corrected pairwise Wilcoxon signed-rank test for post-hoc analysis. We further report Kendall's W effect size and use Cohen's thresholds to classify the effect.

4.4   Results: Synthetic Event Logs

In the following, we report the results for the synthetic event logs.

Subset Separation. The results of our synthetic experiments indicate that LSTMClust and GRUClust performed best regarding F1-BCubed in all settings, followed by HC, Trace2vec, BOA, LED, Case2vec, and autoencoder (see Fig. 3). The approaches perform significantly different ($\chi^2(8) = 7078.453, p < .001, W = .819$) and post-hoc tests confirmed significant differences ($p < .001$) between most approaches except between LSTMClust and GRUClust as well as LED and Trace2vec. A detailed overview of the exact numbers is given in Table 2.

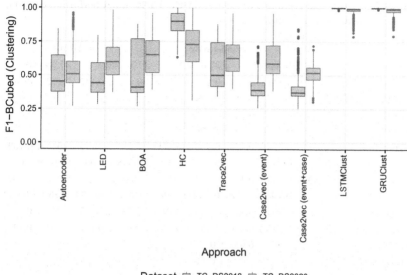

Fig. 3. Average F1-BCubed performance across all event logs grouped by approach.

The HC approach, that uses frequent pattern mining on case attributes and optimizes the process model fitness, performs well on both datasets, but lacks behind LSTMClust and GRUClust. For both datasets, Trace2vec outperformed Case2vec although incorporating attributes. This can be mainly explained by the concatenation of the activity name, event and case attribute such that each combination results in a different word. Consequently, the vocabulary size increases and Case2vec cannot infer the semantic relationships because these combinations occur less frequent in the event log.

A detailed analysis of the results revealed that the vector size of the neural networks had a significant influence ($\chi^2(8) = 7666.676$, $p < .001$, $W = .887$) on the performance with a large effect. The effect was *large* for Case2vec (event+case) ($W = .846$), autoencoder ($W = .605$) and Case2vec (event) ($W = .590$), *moderate* for LSTMClust ($W = .381$) and Trace2vec ($W = .376$), and *small* for GRUClust ($W = .300$). Post-hoc tests showed different significance levels for the different combinations from which we could not draw any clear conclusions. The results show that a vector size between 8 and 32 is sufficient to learn good representations for these datasets.

Furthermore, we analyzed the effect of noise on the performance using the TC-DS2020 dataset. As depicted in Fig. 4, the analysis showed significant influence ($\chi^2(10) = 237.947$, $p < .001$, $W = .991$) on the performance with a large effect. Post-hoc tests confirmed significant influence ($p < .001$) for all approaches with the largest effect for the autoencoder ($W = .996$), and a decrease of a F1-BCubed score from $\mu = .638$ ($\sigma = .130$) to $\mu = .366$ ($\sigma = .041$). The same

Table 2. The mean and standard deviation for the F1-BCubed performance grouped by dataset, clustering algorithm, and epochs.

	Approach	Agglomerative		K-Means	
		10 epochs	25 epochs	10 epochs	25 epochs
TC-DS2018	Autoencoder	0.439 ± 0.134	0.457 ± 0.143	0.432 ± 0.132	0.452 ± 0.142
	BOA	0.518 ± 0.196		-	
	LED	0.487 ± 0.146		-	
	HC	0.891 ± 0.081		-	
	Trace2vec	0.519 ± 0.164	0.520 ± 0.171	0.516 ± 0.166	0.518 ± 0.169
	Case2vec (event)	0.361 ± 0.096	0.370 ± 0.086	0.348 ± 0.091	0.361 ± 0.084
	Case2vec (event+case)	0.338 ± 0.112	0.333 ± 0.108	0.309 ± 0.106	0.308 ± 0.107
	GRUClust	$\mathbf{0.940 \pm 0.129}$	$\mathbf{0.971 \pm 0.079}$	$\mathbf{0.939 \pm 0.130}$	$\mathbf{0.969 \pm 0.082}$
	LSTMClust	0.902 ± 0.174	0.948 ± 0.122	0.901 ± 0.175	0.947 ± 0.124
TC-DS2020	Autoencoder	0.477 ± 0.140	0.489 ± 0.140	0.470 ± 0.142	0.484 ± 0.142
	BOA	0.662 ± 0.156		-	
	LED	0.626 ± 0.144		-	
	HC	0.716 ± 0.154		-	
	Trace2vec	0.560 ± 0.154	0.618 ± 0.152	0.551 ± 0.152	0.614 ± 0.153
	Case2vec (event)	0.500 ± 0.161	0.581 ± 0.159	0.492 ± 0.161	0.578 ± 0.155
	Case2vec (event+case)	0.404 ± 0.099	0.424 ± 0.089	0.384 ± 0.099	0.411 ± 0.090
	GRUClust	0.932 ± 0.094	0.954 ± 0.057	0.924 ± 0.094	0.943 ± 0.063
	LSTMClust	$\mathbf{0.937 \pm 0.089}$	$\mathbf{0.955 \pm 0.063}$	$\mathbf{0.934 \pm 0.090}$	$\mathbf{0.949 \pm 0.065}$

observation was found for HC with a decrease from F1-BCubed of $\mu = .855$ ($\sigma = .065$) down to $\mu = .548$ ($\sigma = .108$).

Process Models. We also evaluated the quality of the process models discovered from each subset. In our experiments, we found that the very simple approaches BOA and LED produce simpler models with a high fitness and precision. However, those approaches do not accurately identify the subsets that were originally inserted into the event logs. LSTMClust and GRUClust also produce process models of high fitness, precision and simplicity but performance is lower than BOA and LED (see Fig. 4). Further analysis revealed that the LSTMClust and GRUClust perform best for very complex and noisy event logs.

We found that only the HC is able to outperform BOA and LED with respect to fitness and simplicity as well as F1-BCubed with less noisy event logs. The HC performance regarding the precision of the models significantly depends on the event logs and only delivers good results when there is only a low percentage of noisy traces. This can be seen specifically in the F-Score (the combined fitness and precision metric) as depicted in Fig. 5.

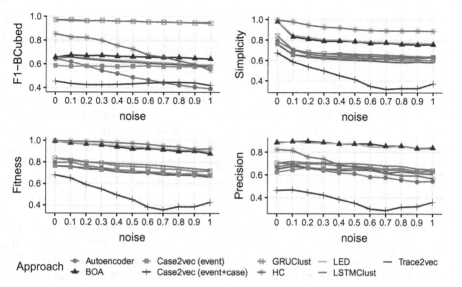

Fig. 4. Average F1-BCubed, Fitness, Precision, and Simplicity of the TC-DS2020 event logs aggregated by noise level with 25 training epochs for neural network approaches.

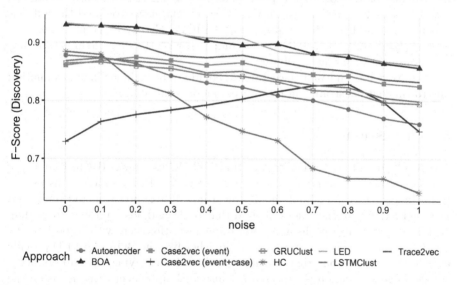

Fig. 5. Average F-Score for the process models of the TC-DS2020 event logs aggregated by noise level with agglomerative clustering and 25 training epochs.

4.5 Results: Real-Life Event Logs

The evaluation of the real-life event logs confirmed the observations for the synthetic evaluation. As shown in Table 3, LSTMClust and GRUClust are the best performing approaches regarding subset identification.

The analysis of the BPIC15 event log confirmed significant differences ($\chi^2(5) = 148.206$, $p < .001$, $W = .823$) between the neural network approaches with a large effect. Post-hoc tests confirmed differences ($p < .001$) between all approaches except between Case2vec (event) and GRUClust, Case2vec (event) and LSTMClust, and GRUClust and LSTMClust ($p > .05$). Different from the observations made in the synthetic evaluation, Case2vec performed better than Trace2vec. Incorporating the executing user lead to a significantly better performance. However, using the case attributes significantly ($p < .001$) decreased performance compared to the same architecture that only considers event attributes. The HC works particularly well regarding the simplicity metric but was not able to provide better process models regarding the F-Score. LSTMClust, GRUClust, and Case2vec (event) are the only approaches that are able to identify the subsets while also providing solid process model performance.

For the BPIC19, we discovered consistent results across the different parameter configurations. Still, there are significant differences ($\chi^2(5) = 140.460$, $p < .001$, $W = .780$) between the neural network approaches. Similar to BPIC15, post-hoc tests confirm significant ($p < .001$) differences between the approaches except between Case2vec (event) and GRUClust, Case2vec (event) and LSTM-Clust, and GRUClust and LSTMClust ($p > .05$). Again, the GRUClust and the LSTMClust produced the best performance regarding subset identification, followed by Case2vec (event+case), Case2vec (event), Trace2vec and the autoencoder. Different from the results of the BPIC15, Case2vec (event+case) performed significantly ($p < .001$) better compared with the same architecture that only considers the event attributes.

Note that certain results (see Table 3) could not be included in our evaluation due to timeout constraints of the process model evaluation.

5   Discussion

The results of our evaluation suggest that LSTMClust and GRUClust are capable of accurately identifying subsets of an event log. Process models discovered from these subsets are of high quality regarding fitness, precision and simplicity. Detailed analysis of the results showed that both methods are robust regarding vector size, training epochs and noisy event logs. However, with respect to the quality of the models, more simpler approaches like the BOA and LED provide even better results but they are not capable of identifying the subsets accurately. This observation is expected because both approaches only focus on the control flow. The other evaluated approaches, i.e., the autoencoder, Trace2vec and Case2vec, show lower performance across all the quality metrics. We believe LSTMClust and GRUClust have a high potential since results are solid although both approaches are not explicitly optimized for process discovery.

Table 3. Best performance of the real-life event logs grouped by approach and corresponding configuration. Results marked with * contain missing results due to process model evaluation timeouts.

Dataset	Approach	Metric	$|V|$	Clusterer	F1-BCubed	F-Score	Simpl.
	Heuristics Miner	-		-	-	0.596	0.723
	Inductive Miner	-		-	-	0.462	0.488
	BOA	-		agglom.	0.287	0.567	0.745
	LED	-		agglom.	0.243	0.594	0.753
	Autoencoder	Euclidean	128	agglom.	0.560	0.308	0.415
BPIC15	Trace2vec	Euclidean	128	k-means	0.294	0.525	0.744
	Case2vec (event)	cosine	128	agglom.	0.984	0.476	0.602
	Case2vec (event+case)	Euclidean	32	agglom.	0.561	0.168	0.241
	HC	-		-	0.478	0.447	0.763
	GRUClust	Euclidean	64	agglom.	0.993	0.475	0.600
	LSTMClust	cosine	64	agglom.	0.986	0.471	0.601
	Heuristics Miner	-		-	-	0.547	0.653
	Inductive Miner	-		-	-	0.159	0.516
	BOA	-		agglom.	0.483	0.766	0.658
	LED	-		agglom.	0.593	0.886	0.660
	Autoencoder	cosine	32	agglom.	0.563	0.787	0.619
BPIC19	Trace2vec	cosine	8	agglom.	0.678	0.275*	0.309*
	Case2vec (event)	Euclidean	4	agglom.	0.667	0.521*	0.467*
	Case2vec (event+case)	Euclidean	3	agglom.	0.718	0.807*	0.619*
	HC	-		-	0.373	0.501	0.768
	GRUClust	cosine	64	agglom.	0.899	0.597	0.498
	LSTMClust	cosine	8	agglom.	0.900	0.850	0.684

The autoencoder, although consuming a single and large one-hot encoded case as the input, can provide good results when trained with a higher number of training epochs, larger vector size, and number of parameters. However, the autoencoder is very sensitive to noisy event logs and performance can drop significantly. Case2vec is sensitive to the selection of the attributes. Attributes that contain random values or do not contribute to the desired cluster result lead to a significant drop in performance. However, when selecting appropriate attributes, Case2vec can outperform Trace2vec significantly as shown in our evaluation. Yet, finding good attributes can still be difficult without prior knowledge.

6 Conclusion and Future Work

In this paper, we presented a novel representation learning technique based on RNNs to obtain vector representations of cases in an event log automatically, which can be used for different process mining techniques. Instead of forming an unsupervised learning problem, we train a neural network in a supervised fashion by using the sequence of activities including event attributes to predict the contextual factors of the corresponding case. Our approach does not rely on any prior knowledge about the process and is able to learn compact representations including contextual factors automatically. This is specifically useful in situations where no additional knowledge about the process is available. The results of the evaluation showed significant performance improvements of our RNN approach regarding the subset identification compared to other methods. Our approach also provides solid and comparable results with respect to the quality of the process models discovered from each of the subsets. Resulting process models have high fitness, precision and are simpler to understand for humans.

For future work, we would like to evaluate if our vector representations are also useful for other process mining techniques such as anomaly detection or conformance checking. It is interesting to investigate whether it is possible to train the neural network such that the quality of the process models are considered, leading to a more quality-driven approach as provided by the hybrid-clusterer [22] approach. Furthermore, the concept of transformer neural networks might also be useful in the area of process mining to better learn case and/or process representations. Transformer networks, like word embeddings, stem from the field of NLP, and are optimized to handle the sequential aspect of language. This would potentially reconcile the embedding and RNN approach. A different direction are graph neural networks that may be able to identify a set of local process models, small models that combined together provide a more explainable view on the entire process.

In conclusion, the internal state of recurrent neural networks is useful to obtain process representations for tasks like trace clustering in process mining. The sequential property of the process data as well as the contextual factors are included automatically, and thus our approach is applicable to any event log without the need to know the exact details of the process.

References

1. Appice, A., Malerba, D.: A co-training strategy for multiple view clustering in process mining. IEEE Trans. Serv. Comput. **9**, 832–845 (2016)
2. Bose, R.P.J.C., van der Aalst, W.M.P.: Context aware trace clustering: towards improving process mining results. In: International Conference on Data Mining (SIAM), pp. 401–412 (2009)
3. Bose, R.P.J.C., van der Aalst, W.M.P.: Trace clustering based on conserved patterns: towards achieving better process models. In: BPM Workshops, pp. 170–181 (2010)
4. Bui, H.N., Vu, T.S., Nguyen, T.T., Nguyen, T.C., Ha, Q.T.: A compact trace representation using deep neural networks for process mining. In: International Conference on Knowledge and Systems Engineering (2019)
5. Cho, K., et al.: Learning phrase representations using RNN encoder-decoder for statistical machine translation. In: Conference on Empirical Methods in Natural Language Processing, pp. 1724–1734, October 2014
6. De Koninck, P., De Weerdt, J.: Scalable mixed-paradigm trace clustering using super-instances. In: ICPM (2019)

7. De. Koninck, P., vanden Broucke, S., De. Weerdt, J.: act2vec, trace2vec, log2vec, and model2vec: representation learning for business processes. In: Weske, M., Montali, M., Weber, I., vom Brocke, J. (eds.) BPM 2018. LNCS, vol. 11080, pp. 305–321. Springer, Cham (2018). https://doi.org/10.1007/978-3-319-98648-7_18
8. van Dongen, B.: BPI Challenge 2015 (2015). https://doi.org/10.4121/uuid: 31a308ef-c844-48da-948c-305d167a0ec1
9. van Dongen, B.: BPI Challenge 2019 (2019). https://doi.org/10.4121/uuid: d06aff4b-79f0-45e6-8ec8-e19730c248f1
10. Evermann, J., Rehse, J.R., Fettke, P.: Predicting process behaviour using deep learning. Decis. Support Syst. **100**, 129–140 (2017)
11. Evermann, J., Thaler, T., Fettke, P.: Clustering traces using sequence alignment. In: Reichert, M., Reijers, H.A. (eds.) BPM 2015. LNBIP, vol. 256, pp. 179–190. Springer, Cham (2016). https://doi.org/10.1007/978-3-319-42887-1_15
12. Greco, G., Guzzo, A., Pontieri, L., Sacca, D.: Discovering expressive process models by clustering log traces. IEEE Trans. Knowl. Data Eng. **18**, 1010–1027 (2006)
13. Hochreiter, S., Schmidhuber, J.: Long short-term memory. Neural Comput. **9**, 1735–1780 (1997)
14. Jablonski, S., Röglinger, M., Schönig, S., Wyrtki, K.M.: Multi-perspective clustering of process execution traces. Enterp. Model. Inf. Syst. Archit. **14**(2), 1–22 (2019). https://doi.org/10.18417/emisa.14.2
15. Junior, S.B., Ceravolo, P., Damiani, E., Omori, N.J., Tavares, G.M.: Anomaly detection on event logs with a scarcity of labels. In: ICPM (2019)
16. Lu, X., Tabatabaei, S.A., Hoogendoorn, M., Reijers, H.A.: Trace clustering on very large event data in healthcare using frequent sequence patterns. In: Hildebrandt, T., van Dongen, B.F., Röglinger, M., Mendling, J. (eds.) BPM 2019. LNCS, vol. 11675, pp. 198–215. Springer, Cham (2019). https://doi.org/10.1007/978-3-030-26619-6_14
17. Luettgen, S., Seeliger, A., Nolle, T., Mühlhäuser, M.: Case2vec: advances in representation learning for business processes. In: Leemans, S., Leopold, H. (eds.) ICPM 2020. LNBIP, vol. 406, pp. 162–174. Springer, Cham (2021). https://doi.org/10. 1007/978-3-030-72693-5_13
18. Nolle, T., Luettgen, S., Seeliger, A., Mühlhäuser, M.: Analyzing business process anomalies using autoencoders. Mach. Learn. **107**(11), 1875–1893 (2018). https:// doi.org/10.1007/s10994-018-5702-8
19. Nolle, T., Luettgen, S., Seeliger, A., Mühlhäuser, M.: BINet: multi-perspective business process anomaly classification. Inf. Syst. 101458 (2019, in press, corrected proof). https://doi.org/10.1016/j.is.2019.101458
20. Peeperkorn, J., vanden Broucke, S., De. Weerdt, J.: Conformance checking using activity and trace embeddings. In: Fahland, D., Ghidini, C., Becker, J., Dumas, M. (eds.) BPM 2020. LNBIP, vol. 392, pp. 105–121. Springer, Cham (2020). https:// doi.org/10.1007/978-3-030-58638-6_7
21. Sánchez-Charles, D., Carmona, J., Muntés-Mulero, V., Solé, M.: Reducing event variability in logs by clustering of word embeddings. In: Teniente, E., Weidlich, M. (eds.) BPM 2017. LNBIP, vol. 308, pp. 191–203. Springer, Cham (2018). https:// doi.org/10.1007/978-3-319-74030-0_14
22. Seeliger, A., Nolle, T., Mühlhäuser, M.: Finding structure in the unstructured: hybrid feature set clustering for process discovery. In: Weske, M., Montali, M., Weber, I., vom Brocke, J. (eds.) BPM 2018. LNCS, vol. 11080, pp. 288–304. Springer, Cham (2018). https://doi.org/10.1007/978-3-319-98648-7_17

23. Song, M., Günther, C.W., van der Aalst, W.M.P.: Trace clustering in process mining. In: Ardagna, D., Mecella, M., Yang, J. (eds.) BPM 2008. LNBIP, vol. 17, pp. 109–120. Springer, Heidelberg (2009). https://doi.org/10.1007/978-3-642-00328-8_11

24. Tax, N., van Zelst, S.J., Teinemaa, I.: An experimental evaluation of the generalizing capabilities of process discovery techniques and black-box sequence models. In: Gulden, J., Reinhartz-Berger, I., Schmidt, R., Guerreiro, S., Guédria, W., Bera, P. (eds.) BPMDS/EMMSAD -2018. LNBIP, vol. 318, pp. 165–180. Springer, Cham (2018). https://doi.org/10.1007/978-3-319-91704-7_11

25. Taymouri, F., Rosa, M.L., Dumas, M., Maggi, F.M.: Business process variant analysis: survey and classification. Knowl.-Based Syst. **211**, 106557 (2021)

26. Thaler, T., Ternis, S., Fettke, P., Loos, P.: A comparative analysis of process instance cluster techniques. In: Wirtschaftsinformatik, pp. 423–437 (2015)

27. Zandkarimi, F., Rehse, J.R., Soudmand, P., Hoehle, H.: A generic framework for trace clustering in process mining. In: ICPM (2020)

Extracting Process Features from Event Logs to Learn Coarse-Grained Simulation Models

Mahsa Pourbafrani$^{(\boxtimes)}$ and Wil M. P. van der Aalst

Chair of Process and Data Science, RWTH Aachen University, Aachen, Germany
{mahsa.bafrani,wvdaalst}@pads.rwth-aachen.de

Abstract. Most process mining techniques are backward-looking, i.e., event data are used to diagnose performance and compliance problems. The combination of process mining and simulation allows for forward-looking approaches to answer "What if?" questions. However, it is difficult to create fine-grained simulation models that describe the process at the level of individual events and cases in such a way that reality is captured well. Therefore, we propose to use coarse-grained simulation models (e.g., System Dynamics) that simulate processes at a higher abstraction level. Coarse-grained simulation provides two advantages: (1) it is easier to discover models that mimic reality, and (2) it is possible to explore alternative scenarios more easily (e.g., brainstorming on the effectiveness of process interventions). However, this is only possible by bridging the gap between low-level event data and the coarse-grained process data needed to create higher-level simulation models where one simulation step may correspond to a day or week. This paper provides a general approach and corresponding tool support to bridge this gap. We show that we can indeed learn System Dynamics models from standard event data.

Keywords: Process mining · Quantifying processes · Process variable extraction · Scenario-based simulation · System dynamics

1 Introduction

As a business owner, the ability to know the process behavior in different situations is a crucial requirement to improve the process and foresee the upcoming problems. Process mining is a set of data-driven techniques that paves the way to this aim and describes the processes from different aspects [1]. The next step in process mining is to answer the questions regarding the future of processes. Simulation and prediction techniques in process mining are introduced to address this goal [2]. It is possible to perform "what-if" analyses and apply different scenarios on the systems, using fine-grained simulation models that behave close to the real systems. Such models are difficult to create and it is hard to explore alternative scenarios. For example, workers who are involved in multiple processes

© Springer Nature Switzerland AG 2021
M. La Rosa et al. (Eds.): CAiSE 2021, LNCS 12751, pp. 125–140, 2021.
https://doi.org/10.1007/978-3-030-79382-1_8

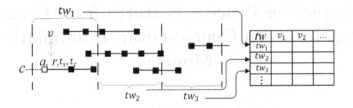

Fig. 1. Transforming fine-grained event logs into the quantitative variables to produce coarse-grained process logs. Time window (tw) indicates the time step, i.e., a specific period of time, and v represents the generated quantitative variable.

may seem under-utilized while being overloaded with work. Different aggregation levels of the states of a process are required for high-level decisions and investigating different scenarios. For instance, the average service time of cases per day plays a more important role than the service time of a single case in deciding on the number of resources to be allocated. As Fig. 1 shows, by looking at event data over a specific period of time, tw, different aspects of the process can be aggregated as process variables such as cases, time-related variables, resources, and activities. The aggregated state of the process and its behavior at that level directly affect every single instance in the process. The resulting coarse-grained process log has a value for each process variable per time window and is used to create a system dynamics model. System dynamics is an aggregated simulation technique that represents a system using the relationships between its variables [15]. System dynamics techniques are able to capture external factors, e.g., the effect of advertisements on the arrival rate of new customers, and simulate the general system without simulating low-level events, e.g., looking at the system at the aggregated level per day instead of taking every single event into consideration. Therefore, unlike traditional discrete event simulations, they are a good match to simulate processes at higher abstraction levels.

In [8], the idea of combining process mining techniques and system dynamics for the purpose of the scenario-based analyses was first presented. In this paper, we propose an approach to extract all the possible measurable aspects of a process systematically for creating coarse-grained process logs. As a result, we can generate default simulation models to be used by system dynamics techniques. The ultimate goal is to bridge the gap between the fine-grained event log and the coarse-grained process log. To do so, we extract *forward-looking* scenarios focusing on the performance aspect w.r.t. the existing attributes in the event log. These questions, i.e., scenarios, are the design choices that come from the process mining insights. For instance, the process shows a bottleneck in an organization, or a long waiting time for a specific part of the process, i.e., a set of activities. We map event logs into the part of the process which we want to focus on and analyze the filtered event logs. We split the filtered logs into the time steps, then we calculate measurable elements over each time step. The remainder of this paper is organized as follows. In Sect. 2, we present the related works. In Sect. 3, we introduce background concepts and notations. In Sect. 4, we present our main approach. We evaluate the approach in Sect. 5 by designing simulation models and Sect. 6 concludes this work.

2   Related Work

Several authors have explored approaches to use simulation in the context of process mining. In [13], the authors introduced an approach to design and generate discrete event simulation models from event logs in the form of Colored Petri Nets including many details such as resource pooling. In [5], the simulations are mainly focused on the activity-flow level presented by Petri nets. Other simulation techniques are based on BPMN models for simulating business processes. In [3], business process simulation including user interaction is proposed.

However, several challenges have not been addressed in the current simulation techniques. In many cases, simulation results are not accurate enough. This is due to the lack of sufficient historical information and not incorporating external factors. The simulation of business processes can be improved by exploiting the event logs and process mining techniques as proposed in [2]. Despite detailed simulation techniques such as discrete event simulation, system dynamics simulation techniques are able to capture a system at a higher level of aggregation as well as affecting the effect of external variables on the system [15]. Techniques such as system dynamics are able to capture external factors and influences. The combination of system dynamics and business processes is proposed in [4]. Authors in [12] mention the possibility of designing system dynamics models for the business processes. However, in the presented work the model generation and simulation are not supported by the data and it is based on the domain knowledge of the process.

The recently proposed approach in [8] introduces the idea of designing system dynamics models using process mining insights. The main goal is to capture the effects of the external variables in the simulation, e.g., the efficiency of users. However, only a proof of concept was provided to show the potential of the combination. Also, one of the applications of the approach, i.e., the production line, is shown in [11]. Furthermore, the extracted values for different variables are exploited to form the models [10]. Besides the hidden relationships between the variables, the granularity of the time step to extract the values highly affects the quality of the simulation results which is addressed in [9] by applying time-series analyses. In this paper, we propose a framework to define, generate and capture all the possible process variables and their quantitative values for answering "what-if" questions in the processes at different levels of aggregation. Our approach addresses designing, extracting, and calculating the required aggregate-simulation variables from event logs based on process mining insights.

3   Preliminaries

In this section, we define process mining and system dynamics concepts and the functions which are used in the proposed approach.

Process mining uses past executions of processes in the form of event logs. An event log captures events which include, case id, timestamps, activity, resource, and other possible attributes.

Table 1. Sample event log of a hospital. Each row is an event. For each unique patient (case) in the process, a specific activity at a specific time is performed by a specific resource.

Case ID	Activity	Age	Start timestamp	Complete timestamp	Resource
116	Registration	28	1/1/2020 10:29	1/1/2020 10:47	John
117	Registration	65	1/1/2020 10:29	1/1/2020 10:29	Sarah
116	First visit	35	1/1/2020 10:30	1/1/2020 10:50	Sam
118	Registration	78	1/1/2020 10:31	1/1/2020 10:49	Sarah
116	Examine	54	1/1/2020 10:31	1/1/2020 10:31	Carl
...	...	...	...	...	...

Definition 1 (Event Log). *An event is a tuple $e=(c,a,r,t_s,t_c)$, where $c\in\mathcal{C}$ is the case identifier, $a\in\mathcal{A}$ is the corresponding activity for the event e, $r\in\mathcal{R}$ is the resource, $t_s\in\mathcal{T}$ is the start time, and $t_c\in\mathcal{T}$ is the complete time of the event e. We call $\xi=\mathcal{C}\times\mathcal{A}\times\mathcal{R}\times\mathcal{T}\times\mathcal{T}$ the universe of events. We also define projection functions, $\pi_C\colon\xi\to\mathcal{C}$, $\pi_A\colon\xi\to\mathcal{A}$, $\pi_R\colon\xi\to\mathcal{R}$, $\pi_{T_S}\colon\xi\to\mathcal{T}$ and $\pi_{T_C}\colon\xi\to\mathcal{T}$ for attributes of events. We assume that events are unique and an event log L is a set of events, i.e., $L\subseteq\xi$.*

For event log $L\subseteq\xi$, $p_s(L)=\min_{e\in L}\pi_{T_S}(e)$ and $p_c(L)=\max_{e\in L}\pi_{T_C}(e)$ return the minimum start timestamp and maximum complete timestamp in L.

A sequence of events with the same case identifier and ordered in time represents a process instance, i.e., a trace.

Definition 2 (Trace). *A trace $\sigma\in\xi^*$ is a finite sequence of events $\sigma=\langle e_1,...,e_n\rangle$, where each $e_i\in\sigma$ happens at most once and for each $e_i,e_j\in\sigma, \pi_C(e_i)=\pi_C(e_j)\wedge\pi_{T_S}(e_i)\leq\pi_{T_S}(e_j), if\ i<j$. For $\sigma\in\xi^*$, $\tilde{\sigma}=\{e\in\sigma\}$ is the set of events in σ. We denote $\overline{L}$ as the set of all traces in the event log L.*

For instance, for a patient in an event log of a hospital in Table 1, the first event e represents that for the patient with case id *116* (c), the activity *registration* (a) was started at timestamp *10:29 01.01.2020* (t_s) by resource *John* (r) and was completed at timestamp *10:47 01.01.2020* (t_c). For the same patient, the sequence of events w.r.t. time is called a trace in the process, e.g., the sequence of activities is *registration, first visit, examine, second visit*.

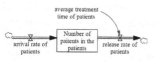

System Dynamics. System dynamics techniques model dynamic systems and their interaction with their environment [16]. The stock-flow diagram is one of the main modeling notations in system dynamics. Systems are modeled w.r.t. three different elements, i.e., stocks, flows, and variables. Stocks are accumulative variables over time, flows manipulate the stock values and variables influence the values of flows and other variables over time. A simple stock-flow diagram for the hospital example is shown in Fig. 2. For instance, the *arrival rate* of the patients and the *release rate* of the patients as flows add/remove to/from the values of the *number of patients in the hospital* as a stock, also, *average treatment time* as a variable affects the release rate. Considering one day as the step of time w.r.t. Figure 2, on average 160 patients, enter the process in the hospital, i.e., the arrival rate, and on average the process takes 8 hours, i.e., average service time. Therefore, simulating the release rate and the number of patients in the hospital per day is possible. The number of patients in the tth day of the simulation is equal to the initial number of patients in the hospital at the beginning of the simulation added by

Fig. 2. The value of the stock *number of patients in the hospital* is calculated based on the *arrival rate of patients* and *finish rate of patients* flows (per time step). The value of *finish rate of patients* is affected by the *average treatment time of patients*.

$$\int_0^t (+arrival\ rate\ of\ patients - release\ rate\ of\ patients)dt.$$

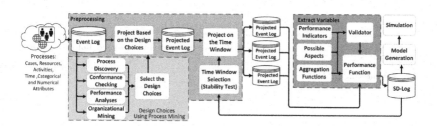

Fig. 3. The main framework to generate possible process variables which describe the process over the steps of time, i.e., SD-Logs. These results are used to form simulation models.

4 Approach

Our approach includes three main modules, as shown in Fig. 3, i.e., applying *Design Choices*, *Preprocessing* step, and *Extract Variables*. Using our approach process behavior is described at different levels. We generate process variables describing the process quantitatively. The transformed process log (SD-Log) provides a coarse-grained view of the observed behavior. These variables are used to generate high-level simulation models to answer what-if questions.

Questions and scenarios are based on the design choices, which are highlighted by the process mining insights. As shown in Fig. 3, process discovery [1], conformance checking [6], performance analysis, and organizational mining [14] results enable designing the simulation scenarios and models. These insights should be quantified in order to be put into action. Based on these results, the focus of the simulation models is either a set of activities, resources, or cases. Therefore, we use the projected event logs on the events including the specified aspects. The focus can be on the whole process, the organizational level, or a part of activity-flow in the process, e.g., workflow pattern structures. For instance, organizational mining shows low efficiency for one of the organizations in the process, therefore, simulation models w.r.t. this knowledge can be designed, e.g., does the resource allocation from the other organization improve the efficiency?

To describe the process over the steps of time, we aggregate the event logs at the time level, i.e., looking at the process in a specific period of time using *Preprocessing* module. The process event log is prepared w.r.t. the design choices from *Design Choice* and the selected time window, the next step is to extract the variables. The *Extract Variables* module defines and calculates possible variables over the steps of time. These variables are the main components of the simulation models for answering what-if questions.

Table 2. Possible design choices for generating simulation models using process mining techniques. *Discovery* and *Conformance Checking* techniques help in selecting a set of activities, resources, organizations, and cases based on the process event log L and the process model M.

PM Techniques	Insights						
	Set of cases	Set of activities		Set of resources			
		Activity	Workflow patterns	Resource	Roles	Organizations	
Discovery (L)	+	+	+	+	+	+	
Conformance checking (L, M)	+	+	+	+	+	+	

4.1 Event Log Preparation

We break down the "forward-looking" analysis into the measurable elements which can be measured over time. We refer to these measurable elements of the scenarios/questions as process variables. These variables are either in the process or in the process environment which some are captured in the event log. To extract possible process variables over time steps, the first step is to form an event log based on the focus of the scenarios/questions and generating different event logs of the process for each time step.

Using the defined *Time Window Projection* and *Design Choices Projection* functions, different levels of what-if analyses are achievable, and the *Performance Function* generates the values of the performance variables.

Design Choices Using Process Mining. The insights provided by the process mining techniques indicate the focus of the modeling. Process discovery, conformance checking, performance analyses, and organizational analyses result in specific parts of a process to be simulated.

Table 2 presents possible insights from different process mining techniques. A set of cases, activities, and resources are possible targets of scenario-based analyses. For instance, for the given example, there is an XOR choice between two activities, *examine* and *radiology* in the process, and the involved activities can be a bottleneck based on the performance analysis and process discovery results, or conformance checking reveals a skipped path for a specific type of cases, e.g., *second visit* is not performed for young patients.

In order to apply the discovered design choices to the simulation model generations, the first step is to use them for process variable extraction. To do so, we define *Design Choice* projection which projects an event log based on the design choices in Table 2. The projected event log includes the corresponding events for the selected insights, e.g., a set of activities.

Definition 3 (Design Choice Projection). *Let ξ be the universe of events and $R{\subseteq}\mathcal{R}$, $C{\subseteq}\mathcal{C}$, and $A{\subseteq}\mathcal{A}$ be the selected sets of resources, cases, and activities, respectively. $DC{\subseteq}2^R{\times}2^C{\times}2^A$ is the universe of design choices. $\Pi_{(R,C,A)} : 2^\xi{\nrightarrow}2^\xi$ is a function that projects a set of events on the given design choice $(R,C,A) \in DC$. For $L{\subseteq}\xi$, $\Pi_{(R,C,A)}(L){=}\{e{\in}L|\pi_\mathcal{R}(e) \in R \wedge \pi_C(e) \in C \wedge \pi_\mathcal{A}(e) \in A\}$.*

For example, in our running example, the process performance analysis shows that the first activity for the patient, *registration*, is the bottleneck of the process. Projecting the event log of the hospital to that specific part structures the simulation model. Therefore, the projected event log only includes the events containing the *registration* activity.

Preprocessing. The design choices indicate which parts of the process should be considered for simulation modeling. The projection functions return an event log in which the events are only from the specified set of insights. Moreover, we define a time projection function to capture the provided event logs between two specific timestamps, e.g., indicated as tw in Fig. 1.

Definition 4 (Time Window Projection). *Let ξ be the universe of events and T be the universe of timestamps. For $t{\in}T$ and $\delta{\in}\mathbb{N}$, given $L{\subseteq}\xi$, we define $Event_{t,t+\delta}(L){=}\{e{\in}L|t{\leq}\pi_{T_S}(e){\leq}t + \delta\}$ and $CaseEvent_{t,t+\delta}(L){=}\{e{\in}L|\exists_{\sigma\in\overline{L}}e \in \sigma \wedge \exists_{e'\in\sigma}t \leq \pi_{T_S}(e') \leq t + \delta\}$. The projection function $P_{t,t+\delta} : 2^\xi{\nrightarrow}2^\xi$ returns a set of events, such that, $P_{t,t+\delta}(L){=}Event_{t,t+\delta}(L) \cup CaseEvent_{t,t+\delta}(L)$.*

An event log can be broken down into smaller ones per time period, e.g., instead of an event log of 10 days in an organization, 10 event logs for each day exist. Before extracting the variables on top of the projected event logs, it is important to consider the overlapping events in different time steps, i.e., between every t and $t+\delta$ (a window of time tw). To address this issue, for $k \in \mathbb{N}$ as the number of times steps using δ as time window, two functions, *Event* and

CaseEvent in Definition 4 are defined. Using $Event_{t,t+\delta}$, all the events started and finished in i^{th} step are captured. For instance, assume δ to be one day, an event started in one day and finished the next day is only considered in the step that it has started in, i.e., the first day. *CaseEvent* returns all the events related to the cases that one of their events happened at i^{th} time step.

4.2 Variable Extraction (SD-Log Generation)

For each of the provided event logs as a result of applying *Time Window Projection* in Definition 4, the process variables should be designed. To design the process variables for the given event logs, i.e., process describers over time steps, performance indicators should be determined.

Process performance indicators can be derived from the timestamp attributes t_s and t_c for the cases, activities, and resources at different levels, which all are considered as aspects. For instance, *service time* of a case, an activity or a resource, *waiting time* of a case, and *time in process* of a case are the possible performance indicators. The aggregation functions also can be applied on top of the performance indicators. These functions can be chosen between mathematical functions such as average, median, and sum. For instance, the average service time of cases in an event log, i.e., paints in the hospital, is calculated using *average* as the aggregation function, *case* as the aspect, and *service time* as the performance indicator. Note that for calculating the performance indicators related to the case aspect, *CaseEvent* makes it possible to capture the related events from the present cases in that time window.

Process Variable in Definition 5 defines process variables by assessing the validity of combining different possible process aspects, performance indicators, and aggregation functions. First, we define a set of possible combinations as shown in Table 3. Based on the design choices and different parameters, i.e., possible process features, process variables are designed. The process variables values are calculated by Definition 6.

Table 3. The validator table, which shows the possibility of applying different Aggregation Functions (AF) on top of the Performance Indicators (IN) for different Aspects (AS). The valid combinations provide process features which along with the selected design choices form process variables.

Validator	IN												
	Value	Count					Service time			Waiting time			Time in process
AF / AS	Numerical variable	Categorical variable	Numerical variable	Case	Resource	Activity	Case	Resource	Activity	Case	Resource	Activity	Case
Sum	True	False	True	False	False	False	True	True	True	True	True	True	True
Average	True	False	True	False	False	False	True	True	True	True	True	True	True
Median	True	False	True	False	False	False	True	True	True	True	True	True	True
⊥	False	True	False	True	True	True	False	False	False	False	False	False	False

Definition 5 (Process Variable). *Let AF={average, median, sum, ⊥} be the set of aggregation functions, IN = {service time, waiting time, time in process, count, value} be the set of performance indicators and AS = {case, resource, activity, numerical attributes, categorical attributes} be the set of process aspects. We denote $\mathcal{F}$=AF × IN × AS as the set of process features (Table 3). $\mathcal{V}$=DC × $\mathcal{F}$ is denoted as the set of process variables. For the given design choice $(R, C, A) \in DC$ and the process feature $f \in \mathcal{F}$, v=$((R, C, A), f) \in \mathcal{V}$ is a process variable.*

Table 3 shows the possibility of combining different parameters to generate valid process features, e.g., it is not possible to apply the average function (af=$average$) on the number (in=$count$) of activities (as=$activity$) in an event log. These possible features are used to form process variables using the design choices in Definition 3.

Definition 6 (Performance Function). *Let ξ be the universe of events and $\mathcal{V}$ be the set of process variables. Φ:$\mathcal{V} \times 2^{\xi} \rightarrow \mathbb{R}_{\geq 0}$ generates the value of the process variable of an event log.*

We generate the set of sequential states of the process with *Time Window Projection* function in Definition 4 and define *Performance Variable* in Definition 5. The next step is to generate the values of the process variables by applying *Performance Function* on the projected event logs as defined in Definition 6.

For instance, let L be the event log of the running example, f=(af, in, as) be a process feature where af=$average$, in=$time\ in\ process$, and as=$case$, based on Table 3, the combination is valid. For the design choice (R, C, A), consider R={$\pi_{\mathcal{R}}(e)|e \in L$}, C={$\pi_{\mathcal{C}}(e)|e \in L$}, and A={$\pi_{\mathcal{A}}(e)|e \in L$}, i.e., the sets of all the resources, cases, and activities in L, respectively. Therefore, $v = ((R, C, A), f)$ is the average time that all cases (patients) spend in the hospital. $\Phi(v, L)$ represents the value of this process variable, i.e.,

$$\Phi(v, L) = \frac{\sum_{i=1}^{|L|} p_c(\tilde{\sigma}_i) - p_s(\tilde{\sigma}_i)}{|L|}.$$

The calculated values of variables form a coarse-grained process log, referred to as SD-Log, over time. The values define the process over time at a higher level of aggregation and can be used for designing the simulation models. Definition 7 defines an SD-Log and Algorithm 1 transforms an event log to an SD-Log.

Definition 7 (SD-Log). *Let $L \subseteq \xi$ be an event log, $\mathcal{V}$ be a set of process variables, $\delta \in \mathbb{N}$ be the selected time window, and k=$\lceil \frac{(p_c(L) - p_s(L))}{\delta} \rceil$ be the number of time steps in the event log w.r.t. δ. The SD-Log of a given L and δ is $sd_{L,\delta}$:{1, ..., k}×$\mathcal{V} \rightarrow \mathbb{R}_{\geq 0}$, such that $sd_{L,\delta}(i, v)$ represents the value of performance function $\Phi(L, v)$ in the ith-time window $(1 \leq i \leq k)$.*

Table 4(a) shows a sample SD-Log with $\delta = 1\ day$ that includes different process variables for the sets of all the resources (R), cases (C), and activities (A) in the sample event log of the hospital, e.g., f=$(average, service\ time, case)$ and $((R, C, A), f)$ represents the process variable v, average service time for all the cases, i.e., patients, and $\Phi(v, L)$ calculates the value of v in each day in the sample log L. Also, in Table 4(a), *number of resources* in the hospital per day

---

Algorithm 1: Variable extraction algorithm w.r.t. the given design choices, which generates SD-Logs for scenario-based analysis.

Input: *event log L, set of process variables $\mathcal{V}$, time window δ, design choice des*

Output: *SD−Log sd*

1 $L'=\Pi_{des}(L)$
2 $t_S=p_s(L')$(start time of the event log)
3 $t_C=p_c(L')$(complete time of the event log)
4 $k=\lceil \frac{(t_C-t_S)}{\delta} \rceil$
5 **foreach** $i \in [1,k]$ **do**
6 $\quad$ $L''=P_{t_S,t_S+\delta}(L')$
7 $\quad$ $t_S=t_S + \delta$
8 $\quad$ **foreach** $v \in \mathcal{V}$ **do**
9 $\quad\quad$ | $\quad$ add $\Phi(v,L'')$ to $sd(i,v)$
10 $\quad$ **end**
11 **end**
12 **return** *sd*;

Table 4. A part of two sample SD-Logs of the running example with a time window of 1 day using different design choices. Each row shows a time step, here 1 day, cell-values represent the process variables' values and columns represent the process variables.

(a)					(b)			
Time Window (Daily)	Arrival rate of cases	Number of resources	Average service time	Average waiting time in process	Time Window Daily	Number of resources *(registration)*	Average service time *(registration)*	Average waiting time in process (registration)
1	180	6	0.359	0.609	1	2	0.425	0.237
2	147	6	0.415	0.540	2	1	0.120	0.483
3	160	6	0.401	0.596	3	1	0.806	0.506
⋮	⋮	⋮	⋮	⋮	⋮	⋮	⋮	⋮

represents the process variable $v = ((R,C,A),(\bot,count,resource)) \in \mathcal{V}$, where R,C, and A are the sets of all the resources, cases and activities in the log, $R=\{\pi_R(e)|e \in L\}$, $C=\{\pi_C(e)|e \in L\}$, and $A=\{\pi_A(e)|e \in L\}$. For generating Table 4(b), $A=\{registration\}$ and R and C are the same as (a).

Based on the design choices, the whole process or specific parts of the process are selected to be modeled and the *Time Window Projection* function generates all the steps of the time for the given time window. The rest of the algorithm is calculating the values of the variables and forming the SD-Log.

Then investigating the relationships between process variables with each other will result in a system dynamics model [10]. The simulation model can be populated with the values of the process variables. Hence, we have a model on which different scenarios for a process can be played. For each question, the components of the question, i.e., process variables, can be the target of the question like the number of finished cases per day or the ones influencing the target of the question such as the number of resources available per day in this example.

5   Evaluation

Our goal is to design higher-level simulation models of processes using the proposed approach. With the models and the extracted SD-Logs which include process variables over time, we assess the validity of the designed models based on the simulated values. To do so, we start with presenting the possible valid models, i.e., system dynamics models for the processes. We use the event logs with common attributes to perform what-if analysis. A real event log, BPI Challenge 2012, is considered to evaluate the approach, i.e., designing the models and extracting the process variables of the process, SD-Log. The possible scenarios considered in the designed model for evaluation are presented in Sect. 5.1. We use one of the scenarios as an example to show the evaluation of the approach.

Extracting the corresponding SD-Log from the event log based on the defined process variables to populate and run the models is the next step. In the last step, the simulation results are compared to the real values inside the SD-Logs, e.g., the simulated number of cases per day in the process and the values in the SD-Log which are derived from the event log. Finally, we discuss the evaluation results, limitations, and possible improvements.

5.1   Designing Simulation Models

To design the simulation models, capturing the relationship between variables directly influences the validity of the models. Either the relations are known beforehand which can be proven by the data or it is an assumption that can be supported or rejected by values of variables over time. For instance, it is known that the number of cases in the process is directly affected by the arrival rate of the cases per hour and the process finish rate. Based on the process and the domain knowledge, the relationship between the number of resources and the arrival rate is expected to be seen, and the variables in the SD-Log can support or reject this assumption.

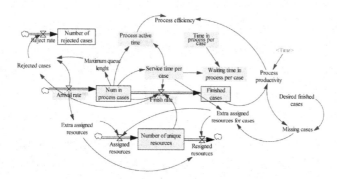

Fig. 4. The sample stock-flow diagram model for the business processes including multiple scenarios. The process variables directly extracted from the event logs are highlighted (blue). The model includes known and expected relationships inside a process at an aggregated level and can be customized for different levels, e.g., one organization. (Color figure online)

We design the basic model shown in Fig. 4 (highlighted elements), for the general process which is possible for validation since the variables can be extracted from the event logs' attributes. We extend the model with the possible external variables for possible business scenarios to answer more questions. This model can be used for different levels in the process, from an activity level to the general process based on the design choices. Common scenarios are inserted into the base model as follows:

- Process efficiency is the number of finished cases in the active time of the process per unit of time. Process efficiency gets affected by the number of cases in the process and the finish rate of the process.
- The effect of the arrival rate on adjusting the number of resources dynamically. An increase in the number of cases arriving in the process leads to an increase in the number of resources assigned to the process.
- Adjusting resources to achieve the desired number of finished cases per unit of time. In case that the finish rate is below the desired number per specified window of time, the resources can be increased or in the opposite situation, the unnecessary resources can be released.
- The effect of the desired capacity of the process on the number of rejected cases. The capacity of the process for handling the cases can be adjusted with the amount of possible rejected cases by the process.
- The effect of cases in the process per unit of time on the average service time of cases. The average service time can be decreased since the resources work faster under a specific amount of workload.

Figure 4 shows the designed model which can be applied in the process at different levels, e.g., one activity or one organization. It covers all the described scenarios and the performance variables presented in the can be validated.

Organizational/Process Blocks. The introduced models and scenarios can be applied to the organizations, activities, and resources in the processes.

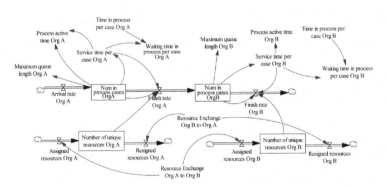

Fig. 5. The designed model for two organizations in the process which hand-over the tasks. Assessing possible scenarios such as how to share the resources between two organizations A and B for smaller queues is possible.

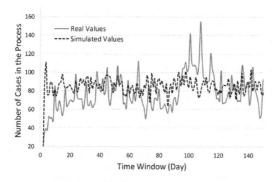

Fig. 6. The real and simulated values of the number of cases in the process only including the set of activities that were performed by the resources in BPI Challenge 2012.

Moreover, the extended models can be designed to capture the interaction between different parts of the process, e.g., two organizations which hand-over the work or the flow of cases, e.g., items in a production line or between different activities in the process. The most common scenario is that organizations sharing the flow of cases, therefore, organizations can exchange the resources and it can be modeled as shown in Fig. 5.

5.2 Evaluation Results

In this section, we assess the validity of the designed general models for the real processes using the provided tool [7] which is publicly available. As indicated in Sect. 5.1, models with variables outside the captured information in event logs are not possible to be validated completely. Therefore, we use the basic default models, highlighted part in Fig. 4 for this section to show the validity of the simulation models and their results. In the BPI Challenge 2012 event log, three different types of activities exist, i.e., performed by users, performed by the system, and performed by the resources. Performance analysis of the process reveals that the most time-consuming part of the process is the flow of tasks including the third type of activities, i.e., employees' tasks. The system-related tasks such as the submission of a request are instance tasks, i.e., the duration is zero, and not related to the efficiency and speed of the employees inside the organization. Therefore, we use the process which only includes the activities and tasks performed by the employees, i.e., their speed and efficiency affect the process. Using the *Design Choice* function, we created the projected event log only including the corresponding events to the third category of activities, i.e., design choice $=(R, C, A)$, where $R=$ the set of all resources in the log, $C=$ the set of all cases in the log, and $A=$ list of activities (employees' task).

Based on the time series analysis approach presented in [9] for time window selection, we chose a *one day* time window and focus on the general model for the simulation of the process in BPI Challenge 2012. We use the extracted variables

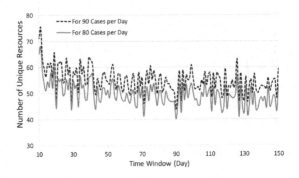

Fig. 7. The number of required unique resources using the dynamic assigning resources based on the desired number of finished cases per day. As shown, exploiting the extended model Fig. 4, on average 9% more resources per day is required to cover 90 finished cases instead of 80 cases.

to define the underlying equations inside the simulation models as proposed in [10]. The populated model with the equations and the values from SD-Log is simulated for 150 steps (days).

The results for the variable *number of cases in the process* in each time window are shown in Fig. 6. Calculating the average pair-wise error of the steps shows 24%. In order to form the stock-flow model, we used the functions that generate the random values for the variables such as the arrival rate using their discovered distribution. The validated model and the values of variables from the SD-Log can be used to exploit further scenarios for the extended model. For instance, in order to see the effect of an increase in the number of desired finished cases from 80 per day to 90 cases, using the model in Fig. 4, the simulation results show that on average 9% increase in the number of unique resources per day is required. Figure 7 represents the results for the two scenarios. The dynamic adjusting of the resources is done by captured relations among the variables, i.e., *assigned resources*, *number of missing cases*, and *average service time*.

Discussion. Using an event log, SD-Logs can be generated which are used to design and populate the corresponding system dynamics models. Inserting the effect of external factors increases the possibility of what-if analysis. However, by adding external factors from outside the event logs into the simulation models, the pair-wise evaluation is not possible, e.g., consider models including variables such as resources expertise, or their efficiency. Therefore, we start with generating models including the variables extracted from event logs and evaluate those, after that, we introduce the external factors to the models for further simulations and what-if analyses. Moreover, capturing the dynamic behavior of processes over windows of time is not always a straightforward task. For instance, in the event log of an emergency room, it is difficult to capture similar patterns in a daily manner for the process variables such as the arrival rate. Therefore, the evaluation of the results of the system dynamics simulation is not accurate enough, and it depends on the time window.

Generating SD-Logs and simulation models using bigger windows of time, e.g., one week instead of a daily manner, can increase the accuracy of the models w.r.t. the pair-wise comparisons of results. Given the above-mentioned concerns, applying the approach on the case studies with known influential external factors, e.g., the amount of money spent on the advertisement and the duration of the advertisement in a process, verifies the approach in practice. In principle, the quality of the captured data from event logs and the process domain knowledge affect the quality of the models.

6 Conclusion

In this paper, we presented an approach to capture the processes in a quantified manner over time. Describing the processes using process variables makes designing valid simulation models possible. We started from event logs and by exploiting process mining techniques the possible design choices are identified. All the possible process variables which represent the process over time w.r.t. different aspects are extracted. The provided functions imply how the design choices can be taken into action using the provided insights by process mining. These design choices are applied to the event logs. Moreover, performance functions are introduced regarding the existed aspects and levels in the event logs. The derived coarse-grained process logs, called SD-Logs, are created based on the performance functions for the generated variables over time and are used to form simulation models for "what-if" analyses. Furthermore, the general models are presented as guidelines for designing possible scenarios which can be customized based on the process variables and scenarios for different processes. We assessed the validity of the designed model using real event logs. The next step is to focus on the underlying equations between variables. These equations are used as a baseline of more accurate stock-flow diagrams in system dynamics modeling for simulation purposes.

Acknowledgments. Funded by the Deutsche Forschungsgemeinschaft (DFG, German Research Foundation) under Germany's Excellence Strategy– EXC 2023 Internet of Production- Project ID: 390621612. We also thank the Alexander von Humboldt (AvH) Stiftung for supporting our research.

References

1. van der Aalst, W.M.P.: Process Mining - Data Science in Action, 2nd edn. Springer, Heidelberg (2016). https://doi.org/10.1007/978-3-662-49851-4
2. van der Aalst, W.M.P.: Process mining and simulation: a match made in heaven! In: Proceedings of the 50th Computer Simulation Conference, SummerSim 2018, pp. 4:1–4:12 (2018)
3. Camargo, M., Dumas, M., González, O.: Automated discovery of business process simulation models from event logs. Decis. Support Syst. **134**, 113284 (2020)

4. Duggan, J.: A comparison of Petri net and system dynamics approaches for modelling dynamic feedback systems. In: 24th International Conference of the Systems Dynamics Society (2006)
5. Khodyrev, I., Popova, S.: Discrete modeling and simulation of business processes using event logs. In: Proceedings of the International Conference on Computational Science, pp. 322–331 (2014)
6. Munoz-Gama, J.: Conformance Checking and Diagnosis in Process Mining - Comparing Observed and Modeled Processes. Lecture Notes in Business Information Processing, vol. 270. Springer, Heidelberg (2016). https://doi.org/10.1007/978-3-319-49451-7
7. Pourbafrani, M., van der Aalst, W.M.P.: PMSD: data-driven simulation using system dynamics and process mining. In: Proceedings of Demonstration at the 18th International Conference on Business Process Management, pp. 77–81 (2020), http://ceur-ws.org/Vol-2673/paperDR03.pdf
8. Pourbafrani, M., van Zelst, S.J., van der Aalst, W.M.P.: Scenario-based prediction of business processes using system dynamics. In: Panetto, H., Debruyne, C., Hepp, M., Lewis, D., Ardagna, C.A., Meersman, R. (eds.) OTM 2019. LNCS, vol. 11877, pp. 422–439. Springer, Cham (2019). https://doi.org/10.1007/978-3-030-33246-4_27
9. Pourbafrani, M., van Zelst, S.J., van der Aalst, W.M.P.: Semi-automated time-granularity detection for data-driven simulation using process mining and system dynamics. In: Dobbie, G., Frank, U., Kappel, G., Liddle, S.W., Mayr, H.C. (eds.) ER 2020. LNCS, vol. 12400, pp. 77–91. Springer, Cham (2020). https://doi.org/10.1007/978-3-030-62522-1_6
10. Pourbafrani, M., van Zelst, S.J., van der Aalst, W.M.P.: Supporting automatic system dynamics model generation for simulation in the context of process mining. In: Abramowicz, W., Klein, G. (eds.) BIS 2020. LNBIP, vol. 389, pp. 249–263. Springer, Cham (2020). https://doi.org/10.1007/978-3-030-53337-3_19
11. Pourbafrani, M., van Zelst, S.J., van der Aalst, W.M.P.: Supporting decisions in production line processes by combining process mining and system dynamics. In: Ahram, T., Karwowski, W., Vergnano, A., Leali, F., Taiar, R. (eds.) IHSI 2020. AISC, vol. 1131, pp. 461–467. Springer, Cham (2020). https://doi.org/10.1007/978-3-030-39512-4_72
12. Rosenberg, Z., Riasanow, T., Krcmar, H.: A system dynamics model for business process change projects. In: International Conference of the System Dynamics Society, pp. 1–27 (2015)
13. Rozinat, A., Mans, R.S., Song, M., van der Aalst, W.M.P.: Discovering simulation models. Inf. Syst. 34(3), 305–327 (2009)
14. Song, M., van der Aalst, W.M.P.: Towards comprehensive support for organizational mining. Decis. Support Syst. 46(1), 300–317 (2008)
15. Sterman, J.D.: Business Dynamics: Systems Thinking and Modeling for a Complex World. McGraw-Hill, New York (2000)
16. Sterman, J.D.: All models are wrong: reflections on becoming a systems scientist. Syst. Dyn. Rev. J. Syst. Dyn. Soc. 18(4), 501–531 (2002)

All that Glitters Is Not Gold

Towards Process Discovery Techniques with Guarantees

Jan Martijn E. M. van der Werf[1]([⊠]), Artem Polyvyanyy[2],
Bart R. van Wensveen[1], Matthieu Brinkhuis[1], and Hajo A. Reijers[1]

[1] Utrecht University, Princetonplein 5, 3584 CC Utrecht, The Netherlands
{j.m.e.m.vanderwerf,m.j.s.brinkhuis,h.a.reijers}@uu.nl,
bart@architecturemining.org
[2] The University of Melbourne, Parkville, VIC 3010, Australia
artem.polyvyanyy@unimelb.edu.au

Abstract. The aim of a process discovery algorithm is to construct
from event data a process model that describes the underlying, real-
world process well. Intuitively, the better the quality of the input event
data, the better the quality of the resulting discovered model should
be. However, existing process discovery algorithms do not guarantee this
relationship. We demonstrate this by using a range of quality measures
for both event data and discovered process models. This paper is a call
to the community of IS engineers to complement their process discovery
algorithms with properties that relate qualities of their inputs to those
of their outputs. To this end, we distinguish four incremental stages for
the development of such algorithms, along with concrete guidelines for
the formulation of relevant properties and experimental validation. We
use these stages to reflect on the state of the art, which shows the need
to move forward in our thinking about algorithmic process discovery.

Keywords: Process mining · Process discovery · Formal guarantees ·
Properties

1 Introduction

Process mining focuses on the extraction of process-related information from
event logs, a collection of sequences of actions, each encoding a historical process execution [1]. Process discovery is a core area in process mining. It studies algorithms that, given an event log, construct process models that aim to
describe the corresponding true process that induced the event log as closely as
possible. One of the main challenges in process discovery is that the true process
is unknown, and has to be inferred from a *sample* observed and recorded in the
event log [11].

An algorithm is a sequence of computational steps that transform a given
input into some *output* [12]. Different algorithms exhibit different properties, for
example, correctness, finiteness, definiteness, effectiveness, and efficiency. Such

© Springer Nature Switzerland AG 2021
M. La Rosa et al. (Eds.): CAiSE 2021, LNCS 12751, pp. 141–157, 2021.
https://doi.org/10.1007/978-3-030-79382-1_9

properties allow us to choose an algorithm that fulfills a certain need, such as performing a guaranteed correct computation within the desired time bounds. A process discovery algorithm transforms a given input event log into an output process model. We usually expect that a process discovery algorithm is finite (terminates after a finite number of computational steps), definite (each computational step is unambiguous), effective (each computational step can be performed correctly in a finite amount of time), and efficient (the fewer or faster computation steps can be executed the better). However, process discovery algorithms treat quality as a *goal* rather than a guarantee. That is, process discovery algorithms are designed to construct a "good" process model from the input event log [1], where the "goodness" of the model is not established by the internals of the algorithm, but by external measures, e.g., precision and recall.

In this paper, we recommend refining the process discovery goal. Our recommendation is triggered by the observation that a process discovery algorithm can construct a good model from an event log yet discover a worse model from another event log of better quality [24]. We argue that process discovery algorithms should come with guarantees formulated in terms of the relationship between the quality of its inputs and outputs. The present paper makes these contributions:

o We propose measures for the quality of event logs, both in the presence and absence of a true process. In the former case, we use standard conformance checking measures, while in the latter case we rely on sampling techniques and measures as studied in statistics;

o We provide empirical evidence that existing process discovery algorithms can construct good models from event logs and, at the same time, produce poor models from better logs;

o We propose four stages for process discovery algorithms to guarantee the intuitively appealing dependency between the quality of input event logs and the quality of output process models.

We believe that a next step in the evaluation of process discovery algorithms is necessary for the field to advance. Several benchmarks (cf. [6]) have identified process discovery algorithms that "glitter", that is, algorithms that produce high-quality models on a limited collection of event logs. We argue that such benchmarks should be complemented with formal analyses to provide quality guarantees with the algorithms, extending the current state-of-the-art evaluation with statistical methods to establish a relation between log and model quality. We invite the process mining community to contribute to the discussion of the maturity of process discovery algorithms. In addition, we encourage the authors of existing and future discovery techniques to establish the proposed guarantees.

The remainder of the paper is structured as follows. The next section introduces the intuition why process discovery algorithms need to provide guarantees. A statistical approach to establish event log quality is introduced in Sect. 3. The proposed four stages of process discovery algorithms are presented in Sect. 4, together with empirical evidence that algorithms do not provide such guarantees yet. Last, Sects. 5 and 6 are devoted to related work, and conclusions, respectively.

2 Setting the Stage

2.1 Process Discovery and Conformance Checking

Process mining projects often start by assuming that some underlying process generates an event log that can be observed, recorded, and used for process discovery. We refer to this underlying entity as the *true process*. The true process is, however, often unknown [11]. Hence, it can only be approximated. Therefore, based on the observed log, process discovery algorithms aim to construct a process model that describes the true process well. Formally, given a set of activities A, an event log L is defined as a multiset over finite sequences, called *traces*, over A. A discovery algorithm disc can be described as a relation disc $\subseteq \mathcal{L}(A) \times 2^{\mathcal{M}(A)}$, where $\mathcal{L}(A)$ and $\mathcal{M}(A)$ are the universe of all possible logs and the universe of all models over A, respectively. Some algorithms, such as the ILP-miner [31], are non-deterministic, i.e., applying a process discovery algorithm may yield different results for the same input log.

To measure how well the discovered process models describes the behavior recorded in the event log, different conformance measures have been proposed [3]. *Precision* is a function prec : $\mathcal{L}(A) \times \mathcal{M}(A) \to [0, 1]$ that quantifies the fraction of behavior allowed by the model that was actually observed. *Recall* is a function rec : $\mathcal{L}(A) \times \mathcal{M}(A) \to [0, 1]$ that quantifies the observed behavior allowed by the model. For both measures, the value of one denotes perfect conformance between the log and model. As shown in [24,27], the entropy-based precision and recall measures satisfy all the requirements for this class of measures proposed in [3,24,27,28].

Process discovery algorithms are often designed with a specific quality goal in mind. Several algorithms have *rediscoverability* as their goal: if the unknown, true process that generated the event log has specific properties, and the event log satisfies certain criteria, then the algorithm discovers the true process. For example, the α-miner has the rediscoverability property for structured workflow nets, imposing log completeness as criterion [4]. Similarly, the Inductive Miner [18] can rediscover process trees under the assumption of activity completeness, i.e., every leaf in the tree should occur at least once in the event log. Other algorithms take different approaches, e.g., to return a model that scores best on one or more conformance measures (e.g., [14,29,31]).

2.2 Relating Log Quality and Model Quality

Event logs used as inputs to process discovery algorithms are often assumed to be faithful representations of the true processes. Let us reflect on the consequences of this assumption. Consider Fig. 1. Assume some event log L is a faithful representation of some true process TP. In other words, L has a high

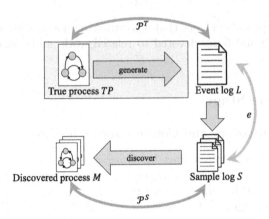

Fig. 1. A true process TP generates an event log L with unkown quality $\mathcal{P}^T$. Any sample S drawn from L has some error e. Discovering a model from S results in a model with quality $\mathcal{P}^S$.

model quality $\mathcal{P}^T$, measured in terms of precision and recall between L and TP. The true process TP is executed continuously, thus generating a stream of events, from which L is a snapshot [3,17]. Therefore, L can be seen as a sample from this stream. Potentially, samples of L can be faithful representations of TP as well. Let S be a sample of L. As it is a sample, the field of statistics provides methods to assess the quality e of the sample with respect to L. And, because S is an event log itself, it can be used to discover some model M, which has quality $\mathcal{P}^S$, again measured in terms of precision and recall, but this time between S and M. Then, if S is a good representation of log L, a process discovery algorithm should construct a model with a quality that approaches $\mathcal{P}^T$.

Now, draw two samples from L, say S_1 and S_2. For S_1, model M_1 is discovered, with model quality $\mathcal{P}^{S_1}$, and for S_2 a model M_2 is discovered, with model quality $\mathcal{P}^{S_2}$. Suppose S_1 has a higher sample quality than S_2. In other words, S_1 is a better representation for L than S_2. Intuitively, the quality of M_1 should then also be closer to $\mathcal{P}^T$ than the quality of M_2. In other words, if $e(S_1) \geq e(S_2)$ then one should expect that $\mathcal{P}^{S_1} \geq \mathcal{P}^{S_2}$. Hence, it is desirable that the process discovery algorithm guarantees that better quality logs result in better quality models. In real-life situations, the true process that generated the event log is unknown. In most process mining methods (cf., [10,15]) the event log is prepared, and then process discovery techniques are applied to unravel a process model. An important concern that these methods do not address relates to the internal validity of process mining projects: if the process is repeated on a new observation, i.e., a new event log, to what degree do the results agree between the analyses? For this property, i.e., test-retest reliability, the guarantees of a process discovery algorithm come into play. If the different samples are of similar quality, then the constructed models should be of similar quality. However, current process discovery algorithms do not explicitly claim to provide such guarantees.

3   Sampling to Measure Log Quality

A necessary step in providing guarantees on the results of process discovery algorithms is to establish measures for log quality. We argue that any event log can be studied as a random sample of traces generated by the true process. Similar to [3], the true process can be represented as a set of traces with some trace likelihood function that assigns a probability to each trace. Consequently, any sample of an event log is again a sample of the true process, as proposed in [17]. We consider a sample log S of an event log L to be a subset of the traces observed in the event log, i.e., $S(\sigma) \leq L(\sigma)$, for all traces $\sigma \in L$, and $S(\sigma) = 0$ if $\sigma \notin L$. This allows drawing different samples from a given event log, and then comparing these samples with the event log to analyze the quality of these samples. Currently, little is known about the representativeness or quality of random samples in process mining [17,30]. In the remainder of this section, we propose random sampling techniques to be used in process mining and provide measures to analyze the quality of a sample with respect to the original event log.

3.1   Sampling Techniques

In this section, we propose three probability sampling techniques that can be used to draw a sample from an event log, where each trace in the event log has equal probability of being sampled. Consequently, samples from these techniques can be used to estimate characteristics of the event log, and, thus, of the true process.

The first technique is *simple random sampling*, where a sample is created by randomly including traces with a predetermined sampling ratio. The second technique is *stratified sampling*, where the data is divided into unique groups, called strata. For process discovery, these groups can be formed based on unique traces. Then, a simple random sample is taken from each group. In theory, this sampling technique would give more representative samples because of stratification on unique traces. However, one has to be careful when applying stratified sampling: as only a natural number of traces can be added to a sample, a trace can only be added fully or not at all. Hence, a problem occurs if a stratum contains fewer traces than there are expected to be sampled. To solve this, rounding using the half to even rule (cf. IEEE 754) can be used, which rounds halves to the nearest even integer, while still rounding other decimal numbers to the nearest integer. No literature exists on the topic of using stratified sampling in the area of process discovery [30].

An extension of stratified sampling is an approach we call *stratified squared* sampling. First, a stratified sample is drawn. Then the number of sampled traces is compared to the number of expected traces based on the sampling ratio. Due to rounding, the number of expected traces can be greater than the number of actually added traces. If this happens, the uncovered strata are sorted based on their frequency, and a trace of each of these strata is added, until the number of sampled traces matches the expected number of traces, or all strata are covered.

3.2   Towards Sample Quality Measures for Process Mining

Event logs describe the behavior of a system in terms of traces of events. As in [17], we define behavior as the directly-follows relation induced from the event log L. The directly-follows relation $>_L$ is defined on pairs of events a and b, such that $a >_L b$ iff the event log L contains a trace in which the two activities a and b occur consecutively. A first measure to compare a sample to its original event log is existential completeness, i.e., the extent to which all possible directly-follows relations are present. This results in the first sample quality measure: *coverage*, which is defined by the proportion of unique directly-follows relations present in the sample and the number of unique directly-follows relations in the event log.

Coverage does not take the occurrence frequency of behavior into account. Different methods exist to measure frequency representativeness. In statistics, error measures are used to quantify the error between the expected values and the real occurrences. We propose to adapt these error measures to quantify the error between the behavior observed in a sample, and the expected behavior from the event log based on the sampling ratio. This results in several measures for sample quality, where $\mathbf{e}$ denotes the expected behavior, and $\mathbf{s}$ denotes the sampled behavior as vectors of length n:

The Normalised Mean Absolute Error (NMAE) calculates the normalized absolute deviation (i.e. error) of the number of occurrences of each unique directly-follows relation of the sample from their respective expected frequency:

$$\text{NMAE} = \frac{\text{MAE}}{\text{avg}\,\mathbf{e}} = \frac{\sum_{i=1}^{n} |\mathbf{s}_i - \mathbf{e}_i|}{\sum_{i=1}^{n} \mathbf{e}_i} \tag{1}$$

Normalised Root Mean Square Error (NRMSE) is similar to NMAE, but uses the root of the squared values, instead of the absolute values, thus penalising large deviations more heavily:

$$\text{NRMSE} = \frac{\text{RMSE}}{\text{avg}\,\mathbf{e}} = \frac{\sqrt{\frac{1}{n} \sum_{i=1}^{n} (\mathbf{s}_i - \mathbf{e}_i)^2}}{\frac{1}{n} \sum_{i=1}^{n} \mathbf{e}_i} \tag{2}$$

The Symmetric Mean Absolute Percentage Error (sMAPE) is a symmetric variation of the NMAE, expressed as a percentage error, with the advantage that the undersampling of behavior is penalised more heavily:

$$\text{sMAPE} = \frac{1}{n} \sum_{i=1}^{n} \frac{|\mathbf{e}_i - \mathbf{s}_i|}{\mathbf{e}_i + \mathbf{s}_i} \tag{3}$$

The Symmetric Root Mean Square Percentage Error (sRMSPE) is similar to sMAPE, using the root mean square error instead of the mean absolute error, thus penalising large deviations more heavily:

$$\text{sRMSPE} = \sqrt{\frac{1}{n} \sum_{i=1}^{n} \left(\frac{\mathbf{e}_i - \mathbf{s}_i}{\mathbf{e}_i + \mathbf{s}_i} \right)^2} \tag{4}$$

For a detailed evaluation of the above measures, we refer the reader to [30]. These measures assess the behavioral quality of a sample with respect to the event log it is drawn from. In other words, these measures provide ways to establish the quality of the input of process discovery algorithms.

4   Designing Process Discovery Algorithms with Guarantees

As observed in a study on the quality of conformance measures [24], some process discovery algorithms have a large variability in the quality of the constructed process models, though the used measures satisfy the properties proposed in [3, 28]. In particular, given different samples of a single event log, the same algorithm sometimes provides good results on small samples, while on larger samples, the algorithm discovers worse models. On further inspection, these algorithms are state of the art, and do not perform any major "process mining crimes" [25]. In addition, they "glitter" in the benchmark study reported in [6].

We consider this observation a threat to the application of process mining, particularly for its repeatability and, hence, the reliability of its results. Suppose for a true process several event logs are captured and analyzed, and the results do not agree, i.e., they differ largely in quality. Several explanations for this phenomenon are possible. A first explanation could be the quality of the input, i.e., the quality of the event logs differed significantly. However, as the observation highlights, another plausible – yet undesirable – explanation lies in the process discovery algorithm itself. In other words, if the process discovery algorithm does not provide any guarantees on the quality of the resulting models, it is impossible to exclude the algorithm as a root cause.

Consequently, we advocate process discovery algorithms to provide guarantees on the quality of the produced results. To this end, we propose to distinguish four stages during the introduction of a process discovery algorithm:

1. The algorithm is well designed;
2. The algorithm is validated on real-life examples;
3. The algorithm has an established relationship between log and model quality;
4. The algorithm is effective.

Though the first two stages are basic, not all algorithms make it to the second stage, as illustrated later. Arguably, algorithms that are shown not to pass the second stage should not be used in empirical studies. The third and fourth stages are entirely novel for process discovery. Once the algorithm is shown to be applicable on real-life examples, the authors should study which guarantees their algorithm provides in a controlled setting where the true process is known. To pass the last stage, the algorithm should provide evidence that in settings where the true process is unknown, the algorithm provides the guarantees stated at stage 3.

4.1   Stage 1: The Algorithm Is Well Designed

In the first stage, the developers of a process discovery algorithm should properly introduce their algorithm. For this, the developers need to provide the following:

o The class of process models the algorithm constructs;
o Evidence for meeting the quality goals of the algorithm;
o Criteria on the logs, e.g., requirements on the true process that generates the logs;
o An initial evaluation on artificial data sets.

Most process discovery algorithms satisfy the requirements of this stage. For example, the ILP-miner [31] is designed for the class of classical Petri nets with interleaving semantics. It is proven to always return a Petri net with a perfect recall score. It imposes no requirements on the input event logs and is tested on artificial logs. Also, the α-miner [4] algorithm is at least in this stage. It is designed for well-structured Workflow nets with rediscoverability as a goal. It imposes two requirements on an input event log: it should contain all directly-follows relations present in the true process, and the true process should be block-structured. A similar argument holds for the Inductive Miner [18].

4.2   Stage 2: The Algorithm Is Validated

Even though an algorithm may be well designed, i.e., it passes stage 1, it is not guaranteed that it works in practice. The second stage in introducing the algorithm is, therefore, the validation of the algorithm on a collection of real-life event logs, such as used in the benchmark reported in [6]. Several algorithms fail to reach this stage. For example, the α-miner is theoretically a robust algorithm, but the requirements it imposes on the true process are too strong for application in real-life situations. Similarly, the ILP-miner is designed from a theoretical point of view and has limitations for practical use, primarily because of its guaranteed recall and runtime performance. Other algorithms, such as the Inductive Miner [18], the Declare Miner [20] and the Split Miner [5] have been applied successfully on several real-life event logs, and thus pass this stage.

4.3   Stage 3: An Established Relationship Between Log and Model Quality

Although passing stage two shows the algorithm's capabilities, this does not provide any guarantees on the quality of the algorithm's output. As a first step in establishing a relationship between the log and model quality, it needs to be shown to what degree the algorithm satisfies the guarantees as sketched in Fig. 1. In other words, the designers need to show that if an event log is a faithful representation of a true process, as per measure $\mathcal{P}^T$, then the algorithm should satisfy properties similar to those listed below:

Algorithm 1: Establish Relation

```
1  while True do
2  │  TP ← GenerateModel(M, A);
3  │  foreach i ∈ [1..N] do
4  │  │  L ← GenerateLog(TP, T);
5  │  │  P^T ← calcModelQuality(L, TP);
6  │  │  foreach r ∈ ratios do
7  │  │  │  foreach j ∈ [1..K] do
8  │  │  │  │  S ← DrawSample(L, r);
9  │  │  │  │  e ← calcSampleQuality(L, S);
10 │  │  │  │  M ← DiscoverModel(S);
11 │  │  │  │  P^S ← calcModelQuality(S, M);
```

Algorithm 2: Test Effectiveness

```
1  foreach L ∈ Benchmark do
2  │  foreach r ∈ ratios do
3  │  │  foreach j ∈ [1..K] do
4  │  │  │  S ← DrawSample(L, r);
5  │  │  │  e ← calcSampleQuality(L, S);
6  │  │  │  M ← DiscoverModel(S);
7  │  │  │  P^S ← calcModelQuality(S, M);
```

P1. For a sample log S that approaches the perfect quality, the quality $\mathcal{P}^S$ of the discovered model from S approaches $\mathcal{P}^T$;

P2. For two samples S_1 and S_2, if sample S_1 has a higher quality than S_2, then the model quality $\mathcal{P}^{S_1}$ is higher than $\mathcal{P}^{S_2}$.

Algorithm designers can choose different strategies to provide evidence for these properties. The most potent form of evidence is a formal proof that the algorithm satisfies these properties for specific instantiations of log and model quality measures. In that way, a relationship between an input log quality and the resulting model quality can be established. We also encourage algorithm designers to define algorithm-specific log quality measures. If a formal proof is not feasible, instead, statistical evidence of these properties can be provided. For this, we propose a controlled experiment as outlined in Algorithm 1. Such a controlled experiment follows the approach shown in Fig. 1. It requires the algorithm designers to have a model generator for the class of true processes the algorithm accepts. The algorithm then generates repeatedly for a true process one or more event logs, and for each event log a set of samples.

We propose to use statistical tests to evaluate the two properties. Property P1 needs an analysis of the relation between the expected $\mathcal{P}^T$ and the observed $\mathcal{P}^S$. For property P2, the Spearman rank correlation can be used to test whether there is a strong correlation between the sample quality and the model quality. If this is the case, then statistical evidence has been provided for the relationship between log and model quality.

Example Evaluation. As an example, the controlled experiment has been implemented in ProM[1] for the Inductive Miner [18]. To calculate precision and recall, an implementation of exact matching entropy-based measures in Entropia is used [22]. For each true process, a single event log with 5,000 traces has been

---

[1] The source code is available on: https://github.com/ArchitectureMining/SamplingFramework.

Table 1. Results of the controlled experiment. The last 10 columns show the Spearman rank correlation between the error measures, and precision and recall. All bold values are statistically significant ($p < 0.001$).

Model	True process Prec.	Recall	Precision Cov.	sMAPE	sRMSPE	NRMSE	NMAE	Recall Cov.	sMAPE	sRMSPE	NRMSE	NMAE
1	0.538	1.000	**0.658**	**−0.988**	**−0.986**	**−0.988**	**−0.989**	**0.338**	**−0.356**	**−0.354**	**−0.354**	**−0.356**
2	0.797	1.000	**0.470**	**−0.986**	**−0.985**	**−0.901**	**−0.954**	0.154	−0.051	−0.052	0.012	−0.004
3	0.935	1.000	**0.781**	**−0.990**	**−0.989**	**−0.975**	**−0.984**	**0.637**	**−0.406**	**−0.417**	**−0.410**	**−0.412**
4	0.953	1.000	**0.705**	**−0.991**	**−0.992**	**−0.984**	**−0.987**	−0.103	0.105	0.108	0.081	0.090
5	0.988	1.000	**0.540**	**−0.983**	**−0.981**	**−0.980**	**−0.986**	**0.437**	**−0.201**	**−0.206**	**−0.207**	**−0.201**
6	0.871	1.000	**0.532**	**−0.934**	**−0.938**	**−0.917**	**−0.926**	**−0.529**	**0.973**	**0.962**	**0.963**	**0.968**
7	0.943	1.000	**0.511**	**−0.991**	**−0.989**	**−0.986**	**−0.989**	**0.456**	**−0.242**	**−0.240**	**−0.228**	**−0.231**
8	0.616	1.000	**0.773**	**−0.992**	**−0.991**	**−0.989**	**−0.990**	0.114	−0.148	−0.154	−0.156	−0.157
9	0.710	1.000	**0.519**	**−0.981**	**−0.978**	**−0.970**	**−0.973**	**0.518**	**−0.327**	**−0.330**	**−0.340**	**−0.341**
10	0.883	1.000	**0.703**	**−0.982**	**−0.982**	**−0.977**	**−0.976**	0.116	−0.022	−0.027	−0.016	−0.023

generated. The event logs were 10 times sampled for 12 sampling ratios: 0.01, 0.02, 0.05, and 0.1 up to 0.9.

The results are shown in Table 1 and Fig. 2. From Fig. 2 we conclude that property P1 holds for precision and recall. For each model that describes the true process, the Spearman rank correlation is calculated between each of the log quality measures and precision, and similarly for recall. As for the measures sMAPE, sRMSPE, NRMSE, and NMAE, 0 is the best quality, a negative correlation indicates the required guarantee that samples of higher quality result in better discovered models, whereas for coverage, a positive correlation indicates this result. As can be seen in the table, the experiment generates mixed results. Though property P2 holds for precision, it is not satisfied for recall. Hence, we can conclude that the Inductive Miner satisfies the two properties for precision, but fails to do so for recall on the second property.

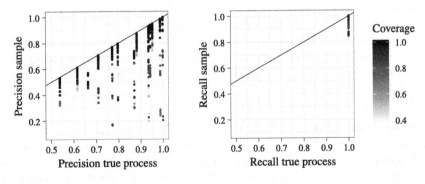

Fig. 2. Relation between the quality of the true process and the quality of the discovered models, for precision (left) and recall (right). Darker points represent a higher coverage.

4.4   Stage 4: The Algorithm Is Effective

An established relationship between log and model quality, the essence of stage 3, does not guarantee the algorithm to be effective in real-life situations. The main caveat in the controlled environment of the previous stage is that the true process is known. Each event log is generated from the known true processes. In real-life situations, the true process is unknown, and, hence, may invalidate assumptions of the discovery algorithm. For example, the Inductive Miner assumes event logs to be generated from process trees. However, no criteria are given to test whether an event log is generated by a process tree, nor does the algorithm provide any details on the model quality if the assumption is invalid.

In this stage, the algorithm designer has to validate how effective the algorithm is in real-life situations. One way to obtain insights into the effectiveness of the algorithm is to apply sampling on a benchmark. This benchmark can be a set of well-known real-life event logs as used in [6], or can be generated automatically, if the designers ensure that the class of generated models is larger than the class of true processes studied in the previous stage. The algorithm designers need to analyze property P2 in the absence of a true process. In other words, even if the true process is unknown, event logs of better quality should return better quality models. This may result in an experiment as outlined in Algorithm 2.

The analysis of property P2 in the absence of a true process can have two possible outcomes. Either it is shown that the algorithm has the desired property, or, if this is not possible, the algorithm should be further improved, or provide additional log quality measures, that guarantee that an event log satisfies the assumptions of the process discovery algorithm.

Example Evaluation. As an example of the analysis in stage 4, we conducted the proposed experiment on the Inductive Miner [18]. Two real-life event logs have been selected, the Road Traffic Fine event log [13] and the Sepsis event log [21]. The Road Traffic Fine log has in total 150,370 traces and 561,470 events. There are 231 unique traces and 11 unique event types. The Sepsis log consists of 1,049 traces, of which 845 are unique, and 15,190 events with 16 unique event types. Sampling was done at the same sampling ratios as before: 0.01, 0.02, 0.05, and 0.1 up to 0.9. For each ratio, ten samples were drawn.

The sample quality measures for the Road Traffic Fine log are shown on the left in Fig. 3. As the plot shows, the larger the sampling ratio, and thus the log size, the better the quality is (error measures: $\rho < -0.9$, $p < 0.001$, coverage: $\rho = 0.96$, $p < 0.001$). Sample size and the conformance measure on precision (Fig. 4) show a moderate positive correlation ($\rho = 0.56$, $p < 0.001$), while there is no correlation between sampling ratio and recall ($\rho = 0.03$, $p = 0.72$). Analyzing the quality measures with the conformance measures shows a different story. In Fig. 4, the coverage is plotted against the precision, indicating there is no correlation between coverage and precision. Further analysis revealed no correlations between the sample quality measures and precision (sMAPE: $\rho = -0.19$, $p = 0.03$, sRMSPE: $\rho = -0.18$, $p = 0.051$, NRMSE: $\rho = -0.21$,

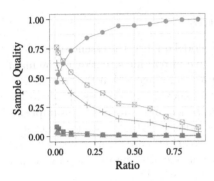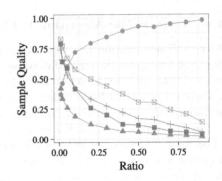

Fig. 3. Plot of ratio and the sample quality measures coverage (●), sMAPE (+), sRM-SPE (⊠), NRMSE (■) and NMAE (▲) for the Road Traffic Fine log (left) and the Sepsis log (right).

$p = 0.02$, NMAE: $\rho = -0.20$, $p = 0.03$, coverage: $\rho = 0.17$, $p = 0.06$). The correlations found for recall show that samples of worse quality result in better models (sMAPE: $\rho = 0.80$, $p < 0.001$, sRMSPE: $\rho = 0.79$, $p < 0.001$, NRMSE: $\rho = 0.77$, $p < 0.001$, NMAE: $\rho = 0.78$, $p < 0.001$, coverage: $\rho = -0.79$, $p < 0.001$).

For the Sepsis log, similar results are found. As indicated by the plots at the right hand side of Fig. 3, a correlation is found between the sampling ratio and the log quality measures (for all error measures: $\rho < -0.9$, $p < 0.001$, coverage: $\rho = 0.59$, $p < 0.001$). The larger the sampling ratio, the higher the precision is ($\rho = 0.57, p < 0.001$), but no correlation was found between sampling ratio and recall ($\rho = 0.03$, $p = 0.72$). A moderate negative correlation was found between the log quality measures and precision (for the error measures: $-0.60 < \rho < -0.50$, $p < 0.001$, coverage: $\rho = 0.59$, $p < 0.001$), while the log quality measures did not show any correlation with recall (for all measures: $-0.04 < \rho < 0.02, p > 0.70$).

As the results suggest, there is no clear relation between log and model quality. Hence, it is with the current measures not possible to conclude that the Inductive Miner is guaranteed to be effective in real-life situations. As a next step, new log quality measures should be developed that do establish the required relationship between log and model quality. The process can then be repeated until sufficient guarantees can be provided on the effectiveness of the algorithm.

5   Related Work

The statistical approach we propose to establish a relation between log and model quality relates to event data quality in general, builds upon established properties of conformance measures, and requires sampling techniques on event logs. This section reviews literature on these topics, and shows how our approach relates to them.

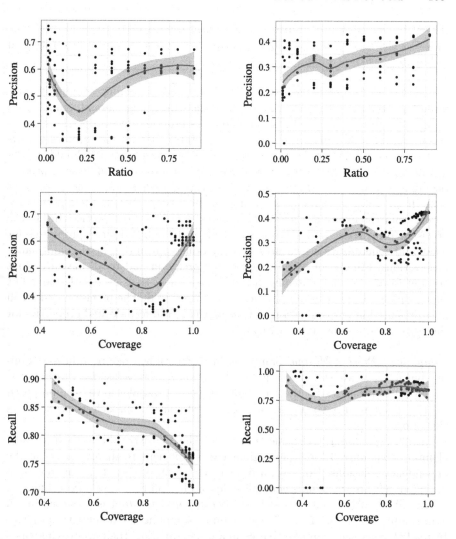

Fig. 4. Plots of ratio and precision, and coverage with precision and recall for the Road Traffic Fine log (left) and the Sepsis Log (right).

Measuring Log Quality. As the process mining manifesto articulates, process mining treats data as first-class citizens [2], and defines four data qualities, of which *completeness* is studied mostly. For example, [9] identifies four categories of process characteristics and 27 classes of event log quality issues. Most studies on event log quality focus on the incompleteness of the data. Examples include not having enough information recorded in the event log (e.g., missing cases or events) [1,9], not having recorded enough behavior in the event log [16], or the traces not being representative of the process [16], and noise. Different notions of noise are studied, such as infrequent behavior that is either incorrect or rare [14].

However, event logs are studied in isolation in these studies. Instead, we argue to assess the quality of event logs relative to other event logs, using statistical techniques based on sampling.

Properties of Conformance Measures. The process mining community has recently initiated a discussion on which formal properties should "good" conformance measures satisfy. In [28], the authors proposed five properties for precision measures. For instance, one property states that for two process models that describe all the traces in the log, a less permissive model should not be qualified as less precise. By demonstrating that a measure fulfills such properties, one establishes its usefulness. In [24], the authors strengthened the properties from [28]. For example, according to these properties, the less permissive model from the example above should be classified as more precise. In [3], the precision properties from [28] were refined, and further desired properties for recall and generalization measures were introduced, resulting in 21 conformance propositions. Finally, in [23], properties for precision and recall measures that account for the partial matching of traces, i.e., traces that are not the same but share some subsequences of activities, were introduced. The precision and recall measures used in our evaluations satisfy all the introduced desired properties for the corresponding measures [3, 24, 27, 28].

Sampling in Process Mining. Sampling has been studied before in process mining, but never as a systematic approach to evaluate process discovery techniques. A first set of measures for the representativeness of samples have been proposed in [17]. Their results show the need for a systematic approach as proposed in this paper.

In [8], a sampling technique specific for the Heuristics Miner is described, claiming that only 3% of the original log is sufficient to discover 95% of the dependency relations. However, a proper evaluation of this claim has not been provided, nor are the results generalizable to other process discovery techniques.

A statistical framework based on *information saturation* is proposed in [7]. Their approach differs from the probability sampling techniques we propose. Instead of generating samples that estimate the event log, their approach focuses on creating a sufficiently small sample that contains as much information from the event log as possible. Consequently, this approach cannot be used to measure sample quality with respect to the event log.

Several biased sampling techniques are described in [26]. These techniques have been evaluated on six real-life event logs and three discovery techniques. The evaluation showed that sampling sometimes improves the F-measure for some of the models. A similar result on the F-measure was obtained in [19]. Their study applied the Google PageRank algorithm on event logs to create a representative sample, which reduced the execution time of the Inductive Miner by half without decreasing the F-measure. As the F-measure harmonizes precision and recall, and no analysis was performed on the reasons behind the improvements, it is unclear how sampling influenced the process discovery results of both studies. Instead of using sampling to improve the quality of the output, we propose to use probability sampling to analyze the input of algorithms, and to establish a relationship between log and model quality. This relationship then allows one to explore why some samples give better models than other samples.

6   Conclusion

This paper identifies the need for process discovery algorithms with guarantees that characterize the dependency between the quality of input event logs and the quality of the process models constructed from these event logs. In particular, we argue that process discovery algorithms should produce better models from better input logs. Currently, process discovery algorithms have never provided such guarantees, since, so far, we, as a community, lacked a theoretical foundation to establish such a relationship. In this paper, for the first time, measures for the statistical sample quality for ranking the quality of event logs are proposed. We recommend using grounded conformance checking measures for assessing the quality of the discovered models. Combining log quality measures with conformance measures provides a framework to formally define properties that express the desired guarantee that better event logs result in better models. These properties can be instantiated with various measures for quality of event logs and process models and be less or more pronounced, for example, imposing a strictly increasing or non-decreasing relation, or requiring a statistical association of a certain degree between the qualities of the corresponding logs and models. To overcome this problem, we propose four stages in the design of an algorithm. Each design comes with additional properties and obligations to establish effective algorithms with guarantees.

We invite the process mining community to further contribute to the discussion of desired qualities for process discovery algorithms to ensure that state-of-the-art algorithms fulfill them, and in this way, advance the field of process discovery as well as the design and evaluation of such algorithms.

Acknowledgments. Artem Polyvyanyy was in part supported by the Australian Research Council project DP180102839.

References

1. van der Aalst, W.M.P.: Process Mining-Data Science in Action, 2nd edn. Springer, Heidelberg (2016). https://doi.org/10.1007/978-3-662-49851-4
2. van der Aalst, W., et al.: Process mining manifesto. In: Daniel, F., Barkaoui, K., Dustdar, S. (eds.) BPM 2011. LNBIP, vol. 99, pp. 169–194. Springer, Heidelberg (2012). https://doi.org/10.1007/978-3-642-28108-2_19
3. van der Aalst, W.M.P.: Relating process models and event logs–21 conformance propositions. In: ATAED, volume 2115 of CEUR Workshop Proceedings, pp. 56–74. CEUR-WS.org (2018)
4. van der Aalst, W.M.P., Weijters, A.J.M.M., Maruster, L.: Workflow mining: discovering process models from event logs. Knowl. Data Eng. **16**(9), 1128–1142 (2004)

5. Augusto, A., Conforti, R., Dumas, M., La Rosa, M.: Split miner: discovering accurate and simple business process models from event logs. In: ICDM 2017, pp. 1–10. IEEE (2017)

6. Augusto, A., et al.: Automated discovery of process models from event logs: review and benchmark. IEEE Trans. Knowl. Data Eng. **31**(4), 686–705 (2019)

7. Bauer, M., Senderovich, A., Gal, A., Grunske, L., Weidlich, M.: How much event data is enough? A statistical framework for process discovery. In: Krogstie, J., Reijers, H.A. (eds.) CAiSE 2018. LNCS, vol. 10816, pp. 239–256. Springer, Cham (2018). https://doi.org/10.1007/978-3-319-91563-0_15

8. Berti, A.: Statistical sampling in process mining discovery. In: eKNOW 2017, pp. 41–43. IARIA (2017)

9. Bose, J.C., Mans, R.S., van der Aalst, W.M.P.: Wanna improve process mining results? In: CIDM 2013, pp. 127–134. IEEE (2013)

10. Bozkaya, M., Gabriels, J.M.A.M., van der Werf, J.M.E.M.: Process diagnostics : a method based on process mining. In: eKNOW 2009, pp. 22–27. IEEE (2009)

11. Buijs, J.C.A.M., van Dongen, B.F., van der Aalst, W.M.P.: Quality dimensions in process discovery: the importance of fitness, precision, generalization and simplicity. Int. J. Coop. Inf. Syst. **23**(1), 1440001 (2014)

12. Cormen, T.H., Leiserson, C.E., Rivest, R.L., Stein, C.: Introduction to Algorithms. MIT Press Ltd, Cambridge (2009)

13. de Leoni, M., Mannhardt, F.: Road Traffic Fine Management Process, February 2015. https://doi.org/10.4121/uuid:270fd440-1057-4fb9-89a9-b699b47990f5

14. de Medeiros, A.K.A., Weijters, A.J.M.M., van der Aalst, W.M.P.: Genetic process mining: an experimental evaluation. Data Min. Knowl. Discov. **14**(2), 245–304 (2007)

15. van Eck, M.L., Lu, X., Leemans, S.J.J., van der Aalst, W.M.P.: PM^2: a process mining project methodology. In: Zdravkovic, J., Kirikova, M., Johannesson, P. (eds.) CAiSE 2015. LNCS, vol. 9097, pp. 297–313. Springer, Cham (2015). https://doi.org/10.1007/978-3-319-19069-3_19

16. Günther, C.: Process mining in flexible environments. Ph.D. thesis, Eindhoven University of Technology (2009)

17. Knols, B., van der Werf, J.M.E.M.: Measuring the behavioral quality of log sampling. In: ICPM 2019, pp. 97–104. IEEE (2019

18. Leemans, S.J.J., Fahland, D., van der Aalst, W.M.P.: Scalable process discovery with guarantees. In: Gaaloul, K., Schmidt, R., Nurcan, S., Guerreiro, S., Ma, Q. (eds.) CAISE 2015. LNBIP, vol. 214, pp. 85–101. Springer, Cham (2015). https://doi.org/10.1007/978-3-319-19237-6_6

19. Liu, C., Pei, Y., Zeng, Q., Duan, H.: LogRank: an approach to sample business process event log for efficient discovery. In: Liu, W., Giunchiglia, F., Yang, B. (eds.) KSEM 2018. LNCS (LNAI), vol. 11061, pp. 415–425. Springer, Cham (2018). https://doi.org/10.1007/978-3-319-99365-2_36

20. Maggi, F.M., Bose, R.P.J.C., van der Aalst, W.M.P.: Efficient discovery of understandable declarative process models from event logs. In: Ralyté, J., Franch, X., Brinkkemper, S., Wrycza, S. (eds.) CAiSE 2012. LNCS, vol. 7328, pp. 270–285. Springer, Heidelberg (2012). https://doi.org/10.1007/978-3-642-31095-9_18

21. Mannhardt, F.: Sepsis Cases - Event Log, December 2016. https://doi.org/10.4121/uuid:915d2bfb-7e84-49ad-a286-dc35f063a460

22. Polyvyanyy, A., et al.: Entropia: a family of entropy-based conformance checking measures for process mining. In: ICPM Doctoral Consortium and Tool Demonstration, volume 2703 of CEUR, pp. 39–42. CEUR-WS.org (2020)

23. Polyvyanyy, A., Kalenkova, A.A.: Monotone conformance checking for partially matching designed and observed processes. In: ICPM 2019, pp. 81–88 (2019)
24. Polyvyanyy, A., Solti, A., Weidlich, M., Di Ciccio, C., Mendling, J.: Monotone precision and recall measures for comparing executions and specifications of dynamic systems. ACM Trans. Softw. Eng. Methodol. **29**(3), 17:1–17:41 (2020)
25. Rehse, J.-R., Fettke, P.: Process mining crimes – a threat to the validity of process discovery evaluations. In: Weske, M., Montali, M., Weber, I., vom Brocke, J. (eds.) BPM 2018. LNBIP, vol. 329, pp. 3–19. Springer, Cham (2018). https://doi.org/10.1007/978-3-319-98651-7_1
26. Fani Sani, M., van Zelst, S.J., van der Aalst, W.M.P.: Improving the performance of process discovery algorithms by instance selection. Comput. Sci. Inf. Syst. **17**(3), 927–958 (2020)
27. Syring, A.F., Tax, N., van der Aalst, W.M.P.: Evaluating conformance measures in process mining using conformance propositions. In: Koutny, M., Pomello, L., Kristensen, L.M. (eds.) Transactions on Petri Nets and Other Models of Concurrency XIV. LNCS, vol. 11790, pp. 192–221. Springer, Heidelberg (2019). https://doi.org/10.1007/978-3-662-60651-3_8
28. Tax, N., Lu, X., Sidorova, N., Fahland, D., van der Aalst, W.M.P.: The imprecisions of precision measures in process mining. Inf. Process. Lett. **135**, 1–8 (2018)
29. Weijters, A.J.M.M., Ribeiro, J.T.S.: Flexible heuristics miner (FHM). In: CIDM 2011, pp. 310–317. IEEE (2011)
30. van Wensveen, B.R.: Estimation and analysis of the quality of event log samples for process discovery. Master's thesis, Utrecht University (2020). https://dspace.library.uu.nl/handle/1874/400143
31. van der Werf, J.M.E.M., van Dongen, B.F., Hurkens, C.A.J., Serebrenik, A.: Process discovery using integer linear programming. Fundamenta Informaticae **94**(3–4), 387–412 (2009)

Patterns

Reusable Abstractions and Patterns for Recognising Compositional Conversational Flows

Sara Bouguelia[1]([⊠]), Hayet Brabra[1], Shayan Zamanirad[2],
Boualem Benatallah[2,1], Marcos Baez[1], and Hamamache Kheddouci[1]

[1] LIRIS – University of Claude Bernard Lyon 1, Villeurbanne, France
{sara.bouguelia,hayet.brabra,marcos.baez,
hamamache.kheddouci}@univ-lyon1.fr
[2] University of New South Wales (UNSW), Sydney, Australia
{shayanz,boualem}@cse.unsw.edu.au

Abstract. Task-oriented conversational bots allow users to access services and perform tasks through natural language conversations. However, integrating these bots and software-enabled services has not kept pace with our ability to deploy individual devices and services. The main drawbacks of current bots and services integration techniques stem from the inherent development and maintenance cost. In addition, existing Natural Language Processing (NLP) techniques automate various tasks but the synthesis of API calls to support broad range of potentially complex user intents is still largely a manual and costly process. In this paper, we propose three types of reusable patterns for recognising compositional conversational flows and therefore automatically support increased complexity and expressivity during the conversation.

Keywords: Conversational bots · Compositional conversational flows · Dialogue patterns · Nested intent · Slot value inference

1 Introduction

Task-oriented conversational bots (or simply chatbots) emerged as a paradigm to naturally access services and perform tasks through natural language conversations with software-enabled services and humans. They enable the understanding of user utterances, expressed in natural language, and on fulfilling such needs by invoking the appropriate backend services (e.g., APIs) [22]. However, allowing users to converse naturally with services and perform their tasks effectively is challenging. The main challenge arises from utterance variations in open-end human-bot interactions and the large space of services potentially unknown at development time. Traditional business process and service composition modeling and orchestration techniques are limited to support such conversations because they usually assume a priory expectations of what information and

© Springer Nature Switzerland AG 2021
M. La Rosa et al. (Eds.): CAiSE 2021, LNCS 12751, pp. 161–176, 2021.
https://doi.org/10.1007/978-3-030-79382-1_10

applications will be accessed and how users will explore these sources and services. Limiting conversations to a process model means that we can only support a small fraction of possible conversations [13]. While existing advances in NLP, rule-based and machine learning (ML) techniques automate various tasks such as intent and slot recognition [5], the synthesis of API calls to support broad range of potentially complex user intents is still largely a manual, ad-hoc and costly process [24]. Our goal is to bridge this gap by dynamically and incrementally synthesizing executable conversation models from natural language conversations. In our previous work, we developed a framework and techniques in this direction [23] including: (i) a word-embedding based API element (e.g. API methods, method parameter) vector space model to support natural language calls to individual APIs [22] and (ii) a hierarchical state machine based model to track and represent human-bot interactions in API-enabled bots [23].

Informed by prior research and literature on conversational systems [5], in this paper, we identify and characterize 3 types of conversation patterns to automatically translate complex user utterances into operations that create composite (nested) states in a bot state machine model: *slot-value-flow*, *nested-intent*, and *API-calls-ordering* patterns. The first pattern allows the bot to resolve a missing value of an intent parameter by extracting it from values of other parameter calls in the conversation history (e.g., a value of output parameter of an already used API call). The second pattern allows the bot to resolve a missing value of an intent parameter by triggering another intent (e.g., a user who wants to schedule a meeting forgets to specify the date. The bot asks for the date and the user responds by a new intent *"Show me my availabilities this week"*). The third pattern allows the bot to map a user intent to a sequence of API calls to satisfy order constraints between two methods of an API (e.g., to fulfil the intent buy a book the bot needs to first call *searchBook* method then *buyBook* method of a *Bookstore* API). These patterns mimics how a developer would have constructed workflows, leveraging conversation knowledge (i.e., slot values and API element vectors), to realise some complex and decomposable user intents. Our approach is motivated by the observation that incorrect inference of conversation flows arises from uncertainty about slot values and relationship between API elements across heterogeneous APIs (e.g., one intent uses *city* as a parameter while another use *location* as a parameter) and complex conversations. More specifically, contributions in this work are summarized as:

– We identify and characterize state machine transformation patterns to support complex user intents. These patterns endow bot platforms with reusable functionality to recognise compositional conversational flows, that would otherwise have to be implemented by bot developers.
– We develop a conversation management service that is augmented with a Context Knowledge Service to support the proposed patterns. This knowledge consists of a graph that represents: (i) slots values relationships and (ii) API methods relationships. It is incrementally derived from conversation utterances and API parameter embeddings.

– Empirical evidence showing the effectiveness of the proposed patterns. The user study showed that these patterns naturally occur when conversing with services, and highlighted the benefits of seamlessly supporting complex user utterances, as perceived by users and confirmed by performance metrics.

In what follows we describe the proposed abstractions, dialog patterns and supporting infrastructure, as well as preliminary evaluation.

2   Related Work

A number of techniques have been proposed to build chatbots, including rule-based [2] and probabilistic models [8]. Main platforms[1] such as Chatfuel and FlowXO provide flow-based solutions to develop chatbots with zero coding using UI elements. Research in this context includes the work by Lopez et al. [13], who propose a system that takes a business process model and generates a list of dialog management rules to deploy the chatbot. Other platforms[2] such as DialogFlow, Wit.ai, Amazon Lex and IBM Watson Assistant, on the other hand, provide machine learning (ML) based solutions. In addition to these solutions, a variety of ML models have emerged in research following two common architectures: *pipeline* and *end-to-end*. A *pipeline-based* model is built with a set of components, each responsible for a specific task such as tracking of intent/slot during conversations [6,15], learning next action [17], etc. *End-to-end* models including end-to-end memory networks [25] and sequence-to-sequence models [14] read directly from a user utterance and produces a system action.

We identified a set of main limitations in the works above: First, rules-based approaches lack flexibility and require considerable development effort. Second, the use of existing probabilistic approaches and ML models such as memory networks becomes prohibitive due to the need for collecting huge and high quality training data. Third, flow-based approaches require the explicit definition of workflow, which is clearly unrealistic in large scale and evolving environments. Furthermore, while ML approaches and platforms provide sophisticated support in term of intent/entities recognition and state tracking, they still far to handle conversations as either structured or unstructured processes. This is because they do not yet automatically support complex and decomposable user intents, where handling of intent requires information that is resulted from other intents either already processed or need to be. In addition, handling conversations as processes requires an advanced understanding of conversation context towards natural and straightforward dialogue experiences.

Similar to our approach, some advanced techniques like DEVY [3] and Lu et al. [6] focus on more understanding of context especially by tracking required slots values from conversations history. However, since these graphs are derived only from conversation utterances they do not consider the knowledge of the

---

[1] Chatfuel: https://chatfuel.com/; FlowXO: https://flowxo.com/.

[2] DialogFlow: https://dialogflow.com/, Wit.ai: https://wit.ai/, Amazon Lex: https:// aws.amazon.com/lex/, IBM Watson https://www.ibm.com/watson/.

heterogeneous APIs being used to converse with a wide variety of enabled processes. This aspect is crucial to perform slot values inference accurately. In addition, these works do not propose any pattern that automates the identification of composite conversation flows. While existing co-reference techniques [9] can be used to support slot-value-flow pattern, again such techniques do not employ API knowledge. Systems like Ava [12] and PLOW [1] can support slot-value-flow pattern in conversations, but by hardcoding variables that refer to values from previous tasks. They also do not provide any automated support for nested-intent and API-calls-ordering. IRIS [7], on the other hand, can enable atomic identification of nested-intent and slot-value-flow patterns, but only to accomplish complex tasks in the data science domain. In addition, such automation is supported by dedicating an API that dynamically adds variables as the conversation progresses to save the result of each dialog task for future use. The key contribution of our approach over these works is greater automation, by enabling the automatic support of conversation patterns through a context knowledge graph that is incrementally derived from conversation history and API knowledge.

3   Overview

A conversation is mainly a sequence of user utterances and bot responses (refers to Fig. 1). In addition, studies on human-bot dialogue patterns [10] reveal that conversations are multi-turn (e.g., in Fig. 1 there are two turns to accomplish *BookTaxi* intent) and multi-intent meaning that during a conversation user's intent continuously changes as shown in Fig. 1. In order to support multi-turn multi-intent conversations, we proposed in our previous work [23] a conversational model that leverages Hierarchical State Machines (HSMs) [21]. HSMs allow to reduce complexity that may be caused by the number of states that are needed to specify interactions between users, chatbots and services.

Inspired by existing workflow management systems and linguistic theory, in this paper, we propose to support greater complexity and expressiveness during conversations by identifying 3 types of dialogue patterns (i.e., *slot-value-flow, nested-intent,* and *API-calls ordering*) to realise some complex and decomposable user intents. These transformation patterns along with the conversational state machine model [23] allows to drive incrementally the workflow that steers the conversation with users. We also develop a conversation manager service that aims at initiating and controlling conversations by using a set of services to communicate with users, manage the hierarchical state machine, and invoke APIs. This conversation manager service is augmented with a context knowledge graph to support the proposed transformation patterns. In this section, we give a brief overview of the conversational state machine then, we explain how the conversation manager service manages the conversation flow.

Conversational State Machine. It contains a set of states called *"intent-states"* representing user intents (e.g., *FindRestaurant*), their slots (e.g., *city, food*) and actions such as API invocations (e.g., call *SearchBusinesses* method) to realise them. Inside each intent-state there are states that represent situations

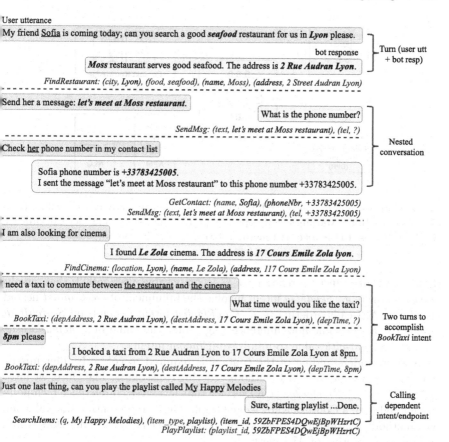

User utterance

My friend <u>Sofia</u> is coming today; can you search a good *seafood* restaurant for us in **Lyon** please.

bot response

Moss restaurant serves good seafood. The address is **2 Rue Audran Lyon.**

} Turn (user utt + bot resp)

FindRestaurant: (city, Lyon), (food, seafood), (name, Moss), (address, 2 Street Audran Lyon)

Send her a message: ***let's meet at Moss restaurant.***

What is the phone number?

SendMsg: (text, let's meet at Moss restaurant), (tel, ?)

Check <u>her</u> phone number in my contact list

Sofia phone number is **+33783425005.**
I sent the message "let's meet at Moss restaurant" to this phone number +33783425005.

} Nested conversation

GetContact: (name, Sofia), (phoneNbr, +33783425005)
SendMsg: (text, let's meet at Moss restaurant), (tel, +33783425005)

I am also looking for cinema

I found **Le Zola** cinema. The address is **17 Cours Emile Zola lyon.**

FindCinema: (location, Lyon), (name, Le Zola), (address, 117 Cours Emile Zola Lyon)

I need a taxi to commute between <u>the restaurant</u> and <u>the cinema</u>

What time would you like the taxi?

BookTaxi: (depAddress, 2 Rue Audran Lyon), (destAddress, 17 Cours Emile Zola Lyon), (depTime, ?)

8pm please

I booked a taxi from 2 Rue Audran Lyon to 17 Cours Emile Zola Lyon at 8pm.

} Two turns to accomplish BookTaxi intent

BookTaxi: (depAddress, 2 Rue Audran Lyon), (destAddress, 17 Cours Emile Zola Lyon), (depTime, 8pm)

Just one last thing, can you play the playlist called My Happy Melodies

Sure, starting playlist ...Done.

} Calling dependent intent/endpoint

SearchItems: (q, My Happy Melodies), (item_type, playlist), (item_id, 59ZbFPES4DQwEjBpWHzrtC)
PlayPlaylist: (playlist_id, 59ZbFPES4DQwEjBpWHzrtC)

Fig. 1. Example of multi-turn multi-intent conversation. After each turn we illustrate the intent and its set of (slot, value) pairs. The red slots are required input slots, the blue slots are output slots, and the green values are inferred values. (Color figure online)

that a bot may occupy in a given conversation (e.g., a bot-to-user question to resolve the value of a missing intent slot). Transitions between intent-states automatically trigger actions to perform desired intent fulfillment operations.

Conversation Manager. Figure 2 presents the architecture of the conversation manager service where new main services to support the proposed patterns have a red border. The tracker represents the core service that coordinates the information flow in the conversation. When the chatbot receives a new utterance from the user, the *Natural Language Understanding (NLU)* service extracts user intent and (slot, value) pairs from this utterance and sends them to the tracker.

The main objective of the *Dialogue Pattern Recogniser (DPR)* service is to identify compositional conversations (i.e., complex user utterances) and automatically transform them into operations that generate states and transitions in the conversational state machine. In other words, this service checks whether

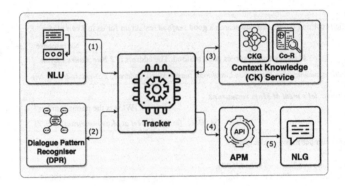

Fig. 2. Conversation Manager Architecture. **(1)** Extract intent and (slot, value) pairs. **(2)** Generate State Machines (SM) operations. **(3)** Infer slot value/Get call ordering of API methods. **(4)** Invoke API method. **(5)** Generate human-like response.

the current utterance is related to a decomposable user intent that involve nested-intent (e.g., *SendMsg* intent involve the fulfillment of *GetContact* nested-intent), or API-calls ordering (e.g., *PlayPlaylist* intent depends on *SearchItems* intent), or a slot-value-flow inference (e.g., infer the value of *Cinema-location* from *Restaurant-city* value to fulfill *FindCinema* intent).

A good understanding of the context is required to correctly infer missing slots' values and identify API methods ordering constraints. Therefore, we introduce the *Context Knowledge (CK)* service that leverages co-reference techniques augmented with a Context Knowledge Graph (CKG) representing slot-value and API methods relationships. This service allows the chatbot to infer slots' values and get call ordering of API methods.

Once the tracker collects all required information for the current intent-state, it calls the *API Manager* (APM), which maps the intent-state and (slot, value) pairs to an API method invocation. Finally, the *NLG* service produces a human-like response based on the *APM* output. In the next sections, we describe in detail the *DPR* and the *CK* services.

4   Dialogue Pattern Recogniser

In this section, for each of the three patterns *slot-value-flow*, *Nested-intent* and *API-calls ordering*, we give (i) a description and (ii) an example of how the pattern can automatically recognise compositional conversation flows and transform them into operations in the conversational State Machine (SM).

4.1   Slot-Value-Flow Pattern

Description. The *slot-value-flow* pattern is a known phenomenon in linguistic theory called Anaphora [16]. Anaphora is the use of an expression whose interpretation depends upon another expression mentioned in the conversation history.

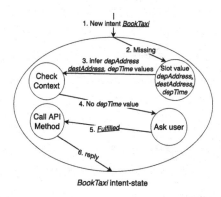

Fig. 3. Slot-value-flow. The SM operations related to BookTaxi intent fulfilment.

e.g., in Fig. 1, the underlined pronoun *"her"* refers to the entity *"Sofia"*). For
chatbots, these expressions are slots' values of previous fulfilled intents that can
be reused by the missing slots' values of the current intent.

Example. Figure 3 illustrates an example of how the *slot-value-flow* pattern can
be supported in a conversational state machine. Considering the user request *"I
need a taxi to commute between the restaurant and the cinema"* in Fig. 1, the
chatbot detects three missing slots' values (*depAddress, destAddress, depTime*)
in the intent *BookTaxi* (1)(2). The *DPR* service adds a call to a context state
to infer the missing slots' values (3). Here the chatbot leverages on the *CK*
service to infer the missing values from previous fulfilled intents (e.g., it infers
the value of *Taxi-depAddress* from *Restaurant-address* value). If a missing slot
value cannot be inferred (*depTime*), the *DPR* service creates a *"Ask User"* state
and the bot asks the user *"What time would you like the taxi?"* (4). The user
answers *"8 pm please"*. Once all required slots for *BookTaxi* intent are fulfilled,
the *DPR* invokes the corresponding API method (5) and the bot responds to
the user (6).

.2   Nested-Intent Pattern

Description. The *nested-intent* pattern is inspired from linguistic theory. In
daily life, people have the capability of using nesting conversations [7]. When a
friend says *"For when should I book the restaurant?"*, we might respond *"The day
Marcos gets back from Milan"*. To automatically translate this linguistic pattern
to workflow pattern the *DPR* needs to recognise the *nested-intent* state. There is
a nested-intent state when the user wants to accomplish an intent but instead of
giving the required slot value, she/he gives another utterance related to another
intent that will return the required value to fulfill the parent intent.

Example. Figure 4 illustrates an example of how the nested-intent pattern can
be supported in a conversational state machine. Considering the user request in
Fig. 1 *"Send her a message: let's meet at Moss restaurant."*, the chatbot detects

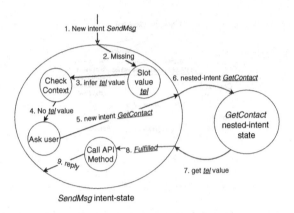

Fig. 4. Nested-intent pattern. The SM operations related to sendMsg intent fulfilment.

one missing slot value *tel* in the new intent *SendMsg* (1)(2). The *DPR* service adds a call to a context state to infer *tel* value (3). If the value cannot be inferred so the *DPR* service creates the *"Ask User"* state and the bot asks the user *"What is the phone number?"* (4). The user replies by a new utterance *"Check her phone number in my contact list"* related to a new intent *GetContact* (5). Based on the *CK* service the *DPR* can identify that the output slot of *GetContact* has a similar type as the missing slot *tel* (i.e., both represent phone number) therefore there is a high probability that *GetContact* is a nested-intent. the *DPR* creates the nested-intent state *GetContact* (6), gets the required value (*tel* value) and comes back to the parent intent *SendMsg* (7) to call the corresponding API method (8) and respond to the user (9).

4.3   API-Calls Ordering Pattern

Description. We identify a completely new pattern called *"API-calls ordering"* pattern. This pattern is related to REST API design patterns that ensure the discoverability of resources and the ability to access data they refer to [18]. From REST API design perspective, there are some methods that require an API generated string, called *"id"*, as an input parameter to access the needed data. This *id* is an output of another method in the same API.

For example, in *Spotify API*, *SearchItems* method returns an item Spotify Catalog information (e.g., owner, Spotify id, etc.) given the item type (e.g., playlist, albums) and a keyword. On the other hand, *PlayPlaylist* is another *Spotify API* method that requires the returned *Spotify id* to play the corresponding playlist. When the user says *"Play the playlist called My Happy Melodies"*, two scenarios are possible from user perspective. **Scenario 1.** The bot asks the user *"What is the playlist id?"*, but it is unlikely for her/him to know the *id* value because it is a *Spotify API* generated string. To get this *id* the user needs to know that it can be obtained from *SearchItems* method otherwise she/he will

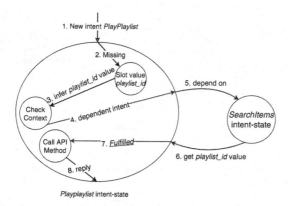

Fig. 5. API-calls ordering. The SM operations related to PlayPlaylist intent fulfilment.

not be able to fulfill *PlayPlaylist* intent. She/He says to the bot *"Search for the playlist named 'My Happy Melodies' on Spotify Catalog"*. The bot fulfills the *SearchItems* intent and returns the *id* value. The user asks again *"Can you start the playlist with this id 59ZbFPES4DQw..."*. In this scenario, the user is forced to adapt to the technology. **Scenario 2.** The bot responses directly to the user saying *"Sure, starting playlist... Done."*. To support this scenario a bot developer needs to implement an intermediately endpoint that combines *SearchItems* and *PlayPlaylist* endpoints. The implementation of new endpoints could grow exponentially if the bot developer have to account for all endpoints pairs. In the following, we explain through the same example how this *API-calls ordering* pattern can be automatically supported in state machines.

Example. In Fig. 5, when the user says *"Play the playlist called My Happy Melodies"*, the *DPR* creates a new intent-state called *PlayPlaylist* (1). It detects that the *id* value is missing (2) and adds a call to a context state (3). Using *CK* service, the *DPR* recongnises that *PlayPlaylist* intent depends on *SearchItems* intent (4). In consequence, it creates the *SearchItems* intent-state (5) and fulfills it to get the *id* value (6). Then, the *DPR* comes back to *PlayPlaylist* to call the corresponding API (7) method and respond to the user (8).

5 Context Knowledge Service

Context can be defined as any information that can be leveraged from previous turns or external knowledge [11]. Maintaining the context is necessary in chatbots as it allows to keep continuity in the dialogue and avoid repetition, making interactions more natural [11]. However inferring information from the conversation context is challenging due to multi-turn multi-intent conversations and heterogeneous APIs. There are several parameters among multiple APIs methods that can share all or some of their values during the conversation [19].

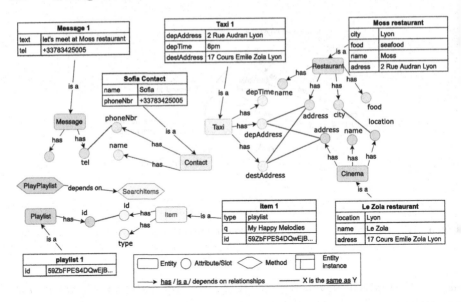

Fig. 6. Example of a context knowledge graph related to the conversation in Fig. 1.

To tackle this challenge, we propose the *Context Knowledge (CK)* Service that aims at accumulating a part of the conversation context. The *CK* service uses a co-reference system to resolve a potentially referenced slot value (e.g., *Contact-name* value is referenced by the pronoun *"her"* in the utterance *"Check her phone number"*). This system links together mentions that relates to entities given the previous turns. In our approach, we choose to use *Neuralcoref* [9], a state-of-the-art coreference resolution system based on neural networks.

In some cases, the co-reference system is not able to infer the correct slot value. For example in Fig. 1, when user says *"I need a taxi to commute between the restaurant and the cinema"*, the co-reference will replace the mention *"the restaurant"* by the entity *"Moss restaurant"* which is a wrong value for the *Taxi-depAddress* slot because it should be an address. To have more accurate slot value inference, we augment the co-reference system with a *Context Knowledge Graph (CKG)* that represents: (i) slots values relationships and (ii) API methods relationships including call-ordering constraints. Figure 6 shows the *CKG* instance related to the conversation in Fig. 1.

Context Knowledge Graph. We denote the graph as $G = (N, E)$, where N and E are the set of nodes and the set of edges respectively. In this graph there are 4 node types: entity (e.g., *Cinema*), attribute/slot (e.g., *city*), entity instance (e.g. *Le Zola cinema*), and methods (e.g., *PlayPlaylist*). There are 4 edges types: *"has"*, *"is a"*, *"depends on"*, and *"same as"*. The relationship *"has"* is generated between an entity and an attribute based on a predefined ontology. The relationship *"is a"* is generated between an instance and its entity (i.e., node *is an* instance of). Both *entity instances* and *is a* edges are incrementally derived

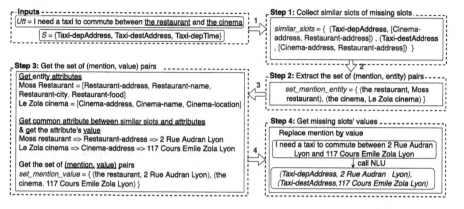

Fig. 7. Example of inferring slots' values.

from the conversation. The relationship *"depends on"* denotes that a method *depends on* another method to get the required *id* value. The computation of this *"depends on"* edge can be done from API reference documentation using the open information extraction methods proposed by [20]. The *"same as"* edge is generated between two similar slots (e.g., in Fig. 6 there is an edge between *Cinema-address* and *Taxi-depAddress*, because the taxi departure may be the cinema's address). The computation of the *"same as"* edge is based on the semantic similarity between the *slots vectors* embedding. A *slot vector* is the average of the vectors values embedding. These values represent the possible values that each slot can take. We acquire such possible values by querying API-KG Web Service[3] that returns a list of values for a given API method parameter. Then, we compute the cosine similarity between each slot pair and compare this similarity with a threshold predefined by the bot developer. If the similarity is greater than the threshold, an edge is created between the two slots.

Slot Value Inference. Figure 7 shows an example of the main steps to infer a missing slots' values { *depAddress, destAddress, depTime* } from a given utterance *"I need a taxi to commute between the restaurant and the cinema"* based on the CKG.

Step 1. We collect the set of similar slots based on the *"same as"* edges. If a missing slot value has only one similar slot (e.g., *Cinema-location* has only *Restaurant-city*), we reuse directly the similar slot's value. *Taxi-depTime* is not considered in next steps because it doesn't have any similar slot.

Step 2. The co-reference system extracts (mention, entity) pairs from *Utt*.

Step 3. For each entity returned by the co-reference system, we get its list of attributes. Next, we get the common attribute using intersection between the list of similar slots and the list of entity attributes. Finally, we get the value of each common attribute and link it to the corresponding mention.

---

[3] https://apikg.ap.ngrok.io/api/docs/.

Step 4. Lastly, each mention in *Utt* is replaced by its corresponding value. The utterance *Utt* is sent to the NLU service to extract the missing slots' values.

6   Evaluation

In this section we describe a study aiming at understanding the need, benefits, and effectiveness of supporting the proposed patterns. We investigate whether the proposed patterns naturally occur when conversing with services, perform a comparative analysis with alternative approaches focusing on the user experience, to then analyse the support provided based on performance metrics.

6.1   Methods

Experimental Design. Participants were recruited from the extended network of contacts of the authors. Invitations were sent via email, asking for volunteers, resulting in a total of 12 participants. We followed a within-subjects design[4] to evaluate the proposed dialog patterns and supporting services. Participants were tasked with interacting with three different chatbots, which were developed to capture the following experimental conditions:

– *DF-Baseline* : The baseline implements the standard conversational management support of traditional chatbot development platforms. It is developed using the underlying techniques of DialogFlow, including the DF NLU model, conversational model, and the Input-Output context mechanism.
– *SM-NeuralCoref* : it relies on the State Machine conversational model but supporting only the NeuralCoref model [9]. The aim of this setup is to emphasize the need for the Context Knowledge Graph.
– *SM-Patterns* : it includes all of our services to support the new proposed conversation patterns and relies on the State Machine conversational model.

Besides the differences highlighted above, all three chatbots were built on the same foundation. They supported 15 intents collected from the DSTC8 dataset [15]. For all three chatbots, we use DialogFlow NLU service as NLU model because it is one of the most complete NLU models [4] to train chatbots.

We devised three main tasks, each comprising representative scenarios that catered to the proposed dialog patterns. Task 1, on the slot-value-flow pattern (T1), required participants to plan a day program by interacting with services that would benefit from leveraging the ongoing context of the conversation (e.g., reusing same locations or date). Task 2, on the nested-intent pattern (T2), asked participants to schedule a doctor's appointment on the first available spot. The dependency between the involved services favored the use of a nested pattern. Task 3, on the API-calls ordering pattern (T3), invited users to look for a restaurant with good ratings, requiring them to interact with services (search, reviews)

---

[4] Study materials and in-depth results available at https://tinyurl.com/25ad8jv6.

linked by an ID. It is important to note that each scenario suggested the need for relevant services without imposing any specific conversation style or order.

Procedure. The study was conducted online with the support of an online form aggregating all the instructions. Before starting, participants provided their consent to participate and for their interactions with the chatbots to be recorded. After providing background information, participants then proceeded to perform the tasks with the three chatbots, in a randomised order to avoid positional bias. For each task, participants were asked to describe the pros and cons of their experience with each chatbot, and to specify which one provided the better experience and why. The duration of the experiment was between 45–90 min.

Data Processing and Analysis. We performed a qualitative and quantitative analysis of the experience with each chatbot. We performed a thematic analysis of the open-ended participant feedback so as to identify emerging themes in their experience with the chatbots, and better characterise the reasons behind their preferred design. The conversation logs were also analysed to i) understand if participants naturally engage in conversations that leverage the proposed dialog patterns, and ii) assess the performance of the chatbots. We analyse the performance in relation to the optimal reference scenario (e.g., the most efficient scenario for the conversation style adopted by the participant) by considering the following metrics: number of (M1) conversation turns, (M2) prompts asking for missing slot values, and (M3) missing slot values correctly inferred.

5.2   Results

T1. Slot-Value-Flow Pattern. The large majority of participants (9/12) reported having a superior experience when interacting with the *SM-Patterns* chatbot as compared to the alternatives. The qualitative analysis of participant feedback revealed two main reasons behind this preference. The dominant theme was the **efficiency of interactions** (9 participants), with participants expressing the *SM-Patterns* chatbot being *"quicker in getting an answer"* (P12) and being able to correctly infer missing values (e.g., *"I liked that it correctly understood my destination and I didn't have to input the address [from a previous turn]"*, P10). Another salient theme was the ability to enable more **natural conversations** (6 participants), with participants explicitly stating the *"experience of the conversation [being] more natural and human-like"* (P14). Participants also suggested improvements, notably in terms of being transparent (2 participants) about what information the chatbot was inferring from the context.

The analysis of the conversation logs showed that the majority of participants (9 participants) engaged in conversations styles that took full advantage of this pattern, successfully referencing the context at least twice. Interestingly, the participants who showed preference towards the other chatbots engaged in conversation styles that to a lesser degree benefited of the slot-value-flow pattern, and instead formulated utterances that provided actual slot values in the requests (e.g., U: *"I want a taxi to [address]"*) instead of leveraging the context.

The quantitative analysis of chatbot performance (Table 1) confirms the qualitative observations, putting the support by SM-Patterns as the closest to the

Table 1. Evaluation of chatbots according to performance metrics. Arrows indicate lower values better (↓) and higher better (↑), and bold face best performance. Percentages denote the relative performance with respect to the reference (optimal) scenario.

Metric	Reference	DF-Baseline	SM-Patterns	SM-NeuralCoref
M1 ↓ (TURNS)	**8,42**	9,92 (18%)	**8,67 (3%)**	10,83 (29%)
M2 ↓ (PROMPTS)	**4,25**	5,58 (31%)	**4,42 (4%)**	6,33 (49 %)
M3 ↑ (SLOTS)	**3,33**	1,33 (−60%)	**3,17 (−5%)**	0,08 (−98%)

optimal performance (reference scenario) for the three metrics under evaluation. In contrast, the simple support by DF-Baseline resulted in longer conversations and required more input from the users. Interestingly, SM-NeuralCoref performed the poorest even when supporting co-reference techniques, but this can be attributed to its inability to accurately infer missing slot values (M3).

T2. Nested-Intent Pattern. As in the previous task, the majority of participants expressed their preference for *SM-Patterns* (9/12 participants). The qualitative analysis of the feedback identified four main themes behind this preference. Participants referred to the chatbot's ability to **keep track of the user goal** (6 participants), stating that when engaging in a nested intent *"[the chatbot] remembered that I wanted to book appointment with a dentist (user goal)"* (P4) while the baseline would *"forget totally [what] I wanted"* (P3). Providing a **natural flow** was another emerging quality attribute (4 participants), with participants expressing that the experienced *"flow felt natural"* (P6) while the baseline would force them to plan ahead. The chatbot was also perceived as **efficient** (5 participants), requiring *"less input for a correct answer"* (P14), while for a few it simply came down to being **effective** (2 participants), i.e., able to complete their task with the conversation styles they engaged in.

An analysis of the conversation logs revealed that most participants (7/12) had naturally described a nesting-intent pattern in their interactions. Looking into the conversation logs of those who expressed preference for the baseline (3 participants) provided further insights. Interestingly 2 of these participants had not actually engaged in a nested-intent pattern, while the one who did had experienced problems in the formulation of the nested intent (i.e., the framing of the nested intent was not recognised by the NLU). This highlights the need for integrating conversation repair strategies into this pattern.

T3. API-Calls Ordering Pattern. All participants (12/12) reported having a better experience with the *SM-Patterns* chatbot. Not surprisingly, the majority of participants (8 participants) commented on the ability to **hide technical details** as one of the main reasons for their preference, one participant citing that in the proposed scenario *"it successfully understood that I wanted a review from the selected restaurant without asking for the business ID"* (P7), whereas the technical details of the service as exposed by the baseline chatbot made it *"difficult to understand for someone who doesn't know what that means"* (P3).

Providing a **smooth conversation flow** was another theme that emerged from the feedback on *SM-Patterns* , with participants mentioning that in comparison, interacting with the baseline chatbot felt like being *"caught in a loop"* (P8). Some participants summarised the positive experience by simply stating that the chatbot was **effective**, working correctly or as expected.

The analysis of conversation logs showed that all but one participant (who deviated from the proposed scenario) described interactions that benefited from the API-calls ordering pattern. What this tells us is this pattern greatly aligns with the conversation styles and expectations of users.

7   Conclusions and Future Work

In this paper, we identified and characterized 3 types of dialog patterns that endow bot platforms with reusable functionality to recognise compositional conversational flows and reduce the development complexity. Our work also comes with its own limitations and space for possible improvements.

While we provide empirical support for the proposed dialog patterns, the evaluation is still limited in the number of participants, and so we plan to run larger scale evaluations. In addition, in this work we only focused on Intent-SingleAPI interaction pattern, and we plan to investigate other patterns such as Intent-CompositeAPI, where user utterance may involve more than one intent.

References

1. Allen, J., et al.: PLOW: a collaborative task learning agent. AAAI (2007)
2. Banchs, R.E., Jiang, R., Kim, S., Niswar, A., Yeo, K.H.: AIDA: artificial intelligent dialogue agent. In: Proceedings of the SIGDIAL 2013, pp. 145–147 (2013)
3. Bradley, N., Fritz, T., Holmes, R.: Context-aware conversational developer assistants. In: 40th International Conference on Software Engineering (ICSE) (2018)
4. Canonico, M., De. Russis, L.: A comparison and critique of natural language understanding tools. Cloud Comput. **2018**, 120 (2018)
5. Chen, H., Liu, X., Yin, D., Tang, J.: A survey on dialogue systems: recent advances and new frontiers. ACM Sigkdd Explor. Newsl. **19**(2), 25–35 (2017)
6. Chen, L., al.: Schema-guided multi-domain dialogue state tracking with graph attention neural networks. In: Proceedings of the AAAI 2020, vol. 34, pp. 7521–7528 (2020)
7. Fast, E., et al.: Iris: a conversational agent for complex tasks. In: CHI 2018 (2018)
8. Henderson, M.S.: Discriminative methods for statistical spoken dialogue systems. Ph.D. thesis, University of Cambridge (2015)
9. Hugging-Face: Fast coreference resolution in spacy with neural networks. https:// spacy.io/universe/project/neuralcoref. Accessed 15 Nov 2020
10. Hutchby, I., Wooffitt, R.: Conversation analysis. Polity (2008)
11. Jain, M., Kota, R., Kumar, P., Patel, S.N.: Convey: exploring the use of a context view for chatbots. In: Proceedings of the CHI 2018, pp. 1–6 (2018)
12. John, R.J.L., Potti, N., Patel, J.M.: Ava: from data to insights through conversations. In: 8th Biennial Conference on Innovative Data Systems Research (2017)

13. López, A., Sànchez-Ferreres, J., Carmona, J., Padró, L.: From process models to chatbots. In: Giorgini, P., Weber, B. (eds.) CAiSE 2019. LNCS, vol. 11483, pp. 383–398. Springer, Cham (2019). https://doi.org/10.1007/978-3-030-21290-2_24

14. Manning, C.D., Eric, M.: A copy-augmented sequence-to-sequence architecture gives good performance on task-oriented dialogue. In: EACL (2017)

15. Rastogi, A., et al.: Towards scalable multi-domain conversational agents: the schema-guided dialogue dataset. arXiv e-prints arXiv:1909.05855, September 2019

16. Reinhart, T.M.: The syntactic domain of anaphora. Ph.D. thesis, MIT (1976)

17. Su, P., et al.: Continuously learning neural dialogue management. CoRR (2016)

18. Ebert, J.: SOA with REST: principles, patterns & constraints for building enterprise solutions with REST by Thomas Erl, Benjamin Carlyle, Cesare Pautasso, Raj Balasubramanian. ACM SIGSOFT Softw. Eng. Notes **38**(3), 32–33 (2013)

19. Wu, C.S., et al.: Transferable multi-domain state generator for task-oriented dialogue systems. arXiv preprint arXiv:1905.08743 (2019)

20. Xiaoxue, R., et al.: API-misuse detection driven by fine-grained API-constraint knowledge graph (2020)

21. Yannakakis, M.: Hierarchical state machines. In: van Leeuwen, J., Watanabe, O., Hagiya, M., Mosses, P.D., Ito, T. (eds.) TCS 2000. LNCS, vol. 1872, pp. 315–330. Springer, Heidelberg (2000). https://doi.org/10.1007/3-540-44929-9_24

22. Zamanirad, S.: Superimposition of natural language conversations over software enabled services. Ph.D. thesis, University of New South Wales, Australia (2019)

23. Zamanirad, S., et al.: Hierarchical state machine based conversation model and services. In: Proceedings of the CAiSE (2020)

24. Zamanirad, S., et al.: Programming bots by synthesizing natural language expressions into API invocations. In: Proceedings of the ASE 2017, pp. 832–837. IEEE (2017)

25. Zhang, Z., et al.: Memory-augmented dialogue management for task-oriented dialogue systems. ACM Trans. Inf. Syst. **37**(3), 1–30 (2019)

Design Patterns for Board-Based Collaborative Work Management Tools

Joaquín Peña[1]([⊠]) [iD], Alfonso Bravo[1] [iD], Adela del-Río-Ortega[1,2] [iD], Manuel Resinas[1,2] [iD], and Antonio Ruiz-Cortés[1,2] [iD]

[1] I3US Institute, Universidad de Sevilla, Sevilla, Spain
{joaquinp,adeladerio,resinas,aruiz}@us.es, alfbralla@alum.us.es
[2] SCORE Lab, Universidad de Sevilla, Sevilla, Spain

Abstract. Board-based software tools for managing collaborative work (e.g. Trello or Microsoft Planner) are highly configurable information systems. Their structure is based on boards that contain cards organized in lists. This structure allows users to organize a wide variety of formal or informal information and work processes in a very flexible way. However, this flexibility means that in every situation the user is required to make decisions to design a new board from scratch, which is not a straightforward task, specially if performed by non-technical users. In this paper, we carried out a study following an inductive approach consisting of analyzing 91 Trello board designs from both research works and board templates proposed by Trello users, which cover a wide variety of domains and use cases. The result is twofold. First, we propose a metamodel for designing boards that takes into account not only the structure of the board but also other decisions like the type of information cards manage and behavioural aspects of how cards flow. Second, we use this metamodel to identify and characterize 8 patterns that are commonly used in board designs. These results, applicable to all board-based tools, provide insights that can be useful for users to design solutions more effectively and efficiently and help us to better understand the roles that these information systems may play in the current enterprise information systems ecosystem.

Keywords: Collaborative work · Design patterns · Digital transformation · Kanban-based software

1 Introduction

Board-based collaborative work management tools, like Trello, Asana or Planner[1], are largely spreading as a way to organize a wide variety of formal

---

[1] https://trello.com, https://asana.com, https://tasks.office.com/.

This work has received funding from grants RTI2018-101204-B-C22 (OPHELIA) and RTI2018-101204-B-C21 (HORATIO) (MCI/AEI/FEDER, UE), and P18-FR-2895 (EKIPMENT PLUS) from the Andalusian government.

or informal information and work processes. These tools allow creating boards where users can add information or actions in form of cards and distribute them into compartments or columns usually called lists or buckets. Depending on the tool, the user can also add labels, descriptions or due dates to cards, assign cards to certain users or define checklists inside cards.

The main purpose with which these tools have been conceived is to manage collaborative tasks. Nevertheless, as shown in the existing literature, their use expands to other scenarios like sharing knowledge, managing shared informal processes or representing shared schedules [2,6,7,10–12,14,15,17]. These different uses are possible because of the different meanings that lists and cards can be given in each board as well as the different ways they can be used (e.g. how cards can be moved between lists). The use of these tools can be divided into two phases. The first one is the board design phase, which involves, first, making decisions about how the board should be used and the meaning of lists and cards, and second, defining an initial set of lists and maybe cards. Once the board is designed, then the board execution phase begins. This phase involves using the board for the predetermined purpose usually by adding, removing or moving cards between lists.

Designing boards is not a straightforward task, specially if it is performed by non-technical users, as commonly occurs in these tools. In an attempt to give support in this endeavour, many of these tools provide the possibility of reusing board designs for specific tasks like human resources onboarding, or SCRUM-based project management by defining board templates or reusing previous boards[2]. All of the research performed around these tools has also been focused on this direction and details reusable board designs that solve specific problems [2,6,11,14,15,17].

In this paper, instead, we want to analyze these tools from a broader perspective. Our goal is to analyze the different purposes for which these tools are used and to characterize the main principles and decisions that lay behind the board designs used for each purpose.

To do so, we carried out a study following an inductive approach analyzing both, the existing literature and the 91 board templates proposed by Trello users that were available when this analysis was made[3] and that cover a wide variety of domains and use cases. As a result, we present a twofold contribution. First, we propose a metamodel for defining board designs that goes beyond the well-known structure of boards, lists and cards, and makes most of the main decisions made during board design explicit. Second, using the proposed metamodel, we identify and characterize a catalogue of 8 patterns of board design. All the board designs of the templates analyzed fit at least in one of these 8 patterns.

These results provide valuable insights for both research and practice. Concerning the former, the metamodel makes it explicit design decisions about the use of these tools that are currently implicit. This opens up new possibilities to reason about them and to provide a more automated support to the design and

---

[2] For instance, https://trello.com/templates or https://asana.com/uses.

[3] Their number at https://trello.com/templates is constantly growing.

execution phases. As for the latter, by relying on the well-grounded notion of patterns as a way to promote reuse, we provide a tool that can help users to design boards more effectively and efficiently since much of the knowledge that used to be spread over a catalogue of 91 domain-specific templates is now synthesized into 8 domain-independent patterns. Furthermore, they give hints on the different roles these information systems can play or the different ways they can be used to address challenges on current enterprise information systems [18].

The rest of the paper is organized as follows. Section 2 introduces some background and discusses related work. The metamodel is presented in Sect. 3 and the catalog of board design patterns is described in Sect. 4. Section 5 discusses the application of the identified patterns in the analyzed templates. Finally, Sect. 6 concludes the paper, provides the implications for research and practice and describes the main limitations identified as well as proposes some future research directions to address some of them.

2   Background and Related Work

The initial idea of board-based collaborative work management tools like Trello, Assana or Planner bases on the principles of Kanban, a method of visualizing workflows to provide an overview of a project from start to finish. To do so, they provide three main elements: boards, lists, and cards. According to this common use of these tools, for each project, like the production of an article, a corresponding board is created. Each board includes a set of lists that may, for example, indicate the progress of a project. Finally, lists contain cards that hold information on a specific task. Figure 1 shows a screenshot of Trello of such a board. Many of these tools also provide other elements such as people, labels, due dates, or checklists that can be assigned to cards.

Besides the static structure, a relevant aspect of a board is how to use it. Commonly, cards are moved from list to list while the board is used. The meaning of moving a card from one list to another depends on the board. For instance, in a board like the one in the example, a card is moved when completed. But other behaviors are also possible.

The use of a board can be divided into two phases, namely: board design and board execution. During board design decisions about the static structure, the dynamic use, and the meaning of the different elements (lists and cards) are made based on the purpose the board is intended to have. In our example, this

Fig. 1. Screenshot of a Trello board of an article production.

involves deciding that cards represent papers, lists represent states of the paper, and moving a paper from one list to another represents transitioning the paper from one state to another. It also involves deciding and creating the lists that represent each of the states of the paper.

During board execution, the board is used based on the decisions made during design. This involves adding, removing, editing, or moving cards. Also, depending on the features of the tool, the use includes assigning people to cards, adding or completing checklists, or defining due dates amongst others. In our example, this involves creating cards as new papers come into our pipeline, and moving them throughout the different lists until reaching the "Accepted" list, hopefully, or "Rejected" in the worst case.

In recent years, a large number of research that report on the use of Trello in different domains, from education or libraries to software development has been published [10–12,14,15,17]. In this research body, it is quite common that authors propose a board design to model a solution to a specific problem:

We can find Kanban-based solutions in the context of education and libraries like in [14,15,17], board designs for SCRUM agile methodology [12,15], or other solutions specific to certain domains like an editorial calendar [6] or a farm [2].

This need to provide a board design to specific problems avoiding to start from scratch every time has also been identified at a practical level. Trello provides a set of public templates categorized according to different domains (like personal, business, or education) and scenarios (like wedding planning, new year resolutions or book club inside of the personal domain)[4]. Many of them are actually proposals by users of Trello. However, a template is just a board that includes a set of predefined lists and may include some predefined cards either to illustrate the use of the board or to provide some information that is reused between boards. It also includes a description in natural language that explains how the boards copied from it should be used (e.g. how cards should move between lists). To the best of our knowledge, none of the existing tools of this type allows the definition of the way to use a specific type of board in a structured and systematic manner.

Unlike existing research, the goal of this paper is not to propose a specific board design, but to identify and characterize which are the patterns that commonly appear in these designs. According to [5], "Patterns, in general, are vehicles for encapsulating knowledge. They are considered one of the most effective means for naming, organizing, and reasoning about design knowledge" in the broader sense of Design knowledge. The concept of patterns has been widely applied and has proven to be useful in a multitude of different domains. In the software development domain, the roots can be found in the well-known analysis [8] and design patterns [9], but they have spread to many other related domains like patterns for different perspectives of business processes: control-flow [1], data [21], resources [20], performance [19], or compliance [23], ontology patterns [5], or organizational patterns for B2B environments [13], to name a few.

---

[4] https://trello.com/templates shows the current existing templates.

We aim to apply the same concept of pattern for the creation of board designs, based on an analysis performed on the common use of Trello. Actually, it would also be applicable to other similar tools. To the best of our knowledge, there exists no previous work in this direction.

3   A Metamodel for Board Design

Before describing the patterns for designing boards, we first need to characterize which are the main elements of a board design. We do that by means of the metamodel for board design, shown in Fig. 2. We have obtained this metamodel based on our analysis of both the research papers mentioned in the related work [2,6,10–12,14,15,17] and the board design of the templates provided by Trello. To do so, we first developed a web scrapper that extracted the main information (template name, description, link) about the 91 board templates proposed by Trello users available at that moment (early 2020) and collected it into an Excel stylesheet. Three researchers from the author team analyzed the collected data and aimed to recognize different aspects that could help to identify categories among the templates. The aspects considered by these researchers, especially the use of Trello features like lists, cards, or labels, were different from one to another. They then decided to perform the categorization according to the use of the basic features that are common to all board-based tools, i.e. boards, lists, and cards, ignoring other features that may be specific to Trello. This resulted in a first version of the metamodel as well as a first categorization of the board templates. Unfortunately, not all templates fit into the defined categories. Therefore, another round was necessary. In this final round, not only the template static structure used in the previous round, but also its behaviour, i.e. the dynamic use and the meaning of the different elements of the board, were taken into account. This yielded the metamodel we present here as well as the catalog of 8 patterns described in Sect. 4. In this case, the categorization covered all the templates analyzed, the 91 Trello templates as well as the templates proposed in the analyzed related literature. Note that both the metamodel and the patterns are general and applicable to all board-based tools. In the following, we describe the metamodel in detail.

The static structure of a board design is modelled by means of three elements: Board, List and Default card. A Board represents the panel in which lists and cards are contained. Boards are composed by an ordered set of Lists, which are the divisions of the boards in the different containers where we will stock the content. Lists are also known as "buckets" or "columns," depending on the nomenclature. The order of the lists represents the visual order in which they appear in the board from left to right. Finally, Default Cards represent the content that appears on the lists, also visually ordered. We use the term Default card instead of just Card to emphasize the fact that we are modelling a board design with a predefined set of cards, and they do not refer to the cards that will be added to the board during its execution phase.

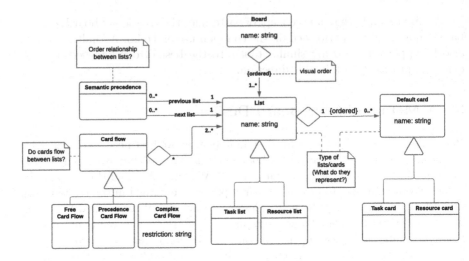

Fig. 2. A metamodel for board designs

However, as we have mentioned before, a board design is not only the static structure. All board designs that appear in templates include additional information collected in natural language about their semantics and how they should be used. Particularly, it is interesting to note how the meaning of cards and their possible behaviour varies from one design to another. While in some of them cards are conceived as tasks or work items, in others, they represent pieces of information or resources. In some cases, cards flow among lists, while in others cards always stay in the same list. Finally, in some cases there is an implicit order relationship between lists (e.g. if lists represent states of a lifecycle), whereas in others this relationship does not exist (e.g. if lists represent people or groups of people). These three elements together characterize how a board design must be used and are included in the metamodel as follows.

Based on the analysis performed, the meaning of cards can be divided into two broad categories. On the one hand, cards may represent tasks or work items. We use the term work item with the same meaning as in [20]. They represent an action or activity and its name (if it is well defined) is usually a verb. On the other hand, cards may also represent resources or, in general, pieces of information. In this case, their name is usually a noun. An example of this type of card can be found in the example of Fig. 1, where a card represents a publication. These two types of cards are represented in the metamodel by means of classes Task card and Resource card respectively.

Furthermore, the analysis also shows that all lists collect cards of the same type either tasks or resources. For this reason, we also apply the same categorization to lists. A Task List is a list that only contains task cards. Similarly, a Resources List is a list that only contains resources cards.

The second aspect that characterizes board designs is whether there exists an order relationship between lists. Inspired by the approach followed by BPMN with the sequence flow definition in its metamodel, this is modeled by means of a class called `Semantic Precedence`. When we say that there is semantic precedence between two lists in a board we are specifying that there is some high-level connection between them, besides their visual representation. For example, we can have an order relationship between the phases of a project (requirements before execution), the states of a task lifecycle (doing before done), or just numeric order (day 1 before day 2).

As we discuss in the following section, having an order relationship between two lists does not mean that cards can be moved between them. Therefore, it is necessary an additional concept to specify the lists among which cards can flow, namely class `Card flow`. This class specifies the set of lists between which cards can flow. The meaning of a card flowing between lists depends on the specific board. For instance, a board in which lists represent people and cards are tasks, moving a card from one list to another means assigning a task to a person. Instead, a board in which lists represent states and cards are resources, moving a card from one list to another means changing the state of the resource. Another example with precedence but without flow is cascade software project, where lists represent states (requirement, analysis, etc.) and cards tasks to be done in every step; cards don't flow between phases, but there is an order between them. A board may also have several card flows, for instance, because it contains different types of lists: some containing information and others containing tasks.

Besides specifying that cards flow between a set of lists, we can also specify if there is any restriction about this card flow. In this paper, we define three different types of restrictions:

- **Free Card Flow**: Cards can move between lists without any type of restriction. For example, cards can move back to previous lists, or they can skip some intermediate list.
- **Precedence Card Flow**: Cards can only flow through the buckets following the precedence detailed in the semantic precedence item previously described. For example, if the semantic precedence represents numeric order, cards will be only allowed to move following that order (cards cannot move from list 2 to list 1, for example).
- **Complex Card Flow**: The movement of cards between lists is restricted by some criteria that must be specified (see restriction item in the metamodel). For example, a complex card flow could allow the movement of cards following a rule different to (and more complex than) the semantic precedence. Another example is to specify that a card cannot be moved into a list if there are more than n cards in that list already. Inspired by the approach followed by BPMN to define complex gateways, the metamodel does not provide any specific detail about how this complex card flow can be defined. However, we envision that a language (or several languages) to model this kind of relationship could be defined.

The restrictions specified in the card flow can also be hard or soft. Restrictions are hard if the tool actually prevents moving the card if they are not followed. Instead, restrictions are soft if restrictions are understood as recommendations.

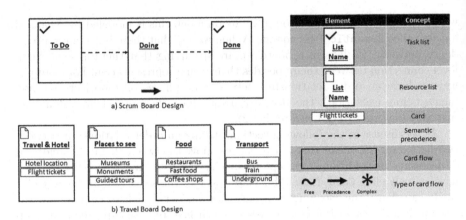

Fig. 3. Examples of board designs modelled using the metamodel

In this case, the tool allows the user to move the cards to any list regardless of the restrictions and it is the user the one who should enforce them. Trello, for instance, does not allow the definition of hard card flows. It is also important to note that a tool might provide some mechanisms to notify the user in case a soft restriction has not been met.

We are going to illustrate how this metamodel can be used to model board designs by means of two examples. Figure 3.a shows a Scrum board design that models three possible states of a project task ("To Do", "Doing" and "Done") by means of three Lists (depicted as rectangles). They are Task lists because they store cards that represent tasks. We represent it with a tick in the upper-left corner of each list. In this board, there is clearly a Semantic precedence defined between "To Do" and "Doing", and between "Doing" and "Done." This is depicted by means of a dashed arrow that links the two corresponding lists. Finally, when using the board, cards will move between the lists to signal that we have started performing a task (move from "To Do" to "Doing") and that we have finished a task (move from "Doing" to "Done"). Therefore, there is a Card flow between the three lists, which is represented by means of a rectangle that groups them. An icon at the bottom of the rectangle indicates the type of Card Flow, which can be either free, precedence, or complex (represented by a tilde, an arrow , or an asterisk, respectively). In this case, the movement will be according to the semantic precedence defined by the context of the problem.

The second example (Fig. 3.b) depicts a board design to organize information related to a trip. There are four lists ("Travel & Hotel", "Places to see", "Food", and "Transport") that contain information or resources, as indicated by the document icon in the upper left corner of each list. In this case, lists are independent of each other, so there is no semantic precedence between them. Furthermore, cards do not flow between lists. Instead, this board design includes some default cards as examples of the information that can be added in two of the four lists ("Places to see" and "Transport"). They are represented by means of rectangles inside the list.

It is important to note that, except for the name of the lists and the default cards contained in them, all the information about the board designs described above is currently specified in natural language in the description of the template or some predefined cards with information about how to use the board. Therefore, one advantage of the metamodel is that it makes this information explicit in a structured way, and hence, it can be used as a foundation to automate parts of its management like the card flow.

4   Patterns for Board Design

After analyzing the board designs of the templates using the elements defined in the metamodel, we have identified 8 different patterns that repeat across them (summarized in Table 1). These patterns represent different ways of designing the lists of a board (or a subset of them) based on the elements of the metamodel. Like all patterns, several of them can be used together on the same board. The patterns are characterized by the three elements of the metamodel related to the semantics of the cards and how they should be used, namely: what cards represent in Lists (column *List/Card type* of Table 1) i.e. tasks (Task list) or information or resources (Resource list); whether there is semantic precedence relationship between lists (column *Semant. prec.*), and whether cards flow between lists (column *Card flow*). A full pattern description template for each pattern can be found at [16] and at http://www.collaborativetoolspatterns.org. Each pattern includes a description of the problem, a detailed motivation, a graphical representation of the pattern, real examples (Trello templates) where the pattern is used, and a discussion of related patterns. In the following we briefly describe each of these eight patterns.

- *Information/Resource Lifecycle.* **Problem:** Managing the lifecycle of several resources and to know in which step every resource is. **Solution:** Lists represent sequenced and ordered steps or states to follow, and the cards, which represent the resources, flow between them. Each card can also contain additional information about the resource. This information can change as the card passes through the different lists. **Example:** The publication lifecycle described in Fig. 1, where cards represent publications and the lists are the states publications go through. Another example is a human resource boarding process.
- *Ordered/Structured Information.* **Problem:** Organizing information in lists that follow some kind of sorting criteria. **Solution:** Cards represent pieces of information and lists represent the topics used to organize these pieces of information. These topics have some order relationship between them according to some criteria. Cards do not change their topic over time (i.e., cards do not flow). For this reason, this pattern is commonly used to publish information to others. **Example:** A board that publishes information to the students about the syllabus of a course. Each list represents a topic covered by the course organized by the temporal sequence in which they are taught and each card represents a piece of information regarding that topic.

Table 1. 8 patterns description table

Pattern	Problem	List/Card type	Semant. prec.	Card flow	Trello template examples	# Tot.	# Pure	# Comb.
Information/ Resources Lifecycle	Management of the lifecycle of several resources at the same time	Resource	Yes	Yes	"Bike Repair Pipeline" "Customer Success Board"	23	23	0
Ordered Information	Organize information in lists that follow some kind of sorting criteria	Resource	Yes	No	"Annual Email Marketing Calendar" "Freelance Branding Project"	12	11	1
Kanban	Manage tasks, handling how they evolve, and monitor them	Task	Yes	Yes	"Planning Your Day" "Kanban Template"	31	19	12
Process Tasks	Provide a sequenced task guide, divided according to the different stages that make up the project	Task	Yes	No	"Design Sprint" "Project Based Learning"	8	5	3
Assigned Information / Resources	Organize information or resources whose classification could change over time	Resource	No	Yes	"Book Clubs" "Setlist Organizer"	2	2	0
Categorized Information	Categorize information by any criteria, but unlike in the previous pattern, information does not change its category over time	Resource	No	No	"Align Your Team With V2MOM" "Customer Support Knowledge Base"	31	21	10
Assigned Tasks	Manage multiple tasks by changing the container to which it belongs, usually to represent that the task is assigned to one person or another	Task	No	Yes	"Team Tasks (5 Things Workflow)"	1	1	0
Categorized Tasks	Manage multiple to-do lists	Task	No	No	"8 Creative Habits" "Personal and Work Goals"	4	4	0

- **Kanban.** **Problem:** Managing tasks, handling how they evolve, and monitoring them. **Solution:** Cards represent tasks and lists represent different states in which tasks can be. Therefore, it allows one to control and easily know the status of each task at any given moment. **Example:** A board with three lists "To Do", "Doing," and "Done" as the one used in Fig. 3.a. However, more advanced lifecycles for tasks can be used that includes states like allocated, started, suspended, or failed as discussed in [20].
- **Process Tasks.** **Problem:** Providing a sequenced task guide, divided according to the different stages that make up the project. **Solution:** Lists represent ordered stages of a project and cards represent tasks to complete at each stage of the project. Therefore, cards do not flow. When all tasks of all stages are completed, the project will be finished. **Example:** A waterfall engineering process where we have lists for requirements, analysis, etc. and cards for the tasks to be done in each stage.
- **Assigned Information/Resources.** **Problem**: To organize information or resources whose classification could change over time. **Solution:** Cards represent pieces of information or resources and lists represent categories that group them. These categories do not have any order relationship between them and cards can flow between lists. **Example:** If lists represent work departments and cards represent employees, we can use this pattern to represent and manage the structure of an organization. In it, cards moving to a different list could happen if employees change their departments
- **Categorized Information.** **Problem:** Categorizing information by any criteria, but unlike in the previous case, information does not change its category over time. **Solution:** Cards represent pieces of information and lists represent categories used to group them. These categories are independent of each other, i.e. there is no ordering relationship between them, and cards do not flow between lists. **Example:** A board that works like a school notebook, where lists are subjects and in each of them, we will stock cards that represent the different notes (text) of that subject. In a work context, lists could represent, for instance, projects. This is also the pattern used in the example of a travel board design of Fig. 3.b.
- **Assigned Tasks.** **Problem:** Managing multiple tasks by changing the list to which it belongs, usually to represent that the task is assigned to one person or another. **Solution:** Cards represent tasks and lists represent a resource to which tasks are assigned. Cards flow to change task assignment. **Example:** Each list represents an employee and contains her assigned tasks. When she finishes her part of the task, it will flow to another employee that will continue working on the same task.
- **Categorized Tasks.** **Problem:** Managing multiple to-do lists. **Solution:** Cards represent tasks that are assigned to a specific list according to the criteria defined by the problem context. For example, task duration, project to which it belongs, or deadline date. Lists are independent of each other and cards do not flow between them. **Example:** A typical set of to-do lists, where each list groups tasks by the context in which they have to be done (e.g., at the phone, at work, at home, at the computer) as proposed by a personal productivity methodology like Getting Things Done [3].

A conclusion of this description is that, in several cases, two different patterns can serve to represent the same information, but emphasizing different aspects depending on the use case the user wants to highlight. For instance, both Kanban and Assigned Tasks are useful to collaboratively manage a set of tasks. However, Kanban is better if you want to have an overview of the global state of all tasks (for instance, if the tasks are complex and need to go through lots of different states), and Assigned Tasks is better if you want to focus on who has each task assigned and if the workload of all members of the team is balanced (the longer the list, the higher the workload). A detailed discussion on the relationships between patterns can be found in the pattern description templates that are available in [16].

5 Application of Patterns in the Templates

All 8 patterns identified have been found applied in practice in different domains in at least one Trello template proposed in the 91 templates analyzed. The details about this classification can be found at [16]. Table 1 summarizes this information. Column *Trello Template Examples* includes a couple of Trello templates in which each pattern is used. Columns *# Tot.*, *# Pure*, and *# Comb.* refer to the total number of times each pattern is found in the board design of the templates, the number of times each pattern is the only one found, and the number of times each pattern is found combined with another pattern, respectively.

A first conclusion of the analysis is that each pattern appears in the templates applied to different domains, which shows how they are generalized solutions that can be applied to a variety of specific domains. For example, as shown in the previous section, the Process Tasks pattern can be used in the software engineering domain for modelling a waterfall process, but it is also used in the template "Design Sprint" to represent a graphical design process.

Another conclusion is that there are three patterns that appear with a much higher frequency than the others. Two of them, Kanban and Information Lifecycle, represent the typical main use case for which board-based tools were initially created. The only difference between them is the meaning of the cards (tasks and information or resources, respectively). For this reason, it is not surprising that together they appear in almost half of the board designs. The case of the Categorized Information pattern, which is the other one, is more interesting. Our hypothesis is that once you have a Kanban-based board, you may find it useful to have a place to share relevant information using the same tool that is already used for managing the tasks. This is implemented using lists for classifying information, which is the purpose of the Categorized Information pattern.

Regarding the other patterns, they are less frequent probably because their purpose differs more from the best-known purpose of board-based tools. In any case, we can find at least one board design in the set of templates analyzed that matches with one of our proposed patterns. We expect that after making explicit this catalog of patterns, some patterns like Assigned Information, Assigned Tasks, or Categorized Tasks (the least used) could increase their use.

Finally, patterns are not mutually exclusive and several of them can be found together in the same board. The analysis performed shows some evidence of this. The most common combination is the Kanban pattern used together with the Categorized Information pattern that occurs 8 times. The reason for combining these two patterns is to have together in the same board the state of the tasks of the project as well as other relevant information to the project.

6 Conclusions and Future Work

In this paper, we analyzed 91 Trello board designs from both research works and board templates proposed by Trello users. Based on this analysis, we presented, first, a metamodel for defining board designs that goes beyond the well-known structure of boards, lists and cards. It makes explicit most of the main decisions made during board design, including the dynamic use and the meaning of the different elements (lists and cards). In addition, using this metamodel and based on the analysis conducted, we identified and characterized a catalog of 8 patterns of board design.

These two results have implications for both research and practice. Regarding the former, our metamodel opens up a range of possibilities. First, it is possible to create an editor of board designs based on the metamodel and the notation illustrated in Fig. 3. Having board designs modelled with the metamodel brings two advantages: (1) it is possible to have a repository of reusable board designs that are independent of the specific board-based tool (Trello, Planner, Asana). Since all of these tools offer APIs to automatically create boards, it is easy to develop a tool that can instantiate these board designs in the tool of your choice, and (2) the metamodel provides a structured way to make explicit information about the design decisions involved in the use of these tools that were up to now implicit or informally explained using natural language (e.g. whether cards should move from one list to another). This means that it can be used as the input of a compliance monitoring tool that automatically notifies (or even enforces) the user if the board is not being used according to the definition of the metamodel (e.g. if the user is moving the card to a list she is not allowed to).

From a practical point of view, the catalog of 8 patterns constitutes an advantageous tool for users to design boards more effectively and efficiently. As it has been proven in many domains, patterns promote reuse, enhance design effectiveness, reduce the errors derived from incomplete or incorrect solutions, and speed up the development process, avoiding the need to reinvent the wheel [4,22]. In our context, we now provide in 8 patterns information that was spread over 91 templates. Furthermore, there is a relevant difference between patterns and templates. Like two organizations need to adapt their processes and information systems to the way they work, the same applies to board designs derived from some pre-existing template. The knowledge of board-based patterns can help organizations customize these boards to their needs even if the starting point of the board is a Trello template. For instance, organizations that use a scrum template that follows the Kanban pattern could be aware that this pattern can be used together with Categorized Information if they want to include in the same board relevant information about the project. Nevertheless, an empirical study on board-based tools users should be conducted to validate the benefits of using patterns. Finally, the catalog of patterns gives us some hints on the different roles these information systems can play or the different ways in which they can be used in the current enterprise information systems ecosystem.

There are still some limitations to the work presented here. In our approach for defining the metamodel, for the sake of generality, we considered the more basic features offered by all board-based tools (mainly boards, lists, cards, and their order and flow). However, we did not take into account other more advanced features like labels, due dates, or human resource assignments. Considering these features may lead to identify additional patterns. Also, lower-level patterns that provide more specific solutions might be identified. For example, one such pattern could be defined as "in a board where cards are tasks, there could be a predefined list *done* where cards would move once the corresponding tasks are finished." This is a concept similar to what happens in software development, where we have the architectural patterns, and then, at a lower level, the design patterns. This is a clear direction for future work.

Finally, the metamodel and catalog of patterns were obtained from the analysis we conducted. This means that on the one hand, there might be uses of Trello not included in the board templates analyzed and, thus, they are not supported or included in our approach. On the other hand, although our results are valid for all board-based tools, we just analyzed Trello templates, so it could be interesting to see if similar results are found when analyzing templates from other board-based tools. In any case, the two assets provided in this paper could be easily extended when new scenarios were identified.

Verifiability

For the sake of verifiability, all the information required for the replication of our analysis and the detailed pattern catalgoue is available online and can be found at [16].

References

1. van der Aalst, W.M.P., ter Hofstede, A.H.M., Kiepuszewski, B., Barros, A.P.: Workflow patterns. Distrib. Parallel Databases **14**(1), 5–51 (2003)
2. Ault, A., Krogmeier, J., Buckmaster, D.: Mobile, cloud-based farm management: a case study with trello on my farm. In: American Society of Agricultural and Biological Engineers (2013)
3. Allen, D.: Getting Things Done: The Art of Stress-Free Productivity. Penguin, New York (2015)
4. Buschmann, F., Henney, K., Schmidt, D.C.: Pattern-Oriented Software Architecture, On Patterns and Pattern Languages. vol. 5, Wiley, Chichester (2007)

5. Falbo, R.A., Guizzardi, G., Gangemi, A., Presutti, V.: Ontology patterns: Clarifying concepts and terminology. In: 4th International Workshop on Ontologies and Semantic Patterns (WOP 2013), pp. 1–13 (2013)
6. Fic, P.: Moved to published: using trello in content management. Dianoia **3**(1), 15–23 (2019)
7. Finch, M.: Using zapier with trello for electronic resources troubleshooting workflow. Code4Lib J. (26) (2014). https://journal.code4lib.org/issues/issues/issue26
8. Fowler, M.: Analysis Patterns: Reusable Object Models. Object Technology Series. Addison-Wesley, Menlo Park (1996)
9. Gamma, E., Helm, R., Johnson, R., Vlissides, J.: Design Patterns: Elements of Reusable Object-Oriented Software. Addison-Wesley, Boston (1995)
10. Gould, E.M.: Workflow management tools for electronic resources management. Ser. Rev. **44**(1), 71–74 (2018)
11. Naik, N., Jenkins, P.: A web based method for managing prince2 projects using trello. In: 2019 International Symposium on Systems Engineering (ISSE), pp. 1–3 (2019). https://doi.org/10.1109/ISSE46696.2019.8984516
12. Naik, N., Jenkins, P., Newell, D.: Learning agile scrum methodology using the groupware tool trello through collaborative working. In: Complex, Intelligent, and Software Intensive Systems, pp. 343–355 (2020)
13. Niwe, M., Stirna, J.: Organizational patterns for B2B environments –validation and comparison. In: Halpin, T., et al. (eds.) BPMDS/EMMSAD -2009. LNBIP, vol. 29, pp. 394–406. Springer, Heidelberg (2009). https://doi.org/10.1007/978-3-642-01862-6_32
14. Ostergaard, K.: Applying kanban principles to electronic resource acquisitions with trello. J. Electr. Resour. Librarianship **28**(1), 48–52 (2016)
15. Parsons, D., Thorn, R., Inkila, M., MacCallum, K.: Using trello to support agile and lean learning with scrum and kanban in teacher professional development. In: 2018 IEEE International Conference on Teaching, Assessment, and Learning for Engineering (TALE), pp. 720–724 (2018). https://doi.org/10.1109/TALE.2018.8615399
16. Peña, J., Bravo, A., del Río-Ortega, A., Resinas, M., Ruiz-Cortés, A.: Catalogue of patterns for board-based tools. Technical report (2021). https://doi.org/10.5281/zenodo.4609894
17. Ray, N.: Prioritize, plan, and maintain motivation with trello. Agric. Educ. Mag. **88**(6), 16 (2016)
18. del Río-Ortega, A., Peña, J., Resinas, M., Ruiz-Cortés, A.: Productivity challenges in digital transformation and its implications for workstream collaboration tools. In: 54th Hawaii International Conference on System Sciences, HICSS 2021. In press, pp. 1–10. ScholarSpace / AIS Electronic Library (AISeL) (2021)
19. del Río-Ortega, A., Resinas, M., Durán, A., Ruiz-Cortés, A.: Using templates and linguistic patterns to define process performance indicators. Enter. Inf. Syst. **10**(2), 159–192 (2016). https://doi.org/10.1080/17517575.2013.867543
20. Russell, N., van der Aalst, W.M.P., ter Hofstede, A.H.M., Edmond, D.: Workflow resource patterns: identification, representation and tool support. In: Pastor, O., Falcão e Cunha, J. (eds.) CAiSE 2005. LNCS, vol. 3520, pp. 216–232. Springer, Heidelberg (2005). https://doi.org/10.1007/11431855_16
21. Russell, N., ter Hofstede, A.H.M., Edmond, D., van der Aalst, W.M.P.: Workflow data patterns: identification, representation and tool support. In: Delcambre, L., Kop, C., Mayr, H.C., Mylopoulos, J., Pastor, O. (eds.) ER 2005. LNCS, vol. 3716, pp. 353–368. Springer, Heidelberg (2005). https://doi.org/10.1007/11568322_23

22. Sales, T.P., Roelens, B., Poels, G., Guizzardi, G., Guarino, N., Mylopoulos, J.: A pattern language for value modeling in ArchiMate. In: Giorgini, P., Weber, B. (eds.) CAiSE 2019. LNCS, vol. 11483, pp. 230–245. Springer, Cham (2019). https://doi.org/10.1007/978-3-030-21290-2_15
23. Turetken, O., Elgammal, A., van den Heuvel, W., Papazoglou, M.P.: Capturing compliance requirements: a pattern-based approach. IEEE Softw. **29**(3), 28–36 (2012). https://doi.org/10.1109/MS.2012.45

ADAMAP: Automatic Alignment of Relational Data Sources Using Mapping Patterns

Diego Calvanese[1,2], Avigdor Gal[3], Naor Haba[3], Davide Lanti[1(✉)],
Marco Montali[1], Alessandro Mosca[1], and Roee Shraga[3]

[1] Free University of Bozen-Bolzano, Bolzano, Italy
{calvanese,lanti,montali,mosca}@inf.unibz.it
[2] Umeå University, Umeå, Sweden
[3] Technion – Israel Institute of Technology, Haifa, Israel
avigal@technion.ac.il, {naor-haba,shraga89}@campus.technion.ac.il

Abstract. We propose a method for automatically extracting semantics from data sources. The availability of multiple data sources on the one hand and the lack of proper semantic documentation of such data sources on the other hand call for new strategies in integrating data sources by extracting semantics from the data source itself rather than from its documentation. In this work we focus on relational databases, observing they are created from semantically-rich designs such as ER diagrams, which are often not conveyed together with the database itself. While the relational model may be semantically-poor with respect to ontological models, the original semantically-rich design of the application domain leaves recognizable footprints that can be converted into *ontology mapping patterns*. In this work, we offer an algorithm to automatically detect and map a relational schema to ontology mapping patterns and offer an empirical evaluation using two benchmark datasets.

1 Introduction

Modern industrial processes and business processes require intensive use of large-scale data alignment and integration techniques to combine data from multiple heterogeneous data sources into meaningful and valuable information. Such integration is performed on structured and semi-structured data sets from various sources such as SQL and XML schemata, entity-relationship (ER) diagrams, ontology descriptions, process models, and web forms. Data integration plays a key role in a variety of domains, including data warehouse loading and exchange, aligning ontologies for the Semantic Web, semantic process model matching [16], and business document format merging (*e.g.*, orders and invoices in e-commence) [21]. As an example, consider an application that keeps track of funded project applications, managing the review process through panel meetings.

One of the main challenges of data integration is to create a common semantic understanding from the multiple available data sources. In ontology-based

© Springer Nature Switzerland AG 2021
M. La Rosa et al. (Eds.): CAiSE 2021, LNCS 12751, pp. 193–209, 2021.
https://doi.org/10.1007/978-3-030-79382-1_12

data access (OBDA) and integration [20], this is achieved through two main components: *(i)* an ontology that captures the relevant concepts and relations of the domain of interest at a high level of abstraction, in turn acting as a vehicle for reaching a semantic consensus; and *(ii)* a mapping specification that dictates how the data in relational sources can be used to (virtually) populate the classes and properties of the ontology.

A major impediment towards the adoption of OBDA is that data sources typically lack a proper semantic documentation, which makes it extremely difficult and error-prone to obtain both the ontology and the mapping. Consider, in particular, the case of relational databases, where well-established conceptual modeling principles and methodologies can be employed to design their schemata so as to suitably reflect the application domain at hand. This design phase is centered around the usage of semantically-rich representations such as ER diagrams. However, these representations typically get lost during deployment, since they are not conveyed together with the database itself, or quickly get outdated due to continuous adjustments triggered by changing requirements. This may lead to loss of information regarding concept hierarchies, which are flattened in the corresponding relational schema.

In this work, we aim at reconstructing such lost domain semantics by inspecting relational data sources, without any additional documentation. To do so, we start from the key observation that while the relational model may be semantically-poor with respect to ontological models, the original semantically-rich design of the application domain leaves recognizable footprints that can be converted into the aforementioned ontological patterns. Therefore, we propose to use *ontology mapping patterns* (*mapping patterns* for short) [8], which systematically collect recurring ways of linking relational data sources to ontologies via mapping specifications. A mapping pattern relates a relational schema fragment to a corresponding ontology fragment, establishing the mapping between the two. Mapping patterns, therefore, provide a form of a conceptual middleware that describes a shared set of abstractions that facilitates interoperability.

Specifically, we propose an algorithmic technique called ADAMAP that, given a relational data source, automatically determines how suitable fragments of its schema align with corresponding mapping patterns. Once mapping patterns are suitably instantiated on a given data source, they can be employed for a number of downstream data engineering tasks, *e.g.*, *ontology bootstrapping* [13,17,19,24] and *schema cover* [22].

Given a data source, there are in general multiple, sound ways to identify which patterns are relevant, and how they match. Consequently, to assess the usefulness and efficacy of ADAMAP, we comparatively evaluate the results it produced in two real-world case studies against a set of pattern applications manually identified by a human expert. This shows that most of the time the algorithm and the expert agree, which is particularly significant considering that the mapping patterns turn out to cover a large portion of the data sources at hand.

The contribution of this work is twofold. On a conceptual level, we offer an approach to enrich a relational model with semantics through the identification of the footprints that were left by the conceptual model on which the relations are based. We then offer an algorithmic solution to the mapping problem using mapping patterns. Our empirical evaluation demonstrates the effectiveness of the approach.

The rest of the paper is organized as follows. Section 2 presents the building blocks of our proposed model, namely the OBDA approach and the mapping patterns, and provides the problem definition. Our algorithmic solution, ADaMaP, is described in Sect. 3 followed by an empirical evaluation (Sect. 4). The paper is concluded with related work (Sect. 5) and concluding discussion (Sect. 6). An appendix, offering more in detail discussions and details to support replicability are provided in an online repository.[1]

2   Model

We now detail the building blocks for our proposed method. We begin by presenting the OBDA framework, which we rely on in this work, (Sect. 2.1). Then, Sect. 2.2 provides an overview of mapping patterns, which represent the inherent semantics of a data source. Finally, in Sect. 2.3 we formally define the problem. Throughout, we shall use an example that is based on a database developed by SIRIS Academic S.L., a consultancy company specialized in higher education and research, based on the European CORDIS repository.[2]

2.1   OBDA Framework

In this work, we rely on the OBDA framework of [20]. We use **bold** font to denote tuples, *e.g.*, **x**, **y**, treat tuples as sets, and allow the use of set operators on them. An *OBDA specification* is a triple $\langle \mathcal{T}, \mathcal{M}, \mathcal{S} \rangle$ where $\mathcal{T}$ is an *ontology TBox*, $\mathcal{M}$ is a set of *mappings*, and $\mathcal{S}$ is the schema of a database. The schema of the databse is a pair (Σ, Γ) where the signature Σ is a set of table schemata, and Γ is a set of database constraints, including keys and foreign keys.

The ontology $\mathcal{T}$ is formulated in OWL 2 QL [18], whose formal counterpart is the description logic *DL-Lite*$_\mathcal{R}$ [7], which notation is adopted in this work. An OWL 2 QL *TBox* $\mathcal{T}$ is a finite set of axioms of the form $B \sqsubseteq C$ or $r_1 \sqsubseteq r_2$, where B, C are *classes* and r_1, r_2 are *object properties*, according to the following grammar (where A is a *class name*, d is a *data property name*, and p is an *object property name*):

$$B \rightarrow A \mid \exists r \mid \exists d \qquad C \rightarrow B \mid \neg B \qquad r \rightarrow p \mid p^-$$

For presentation simplicity we discard datatypes, which are also part of OWL 2 QL.

---

[1] https://github.com/ontop/ontop-examples/tree/master/caise-2021-patterns.
[2] https://cordis.europa.eu/projects/en.

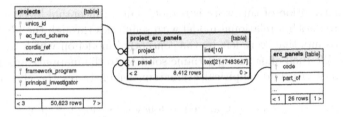

Fig. 1. Fragment of the CORDIS database.

Mappings specify how to populate classes and properties of the ontology with individuals and values, starting from the data in the underlying database. In OBDA, the standard language for mappings is R2RML [9], which we replace here with a more convenient abstract notation, as follows. A *mapping m* is an expression of the form

$$s : Q(\mathbf{x}) \qquad t : \mathbf{L}(t(\mathbf{x}))$$

where $Q(\mathbf{x})$ is a SQL query over the database schema Σ, called *source query*, and $\mathbf{L}(t(\mathbf{x}))$ is a list of *target atoms* of the form $C(t_1(\mathbf{x_1}))$, $p(t_1(\mathbf{x_1}), t_2(\mathbf{x_2}))$, or $d(t_1(\mathbf{x_1}), t_2(\mathbf{x_2}))$, where $t_1(\mathbf{x_1})$ and $t_2(\mathbf{x_2})$ are terms that we call *templates*. In this work we express source queries using *relational algebra* notation, omitting answer variables under the assumption that they coincide with the variables used in the target atoms. Intuitively, a template $t(\mathbf{x})$ in a target atom of a mapping corresponds to an *R2RML template*, and is used to generate object *IRIs* (Internationalized Resource Identifiers) or RDF *literals*, starting from database values retrieved by the source query in that mapping.

In our examples, we use the concrete mapping syntax adopted by the OBDA system Ontop [6], in which the source query is expressed in SQL and each target atom is expressed as an *RDF triple pattern with templates*. The answer variables of the source query are indicated in a target atom by enclosing them in curly brackets ({ · · · }). A mapping example for the fragment of Fig. 1, expressed in such syntax, is the following:

```
target    :Project-{p_id} a :EC-Project . :Project-{p_id} :cordisRef {cordis_ref} ...
source    SELECT p.unics_id AS p_id, p.cordis_ref AS cordis_ref
          FROM    unics_cordis.projects p
```

The effect of such a mapping, when applied to a database instance $\mathcal{D}$ for Σ, is to instantiate, for each answer tuple returned by the source query, each (RDF) triple pattern with templates in the target to an actual RDF triple. This is done using IRIs and literals that are constructed from the assignments to the answer variables p_id and cordis_ref, obtained when the source query is evaluated over $\mathcal{D}$.

Table 1. Portion of schema-driven patterns from [8]

E-R DIAGRAM	DB SCHEMA	MAPPING PATTERN	ONTOLOGY
Schema Entity (SE)			
	$T_E(\underline{K}, A)$	$s: T_E$ $t: C_E(t_E(K)),$ $\{d_A(t_E(K), A)\}_{A \in K \cup A}$	$\{\exists d_A \sqsubseteq C_E\}_{A \in K \cup A}$
Schema Relationship (SR)			
	$T_E(\underline{K_E}, A_E)\ \ T_F(\underline{K_F}, A_F)$ $T_R(\underline{K_{RE}, K_{RF}})$	$s: T_R$ $t: p_R(t_E(K_{RE}), t_F(K_{RF}))$	$\exists p_R \sqsubseteq C_E$ $\exists p_R^- \sqsubseteq C_F$

In case of (_, 1) cardinality on role R_E (resp., R_F), the primary key for T_R is restricted to the attributes K_{RE} (resp., K_{RF}).

2.2 Mapping Patterns

(Ontology) mapping patterns [8] emerge when mapping a database to a *domain ontology*, and explain the link between the conceptualization behind the database design and the domain ontology. To justify our formalization of patterns, we make the following two fundamental observations: *(i)* a conceptual schema may have more than one admissible relational mapping, according to the applied methodology, as well as to considerations about efficiency, performance optimization, and space consumption on the final information system; *(ii)* given the logical schema of a relational database, regardless of its normal form, multiple conceptual schemata can provide (admissible) alternative representations of its domain. By *(i)* and *(ii)*, we explicitly associate a conceptual schema to each database schema in order to disambiguate among possible conceptualizations of the database schema, unlike bootstrapping-oriented approaches, *e.g.,* [13].

Formally, a mapping pattern is a quadruple $(\mathcal{C}, \mathcal{S}, \mathcal{M}, \mathcal{O})$, where $\mathcal{C}$ is a conceptual schema, $\mathcal{S}$ is a database schema, $\mathcal{M}$ is a set of mappings, and $\mathcal{O}$ is an ontology. In such mapping pattern, the pair $(\mathcal{C}, \mathcal{S})$ is the *input*, putting into correspondence a conceptual representation to one of its (many) admissible (*i.e.,* formally sound) database schemata. Such variants are due to differences in the applied methodology, considerations about efficiency, performance optimization, and space consumption of the final database. The pair $(\mathcal{M}, \mathcal{O})$, instead, is the *output*, where the *database schema ontology* $\mathcal{O}$ [25] is the OWL 2 QL encoding of the conceptual schema $\mathcal{C}$, and the set $\mathcal{M}$ of *database schema mappings* provides the link between $\mathcal{S}$ and $\mathcal{O}$. Database schema ontology refers to an ontology whose concepts and properties reflect the constructs of the conceptual schema, mirroring the structure of the relational database.

Table 1 shows two examples of patterns, namely, **Schema Entity** (SE) and **Schema Relationship** (SR). SE is a fundamental pattern that considers a single table T_E with primary key **K** and other attributes **A**. The pattern captures how T_E is mapped into a corresponding class C_E. The primary key of T_E is employed to construct the objects that are instances of C_E, using a template t_E specific for that class. Each relevant attribute of T_E is mapped to a data property of C_E.

Example. The `projects` table (Fig. 1) contains ids of projects (attribute `unics_id`), together with their funding scheme, their reference in the CORDIS portal[3], *etc.* It is mapped to the :EC-Project class using `unics_id` to construct its objects. In addition, every attribute in the table is mapped to a corresponding data property.

SR considers three tables T_R, T_E, and T_F, in which the primary key of T_R is partitioned into two parts $\mathbf{K}_{RE}$ and $\mathbf{K}_{RF}$ that are foreign keys to T_E and T_F, respectively. T_R has no additional attributes. The pattern captures how T_R is mapped to an object property p_R, using the two parts $\mathbf{K}_{RE}$ and $\mathbf{K}_{RF}$ of the primary key to construct respectively the subject and the object of each triple in p_R.

Example. The table `project_erc_panels` (Fig. 1) connects through two foreign keys the projects to their corresponding ERC panel. Such table is mapped to an :ercPanel object property, for which the ontology asserts that the domain is the class :Project and the range is an additional class :ERC-Panel, which correspond to the `erc_panels` table.

2.3 The Alignment of Data Sources with Mapping Patterns Problem

Let $\mathcal{P}$ be a set of mapping patterns, representing the elementary semantics of an application domain. For the scope of this paper, $\mathcal{P}$ is composed of the patterns proposed by Calvanese *et al.* [8] and illustrated in Sect. 2.2. In addition, recall that $\mathcal{S}$ is a database schema (see Sect. 2.1) composed of $\Sigma = \{T_1, T_2, \ldots, T_n\}$ and Γ, which captures database constraints, including primary and foreign keys. We assume that $\mathcal{S}$ was created from some conceptual model (*e.g.*, the way a relational database schema is created from an ER diagram) and that $\mathcal{P}$ represents the mapping patterns whose inputs are in line with what a designer used when transforming such conceptual model to a database schema. The problem we address in this paper is a reverse engineering one, essentially aligning the tables of Σ with the mapping patterns in $\mathcal{P}$ using Γ.

Formally, we denote by $M(\mathcal{S}, \mathcal{P}) \subseteq \mathcal{S} \times \mathcal{P}$ (M, for short) an alignment between a database schema $\mathcal{S} = (\Sigma, \Gamma)$ and a set $\mathcal{P}$ of mapping patterns. An *alignment* M is a set of correspondences (S, p), each representing an assignment of a schema S to a mapping pattern p whose input database schema can be instantiated to S. Note that a schema S may be involved in more than one correspondence. An alignment consists of a subset of all mapping patterns whose input is in line with the design of the database and we are interested in a *maximal alignment* that represents the full set of such mapping patterns.

Problem 1 (alignment of data sources with mapping patterns). *Let* $\mathcal{S} = (\Sigma, \Gamma)$ *be a database schema and* $\mathcal{P}$ *a set of mapping patterns. The* alignment of data sources with mapping patterns *problem aims to find a maximal alignment* $M(\mathcal{S}, \mathcal{P})$, *such that, for each pair* $(S, p) \in M(\mathcal{S}, \mathcal{P})$, *the input database schema of* p *can be instantiated to* S.

---

[3] https://cordis.europa.eu/projects/en.

3 Extracting Semantics from Data Sources with ADAMAP

We are now ready to describe the proposed ADAMAP algorithm (Sect. 3.1) and discuss some possible usages of the discovered alignment (Sect. 3.2).

3.1 ADAMAP: Automatically Extracting Semantics from Data Sources

We now introduce ADAMAP, an iterative algorithm that automatically aligns a relational data source to mapping patterns (see Sect. 2.2 and a summarization of abbreviations in Table 2). ADAMAP is applied to each table $T \in \Sigma$ separately, aiming to determine the most suitable set of mapping patterns. The utilization of the mapping patterns requires some or all of the following properties in the definition of a relational data source schema design: (1) primary keys, (2) foreign keys, and (3) unique constraints [8]. For the scope of this paper we assume that such properties are well defined and note that in the absence of such properties, discovery methods may be applied, for example, randomness [26] can be used to recover foreign keys.

Given a table T, the inference of ADAMAP is divided into four cases, each targeting a different amount of table relationships with respect to Σ. The table-based inference is illustrated in Fig. 2. We denote T's primary key by $\mathbf{K}_T$ and its foreign key(s) by $\mathbf{FK}_T$.

Whenever a table does not have foreign keys, the corresponding mapping pattern is set to be Schema Entity (SE) as shown in Fig. 2a. Intuitively, this means that in the absense of known relationships, the table should be mapped into an entity set. If a table has a single relationship with a reference table R, ADAMAP applies the inference in Fig. 2b and checks whether the primary key of R, $\mathbf{K}_R$, is the same as the foreign key $\mathbf{FK}_R$. If not, we return to the case of SE. If it is, we check the same condition for the examined table T. If $\mathbf{K}_T$ is a foreign key in T, we assign T with a Schema Hierarchy (SH), *i.e.,* recognizing that the entity set corresponding to the table T is a sub-class of the entity set corresponding to R. If not, we check whether the foreign key is a key in T and decide between adding a correspondence of T with SHa (requiring an identifier alignment in case it is) and adding two correspondences to the alignment, (T, SRm) and (T, SE), meaning that T and R should be merged into a single entity.

For a table T with two foreign keys, $\mathbf{FK}_T^1$ referring to table R_1 and $\mathbf{FK}_T^2$ to table R_2 (Fig. 2c), We denote $\mathbf{FK}_T = \mathbf{FK}_T^1 \cup \mathbf{FK}_T^2$. We first check whether $\mathbf{K}_T == \mathbf{FK}_T$. In case of a negative answer, as in most other negative answers in Fig. 2c, we roll back to use the inference in Fig. 2b for each of the foreign keys in T, *i.e.,* as if T has a single foreign key. Then, regardless of the former answer, we check whether the primary keys of R_1 and R_2 are the same as the respective foreign keys $\mathbf{FK}_{R_1}$ and $\mathbf{FK}_{R_2}$. The final check in Fig. 2c is conditioned on whether one of the referenced tables contains a foreign key that identifies (id. in the figure) the table. We note here that in case we do not roll back to Fig. 2b, the inference of Fig. 2c may obtain a correspondence between T and one of the following schema relationship patterns: 1) a "simple" relationship

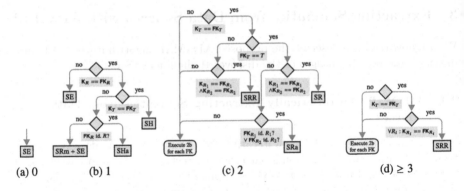

Fig. 2. ADAMAP inference for a table T by the number of foreign keys it contains.

between R_1 and R_2 (SR) if T is only composed of the foreign keys, 2) a reified relationship (SRR), where all the tables are identified by their foreign keys and may have additional attributes, and 3) a relationship that requires an alignment of attributes (SRa) in either R_1 or R_2.

In another special case, a table has three or more references to other tables. The inference of this case, illustrated in Fig. 2d, is quite similar to the path in Fig. 2c resulting in SRR. The idea is that T represents a relationship between multiple tables in DB, each identified by the foreign key to T and may include additional attributes.

Finally, by applying the rules illustrated in Fig. 2 for every T in Σ, we obtain an alignment M as a solution to Problem 1.

Table 2. Patterns abbreviations

Pattern	Abbreviation
Schema entity	SE
Schema relationship	SR
→with identifier alignment	SRa
→with merging	SRm
Schema reified Relationship	SRR
Schema hierarchy	SH
→with identifier alignment	SHa

We now illustrate the execution of ADAMAP using the tables in Fig. 1.

Example. Both `projects` and `erc_panels` (see Fig. 1) do not contain a foreign key constraint and thus ADAMAP creates a correspondence between these tables and an SE pattern according to Fig. 2a. `project_erc_panels` has two foreign keys and accordingly we use the inference of Fig. 2c. However, since the union of foreign keys (`project`, `panel`) is not the primary key in `project_erc_panels`, we roll back to the inference in Fig. 2b. In both tables the foreign key refers to a primary key (`unics_id` in `projects` and `code` in `erc_panels`), satisfying the first condition. As for the second condition, we observe that `project` (the foreign key from `projects`) is a primary key in `project_erc_panels`. However, `panel` (the foreign key from `erc_panels`) is not. In the case of `projects` we obtain a correspondence with SH and for `erc_panels`, since `panel` does not identify `project_erc_panels` we resolve a correspondence with two patterns, namely, SRm and SE. The output of ADAMAP is therefore {(`projects`, SE), (`erc_panels`, SE) (`project_erc_panels`, SH), (`project_erc_panels`, SRm), (`project_erc_panels`, SE)}.

3.2 Usage of Aligning Data Sources with Mapping Patterns

ADaMaP provides an automatic approach to enriching a database with semantics using matching patterns. We now describe two possible usages of such a method.

Bootstrapping. In this setting, we only have a conceptual schema of the domain. Using ADaMaP, a database schema can be transformed into a set of patterns. Once the patterns are aligned with the tables in the database schema, they can be used to (semi-)automatically bootstrap a set of mappings, which can then be further refined and extended manually, possibly exploiting again the discovered patterns. These mappings, in turn, may also be applied to bootstrap an ontology, providing the application domain with an additional level of abstraction.

Schema Cover. The idea of schema cover was first introduced by Saha *et al.* [22], promoting reuse and collaboration among data source providers. Such reuse is based on a repository of information building blocks, referred to as concepts, representative of entities in the domain of discourse (*e.g.*, ERC panels). Schemata are mapped against a set of concepts in a process termed schema cover. The idea is to "cover" a schema and thereby interpret the schema in terms of known concepts. This way, the schema is integrated into an existing body of information and knowledge. For example, consider a network of researchers that represent diverse interdisciplinary research skills and cooperate to submit joint research proposals. The analysis of capabilities does not follow a common format or standard. The aim of schema cover is to allow creating in this case research consortia in response to specific call for proposals.

4 Empirical Evaluation

In this section we provide an empirical evaluation of ADaMaP. Experimental settings are given in Sect. 4.1 and the empirical results are analyzed in Sect. 4.2.

4.1 Experiments Setting

Considered Scenarios. The first aspect to consider is the choice of the experimental scenarios. To assess the feasibility of the approach in practice, we focus on non-trivial and real-world scenarios. Such real-world scenarios should be built around reasonably well-designed database schemata, providing the (primary-key and foreign-key) constraints that are needed by our approach, and any bootstrapping approach in general. We identified two such scenarios, provided in an online repository,[4] and detailed next.

NPD Benchmark (NPD). [15] This scenario is built around the domain of oil and gas extraction, presenting a high number of mappings (>1k). Most mappings were automatically generated, but there are numerous complex manually-written mappings as well. The ontology falls in the OWL 2 QL profile, and consists of

---

[4] https://github.com/ontop/ontop-examples/tree/master/caise-2021-patterns.

4176 TBox axioms over 343 classes, 142 object properties, and 238 data properties. The database schema consists of 70 tables, 962 columns, and 89 foreign key constraints. The database schema has a structure, but was not designed according to common conceptual modeling practices. In fact, it was automatically generated out of unstructured data as CSV files [14].

CORDIS. This setting is designed around the domain of competitive research projects, provided by SIRIS Academic S.L.[5], a consultancy company specializing in higher education and research. The mappings were manually-written, and they amount to 120. The ontology, expressed in OWL 2 QL, consists of 186 TBox axioms over 24 classes, 24 object properties, and 30 data properties. The database schema is quite well-structured and consists of 19 tables, 6 views, 95 columns, and 20 foreign-key constraints.

Table 3. Coverage analysis

Pattern	#usages	#mappings		Pattern	#usages	#mappings
SE	13	60		SE	61	454
SR	3	3		SRm	74	74
SRm	3	3		SRR	1	12
SRR	1	16		SH	3	132
Covered Mappings: 89 (out of 120)				Covered Mappings: 672 (out of 1173)		
(a)CORDIS Coverage				(b)NPD Coverage		

Database Schema Ontology vs. Domain Ontology. Recall that a mapping pattern puts into correspondence a database schema $\mathcal{S}$, together with its intended conceptualization $\mathcal{C}$, to a pair $(\mathcal{M}, \mathcal{O})$, where $\mathcal{M}$ is a set of database schema mappings and $\mathcal{O}$ is a database schema ontology. Differently from an arbitrary *domain* ontology, $\mathcal{O}$ provides an information-preserving encoding of $\mathcal{C}$, *modulo* the expressivity of OWL 2 QL.

In real-world scenarios, however, it is usually the case that the domain ontology is developed independently from the relational data-source. The NPD and CORDIS scenarios we consider here are no exception to this. This results in a misalignment between the domain ontology and the conceptual schema used for the database, which in turn results in a misalignment between the database schema ontology and the domain ontology. *In our experimental evaluation we shall provide a quantitative measure over this misalignment, for both the NPD and CORDIS scenarios.*

Applied vs. Discovered Patterns. The conceptual schema of a database, which serves in the design of our patterns, is typically discarded after the design and deployment phases, and therefore it is actually not available as input to ADAMAP. As a result, the algorithm cannot disambiguate all the possible conceptualizations corresponding to the same database schema, but instead chooses one of them (literally, it operates according to the "most-typical" application of a pattern as per [8]).

---

[5] https://www.sirisacademic.com/wb/.

To check the efficacy of this approach, we have manually analyzed the scenarios and categorized the mappings according to the schema-driven mapping patterns that were actually used in such scenarios.

Evaluation Measures. We use quantitative evaluation measures to measure the differences between ADAMAP's results and the manual analysis. The latter serves as a reference model when comparing the automatically generated and manually extracted reference alignments. M denotes the output of ADAMAP and M^* denotes a manually extracted reference alignment. We use the terms *coordinated positive* and *coordinated negative* to represent agreement between M and M^* on the presence and absence of correspondences, respectively. Disagreements are marked as *discoordinated positive* for correspondences that were identified by the algorithm but not part of the manual alignment and *discoordinated negative* for the opposite situation. We use the well-known precision and recall measures to measure ADAMAP's success in aligning a database schema with a set of mapping patterns, with respect to a manually extracted alignment. Precision (P) measures the ratio of coordinated positive correspondences out of all correspondences assigned by the algorithm. On the other hand, Recall (R) measures the number of coordinated positive correspondences from all the correct correspondences as given in the reference alignment. P and R are formally defined as follows:

$$P_{M^*}(M) = \frac{|M \cap M^*|}{|M|}, \qquad R_{M^*}(M) = \frac{|M \cap M^*|}{|M^*|} \qquad (1)$$

We use precision and recall to define the F1-measure, $F_{M^*}(M)$, calculated as the harmonic mean of $P_{M^*}(M)$ and $R_{M^*}(M)$.

4.2   Results

Coverage Analysis. To analyze to what extent the database schema ontology is aligned with the domain ontology, we check how many mappings in the analyzed scenarios can be explained through the mapping patterns in [8]. A mapping that cannot be justified this way suggest a misalignment between the database schema and the domain ontology.

Tables 3(a) and 3(b) report on the number of schema-driven mapping-pattern applications that were manually reported in CORDIS and NPD, respectively, as well as the total number of mappings that are covered by these patterns. For CORDIS, 89 out of 120 mappings (74.16%) can be explained by a schema-driven pattern, whereas for NPD the situation is slightly worse, with only 672 out of 1173 mappings (57.29%). This can be attributed to the fact that the database schema of NPD was not designed according to well-known good practices of conceptual modeling, but was rather automatically generated out of CSV's semi-structured data [14]. The remaining mappings, non explainable through schema-driven patterns, fill the gap between the abstraction levels used in the database schema and the domain ontology.

Table 4. Portion of schema-driven patterns from [8]

E-R DIAGRAM	DB SCHEMA	MAPPING PATTERN	ONTOLOGY
Schema Relationship with Merging (SRm)			
	$T_F(\underline{K_F}, A_F)$ $T_E(\underline{K_E}, \overline{K_{EF}}, A_E)$	$s\!: T_E$ $t\!: p_{EF}(t_E(K_E), t_F(K_{EF}))$	$\exists p_{EF} \sqsubseteq C_E$ $\exists p_{EF}^- \sqsubseteq C_F$
Schema Hierarchy (SH)			
	$T_E(\underline{K_E}, A_E)$ $T_F(\underline{K_{FE}}, A_F)$	$s\!: T_F$ $t\!: C_F(t_E(K_{FE}))$, $\{d_A(t_E(K_{FE}), A)\}_{A \in A_F}$	$C_F \sqsubseteq C_E$ $\{\exists d_A^- \sqsubseteq C_F\}_{A \in A_F}$

Mismatches Analysis. The following relates separately to CORDIS and NPD, with reference to Fig. 3.

CORDIS. We observe that the algorithm and the manual analysis disagree on 7 instances, with 5 discoordinated positives and 2 discoordinated negatives. In terms of precision (P), recall (R), and F1-measure (F), ADaMaP obtains the following results:

$$P_{M^*}(M) = R_{M^*}(M) = F_{M^*}(M) = 0.8$$

ADaMaP discovered 80% of the manually assigned correspondences (recall) and 80% of the correspondences assigned by ADaMaP were also assigned manually (precision). Overall, ADaMaP and the manual extraction have 20% of disagreements. All but one disagreement stem from the fact that multiple conceptual schemata can correspond to the same database schema, as observed above. The algorithm cannot determine which of these equally valid choices is actually the one that was adopted by the human designer.

For the table `project_erc_panels` depicted in Fig. 1, the algorithm identifies two applicable patterns, namely SH and SRm from Table 4. The application of SH is justified by the foreign key `project` that coincides with the primary key of table `project_erc_panels`. Under this plausible modeling point of view, projects having an ERC panel are a subclass of projects. The application of *SRm*, instead, is justified by the foreign key `panel`, *i.e.*, the 1-N relationship between `project_erc_panels` and `erc_panels` has been merged into the former.

However, as introduced in Sect. 2, such table may also match the less typical pattern SR, which is actually the one we observed in the CORDIS scenario. For such reason, the two findings by the algorithm have been categorized as discoordinated positives since the algorithm applied (still suitable) patterns that are different from the one that was chosen in the manual alignment.

```
target    :NUTS2-{nuts_code} a :NUTS2 ; :extendedName {nuts_desc} .
source    SELECT etu.nuts_code AS nuts_code, etu.description AS nuts_desc
          FROM unics_cordis.eu_territorial_units etu
          WHERE etu.nuts_level=2

target    :NUTS3-{nuts_code} a :NUTS3 . :extendedName {nuts_desc} .
source    SELECT etu.nuts_code AS nuts_code, etu.description AS nuts_desc
          FROM unics_cordis.eu_territorial_units etu
          WHERE etu.nuts_level=3
```

Another mismatch, shown above, relates to the table eu_territorial_units, which has not been modeled as a separate entity, but rather as a *clustering* of different classes based on the value of attribute nuts_level. In these two mappings, two classes are created: :NUTS2 captures all the *nomenclatures of territorial units for statistics* having *level of division* equal to 2 and :NUTS3 captures the case where the level of division is 3.

Such clustering cannot be recognized by working at the schema level, but rather requires to inspect the actual data. Consequently, it cannot possibly be discovered by ADaMaP. This calls for an interesting extension of our algorithm, where also this and other forms of *data-driven mapping patterns* [8] are supported.

CORDIS

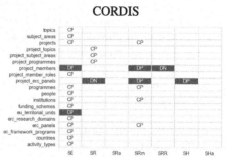

NPD. For the NPD scenario, we observe that the algorithm and the manual analysis disagree on 35 instances, with 14 discoordinated positives and 21 discoordinated negatives. In terms of precision (P), recall (R), and F1-measure (F), ADaMaP obtains the following results:

$$P_{M^*}(M) = 0.88, R_{M^*}(M) = 0.82,$$
$$F_{M^*}(M) = 0.85$$

Compared to the CORDIS scenario, ADaMaP obtains better results. This is because a portion of mappings for NPD were automatically bootstrapped, which results in the most-typical pattern being applied. Also, in the case of NPD, we observe that ADaMaP showed higher precision than recall, suggesting that ADaMaP may be better in obtaining an agreement with the manual alignment than covering the full scope of correspondences.

The reasons for the disagreements are totally analogous to those we observed for CORDIS. Something

NPD

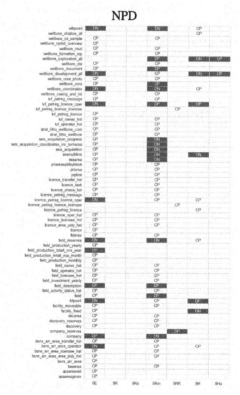

Fig. 3. Algorithm vs Manual analysis

peculiar about this scenario, that we did not observe in CORDIS, is the presence of mistakes both at the level of the database schema and at the level of patterns application. For the former, tables `seaArea`, `seis_acquisition`, `wellbore_core_photo`, and `apaAreaNet` declare non-minimal superkeys[6] as primary keys. Database design theory tells us that this is a conceptual modeling error. Such mistakes in the schema led to "non-conventional" applications of mapping patterns, such as the following:

- `seis_acquisition`: URIs are not built from the primary key of that table, but rather from a proper subset of the primary key that is declared as UNIQUE.
- `wellbore_core_photo`: `wellbore_core_photo_id` is UNIQUE, strictly contained in the primary key while URIs are built from the (non-minimal) primary key.
- Similar choices to the one above are taken for tables `apaAreaNet` and `wellbore_mud`.

Altogether wrong applications of a pattern are present as well. For instance, for table `seaArea`, the primary key is the pair of attributes (`seaArea_id`, `seaSurveyName`). However, attribute `seaArea_id` is declared as UNIQUE in the schema. This implies that the primary key is, again, a non-minimal superkey. However, the mapping-designer here has chosen, for building URIs, neither the primary key, nor the unique attribute, but actually the non-key attribute `seaSurveyName`. This breaks the principle of lossless transformation: the 1-1 correspondence between table rows and individuals in the ontology is lost.

5   Related Work

Multiple tools and approaches deal with the problem of extracting an ontology from a relational data source [2,5,11,13,17,19,23,24] have been proposed. The addressed application scenarios span from OBDA and Virtual Knowledge Graph (VKG) systems construction, reverse engineering, data integration, ontology learning, reasoning-based constraints checking, *etc.*. They differ mainly in the ontology languages they support and the required level of automation yet only a few come with a systematic categorization of the mappings that they produce as declarative connection between the data sources and the ontology [2,13,17,23]. The comparison of mapping patterns to alternative categorizations is out of this paper scope (see [8]) and we argue that ADaMAP is agnostic with respect to the mapping patterns nature in place and can, in principle, be fed with any catalog of patterns with a proper formal specification.

The analysis of real-world OBDA scenarios offered in this paper represents an original contribution to the current literature on ontology and mapping extraction from relational data sources, and a novel way to evaluate the performances of an algorithm such as ADaMAP, which is meant to support the identification of suitable and semantic-preserving patterns from relational schemata. To the best of our knowledge, none of the former approaches aim at showing that the mapping patterns (and the ontologies) they produced are sufficiently sound and

---

[6] Recall that in database theory, a key is a minimal superkey.

complete to reflect the real design choices and conceptual modeling practices that are used by expert designers on real-world scenarios.

The term *ontology mapping patterns*, used in this work to describe semantics, should not be confused with *ontology design patterns* (ODP). In ontology engineering, the latter provides solutions to recurrent modeling issues, and their adoption improves quality in terms of the ontology axioms specification [12]. Ontology mapping patterns stem from observation and categorization of typical relational database structures, their associated constraints and conceptual models.

6 Conclusions

We have introduced ADAMAP, an algorithmic technique that extracts semantics from a relational data source, by automatically identifying how ontology mapping patterns are applied to fragments of its schema. With such identification process each fragment gets projected into a set of ontological axioms, together with mapping rules capturing the schema-to-ontology correspondence. Thanks to ADAMAP, the creation of the ontology and of the mapping rules is no longer completely manual, error-prone effort. The validation of ADAMAP in two real-world case studies confirms that the identified patterns by-and-large agree with those detected by a human expert.

The patterns identified by ADAMAP provide a solid basis that can be manually improved by human experts, overcoming the "blank-page" syndrome when setting up ontology-based data access and integration systems. In addition, the identified patterns can be instrumental in a number of consequent tasks: in data engineering, tackling central problems such as ontology bootstrapping and schema cover, and in process mining, where the increasing focus on artifact-centric [10] and object-centric [1,3] processes requires to reconstruct conceptual data models from event data [4].

As discussed, ADAMAP comes with some limitations that should be tackled. First and foremost, for a given relational schema there are in general many possible combinations of mapping patterns that are, in principle, equally valid. While the current version of ADAMAP returns the "most typical" of such combinations, it would be interesting to allow ADAMAP to incrementally explore multiple possibilities, for example by iteratively generating and recommending alternatives that could then be inspected and further explored by human experts. Second, currently ADAMAP only focuses on the schema of the data source, without exploiting the data stored therein. In a number of situations, determining whether a given mapping pattern can be suitably applied requires to simultaneously inspect the schema, the data, and potential additional constraints that can be inferred from such data. We wish to enrich ADAMAP with data-driven features, allowing it to account not only for the schema-driven mapping patterns considered in this work, but also for the data-driven mapping patterns categorized in [8].

Acknowledgements. This research has been partially supported by the EU H2020 project INODE (grant agreement No 863410), by the Italian PRIN project HOPE, by the European Regional Development Fund (ERDF) Investment for Growth and Jobs Programme 2014–2020 through the project IDEE (FESR1133), and by the Free University of Bozen-Bolzano through the projects QUADRO, KGID, GeoVKG, and STyLoLa. Diego also acknowledges the support of the Wallenberg AI, Autonomous Systems and Software Program (WASP) funded by the Knut and Alice Wallenberg Foundation and Gal the support of the Benjamin and Florence Free Chair. We thank Kurt Stockinger for his feedback.

References

1. Aalst, W.M.P.: Object-centric process mining: dealing with divergence and convergence in event data. In: Ölveczky, P.C., Salaün, G. (eds.) SEFM 2019. LNCS, vol. 11724, pp. 3–25. Springer, Cham (2019). https://doi.org/10.1007/978-3-030-30446-1_1

2. Arenas, M., Bertails, A., Prud'hommeaux, E., Sequeda, J.: A direct mapping of relational data to RDF. W3C Recommendation, World Wide Web Consortium (September 2012)

3. Artale, A., Kovtunova, A., Montali, M., van der Aalst, W.M.P.: Modeling and reasoning over declarative data-aware processes with object-centric behavioral constraints. In: Hildebrandt, T., van Dongen, B.F., Röglinger, M., Mendling, J. (eds.) BPM 2019. LNCS, vol. 11675, pp. 139–156. Springer, Cham (2019). https://doi.org/10.1007/978-3-030-26619-6_11

4. Bano, D., Weske, M.: Discovering data models from event logs. In: Dobbie, G., Frank, U., Kappel, G., Liddle, S.W., Mayr, H.C. (eds.) ER 2020. LNCS, vol. 12400, pp. 62–76. Springer, Cham (2020). https://doi.org/10.1007/978-3-030-62522-1_5

5. Bizer, C., Seaborne, A.: D2RQ: treating non-RDF databases as virtual RDF graphs. In: Proceedings of the 3rd International Semantic Web Conference (ISWC). LNCS, vol. 3298. Springer, Heidelberg (2004)

6. Calvanese, D., et al.: Ontop: answering SPARQL queries over relational databases. Semantic Web J. **8**(3), 471–487 (2017)

7. Calvanese, D., De Giacomo, G., Lembo, D., Lenzerini, M., Rosati, R.: Tractable reasoning and efficient query answering in description logics: the DL-Lite family. J. Automat. Reasoning **39**(3), 85–429 (2007) https://doi.org/10.1007/s10817-007-9078-x

8. Calvanese, D., Gal, A., Lanti, D., Montali, M., Mosca, A., Shraga, R.: Mapping patterns for virtual knowledge graphs. CoRR Technical Report arXiv:2012.01917, arXiv.org e-Print archive (2020), https://arxiv.org/abs/2012.01917

9. Das, S., Sundara, S., Cyganiak, R.: R2RML: RDB to RDF mapping language. W3C Recommendation, World Wide Web Consortium (September 2012)

10. Fahland, D.: Artifact-centric process mining. In: Encyclopedia of Big Data Technologies. Springer, Heidelberg (2019) https://doi.org/10.1007/978-3-319-77525-8_93

11. Gupta, S., Szekely, P., Knoblock, C.A., Goel, A., Taheriyan, M., Muslea, M.: Karma: a system for mapping structured sources into the Semantic Web. In: Proceedings of the Extended Semantic Web Conference (ESWC) (2012)

12. Hitzler, P., Gangemi, A., Janowicz, K.: Ontology Engineering with Ontology Design Patterns: Foundations and Applications, vol. 25. IOS Press, Amsterdam (2016)

13. Jiménez-Ruiz, E., et al.: BOOTOX: practical mapping of RDBs to OWL 2. In: ArenasArenas, M., et al. (eds.) ISWC 2015. LNCS, vol. 9367, pp. 113–132. Springer, Cham (2015). https://doi.org/10.1007/978-3-319-25010-6_7

14. Kharlamov, E., et al.: Optique 1.0: Semantic access to Big Data: The case of Norwegian Petroleum Directorate's FactPages. In: Proceedings of the 12th Int. Semantic Web Conference, Posters & Demonstrations Track (ISWC). CEUR Workshop Proceedings, vol. 1035, pp. 65–68 (2013) http://ceur-ws.org/

15. Lanti, D., Rezk, M., Xiao, G., Calvanese, D.: The NPD benchmark: Reality check for OBDA systems. In: Proceedings of the 18th International Conference on Extending Database Technology (EDBT), pp. 617–628 (2015)

16. Leopold, H., Niepert, M., Weidlich, M., Mendling, J., Dijkman, R., Stuckenschmidt, H.: Probabilistic optimization of semantic process model matching. In: Barros, A., Gal, A., Kindler, E. (eds.) BPM 2012. LNCS, vol. 7481, pp. 319–334. Springer, Heidelberg (2012). https://doi.org/10.1007/978-3-642-32885-5_25

17. de Medeiros, L.F., Priyatna, F., Corcho, O.: MIRROR: automatic R2RML mapping generation from relational databases. In: Cimiano, P., Frasincar, F., Houben, G.-J., Schwabe, D. (eds.) ICWE 2015. LNCS, vol. 9114, pp. 326–343. Springer, Cham (2015). https://doi.org/10.1007/978-3-319-19890-3_21

18. Motik, B., Cuenca Grau, B., Horrocks, I., Wu, Z., Fokoue, A., Lutz, C.: OWL 2 Web Ontology Language profiles (second edition). W3C Recommendation, World Wide Web Consortium (December 2012)

19. Pinkel, C., Binnig, C., Kharlamov, E., Haase, P.: IncMap: pay as you go matching of relational schemata to OWL ontologies. In: Proceedings of WS on Ontology Matching. CEUR Workshop Proceedings, vol. 1111 (2013) http://ceur-ws.org/

20. Poggi, A., Lembo, D., Calvanese, D., De Giacomo, G., Lenzerini, M., Rosati, R.: Linking data to ontologies. J. Data Seman. **10**, 133–173 (2008)

21. Rahm, E., Bernstein, P.A.: A survey of approaches to automatic schema matching. VLDB J. **10**, 334–350 (2001) https://doi.org/10.1007/s007780100057

22. Saha, B., Stanoi, I., Clarkson, K.L.: Schema covering: a step towards enabling reuse in information integration. In: Proceedings of the 26th IEEE International Conference on Data Engineering (ICDE), pp. 285–296. IEEE Computer Society (2010)

23. Sequeda, J., Priyatna, F., Villazón-Terrazas, B.: Relational database to RDF mapping patterns. In: Proceedings of the 3rd International Conference on Ontology Patterns, WOP 2012, vol. 929. pp. 97–108. CEUR-WS.org, Aachen, DEU (2012)

24. Sequeda, J.F., Miranker, D.P.: Ultrawrap mapper: a semi-automatic relational database to RDF (RDB2RDF) mapping tool. In: Proceedings of the 14th International Semantic Web Conference, Posters & Demonstrations Track (ISWC). CEUR Workshop Proceedings, vol. 1486 (2015) http://ceur-ws.org/

25. Spanos, D.E., Stavrou, P., Mitrou, N.: Bringing relational databases into the semantic web: a survey. Semantic Web J. **3**(2), 169–209 (2012)

26. Zhang, M., Hadjieleftheriou, M., Ooi, B.C., Procopiuc, C.M., Srivastava, D.: On multi-column foreign key discovery. Proc. VLDB Endowment **3**(1–2), 805–814 (2010)

Data and Task Management

A Metadata Model to Connect Isolated Data Silos and Activities of the CAE Domain

Julian Ziegler[1,3(✉)], Peter Reimann[1,2], Florian Keller[3], and Bernhard Mitschang[2]

[1] Graduate School of Advanced Manufacturing Engineering (GSaME), University of Stuttgart, Stuttgart, Germany
Julian.Ziegler@ipvs.uni-stuttgart.de
[2] Institute for Parallel and Distributed Systems (IPVS), University of Stuttgart, Stuttgart, Germany
[3] MANN+HUMMEL GmbH, Ludwigsburg, Germany

Abstract. Computer-aided engineering (CAE) applications support the digital transformation of the manufacturing industry. They facilitate virtual product development and product testing via computer simulations. CAE applications generate vast quantities of heterogeneous data. Domain experts struggle to access and analyze them, because such engineering data are not sufficiently described with metadata. In this paper, we characterize the CAE domain and identify unsolved challenges for a tailored data and metadata management. For instance, work activities in product development projects and their relationships to data are not represented explicitly in current metadata models. We propose a metadata model that addresses all challenges and provides a connected view on all CAE data, metadata, and work activities of development projects. We validate the feasibility of our metadata model through a prototypical implementation and its application to a real-world use case. This verifies that our metadata model addresses the CAE-specific challenges and this way eases the task of domain experts to exploit relevant data.

Keywords: Metadata models · Graphs · Computer-aided engineering

1 Introduction

Due to the advancing digitization, companies are increasingly adopting computer-aided technologies. Especially in product development, computer-aided engineering (CAE) enables a gradual shift from physical to virtual prototypes. This shift towards virtual product development, simulation, testing, and optimization reduces costs and time needed for these tasks [22]. Companies with strong activities in the field of CAE generate large amounts of heterogeneous data. The diversity in the structure and formats of CAE data makes it difficult for domain experts to analyze them. Yet, control over data discovery and analysis tasks should be in the hands of domain experts, as claimed by Viaene [21].

© Springer Nature Switzerland AG 2021
M. La Rosa et al. (Eds.): CAiSE 2021, LNCS 12751, pp. 213–228, 2021.
https://doi.org/10.1007/978-3-030-79382-1_13

In addition, Gray et al. [8] consider metadata as key enabler for data discovery, data exploration, and data analyses. All this calls for an adequate data and metadata management that is able to cope with the significant data heterogeneity in the CAE domain and that empowers domain experts to discover and access data for further analyses.

This data and metadata management has to address specific challenges imposed by the CAE domain and by its primary users, i. e., domain experts such as CAE engineers. However, product development is supported by other computer-aided disciplines, and CAE is only one part of a modern *Digital Engineering* landscape [5]. So, the *CAE domain* does not only cover data from CAE applications, but also from all other related disciplines, i. e., computer-aided design (CAD) and computer-aided testing (CAT). To derive relevant challenges, we characterize the CAE domain, analyze a use case for modern product development of a partner company, and combine this with a literature review.

One challenge is that product development projects involve the collaboration of multiple organizational units in a company. Usually, different organizational units store their data in their own isolated data silos. This isolation of data limits access and hinders cross-organizational data analyses by domain experts. This is even aggravated by the heterogeneity of data in the CAE domain that limits their annotation with metadata. Furthermore, a metadata model needs to describe not only data with metadata, but also the work activities of product development projects that produce and consume these data. Likewise, it has to cover input/output relationships between data and activities. This allows to represent the dataflow in product development projects. It makes a metadata model familiar to domain experts, as this dataflow corresponds to the way they work in their projects. It also helps domain experts to better compare and reproduce data, as well as to interpret and assess data quality more easily [6,10].

Literature comprises various generic metadata models for heterogeneous data. However, they do not address all challenges that are relevant to the CAE domain. While domain-specific metadata models exist, Willis et al. highlight that these hinder interdisciplinary work and create separation between different areas of virtual product development [23]. In this paper, we hence propose a metadata model that offers a tailored approach to manage data and metadata for the CAE domain. This is based on an architecture with a data lake as storage back end to handle heterogeneous data in large volumes [7]. Our metadata model is realized on top of this data lake and provides the means to describe all data and work activities of product development projects in an interconnected structure. This eliminates data silos and provides a connected view on all data, metadata, and activities across organizational units. The explicit representation of work activities and their relationships to data and metadata represents the dataflow of development projects in a native way as it is familiar to domain experts. We implemented a prototype of our architecture and metadata model and validate its feasibility by applying it to a real-world use case. This shows that our metadata model facilitates domain experts to access data from the whole CAE domain and use it for data analyses to optimize their products.

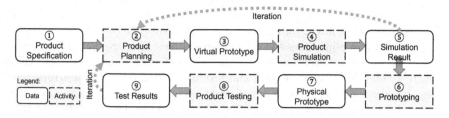

Fig. 1. Illustration of a simplified product development project involving computer-aided product simulations (steps 3 to 5) and product testing (6 to 9).

This paper is organized as follows: The use case of our partner company and the challenges prevalent in the CAE domain are presented in Sect. 2. Section 3 discusses related work. We introduce our conceptual metadata model and a graph-based logical realization in Sect. 4. Section 5 describes our prototype and the results of our validation. Section 6 concludes and lists future work.

2 Challenges for Data Management in the CAE Domain

To identify relevant challenges for data and metadata management in the CAE domain, we partnered with MANN+HUMMEL GmbH, which actively pushes virtual product development. Their core business is filtration and their products cover a wide range of applications, including the areas transport and life sciences. This has been backed up by a literature review for challenges. In Sect. 2.1, we outline a generic workflow in virtual product development projects. In Sect. 2.2, we present a real-world use case that may benefit from digitized product development. We end in Sect. 2.3 with a consideration of domain-specific challenges for data and metadata management.

2.1 Product Development Project Workflow

Together with engineers from MANN+HUMMEL, we identified a generic workflow for product development projects that combines various internal data sets from different organizational units of the company. This workflow also aligns with a more universal definition of virtual product development [11]. Figure 1 represents this workflow with its individual steps, numbered from 1 to 9. The white boxes represent data sets, while the gray boxes with a dotted line represent work activities, i. e. steps performed by employees in the project.

The workflow starts with a product specification (step 1) that is then used by domain experts to plan the product and to design a virtual prototype (steps 2–3). In the next activity, this virtual prototype is simulated with a CAE application (step 4). The resulting simulation data (step 5) are then used to draft a design plan for a physical prototype (steps 6–7), which is tested with a CAT application (steps 8–9). If the original specification is met, the newly developed product can be transferred to production planning. To reach this point, several iterations of repeated product planning, simulation, and prototyping steps may be necessary.

This workflow illustrates the various disciplines in a product development project that generate large amounts of heterogeneous data, i.e., product design (CAD), product simulation (CAE), and product testing (CAT). The strong data heterogeneity is further increased by a wide range of competing computer applications, which rarely meet open standards with regard to data. Simulation applications typically require large 3D CAD geometries as input. Their output data are large application-specific binary files that need further processing to derive user-desired metrics such as product characteristics. CAT data formats depend on the test benches they are produced with. Here, different suppliers rely on their own data formats, which are usually binary or text-based file formats.

2.2 Use Case: Feedback in Virtual Product Development

Data from the disciplines CAD, CAE and CAT are often stored in separate data silos, each of which is managed by a specific organizational unit of a company. As noted by Che et al., such data silos limit the potential for gaining insights through data analysis, since each silo can only be analyzed in isolation [4]. To identify relevant connections between data sets from multiple silos, domain experts need context that describes the data. Context may be provided by metadata that describe properties of data, such as the dimensionality of a CAD geometry. In addition, information about the origin of a data set can describe which computer applications and which parameters were used for data creation, e.g., the name of a simulation software or the numerical calculation models used.

Related to the workflow shown in Fig. 1, connecting data from the two silos product testing (CAT) and simulation (CAE) can reduce the number of necessary iterations and thus reduce the duration and costs of product development. If simulation or test results (steps 5 or 9) indicate that the product specification cannot be met, it is necessary to start a new iteration with the planning step 2. The goal is to make the decision to start a new iteration as early as possible, i.e., based on the simulation results in step 5. This can avoid expensive and time-consuming product tests, i.e., all steps from 6 to 9. However, this is only possible if the simulation models accurately simulate the real physical tests.

Data and metadata management which offers a connected view on both silos of CAE and CAT data may help to optimize simulation models. We may use the numerous data from historical physical product tests (step 9) to increase the accuracy of the simulation results (step 5) in a feedback loop. For instance, Gaussian Process regression on historical testing data may indicate how to calibrate predefined input constants of the simulation models. This enables domain experts to decide more reliably and thus more frequently at an earlier stage after step 5 whether a product requires an iteration back to the planning step 2.

2.3 Challenges for CAE Data and Metadata Management

In the following, we present three challenges C_1, C_2, C_3, which need to be addressed for the management of data and metadata of the CAE domain.

C_1 **Isolated Data Silos with Heterogeneous Data Sets:** A metadata model must be able to provide a connected view of all data of product development projects across the boundaries of various organizational units. Such a connected view allows domain experts to access data sets that were previously stored in data silos to which they had no access. Data in the CAE domain exist in different formats and structures, which are often not known to the users [4]. Hence, a level of abstraction is required that allows metadata to be linked to all heterogeneous data. Furthermore, the metadata model needs to be flexible to handle temporary changes of data schemes and formats. For example, when a software used in product development is updated, new metadata may become available or previously available metadata may disappear. It is also desirable if the metadata model does not require low-level database knowledge so that it can be understood and used by domain experts with as little training as possible.

C_2 **Activities have to be Represented as First-Class Entities with Their Own Metadata:** We define activities as all work activities in product development projects that produce or consume data. They represent the actual work done by the employees in a company. These employees may process data either indirectly, e.g., by running a computer simulation which generates data, or directly by manually processing data using spreadsheets or similar tools. Since such activities are a core element of a product development project, domain experts consider them as important as the data sets themselves. These activities hence have also to be associated with numerous metadata that are relevant for subsequent processing and interpretation of data sets. Such metadata include, e.g., the numerical calculation model used for a simulation. Capturing the activities with their metadata improves comparability and reproducibility of data sets, since the activities that produced them can be analyzed explicitly [6,10].

C_3 **Relationships Between Data and Activities have to be Represented:** The representation of relationships in a metadata model makes it possible to directly link all data with the activities that produce or consume this data. This makes it possible to accurately represent the dataflow of product development projects, e.g., in a similar way as the dataflow shown in Fig. 1. Such a dataflow represents which data is related to which activities and thus depicts the project progression in a way as it is known to the domain experts working on it. Thus, they can intuitively navigate through such a metadata model and easily find desired data. Furthermore, explicit descriptions of relationships between data, activities, and metadata allow domain experts to see the data lineage, i.e., how data was created and how it has been processed over time. This simplifies the interpretation and assessment of the data by domain experts [2,8].

3 Related Work

We identified three groups of related work: metadata models, workflow modeling techniques, and commercial computer applications. The metadata models are further divided into generic models, which attempt to support metadata of

Table 1. Summary of related work. ● = fulfilled; ◗ = partially fulfilled; ○ = not fulfilled.

	C_1	C_2	C_3
Generic metadata models ([9,15,18]	●	○	○
Specialized metadata models ([12,19,20]	◗	○	○
Workflow modeling techniques (e.g., BPMN [14])	◗	◗	●
Commercial computer applications	◗	○	○

any domain, and specialized models, which are tailored to specific use cases in simulation and scientific data management. A summary is compiled in Table 1.

Generic Metadata Models. Sawadogo et al. propose a *MEtadata model for DAta Lakes* (MEDAL) based on a hypergraph, i.e., consisting of hypernodes and hyperedges [18]. Each hypernode represents a data object and contains a simple graph, whose nodes represent different versions of this data object. Hyperedges connect multiple hypernodes to group and aggregate data objects. Hellerstein et al. developed another model called *Ground* [9] that also associates each data object with its own graph. Instead of a hypergraph, Ground uses three distinct graphs that are interconnected: version graphs track versions of data objects, model graphs describe dependencies between data objects, and lineage graphs attribute provenance information. The *Generic and Extensible Metadata Management System* (GEMMS) proposed by Quix et al. is specifically designed to ease data integration in data lakes [15]. It categorizes the metadata as structural or semantic abstractions of files that make them queryable.

All three metadata models provide abstractions to attribute heterogeneous data with metadata (C_1). However, they all lack the ability to represent work activities of a CAE domain as first-class entities and to explicitly associate them with metadata (C_2). Likewise, they cannot describe the relationships between data and activities in a way that represents the dataflow in product development projects (C_3). GEMMS cannot represent work activities and relationships between data at all. Both graph-based approaches (MEDAL, Ground) can attribute relationships among data objects with metadata, but these relationships do not represent a dataflow between work activities. Ground's lineage metadata are only attributed to single data objects and cannot describe input-output relationships between data objects and activities. MEDAL can describe transitions from one version to another with relationships, but it does not allow for explicitly describing the activities carrying out these version transitions.

Specialized Metadata Models. Vasilakis et al. focus on specific event simulations and suggest to store simulation output data in a data warehouse [20]. The approach proposed by Valle et al. is tailored to the specific problem of CFD simulations [19]. Their *Scientific Data Bag* (SDB) is a container format that stores semantic information as metadata to describe heterogeneous files. Matthews et al. introduce the *Core Scientific Metadata Model* (CSMM) aimed at representing data generated by scientific studies as well as accompanying metadata [12]. All three proposed solutions are tailored to specific use cases or problem domains. They are limited to their respective data silo and do not allow to connect data across boundaries of different silos and organizational units (C_1). Furthermore, the proposals have a strict focus on describing data, but they do not allow to explicitly represent work activities (C_2) and thus also not relationships between data and these activities (C_3).

Workflow Modeling Techniques. Approaches from a different angle are techniques to represent workflows or business processes. The *Business Process Model and Notation* (BPMN) is the major representative of such techniques [14]. BPMN represents process steps as so-called *tasks*, which may be used to model the work activities and the dataflow between them (C_3). Furthermore, it allows for associating these tasks with abstract representations of any data set. However, it is not possible to attribute data or tasks with arbitrary metadata (C_1, C_2). While BPMN annotations could be re-purposed for metadata, this has several drawbacks. BPMN has no metadata definitions in its core. This requires domain experts to spend much effort to decide on structures themselves. Moreover, it lacks the flexibility to express more than simple one-to-one relations.

Commercial Computer Applications. Management of CAE data is a large field where various commercial off-the-shelf computer applications are available, e. g., Dassault Systèmes SIMULIA[1] or T-Systems Medina/SDM[2]. These offerings are familiar to domain experts due to their presence in industry. However, they are tightly coupled with dedicated simulation software for CAE applications. Hence, they are less suited to create a connected view that includes data sets from other areas, such as CAT (C_1). They also lack the capability to describe arbitrary work activities (C_2) or relationships between data and activities (C_3).

4   Grab'MeMo: A Graph-Based Metadata Model

Due to the high heterogeneity of data in the CAE domain, our approach separates storage of data from metadata. This means we store data files in their raw formats in a data lake, acting as storage back end [7]. Grab'MeMo, our **graph-based metadata model**, serves as a way to index files in this storage back end. The following Sect. 4.1 introduces our conceptual metadata model. Section 4.2 describes how to realize it via a graph-based logical model.

4.1   Conceptual Metadata Model

Figure 2 depicts our conceptual metadata model as UML class diagram. In its core, the model consists of three main elements: data containers, activities, and contextual metadata. In the following, we detail on these elements and discuss how our metadata model addresses the challenges introduced in Sect. 2.3.

---

[1] SIMULIA: https://www.3ds.com/products-services/simulia/products.

[2] Medina/SDM: https://plm.t-systems-service.com/en/medina-sdm.

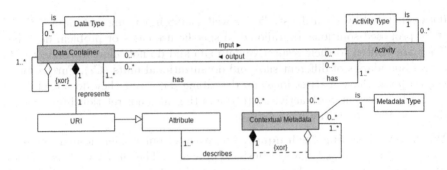

Fig. 2. Conceptual metadata model as UML class diagram. The core elements are shown as gray boxes. White boxes show generalizations or composites of core elements.

A *data container* is an abstraction of an identifiable collection of data located in a storage back end [16]. This level of abstraction allows our metadata model to represent data files independently of their format or structure. This way, we may attribute heterogeneous data originating from any data silo involved in product development projects (C_1). Each data container is composed with exactly one URI that points to its storage location, e. g., to a file in the underlying data lake.

An *activity* element is an abstraction of a work activity that produces, consumes, or processes data in a product development project. Such an activity may be the creation of a product design in a CAD application or the calculation of a computer simulation. In the same way as with data containers, this level of abstraction for activities allows to conceptually represent all activities in product development projects as first-class entities in a metadata model (C_2). Input and output relationships associate an activity with the data containers it takes as input and/or produces as output. These associations between data containers and activities describe the dataflow of a product development project (C_3). They have many-to-many cardinalities to reflect all kinds of activities occurring in practice. Many activities both consume and produce at least one data container, e. g., a computer simulation that takes a product design to simulate the properties of this product. Nevertheless, some activities produce several data containers, but not consume any, or vice versa.

Neither data containers nor activities directly contain a form of metadata. Instead, they may be associated with an arbitrary number of *contextual metadata* elements. This indirection makes it possible to attribute data and activities with any metadata regardless of their heterogeneity (C_1, C_2). Each metadata element is composed of at least one *attribute* that represents descriptive information for the associated data containers or activities. An example attribute is the name of an employee who performed an associated activity. The URI of a data container is modeled as a specialization of such an attribute to ensure that any data container has such an identifier as metadata. The composition of attributes to metadata elements allows to group multiple related attributes in one metadata element and still maintain the needed flexibility (C_1). In case of a product design, a contextual metadata element may contain multiple attributes that characterize one of the materials the product is constructed of. Due to version changes of the utilized CAD application, the number of available attributes for material characterization may increase or decrease over time. In such a case, we just need to add or remove attributes to or from a metadata element, but this metadata element itself and its associations to data or activities may remain unchanged.

Our metadata model contains special forms of aggregation for data containers and contextual metadata. This aggregation allows a data container or metadata element to represent a collection of other data containers or metadata elements, respectively. This may be used to create virtual abstractions of multiple data containers. Domain experts can use this aggregation to create hierarchical data structures comparable to those they are working with, e. g., an abstract data container may represent a folder of multiple files on their local disk. Note that such a container of containers must not have an URI, as it does not represent physical data. Hence, an $\{xor\}$ constraint prohibits that a data container may both aggregate other containers and be composed with an URI. Aggregation of contextual metadata further increases flexibility and enables hierarchical grouping based on, e. g., the topic of their attributes. In case one contextual metadata element contains attributes for time (hours, minutes) and another one for a date (year, month, day), both may be aggregated to have all timestamp-related metadata in one place. In a similar way to data containers, an aggregating contextual metadata element must not have attributes of its own.

The three core elements (data containers, activities, contextual metadata) are associated with exactly one individual *type*. This type allows to add domain-specific semantics to this otherwise abstract metadata model. For instance, it may be used to model the various computer applications used in CAE as types of activities. Thereby, a type may identify whether a simulation activity is implemented by OpenFOAM[3] or SU2[4], which are two popular open source software suits for computer simulations. In a conceptual model, this type element may refer to parts of a domain-specific concept model, a business glossary, or more expressive ontologies, e. g., the *Product Design Ontology* [3]. This ontology is designed for CAD data and CAE input data. It defines the types of data files that exist, what metadata they may have, and establishes a common vocabulary that improves interdisciplinary work between different areas of virtual product development.

4.2   Graph-Based Logical Model

We propose to use a graph structure to design the logical level of our conceptual metadata model. As summarized by Angles et al., graphs have multiple advantages compared to other database models, such as relational, network and object-oriented models [1]. For instance, graphs provide a simple structure that allows domain experts to intuitively model and access data. Furthermore, they

---

[3] OpenFOAM: https://www.openfoam.com/.
[4] SU2: https://su2code.github.io/.

Table 2. Mapping of conceptual metadata model to a property graph data model.

Conceptual element	Node	Edge	Label	Property
Data container, Activity, Contextual metadata	✗			
Types of Data/Activity/Metadata			✗	
Attribute/URI				✗
Input/Output and *has* associations		Directed		
Aggregation		Directed		

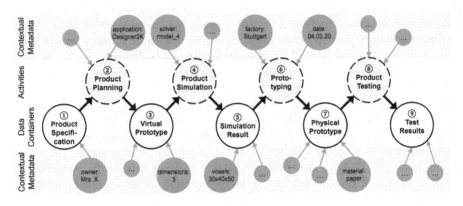

Fig. 3. Illustration of a graph structure representing data, activities, and metadata for the product development project depicted in Fig. 1.

natively support relationships between data and enable users to discover data having certain kinds of relationships. We propose to use a *property graph* data model [17]. A property graph is a directed multi-graph that can store values within its nodes and edges as properties and labels.

Table 2 summarizes how we map individual elements of our conceptual model to elements of a property graph in the logical model. Instances of the core elements (data containers, activities, contextual metadata) are each represented by a node in our graph. Each node has a label that corresponds to the conceptual type of the relevant data, activity, or metadata element. An attribute of a metadata element is represented by a property of the corresponding node in the graph. Thereby, activity and data container nodes are described by associated contextual metadata nodes that carry a property for each of their attributes. In addition, data container nodes get a dedicated property for their URI attribute.

Directed edges between data container and activity nodes represent their *input/output* relationships (C_3). The *has* associations that connect contextual metadata nodes to data container or activity nodes are represented via directed edges as well. An aggregation of data container nodes or metadata nodes is realized with a directed edge pointing from the aggregating node to the aggregated nodes. These aggregating nodes then must not carry any properties. The *is, rep-*

resents, and *describes* associations in the conceptual model are all part of nodes as their labels or properties. Hence, they do not need an explicit mapping.

Figure 3 shows an example instantiation of the graph structure realizing our conceptual metadata model for the workflow of a product development project shown in Fig. 1. The workflow is represented by a set of interconnected data container nodes (1, 3, 5, 7, 9) and activity nodes (2, 4, 6, 8). Various contextual metadata nodes are connected to data container or activity nodes to further describe them with their properties, e.g., the owner of a product specification or the application used for product planning (C_1, C_2). The directed edges connecting these nodes represent the dataflow between data containers and activities (C_3). For the sake of clarity, URIs and labels are not depicted in Fig. 3.

5 Implementation and Validation

We deployed a prototype that implements our graph-based metadata model and uses a data lake for data storage. Section 5.1 discusses its architecture and design considerations. We also implemented our use case (Sect. 2.2) and use it to validate our metadata model and discuss its advantages in Sect. 5.2 .

5.1 Prototypical Implementation and Design Considerations

We chose a layered architecture for our prototypical implementation, as shown in Fig. 4. The three layers separate data sources (source layer), a data lake and a graph database implementing our metadata model (data provisioning layer), as well as client applications using the metadata (application layer). The data provisioning layer ingests data from the source layer, stores them as files in the data lake, and generates appropriate metadata nodes that are stored in the graph database. Example client applications provide reports, data analyses results, or facilitate graphical data exploration for domain experts.

We chose a data lake for data storage due to the nature of heterogeneous and large data in the CAE domain. A data lake is a concept for primarily, but not exclusively, storing raw data [7]. It is generally associated with a large and scalable storage based on low-cost commodity hardware. For data of the CAE domain, we require a storage solution that additionally supports data having varying data structures that are not known in advance, e.g., in case of proprietary file formats. Multiple storage solutions with such capabilities are available. For example, Amazon S3[5] is a cloud-based storage solution that supports structured and unstructured data, is scalable, and fault tolerant. We selected HDFS (Hadoop Distributed File System[6]), mainly because companies and other stakeholders in the CAE domain may prefer an on-premise solution due to information exchange policies of their customers. If cloud-based data storage is desired,

---

[5] Amazon S3: https://aws.amazon.com/products/storage/data-lake-storage/.
[6] Apache Hadoop: https://hadoop.apache.org.

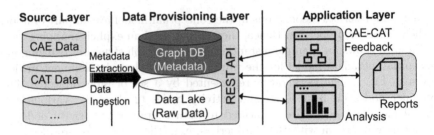

Fig. 4. Architecture of the prototypical implementation of our metadata model.

HDFS can be deployed on all major cloud platforms. Another major benefit is Hadoop's extensive environment that allows to add more functionality if desired, such as data processing and analytics with MapReduce and Apache Spark or data warehouse capabilities with Apache Hive.

We realized the logical model of our metadata model with a property graph. Therefore, a graph database that supports the property graph data model is a straightforward solution to store our metadata structure. Multiple options for graph databases are available, many even support a data model that extends a regular property graph. Azure Cosmos DB[7] and Amazon Neptune[8] are both cloud-based databases that support multiple data models, including property graphs. We selected Neo4j as graph database that is specifically tailored to support the property graph model [13]. It is a widely supported database, features scalability, high availability setups, and ACID-compliant transactions.

To orchestrate both components HDFS and Neo4J, we implemented a Java-based server application using Apache Tomcat[9]. It provides our REST (Representational State Transfer) style API to clients on the application layer and manages connections to HDFS and Neo4j. It provides classic CRUD (create, read, update, and delete) functionality to client applications and allows them to access nodes and edges of our metadata structure as resources. Furthermore, data files associated with data container nodes can be uploaded and downloaded. For more complex queries, our API allows to pass Cypher queries directly to Neo4j. Cypher is a declarative query language for graphs that resembles SQL.

A client application can upload data and assign a label as its type via our API, which then automatically stores the file in the data lake and creates a corresponding data container node in our metadata structure. Activity nodes can be created via another call to a corresponding API endpoint. Moreover, our API offers an endpoint to create contextual metadata nodes with their properties and label and to associate these metadata nodes to either data container or activity nodes. Further properties can be added, altered, or removed by updating such a metadata node. An API endpoint for relationships allows to create edges between two given nodes, delete edges, and list all incoming or outgoing edges of a node.

---

[7] Azure Cosmos DB: https://azure.microsoft.com/services/cosmos-db/.

[8] Amazon Neptune https://aws.amazon.com/neptune/.

[9] Apache Tomcat: https://tomcat.apache.org.

To retrieve data, a client can traverse the metadata structure until it encounters a desired node. The client may then retrieve the properties and label of the node. In case of data container nodes, an API endpoint allows to download the data files using the URI associated with these nodes. Through Cypher queries, large sets of nodes can be retrieved with a single API call. Cypher queries may also be used for more complex queries, e. g., with filter predicates or pattern matching. As an example, a query may select all data container nodes that are the output of an activity node, representing a specific simulation application, but only for recent versions (> 2.5) of this application:

```
MATCH (n:SpecificSimulationApplication)-[:output]->(m:ResultData)
WHERE n.version > 2.5
RETURN m
```

5.2   Use Case: CAE-CAT Feedback

In the general workflow for product development projects presented in Fig. 1, multiple iterations of product planning, simulation, prototyping and testing may be needed until a satisfying product is developed. With increasing accuracy of simulations, more insufficient products can be canceled directly after step 5 of this workflow, i. e., before costly physical prototypes are created and tested. By leveraging historical data from physical product tests (CAT data), we can automatically optimize simulation models (CAE data). Therefore, we implemented two Python applications that act as clients in our application layer in Fig. 4.

The first client application is responsible for ingesting our source data into the data provisioning layer and for creating the corresponding metadata nodes. Due to missing standards for the various data formats and metadata in the CAE domain, no practical and mature approach exists in literature to extract relevant metadata from CAE files. We hence see this domain-specific kind of metadata extraction as an open research problem and therefore provide a first prototype solution that is tailored to our specific use case of a CAE-CAT feedback loop. We implemented a modular framework that comprises several modules and adapters to extract metadata from our specific CAT and CAE files. Based on the extracted metadata, our client creates nodes, properties, and relationships between nodes through the REST API. An example of the resulting graph can be seen in Fig. 3. Our framework can easily support more file types by simply adding more modules or adapters.

The second client application queries fine-grained subsets of the previously ingested data that can then be used to optimize and validate simulation models. This optimization can be achieved, e. g., by calibrating predefined constants in a simulation model. Our client application obtains these calibration constants via a Gaussian Process regression model, trained on historical testing data. The testing data has to be selected in dependence of various parameters and the problem area itself: materials, product dimensions, intended purpose, and many more. All permutations require their own specifically trained regression model. For instance, to improve a simulation model that simulates products made of cellulose fibres, we may fetch test results that were conducted with physical prototypes also made of cellulose fibres. Our client application uses activities and contextual metadata to select those historical test results that are relevant to the simulation model it wants to improve. The selected test results are downloaded from the data provisioning layer and used to train a Gaussian Process regression which is then used to determine better calibration constants for the simulation model. This way, the accuracy of the simulation is increased and aligned to the results from physical product testing.

The flexibility of a data lake allows to seamlessly store data and metadata from computer-aided simulation applications (CAE) as well as results from computer-aided product testing (CAT) together in their respective raw file formats. So, we may integrate different kinds of data from two data silos (CAE and CAT) and treat these heterogeneous data sets equally in our metadata model (C_1). Our second client application can examine metadata from one CAE data set and use it to create queries to fetch data from a CAT data set. With activities and their metadata as first-class entities, our second client application has additional context for more fine-grained data selection. For instance, it may select test results from products designed with a specific material or even with a specific version of a CAD application (C_2). This is further supported by the relationships between data, activities, and their related metadata (C_3). They enable us to connect, e.g., a design activity in early stages of product development with later test results of the correspondingly designed product. In addition, this dataflow between related work activities provides information about data lineage, which may itself be mined to gain additional insights on projects. As example, the progress of projects can be analyzed to find patterns that influence KPIs, such as the duration and costs of development projects. In this use case, the improved simulation accuracy allows us to start a new iteration earlier in future product development projects, reducing project duration and cost. Furthermore, with simulation models of higher quality, it is possible to enrich data sets from product testing that previously were too sparse to be used for feedback purposes. Such enriched data sets also enable more comprehensive data analyses on larger amounts of data. We also gain knowledge about the reliability of the simulation results and their deviation, which further supports decision-making in the course of a product development project, as domain experts can better assess the available results.

6   Conclusion

In this paper, we propose a metadata model that offers a tailored approach to data management in the CAE domain by addressing three domain-specific challenges. It eliminates data silos by providing a connected view on all heterogeneous data, metadata, and activities in virtual product development. Work activities are explicitly modeled as first-class entities alongside data. This allows us to describe them with metadata and improve comparability and reproducibility for domain experts. Furthermore, the metadata model explicitly represents relationships between data and activities that reflect the dataflow of product development projects. This brings in valuable context that makes our metadata model familiar to domain experts. Our prototypical implementation for a real-world use case shows that this empowers domain experts to interpret, access, and analyze their data. For instance, it facilitates them to retrieve CAT data that is necessary to increase the accuracy of CAE simulation models.

For future work, we are going to incorporate means to automatically capture data lineage and other metadata in order to populate our graph structure.

Acknowledgements. The authors thank the German Research Foundation (DFG), the Ministry of Science, Research and Arts of the State of Baden-Wurttemberg, and the MANN+HUMMEL GmbH for financial support within the Graduate School of Excellence advanced Manaufacturing Engineering.

References

1. Angles, R., Gutierrez, C.: Survey of Graph Database Models. ACM Comput. Surv. **40**(1), 1–39 (2008)
2. Bose, R.: A conceptual framework for composing and managing scientific data lineage. In: Proceedings of the 14th International Conference on Scientific and Statistical Database Management, pp. 15–19. Edinburgh, Scotland, UK (2002)
3. Catalano, C.E., et al.: A product design ontology for enhancing shape processing in design workflows. J. Intell. Manuf. **20**(5), 553–567 (2009)
4. Che, D., Safran, M., Peng, Z.: From big data to big data mining: challenges, issues, and opportunities. In: DASFAA 2013, Wuhan, China (2013)
5. Dankwort, C.W., et al.: Engineers' CAx education-it's not only CAD. Comput. Aided Des. **36**(14), 1439–1450 (2004)
6. Davidson, S.B., Freire, J.: Provenance and scientific workflows: challenges and opportunities. In: Proceedings of SIGMOD, pp. 1345–1350. Vancouver, Canada (2008)
7. Fang, H.: Managing data lakes in big data era: what's a data lake and why has it became popular in data management ecosystem. In: IEEE-CYBER 2015 (2015)
8. Gray, J., et al.: Scientific data management in the coming decade. SIGMOD Rec. **34**(4), 34–41 (2005)
9. Hellerstein, J.M., et al.: Ground: a data context service. In: Proceedings of the 8th Biennial Conference on Innovative Data Systems Research, Chaminade, CA, USA (2017)
10. Herschel, M., Diestelkämper, R., Ben Lahmar, H.: A survey on provenance: what for? what form? what from? VLDB J. **26**, 881–906 (2017)
11. Hirz, M., et al.: Overview of virtual product development. In: Integrated Computer-Aided Design in Automotive Development, pp. 25–50. Springer, Berlin, Heidelberg (2013) https://doi.org/10.1007/978-3-642-11940-8_2
12. Matthews, B., et al.: Using a core scientific metadata model in large-scale facilities. Int. J. Digital Curation **5**(1), 106–118 (2010)
13. Miller, J.J.: Graph database applications and concepts with Neo4j. In: Proceedings of the Southern Association for Information Systems Conference, Atlanta, GA, USA (2013)
14. Object Management Group: Business Process Model and Notation (2014). https://www.omg.org/spec/BPMN/

15. Quix, C., Hai, R., Vatov, I.: Metadata extraction and management in data lakes with GEMMS. Complex Syst. Inf. Model. **9**, 67–83 (2016)
16. Reimann, P., et al.: SIMPL - a framework for accessing external data in simulation workflows. In: BTW 2011, Kaiserslautern, Germany (2011)
17. Rodriguez, M.A., Neubauer, P.: Constructions from Dots and Lines. Bull. Am. Soc. Inf. Sci. Technol. **36**(6), 35–41 (2010)
18. Sawadogo, P., et al.: Metadata systems for data lakes: models and features. In: ADBIS 2019 (2019)
19. Valle, M., et al.: Scientific data management for visualization implementation experience. In: Simulation und Visualisierung 2005 (SimVis 2005), pp. 347–354. SCS Publishing House e.V., Magdeburg, Germany (2005)
20. Vasilakis, C., et al.: A data warehouse environment for storing and analyzing simulation output data. In: Proceedings of of the WSC, vol. 1 (2004)
21. Viaene, S.: Data scientists aren't domain experts. IT Prof. **15**(6), 12–17 (2013)
22. Vinodh, S., Kuttalingam, D.: Computer-aided design and engineering as enablers of agile manufacturing. J. Manuf. Tech. Manage. **22**, (2011)
23. Willis, C., Greenberg, J., White, H.: Analysis and synthesis of metadata goals for scientific data. JASIST **63**(8), 1505–1520 (2012)

Challenges and Perils of Testing Database Manipulation Code

Maxime Gobert[1]([✉]), Csaba Nagy[2], Henrique Rocha[3], Serge Demeyer[3,4], and Anthony Cleve[1]

[1] Namur Digital Institute, University of Namur, Namur, Belgium
maxime.gobert@unamur.be
[2] Software Institute, Università della Svizzera Italiana, Lugano, Switzerland
[3] Department Computer Science, University of Antwerp, Antwerp, Belgium
[4] Flanders Make vzw, Lommel, Belgium

Abstract. Software testing enable development teams to maintain the quality of a software system while it evolves. The database manipulation code requires special attention in this context. However, it is often neglected and suffers from software maintenance problems. In this paper, we investigate the current state-of-the-practice in testing database manipulation code. We first analyse the code of 72 projects mined from Libraries.io to get an impression of the test coverage for database code. We confirm that the database is poorly tested: 46% of the projects did not cover with tests half of their database access methods, and 33% of the projects did not cover the database code at all. To understand the difficulties in testing database code, we analysed 532 questions on StackExchange sites and deduced a taxonomy. We found that developers mostly look for insights on general best practices to test database access code. They also have more technical questions related to DB handling, mocking, parallelisation or framework/tool usage. This investigation lays the basis for future research on improving database code testing.

Keywords: Testing · Database manipulation code · Empirical study

1 Introduction

Database manipulation code is usually seen as an outsider in the codebase of an information system. It lies between the programs and the database, so it belongs partially to both, but not entirely to one. It can also involve multiple development teams. For example, in larger systems, a complex database requires a department of database administrators (DBAs) separated from the group of software engineers who maintain the application code. Both groups are in charge of maintaining their own side, but they need to share responsibilities as far as program-database communication is concerned.

However, shared responsibilities come at a price, and the *dual role* of database manipulation code leads to software maintenance problems. Stonebraker *et al.*

M. La Rosa et al. (Eds.): CAiSE 2021, LNCS 12751, pp. 229–245, 2021.
https://doi.org/10.1007/978-3-030-79382-1_14

argue that it is the most significant factor of database or application decay [26]. As they say, evolving requirements result in changes in the schema, which in turn require adjustments in the database manipulation code. Developers tend to minimise their effort to implement modifications, and the application or the database quality suffers the consequences.

Several researchers have proposed approaches addressing the evolution of database-centric systems [7–9,17,18,21,31]. Other authors developed methods specifically designed for testing database applications, with a focus on test case generation [6], test data generation [5], test case prioritisation [11], and regression testing [24]. Despite the undeniable benefits of these methods, *no research work has investigated how developers test database access code in practice* – which could direct researchers where automated assistance is needed the most.

To provide such guidance, we investigated the current state-of-the-practice in testing database manipulation code addressing our research question: *What are the main challenges/problems when testing database manipulation code?*

As a motivational study, we analysed a set of open-source systems that rely on database access technologies and implement automated tests. We mined 6,626 projects from Libraries.io and found automated tests along with database manipulation code in only 332. Out of these, we examined 72 projects, for which we could collect coverage reports of test executions. We observed how tests cover the database access code in these projects. We found that overall *the database manipulation code is poorly tested.* 46% of the projects did not test half of their DB methods, and 33% of the projects did not even test DB communication.

To understand the reasons for such poor coverage, we qualitatively analysed 532 questions from popular StackExchanges websites and *identified the problems that hamper developers when writing tests.* We distilled the results in a comprehensive taxonomy of 83 issues grouped into 7 main categories. For each category, we discuss critical issues and solutions proposed by StackExchange users. Besides our contributions of (i) exploratory evidence of poorly tested database manipulation code and (ii) an extensive taxonomy of database testing problems, (iii) we infer actionable directions both for researchers and practitioners. Our study – being the first of its kind in this field – lays the foundation for future research on improving the maintenance of database code through automated testing.

2   Motivational Study

We first explore how developers test their database manipulation code in practice. Figure 1 depicts an overview of the three main steps we followed during this exploration: (1) we selected a set of open-source projects using databases, (2) we identified which part of their source code was involved in database communication and (3) we analysed how automated tests covered it.

During step ① *Project Selection*, we mined open-source systems from Libraries.io,[1] which we chose because (i) it monitors a broad set of projects (not just libraries), and (ii) it has a large database of dependencies among projects.[2]

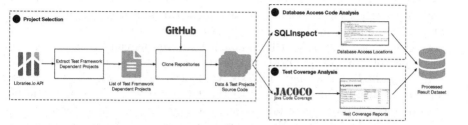

Fig. 1. Overview of the main steps for test coverage analysis of database access code

We specifically looked for applications using databases and automated testing technologies. Libraries.io provides us with the possibility of searching for such projects through their dependencies. Selected projects had to satisfy four inclusion criteria: (i) *be written in Java*, since we rely on tools that support only Java (*i.e.*, to identify database code and measure test coverage); (ii) *use JUnit*[3] *or TestNG*,[4] i.e., the top Java testing frameworks according to the usage statistics of Maven central;[5] (iii) *use database access technologies*, e.g., `java.sql` or `javax.persistence`; (iv) *have executable test suites*, as required by JaCoCo,[6] the test coverage tool we rely on.

We relied on version 1.4.0 of Libraries.io dataset published in December 2018, as it was the most recent at the time of conducting the survey. We cloned 6,626 systems satisfying a search query for Java projects with testing framework dependencies. Then we filtered them looking for imports of database communication libraries. The list of imports can be found in our replication package [1]. At this stage, we identified 905 projects.

In step ② *Database Access Code Analysis*, we identified the part of the source code involved in database communication. We used SQLInspect[7] for this purpose – a static code analyser for Java applications using JDBC, Hibernate, or JPA. This tool looks for locations in the source code where queries are sent to a database, extracts these queries, and analyses them for further inspection (*e.g.*, smell detection). In the remaining of the paper, we call *database access methods* all methods that construct or execute a DB query. We selected SQLInspect

[1] https://libraries.io/data.

[2] At the time of writing, it has 2.7M unique packages, 33M repositories, and 235M interdependencies between them.

[3] https://junit.org/.

[4] https://testng.org/.

[5] https://mvnrepository.com/open-source/testingframeworks.

[6] https://www.jacoco.org.

[7] https://bitbucket.org/csnagy/sqlinspect.

because (i) it supports popular database access technologies, (ii) it returns all the database access methods of the project under analysis, and (iii) it relies on a technique reaching a precision of 88% and a recall of 71.5% [18].

From the 905 projects selected at the first stage, SQLInspect identified database access methods in 332 of them. In the other projects, it did not detect database accesses. The reason for this is that SQLInspect looks for SQL, Hibernate, or JPA queries in the source code. An import does not necessarily imply query executions, and other DB communication means can be used (*e.g.,* an object-relational mapping; ORM) too, or the packages may not be used at all.

In step ③ *Test Coverage Analysis,* we looked at the way the DB access methods are *covered by tests.* We used the JaCoCo Maven plugin that can be integrated with a project's tests to collect coverage data at different granularity levels (*e.g.,* method or line). We implemented a script modifying the pom files of the 332 projects to execute tests with JaCoCo. Maven compilation or test execution failures prevented the generation of a test report file for 178 projects. Many projects (82) did not have a pom file or tests at all, despite having a dependency on a test framework. In the end, we collected test coverage data for 72 systems. Then we processed the reports along with the results of step ②.

Table 1. Overview of the projects

Metric	Min	Q1	Med	Q3	Max
Java LOC (effective)	225	1,476	3,198	12,929	133,331
GitHub stars	0	0	2	10	9,152
Methods	11	110	278	1,057	15,188
DB access methods (in prod. code)	1	2	4	7	80

Table 1 summarises the main characteristics (with minimum, quartiles, median, and maximum values) of the analysed projects. The projects are of various sizes ranging from 225 LOC up to 133 kLOC. The biggest project is

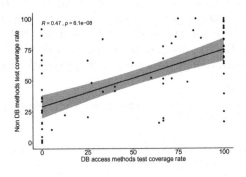

Fig. 2. Non-DB access methods vs DB access methods test coverage rate

Speedment,[8] a Java Stream ORM. The most popular project is MyBatis[9] with 9,152 stars. Regarding database access code, we only considered methods in production code (*i.e.,* test classes excluded). We intentionally did not set a minimum threshold for the projects' size or database methods. Our goal was to see whether they test database access code or not in real-life projects. If the project had only one method communicating with the DB, we wanted to see the tests for it.

Figure 2 shows a scatter plot of all projects and their respective test coverage rates. In total, 24 projects do not test database access communication at all. Also, a significant number of projects with the highest coverage rate have, in fact, full coverage. We found a mean value of 2.8 database methods for projects with full coverage. There are slightly fewer projects (48.6%) in the figure with lower coverage for database methods. However, considering only the projects above the median (*i.e.,* with at least five database methods), there is a bigger difference: 59% of them have a smaller coverage for database methods than for regular methods. Similarly, while 46% of the projects cover less than half of their database methods, this number increases to 53% for projects above the median. Moreover, 33% of the projects do not test the database code at all, and it increases again to 35% for projects with at least five database methods.

We assessed the relationship between the test coverage rates of DB access methods vs regular methods using the Kendall correlation, as the Shapiro-Wilk normality test showed a significant deviation from the normal distribution. The result was a moderate positive correlation with a high statistical significance ($\tau = 0.47$, $p < 0.0001$).

In summary, we found a statistically significant correlation between the test coverage of regular and database access methods, but it is a weak-moderate correlation, and there can be important differences between the two. As our closer look at the sample set showed, the coverage of database code is poor in general together with regular methods. But when it comes to more complex database access code, it is even more neglected.

3 Challenges and Problems When Testing DB Access Code

The goal of our main research question is to understand the reasons holding back the developers to consider database access code in their test cases. We decided to study their most common problems on popular question-and-answer (Q&A) websites of the StackExchange network. The outcome of this qualitative study is a hierarchical taxonomy of common issues faced by developers.

3.1 Context and Data Collection

---

[8] https://github.com/speedment/speedment.
[9] https://github.com/mybatis/ mybatis-3.

Identification and Extraction of Questions. We targeted popular web sites of the StackExchange network for data collection: StackOverflow,[10] SoftwareEngineering[11] and CodeReview.[12] StackOverflow is the largest Q&A website in software engineering, making it a popular target of mining studies. At the time of our analysis, it included over 20M questions and 29M answers for software developers. Questions can be asked about specific programming problems, algorithms, tools used by programmers, and practical problems related to software development. Testing the database access code also falls into these categories. However, the guidelines of StackOverflow say that the best "*questions have a bit of source code in them.*" So more generic questions, not closely related to source code, are often discouraged as out-of-scope or opinion-based. General discussions are preferred on the SoftwareEngineering site of StackExchange. We included this site as we were interested in higher, conceptual-level problems as well; not only those related to the source code. Another valuable source for discussions in the StackExchange network is CodeReview. There, developers can ask for suggestions on a given piece of code. As they often include test code, we considered questions from CodeReview as well.

From these three Q&A websites, we selected our candidate questions according to the following criteria:

(a) *Scope.* We decided to select questions if (i) they explicitly mention testing in their title, and (ii) they use database access terms in their description (*e.g.,* DAO, SQL). For this filtering, we loaded the dumps of StackExchange sites into a database. We created full-text indices on both the titles and question bodies. Then we queried them, so the description had to match (`database | (data & access) | sql | dao | pdo) & test` and the title had to match `test`. The full-text search handled normalised text so stemmed words were also considered (*e.g.,* test-*ing*, database-*s*). Notice that StackOverflow has a tagging system for classification. However, the use of these tags is up to the user, who can easily omit them. Besides, the tagging system is different for the three sites considered, which led us to our alternative approach.

(b) *Impact and quality.* Due to the potentially large number of questions and our limited resources, we targeted posts with higher impact and better quality. For this reason, we relied on the scoring system of StackExchange. No upvotes or a negative score indicates problems, *e.g.,* an unclear, or out-of-scope question. Therefore we excluded posts with zero or negative ratings.

We used the StackOverflow dump published by StackExchange in December 2019, and the dumps of SoftwareEngineering and CodeReview published in March 2020. A total number of 1,837 questions matched the criteria: 41 on CodeReview, 174 on SoftwareEngineering and 1,622 on StackOverflow (see Table 2). We did a first manual screening of questions on the different sites. We

---

[10] http://stackoverflow.com.

[11] http://softwareengineering.stackexchange.com.

[12] http://codereview.stackexchange.com.

observed that questions on CodeReview and SofwareEngineering were closer to our scope. Therefore, we decided to select more questions from these sites and to aim at a higher quality. To reach a 99% confidence level with a 5% margin of error, we set a threshold for a minimum score of 1 for CodeReview, 3 for SoftwareEngineering, and 13 for StackOverflow.

Table 2. Overview of the questions selected from StackExchange sites

Source	Candidate questions	Selected questions	False positives
CodeReview	41	41	3
SoftwareEngineering	174	140	25
StackOverflow	1,622	351	86
Total	1,837	532	114

Manual Classification of Database Testing Issues. After collecting the 532 questions, we manually inspected them. We followed an open coding process often applied to construct taxonomies or systematic mapping studies [20,29]. In this approach, participants apply labels to concepts found in the text of artefacts. Then the tags are organised into an overall structure. During the process, labels and categories might be merged and renamed [20]. We performed the classification process in three main rounds. First, we did a trial round with a random set of 100 questions, wherein two of the authors assigned labels to the artefacts. The goal was to see whether we need to apply changes to our selection criteria and to test the classification platform that we implemented for this purpose. After the first round, we implemented a few adjustments to our platform. For the second round, we labeled the remaining questions with the help of two more authors. In the last round, we resolved conflicts where needed.

Each artefact was labeled by two of the four participants, randomly assigned to them. The platform showed the question and its relevant metadata (score, timestamp, tags) along with a link to the original discussion thread for further inspection. We followed a multi-label approach. Each participant could assign multiple labels to the artefact from the list of existing labels in the database. If needed, they could create new tags too. In principle, existing labels should not be shown to participants. But as we expected a high number of tags, showing the existing ones could help us using consistent naming without introducing substantial bias. Indeed, the participants were not aware of the assignments.

After the second round, all 532 questions were labeled by two participants. At this point, one author reviewed all the tags and proposed the merging of those with identical meaning. This merging was discussed among authors and applied to the database. We finally agreed and used identical tags for 147 questions; partially agreed for 77 posts (only a subset of identical labels), and used entirely different tags for 308 questions. The high number of unique tags explains this relatively high number of conflicts (72.37%). Indeed, at this point, the database had 290 different labels. Thus, participants took advantage of the multi-label classification and captured various aspects of questions.

To resolve conflicts, a third tagger was assigned to review each conflicting artefact. This third person was a randomly selected author who took part in the classification but did not label the same question beforehand. The system showed the labels of the previous taggers, and the reviewer could accept or discard them. Minor modifications were also allowed, if necessary.

At the end of this process, one author carefully reviewed all the tags and organised them into categories. This categorisation was then discussed among the authors in multiple rounds. As an outcome, a taxonomy was constructed with 83 database testing issues in 7 main categories. In the rest of this section, we present this taxonomy together with qualitative examples.

3.2   Taxonomy of Database Testing Issues

Usman *et al.* reviewed taxonomies in software engineering and found the hierarchical form the most frequently used classification structure [29]. We adopted this representation as an efficient approach to organise our findings. In this form, there is a parent-child (*is-a*) relationship between categories, and one category has additional subcategories. Categories correspond to issues or problems raised in the question, and subcategories represent subtypes of a problem. Consider, *e.g.*, *Mocking Persistence Layer* as a specialised type of *Mocking*-related issues.

Figure 3 shows the final structure of the taxonomy. There are a total number of 83 leaf issues organised in 7 main (root) categories. For each root category, we show the total number of questions labelled with such problems. The distribution of the corresponding questions over the three sites is also provided. For example, the *Mocking* category had 54 questions including 8 from CodeReview, 17 from StackExchange, and 29 from StackOverflow. Recall that we had a multi-label approach, so one question could represent mixed problems. Thus, a question can belong to more categories in the hierarchical taxonomy.

We observe intriguing technical and conceptual difficulties, and we differentiate between them in Fig. 3. We mark the technical problems with ⚡ and the conceptual ones with 🎓. It is interesting to observe the origin of questions for those abstraction levels. Higher-level, conceptual problems mainly originate from SoftwareEngineering, especially for *Maintainability/Testability* or *Method*. Technical problems are closer to the source code and mostly originate from *StackOverflow*, especially for the *Framework/Tool Usage* category. Questions from CodeReview cover both abstraction levels, but most of them relate to the general *Best Practices* category. None of them deals with *Framework/Tool Usage*. Below, we describe and illustrate each main problem category. We cite posts on StackExchange sites with *SE* notation. Due to space limitation, these references can be found in our replication package [1].

⚡ **DB Handling.** The most prevalent technical issues are related to the management of the database: we found 145 questions in this category. Indeed, many

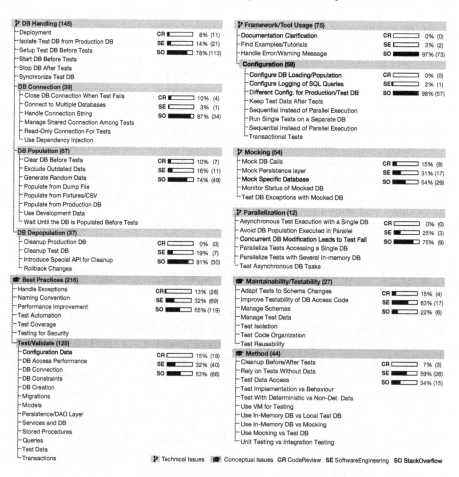

Fig. 3. Taxonomy of issues faced by developers when testing database access code

have problems initialising the database before executing the tests. This includes starting the database, configuring it, and populating it with test data. The test database population was often mentioned as a root cause of performance issues. These initialisation steps are critical as they have to be performed before test executions. As a developer complained: "*This whole thing takes quite some time (...). Having this run as part of our CI (...) is not a problem, but running locally takes a long time and really prohibits running them before committing code*" *SE1*. Solutions often include performance tweaks, *e.g.,* having an in-memory DB for local tests or ensuring that time-critical parts of the initialisation are executed only when needed. Instead of re-initialising the database before running the tests, an alternative is to clean it up *after* running the tests. This ensures that a failing test does not leave the environment in an inconsistent state *SE2*. Many recommend transactional tests (*i.e.,* wrap tests in transactions) for this purpose, so that a rollback can recover the initial state of the database. An advantage is that it can be significantly cheaper than recreating it. This, however, is not possible for testing DB access that already relies on transactions. As a desired feature, this is also supported by many testing frameworks. Some questions came from situations when the design does not support data deletion *SE3*. Others faced issues keeping a test DB in synch with a production or development DB *SE4*; while many had problems handling the connection to a test DB *SE5, SE6, SE7*.

🝆 **Framework/Tool Usage.** A large number of problems (75) concern the use of a concrete tool or framework. Most of them relate to configuring a framework for a dedicated database in a test/development or production environment *SE8, SE9*. These questions have high scores suggesting that many developers suffer from such issues. For example, a question to configure Django *SE9* was voted up 59 times and stared by 16 users. Similarly, developers ask help for different DB initialisation (*e.g.,* running scripts, using dumps or fixtures), or cleanup configurations *SE10*. Interestingly, in some cases, they want to keep the test database after running their tests for debugging purposes *SE11*. Many also ask for guidance to solve a particular error message in the testing framework, *e.g.,* misusing transactional tests *SE12*, or to configure in-memory databases *SE13*.

🝆 **Mocking.** Mocks can help by isolating the tests (*i.e.,* cutting off dependencies), and by avoiding the performance drawbacks of databases (*e.g.,* avoiding IO). Many questions indicate that developers need help in mocking the persistence layer. As a first step, an important design decision they have to make is the level at which they implement the mocks. For example, a developer reasoned in a question as follows: "*I could either mock this object at a high level (...), so that there are no calls to the SQL at all (...) Or I could do it at a very low level, by creating a MockSQLQueryFactory that instead of actually querying the database just provides mock data back*" *SE14*. Recommendations depend on the objectives, as an answer says: "*Higher level approaches are more appropriate for unit testing. Lower-level approaches are more appropriate for integration testing.*" Broader questions were also asked about the benefits of mocking *SE15*, or guidelines to mock the data access layer *SE16, SE17*. Technical questions tackled, for example, emulating exceptions in a mocked database *SE18*. When mocking is unfeasible, it can indicate poor software design *SE19*. Stored procedures *SE20* and views *SE21* also made mocking impossible in other systems.

🝆 **Parallelization.** We observed some (12) technical problems related to parallel test executions. These were closely related, so we grouped them in this category. One of the highest-rated questions was about turning off the parallel execution of tests in *sbt* (a build tool for Scala and Java) *SE22*. The developer complained that a project "*mutates state in a test database concurrently, leading to the test to fail.*" Likewise, asynchronous or lazy calculations led to challenging bug hunts *SE23* They also asked for advice to make test execution parallel, *e.g.,* to handle a dedicated in-memory database per thread *SE24*.

☛ **Best Practices.** The most frequently used labels were about testing best practices for DB applications. Developers either look for general advice or explicitly want to know about best practices. The highest-rated question has 331 upvotes entitled "*What's the best strategy for unit-testing database-driven applications?*" *SE25*. It generates discussion on mocking vs testing against an actual database. In the answers, mocking is mostly recommended for unit testing, while a copy of the database is favoured for more complex databases. In other cases, a combined approach might be needed: "*Ideally I want to test the data access layer using mocking without the need to connect to a database and then unit test the store procedure in a separate set of tests*" *SE16*. Best practices are also sought for performance improvements *SE26, SE1, SE27*. In particular, where mocking is not an option, solutions mostly advise the use of in-memory databases to reduce IO operations. Other topics include testing for security vulnerabilities, *e.g.,* looking for static analysers to spot SQL injection attacks *SE28*. Likewise, some questions look for tools to measure test coverage. They want to know, for example, the coverage of executed queries in test cases *SE29*. A majority of these questions were grouped under *Test/Validate*. These are looking for advice on testing or validating a specific code or DB entity. For example, SQL queries embedded in code *SE30*, database migration *SE31* or transactions *SE32*.

📌 **Maintainability/Testability.** Several questions tried to address maintainability problems or the testability of the database access code. In a question, a developer struggled with a system that validated RESTful APIs with SQL queries in its integration tests *SE33*. As he summed up his root problem: "*a small change in the DB structure often results in several man days wasted on updating the SQL and the SQL building logic in the integration tests.*" The developer wanted to wipe out the SQL code from the tests entirely. In the answer, they discouraged him from doing so. They acknowledged that relying on the queries can be a good practice to verify the database state. Instead, it was recommended to improve the maintainability of the tests: (i) by reducing the coupling inside the codebase (one table per module), and (ii) by splitting the tests into smaller pieces. In another question, a developer wanted to reduce the maintenance effort by omitting the tests of the ORM layer. He was, however, afraid of giving up on aiming for a 100% coverage. As he wrote it, "*Our test databases are a bit messy and are never reseted, hence it's impossible to validate any data (and that is out of my control).*" In the answers, they supported him that it is important to balance coverage and prioritise efforts then suggested generating the tests for the ORM layer. Others pointed out that preparing the environment of testing the database access code is also troublesome. For example, a developer complained: "*The problem I ran into was that I spent a lot of time maintaining the code to set up the test environment more than the tests*" *SE34*. Many questions were also related to the management of changing schema or test data. As a general guideline, a recommendation said: "*I would apply a single rule: keep your test data close to your test. Test is all about maintenance: they should be designed with maintenance in mind, hence, keep it simple*" *SE35*.

📌 **Method.** Many developers were concerned about the problems of their testing method. The most frequent arguments were whether DB-dependent code should be tested via unit or integration tests *SE36,SE37,SE38,SE39,SE25*. A regular claim was that "*unit tests should not deal with the database, integra-*

tion tests deal with the database" SE37. Recommendations target to maximise the isolation of unit tests and decouple the database, *e.g.,* through mocking. In contrast, integration tests aim to test more complex structures by relying on the database. Interesting questions related to populating a database before tests, *e.g.,* whether data should be dynamically generated or pre-populated beforehand *SE40.* A re-occurring discussion was on the use of an in-memory database versus a mocking strategy *SE41.* When performance or decoupling the tests from the database was more critical, the choice was to mock. Otherwise, we could see cases where mocking was not possible (*e.g.,* because of stored procedures or views). The in-memory database was then considered as a good compromise to test the database access. It indeed solves the portability issues of testing against an actual DB and improves the performance. Compared to mocking, the testing can be more extensive, *e.g.,* it enables the tests to validate embedded SQL queries. In some cases, however, the in-memory database differs significantly from the production database. This can be a problem as some DB-specific features cannot be tested, *e.g.,* a special SQL syntax *SE42.*

3.3   Discussion and Implications

Below, we discuss the main observations we made in our investigation, together with actionable directions for researchers and practitioners.

Maintainability of DB Tests. A frequent issue was to keep tests in sync with database schema changes, as developers hardly get any support for this task. Many also struggled with isolating tests. Our study is exploratory by nature, and more studies are needed to understand the factors affecting the maintainability of database-related test code. Understanding more from the practices of the developers, and good, maintainable database test code [2,23] is a promising direction. Alternatively, automated approaches could help in regular tasks of developers. Some approaches aim to identify the system fragments impacted by schema changes [16,17]. Such methods could be extended to the testing context, *e.g.,* to maintain a mapping between schema elements and mocks.

In-Memory DB vs Actual DB vs Mocking. We have seen many points in favour and against whether tests should rely on mocking, in-memory databases, or the actual database. In the systems analyzed in our motivational study, we found that 19 out of the 72 projects (26%) used mocks: 17 had Mockito,[13] and 2 had EasyMock tests.[14] This low number surprised us, as mocking was *the* recommended approach for unit tests to decouple them from the DB. This is in line with the findings of Trautsch and Grabowski [27] who observed only a small amount of unit tests in open source Python projects, especially with mocks. A potential explanation is that it is easier to set up an in-memory database and rely on integration tests; instead of bothering with the implementation of mocks, despite its advantages. In any respect, developers need help in the implementation of database-related tests. They would benefit from automated support in

---

[13] https://site.mockito.org/.
[14] https://easymock.org/.

this context. Some authors already explored the generation of tests with mocks [3,19]. The emergence and initial success of such tools (*e.g.,* EasyMock,[14] Mock-Neat[15]) is encouraging to develop similar approaches.

DB Support in Testing Frameworks. In our motivational study, we excluded projects with failing tests. Many failures were due to misconfigured testing environments. The systems either (i) relied on an external database for their tests, or (ii) used in-memory databases, but did not set them up correctly. We observed related problems in our qualitative study: many developers struggle to configure frameworks with multiple database connections. Testing frameworks could better support developers in this task with DB-dedicated features, especially if these are configurable from the build systems. Some frameworks already provide similar functionalities. For example, *Spring Test* has *JdbcTestUtils,*[16] a collection of JDBC-related functions. It also provides support for test fixtures and transactional tests. Another framework, Rails, offers similar features. We observed that the most desired features are related to the initial configuration of databases, and the efficient recovery of the database state between successive tests. Developers' needs remain unexplored in this field, and further research is necessary to improve testing practices as far as DB access is concerned.

4   Threats to Validity

Construct Validity. In our motivational study, we rely on SQLInspect to identify the database access methods of projects, *i.e.,* methods involved in querying the database. As a static tool, it may miss some DB methods, particularly in case of highly dynamic query construction. For test coverage, we rely on JaCoCo, a state-of-the-art tool used in industry and academia [14]. It might miss execution paths, and its configuration can influence the coverage results (*e.g.,* due to missing classes from the classpath). To avoid this, we executed tests according to Maven standards and excluded projects with failing tests.

Internal Validity. In our qualitative analysis, the manual classification of StackExchange questions is exposed to subjectiveness. To mitigate this risk, two authors examined each post independently, and a third author resolved conflicts.

External Validity. Our motivational study is exploratory by nature. It considers various types of projects in terms of application domain, size, and intensity of DB interactions. They are, however, all from Libraris.io and limited to the Java programming language. Projects not considered in our study might lead to other results. In our qualitative study, we extracted questions from three different StackExchange sites, intending to reach a higher level of diversity. We selected higher-ranked questions which are likely to influence more developers. This might introduce a bias towards the posts we selected. In reality, developers might face even more diverse challenges when (not) testing database code.

---

[15] https://github.com/nomemory/mockneat.

[16] https://docs.spring.io/spring/ docs/current/spring-frameworkreference/testing. html.

5   Related Work

Our research work got motivated and inspired by more general studies analysing testing practices and related maintainability issues. Beller *et al.* [4] conducted a large-scale field study on testing practices, monitoring 5 months of activities from 416 software engineers. They observed, among others, that (i) developers rarely run tests in the IDE; (ii) Test-Driven Development is not widely spread among the participants; and (iii) developers usually spend 25% of their time on testing. Gonzalez *et al.* [12] analysed over 80K open-source projects and found that (i) only 17% of those projects included test cases, and (ii) 76% of them did not implement testing patterns that would ease maintainability.

Several researchers have proposed approaches for testing database applications. Deng *et al.* [10] propose a white-box testing approach for web applications. They extract URLs from the application source code to create a path graph, from which they then generate test cases. Ran *et al.* [22] propose a similar framework, but for black-box testing web applications. They use a directed graph of the webpage transitions and database interactions as input for generating test sequences, and for capturing how the database updates along with the test cases. Kapfhammer and Soffa [15] present a test coverage technique that monitors database interactions. They employ instrumentation of the application and test cases to capture when SQL is used. Tuya *et al.* [28] define a criterion to measure SQL query coverage. They argue that SQL queries embedded in code are not taken into account for test design.

In this paper, we collect and classify questions in StackExchange sites, through a multi-tagging approach, itself inspired by previous work in our field. Gonzalez *et al.* [13] propose a 5-way classifier approach that assigns multiple tags to StackOverflow questions. They use a dataset composed of a training set of over 3 million questions and a test set of 20 thousand questions. Vasilescu *et al.* [30] investigate the relationships on StackOverflow questions/answers and GitHub commits. They find a positive correlation indicating that the activity of developers on StackOverflow affects their commit activity on GitHub.

Our qualitative analysis revealed that many StackExchange questions were related to Mocking, a testing technique to simulate dependencies, often used to isolate the component under test. Spadini *et al.* [25] empirically analyse the usage of mocking dependencies on testing. They analyse 4 projects with a total of 2,178 test dependencies and they survey 105 developers on their findings. The results indicate that mocking is often used on dependencies that would have made testing difficult to depend on external resources. Other popular topics we found in StackExchange questions were related to best practices of testing database code, specially understandability. Alsharif *et al.* [2] study the understandability of auto-generated database tests. They argue that studies focusing on creating database tests do not take into account the human cost to understand such tests.

In summary, the analysis of related research shows that DB access code is sufficiently different from normal code to warrant specialised approaches. Several proposals were made to support database access code testing. Nevertheless, no research work has investigated *how* developers test DB access code *in practice*, nor the main *issues* they face in this context.

6 Conclusion

We present a study of the challenges faced by developers when testing database access code in practice. As a motivational study, we first studied the extent to which database code is covered by tests by analysing 72 open-source Java projects. We found that 46% of those projects did not test half of their database methods and 33% of them did not test the database communication at all.

We then conducted a qualitative study to understand the poor test coverage of database access code. We analysed 532 StackExchange questions related to database code testing and identified a total of 83 issues, classified in a taxonomy of 7 main categories. We found that developers mostly look for insights on general best practices to test DB access code. Concerning technical issues, they ask mostly about DB handling, mocking, parallelisation, or framework/tool usage.

We address an unexplored field of understanding testing practices of database communication and to identify the main difficulties that hamper developers. Our findings can serve as a starting point to direct researchers where practitioners need assistance. They open the door to complementary studies focused on particular categories of issues as well as their link with actual bugs. Further investigation is needed, however, such as the validation of the taxonomy with testing practitioners, or the analysis of the *answers* given to forum questions about database code testing. Immediate feedback of practitioners and answers may contain solutions to the issues we identified in this paper, that could guide researchers towards dedicated techniques and tools to assist developers when testing DB access code.

✎ Replication Package. We made all data, scripts, and detailed results of our study publicly available in a replication package [1].

Acknowledgements. This work is supported by (a) the F.R.S.-FNRS and FWO-Vlaanderen via the EOS project 30446992 SECO-ASSIST and (b) Flanders Make vzw.

References

1. Repl. pkg. https://github.com/csnagy/caise2021-db-manipulation-testing
2. Alsharif, A., et al.: What factors make SQL test cases understandable for testers? a human study of automated test data generation techniques. In: ICSME (2019)
3. Arcuri, A., Fraser, G., Just, R.: Private API access and functional mocking in automated unit test generation. In: Proceedings of ICST (2017)
4. Beller, M., Gousios, G., Panichella, A., Zaidman, A.: When, how, and why developers (do not) test in their ides. In: Proc. ESEC/FSE (2015)
5. Castelein, J., Aniche, M., Soltani, M., Panichella, A., van Deursen, A.: Search-based test data generation for SQL queries. In: Proceedings of ICSE (2018)
6. Chays, D., Dan, S., Frankl, P.G., Vokolos, F.I., Weber, E.J.: A framework for testing database applications. In: Proceedings of ISSTA (2000)

7. Chen, T.H., Shang, W., Hassan, A.E., Nasser, M., Flora, P.: Detecting problems in the database access code of large scale systems. In: Proceedings of ICSE (2016)
8. Cleve, A., Brogneaux, A., Hainaut, J.: A conceptual approach to database applications evolution. In: Proceedings of ER (2010)
9. Delplanque, J., Etien, A., Anquetil, N., Ducasse, S.: Recommendations for evolving relational databases. In: Proceedings of CAiSE (2020)
10. Deng, Y., Frankl, P., Wang, J.: Testing web database applications. SIGSOFT Softw. Eng. Notes 29(5), 1–10 (2004)
11. Garg, D., Datta, A.: Test case prioritization due to database changes in web applications. In: Proceedings of ICST (2012)
12. Gonzalez, D., Santos, J.C.S., Popovich, A., Mirakhorli, M., Nagappan, M.: A large-scale study on the usage of testing patterns that address maintainability attributes: patterns for ease of modification, diagnoses, and comprehension. In: MSR (2017)
13. González, J.R.C., Romero, J.J.F., Guerrero, M.G., Calderón, F.: Multi-class multi-tag classifier system for stackoverflow questions. In: Proceedings of ROPEC (2015)
14. Ivanković, M., Petrović, G., Just, R., Fraser, G.: Code coverage at Google. In: Proceedings of ESEC/FSE (2019)
15. Kapfhammer, G.M., Soffa, M.L.: Database-aware test coverage monitoring. In: Proceedings of the 1st India Software Engineering Conference (2008)
16. Maule, A., Emmerich, W., Rosenblum, D.: Impact analysis of database schema changes. In: Proceedings of ICSE 2008 (2008)
17. Meurice, L., Nagy, C., Cleve, A.: Detecting and preventing program inconsistencies under database schema evolution. In: Proceedings of QRS (2016)
18. Meurice, L., Nagy, C., Cleve, A.: Static analysis of dynamic database usage in java systems. In: Proceedings of CAiSE (2016)
19. Pasternak, B., Tyszberowicz, S., Yehudai, A.: Genutest: a unit test and mock aspect generation tool. In: Hardware and Software: Verification and Testing (2008)
20. Petersen, K., Vakkalanka, S., Kuzniarz, L.: Guidelines for conducting systematic mapping studies in software engineering: an update. IST 64, 1–18 (2015)
21. Qiu, D., Li, B., Su, Z.: An empirical analysis of the co-evolution of schema and code in database applications. In: Proceedings of ESEC/FSE (2013)
22. Ran, L., et al.: Building test cases and oracles to automate the testing of web database applications. Inf. Softw. Technol. 51(2), 460–477 (2009)
23. Riaz, M., Mendes, E., Tempero, E.: Towards maintainability prediction for relational database-driven software applications: evidence from software practitioners. In: Proceedings of Advances in Software Engineering (2010)
24. Rosero, R.H., Gómez, O.S., Rafael, G.D.R.: Regression testing of database applications under an incremental software development setting. IEEE Access 5, 18419–18428 (2017)
25. Spadini, D., Aniche, M., Bruntink, M., Bacchelli, A.: Mock objects for testing java systems. Empirical Softw. Eng. 24(3), 1461–1498 (2018). https://doi.org/10.1007/s10664-018-9663-0
26. Stonebraker, M., Deng, D., Brodie, M.L.: Application-database co-evolution: a new design and development paradigm. In: New England Database Day (2017)
27. Trautsch, F., Grabowski, J.: Are there any unit tests? an empirical study on unit testing in open source python projects. In: Proceedings of ICST (2017)
28. Tuya, J., Suárez-Cabal, M.J., de la Riva, C.: Full predicate coverage for testing SQL database queries. Softw. Testing, Verification Reliab. 20, 237–288 (2010)
29. Usman, M., Britto, R., Börstler, J., Mendes, E.: Taxonomies in software engineering: a systematic mapping study and a revised taxonomy development method. Inf. Softw. Technol. 85, 43–59 (2017)

30. Vasilescu, B., Filkov, V., Serebrenik, A.: Stackoverflow and github: Associations between software development and crowdsourced knowledge. In: Proceedings of ICSC (2013)
31. Vassiliadis, P., Zarras, A.V.: Survival in schema evolution: Putting the lives of survivor and dead tables in counterpoint. In: Proceedings of CAiSE (2017)

Semi-contingent Task Durations: Characterization and Controllability

Marco Franceschetti$^{(\boxtimes)}$ [ID] and Johann Eder [ID]

Department of Informatics-Systems, Universität Klagenfurt, Klagenfurt, Austria
{marco.franceschetti,johann.eder}@aau.at

Abstract. Traditionally, process designers distinguish between two categories of task durations: contingent and non-contingent. The duration of contingent tasks can only be observed by the controlling agent, the process manager, but not controlled. The duration of non-contingent tasks, instead, is fully under the control of the controlling agent - from the start of the task, until it terminates. In many applications we found, nevertheless, a third category, which we call semi-contingent. A semi-contingent task duration is controllable by the agent, but only until the task starts. We characterize and formally define this additional category of duration. We propose a novel procedure based on constraint propagation to check the dynamic controllability of processes featuring contingent, non-contingent and semi-contingent durations. We formally prove that this procedure is sound and complete, and experimentally show its feasibility.

Keywords: Process scheduling · Task durations · Dynamic controllability

1 Introduction

Modeling and verifying temporal aspects of a business process are essential tasks for effective process management. Modeling temporal aspects includes defining deadlines, durations, and other temporal constraints [4,7]. Verification of the temporal qualities aims at checking whether a given process model meets specific quality criteria. In particular, it is essential to know beforehand whether time failures can be avoided, or whether a process controller can steer a process execution, so that no temporal constraint is violated [5].

Research in the field aims at introducing modeling constructs allowing the adequate representation of relevant temporal aspects, and developing algorithms for reasoning about relevant temporal properties of process models. In recent years, there has been increasing awareness on the distinction between activities whose duration is under the control of an agent, a process controller, and activities whose duration cannot be controlled but merely observed at run-time [24]. These uncontrollable durations are called *contingent*, e.g., bank money transfers within the EU, which are guaranteed to take from 1 to 4 working days, but the

© Springer Nature Switzerland AG 2021
M. La Rosa et al. (Eds.): CAiSE 2021, LNCS 12751, pp. 246–261, 2021.
https://doi.org/10.1007/978-3-030-79382-1_15

client cannot control the actual duration. In contrast, durations under the control of the agent are known as *non-contingent*, e.g., upon receipt of an invoice with 30 d time of payment, it is at the client's discretion when to settle it within the next 30 d.

While the distinction of contingent and non-contingent durations as modeling notions is well established, it does not sufficiently cover a relevant class of activities, which we call *semi-contingent*. An agent may control the semi-contingent duration of an activity, but only until this activity starts. An example of such an activity is a delivery, which lasts between 1 and 7 d, as selected by the client; however, once the shipping starts, it cannot be changed to a faster or slower option.

Contingent activities in processes led to the formulation of *dynamic controllability* [5,24] as the preferred criterion for temporal correctness. Dynamic controllability requires the existence of a dynamic schedule, which assigns timestamps for starting and finishing activities in a reactive manner, in response to the actual durations of contingent activities observed at run-time. Nevertheless, this falls short in the presence of semi-contingent durations.

Treating semi-contingent durations as contingent is stricter than necessary, and might reject viable process definitions as not dynamically controllable. Treating semi-contingent durations as non-contingent, instead, is too weak to exclude time failures: it might admit processes, where each admissible dynamic schedule requires some activities to start without knowing when they need to complete, thus forcing their durations to be adjusted while they execute. We described such particular behavior as the *sudden termination problem* in [8], where we analyzed constellations of constraints leading to this problem in depth. Here we generalize this notion of semi-contingent duration, and provide a novel way of checking for dynamic controllability in the presence of non-, semi-, and contingent durations by applying rules for constraint propagation.

To this end, with this paper, we provide the following contributions:

– The precise characterization of semi-contingent activity duration;
– A process model which captures all contingent, non-contingent, and semi-contingent durations;
– The STNSU, a novel type of Temporal Constraint Network for expressing semi-contingent durations;
– A procedure to check whether a process model is dynamically controllable, based on a constraint propagation approach for the STNSU.

These contributions aim to capture the temporal properties of information systems, their context, and the temporal requirements for process execution more accurately, and to provide process controllers with better means to meet these requirements.

The remainder of this paper is structured as follows: in Sect. 2 we characterize semi-contingent durations. In Sect. 3 we introduce a lean process model that allows the modeling of semi-contingent activities. In Sect. 4 we introduce the STNSU, formalize dynamic controllability, and define a checking procedure. In Sect. 5 we discuss the evaluation of the checking procedure. In Sect. 6 we discuss related work, and in Sect. 7 we draw conclusions.

2   Characterization of Semi-contingent Durations

We call an activity resp. its duration *semi-contingent*, if the controller might decide the duration (resp., the time-point of the activity's termination) only until the activity starts, generalizing our previous work in [8]. We claim that catering for *semi-contingent* durations is necessary to correctly represent temporal properties of processes. Let's consider, as an example, a process for kitchen manufacturing, in which the producer of custom made kitchens stipulates a contract with a supplier of glass panels for cabinets. The manufacturer may choose the time of procurement of the panels in a time window between 6 and 8 weeks after placing the order. Such a choice is made in coordination with the other kitchen manufacturing activities. However, once the exact procurement date is fixed (e.g., after 48 d), it cannot be changed, as also the supplier needs to coordinate the glass production and procurement of materials with other activities. Thus, here procurement is a semi-contingent activity, since the kitchen producer can fix its duration only until it starts.

We argue the relevance of semi-contingent durations with a selection of examples from different domains which inherently have this property:

- Shipping products with express delivery or regular delivery: once a product is handed over to the courier, shipping time cannot be changed anymore.
- Fixing the number of DNA amplification cycles for a COVID-19 PCR test: once the number of cycles is fixed, the duration of the test is determined.
- Administering a sedative drug: some are effective faster, others have longer activation times. As only one can be administered per day, once the drug is administered, the sedation time is fixed.
- Running computations on a configurable cloud VM: once the VM configuration is chosen and the job is launched, its duration is determined.

Now we argue why these types of activities should not be modeled as contingent or non-contingent. Figure 1 shows a minimal example with three activities: A and B are executed concurrently, followed by C. Activity A is contingent, with a duration between 10 and 15 time units. Activity B is semi-contingent, with a duration between 10 and 15 time units. Activity C is semi-contingent, with a duration between 2 and 7 time units. A and B must be synchronized, i.e. start at the same time (constraint $c0$), and end at the same time (constraint $c1$); the process may last up to 21 time units (constraint $c2$).

If we treat activity B as non-contingent, the process is considered as dynamically controllable - whenever A terminates, the controller can set the termination of B. However, when B is semi-contingent, and it is about to start at the same time when A starts, the controller does not yet know how long A will last, and hence which duration of B to choose to meet constraint $c1$. So, if B is semi-contingent, the process is not dynamically controllable. Hence, considering semi-contingent activities as non-contingent leads to wrong results.

If we treat C as a contingent activity, the process is not dynamically controllable because the sequence of A and C might take more than the deadline

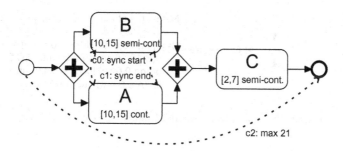

Fig. 1. BPMN-like notation for a minimal process with A contingent, and B, C semi-contingent activities, and temporal constraints.

from $c2$. However, as the controller might decide the duration of C after the termination of A, she can guarantee that all constraints are observed, and the process is dynamically controllable.

To summarize: regarding semi-contingent activities as non-contingent leads to wrongly considering processes as dynamically controllable while they are not. Regarding semi-contingent activities as contingent is too strict, and wrongly considers processes as not dynamically controllable.

3 Modeling Processes with Semi-contingent Durations

3.1 Process Model

For most general applicability, here we introduce a minimal process model, which is sufficient to capture the various duration types and temporal constraints.

We consider the most common control-flow patterns: sequence, inclusive and disjunctive splits, and the corresponding joins. We consider activity durations, process deadline, and upper- and lower-bound constraints between events (start and end of activities). We measure time in *chronons*, representing, e.g., hours, days, ..., encoded as natural numbers forming a time axis starting at *zero*. A duration is defined as the distance between two time-points on the time axis.

We distinguish between non-contingent, semi-contingent, and contingent activities. The duration of contingent activities cannot be controlled; thus, it cannot be known when they will actually terminate. The process controller may, however, control the duration of non-contingent activities at any time. A semi-contingent activity, in contrast, requires to know, at its start time, when it has to terminate: the process controller can set its duration until it starts.

Definition 1 (Process Model). *A process P is a tuple (N, E, C, Ω), where:*

- *N is a set of nodes n with $n.type \in \{start, activity, xor - split, xor - join, par - split, par - join, end\}$. Each $n \in N$ is associated with $n.s$ and $n.e$, the start and end event of n. From N we derive $N^e = \bigcup\{n.s, n.e | n \in N\}$.*
- *E is a set of edges $e = (n1, n2)$ defining precedence constraints.*

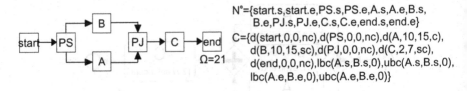

Fig. 2. Example process model from the process of Fig. 1.

- C is a set of temporal constraints:
  - duration constraints $d(n, n_{min}, n_{max}, dur)$ $\forall n \in N$, where $n_{min}, n_{max} \in$ $\mathbb{N}$, $dur \in \{c, sc, nc\}$, stating that n takes some time in $[n_{min}, n_{max}]$. n can be contingent ($dur = c$), semi-contingent ($dur = sc$), non-contingent ($dur = nc$);
  - upper-bound constraints $ubc(a, b, \delta)$, where $a, b \in N^e$, $\delta \in \mathbb{N}$, requiring that $b \leq a + \delta$;
  - lower-bound constraints $lbc(a, b, \delta)$, where $a, b \in N^e$, $\delta \in \mathbb{N}$, requiring that $b \geq a + \delta$.
- $\Omega \in \mathbb{N}$ is the maximum process duration.

Figure 2 shows the process model defined after Definition 1 for the process of Fig. 1.

We now define the temporal semantics of the process model.

3.2   Temporal Semantics

We define the temporal semantics of temporally constrained process definitions by defining which scenarios are valid. A scenario is a run of the process (a process instance) with timestamps when each event (starting and ending of process steps) occurred. A scenario is *valid* if it satisfies all temporal constraints.

Definition 2 (Valid Scenario). Let $P(N, E, C, \Omega)$ be a process model. Let σ be a scenario for P, assigning to each time-point t a timestamp $\bar{t}$. σ is a valid scenario for P iff:

1. $\forall (n1, n2) \in E$, $\overline{n1.e} \leq \overline{n2.s}$;
2. $\forall d(n, n_{min}, n_{max}, [c|sc|nc]) \in C$, $\overline{n.s} + n_{min} \leq \overline{n.e} \leq \overline{n.s} + n_{max}$;
3. $\forall ubc(a, b, \delta) \in C$, $\bar{b} \leq \bar{a} + \delta$;
4. $\forall lbc(a, b, \delta) \in C$, $\bar{a} + \delta \leq \bar{b}$;
5. $\overline{end.e} \leq \overline{start.s} + \Omega$.

It is easy to see that the scenario for the process in Fig. 2 given by: $\overline{start.s} = \overline{start.e} = \overline{PS.s} = \overline{PS.e} = 0, \overline{A.s} = \overline{B.s} = 2, \overline{A.e} = \overline{B.e} = 15, \overline{PJ.s} = \overline{PJ.e} = 18, \overline{C.s} = 19, \overline{C.e} = \overline{end.s} = \overline{end.e} = 21$ is valid.

A valid scenario represents a run of the process without time failures. In the next section we discuss when a controller can guarantee execution without time failures despite uncertainties.

4 Controllability of Processes with Semi-contingent Durations

An execution strategy (schedule) for a process states when each activity should be started and when non- and semi-contingent activities should be terminated. If an execution strategy exists, we call the process controllable. Controllability is often considered too strict, e.g., it would not admit an activity to start immediately after the end of a contingent activity [5]. Dynamic controllability requires the existence of a dynamic execution strategy, where the observation of actual durations can influence the start- and end-time of subsequent activities. In the following we develop a method for checking whether a process model is dynamically controllable.

4.1 Simple Temporal Network with Semi-contingency and Uncertainty (STNSU)

Temporal Constraint Networks (TCNs) have been adopted in previous work (e.g., [5,22,25]) to check the temporal correctness of process models, in particular in the form of dynamic controllability of a Simple Temporal Network with Uncertainty (STNU) [20]. Following the considerations in Sect. 2, we argue that the STNU and the usual notions for temporal correctness fall short when a process model features semi-contingent durations. Therefore, we introduce a new TCN with increased expressiveness to cope with semi-contingent durations and show how to check its temporal correctness. We introduce here the Simple Temporal Network with Semi-Contingency and Uncertainty (STNSU), as a STNU extended with semi-contingent nodes and edges.

Definition 3 (Simple Temporal Network with Semi-Contingency and Uncertainty (STNSU)). *A STNSU is a tuple $\langle \mathcal{N}, \mathcal{E} \rangle$, where:*

- *$\mathcal{N}$ is a set of nodes, partitioned in:*
  - *$\mathcal{N}_n$ the set of non-contingent nodes;*
  - *$\mathcal{N}_c$ the set of contingent nodes;*
  - *$\mathcal{N}_s$ the set of semi-contingent nodes;*
- *$\mathcal{E}$ is a set of edges, partitioned in:*
  - *$\mathcal{E}_n$ the set of non-contingent edges of the form (A, B, δ), where $A \in \mathcal{N}$, and $B \in \mathcal{N}_n \cup \mathcal{N}_s$;*
  - *$\mathcal{E}_c$ the set of contingent edges of the form (A^C, l, u, C), where $A \in \mathcal{N}_n$, $C \in \mathcal{N}_c$, and $0 < l(e) < u(e)$;*
  - *$\mathcal{E}_s$ the set of semi-contingent edges of the form (A, a, b, S), where $A \in \mathcal{N}_n$, $S \in \mathcal{N}_s$, and $a \leq b$. A semi-contingent edge is a pair of non-contingent edges $(A, S, b), (S, A, -a) \in \mathcal{E}_n$.*

A STNSU is a directed weighted graph in which nodes represent time-points, and edges represent constraints between time-points. A special time-point *zero* marks the reference in time, after which all other time-points occur. Nodes and edges can be contingent, non-contingent, or semi-contingent: a node is contingent if it is the target of a contingent edge. A non-contingent edge of the form (A, B, δ) from A to B represents a constraint $B \leq A + \delta$ to be fulfilled. A contingent edge (or *link*) of the form (A^C, l, u, C) from A^C to C represents a constraint which is guaranteed to hold: in particular, that time-point C will be observed to take a value between l and u after time-point A^C.

Each semi-contingent node $S \in \mathcal{N}_s$ is associated to exactly one non-contingent node $A \in \mathcal{N}_n$ by a semi-contingent link $e = (A, a, b, S) \in \mathcal{E}_s$, which is a shorthand for a pair of non-contingent edges $(A, S, b), (S, A, -a)$. For brevity, we define $\alpha : \mathcal{N}_s \rightarrow \mathcal{N}_n$ as the function returning, for a semi-contingent node S, the non-contingent node A such that $e = (A, a, b, S) \in \mathcal{E}_s$: $\alpha(S) = A$. We call A the *dispatcher* of S.

4.2 Mapping Processes into STNSUs

Checking temporal qualities of processes is often based on mapping them into some TCN [5,22,25]. We can map a process model $P(N, E, C, \Omega)$ with semi-contingent durations into a STNSU $\langle \mathcal{N}, \mathcal{E} \rangle$ with the following mapping rules:

- Each $n.s \in P.N^e$ is mapped into a node in $\mathcal{N}_n$;
- Each $n.e \in P.N^e : d(n, n_{min}, n_{max}, nc) \in P.C$ is mapped into a node in $\mathcal{N}_n$;
- Each $n.e \in P.N^e : d(n, n_{min}, n_{max}, c) \in P.C$ is mapped into a node in $\mathcal{N}_c$;
- Each $n.e \in P.N^e : d(n, n_{min}, n_{max}, sc) \in P.C$ is mapped into a node in $\mathcal{N}_s$;
- Each $(n1, n2) \in P.E$ is mapped into an edge $e = (n2.s, n1.e, 0) \in \mathcal{E}_n$; $e_0 = (start.s, zero, 0)$ is added to $\mathcal{E}_n$;
- Each non-contingent duration constraint $d(n, n_{min}, n_{max}, nc) \in P.C$ is mapped into a pair of non-contingent edges $e_{max} = (n.s, n.e, n_{max})$ and $e_{min} = (n.e, n.s, -n_{min}) \in \mathcal{E}_n$;
- Each contingent duration constraint $d(n, n_{min}, n_{max}, c) \in P.C$ is mapped into a contingent edge $e = (n.s, n_{min}, n_{max}, n.e) \in \mathcal{E}_c$;
- Each semi-contingent duration constraint $d(n, n_{min}, n_{max}, sc) \in P.C$ is mapped into a semi-contingent edge $e = (n.s, n_{min}, n_{max}, n.e) \in \mathcal{E}_s$;
- For each constraint $ubc(a, b, \delta) \in P.C$ there is an edge $e = (a, b, \delta) \in \mathcal{E}_n$;
- For each constraint $lbc(a, b, \delta) \in P.C$ there is an edge $e = (b, a, -\delta) \in \mathcal{E}_n$;
- $P.\Omega$ is mapped into a non-contingent edge $e_\Omega = (start.s, end.e, \Omega)$.

Semi-contingent durations are mapped into semi-contingent STNSU edges, which are pairs of non-contingent edges, since the controller is allowed to take a decision on how long they may take, although only until they start. The STNSU derived from a process P with the above mapping rules encodes all time-points and constraints of P, i.e. it is *temporally equivalent* to P.

Figure 3 shows the STNSU derived by mapping the process model of Fig. 2. Note that in Fig. 3 we adopted the usual STNU notation with contingent edges dashed, inverted w.r.t. non-contingent edges, and labeled with the contingent time-point name; semi-contingent nodes are shaded. For a more compact presentation, in the figure we did not include nodes resulting from the mapping of the par-split and par-join, and compacted process start and end into single nodes.

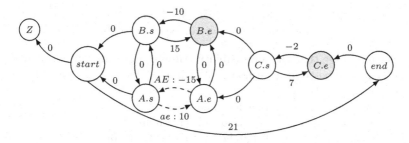

Fig. 3. STNSU derived from the example process shown in Fig. 2.

4.3 Dynamic Controllability of STNSUs

We define and formalize the dynamic controllability of a STNSU based on the definition of dynamic controllability of STNUs. [14] defines dynamic controllability as the existence of a complete, valid, and admissible dynamic execution strategy assigning timestamps to non-contingent nodes. Such a dynamic execution strategy might, in particular, react to the observed duration of contingent activities, however, only for assigning *future* time-points.

An execution strategy for a STNU is complete if it covers every possible combination of durations of contingent activities (for a formalization of this property, we refer to [2,14]); it is valid if it satisfies all temporal constraints; it is admissible if the assignment of a timestamp $\overline{T}$ to a non-contingent node T may depend on the timestamp of a node T' if $\overline{T'} \leq \overline{T}$.

For a complete, valid, and admissible dynamic execution strategy for a STNSU, we require in addition that the assignment of a timestamp to a semi-contingent node only depends on time-points which are before the timestamp of its dispatcher node, i.e. the assignment of a timestamp $\overline{S}$ for a semi-contingent node S may depend on the timestamp of node R, if $\overline{R} \leq \overline{\alpha(S)}$.

We express these admissibility properties formally by requiring that two scenarios assign the same time-point $\overline{T}$ to a non-contingent node T if they are equal up to time-point $\overline{T}$, and they assign the same time-point $\overline{S}$ to a semi-contingent node S if they are equal up to the time-point of the dispatcher of S, $\overline{\alpha(S)}$.

Definition 4 (Dynamic Execution Strategy for STNSU). *Given a STNSU $\langle \mathcal{N}, \mathcal{E} \rangle$. An execution strategy Σ is a set of scenarios σ. A scenario σ is a mapping of the nodes to $\mathbb{N}$: we denote with $\overline{T}_\sigma$ the timestamp assigned to T by σ.*

An execution strategy Σ is complete if it contains a scenario for each possible combination of contingent durations.

An execution strategy Σ is valid if each scenario in Σ is valid.

An execution strategy Σ is admissible if $\forall \tau \in \mathbb{N}$:

(i) For each non-contingent node $T \in \mathcal{N}_n$, $\forall\ \sigma, \sigma' \in \Sigma$, if $\overline{T}_\sigma \geq \tau$ and $\forall\ R \in \mathcal{N}_n \cup \mathcal{N}_s : \overline{R}_\sigma < \tau$ and $\overline{R}_{\sigma'} = \overline{R}_\sigma$, then $\overline{T}_{\sigma'} = \overline{T}_\sigma$.

(ii) For each semi-contingent node $S \in \mathcal{N}_s$, $\forall \sigma, \sigma' \in \Sigma$, if $\overline{S}_\sigma \geq \tau$ and $\forall\ R \in \mathcal{N}_n \cup \mathcal{N}_s : \overline{R}_\sigma < \alpha(S)$ and $\overline{R}_{\sigma'} = \overline{R}_\sigma$, then $\overline{S}_{\sigma'} = \overline{S}_\sigma$.

Definition 5 (Dynamic Controllability). *A STNSU is dynamically controllable, iff it admits a complete, valid and admissible execution strategy.*

It is easy to see that the admissibility criterion for semi-contingent nodes is stricter than for non-contingent nodes. Which constellations of constraints might violate dynamic controllability? An execution strategy has to assign timestamps to semi-contingent time-points when their dispatchers execute. Suppose there is a constraint c between a semi-contingent time-point S and a contingent time-point C, which occurs after dispatcher $\alpha(S)$. Then, for some timestamp value $\overline{S}$ assigned at time $\overline{\alpha(S)}$, and some observed $\overline{C} > \overline{\alpha(S)}$, it may happen that c is violated. So dependencies between semi-contingent and contingent time-points may harm dynamic controllability. If, however, the choice of the timestamp for S does not depend on any contingent time-point observed after the dispatcher is executed, then it is possible to assign S a value without the risk of incurring in a constraint violation due to uncontrollable events.

4.4 Inference Rules for STNSUs

For checking dynamic controllability, we propose a technique based on the propagation of constraints and the check for negative cycles in the graph as an indication of contradictions between constraints. The method is based on combining two constraint propagation systems: RUL [2] and P-rules [10].

For STNUs, recently, the RUL system [2] has been proposed, an elegant and efficient system for the propagation of constraints leading to a sound and complete checking procedure for dynamic controllability of STNUs.

For the propagation of the stricter constraints for semi-contingent edges, we resort to the P-rules of [10], which were developed to derive admissible ranges for temporal parameters. P-rules care to make the satisfaction of constraints independent of the observation of contingent nodes.

Therefore, here we propose to *combine* the P-rules and the RUL system in a set R_S of rules. The application of the rules in R_S depends on the type of STNSU nodes and edges. We list here the rules in R_S with the notation *Rule : antecedent $\Rightarrow$ consequent* as follows:

1. <u>P-Upper:</u> If $S \in \mathcal{N}_s$, $C \in \mathcal{N}_c$ with $(A^C, l, u, C) \in \mathcal{E}_c$, and $\exists e = (S, C, \delta) \in \mathcal{E}_n$,
   $\Rightarrow$ introduce $(S, A^C, \delta - u) \in \mathcal{E}_n$.
2. <u>P-Lower:</u> If $S \in \mathcal{N}_s$, $C \in \mathcal{N}_c$ with $(A^C, l, u, C) \in \mathcal{E}_c$, and $\exists e = (C, S, \delta) \in \mathcal{E}_n$,
   $\Rightarrow$ introduce $(A^C, S, l + \delta) \in \mathcal{E}_n$.
3. <u>P-Relax:</u> If $N, M, L \in \mathcal{N}$, and $\exists e_0 = (N, M, \delta_0) \in \mathcal{E}_n$, $\exists e_1 = (M, L, \delta_1) \in \mathcal{E}_n$,
   $\Rightarrow$ introduce $(N, L, \delta_0 + \delta_1) \in \mathcal{E}_n$.
4. <u>Upper:</u> If $N \in \mathcal{N}_n \cup \mathcal{N}_c$, $C \in \mathcal{N}_c$ with $(A^C, l, u, C) \in \mathcal{E}_c$, $\exists e = (N, C, \delta) \in \mathcal{E}_n$,
   $\Rightarrow$ introduce $(N, A^C, \delta') \in \mathcal{E}_n$, where $\delta' = max\{v - u, -l\}$.
5. <u>Lower:</u>
   - If $R \in \mathcal{N}_n$, $C \in \mathcal{N}_c$ with $(A^C, l, u, C) \in \mathcal{E}_c$, and $\exists e = (C, R, \delta) \in \mathcal{E}_n$, and $\delta \leq 0$, $\Rightarrow$ introduce $(A^C, R, \delta') \in \mathcal{E}_n$, where $\delta' = l + \delta$.

 – If $R \in \mathcal{N}_c$ with $(A^R, l^R, u^R, R) \in \mathcal{E}_c$, $C \in \mathcal{N}_c$ with $(A^C, l, u, C) \in \mathcal{E}_c$, and $R \neq C$, and $\exists e = (C, R, \delta) \in \mathcal{E}_n$ with $\delta \leq u^R$, $\Rightarrow$ introduce $(A^C, R, \delta') \in \mathcal{E}_n$, where $\delta' = l + \delta$.

Rules 1–3 are the P-rules, which have the effect of deriving constraints which are independent of contingent durations, as shown in [10]. To rules 1–2 we added here the requirement that they are applied only for semi-contingent nodes. Rules 3–5 are the rules of the RUL system. Rule 3 (P-Relax) is the rule Relax in RUL. We call a rule *applicable* if the condition expressed in its antecedent holds. With the following lemma, we show that no rule application invalidates the applicability of any other rule in R_S:

Lemma 1 (Commutativity of the Rules). *Let $R_1 : a_1 \Rightarrow c_1$, $R_2 : a_2 \Rightarrow c_2$ be any two rules in R_S, applicable in a STNSU $\langle \mathcal{N}, \mathcal{E} \rangle$. Let $\langle \mathcal{N}, \mathcal{E}' \rangle$ be the STNSU resulting from the application of R_1. Then R_2 is applicable in $\langle \mathcal{N}, \mathcal{E}' \rangle$.*

Proof. It is sufficient to see that: (1) the conditions in all antecedents of the rules require the existence of some nodes and edges with certain properties, but do not test for the absence of nodes or edges. (2) Each rule application introduces new edges and does not remove any existing edge. Thus, the application of any rule does not invalidate the applicability of any other applicable rule. $\square$

We can now define a procedure to check the dynamic controllability of a STNSU based on the inference rules in R_S.

4.5   Checking Dynamic Controllability

To check dynamic controllability, we follow the established approach for checking controllabilities in Temporal Constraint Networks: constraints are propagated until a negative cycle is observed, or no further constraints can be derived [2,20]. We start from a STNSU $\langle \mathcal{N}, \mathcal{E} \rangle$, and apply iteratively any applicable inference rule, which derives an additional edge. The iterations stop when a negative cycle (in the usual graph-theory sense) is found or quiescence (a fix-point) is reached, i.e. no additional constraint can be inferred. If no negative cycle can be derived, the STNSU is dynamically controllable.

The correctness (soundness and completeness) of this procedure follows from soundness and completeness of RUL [2] and the following observations: (1) the P-rules are stricter than the rules of RUL alone, i.e. for every edge derived by RUL, there is an edge derived by the P-rules, which is at least as constraining. So if the application of the P-rules terminates without a negative cycle, there is an execution strategy that satisfies all requirements, with the possible exception of admissibility for semi-contingent nodes. (2) The P-rules, in addition, make any edge e between a semi-contingent node and any contingent node occurring after its dispatcher redundant. If e is redundant, its satisfaction does not depend on the observation of any time-point later than the time-point of the dispatcher. This cares for an admissible dynamic execution strategy, and thus for the soundness of the procedure. We can also show that the introduction of any weaker edge, however, would not make e redundant. Therefore, the procedure is also complete.

Theorem 1 (Soundness and Completeness). *The iterated application of the rules in R_S until quiescence is a sound and complete procedure for checking the dynamic controllability of a STNSU.*

Proof. Soundness: It follows from (i) the soundness of RUL, and (ii) the inference of constraints independent of contingent durations with the P-rules.

(i) Applying the rules from the RUL system results in the check of existence of a dynamic execution strategy, which allows meeting all temporal constraints, i.e. a sound dynamic controllability check [2].

(ii) The P-rules derive non-contingent edges, which make any edge e between a semi-contingent time-point S and a contingent time-point C, with $(A^C, l, u, C) \in \mathcal{E}_c$, redundant [10]. This is achieved by applying either P-Upper or P-Lower to derive a non-contingent edge e':

- P-Upper is applied when $e = (S, C, w)$, and derives $e' = (S, A^C, w - u)$: one can verify that for any $\overline{S}$ such that $\overline{A^C} \le \overline{S} + w - u$ (e' is satisfied), also $\overline{C} \le \overline{S} + w$ (e is satisfied) for any observed $\overline{C} \in [\overline{A^C} + l, \overline{A^C} + u]$.
- P-Lower is applied when $e = (C, S, v)$, and derives $e' = (A^C, S, l + v)$: one can verify that for any $\overline{S}$ such that $\overline{S} \le \overline{A^C} + l + v$ (e' is satisfied), also $\overline{S} \le \overline{C} + v$ (e is satisfied) for any observed $\overline{C} \in [\overline{A^C} + l, \overline{A^C} + u]$.

So any execution strategy which fulfills the constraint encoded by e' entails the fulfillment of the constraint encoded by e, i.e. e' makes e redundant. Thus, the edges introduced by the P-rules make the assignment of semi-contingent time-points independent of contingent time-points, and for any $S \in \mathcal{N}_s$, no contingencies after $\alpha(S)$ need to be observed for assigning $\overline{S}$.

So, applying the rules in R_S results in a sound dynamic controllability check.

Completeness: It is sufficient to add the following consideration on top of the completeness of RUL [2]. Any e' introduced by the P-rules between S and A^C is the least constraining edge, which makes e between S and C redundant [10].

For P-Lower: consider $e = (C, S, v)$ and a less constraining[1] edge e'' is introduced instead of $e' = (A^C, S, l + v)$, e.g., $e'' = (A^C, S, l + v + 1)$. Then, if $\overline{S} = \overline{A^C} + l + v + 1$ (e'' is satisfied) and $\overline{C} = \overline{A^C} + l$, the constraint encoded in e, $S \le C + v$, is not met, i.e. e is not made redundant by e''. It is easy to construct a similar case for P-Upper. Hence, the checking procedure is also complete. $\square$

Theorem 1 provides us with a foundation for checking the dynamic controllability of processes. (1) with the mapping defined in Sect. 4.2 we map a process P into a temporally equivalent STNSU $\langle \mathcal{N}, \mathcal{E} \rangle$. (2) with the iterated application of the rules in R_S, we perform a check for the dynamic controllability of $\langle \mathcal{N}, \mathcal{E} \rangle$. Since $\langle \mathcal{N}, \mathcal{E} \rangle$ is temporally equivalent to P, we conclude that its dynamic controllability coincides with the dynamic controllability of P.

For the STNSU of Fig. 3, applying P-Upper and P-Lower at $A.s$, $A.e$, $B.e$, we derive $(A.s, B.e, 10)$ and $(B.e, A.s, -15)$, which form a negative cycle. Thus the process of Fig. 2 is not dynamically controllable (as argued in Sect. 2).

---

[1] We say that (A, B, δ) is less constraining than (A, B, δ') if $\delta' < \delta$, since in this case $B \le A + \delta' \to B \le A + \delta$.

5   Implementation, Evaluation, and Discussion

Evaluation of this research requires proof of relevance, correctness, and feasibility. Relevance of the notion of semi-contingent durations was given in Sect. 2 through a series of examples, which are demonstrated to be ill-served with mere contingent and non-contingent durations. Correctness of the method for checking the dynamic controllability of STNSUs has been formally proofed in Sect. 4. Here we show that the approach is feasible and appropriate by reporting the implementation of the approach and a series of experiments checking the correctness of the implementation and its scalability.

Correctness: In [8] we identified constraint patterns, which result in the potential sudden termination of a task. For each pattern, we have shown which additional constraints need to be included in a process definition to avoid sudden termination, and demonstrated the correctness of the operation. We applied the dynamic controllability checking procedure to STNSUs derived from processes exhibiting the sudden termination patterns of [8]. The procedure correctly resolved all the patterns, introducing edges encoding the very same constraints needed to avoid sudden termination, as shown in [8]. Thus, we have empirically tested the correctness of the procedure in handling sudden termination, which is a consequence of not adequately treating semi-contingent durations.

Scalability: We ran experiments using the same Windows 10 machine with i7 CPU and 16 GB of RAM, as well as the same set of randomly generated processes we used in [8], setting activities subject to sudden termination as semi-contingent. Test set, demographics, and results are publicly available[2]; algorithm implementations are available upon request. Since, like STNUs, STNSUs do not distinguish between XOR and PAR splits, and our process model does not have loops, only the number of nodes is relevant for measuring execution times. We regard the range of process sizes (from 10 up to 50 nodes) used for the experiments as representative of most of the cases found in practical applications.

We report the average measured execution times for the various process sizes in Fig. 4. On average, the checking procedure for a process of size 10 required 0.06 s; for size 20, 0.40 s; for size 30, 1.51 s; for size 40, 3.89 s; for size 50, 7.35 s.

Our experiments show that checking dynamic controllability requires a short time and scales well, even on common computing equipment. Since the checking procedure can also resolve sudden termination, and here we used the same machinery and data-set of [8], we can compare our results with the scalability results of [8]. From the comparison (see Fig. 4), we observe that the approach we propose here outperforms our previous approach for resolving sudden termination, and we can claim that it is more general, elegant, and efficient.

6   Related Work

Here we provided a definition of semi-contingent durations, which generalizes our previous work in [8]. To the best of our knowledge, our research is the first to

---

[2] Data available at: https://github.com/isys-aau-time/CAiSE2021.

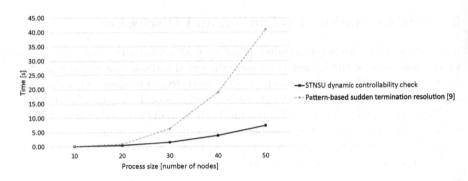

Fig. 4. Results of the evaluation: our STNSU-based approach to check dynamic controllability vs. pattern-based approach [8] to resolve sudden termination.

explore semi-contingent durations. Related work, therefore, comprises (a) formulation of temporal constraints in process models, (b) checking temporal qualities of process models, and (c) scheduling and monitoring of process execution.

General overviews of time management for business processes are provided in [4, 6, 9], as well as in [16]. Despite being extensive, none of these works identified the existence of, and need to represent, semi-contingent durations.

Verification of timed processes was addressed by several previous works, such as [1, 3, 11, 19], resorting on network analysis, scheduling, and Temporal Constraint Networks (TCNs). Here we enrich TCN-based approaches with the notion of semi-contingent duration, and new reasoning procedures.

Time Petri nets [17] are a formalism allowing for the analysis of temporal qualities, based on traditional Petri net properties. While their underlying semantics cater for advanced expressiveness (e.g., for concurrent executions), they do not consider the diversity of duration types, which, as we show here, is essential for faithful representation and reasoning. Further, no approach to check dynamic controllability of such nets has been explored so far.

Rigorous verification of programs may be supported by advanced logics, such as dynamic logic [12], which allows one to formulate correctness specifications, and formally verify whether they are met by a program. However, dynamic logic reasons on predicates expressing states in a sequence (the program execution), and falls short with the quantitative measure of time we consider here.

A consistent body of research (e.g., [13, 18]) explored the monitoring of the compliance of process instances to their process model at run-time. However, to the best of our knowledge, all approaches to monitoring and compliance checking address the notion of satisfiability rather than dynamic controllability, and do not consider the existence of semi-contingent durations for tasks as we do here.

Executed instances may be analyzed with process mining [23], which requires a large number of process logs to extract meaningful temporal information. Thus, it falls short for new, frequently changing, or scarcely executed processes, that are instead supported by our model-based approach.

For defining the novel class of STNSUs, we based on and extended the well-studied STNUs [21]. Major research efforts in the last decades developed several notions of controllability for TCNs, as well as a number of network models [15, 21, 24, 25]. With this work, we contribute to this field of research by introducing a new class of TCN, and formally defining its dynamic controllability.

7   Conclusions

Faithfully capturing the nature of real-world processes is essential for information systems to support the execution of processes. Here we have shown that the established notions of contingent and non-contingent durations and dynamic controllability do not adequately capture the essence of activities, whose duration is chosen at their start by the executor and cannot be changed later. We call these activities and their durations semi-contingent.

We have formalized semi-contingent durations and defined dynamic controllability as a notion for temporal correctness of processes with contingent, non-contingent, and semi-contingent durations. We have shown how to verify whether such a process is dynamically controllable, with the support of the STNSU, a novel class of Temporal Constraint Networks. We demonstrated that dynamic controllability can be efficiently checked at design-time.

With this work, we closed a significant gap in the representation and reasoning on temporal qualities for process models, which, as we demonstrated, are of high relevance in many application domains. This new notion of semi-contingent duration empowers process modelers to model the properties and requirements of process-oriented information systems more accurately. The tools we developed care for analyzing temporal properties of process models at design-time.

References

1. Bettini, C., Wang, X., Jajodia, S.: Temporal reasoning in workflow systems. Distrib. Parallel Databases **11**(3), 269–306 (2002)
2. Cairo, M., Rizzi, R.: Dynamic controllability of simple temporal networks with uncertainty: simple rules and fast real-time execution. Theor. Comput. Sci. **797**, 2–16 (2019)
3. Cardoso, J., Sheth, A., Miller, J., Arnold, J., Kochut, K.: Quality of service for workflows and web service processes. J. Web Semantics **1**(3), 281–308 (2004)
4. Cheikhrouhou, S., Kallel, S., Guermouche, N., Jmaiel, M.: The temporal perspective in business process modeling: a survey and research challenges. Service Oriented Comput. Appl. **9**(1), 75–85 (2014). https://doi.org/10.1007/s11761-014-0170-x
5. Combi, C., Posenato, R.: Controllability in temporal conceptual workflow schemata. In: Dayal, U., Eder, J., Koehler, J., Reijers, H.A. (eds.) BPM 2009. LNCS, vol. 5701, pp. 64–79. Springer, Heidelberg (2009). https://doi.org/10.1007/978-3-642-03848-8_6
6. Combi, C., Pozzi, G.: Temporal conceptual modelling of workflows. In: Song, I.-Y., Liddle, S.W., Ling, T.-W., Scheuermann, P. (eds.) ER 2003. LNCS, vol. 2813, pp. 59–76. Springer, Heidelberg (2003). https://doi.org/10.1007/978-3-540-39648-2_8

7. Eder, J., Franceschetti, M.: Time and business process management: problems, achievements, challenges. In: 27th International Symposium on Temporal Representation and Reasoning. LIPIcs, vol. 178 (2020)
8. Eder, J., Franceschetti, M., Lubas, J.: Scheduling processes without sudden termination. In: Nurcan, S., Reinhartz-Berger, I., Soffer, P., Zdravkovic, J. (eds.) BPMDS/EMMSAD -2020. LNBIP, vol. 387, pp. 117–132. Springer, Cham (2020). https://doi.org/10.1007/978-3-030-49418-6_8
9. Eder, J., Panagos, E., Rabinovich, M.: Workflow time management revisited. In: BPMDS/EMMSAD-2020. LNBIP, vol. 387, pp. 207–213. Springer, Heidelberg (2013). https://doi.org/10.1007/978-3-642-36926-1_16
10. Franceschetti, M., Eder, J.: Negotiating temporal commitments in cross-organizational business processes. In: 27th International Symposium on Temporal Representation and Reasoning (TIME 2020). LIPIcs, vol. 178 (2020)
11. Guermouche, N., Godart, C.: Timed model checking based approach for web services analysis. In: ICWS 2009. IEEE International Conference on Web Services, 2009, pp. 213–221. IEEE (2009)
12. Harel, D., Kozen, D., Tiuryn, J.: Dynamic logic. In: Handbook of Philosophical Logic, pp. 99–217. Springer (2001)
13. Hashmi, M., Governatori, G., Lam, H.-P., Wynn, M.T.: Are we done with business process compliance: state of the art and challenges ahead. Knowledge and Information Systems, pp. 1–55 (2018)
14. Hunsberger, L.: Fixing the semantics for dynamic controllability and providing a more practical characterization of dynamic execution strategies. In: 16th International Symposium on Temporal Representation and Reasoning, pp. 155–162. IEEE (2009)
15. Lanz, A., Posenato, R., Combi, C., Reichert, M.: Controlling time-awareness in modularized processes. In: Schmidt, R., Guédria, W., Bider, I., Guerreiro, S. (eds.) BPMDS/EMMSAD-2016. LNBIP, vol. 248, pp. 157–172. Springer, Cham (2016). https://doi.org/10.1007/978-3-319-39429-9_11
16. Lanz, A., Reichert, M., Weber, B.: Process time patterns: a formal foundation. Inf. Syst. 57, 38–68 (2016)
17. Ling, S., Schmidt, H.: Time petri nets for workflow modelling and analysis. In: 2000 IEEE International Conference on Systems, Man and Cybernetics, vol. 4, pp. 3039–3044. IEEE (2000)
18. Ly, L.T., Maggi, F.M., Montali, M., Rinderle-Ma, S., van der Aalst, W.M.: Compliance monitoring in business processes: functionalities, application, and tool-support. Inf. Syst. 54, 209–234 (2015)
19. Marjanovic, O., Orlowska, M.E.: On modeling and verification of temporal constraints in production workflows. Knowl. Inf. Syst. 1(2), 157–192 (1999)
20. Morris, P., Muscettola, N., Vidal, T.: Dynamic control of plans with temporal uncertainty. In: Proceedings of the 17th International Joint Conference on Artificial Intelligence-Volume 1, pp. 494–499. Morgan Kaufmann Publishers Inc. (2001)
21. Morris, P.H., Muscettola, N.: Temporal dynamic controllability revisited. In: Proceedings of the AAAI, pp. 1193–1198 (2005)
22. Posenato, R., Zerbato, F., Combi, C.: Managing decision tasks and events in time-aware business process models. In: Weske, M., Montali, M., Weber, I., vom Brocke, J. (eds.) BPM 2018. LNCS, vol. 11080, pp. 102–118. Springer, Cham (2018). https://doi.org/10.1007/978-3-319-98648-7_7
23. van der Aalst, W.M., Schonenberg, M., Song, M.: Time prediction based on process mining. Inf. Syst. 36(2), 450–475 (2011)

24. Vidal, T.: Handling contingency in temporal constraint networks: from consistency to controllabilities. J. Exp. Theor. Artif. Intell. **11**(1), 23–45 (1999)
25. Zavatteri, M., Viganò, L.: Conditional simple temporal networks with uncertainty and decisions. Theor. Comput. Sci. **797**, 77–101 (2019)

Constraint Modelling

Referential Integrity Under Uncertain Data

Sebastian Link[✉][iD] and Ziheng Wei

School of Computer Science, The University of Auckland, Auckland, New Zealand
{s.link,z.wei}@auckland.ac.nz

Abstract. Together with domain and entity integrity, referential integrity embodies the integrity principles of information systems. While relational databases address applications for data that is certain, modern applications require the handling of uncertain data. In particular, the veracity of big data and the complex integration of data from heterogeneous sources leave referential integrity vulnerable. We apply possibility theory to introduce the class of possibilistic inclusion dependencies. We show that our class inherits good computational properties from relational inclusion dependencies. In particular, we show that the associated implication problem is PSPACE-complete, but fixed-parameter tractable in the input arity. Combined with possibilistic keys and functional dependencies, our framework makes it possible to quantify the degree of trust in entities and relationships.

Keywords: Computational complexity · Inclusion dependency · Possibility theory · Reasoning · Referential integrity

1 Introduction

Big data has given our community big opportunities and challenges. One of these challenges is to build information systems that accommodate different dimensions of big data, including its veracity. According to an IBM study, one in three managers distrust the data that they use to make decisions[1]. The ability to quantify the degree of uncertainty in data would enable us to found decision making on data that is perceived to be sufficiently trustworthy.

In [15, 17] the authors presented a design framework for relational databases with uncertain data. Based on possibility theory [10], records are assigned a discrete degree of possibility (p-degree) with which they occur in a relation. Intuitively, the p-degree quantifies the level of trust an organization is prepared to assign to a record. The assignment of p-degrees can be based on many factors, specific to applications and irrelevant for developing the framework. In addition, an integrity constraint is assigned a degree of certainty (c-degree) that quantifies to which records it applies. Intuitively, the higher the c-degree of a constraint the lower the minimum p-degree of records to which the constraint applies. For example, a constraint is assigned the highest c-degree to affect all records, and the lowest c-degree to affect only records with the highest p-degree.

---

[1] http://www-01.ibm.com/software/data/bigdata/.

© Springer Nature Switzerland AG 2021
M. La Rosa et al. (Eds.): CAiSE 2021, LNCS 12751, pp. 265–279, 2021.
https://doi.org/10.1007/978-3-030-79382-1_16

The design frameworks of [17] were developed for possibilistic functional dependencies (pFDs) and possibilistic multivalued dependencies (pMVDs) [28].

The work from [17,28] has therefore shown one way of extending Codd's principle of entity integrity from certain to uncertain data. The other principle is that of referential integrity, which ensures that references between data across tables are maintained soundly. So far, referential integrity has not been investigated for applications that accommodate uncertain data. Hence, we currently lack the ability to guarantee that uncertain data are appropriately referenced across tables. While it would be possible to record all data in one table, this would violate other principles of data management, such as the minimization of data redundancy and sources of inconsistency. This strongly motivates research on possibilistic variants of referential integrity constraints. The most expressive class of referential integrity constraints are inclusion dependencies (INDs), which subsume the important special case of foreign keys. It is therefore the main goal of this paper to introduce the class of possibilistic inclusion dependencies (pINDs) as a fundamental notion that extends the principle of referential integrity to the veracity dimension of big data. Previous classes of constraints that have been extended to the possibilistic setting were downward-closed. Here, a class of integrity constraints is downward-closed whenever every constraint in the class that is satisfied by a database instance will also be satisfied by every subset of that instance. Unfortunately, the class of inclusion dependencies is not downward-closed, which raises the challenge of introducing a suitable notion. In addition, we would like pINDs to cover traditional INDs as a special case, but inherit the computational properties of this special case. Hence, we are aiming for a notion that is adequate for uncertain data, while still being computationally attractive.

From a perspective of information systems engineering, the main contribution of our framework is quantifying the degree of trust in entities and relationships. Technically, we can summarize the contributions of the current work as follows.

– We introduce the class of possibilistic inclusion dependencies as a notion fundamental to extending the principle of referential integrity to the veracity of big data, and quantifying the degree of trust in relationships between data elements.
– While pINDs capture traditional inclusion dependencies as the special case where only one degree of uncertainty is permitted, we show that pINDs still inherit the good computational behavior of this special case. More specifically, we establish an algorithm that decides the implication problem in deterministic quadratic space. While we show that the implication problem is PSPACE-complete, it is also fixed-parameter tractable in the arity.

Organization. Section 2 introduces our running application scenario. We discuss related work in Sect. 3. We define a possibilistic data model in Sect. 4. We propose the class of pINDs in Sect. 5. Section 6 establishes the computational properties for our new class of pINDs. Section 7 concludes and comments briefly on future work.

2   Application Scenario

As a running example consider the following database schema that catalogs which parts are available from which supplier at what price.

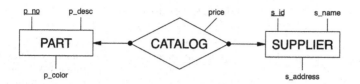

Fig. 1. Entity-relationship diagram for application scenario

- PART={p_no,p_desc,p_color} with key {p_no}
- SUPPLIER={s_id,s_name,s_address} with key {s_id}
- CATALOG={p_no,s_id,price} with key {p_no,s_id} and foreign keys
  - [p_no] ⊆ PART[p_no] and
  - [s_id] ⊆ SUPPLIER[s_id].

The corresponding Entity-Relationship diagram is shown in Fig. 1. Table 1 shows the result of integrating data from three legacy systems of the organization.

Table 1. Data integrated from legacy systems

PART			CATALOG			SUPPLIER		
p_no	p_desc	p_color	p_no	s_id	price	s_id	s_name	s_address
p1	lever	red	p1	s1	2 frogs	s1	Rumpel	Witchery
p2	knob	yellow	p1	s2	1 bat	s2	Pumpel	Wizyard
p3	disc	green	p2	s1	2 toads			
			p3	s3	2 snails			

As we can see, the database satisfies the keys and foreign keys defined by the schema. However, the integrated database does not contain any information about the level of trust associated with the records, based on the sources they have been integrated from. As an example use case of the framework we are proposing, we will now illustrate how the integration process can embed information about the different degrees of uncertainty that might be associated with the records. Note that this is just one specific way of using our framework.

The data shown in Table 1 is the result of integrating three different legacy systems as given in Table 2. While entity integrity in the form of the keys on the schemata is valid on all tables, there are issues with referential integrity.

These issues are simply hidden away in the integrated data set, which lacks a representation of the degrees of trust we should associate with the data. In an attempt to overcome this challenge, we assign possibility degrees (p-degrees) to records. In this example, we do this in the following intuitive way: we assign the highest degree *universal* when a record appears in all three relations of the same relation schema, the second highest degree *common* when a record appears in two of the three relations of the same relation schema, the third highest degree *isolated* when a record only appears in one

Table 2. Legacy databases

PART			CATALOG			SUPPLIER		
p_no	*p_desc*	*p_color*	*p_no*	*s_id*	*price*	*s_id*	*s_name*	*s_address*
p1	lever	red	p1	s1	2 frogs	s1	Rumpel	Witchery
p2	knob	yellow	p1	s2	1 bat	s2	Pumpel	Wizyard
			p2	s1	2 toads			
								Legacy database 1

PART			CATALOG			SUPPLIER		
p_no	*p_desc*	*p_color*	*p_no*	*s_id*	*price*	*s_id*	*s_name*	*s_address*
p1	lever	red	p1	s1	2 frogs	s1	Rumpel	Witchery
p3	disc	green	p1	s2	1 bat	s2	Pumpel	Wizyard
			p3	s3	2 snails			
								Legacy database 2

PART			CATALOG			SUPPLIER		
p_no	*p_desc*	*p_color*	*p_no*	*s_id*	*price*	*s_id*	*s_name*	*s_address*
p1	lever	red	p1	s1	2 frogs	s1	Rumpel	Witchery
p3	disc	green	p2	s1	2 toads			
								Legacy database 3

Table 3. Data integrated from legacy systems with information about uncertainty

PART				CATALOG				SUPPLIER			
p_no	*p_desc*	*p_color*	**trust**	*p_no*	*s_id*	*price*	**trust**	*s_id*	*s_name*	*s_address*	**trust**
p1	lever	red	**universal**	p1	s1	2 frogs	**universal**	s1	Rumpel	Witchery	**universal**
p2	knob	yellow	**common**	p1	s2	1 bat	**common**	s2	Pumpel	Wizyard	**common**
p3	disc	green	**isolated**	p2	s1	2 toads	**common**				
				p3	s3	2 snails	**isolated**				

of the three relations of the same relation schema, and the bottom degree *impossible* when the record does not occur in any relation. In relational databases, the closed world assumption states that any record that is not explicitly listed in a relation is not part of it. The bottom p-degree *impossible* extends the closed world assumption to possibilistic databases, since it is assigned to every record that does not occur in the possibilistic database instance. Table 3 shows the integrated database instance inclusive of the levels of trust associated with the various records.

P-degrees quantify the level of trust we associate with records. There are different methods to assign such degrees. For example, each of the legacy systems may have some associated level of trust, and we simply assign the highest degree of trust among the systems in which the tuple occurs. Another method may assign p-degrees according to the recency of tuples.

Apart from quantifying uncertainty, p-degrees enable us to assign degrees of certainty to integrity constraints. For example, we can assign the highest degree of certainty to a constraint when it holds on the set of all records that are higher than the bottom p-degree, and the bottom degree of certainty when the constraint does not even hold on the set of records that have the highest p-degree. For instance, the key {p_no} holds with the highest degree of certainty on PART, and the key $\{s\_id\}$ holds with the highest degree of certainty on SUPPLIER. Similarly, the key $\{p\_no,s\_id\}$ holds with the highest degree of certainty on CATALOG.

The foreign key $[p\_no] \subseteq$ PART$[p\_no]$ on CATALOG holds on the database that only considers records with the *universal* degree of trust, but not on the database that considers records with the *universal* or *common* degree of trust. Hence, it can only be assigned the second lowest degree of certainty.

Similarly, the foreign key $[s\_id] \subseteq$ SUPPLIER$[s\_id]$ on CATALOG holds on the database that considers only records with the *universal* degree of trust, and on the database that considers records with the *universal* or *common* degree of trust, but not on the database that considers records with the *universal, common* or *isolated* degree of trust. Hence, it can be assigned the second highest degree of certainty.

Denoting the degrees of certainty in this example by $\beta_1 > \beta_2 > \beta_3 > \beta_4$, we can revise our classical database schema as follows:

- PART $= \{$p_no,p_desc,p_color$\}$ with p-key $(\{p\_no\}, \beta_1)$
- SUPPLIER $= \{$s_id,s_name,s_address$\}$ with p-key $(\{s\_id\}, \beta_1)$
- CATALOG $= \{$p_no,s_id,price$\}$ with p-key $(\{p\_no, s\_id\}, \beta_1)$ and foreign keys
  - $([p\_no] \subseteq$ PART$[p\_no], \beta_3)$ and
  - $([s\_id] \subseteq$ SUPPLIER$[s\_id], \beta_2)$.

Figure 2 shows a corresponding Entity-Relationship diagram. Here, we augment some of the edges with indices of certainty degrees that apply to either attributes that form a key or directed edges that represent a foreign key. For example, we have attached the index 1 to attributes p_no of PART and s_id of SUPPLIER to indicate that they form a p-key for these entity types of c-degree β_1. Similarly, the label 2 of the edge from CATALOG to SUPPLIER represents the possibilistic foreign key $([s\_id] \subseteq$ SUPPLIER$[s\_id], \beta_2)$, and the label 3 of the edge from CATALOG to PART represents the possibilistic foreign key $([p\_no] \subseteq$ PART$[p\_no], \beta_3)$.

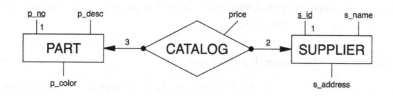

Fig. 2. Entity-relationship diagram representing information about uncertainty

The main aim of this paper is to define possibilistic inclusion dependencies, and to establish axiomatic and algorithmics solutions for their associated implication problem. These provide a foundation for quantifying the levels of trust in data, and hence also for resilience of decision-making in the presence of uncertain data.

3   Related Work

We review results on inclusion dependencies in relational databases, work on relaxed notions of inclusion dependencies, and their impact on data quality in general.

3.1   Classical Inclusion Dependencies

The implication problem is one of the core reasoning problems that is associated with any class of data dependencies [2,25]. Solutions to this problem provide us with a complete understanding of how the data dependencies in this class interact, but also allow us to minimize the overhead spent on enforcing those dependencies that business analysts and data stewards have selected for modeling the integrity of their database. Indeed, if some dependency is implied by a set of dependencies that is valid on a given database instance, then we know that this dependency is also valid - which means we have already validated it implicitly. Vice versa, if a meaningful dependency is not implied, then we do need to validate it after an update occurs. Typically, solutions to the implication problem also allow us to exhaust all possibilities for optimizing the performance of operations on our data. For example, in order to apply some dependency during query optimization it may suffice to check whether it is implied by a given set of dependencies. Similarly, if we observe some inconsistencies with respect to an implied data dependency, we can conclude that there must be an inconsistency with respect to some data dependency that we are meant to enforce.

For these and other reasons, the implication problem for inclusion dependencies has been studied in many data models, in particular first for the relational model of data. Indeed, Casanova et al. [5] showed that finite and unrestricted implication problem coincide for the class of inclusion dependencies, the problem is PSPACE-complete, and enjoys a binary axiomatization. We will extend these results to the possibilistic case in this article. Here, the extension refers to an arbitrary finite scale of possibility degrees where the relational model occurs as the special case where only two possibility degrees are given, namely a top and a bottom degree. In fact, tuples in the current database instance are assigned the top degree, and tuples that are not in the current database instance are assigned the bottom degree.

3.2   Approximate Inclusion Dependencies

In practice it is often difficult to avoid integrity issues completely. For that purpose, more robust notions of constraints are often useful. These permit violations of the constraints up to some degree. For inclusion dependencies, in particular, different kinds of relaxed notions have been considered. An intuitive approximation is given by upper bounds on the proportion of tuples that need removal from the referencing table to satisfy the given inclusion dependency [18]. In addition, sets of (approximate) inclusion dependencies can also be approximated. Intuitively this makes sense for large sets of constraints that can often not be maintained efficiently, or where some of the constraints are not meaningful [20]. Missing values, often represented in the form of null markers, also cause uncertainty in databases. In fact, SQL supports simple and partial semantics for foreign keys on databases with null markers [12]. Under simple semantics tuples with null markers on some foreign key attributes do not require a match in the referenced table, while partial semantics still requires partial matches. Similarly, possibilistic inclusion dependencies also relax the requirement to hold on the entire instance. However, the scope where they need to hold is precisely given by the dual relationship of their associated possibility and certainty degrees.

3.3 Data Quality and Inclusion Dependencies

More generally, inclusion dependencies and their relaxed notions control referential integrity, with important consequences for the quality of data [22, 24, 29] and schema evolution [8, 26]. For example, data quality problems can be controlled by the use of conditional inclusion dependencies [19] that enable users to customize referential integrity to specific patterns of data. Similarly, the use of smart data samples that show the violation of constraints can draw the attention of human experts to data quality problems [21]. The combination of sampling with the discovery of constraints [11] makes it possible to discover meaningful constraints and data quality problems in unison [27]. These approaches offer opportunities for the application of possibilistic inclusion dependencies in the future. Interestingly, our framework of possibility theory has been used to approach the problem of cleaning data from a different perspective [13]. In that perspective, it is not the data that is viewed to be dirty, but it is the degree of trust in the data that is viewed dirty instead. The problem then is to minimally change the p-degrees associated with tuples in order to satisfy the given possibilistic constraints [13].

3.4 Other Classes of Possibilistic Constraints and Approaches to Uncertainty

Our possibilistic framework has been applied to advance entity integrity for uncertain data using classes of constraints such as keys [3], cardinality constraints [23], functional dependencies [15, 16], and multivalued dependencies [28]. The current article is thus the first to extend the framework towards advancing referential integrity for uncertain data.

Recently, primitive data types in OCL/UML have been extended to model the uncertainty of physical measurements or user estimates [4], and also proposed an algebra of operations to propagate them to complex types.

4 Possibilistic Databases

Previous work introduced the model of uncertain data for single relations [15, 17, 28]. Since our primary interest in the current article is on referential integrity, we will extend the model to actual database schemata and instances, since referential integrity constraints express relationships across different tables.

A relation schema, usually denoted by R, is a finite non-empty set of *attributes*. Each attribute $A \in R$ has a *domain* $dom(A)$ of values. A *tuple* t over R is an element of the Cartesian product $\prod_{A \in R} dom(A)$ of the attributes' domains. For $X \subseteq R$ we denote by $t(X)$ the *projection* of t on X. A *relation* over R is a finite set r of tuples over R. A database schema, usually denoted by D, is a finite non-empty set of relation schemata.

A database over D, usually denoted by db, assigns to each relation schema $R \in D$ a relation r over R.

Our running example uses the database schema SUPPLY = {PART, SUPPLIER, CATALOG} with relation schemata PART = {p_no, p_desc, p_color}, SUPPLIER = {s_id, s_name, s_address}, and CATALOG = {p_no, s_id, price}.

We define possibilistic relations as relations where each tuple is associated with some confidence. The confidence of a tuple expresses up to which degree of possibility a tuple occurs in a relation. Formally, we model the confidence as a *scale of possibility*, that is, a finite, strictly linear order $\mathcal{S} = (S, <_k)$ with $k + 1$ elements where k is some positive integer, which we denote by $\alpha_1 >_k \cdots >_k \alpha_k >_k \alpha_{k+1}$, and whose elements $\alpha_i \in S$ we call *possibility degrees* (p-degrees). We sometimes simply write $<_k$ to refer to $\mathcal{S} = (S, <_k)$, and omit the subscript k from $<_k$ when it is fixed. The top p-degree α_1 is reserved for tuples that are 'fully possible' to occur in a relation, while the bottom p-degree α_{k+1} is reserved for tuples that are 'impossible' to occur in the relation at the moment. The use of the bottom p-degree α_{k+1} in our model is the counterpart of the classical closed world assumption. Humans like to use simple scales in everyday life, for instance to communicate, compare, or rank. Simple usually means to classify items qualitatively, rather than quantitatively by putting a precise value on it. Note that classical relations use a scale with two elements, that is, where $k = 1$.

In our running example, we use four different p-degrees that we label $\alpha_1 = $ *universal* for the top degree, $\alpha_2 = $ *common*, $\alpha_3 = $ *isolated*, and $\alpha_4 = $ *absent* for the bottom degree. A tuple is assigned p-degree α_i when it occurs in $4 - i$ legacy instances. For simplicity, we will use the same linear order on all relation schemata. We can also use different orders, but these can either be fused or more involved definitions can be given for our possibilistic referential constraints.

Formally, a *possibilistic relation schema* (p-schema) $(R, <_k)$ consists of a relation schema R and a possibility scale $<_k$. A *possibilistic relation* (p-relation) over $(R, <_k)$ consists of a relation r over R, together with a function $Poss_r$ that maps each tuple $t \in r$ to a p-degree $Poss_r(t)$ in the possibility scale $<_k$. Sometimes, we simply refer to a p-relation $(r, Poss_r)$ by r, assuming that $Poss_r$ has been fixed. For example, Table 3 shows p-relations $(r, Poss_r)$ over $(\text{PART}, <_3)$, $(\text{SUPPLIER}, <_3)$, and $(\text{CATALOG}, <_3)$ where $<_3 = $ *universal* $>_3$ *common* $>_3$ *isolated* $>_3$ *absent*.

A *possibilistic database schema* (pdb-schema) $(D, <_k)$ consists of a set D of relation schemata R, each of which forms a p-schema $(R, <_k)$. A *possibilistic database* (pdb) over $(D, <_k)$, usually denoted by $pdb = (db, Poss)$, assigns to each p-schema $(R, <_k)$ of $(D, <_k)$ a p-relation $(r, Poss_r)$. Again, Table 3 shows a pdb over pdb-schema $(\text{SUPPLY}, <_3)$ with $<_3 = $ *universal* $>_3$ *common* $>_3$ *isolated* $>_3$ *absent*.

Possibilistic databases enjoy a well-founded semantics in terms of possible worlds. In fact, every possible world is itself a classical database. For $i = 1, \ldots, k$ let $db_i = \{r_i \mid r \in db\}$ denote the database that consists of all tuples in db that have a p-degree of at least α_i, that is, $r_i = \{t \in r \mid Poss_r(t) \geq \alpha_i\}$ for all p-relations $(r, Poss_r)$. Indeed, we have $r_1 \subseteq r_2 \subseteq \cdots \subseteq r_k$ for all of the p-relations $(r, Poss_r)$ that constitute pdb. Hence, the p-degree associated with the world db_i is α_i. In particular, db_{k+1} is not a possible world since it includes tuples that are *impossible* to occur. Vice versa, the possibility $Poss_r(t)$ of a tuple $t \in r$ is the possibility of the smallest possible world

Table 4. Chain of possible database worlds

PART			CATALOG			SUPPLIER		
p_no	*p_desc*	*p_color*	*p_no*	*s_id*	*price*	*s_id*	*s_name*	*s_address*
p1	lever	red	p1	s1	2 frogs	s1	Rumpel	Witchery
								Possible World $db1$

PART			CATALOG			SUPPLIER		
p_no	*p_desc*	*p_color*	*p_no*	*s_id*	*price*	*s_id*	*s_name*	*s_address*
p1	lever	red	p1	s1	2 frogs	s1	Rumpel	Witchery
p3	disc	green	p1	s2	1 bat	s2	Pumpel	Wizyard
			p2	s1	2 toads			
								Possible World $db2$

PART			CATALOG			SUPPLIER		
p_no	*p_desc*	*p_color*	*p_no*	*s_id*	*price*	*s_id*	*s_name*	*s_address*
p1	lever	red	p1	s1	2 frogs	s1	Rumpel	Witchery
p3	disc	green	p1	s2	1 bat	s2	Pumpel	Wizyard
			p2	s1	2 toads			
			p3	s3	2 snails			
								Possible World $db3$

in which t occurs. If $t \notin db_k$, then $Poss_r(t) = \alpha_{k+1}$. The top p-degree α_1 takes on a distinguished role: every tuple that is 'fully possible' occurs in every possible world - and is thus - 'fully certain'. This confirms our intuition that pdbs subsume databases (of fully certain tuples) as a special case. Table 4 shows the possible worlds of databases db_1, db_2, and db_3 of our running example.

5 Possibilistic Inclusion Dependencies

We recall the concepts of possibilistic keys and possibilistic functional dependencies from previous work [3, 15]. These form primary mechanisms to address entity integrity for uncertain data. We then introduce the new concept of possibilistic inclusion dependencies as the primary mechanism to address referential integrity for uncertain data.

An FD $X \rightarrow Y$ is satisfied by a relation r whenever every pair of tuples in r that have matching values on all the attributes in X have also matching values on all the attributes in Y [2,25]. If $X \cup Y = R$, we call X a *key* because this case entails that there are no different tuples that match on X. For example, the FD $p\_no, s\_id \rightarrow price$ is satisfied by all the relations over CATALOG in Table 2, but the FD $s\_id \rightarrow price$ is only satisfied by the relations over CATALOG in the second legacy database of Table 2. In particular, $\{p\_no, s\_id\}$ is a key but $\{s\_id\}$ is not a key.

For a given FD σ, the marginal certainty with which σ holds in a p-relation corresponds to the p-degree of the smallest possible world in which σ is violated. Therefore, dually to a scale $\mathcal{S}$ of p-degrees for tuples we use a scale $\mathcal{S}^T$ of certainty degrees (c-degrees) for constraints. We use positive integers as indices of the Greek letter β to denote c-degrees. Formally, the duality between p-degrees in $\mathcal{S}$ and c-degrees in $\mathcal{S}^T$ is defined by the mapping $\alpha_i \mapsto \beta_{k+2-i}$, for $i = 1, \ldots, k+1$. Since the impossible world

r_{k+1} violates every FD, the marginal certainty $C_{(r,Poss_r)}(\sigma)$ with which the FD σ holds on the p-relation $(r, Poss_r)$ is the c-degree β_{k+2-i} for the smallest world r_i in which σ is violated. In particular, if r_k satisfies σ, then $C_{(r,Poss_r)}(\sigma) = \beta_1$.

We can now define the syntax and semantics of pFDs. A pFD over a p-schema $(R, \mathcal{S})$ is an expression $(X \rightarrow Y, \beta)$ where $X, Y \subseteq R$ and $\beta \in \mathcal{S}^T$. A p-relation $(r, Poss_r)$ over $(R, \mathcal{S})$ *satisfies* the pFD (σ, β) if and only if $C_{(r,Poss_r)}(\sigma) \geq \beta$. In our running example we use $\beta_1 >_3^S \beta_2 >_3^S \beta_3 >_3^S \beta_4$, with the interpretations of *certain* for β_1, *quite certain* for β_2, *kind of certain* for β_3 and *not certain at all* for β_4. The marginal certainty of the FD $p\_no, s\_id \rightarrow price$ for the p-relation over CATALOG in Table 3 is *certain*, since the FD holds even in the largest possible world having p-degree α_3. The FD $s\_id \rightarrow price$ is *kind of certain* since the smallest possible world that violates it ($db2$) has p-degree α_2.

We denote by $R, S \in D$ relation schemata in a database schema D and by $X = [A_1, \ldots, A_n]$ and $Y = [B_1, \ldots, B_n]$ sequences of distinct attributes in R and S, respectively, such that for all $m = 1, \ldots, n$, $dom(A_m) = dom(B_m)$ holds. The expression $R[X] \subseteq S[Y]$ a called an *inclusion dependency* (IND) over D. A database db over D with relations r over R and s over S is said to satisfy the IND $R[X] \subseteq S[Y]$ over D if and only if for every tuple $t_r \in r$ there is some tuple $t_s \in s$ such that $t_r[X] = t_s[Y]$. In our running example, the expressions CATALOG$[p\_no] \subseteq$ PART$[p\_no]$ and CATALOG$[s\_id] \subseteq$ SUPPLIER$[s\_id]$ denote INDs over SUPPLY. According to Table 4, the first IND is satisfied by $db1$ and $db3$ but not by $db2$, while the second IND is satisfied by $db1$ and $db2$ but not by $db3$.

We will now introduce the new concept of possibilistic inclusion dependencies.

Definition 1. *Let $(D, <_k)$ denote a pdb-schema and let $R[X] \subseteq S[Y]$ denote an IND over D. For $i \in \{1, \ldots, k+1\}$, we call the expression $(R[X] \subseteq S[Y], \beta_i)$ a possibilistic inclusion dependency (pIND) over $(D, <_k)$. Let $pdb = (db, Poss)$ denote a pdb over $(D, <_k)$ such that $(r, Poss_r)$ and $(s, Poss_s)$ denote p-relations over $(R, <_k)$ and $(S, <_k)$, respectively. The marginal certainty $C_{pdb}(R[X] \subseteq S[Y])$ with which the IND $R[X] \subseteq S[Y]$ holds on $pdb = (db, Poss)$ is the c-degree β_{k+2-i} for the smallest world db_i in which $R[X] \subseteq S[Y]$ is violated. In particular, if db_k satisfies $R[X] \subseteq S[Y]$, then $C_{pdb}(R[X] \subseteq S[Y]) = \beta_1$. We say that pdb satisfies the pIND $(R[X] \subseteq S[Y], \beta_i)$, denoted by $\models_{pdb} (R[X] \subseteq S[Y], \beta_i)$, if and only if $C_{pdb}(R[X] \subseteq S[Y]) \geq_k^S \beta_i$.*

The pdb from Table 3 shows that the smallest possible world that violates the IND CATALOG$[p\_no] \subseteq$ PART$[p\_no]$ is $db2$. Consequently, the marginal certainty of CATALOG$[p\_no] \subseteq$ PART$[p\_no]$ is β_3. Similarly, the smallest possible world that violates the IND CATALOG$[s\_id] \subseteq$ SUPPLIER$[s\_id]$ is $db3$. Hence, the marginal certainty of CATALOG$[s\_id] \subseteq$ SUPPLIER$[s\_id]$ is β_2. We conclude that pdb satisfies the pINDs

- (CATALOG$[p\_no] \subseteq$ PART$[p\_no]$), β_3) and
- (CATALOG$[s\_id] \subseteq$ SUPPLIER$[s\_id]$, β_2),

but satisfies none of the pINDs

- (CATALOG$[p\_no] \subseteq$ PART$[p\_no]$), β_2)
- (CATALOG$[s\_id] \subseteq$ SUPPLIER$[s\_id]$, β_1).

Following Definition 1, pINDs enjoy a possible world semantics. Indeed, for every pdb pdb over every pdb-schema $(D, <_k)$, and for every $i = 1, \ldots, k$, we have that $\models_{pdb}$ $(R[X] \subseteq S[Y], \beta_i)$ if and only if $\models_{db_j} R[X] \subseteq S[Y]$ holds for all $j = 1, \ldots, k+1-i$.

An important difference to pFDs is that the equivalence requires us to check all possible worlds from $j = 1, \ldots, k + 1 - i$, while pFDs only require us to check the largest possible world db_{k+1-i}. The reason for the latter is that FDs are closed downwards in the sense that every FD that is satisfied by a relation will also be satisfied by any sub-relation of the relation. This is not true for inclusion dependencies, which is why we specifically need to require that property in our semantics. This requirement, however, is very natural since values of tuples associated with some p-degree α should never reference tuples that are associated with a p-degree lower than α. Hence, this requirement is a natural extension of Codd's principle of referential integrity to uncertain data.

6 Reasoning About Possibilistic Inclusion Dependencies

The significance of (p)INDs results from their applicability to the most fundamental processing tasks for (uncertain) data. For example, we need to validate that all INDs that govern our data are still satisfied after updates are processed. This validation should impose a minimum overhead in resources. Computing a minimal set of INDs that *imply* all the INDs that govern the data makes it possible to minimize resources. For queries we want to generate a query plan that is likely to return the answer set as efficiently as possible. In attempting to find an optimal query plan, we may need to check whether some candidate IND holds on the given database. Deciding whether this candidate is implied by the set of INDs that are enforced on the data, the resources required to validate the candidate are minimized. Hence, INDs are useful when they can be reasoned about efficiently. We will show that our definition of pINDs cannot only express referential integrity for uncertain data, but also inherits the good computational behaviour from the well-known special case where $k = 1$.

6.1 Correspondence to INDs

We establish a correspondence between instances of the implication problems for pINDs and INDs. Let $\Sigma \cup \{\varphi\}$ denote a set of pINDs over a pdb-schema $(D, <_k)$. We say that Σ *implies* φ, denoted by $\Sigma \models \varphi$, if every pdb $(db, Poss)$ over $(D, <_k)$ that satisfies every pIND in Σ also satisfies φ.

Example 1. Let Σ consist of the pINDs (CATALOG[p_no] $\subseteq$ PART[p_no]), β_3) and (CATALOG[s_id] $\subseteq$ SUPPLIER[s_id], β_2). Let φ_1 denote the pIND (CATALOG[p_no] $\subseteq$ PART[p_no]), β_2) and let φ_2 denote the pIND (CATALOG[s_id] $\subseteq$ SUPPLIER[s_id], β_1). Then Σ implies neither φ_1 nor φ_2. Indeed, the p-database from Table 3 satisfies the two pINDs in Σ but satisfies neither φ_1 nor φ_2.

For a set Σ of pINDs on some pdb-schema $(D, <_k)$ and c-degree $\beta > \beta_{k+1}$, let $\Sigma_\beta = \{\sigma \mid (\sigma, \beta') \in \Sigma \text{ and } \beta' \geq \beta\}$ be the β-cut of Σ. The strength of our framework is engraved in the following result. It says that a pIND (σ, β) with c-degree β is implied by a set Σ of pINDs if and only if the IND σ is implied by the β-cut Σ_β of Σ.

Theorem 1 *[β-cuts]. Let $\Sigma \cup \{(\varphi, \beta)\}$ denote a set of pINDs over p-db schema $(D, <_k)$ and let $\beta > \beta_{k+1}$. Then $\Sigma \models (\varphi, \beta)$ if and only if $\Sigma_\beta \models \varphi$.*

Proof. Let $\beta = \beta_i$ for some $1 \leq i \leq k$.

If $\Sigma \not\models (\varphi, \beta)$, then there is some p-db over $(D, <_k)$ that satisfies all pINDs in Σ but does not satisfy (φ, β). By definition there must exist a smallest possible world that satisfies all INDs in Σ_β but does not satisfy φ.

Vice versa, let db denote a database instance over D such that db satisfies all INDs in Σ_β but violates φ. For $\varphi = R[X] \subseteq S[Y]$ there must exist some tuple $t_r \in r$ such that for all tuples $t_s \in s$ we have $t_r[X] \neq t_s[Y]$. For $\beta = \beta_i$ with $1 \leq i \leq k$ we assign to $t_r \in r$ the p-degree α_{k+1-i} and to all other tuples in db the p-degree α_1. Then the resulting pdb $(db, Poss)$ will satisfy Σ and violate (φ, β).   □

The following example illustrates Theorem 1.

Example 2. For Σ, φ_1, and φ_2 from Example 1 we know that Σ does neither imply φ_1 nor φ_2. This is evident from the pdb in Table 3. Indeed, the smallest possible world which satisfies Σ_{β_2} and violates CATALOG$[p\_no] \subseteq$ PART$[p\_no]$ is the possible world db2. Vice versa, if we take the possible world db2 and assign the p-degree α_2 to the tuple (p2, s1, 2 toads) over CATALOG, and assign the p-degree α_1 to all the other tuples, then the resulting pdb will satisfy Σ but violate φ_1.

A similar argument can be made for Σ and φ_2, with the only difference being that the possible world db3 satisfies Σ_{β_1} and violates CATALOG$[s\_id] \subseteq$ SUPPLIER$[s\_id]$ due to the tuple (p3, s3, 2 snails). Vice versa, assigning p-degree α_3 to this tuple in db3 and assigning p-degree α_1 to any other tuple in this database, results in a pdb that satisfies Σ and violates φ_2.

6.2 Algorithmic Characterization

We would like an algorithm that can decide the implication problem for pINDs efficiently. Using Theorem 1, we can extend the decision procedure for classical INDs to decide the implication problem for pINDs. Algorithm 1 directly returns an affirmative answer whenever the candidate pIND φ has bottom c-degree β_{k+1}. Otherwise, it uses the chase procedure for INDs applied to the β-cut Σ_β. Algorithm 1 runs in non-deterministic linear space. According to Savitch (PSPACE = NPSPACE) the algorithm can be implemented to run in determinstic quadratic space.

Corollary 1. *Algorithm 1 decides pIND implication in deterministic quadratic space.*

Proof. The correctness and complexity of Algorithm 1 follow from that of the algorithm for deciding INDs in the special case $k = 1$, and Theorem 1.   □

Example 3. Let Σ consist of the following two pINDs over the extended pdb-schema SUPPLY that we have been using as a running example:

- (SALES$[s\_id] \subseteq$ CATALOG$[s\_id], \beta_1$)
- (CATALOG$[s\_id] \subseteq$ SUPPLIER$[s\_id], \beta_2$).

Algorithm 1. pIND-chase

Require: Set $\Sigma \cup \{(R_a[A_1,\ldots,A_n] \subseteq R_b[B_1,\ldots,B_n],\beta)\}$ of pINDs over $(D,<_k)$
Ensure: Yes, if Σ implies $(R_a[A_1,\ldots,A_n] \subseteq R_b[B_1,\ldots,B_n],\beta)$, and No, otherwise
1: **if** $\beta = \beta_{k+1}$ **then return** ('Yes')
2: **end if**;
3: $\mathcal{E} := \{R_a[A_1,\ldots,A_n]\}$;
4: **repeat**
5:      **if** $R_i[C_1,\ldots,C_n] \in \mathcal{E}$ and $R_i[C_1,\ldots,C_n] \subseteq R_j[D_1,\ldots,D_m]$ can be inferred from
6:      Σ_β by a single application of $\mathcal{P}'$ **then**
7:          $\mathcal{E} := \mathcal{E} \cup \{R_j[D_1,\ldots,D_m]\}\}$;
8:      **end if**
9: **until** $R_b[B_1,\ldots,B_n] \in \mathcal{E}$ or no change possible
10: **if** $R_b[B_1,\ldots,B_n] \in \mathcal{E}$ **then return** 'Yes'
11: **else**
12:     **return** ('No');
13: **end if**

We use φ to denote $(\text{SALES}[s\_id] \subseteq \text{CATALOG}[s\_id],\beta_2)$ and we use φ' to denote $(\text{SALES}[s\_id] \subseteq \text{CATALOG}[s\_id],\beta_1)$ as two candidate pINDs for which we wonder whether they are implied by Σ.

Let us apply Algorithm 1 to both inputs $\Sigma \cup \{\varphi\}$ and $\Sigma \cup \{\varphi'\}$. For neither of the two inputs does β represent the bottom c-degree β_4. For φ we obtain the β_2-cut Σ_{β_2} of Σ that consists of the two INDs:

- $\sigma_1 = \text{SALES}[s\_id] \subseteq \text{CATALOG}[s\_id]$
- $\sigma_2 = \text{CATALOG}[s\_id] \subseteq \text{SUPPLIER}[s\_id]$.

Starting with $\mathcal{E} = \{\text{SALES}[s\_id]\}$ and applying first σ_1 and then σ_2 we obtain $\mathcal{E} = \{\text{SALES}[s\_id], \text{CATALOG}[s\_id], \text{SUPPLIER}[s\_id]\}$, which means that Algorithm 1 returns an affirmative answer. Starting with $\mathcal{E}' = \{\text{SALES}[s\_id]\}$ and β_1-cut $\Sigma_{\beta_1} = \{\sigma_1\}$, we can only apply σ_1 to obtain $\mathcal{E}' = \{\text{SALES}[s\_id], \text{CATALOG}[s\_id]\}$. This means Algorithm 1 returns a negative answer since $\text{SUPPLIER}[s\_id] \notin \mathcal{E}'$.

6.3 PSPACE-Completeness and Fixed-Parameter Tractability

Corollary 1 shows that the implication problem of pINDs is in PSPACE. In the relational model the implication problem of INDs is also PSPACE-hard [5], and INDs form the special case of pINDs for $k = 1$. Hence, the implication problem of pINDs is also PSPACE-complete. Following [12] the implication problem for INDs is even fixed-parameter tractable (FPT) [9] in the arity of the input. That is, there is a deterministic algorithm that runs in polynomial time when the arity of the input is fixed.

Corollary 2. *The implication of pINDs is* PSPACE-*complete and* FPT *in their arity.*

It also follows from a result about INDs [7] that the implication problem for pINDs with bounded arity is NLOGSPACE-complete.

7   Conclusion and Future Work

Using possibility theory we have proposed a class of inclusion dependencies for uncertain data. Our proposal can express different degrees of certainty by which INDs hold. Since the degrees can be customized to the needs of data owners, our possibilistic INDs are able to enforce referential integrity according to the requirements of applications. This should provide organizations with the ability to quantify the level of trust they have in their data and the relationships between them. This trust will facilitate more confident decision-making under uncertainty. Our proposal inherits the good computational behavior from its special case of certain data.

The research opens up several new questions. When studying the interaction of entity and referential integrity for uncertain data, and their extension to other data models with missing values, such as JSON. It will be important to extend conceptual, logical, and physical design approaches from certain to uncertain data, such as [6,14]. While a headstart has been made [17], inclusion dependencies have not been taken into account yet. Another core reasoning problem is the discovery of possibilistic constraints for a given class that hold on a given possibilistic database. This problem has received much attention in the relational model [1], but not yet for models of uncertain data.

References

1. Abedjan, Z., Golab, L., Naumann, F., Papenbrock, T.: Data Profiling. Synthesis Lectures on Data Management. Morgan & Claypool Publishers (2018)
2. Atzeni, P., De Antonellis, V.: Relational Database Theory. Benjamin/Cummings (1993)
3. Balamuralikrishna, N., Jiang, Y., Koehler, H., Leck, U., Link, S., Prade, H.: Possibilistic keys. Fuzzy Sets Syst. **376**, 1–36 (2019)
4. Bertoa, M.F., Burgueño, L., Moreno, N., Vallecillo, A.: Incorporating measurement uncertainty into OCL/UML primitive datatypes. Softw. Syst. Modeling **19**(5), 1163–1189 (2019). https://doi.org/10.1007/s10270-019-00741-0
5. Casanova, M.A., Fagin, R., Papadimitriou, C.H.: Inclusion dependencies and their interaction with functional dependencies. J. Comput. Syst. Sci. **28**(1), 29–59 (1984)
6. Chen, P.P.: The entity-relationship model - toward a unified view of data. ACM Trans. Database Syst. **1**(1), 9–36 (1976)
7. Cosmadakis, S.S., Kanellakis, P.C., Vardi, M.Y.: Polynomial-time implication problems for unary inclusion dependencies. J. ACM **37**(1), 15–46 (1990)
8. Dimolikas, K., Zarras, A.V., Vassiliadis, P.: A study on the effect of a table's involvement in foreign keys to its schema evolution. In: Dobbie, G., Frank, U., Kappel, G., Liddle, S.W., Mayr, H.C. (eds.) ER 2020. LNCS, vol. 12400, pp. 456–470. Springer, Cham (2020). https://doi.org/10.1007/978-3-030-62522-1_34
9. Downey, R.G., Fellows, M.R.: Fundamentals of Parameterized Complexity. Texts in Computer Science. Springer (2013)
10. Dubois, D., Prade, H.: Possibility theory. In: Meyers, R.A. (ed.) Computational Complexity: Theory. Techniques, and Applications, pp. 2240–2252. Springer, New York (2012)
11. Dürsch, F., et al.: Inclusion dependency discovery: an experimental evaluation of thirteen algorithms. In: Zhu, W., et al. (eds.) Proceedings of the 28th ACM International Conference on Information and Knowledge Management, CIKM 2019, Beijing, China, 3–7 November, 2019, pp. 219–228 (2019)

12. Köhler, H., Link, S.: Inclusion dependencies and their interaction with functional dependencies in SQL. J. Comput. Syst. Sci. **85**, 104–131 (2017)
13. Köhler, H., Link, S.: Possibilistic data cleaning. IEEE Trans. Knowl. Data Eng. (in press)
14. Levene, M., Vincent, M.W.: Justification for inclusion dependency normal form. IEEE Trans. Knowl. Data Eng. **12**(2), 281–291 (2000)
15. Link, S., Prade, H.: Possibilistic functional dependencies and their relationship to possibility theory. IEEE Trans. Fuzzy Syst. **24**(3), 757–763 (2016)
16. Link, S., Prade, H.: Relational database schema design for uncertain data. In: Mukhopadhyay, S., et al. (eds.) Proceedings of the 25th ACM International Conference on Information and Knowledge Management, CIKM 2016, Indianapolis, IN, USA, 24–28 October, 2016, pp. 1211–1220. ACM (2016)
17. Link, S., Prade, H.: Relational database schema design for uncertain data. Inf. Syst. **84**, 88–110 (2019)
18. Lopes, S., Petit, J.-M., Toumani, F.: Discovering interesting inclusion dependencies: application to logical database tuning. Inf. Syst. **27**(1), 1–19 (2002)
19. Ma, S., Fan, W., Bravo, L.: Extending inclusion dependencies with conditions. Theor. Comput. Sci. **515**, 64–95 (2014)
20. De Marchi, F., Petit, J.-M.: Approximating a set of approximate inclusion dependencies. In: Intelligent Information Processing and Web Mining, Proceedings of the International IIS: IIPWM'05 Conference held in Gdansk, Poland, 13–16 June, 2005, pp. 633–640 (2005)
21. De. Marchi, F., Petit, J.-M.: Semantic sampling of existing databases through informative armstrong databases. Inf. Syst. **32**(3), 446–457 (2007)
22. Ordonez, C., García-García, J.: Referential integrity quality metrics. Decis. Support Syst. **44**(2), 495–508 (2008)
23. Roblot, T., Link, S.: Cardinality constraints and functional dependencies over possibilistic data. Data Knowl. Eng. **117**, 339–358 (2018)
24. Sadiq, S.W., et al.: Data quality: The role of empiricism. SIGMOD Rec. **46**(4), 35–43 (2017)
25. Thalheim, B.: Dependencies in relational databases, vol. 126. Teubner, Teubner-Texte zur Mathematik (1991)
26. Vassiliadis, P., Kolozoff, M.-R., Zerva, M., Zarras, A.V.: Schema Evolution and Foreign Keys: Birth, Eviction, Change and Absence. In: Mayr, H.C., Guizzardi, G., Ma, H., Pastor, O. (eds.) ER 2017. LNCS, vol. 10650, pp. 106–119. Springer, Cham (2017). https://doi.org/10.1007/978-3-319-69904-2_9
27. Wei, Z., Link, S.: DataProf: semantic profiling for iterative data cleansing and business rule acquisition. In: Das, G., Jermaine, C.M., Bernstein, P.A. (eds.) Proceedings of the 2018 International Conference on Management of Data, SIGMOD Conference 2018, Houston, TX, USA, 10–15 June, 2018, pp. 1793–1796 (2018)
28. Wei, Z., Link, S.: A Fourth Normal Form for Uncertain Data. In: Giorgini, P., Weber, B. (eds.) CAiSE 2019. LNCS, vol. 11483, pp. 295–311. Springer, Cham (2019). https://doi.org/10.1007/978-3-030-21290-2_19
29. Zhang, R., Indulska, M., Sadiq, S.W.: Discovering data quality problems - the case of repurposed data. Bus. Inf. Syst. Eng. **61**(5), 575–593 (2019)

Uniqueness Constraints on Property Graphs

Philipp Skavantzos, Kaiqi Zhao, and Sebastian Link[(✉)] ⓘ

School of Computer Science, The University of Auckland, Auckland 1010, New Zealand
pska752@aucklanduni.ac.nz, {kaiqi.zhao,s.link}@auckland.ac.nz

Abstract. Graph database are increasingly popular for data management and analytics. As with every data model, managing the integrity of entities is fundamental for data governance but also important for the efficiency of update and query operations. In response to shortcomings of uniqueness and existence constraints in graph databases, we propose a new principled class of constraints that separates uniqueness from existence dimensions, and fully supports multiple labels and composite properties. We illustrate benefits of the constraints on real-world examples by use of the node integrity they enforce for better update and query performance. We establish axiomatic and algorithmic characterizations for reasoning about any set of constraints in our new class. We also give examples of small node samples that satisfy the same constraints as the original data set, and are useful for the elicitation of business rules, and the identification of data quality problems. Finally, we briefly discuss the role of our constraints in the design for data quality, and propose extensions to managing node integrity within graph database systems.

Keywords: Existence constraint · Property graph · Reasoning · Uniqueness constraint

1 Introduction

Uniqueness constraints (UCs) enable the efficient and flexible handling of entity integrity in database management systems [3]. Given a collection of entities, a UC is a set of attributes whose values uniquely identify an entity in the collection. Keys form a special class of UCs where no entity in the database is permitted to have missing values on any attribute of the key. In contrast, UCs only require unique combinations of values for those entities that have no missing value on any attribute of the UC. Both keys and UCs are fundamental for understanding the structure and semantics of data. As such they are fundamental to the entire information systems cycle, from requirements engineering and conceptual modeling to logical and physical design. Indeed, uniqueness constraints enable i) analysts to identify objects such as entities and relationships, ii) designers to transform schemata that exhibit data redundancies to those that minimize them, and iii) users to access information effectively and efficiently. Knowledge about UCs enables us to i) uniquely reference entities across data repositories, ii) minimize data redundancy at schema design time to process updates efficiently at run time, iii) provide better selectivity estimates in cost-based query optimization, iv) provide a

© Springer Nature Switzerland AG 2021
M. La Rosa et al. (Eds.): CAiSE 2021, LNCS 12751, pp. 280–295, 2021.
https://doi.org/10.1007/978-3-030-79382-1_17

query optimizer with new access paths that can lead to substantial speedups in query processing, v) allow the database administrator to improve the efficiency of data access via physical design techniques such as data partitioning or the creation of indexes and materialized views, and vi) provide new insights into application data.

Due to their importance, keys and UCs have been studied for most data models, including graphs. For instance, a notion for keys proposed in academia [5] is very expressive to serve its target application of entity resolution. The notion subsumes keys from XML and conditional constraints [5]. This expressiveness has its price, for example, implication is NP-complete, satisfiability and validation are both coNP-complete to decide [5]. Among a recent surge of graph databases, Neo4j is the most popular one[1]. It employs an expressive property graph model. Objects such as vertices and edges may have properties, which are pairs of an attribute and a value, reflecting the NoSQL nature of graph databases. In this context, Neo4j keys have been investigated recently [8]. These keys require both existence and uniqueness constraints for all vertices.

In this article we develop a flexible and expressive notion of UCs for the property graph model. As existence and uniqueness of properties are often not both achievable for all vertices, UCs offer a more flexible mechanism to manage node integrity than Neo4j keys do. While Neo4j does support UCs, their use is restricted to single labels and single properties. In response, our notion of UCs can take advantage of multiple labels and properties. In contrast to Neo4j UCs, our notion of UCs can separate existence from uniqueness requirements. This allows us to minimize the subset of properties that can uniquely identify all nodes for which a set of properties exist.

In this article we make the following contributions:

- For the flexible management of node integrity in property graphs, we introduce the class of multi-label embedded uniqueness constraints (eUCs). These include various previous notions as special cases.
- We provide real-world examples and use cases that illustrate the benefit of eUCs for graph data management, including updates, indexing, and query optimization.
- We characterize the implication problem of eUCs both axiomatically and algorithmically. Our characterization makes it simple to obtain a set of eUCs that causes a minimal overhead for managing node integrity.
- We outline applications of eUCs in information systems engineering, such as the elicitation of business rules, the identification of data quality problems, and the design for data quality.
- Finally, we give four recommendations for the future use of uniqueness constraints within graph database management systems.

In what follows, we motivate our work with an application scenario in Sect. 2. Section 3 includes a concise review of relevant work. The formal semantics for eUCs over property graphs and their illustration on real-world examples is given in Sect. 4. Use cases of eUCs for efficient updating and querying are discussed in Sect. 5. In Sect. 6, we establish axiomatic and algorithmic characterizations of the implication problem. Applications of eUCs to information systems engineering are illustrated in Sect. 7. Recommendations for the definition and use of uniqueness constraints by graph

---

[1] https://db-engines.com/en/ranking_trend/graph+dbms.

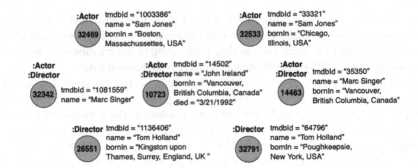

Fig. 1. Real-world vertices, labels, and property-value pairs in *Open Movie Database*

database management systems are given in Sect. 8, before we conclude and briefly comment on future work in Sect. 9.

2 Application Scenario

As a running example, we use the *Open Movie Database*[2]. This dataset is referenced by Neo4j in its user guide. It contains 28,863 nodes and 166,261 edges. We denote the dataset by G_0. Figure 1 shows a few vertices of G_0. For example, the left-most vertex has node identifier *32342*, carries the labels of *Actor* and *Director*, and the properties *tmdbID* = *"1081559"* and *name* = *"Marc Singer"*.

Without looking at the data, we may expect that actors can be identified by their name, and similar for directors. However, the nodes *32469* and *32533* reveal different actors with the same name (*Sam Jones*), while the nodes *26551* and *32791* reveal different directors with the same name (*Tom Holland*). More surprisingly, there appear to be different people that are both actors and directors (with ids *32342* and *14463*), but still share the same name (*Marc Singer*). Hence, even though all nodes with label *Actor* or label *Director* have the property *name*, the three keys {*Actor*}:{*name*}, {*Director*}:{*name*}, and {*Actor,Director*}:{*name*} are all violated.

Due to the existence requirement of keys, adding a property to the key does not help. For example, the key {*Actor,Director*}:{*name,bornIn*} is violated since the vertex *32342* has no property on *bornIn*. In contrast, the UC {*Actor,Director*}:{*name,bornIn*} is satisfied by G_0. That is, there are no different people that are actors and directors, for which properties *name* and *bornIn* exist, and who have matching values on both of those properties. Interestingly, Neo4j only supports UCs with singleton labels and singleton properties, so the UC above cannot be expressed by Neo4j.

However, the property graph G_0 satisfies an even sharper UC. Indeed, there are not even two different people that are both actors and directors, for whom *name* and *bornIn* exist, and who have matching values on just *name*. We call these UCs *embedded* (eUCs), and write $L : (E, U)$ to say that there are no two different vertices with all labels in L, all property attributes in E, and matching values

---
[2] http://www.omdbapi.com.

on all the property attributes in U. Interestingly, neither of the single-label eUCs $\{Actor\}{:}(\{name, bornIn\}, \{name\})$ and $\{Director\}{:}(\{name, bornIn\}, \{name\})$ is satisfied by G_0: The first eUC is violated due to the two actors with name *Sam Jones*, and the second eUC is violated due to the two directors with name *Tom Holland*.

Most interestingly, the validity of $\{Actor,Director\}{:}(\{name, bornIn\}, \{name\})$ suggest that the offending nodes may represent node integrity issues. Indeed, it turns out that the two nodes *32342* and *14463* refer to the same individual *Marc Singer*. Most likely, the issue is that *32342* was entered into the dataset when the property *bornIn* was unavailable, and when it became available the node was not updated but a new node (*14463*) was introduced. This suggests that, ideally, the key $\{Actor,Director\}{:}\{name\}$ should hold. However, without modifying the database, the best we can do is to specify the eUC $\{Actor,Director\}{:}(\{name, bornIn\}, \{name\})$. This is supported by the invalid eUCs $\{Actor\}{:}(\{name, bornIn\}, \{name\})$ and $\{Director\}{:}(\{name, bornIn\}, \{name\})$, and the fact that neither $\{Actor\}{:}\{name\}$ nor $\{Director\}{:}\{name\}$ constitute meaningful keys due to different actors with the same name, and similar for directors.

Our application scenario suggests that eUCs provide a robust notion of constraints that can handle node integrity in the presence of dirty data.

3 Literature Review

We discuss related work on keys and uniqueness constraints from relational databases with missing data, and previous related work on keys for graphs.

While the concept of keys over relational databases with no missing data is unchallenged, various complementary classes of keys and uniqueness constraints exist when some data is missing [7]. Candidate keys require that values on every key attribute exist for every record and that the combination of values on the key attributes is unique for every record. In contrast, UCs only require a unique combination of values for those records for which these values exist for every attribute of the UC. Hence, a set of attributes E is a candidate key when the SQL constraint UNIQUE(E) holds and every attribute in E is defined to be NOT NULL. Recently, eUCs (E, U) have been proposed for relational databases with missing data [10]. Here, the uniqueness of values is only stipulated on a subset $U \subseteq E$ for all records for which values in all attributes in E exist. Indeed, eUCs (E, U) capture SQL UNIQUE as the special case where $E = U$. The benefit of eUCs over SQL UNIQUE in terms of physical data access for more efficient updating and querying has been demonstrated [11].

State-of-the-art graph database management systems provide limited support for node integrity. Similar to candidate keys, Neo4j keys require both existence and uniqueness for all the properties of the key [8]. In [4] the authors propose a class of keys for graphs to perform entity matching. The associated implication problem is NP-complete, and those of satisfiability and validation are coNP-complete [5]. In [6] different ways are discussed for mapping relational databases into an RDF graph, with an emphasis on how to represent the original key and foreign key constraints in the resulting RDF graph. Finally, in [9] the authors put forward some proposals for extending the capabilities of Neo4j in specifying integrity constraints. The authors provide a simple prototype implementation and experiments.

UCs provide a more flexible mechanism for managing node integrity than keys do. However, their current use is limited to single labels and single properties in Neo4j, while composite indices on single labels need to be specified manually. We therefore propose multi-label embedded uniqueness constraints $L : (E, U)$, which subsume Neo4j's UCs as the special case where both $L = \{\ell\}$ and $E = \{e\} = U$ are singleton labels and property attributes, respectively, and Neo4j's composite indices as the special case where $L = \{\ell\}$ is a singleton label and $E = U$. As a running example, the multi-label eUC $\{Actor,Director\}:(\{name,bornIn\}, \{name\})$ is satisfied by the *Open Movie* property graph G_0, frequently used as a showcase by Neo4j. The graph does not satisfy the single-label eUCs $\{Actor\}:(\{name,bornIn\}, \{name\})$ nor $\{Director\}:(\{name,bornIn\}, \{name\})$, as illustrated by G_0. We will formalize our ideas for multi-label eUCs and illustrate their benefits for the effective and efficient management of node integrity in property graphs.

4   Multi-label Embedded Uniqueness Constraints

We recall basics of the property graph model to prepare our formal definition of multi-label embedded uniqueness constraints. Subsequently, we illustrate the new concept of multi-label eUCs on a standard real-world property graph.

4.1   Property Graph Model

We provide the basic definitions for the property graph model [2]. For this we assume that the following sets are pairwise disjoint: $\mathcal{O}$ denotes a set of objects, $\mathcal{L}$ denotes a finite set of labels, $\mathcal{K}$ denotes a set of property attributes, and $\mathcal{N}$ denotes a set of values.

A *property graph* is a quintuple $G = (V, Ed, \eta, \lambda, \nu)$ where $V \subseteq \mathcal{O}$ is a finite set of objects, called *vertices*, $Ed \subseteq \mathcal{O}$ is a finite set of objects, called *edges*, $\eta : E \to V \times V$ is a function assigning to each edge an ordered pair of vertices, $\lambda : V \cup Ed \to \mathcal{P}(\mathcal{L})$ is a function assigning to each object a finite set of labels, and $\nu : (V \cup Ed) \times \mathcal{K} \to \mathcal{N}$ is a partial function assigning values for properties to objects, such that the set of domain values where ν is defined is finite. An example of a property graph is given in Fig. 1.

4.2   Introducing Embedded Uniqueness Constraints

We now formally define the syntax and semantics of embedded uniqueness constraints. These will cover the uniqueness constraints, as used by Neo4j, as a special case.

Before that, we define the subset $V_{\mathfrak{L}} \subseteq V$ of vertices in a property graph that carry at least all the labels of the given set $\mathfrak{L}$ of labels, as follows: $V_{\mathfrak{L}} = \{v \in V \mid \mathfrak{L} \subseteq \lambda(v)\}$.

Definition 1. *For a finite set $\mathcal{L}$ of labels and a finite set $\mathcal{K}$ of property attributes, an* embedded uniqueness constraint *(or eUC) over $\mathcal{L}$ and $\mathcal{K}$ is an expression $L : (E, U)$ where $L \subseteq \mathcal{L}$ and $U \subseteq E \subseteq \mathcal{K}$. For a singleton L we call $L : (E, U)$ a* single-labelled *eUC, and otherwise* multi-labelled. *For a given property graph $G = (V, E, \eta, \lambda, \nu)$ over $\mathcal{O}, \mathcal{L}, \mathcal{K}$, and $\mathcal{N}$ we say that G satisfies the eUC $L : (E, U)$ over $\mathcal{L}$ and $\mathcal{K}$, denoted by $\models_G L : (E, U)$, iff there are no vertices $v_1, v_2 \in V_{\mathfrak{L}}$ such that $v_1 \neq v_2$, for all $A \in E$, $\nu(v_1, A)$ and $\nu(v_2, A)$ are defined, and for all $A \in U$, $\nu(v_1, A) = \nu(v_2, A)$.* □

Neo4j UCs are the special case of eUCs $L : (E, U)$ where $L = \{\ell\}$ and $E = U = \{u\}$, that is, $\{\ell\} : (\{u\}, \{u\})$. Neo4j's composite indices are covered as the special case where $L = \{\ell\}$ and $E = U$, that is, $\{\ell\} : (U, U)$.

4.3   Real-World eUCs for Managing Node Integrity and Node De-Duplication

As real-world examples, Table 1 lists all minimal eUCs $\{Actor, Director\} : (E, U)$ that hold on G_0. Minimal means removal of any attribute from E or U leads to an eUC that is violated by G_0. The eUCs of Table 1 are ranked by their *coverage*, that is, the ratio among all vertices with labels *Actor* and *Director* for which the properties in E exist. The coverage indicates on what ratio of tuples the UC applies. Whenever $E = U$, the eUC denotes a composite UC. The cases where E contains attributes that are not in U are marked in bold font, and indicate eUCs that cannot be expressed as composite UCs. Interestingly, on nodes for people that are both an actor and a director, the *name* uniquely identifies the person as long as one of the properties *bornIn, born*,

Table 1. Minimal eUCs with label set {Actor,Director} satisfied by graph G_0

E	U	*Coverage*
identity	identity	1
tmdbId	tmdbID	1
url	url	1
imdbId	imdbId	0.995893
bornIn, name	**name**	**0.907598**
born, name	**name**	**0.905544**
bornIn, born	*bornIn, born*	*0.891170*
poster, name	**name**	**0.856263**
poster	poster	0.856263
bornIn, died	*bornIn, died*	*0.211499*
born, died	**born**	**0.211499**
died, name	**name**	**0.211499**
poster, died	**died**	**0.197125**

or *poster* exist. Indeed, the UC $\{Actor,Director\}:\{name\}$ is violated. However, the violation only results from the incorrect duplication of nodes for the same individual (*Marc Singer*). In fact, when the values for properties *bornIn, born*, and *poster* became available, a new node (*14463*) was inserted for the same individual rather than updating the existing node (*32342*). This led to duplication. Indeed, if G_0' results from G_0 by removing the old node (*32342*), then G_0' satisfies the key $\{Actor,Director\}:\{name\}$. The example shows that eUCs such as $\{Actor,Director\}:(\{name,bornIn\},\{name\})$ can manage node integrity when dirty data is present (for example when duplication is unknown or unresolvable), or clean dirty data (de-duplicate) and promote UCs such as $\{Actor,Director\}:\{name\}$. Finally, the two composite UCs are marked in italic, and the remaining eUCs are unary UCs.

5   Use Cases

We showcase the use of eUCs on the most common data tasks: updates and queries.

5.1   Updates

A major use case of constraints is to enforce them during updates. This means that every update operation that results in a property graph which would violate some constraint will be rejected (or at least raises some red flag). This is no different for eUCs, but there are important differences to node keys which we will highlight now as well.

Unlike node keys, we can create nodes that miss properties from the eUC, or remove some eUC properties from nodes. Given the key {*Actor,Director*}:{*bornIn,name*}, the operation

```
CREATE   (n:Actor:Director   {name:'Billy Jean'})
```

would not create a new node since a value for the property *bornIn* is not provided. In contrast, the UC {*Actor,Director*}:({*bornIn,name*},{*bornIn,name*}) would permit the creation of this node. Similarly, we may remove the property *bornIn* or *name* from any existing node without violating the eUC, while this is impossible for the node key.

Indeed, eUCs only check uniqueness of the required properties on those nodes for which the required properties exist. Consider the following update operation to the unique node where *tmdbID* = *'1081559'*, see Fig. 1:

```
MATCH (n:Actor:Director {tmdbID: '1081559'})
SET n.bornIn = 'Vancouver' RETURN n.name, n.bornIn
```

This operation creates the property *bornIn* = *"Vancouver"* for this node, without violating the composite UC {*Actor,Director*}:({*bornIn,name*},{*bornIn,name*}) since the only other *:Actor:Director* node that has the same value (*Marc Singer*) on property *name* has a different value on *bornIn* (Vancouver, British Columbia, Canada). In contrast, the same operation will violate eUC {*Actor, Director*}:({*bornIn,name*},{*name*}).

5.2   Indexing for Efficient Updates and Queries

Currently, Neo4j offers two kinds of support for the creation of indices based on uniqueness constraints. Whenever a unary UC with a single label is specified, such as {*l*} : {*u*}, Neo4j will automatically add an index on those property attributes, so such an index cannot be added separately. Currently there is no support for composite uniqueness constraints in Neo4j (not even for single labels). However, composite indices on single labels can be specified manually. For example,

```
CREATE  INDEX  index_Act  FOR  (n:Actor)  ON  (n.bornIn,  n.name)
```

creates an index to enforce the composite UC {*Actor*}:{*bornIn,name*}.

For eUCs there is no support in terms of index structures available. In SQL, eUCs can be enforced using so-called filtered indices, and this should be made available in graph data management systems as well. For example, specifying an eUC such as {*Actor,Director*}:({*bornIn,name*},{*name*}) should automatically create a filtered composite index such as:

```
CREATE INDEX index_Actor_Director FOR (n:Actor:Director)
ON (n.name) WHERE exists(n.bornIn)
```

Note that the index will only be created on nodes n for which the property *name* exists, so exists(n.name) has been omitted from the WHERE clause. The use of such a filtered index would result in speed ups of update operations such as those presented in the last subsection, but also result in speed ups of queries. For instance, executing the following query without an index

$$\text{MATCH (n : Actor : Director)} \tag{1}$$
$$\text{WHERE EXISTS (n.bornIn) AND EXISTS (n.name) RETURN n.name}$$

will do a NodeByLabelScan for the node label *Director*, followed by a filter operation on *Actor*. This query would still take long on realistically-sized property graphs. However, if we create an index as above, the query optimizer use the index and perform an efficient NodeIndexScan search. Illustrating the benefit of these indices, we worked around the index creation by assigning a new label to all nodes that are labeled by *Actor* and *Director* for which the properties *bornIn* and *name* exist, and then created an index on property *name* for nodes with the new label. This is impractical and users must not be burdened with it. As Fig. 2 shows, executing Query (1) results in a total of 15,521 database hits, while utilizing the index will result in a total of 885 hits. Neo4j evaluates the performance of queries by *database hits* as a more accurate measure than query response time. We ran the query ten times without index, followed by ten runs with the index, and their average run time was 8.3 ms without and 2.3 ms with index. Hence, we can clearly recognize the benefit of indexing.

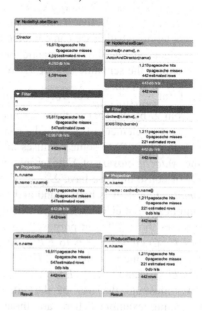

Fig. 2. Performance of Query (1) without (left) and with index

6 Reasoning

We formally define the implication problem associated with eUCs over property graphs, illustrate it on examples, and establish axiomatic and algorithmic solutions.

Given a set $\mathcal{L}$ of labels and a set $\mathcal{K}$ of property attributes, let $\Sigma \cup \{\varphi\}$ denote a set of eUCs over $\mathcal{L}$ and $\mathcal{K}$. The *implication problem* for eUCs is to decide, given $\Sigma \cup \{\varphi\}$, whether Σ implies φ. In fact, Σ *implies* φ, denoted by $\Sigma \models \varphi$, if and only if every property graph G that satisfies all eUCs in Σ also satisfies φ.

The ability to efficiently decide whether some eUC φ is implied by Σ is funda-mental for node integrity management on property graphs. If φ is implied by a mean-ingful set Σ of eUCs, then we do not need to specify φ because it is specified already implicitly. However, if φ is not implied, then failure to specify it explicitly will result in integrity faults that cannot be detected.

6.1 Axiomatic Characterization

We will establish an axiomatization for eUCs. The set $\Sigma^* = \{\varphi \mid \Sigma \models \varphi\}$ denotes the *semantic closure of* Σ, that is, the set of all eUCs implied by Σ. The semantic closure does not tell us whether we can compute it, nevermind how. It is a core reasoning task to investigate whether/how a semantic notion can be characterized syntactically. In fact, we determine the semantic closure Σ^* of a set Σ of eUCs by applying *inference rules* of the form $\dfrac{\text{premise}}{\text{conclusion}}$. For a set $\mathfrak{R}$ of inference rules let $\Sigma \vdash_{\mathfrak{R}} \varphi$ denote the *inference* of φ from Σ by $\mathfrak{R}$. That is, there is some sequence $\sigma_1, \ldots, \sigma_n$ such that $\sigma_n = \varphi$ and every σ_i is an element of Σ or is the conclusion that results from an application of an inference rule in $\mathfrak{R}$ to some premises in $\{\sigma_1, \ldots, \sigma_{i-1}\}$. Let $\Sigma_{\mathfrak{R}}^+ = \{\varphi \mid \Sigma \vdash_{\mathfrak{R}} \varphi\}$ be the *syntactic closure* of Σ under inferences by $\mathfrak{R}$. $\mathfrak{R}$ is *sound* (*complete*) if for every set Σ of constraints we have $\Sigma_{\mathfrak{R}}^+ \subseteq \Sigma^*$ ($\Sigma^* \subseteq \Sigma_{\mathfrak{R}}^+$). The (finite) set $\mathfrak{R}$ is a (finite) *axiomatization* if $\mathfrak{R}$ is both sound and complete. Table 2 shows an inference rule for the implication of eUCs, which we will show to be sound and complete. The extension rule serves three different purposes, covering redundant extensions of the i) label set L to LL', ii) embedding E to EE', and unique property set U to UU'. Note that we implicitly assume here that $L : (E, U)$ and $LL' : (EE', UU')$ are both well-formed, that is, $U \subseteq E$ and $UU' \subseteq EE'$.

We illustrate the use of the inference rules on our running example. There are three distinct ways in which the extension rule $\mathcal{E}$ can be applied. Firstly, we may use it to extend the labels. For instance, the eUC $\{Actor\}:(\{died, name\}, \{name\})$ holds on G_0. Consequently, we can apply $\mathcal{E}$ to infer the eUC $\{Actor, Director\}:(\{died, name\}, \{name\})$. Sec-

Table 2. Axiomatization $\mathfrak{E} = \{\mathcal{E}\}$ of multi-label eUCs with the extension rule $\mathcal{E}$

$$\frac{L : (E, U)}{LL' : (EE', UU')}$$

ondly, we may use $\mathcal{E}$ to extend the embedding E. For instance, the eUC $\{Actor, Director\}:(\{poster, name\}, \{name\})$ holds on G_0. Hence, an application of the extension rule $\mathcal{E}$ allows us to infer the eUC $\{Actor, Director\}:(\{bornIn, poster, name\}, \{name\})$. Finally, we may use $\mathcal{E}$ to extend the property attribute set U. For instance, an application of $\mathcal{E}$ to the eUC $\{Actor, Director\}:(\{bornIn, poster, name\}, \{name\})$ results in the eUC $\{Actor, Director\}:(\{bornIn, poster, name\}, \{poster, name\})$. Since we prove in the following theorem that the extension rule $\mathcal{E}$ is sound, all the inferred eUCs are also satisfied by G_0.

We will now show that $\mathfrak{E} = \{\mathcal{E}\}$ forms indeed a sound and complete set of inference rules for the implication of multi-label eUCs over property graphs.

Theorem 1. *The set* $\mathfrak{E} = \{\mathcal{E}\}$ *forms a finite axiomatization for the implication of multi-label embedded uniqueness constraints over property graphs.*

Proof. For the soundness of $\mathfrak{E}$ we use contra-position to prove that the extension rule $\mathcal{E}$ is sound. For that purpose assume there is a property graph G that violates the eUC $LL' : (EE', UU')$. We need to show that G also violates the eUC $L : (E, U)$. Since G violates $L : (E, U)$, there are vertices $v_1, v_2 \in V_{LL'}$ such that $v_1 \neq v_2$ and for all $A \in EE'$, $\nu(v_1, A)$ and $\nu(v_2, A)$ are defined, and for all $A \in UU'$, $\nu(v_1, A) = \nu(v_2, A)$. Hence, $v_1, v_2 \in V_{LL'} \subseteq V_L$ such that $v_1 \neq v_2$ and for all $A \in E$, $\nu(v_1, A)$ and $\nu(v_2, A)$ are defined, and for all $A \in U$, $\nu(v_1, A) = \nu(v_2, A)$. Consequently, G would also violate the eUC $L : (E, U)$. This means $\mathfrak{E}$ is sound.

We show the completeness of $\mathfrak{E}$ by contra-position. Let $\Sigma \cup \{L : (E, U)\}$ denote a set of eUCs over $\mathcal{L}$ and $\mathcal{K}$ such that $L : (E, U) \notin \Sigma^+$. We will show that Σ does not imply $L : (E, U)$ by defining a property graph G that satisfies all eUCs in Σ and violates $L : (E, U)$.

Table 3. Simplifying $\mathfrak{E}$ for composite indices in Neo4j

$\{l\} : (U, U)$	$\{l\} : U$
$\{l\} : (UU', UU')$	$\{l\} : UU'$

Let us define the property graph $G = (V, Ed, \eta, \lambda, \nu)$ as follows: $V = \{v_1, v_2\}$, $Ed = \emptyset$, and therefore there is nothing to define for η, $\lambda(v_1) = L = \lambda(v_2)$, for all $A \in U$ we define $\nu(v_1, A) = 0 = \nu(v_2, A)$, for all $A \in E$ we define $\nu(v_1, A) = 0$ and $\nu(v_2, A) = 1$, and for all $A \in \mathcal{K} - E$, $\nu(v_1, A)$ and $\nu(v_2, A)$ remain undefined. It follows that G violates $L : (E, U)$ since there are $v_1, v_2 \in V_L$ such that $v_1 \neq v_2$, for all $A \in E$, $\nu(v_1, A)$ and $\nu(v_2, A)$ are defined, and for all $A \in U$, $\nu(v_1, A) = \nu(v_2, A)$. It remains to show that G satisfies every $L' : (E', U') \in \Sigma$. Assume, to the contrary, that G violates some $L' : (E', U') \in \Sigma$. Consequently, $v_1, v_2 \in V_{L'}$ such that $v_1 \neq v_2$, for all $A \in E'$, $\nu(v_1, A)$ and $\nu(v_2, A)$ are defined, and for all $A \in U'$, $\nu(v_1, A) = \nu(v_2, A)$. This is only possible when $L' \subseteq L$, $E' \subseteq E$, and $U' \subseteq U$ hold. This, however, would mean that $L : (E, U) \in \Sigma^+$ by a single application of the extension rule $\mathcal{E}$ to $L' : (E', U') \in \Sigma$. This would contradict our premise that $L : (E, U) \notin \Sigma^+$. Consequently, our assumption that G violates some eUC in Σ must have been wrong. We conclude that G satisfies every eUC in Σ and violates $L : (E, U)$. We conclude that Σ does not imply $L : (E, U)$, which establishes the completeness of $\mathfrak{E}$. □

Suppose Σ consists of the single multi-label UC $\{Actor, Director\}:(\{bornIn, name\}, \{bornIn, name\})$, and φ denotes the multi-label eUC $\{Actor, Director\}:(\{bornIn, name\}, \{name\})$. The property graph in Fig. 3 witnesses that Σ does not imply φ, since the two vertices are both labeled *Actor* and *Director*, both have properties *bornIn* and *name* with matching values on *name* and non-matching values on *bornIn*.

Strictly speaking, UCs in Neo4j are only defined on single labels and only for a single property, that is, $\{l\} : \{u\}$.

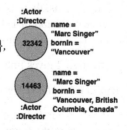

Fig. 3. Witness graph for $\varphi \notin \Sigma^*$

Algorithm 1. Implication of eUCs

Require: Set $\Sigma \cup \{L : (E, U)\}$
Ensure: *TRUE*, if $\Sigma \models L : (E, U)$, and *FALSE*, otherwise
 1: **for all** $L' : (E', U') \in \Sigma$ **do**
 2:     **if** $L' \subseteq L$ and $E' \subseteq E$ and $U' \subseteq U$ **then**   ▷ We found an eUC that implies $L : (E, U)$
 3:         **return** *TRUE*
 4: **return** *FALSE*

In this form, no inference rule is required to achieve completeness. In other words, only those constraints in the class are implied that are explicitly specified. Of course, the Neo4j UCs still imply constraints from other classes, such as composite UCs or eUCs. Table 3 shows how the axiomatization for eUCs becomes simpler for the special case of composite indices, as used by Neo4j. In particular, the separation of E and U is no longer necessary since $E = U$ in this case. For that reason the inference rule on the left-hand side of Table 3 can be written in a more concise form as the inference rule on the right-hand side.

It should be noted that eUCs enjoy a more natural axiomatization than Neo4j's keys from [8]. In particular, the axiomatization for Neo4j keys is binary, while that for eUCs is unary. This means that any eUC that is implied by a given set Σ of eUCs is always implied by a single eUC $\sigma \in \Sigma$. In particular, the implied eUC can be inferred from σ by a single application of the extension rule $\mathcal{E}$.

6.2 Algorithmic Characterization

The axiomatization of eUCs enables us to establish an algorithm that decides implication efficiently. In fact, we can directly prove the following characterization for the implication problem, from which we will derive such an algorithm.

Theorem 2. *For every eUC set $\Sigma \cup \{L : (E, U)\}$ over $\mathcal{L}$ and $\mathcal{K}$, $\Sigma \models L : (E, U)$ if and only if there is some $L' : (E', U') \in \Sigma$ such that $L' \subseteq L$, $E' \subseteq E$ and $U' \subseteq U$.*

Proof. **Sufficiency** ($\Leftarrow$). If there is some $L' : (E', U') \in \Sigma$ such that $L' \subseteq L$, $E' \subseteq E$ and $U' \subseteq U$ hold, then an application of the *extension rule* $\mathcal{E}$ shows that $L : (E, U) \in \Sigma_{\mathfrak{E}}^+$. The soundness of $\mathfrak{E}$ means that $L : (E, U)$ is implied by Σ.

Necessity ($\Rightarrow$). Suppose that for all $L' : (E', U') \in \Sigma$ where $L' \subseteq L$, $E' \subseteq E$, we have $U' \not\subseteq U$. That is, there is some property $A \in U' - U$. This constitutes the main case in the proof of Theorem 1. Hence, the property graph created in that case satisfies Σ and violates $L : (E, U)$. Consequently, $L : (E, U)$ is not implied by Σ. $\square$

Theorem 2 gives linear time decidability for eUC implication.

Corollary 1. *Algorithm 1 decides eUC implication in linear input time.*

Proof. The soundness of Algorithm 1 is a simple application of Theorem 2. Hence, it suffices to scan the input $\Sigma \cup \{L : (E, U)\}$ once to determine whether there is an eUC $L' : (E', U') \in \Sigma$ such that $L' \subseteq L$, $E' \subseteq E$ and $U' \subseteq U$. Consequently, Algorithm 1 runs in time $\mathcal{O}(|\Sigma \cup \{L : (E, U)\}|)$. $\square$

Suppose $\Sigma = \{\sigma\}$ consists of the single multi-label UC $\{Actor,Director\}$:$(\{bornIn, name\},\{bornIn,name\})$, and φ denotes the multi-label eUC $\{Actor,Director\}$:$(\{bornIn, name\},\{name\})$. Here, φ is not implied by Σ. Indeed, while σ and φ share the same labels and embeddings, the property $bornIn$ of σ is not a property of φ. For a different example, let $\Sigma' = \{\sigma'\}$ consists of the eUC $\{Actor,Director\}$:$(\{poster,name\},\{name\})$, and φ' denotes the eUC $\{Actor,Director\}$:$(\{bornIn,poster,name\},\{bornIn,name\})$. Then φ' is indeed implied Σ' due to the soundness of $\mathcal{E}$.

7   Applications in Information Systems Engineering

We highlight how eUCs can be used to identify in parallel i) meaningful business semantics, and ii) data quality problems. In addition, we give an example of how eUCs can be used for the design of graph data models.

7.1   Business Rule Elicitation and Detecting Data Quality Problems

As mentioned, a closer look at the eUC $\{Actor,Director\}$:$(\{bornIn,name\},\{name\})$ suggests the following question: Are there really different people who were actors and directors and have the same name?

Figure 1 shows two different actors with the name *Sam Jones*, and two different directors with the name *Tom Holland*. The multi-label UC $\{Actor,Director\}$:$\{name\}$ is violated due to different nodes with *Marc Singer*. Figure 4 reveals that both nodes refer to the same person. It is simply that this director and actor was recorded with different identifiers and *tmdbIDs*. For one of these nodes, the properties $bornIn$, $born$, and $poster$ do not exist.

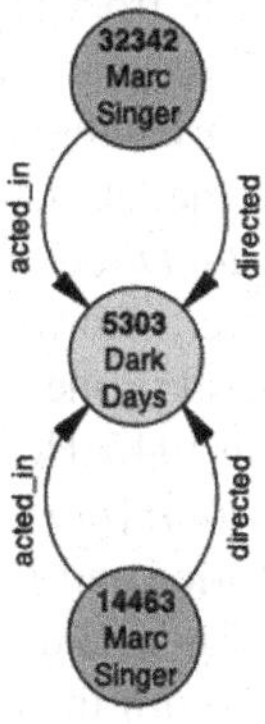

The validity of the eUC $\{Actor,Director\}$:$(\{bornIn,name\},\{name\})$ made us question why the UC $\{Actor,Director\}$:$\{name\}$ does not hold. A closer look showed us that the only violation resulted from duplicating the person Marc Singer. This dirty data makes us realize that no two different people that are actors and directors share the same name. Hence, the UC $\{Actor,Director\}$:$\{name\}$ is a business rule.

Fig. 4. Duplication of Marc Singer

Realizing that constraints express meaningful business semantics and any violations constitute dirty data can be facilitated by mining constraints from data, and letting domain experts inspect node samples. In the perfect case, we find a small number of nodes that satisfy the same eUCs as the original dataset does. This supports domain experts in their task of spotting dirty data and help data stewards realize, as a consequence, which constraints constitute business rules.

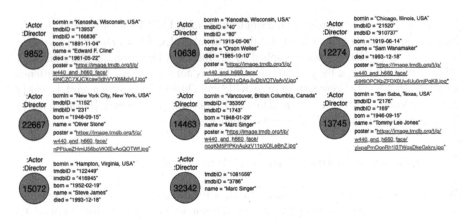

Fig. 5. Perfect node sample for the node set with labels *Actor* and *Director*

Figure 5 shows a perfect node sample that consists of only eight nodes that satisfy exactly the same eUCs with label set {*Actor,Director*} as the original dataset with 487 nodes does. Note that the minimal eUCs from Table 1 cover the set of eUCs with label set {*Actor,Director*} that hold on G_0. In this sense, the eUCs from Table 1 and the node sample from Fig. 5 represent the same information from different points of views. The eUC set is the abstract description of the eUCs that hold, while the perfect sample is a user-friendly view that violates all those eUCs that do not hold.

The UC {*Actor,Director*}:{*bornIn,born*} that holds on G_0 raises the question why {*Actor,Director*}:{*bornIn*} and {*Actor,Director*}:{*born*} are not business rules. For the former, *Edward F. Cline* and *Orson Welles* were both born in Kenosha, Wisconsin, USA. For the latter, *Oliver Stone* and *Tommy Lee Jones* were both born on September 15 in 1946. However, is {*Actor,Director*}:{*bornIn,born*} indeed a minimal UC? In fact, {*Actor*}:{*bornIn,born*} or {*Director*}:{*bornIn,born*} may already be UCs. The twins Maurice and Robin Gibb (the Bee Gees) were also actors, so {*Actor*}:{*bornIn,born*} does not hold. According to G_0, the directors Remy Belvaux and Andre Bonzel were both born in Naumur on 11/10/1966, so {*Director*}:{*bornIn,born*} does not appear to be a business rule either. However, Andre Bonzel was actually born on 13 May 1961 in Paris, so the information in the dataset is wrong. The dataset further says that both directors Danny Pang and Alan Mak were born on 1 January 1965 in Hong Kong. However, Danny Pang was actually born on 11 November 1965, so we have found more data quality problems. Finally, the twins Christoph and Wolfgang Lauenstein were both directors, so the UC {*Director*}:{*bornIn,born*} is not a business rule. However, the eUC {*Director*}:({*poster,bornIn,born*},{*bornIn,born*}) holds on G_0 with a coverage of 0.43. We just saw that {*Actor,Director*}:{*bornIn,born*} is indeed a minimal UC on G_0, and have found some dirty data in the dataset along the way.

7.2 Towards Data Quality-Driven Schema Design

The design for data quality is an unresolved problem in information systems engineering [1]: "The problem of measuring and improving the quality of data has been dealt with in the literature as an activity to be performed a posteriori, instead of during the design of the data. As a consequence, the design for data quality is still a largely unexplored area. In particular, while the data quality elicitation and the translation of data quality requirements into conceptual schemas have been investigated; there is a lack of comprehensive methodologies covering all the phases of design of information systems/databases/data warehouse systems." We understand our data-completeness tailored framework from [12] as a first step towards a comprehensive methodology for data-quality driven schema design.

Our notion of eUCs facilitates an extension of this framework to property graphs. Consider the property graph on the left of Fig. 6, where nodes represent parents that pay a benefit, which is determined by the number of their known children. Based on the embedded functional dependency (eFD) $\{parent, child, benefit\} : parent \rightarrow benefit$ on nodes with label *LiableParent*, both occurrences of *benefit* = 240 are redundant. The eFD is satisfied since for all *LiableParent* nodes with properties *parent*, *child*, and *benefit*, matching values on *parent* imply matching values on *benefit*. The occurrence of *benefit* = *360* does not cause inconsistency since the property *child* is missing on the node. Hence, the eFD facilitates a transformation into the graph on the right of Fig. 6. The data redundancy is removed by forming a collection of all the existing children, which can be understood as a value itself. This is achieved by transforming the eFD into the eUC $\{LiableParent\}:(\{parent, child, benefit\}:\{parent\})$ ensuring that no data redundancy can occur on benefit, whenever the property *child* exists.

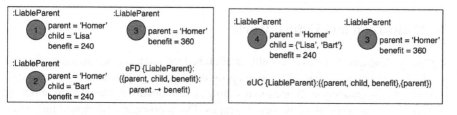

Fig. 6. Removing node redundancy by transforming eFDs into eUCs

8 Recommendations for Graph Database Systems

Finally, we offer some recommendations to enhance the capability of graph database systems in managing the integrity of nodes with uniqueness constraints.

Support Composite UCs. Currently, Neo4j only offers support for UCs on single properties. This is beneficial to natural identifiers, such as employee id or national health identifiers, or surrogate identifiers. The latter invites multiple identifiers for the same entity, creating problems for data analytics and management. The support of composite UCs is not only natural but also beneficial.

Support Multi-label UCs. Currently, Neo4j only supports constraints on single labels. The use of multi-labels is beneficial for at least two reasons. (1) Property graph databases often claim support for multi-labels. While true in terms of data modeling and querying, there are opportunities to improve updates. (2) Constraints on nodes with a single label also apply to nodes with additional labels. However, additional constraints naturally apply to multi-label nodes. For example, G_0 does not satisfy single-label UCs Actor:{bornIn,born} nor Director:{bornIn,born}, but does satisfy the multi-label UC {Actor,Director}:{bornIn,born}.

Support Embedded UCs. Foremost, eUCs separate completeness and uniqueness requirements to clarify the role of each property. This separation translates into more targeted management of node integrity, more efficient updates and query operations, business rule elicitation, de-duplication of nodes, and graph model design.

Support Filtered Composite Indices. Currently, Neo4j only supports composite indices on single labels. An extension to multiple labels is illustrated by

```
CREATE  INDEX  FOR  (n:Actor:Director)  ON  (n.bornIn,  n.name)
```

which supports the UC {Actor,Director}:{name,bornIn}. This is insufficient for eUCs $L : (E, U)$ which require filtering by existence constraints on E, and the specification of properties in U, based on the node set with labels in L. For our example eUC {Actor,Director}:({name,bornIn},{name}), the following is a filtered composite index.

```
CREATE  INDEX  FOR  (n:Actor:Director)  ON  (n.name)  WHERE
        exists  (n.bornIn)  and  exists  (n.name)
```

9   Conclusion and Future Work

We have introduced the class of multi-label embedded uniqueness constraints (eUCs) for the flexible management of node integrity in property graphs. Our class separated existence from uniqueness concerns, resulting in additional benefits for the efficient updating and querying of properties in graphs. Our axiomatic and algorithmic characterization of their associated implication problem shows that eUCs can be reasoned about efficiently, further justifying our recommendations for their use in future graph database management systems.

For future work, we plan to investigate other computational problems associated with eUCs. These include their discovery from property graphs, the computation of perfect samples to facilitate the elicitation of meaningful eUCs and the identification of node integrity faults, and their extreme behavior. The latter refers to the combinatorial problem of characterizing which families of non-redundant eUCs attain maximum cardinality. A solution to this problem will provide us with worst-case bounds for their management, and a better understanding of the search space for the discovery problem.

References

1. Batini, C., Maurino, A.: Design for data quality. In: Liu, L., Özsu, M.T. (eds.) Encyclopedia of Database Systems, 2nd edn. (2018)

2. Bonifati, A., Fletcher, G.H.L., Voigt, H., Yakovets, N.: Querying Graphs. Morgan & Claypool Publishers, Synthesis Lectures on Data Management (2018)
3. Codd, E.F.: A relational model of data for large shared data banks. Commun. ACM **13**(6), 377–387 (1970)
4. Fan, W., Fan, Z., Tian, C., Dong, X.L.: Keys for graphs. PVLDB **8**(12), 1590–1601 (2015)
5. Fan, W., Lu, P.: Dependencies for graphs. ACM Trans. Database Syst. **44**(2), 5:1–5:40 (2019)
6. Lausen, G.: Relational databases in RDF: keys and foreign keys. In: SWDB-ODBIS, pp. 43–56 (2007)
7. Link, S.: Old keys that open new doors. In: Foundations of Information and Knowledge Systems - 10th International Symposium, FoIKS 2018, Budapest, Hungary, May 14–18, 2018, Proceedings, pp. 3–13 (2018)
8. Link, S.: Neo4j keys. In: Conceptual Modeling - 39th International Conference, ER 2020, Vienna, Austria, 3–6 November, 2020, Proceedings, pp. 19–33 (2020)
9. Pokorný, J., Valenta, M., Kovacic, J.: Integrity constraints in graph databases. In: The 8th International Conference on Ambient Systems, Networks and Technologies (ANT 2017) / The 7th International Conference on Sustainable Energy Information Technology (SEIT 2017), 16–19 May 2017, Madeira, Portugal. Procedia Computer Science, vol. 109, pp. 975–981. Elsevier (2017)
10. Wei, Z., Leck, U., Link, S.: Discovery and ranking of embedded uniqueness constraints. PVLDB **12**(13), 2339–2352 (2019)
11. Wei, Z., Leck, U., Link, S.: Entity integrity, referential integrity, and query optimization with embedded uniqueness constraints. In: 35th IEEE International Conference on Data Engineering, ICDE 2019, Macao, China, 8–11 April, 2019, pp. 1694–1697 (2019)
12. Wei, Z., Link, S.: Embedded functional dependencies and data-completeness tailored database design. Proc. VLDB Endow. **12**(11), 1458–1470 (2019)

Refining Case Models Using Cardinality Constraints

Stephan Haarmann[1(✉)], Marco Montali[2], and Mathias Weske[1]

[1] Hasso Plattner Institute, University of Potsdam, Potsdam, Germany
{stephan.haarmann,mathias.weske}@hpi.de
[2] Free University of Bozen-Bolzano, Bolzano, Italy
montali@inf.unibz.it

Abstract. Traditionally, business process management focuses on structured, imperative processes. With the increasing importance of knowledge work, semi-structured processes are entering center stage. Existing approaches to modeling knowledge-intensive processes use data objects but fail to sufficiently take into account data object cardinalities. Hence, they cannot guarantee that cardinality constraints are respected, nor use such constraints to handle concurrency and multiple activity instances during execution. This paper extends an existing case management approach with data object associations and cardinality constraints. The results facilitate a refined data access semantics, lower and upper bounds for process activities, and synchronized processing of multiple data objects. The execution semantics is formally specified by colored Petri nets. The effectiveness of the approach is shown by a compiler translating case models to colored Petri nets and by a dedicated process execution engine.

Keywords: Case management · Execution semantics · Petri nets

1 Introduction

Organizations apply Business Process Management (BPM) to specify, organize, analyze, and enact business processes. Models play an important role in documenting, improving, configuring, and monitoring these processes. Control flow-oriented process modeling languages, such as BPMN [22], are suited for well-structured processes. However, they lack support for semi-structured ones often required for knowledge work [5]. When executing knowledge-intensive processes, knowledge workers make informed decisions choosing from a set of possible continuations for a process. Thereby, they consult and maintain data objects.

Effective models of knowledge-intensive processes must capture flexible and data-centric behavior concisely and comprehensibly. Still, knowledge workers must decide how to progress each case in an ad-hoc manner. To address these requirements, among others, declarative [1,14,24] and artifact-centric modeling approaches [7,16,18] have been proposed. Declarative approaches concisely define

© Springer Nature Switzerland AG 2021
M. La Rosa et al. (Eds.): CAiSE 2021, LNCS 12751, pp. 296–310, 2021.
https://doi.org/10.1007/978-3-030-79382-1_18

processes with many variants through rules that eliminate undesired behavior. Artifact-centric models decompose processes based on data objects, called artifacts, or states thereof and combine the parts dynamically at run-time.

There also exist hybrid approaches such as fragment-based Case Management (fCM) [13,19]. fCM combines traditional BPMN-like control flow with a stronger focus on data objects. Processes are defined through multiple activity-centric process fragments. Each case manages a set of data objects, which can be accessed by all fragments of a given case. Consequently, the data requirements for process activities can lead to sophisticated dependencies among fragments. Data objects and their states are not only used for determining the process execution semantics but also for defining the goal of a case.

While previous works on fCM have focused on the approach from a conceptual perspective, process execution semantics have only been investigated informally. Behavior is specified in fragments, which are loosely coupled through data requirements and shared objects. Notably, these dependencies are not merely based on data objects and their states but also by their mutual associations and their cardinalities. In this paper, we focus on the following research question:

RQ: How can we formally characterize the execution of fCM models while considering data associations and cardinality constraints?

We present a thorough execution semantics for fCM case models, which takes into account process fragments and data objects with their respective states. Cardinality constraints of data objects are captured in the domain model and considered in activities' enablement conditions. The formalization is expressed as a translational semantics mapping fCM case models to colored Petri nets (CPN). It allows us to describe the process behavior precisely, to verify models formally, and to provide IT support during execution. In this regard, we present prototypes of a compiler (fCM to CPN) and a dedicated execution engine.

In Sect. 2, we present the fCM language by example. We specify the execution semantics in Sect. 3. We present our prototypes and a discussion in Sect. 4. Section 5 discusses related work. We conclude our paper in Sect. 6.

2   FCM Syntax and Notation

An fCM case model consists of a domain model, an object life cycle for each class in the domain model, fragments, and termination conditions [13]. We extend case models with data associations and cardinality constraints and thus get a full-fledged but non-hierarchical data model to represent structural aspects.

There is one domain model with associations and cardinality constraints for each case model. In practice, there may be only one domain model for the enterprise. However, the case class and goal cardinality constraints need to be defined for each case model. Domain model are visualized as UML class diagrams. We distinguish two types of cardinality constraints: *global cardinality constraints* must always hold, while *goal cardinality constraints* must hold when the case is closed. This accounts for "transient" states on the way towards the final state and is in the same spirit of what is supported by alternative approaches (cf. [1]).

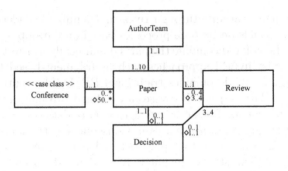

Fig. 1. The domain model of the submission and reviewing phase of an academic conference. Goal cardinality constraints have a leading ◇. They are depicted if and only if they refine the corresponding global constraints.

Consider a process for submitting and reviewing conference papers. The domain model (Fig. 1) contains classes for the conference, papers, authors, reviews, and decisions as well as associations among them. The conference is the case object and instantiated exactly once in each case. The association between the classes Paper and Conference together with its corresponding cardinality constraints requires exactly one conference for each paper and allows arbitrary many papers for each conference (global cardinality constraints). The goal cardinality must be at least 50, even though a conference exists independently of any paper.

For each class in the domain model, the case model has one object life cycle (OLC). An OLC contains a finite set of abstract states and transitions. fCM does not rely on initial and final states as other approaches do. In fact, the knowledge workers decide how to reach the case goal within the constraints given by the case model. A conference object, for example, can be in one of the states scheduled, open for submissions, closed for submissions, and reviewing closed (cf. Fig. 2). OLCs are not always sequences. They can contain disconnected parts in case of alternative initial states and branches in case of alternative state progressions.

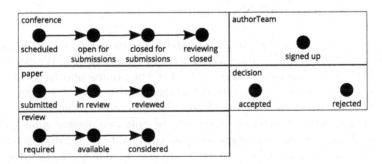

Fig. 2. Object life cycles for each class in the conference example (cf. Fig. 1) depicted as graphs. Each object life cycle consists of a set of states and state transitions between these states. States are represented by labeled circles, transitions by unlabeled arcs.

Objects are created and updated by activities. fCM places activities in acyclic control flow graphs called fragments (Fig. 3), which may additionally include XOR-gateways and start events. Activities read and write data objects, which are partitioned into input- and output sets, respectively. Furthermore, activities can operate on sets of objects[1]. All prerequisites fulfilled, fragments can run repeatedly and concurrently. While our example includes no XOR-gateways and fCM does not support loops and AND-gateways, decisions, concurrency, and loops can be modeled using alternative, concurrent, and repeatable fragments, respectively. In the example shown in Fig. 3, fragments *fb–ff* can be executed multiple times. Furthermore, instances of fragments *fc–ff* can run concurrently.

A case can end if a termination condition is satisfied (a goal is accomplished). For convenience, we define predicates called *object configurations* that require an object of a class in a state, e.g., *conference[scheduled]*. We call a set of object configurations a *data condition*. A termination condition is a data condition. The example has a single termination condition {*conference[reviewing closed]*}.

For fCM's formal definition, we refer to [13] and to our technical report [11].

3   Execution Semantics

A formal semantics is crucial to understand how fragments and objects interact, and for process analysis, execution, and monitoring. We present a semantics for fCM case models with data objects, associations, and cardinality constraints. We describe the execution of the example to provide an intuitive understanding. Then, we define a translational semantics targeting colored Petri nets (CPNs).

3.1   Walk-Through

A new case of the example in Sect. 2 begins once a conference is scheduled (*fa*). The start event creates the case object (conference). In general, non-initial fragments can begin after the start event; in the example, however, no fragment can be instantiated yet because the data prerequisites of their respective first activities are not satisfied. Thus, the conference must be opened for submissions first (*fa*) to fulfill the requirements of "submit paper" (*fb*).

When an author team submits their first paper (input set •, Fig. 3), a paper object and an author team object are created. Both get associated since objects that are created together and whose classes are associated get associated. Papers also get associated with the conference object as objects read get associated with newly created objects if their classes are associated. Global cardinality constraints must hold, i.e., an author team may submit not more than ten papers. Papers can be submitted concurrently (multiple instances of *fb*), but an instance of *fb* handles the submission and notification of only one paper. The submission is closed eventually (*fa*). Since no new papers can be accepted anymore, the conference-to-paper associations must meet the goal cardinality constraint. So, "close submission" requires 50 or more papers and updates them all.

---

[1] Previous fCM versions do not support set objects.

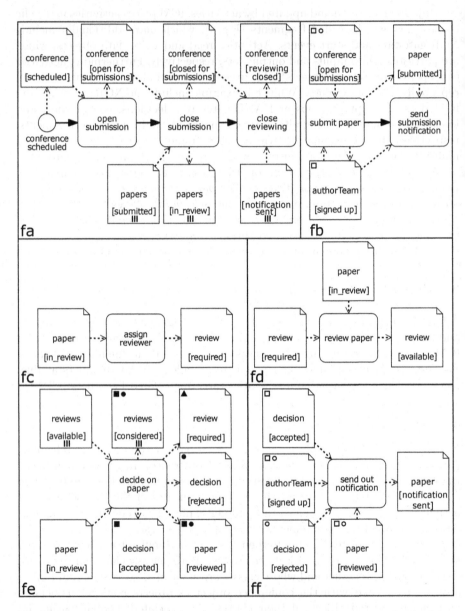

Fig. 3. Process fragments for the conference example. Each fragment is depicted as a graph consisting of BPMN elements. If an activity has more than one input- or output set, we added markers to the data object nodes to indicate the sets (in BPMN these are defined as attributes), e.g., submit paper has the input sets ○ = {*conference* [*open for submissions*]} and □ = {*conference*[*open for submissions*], *authorTeam* [*signed_up*]} differentiating between an author team's first and any consecutive submission. This is visually indicated by the markers ○ and □, respectively.

After the submission has been closed, reviews for each paper are assigned (*fc*) and consequently created (*fd*). At most four reviews can be assigned to each paper (global cardinality constraint). Once all reviews for a given paper have been created, fragment *fe* can be executed: if there are less than three reviews, the outcome is an additional required review (output set ▲); if there are three reviews, the knowledge workers may decide that an additional review is needed or accept/reject the paper (output sets • and ■, respectively); if there are already four reviews, the first option (▲) is no longer applicable. Once a decision for the paper has been created, a notification is sent to the authors (*ff*). Once notifications for all papers have been sent, the reviewing phase is closed (*fa*). The whole case can be closed when the termination condition *conference[reviewing closed]* is fulfilled and all goal cardinality constraints are satisfied.

3.2   A Translational Semantics

As we have shown, the behavior defined in the fragments is significantly refined by the associations and their cardinality constraints. We define a translational semantics for fCM models to CPNs describing the behavior formally.

Assumptions & Preprocessing. To focus on the main aspects of the formalization and to avoid introducing additional complexity, we only support binary associations and at most one association between a pair of classes. This guarantees that, at the fragment level, no ambiguity arises when one wants to create a link between a pair of objects. Also, we assume that all the associations are existential. An association is existential if at least one of the corresponding global cardinality constraints has a positive lower bound. This means that an object of one of the involved classes cannot exist without an object of the other class. We call these objects *dependent* and *supporter*, respectively (in [26] such objects are called *slave* and *master*). Finally, we do not allow many-to-many associations.

To meet these condition, one has to operate on the data model via reification. A violating association is replaced by classes and multiple (compliant) associations. This comes at the price of enriching the vocabulary of the domain as extra classes and associations are added. For example, a many-to-many association A between classes c_1 and c_2 can be reified into a new class c_A related to c_1 and c_2 via two many-to-one associations. In some cases, such as reflexive associations, reification must be performed iteratively.

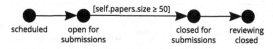

Fig. 4. OLC of the conference augmented with guards. The conference can only change to the state "closed for submissions" if there are at least 50 associated papers. This requirement arises from the goal cardinality constraints and the fragments: eventually, there must be 50 papers, and the fragments do not support adding papers for a conference once it is in the state "closed for submissions".

An activity that creates a *dependent* must read or co-create a *supporter*, i.e., "submit paper" must read the conference to create a paper. Such activities make assumptions about the states of the *supporter* object (i.e., *conference[open for submissions]*). If the state of a *supporter* is irreversibly changed to another, no further *dependents* can be created (i.e., *conference[closed for submissions]*); thus, the goal cardinality constraint must hold. This knowledge is encoded in the OLCs and the fragments: fragments describe the data requirements for each activity; OLCs describe valid state transitions, e.g., the OLC for the conference has no path from *closed for submissions* to *open for submissions*. Thus, we augment state transitions with guards to assert goal cardinality constraints (see Fig. 4).

Translation. We define the formal execution semantics for fCM by mapping case models to CPNs. A CPN is a Petri net with typed places and tokens. Transitions can have guards based on tokens and may derive new tokens from existing ones.

We define types, also called *colorsets*, to represent data objects, associations, and control flow. Objects are of type ID, where an ID consists of a class and an integer (i.e., number of objects of the same class at the point of creation). An association is an unordered pair of IDs. Instead of a token for each association, we use one token for the set of all associations. This representation for associations in CPNs is better suited than individual association tokens, since the content of a token can be queried. Also, places holding sets can be replaced by databases [21]. Additionally, we use a set of IDs as a registry for data objects. The control flow (ControlFlow) colorset has a field of type ID with the initial value NULL for each class. We also use tokens of the integer (INT) colorset and blank tokens (Unit).

The state of a case, including all data objects, associations, and control flow, is captured by tokens. We add places *i*, *r*, and *o* for the case's respective abstract states ready, running, and terminated (Fig. 5). The CPN contains a single place of colorset Set<Association> holding a token with all associations (Fig. 5) and one of colorset Set<ID> holding references to all objects (Fig. 5). We add a place for each object configuration (Fig. 6). An ID token on this place represents a data object. For each class, we add a place with colorset INT holding a token (with initial value 0) counting the number of respective objects (Fig. 6). Considering fragments, we add a ControlFlow place for each control flow (Fig. 7).

Events, activities, gateways, and termination conditions are represented by transitions. The firing of a start event moves a token from *i* to *r*, enables all non-initial fragments, and disables initial ones. Firing a termination condition

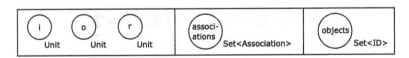

Fig. 5. Places that are created for each case model: an initial place *i*, which holds a single token until a case is started; a place *r*, which holds a single token while the case is running; and a final place *o*, which holds a token after the case has been closed. We add a place *associations* of type Set<Association> and a place of type Set<ID>.

Fig. 6. To support data, two sets of places are added: a place with colorset INT for each class and a place of colorset ID for each object configuration (class and state).

moves a token from r to o. Transitions representing fragments' first activities consume and re-produce a token on r. If an activity has an incoming control flow, a corresponding ControlFlow token is required. A ControlFlow token is produced for outgoing control flow. The ControlFlow token tracks the data objects accessed by the fragment instance. So, this information is carried from activity to activity. After activity "submit paper" (*fb*), the ControlFlow token references the conference, author team, and paper. The next activity, i.e., "send submission notification", must not overwrite this information; thus, the same author team and paper are read. A CPN transition consumes (produces) tokens from (into) the same places every time it fires. However, fCM partitions inputs (outputs) of an activity into multiple alternative sets. To capture the I/O behavior of an activity, we create a transition for each combination of an input set with an output set (see Fig. 8). Such a transition consumes a token for each object configuration required by the input set and produces one for each object that is written or that remains unchanged. If a new object is created, the transition consumes and increments the corresponding counter. Its value is used to create the new object ID. If the created object (*dependent*) depends on another one (*supporter*), the set of associations is updated accordingly. Two potentially associated objects, e.g., author team and paper, can only be read together if they are associated (guard i in Fig. 8). Furthermore, an activity cannot be executed if it would violate the cardinality constraints (guard ii, iii, and iv).

Fragment *fb* (Fig. 3) has the activities "submit paper" and "send submission notification". The first has the input sets □ and ∘ and one output set. It is mapped to two transitions, respectively (Fig. 9). Input set ∘ captures the first submission of an author team: a token for the conference is consumed and reproduced, and new tokens for author team and paper are created. Associations between paper and conference and between author team and paper are established by updating the set of associations. Guard conditions assert the cardinality constraints. All three objects are referenced by the ControlFlow token. The transition for "send submission notification" reads the ControlFlow token and consumes the referenced paper and author team.

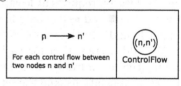

Fig. 7. For each control flow arc, a Control-Flow place is created.

Activities may process sets of objects. Assuming a set of type c_s in the state q_s is required, there must be an associated reference object in the input set. The CPN transition consumes the token for the reference object and one

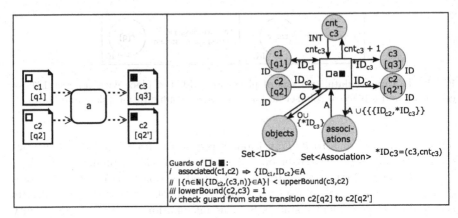

Fig. 8. Activity a with input set $\square$ = $\{c1[q1], c2[q2]\}$ and output set $\blacksquare$ = $\{c2[q2'], c3[q3]\}$. Objects can be read (c1,c2), updated (c2[q2'] with $q2 \neq q2'$), or created (c3). Associations (A) and the object registry (O) are read and updated. We assume an association between c3 and c2. The transition consumes and produces the required tokens. The guard asserts that (i) inputs are associated if applicable and cardinality constraints are met $(ii, iii, \text{and } iv)$. For grey places see the mappings in Figs. 5 and 6.

for the associations to select the objects of class c_s that are associated with the reference object. If all these c_s objects are in the state q_s, the corresponding tokens are consumed. The output is similar to non-batch processing: read objects can be updated or remain unchanged. In any case, tokens for all read objects are produced. New objects may get associated with all objects in the set.

In fragment fe (Fig. 3), knowledge workers decide whether to accept a paper, reject it, or request an extra review based on the paper's available reviews. Each of the output sets ($\blacksquare$, $\bullet$, and $\blacktriangle$) is represented by a transition (Fig. 10). Since a decision requires at least three reviews (cf. Fig. 1), the two corresponding transitions ($\blacksquare$ and $\bullet$) can only fire if the set of reviews has three or four elements (upper bound). In the case of four reviews, the other transition ($\blacktriangle$) is disabled.

We add a transition for each termination condition. It closes the case by moving the token from r to o and consumes tokens for each required predicate, the set of associations, and the set of objects to check goal cardinality constraints.

Due to space limitations, this paper does not include all details of the formalization. Interested readers are referred to our technical report [11].

4   Implementation and Discussion

The encoding of case models into CPNs detailed in Sect. 3 provides a basis for full-fledged enactment of fCM models. In this respect, we present prototypes of i) a compiler translating fCM models to CPNs compatible with CPNTools and of ii) an execution engine. Prototypes, documentation, and screencasts are available at https://github.com/bptlab/fcm2cpn/tree/caise and https://github.com/bptlab/fCM-Engine/tree/caise.

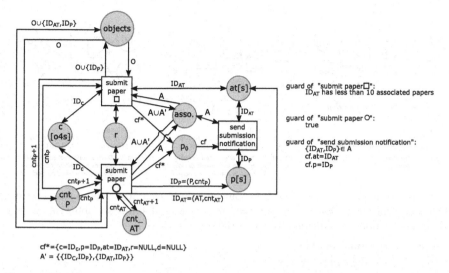

$$cf^* = \{c=ID_C, p=ID_P, at=ID_{AT}, r=NULL, d=NULL\}$$
$$A' = \{\{ID_C, ID_P\}, \{ID_{AT}, ID_P\}\}$$

Fig. 9. CPN formalization of fragment *fb*. Types have been omitted for better readability. Places have been created by the mappings in Fig. 5 and Fig. 6. Transitions represent the activities and are connected to the places. Labels are abbreviated: c[o4s] = conference[open for submissions], at[s] = authorTeam[signed up], and p[s] = paper[submitted]. Initials of the classes are used for places and variables.

Case models can be created using common tools for BPMN and UML modeling. Given a BPMN file describing a set of fragments and a domain model (UML Class diagram without hierarchies) describing the classes of objects used in the case model, the compiler creates a CPN file using Access/CPN. We assume that the fragments conform to the OLCs, which, consequently, can be inferred.

The fCM engine takes the CPN and the corresponding domain model. The engine communicates with CPN-tools to determine the enabled activity and event instances. The domain model is parsed to generate forms for data objects. Data objects' attributes and respective value assignments are managed outside of CPNtools. When a user selects an enabled activity, the engine displays the available input-output set combinations. The user can choose one, and the corresponding

Table 1. Requirements of knowledge-intensive processes [5] fully (+) or partly (○) satisfied by fCM (+). We do not include requirements regarding user management and adaptability.

R1	Data Modeling	+
R4	Synchronized Data Access	○
R5	Data-driven Actions	+
R7	Formalized Rules and Constrains	○
R9	Goal Modeling	+
R11	Support for Different Modeling Styles	+
R12	Visibility of the Process Knowledge	+
R13	Flexible Process Execution	+
R24	Capture and Model External Events	+

form is displayed (see Fig. 11). Once the user completes an action, the engine updates the objects and instructs CPNtools to execute the respective transition.

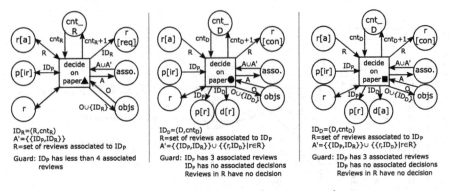

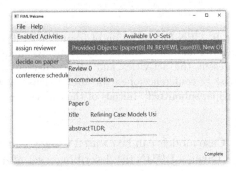

Fig. 10. Formalization of fragment *fe* split into three separated nets to ease comprehension. Types of the places are omitted and classes and states are abbreviated. The set of associations A is queried to derive the set of reviews R.

Table 2. Relevant marking for the CPN, see Fig. 10 for place names.

r	()
p[ir]	(Paper, 0)
r[a]	(Review, 0)
	(Review, 1)
asso	[((Paper, 0), (Review, 0)), ((Paper, 0), (Review, 1))]
objs	[(Paper, 0), (Review, 0), (Review, 1)]
countR	1

Fig. 11. The engine depicting the state from Table 2. A new review is created.

Tools are important to cope with the complexity of the approach and the domain. Our version of fCM contains hidden dependencies [10]: changing one part of a case model (e.g., cardinality constraints) may require adaptation of other parts (e.g., the inputs of activities). Additionally, the execution of fragments depends on the effects that other fragments induce over data objects and their associations. Well-designed tools for modeling, verification, and execution can compensate for some challenges [10]. The presented engine guides users and makes it optional to interpret the intricate models manually at run-time. Furthermore, fCM with its details may prove to be a proper low-code solution used by trained engineers rather than business users to design, implement, and monitor knowledge-intensive processes. However, this work focuses on the concepts and semantics. Notation and usability are left for future work.

We added domain models with associations and cardinality constraints to case models satisfying requirements for knowledge-intensive processes (cf. [5], Table 1): the process model integrates different perspectives each can be used according to their strengths. Furthermore, the process is data-driven—available objects and cardinality constraints determine the enabled activities. Finally, data objects are captured in detail with states, associations, and constraints.

Data cardinality constraints are crucial for formal verification. In general, verifying models combining processes and data is undecidable [4], in particular, because the process may operate on unboundedly many data objects. As shown in [20], a data-aware version of soundness and other data-aware temporal properties can be verified if cardinality constraints with suitable upper bounds and adequately restructured queries are employed. This work takes a first step towards applying techniques studied in [20] and related approaches to the verification of fCM models, which is one of the next steps we want to take.

5 Related Work

We briefly present related work in three categories: fragment-based case management, alternative modeling approaches, and formal models/execution semantics.

fCM is a production case management approach introduced by Meyer et al. [19]. Hewelt and Weske describe fCM, focusing on the language and syntax [13]. Consecutive works propose methods for eliciting [12] and verifying [15] case models. These works do not consider associations or cardinality constraints. We add these to fCM, strengthening the link between data and behavior.

Data-centric process modeling approaches have a long history. Recently, Steinau et al. provided an overview of such approaches [28]. An early approach is MERODE, which interprets data models with existential associations as behavioral specifications [26]. In contrast to MERODE, fCM focuses on case management. Guard stage milestone [17] and CMMN [23] arrange activities in stages with data pre- and post-conditions. PHILharmonicFlows [18] models OLCs, which can be orchestrated into larger processes. Associations and cardinalities can be used to synchronize transitions between sets of objects [27]. BAUML [7] is an artifact-centric UML-based approach: class diagrams model artifacts, state machines the respective OLCs, activity diagrams refine the triggers of the OLCs, and OCL is used for constraints. BAUML is a generic *artifact first* approach. fCM on the other hand is more specific and tailored towards case management. In comparison to both BAUML and PHILharmonicFlows, artifacts are not the primary method of defining the process. Instead, activity-centric fragments define the process that creates, accesses, and alters data objects.

Rather than specifying process variants imperatively, declarative models define constraints to capture multi-variant processes concisely. Two prominent declarative languages are DECLARE [24] and DCR-Graphs [14]. Both use variants of linear temporal logics. While declarative modeling is powerful to model constraints from laws, guidelines, and other rules, imperative models are preferred when explicit control and data flow are important. DCR-KiPM [25] is a hybrid approach combining declarative DCR-Graphs with an imperative notion called KiPM to model knowledge-intensive processes. Object-centric behavioral constraints combine declarative process models with data models [1]. Activities and LTL rules over finite traces are quantified based on data objects and their

associations. Cardinality constraints exist in two flavors: they have to hold globally or eventually. However, no case exists. fCM achieves flexibility by combining
fragments, modeled using elements within the BPMN tradition, dynamically. In
fCM, declarative rules can be asserted through compliance checking [15].

Formal execution semantics are broadly applied in BPM. Dijkman et al.
present a Petri net formalization for BPMN models enabling analysis and verification [6]. Proclets [2] are an extension of Petri nets: a process is composed
of multiple workflow modules that contain synchronization points. They allow
modeling various kinds of processes, such as choreographies and data-centric processes. Fahland introduces cardinality constraints for the synchronization points
enabling many-to-many interactions [8]. DB-Nets assure that a process adheres
to constraints given by a database (such as primary and foreign key constraints)
by incorporating transactional semantics [21]. Catalog nets combine Petri nets
with queryable read-only databases to support synchronization among cases [9].
Translating fCM to these formalisms would be interesting to connect the two
trends of research. Object-centric Petri nets have been used to describe processes
mined from object-centric event logs [3]. It would be interesting to see mining
algorithms targeting fCM. Our semantics are defined using Petri nets, but users
only interact with the fCM model, which hides the formalism's complexity.

6   Conclusion

Knowledge-intensive processes demand flexibility and data-driven actions. Also,
modeling approaches should incorporate various perspectives through suited languages [5]. In this paper, we integrated activity-centric process fragments with
domain models comprising associations and cardinality constraints. While we
use fCM models, our work can benefit traditional processes (e.g., modeled using
BPMN) to determine bounds for loops and multi-instance activities.

We showed that object cardinalities influence the behavior of processes.
Activities are enabled depending on whether certain cardinality constraints hold.
For example, a paper may only be rejected or accepted if three reviews exist
(requirement). On the other hand, only one decision is made for each paper
(bound). Furthermore, cardinality constraints may require batch processing,
where multiple objects of the same type are accessed simultaneously. Additionally, cardinality constraints can refine the goal definition of a case. Not only
do objects need to progress into specific states, but they also need to exist
in specified quantities. This allows defining knowledge-intensive processes more
comprehensively.

We provide a formal semantics using CPNs respecting the behavioral implications of cardinalities. The semantics is the underpinning for many BPM related
tasks, such as process execution, verification, modeling, and mining. Due to the
intricate nature of knowledge-intensive processes, tools are important. During
modeling, a tool may highlight hidden dependencies and aid with the verification. At run-time, engines may guide the knowledge workers making it unnecessary to interpret the model manually. Alternatively, process monitoring may

check compliant actions. While we only focus on the definition of the formal semantics, we lay an important foundation for these future tasks.

We do not consider inheritance. Class hierarchies, where associations and cardinality constraints are the same on all levels, do not require any changes. However, specializing and generalizing associations including cardinality constraints and advanced modeling concepts, e.g., the phase pattern, are interesting for future work and require investigation of conceptual models and algorithms.

Future work may also investigate the role of knowledge workers in detail: they may require relaxed constraints or the ability to adapt the process ad hoc.

Acknowledgments. We thank Leon Bein for his work on the prototypes. Marco Montali acknowledges the UNIBZ CRC Project REKAP.

References

1. van der Aalst, W.M.P., Artale, A., Montali, M., Tritini, S.: Object-centric behavioral constraints: Integrating data and declarative process modelling. In: Proceedings of the 30th International Workshop on Description Logics, Montpellier, France, 18–21 July, 2017 (2017)
2. van der Aalst, W.M.P., Barthelmess, P., Ellis, C.A., Wainer, J.: Workflow modeling using proclets. In: Cooperative Information Systems, 7th International Conference, CoopIS, Eilat, Israel, 6–8 September, 2000, Proceedings, pp. 198–209 (2000)
3. van der Aalst, W.M.P., Berti, A.: Discovering object-centric Petri nets. Fundam. Informaticae **175**(1–4), 1–40 (2020)
4. Calvanese, D., De Giacomo, G., Montali, M.: Foundations of data aware process analysis: a database theory perspective. In: pods-13, pp. 1–12. ACM Press (2013)
5. Ciccio, C.D., Marrella, A., Russo, A.: Knowledge-intensive processes: characteristics, requirements and analysis of contemporary approaches. J. Data Semant. **4**(1), 29–57 (2015)
6. Dijkman, R.M., Dumas, M., Ouyang, C.: Semantics and analysis of business process models in BPMN. Inf. Softw. Technol. **50**(12), 1281–1294 (2008)
7. Estañol, M., Munoz-Gama, J., Carmona, J., Teniente, E.: Conformance checking in UML artifact-centric business process models. Softw. Syst. Model. **18**(4), 2531–2555 (2019)
8. Fahland, D.: Describing behavior of processes with many-to-many interactions. In: Application and Theory of Petri Nets and Concurrency - 40th International Conference, PETRI NETS, Aachen, Germany, June 23–28, 2019, Proceedings, pp. 3–24 (2019)
9. Ghilardi, S., Gianola, A., Montali, M., Rivkin, A.: Petri nets with parameterised data - modelling and verification. In: Business Process Management - 18th International Conference, BPM, Seville, Spain, September 13–18, 2020, Proceedings, pp. 55–74 (2020)
10. Green, T.R.: Cognitive dimensions of notations. People and computers V (1989)
11. Haarmann, S., Montali, M., Weske, M.: Technical report: Refining case models using cardinality constraints (2020)
12. Hewelt, M., Pufahl, L., Mandal, S., Wolff, F., Weske, M.: Toward a methodology for case modeling. Softw. Syst. Model. **19**(6), 1367–1393 (2020)

13. Hewelt, M., Weske, M.: A hybrid approach for flexible case modeling and execution. In: Business Process Management Forum - BPM Forum, Rio de Janeiro, Brazil, 18–22 September, 2016, Proceedings, pp. 38–54 (2016)

14. Hildebrandt, T.T., Mukkamala, R.R.: Declarative event-based workflow as distributed dynamic condition response graphs. In: Proceedings Third Workshop on Programming Language Approaches to Concurrency and communication-cEntric Software, PLACES, Paphos, Cyprus, 21st March 2010, pp. 59–73 (2010)

15. Holfter, A., Haarmann, S., Pufahl, L., Weske, M.: Checking compliance in data-driven case management. In: Business Process Management Workshops - BPM 2019 International Workshops, Vienna, Austria, 1–6 September, 2019, Revised Selected Papers, pp. 400–411 (2019)

16. Hull, R.: Artifact-centric business process models: brief survey of research results and challenges. In: Meersman, R., Tari, Z. (eds.) OTM 2008. LNCS, vol. 5332, pp. 1152–1163. Springer, Heidelberg (2008). https://doi.org/10.1007/978-3-540-88873-4_17

17. Hull, R., et al.: Introducing the guard-stage-milestone approach for specifying business entity lifecycles. In: Web Services and Formal Methods - 7th International Workshop, WS-FM, Hoboken, NJ, USA, 16–17 September, 2010. Revised Selected Papers, pp. 1–24 (2010)

18. Künzle, V., Reichert, M.: PHILharmonicFlows: towards a framework for object-aware process management. J. Softw. Maintenance Res. Pract. 23(4), 205–244 (2011)

19. Meyer, A., Herzberg, N., Puhlmann, F., Weske, M.: Implementation framework for production case management: modeling and execution. In: 18th IEEE International Enterprise Distributed Object Computing Conference, EDOC, Ulm, Germany, 1–5 September, 2014, pp. 190–199 (2014)

20. Montali, M., Calvanese, D.: Soundness of data-aware, case-centric processes. Int. J. Softw. Tools Technol. Transfer 18(5), 535–558 (2016)

21. Montali, M., Rivkin, A.: DB-Nets: on the marriage of colored Petri nets and relational databases. Trans. Petri Nets Other Model. Concurr. 12, 91–118 (2017)

22. Object Management Group: Business Process Model and Notation (BPMN), January 2014. https://www.omg.org/spec/BPMN

23. Object Management Group: Case Management Model and Notation (CMMN), December 2016. https://www.omg.org/spec/CMMN

24. Pesic, M., Schonenberg, H., van der Aalst, W.M.P.: DECLARE: full support for loosely-structured processes. In: 11th IEEE International Enterprise Distributed Object Computing Conference (EDOC), 15–19 October 2007, Annapolis, Maryland, USA, pp. 287–300 (2007)

25. Santoro, F.M., Slaats, T., Hildebrandt, T.T., Baião, F.A.: DCR-KiPN a hybrid modeling approach for knowledge-intensive processes. In: Conceptual Modeling - 38th International Conference, ER, Salvador, Brazil, 4–7 November, 2019, Proceedings, pp. 153–161 (2019)

26. Snoeck, M.: Enterprise Information Systems Engineering - The MERODE Approach. Springer, The Enterprise Engineering Series (2014)

27. Steinau, S., Andrews, K., Reichert, M.: The relational process structure. In: Advanced Information Systems Engineering - 30th International Conference, CAiSE, Tallinn, Estonia, 11–15 June, 2018, Proceedings, pp. 53–67 (2018)

28. Steinau, S., Marrella, A., Andrews, K., Leotta, F., Mecella, M., Reichert, M.: DALEC: a framework for the systematic evaluation of data-centric approaches to process management software. Softw. Syst. Model. 18(4), 2679–2716 (2019)

Process Understanding

Digging for Gold in RPA Projects – A Quantifiable Method to Identify and Prioritize Suitable RPA Process Candidates

Johannes Viehhauser$^{(\boxtimes)}$ and Maria Doerr$^{(\boxtimes)}$

Technical University of Munich, Arcisstraße 21, 80333 Munich, Germany
{johannes.viehhauser,maria.doerr}@tum.de

Abstract. Robotic Process Automation (RPA) is an emerging technology that enables the automation of well-defined and repetitive back office processes by providing a virtual workforce. Even though RPA draws much corporate attention in recent years, many RPA projects fail or lack behind expectations. A major reason is the automation of wrong processes, mainly driven by a lack of objective methods to identify and select suitable process candidates. The goal of this paper is to develop a generalizable method to detect, prioritize, and select process candidates for the automation with RPA. The paper follows the principles of Design Science Research and includes a literature review, expert interviews, and an extensive survey based on the Analytic Hierarchy Process approach with RPA developers, consultants, and end users. As a result, we present a three step approach and a quantifiable model to objectively prioritize suitable RPA process candidates based on suitability values. We empirically show that the most important criteria to select suitable RPA process candidates are a high degree of standardization and high volume.

Keywords: Robotic Process Automation · RPA · Business process management · Decision support model · Process suitability

1 Introduction

The continuous optimization and automation of business processes are regarded as vital parts of corporate activities to increase productivity and competitiveness. However, most companies only automate the peak of the iceberg of their processes, since only structured processes with high case frequencies are economically viable to be automated with traditional heavyweight IT solutions. The predominant number of processes, though, does not justify automation. For some years, an automation revolution has been on the rise to address those processes with medium case frequencies that previously did not justify the use of IT resources: Robotic Process Automation (RPA) [1,25]. RPA constitutes software robots that mimic human activities to digitally perform tasks on the user

© Springer Nature Switzerland AG 2021
M. La Rosa et al. (Eds.): CAiSE 2021, LNCS 12751, pp. 313–327, 2021.
https://doi.org/10.1007/978-3-030-79382-1_19

interface of computer systems [15,21]. The goal of RPA is to automate existing processes without major changes to processes and existing IT infrastructure. It can be regarded as an evolution from basic automation solutions, since it is more robust to changes, allows enriched logic, and supports more complex processes [21]. Therefore, the software is best suited to perform mundane and repetitive "swivel chair" tasks, for example transferring data between systems or manipulating and processing data based on pre-defined rules [15,22].

One of the key challenges of RPA is to select the most promising process candidates, since the automation of unfitting processes drives inefficiencies, increases failure rates, and threatens the success of leveraging RPA technologies [1,6,25]. Various authors point out a lack of standardized methods to analyze and identify suitable RPA processes [e.g., 2,12,26]. In addition, a lack of well-defined guidelines to prioritize automation candidates based on critical factors becomes apparent [e.g., 4,25]. As shown by case studies on RPA in the telecommunications, healthcare, and financial services industries, process selection is often based on "rules-of-thumb" rather than on clearly defined, generalizable, and reliable criteria [7,15,22]. The examined companies select processes based on their complexity and volume but do not further specify or quantify the applied criteria. This increases the risk of poor selection decisions and project failure. The importance of careful process selection is also confirmed by a case study in the banking and energy industry, which puts the automation of unsuitable processes into direct connection with a lack of standardized selection approaches. The misjudgment leads to a significant waste of time and resources [19].

In summary, the existing research on process selection in RPA projects lacks robust, generalizable, and quantifiable selection criteria to identify suitable RPA processes. Thus, we raise the following research question: *How can organizations systematically identify and prioritize the most suitable process candidates for automation with RPA?* The ambition of this research follows the calls for research from the papers [1] and [29], where the authors shed light on the research on process selection for the automation with RPA and, in particular, on the different importance of process characteristics. To answer the research question, we apply an objective centered Design Science Research (DSR) approach to develop an objective and generalizable process selection model [8,20]. Moreover, we use the Analytic Hierarchy Approach (AHP) method in the course of a large-scale survey to derive factor weights for process selection criteria [23].

This paper makes several noteworthy contributions. First, it provides a mathematical model with quantifiable suitability values to assess and prioritize the automation potential of processes for RPA. Moreover, it extends the knowledge of process characteristics for RPA by introducing factor weights based on empirical data. Besides, the findings inform managerial practice by providing guidance to select promising RPA process candidates and therewith increase the overall probability for project success.

The outline of this paper is structured as follows: Sect. 2 introduces the applied research methodology, followed by a discussion of the results of the conducted literature review and expert interviews as well as the deducted selection criteria in Sect. 3. Next, Sect. 4 introduces an RPA process selection model and the empirically derived factor weights. The model is evaluated with real-life case data in Sect. 5. Finally, Sect. 6 concludes with a discussion of key findings, potential limitations, and possible future fields of research.

2   Methodology

To answer the research question of how organizations can systematically assess the automation potential of business processes with RPA, we deploy an objective-centered DSR approach [8,20]. First, the research problem and objective were identified and defined as introduced in Sect. 1. Next, the design and development phase with data collection, analysis, and model development followed. Therefore, a literature review and expert interviews were conducted to derive selection approaches and criteria. The combination of data input from literature and expert interviews allowed for triangulation to avoid biases and to combine theory with practice. Based on the findings, a quantifiable decision support model for RPA process selection was developed. To receive the weighted importance of the selection criteria, a survey, following the principles of AHP, with 134 participants was conducted [23]. Based on a pairwise comparison of decision elements, AHP is suitable to structure complex, multi-attribute decision problems such as process selection in RPA projects [27]. Finally, the developed decision support model was demonstrated, evaluated, and further refined based on real-life data from management accounting to ensure its operability.

3   Identification of Process Selection Criteria

3.1   Literature Review

To derive state-of-the-art knowledge about process selection approaches and criteria, we conducted a systematic literature review [30]. The search was based on the terms *"Robotic Process Automation"*, *"RPA"*, *"Intelligent Process Automation"*, *"Virtual Workforce"*, and *"Software Robots"* and covered Google Scholar, Springer, Elsevier, ResearchGate, IEEE Xplore, AIS eLibrary, and ACM Digital Library . In total, 82 research papers, conference papers, and white papers resulted. A further selection of papers that specifically address RPA and that rely on a peer-review process for high quality journals resulted in a total of 24 case studies on the implementation of RPA, literature reviews on RPA, and papers with focus on the organization of RPA projects as well as RPA process selection.

The organization of RPA projects from project selection to implementation is described in various case studies, whereby most authors propose four to six stage approaches [e.g., 3,10,12,14,25]. All approaches start with process identification and suitability assessment based on, for example, process walk-throughs. The literature review underlines that the selection lacks generally valid selection criteria, ranging from decisions driven solely by process characteristics to a combination of process suitability and minimum expected savings [e.g., 12,15,22].

As an innovative lever to discover processes for the automation with RPA, in [6, 17], the authors introduce robotic process mining to identify mature processes with high automation potential based on logs of interactions. However, both papers do not specify formal characterisations for suitable automation routines, their applicability is limited to the availability of log data, and they only include sub-processes where all prerequisites are fulfilled and that are fully rule-based. After the process selection, in [10], the authors propose a potential modification of processes before implementation. All other authors suggest to start directly with the design and implementation of RPA. The literature review reveals that, even though defined on a high level, research lacks a detailed and universal approach for prioritizing RPA processes which emphasize the need for developing a structured approach to identify, prioritize, and select suitable RPA processes.

Table 1. Overview on identified process selection criteria from literature review.

Selection criteria	Number of mentions	Sources
Standardization	17	E.g., [4, 5, 7, 15, 16, 21, 22]
Volume	16	E.g., [4, 5, 7, 15, 21, 22]
Automation rate	9	[2–4, 6, 7, 10, 13, 18, 19]
Stability and maturity	8	[3, 4, 6, 10, 14, 15, 21, 32]
Digital data input	8	[2, 4, 5, 10, 13–15, 21]
Failure rate	4	[3, 6, 12, 16]
Structured data input	3	[4, 10, 14]

Existing research reveals that it is critical to define appropriate process selection criteria, even though there are differences in terms of which criteria are applied. In general, process identification is based on two to four selection criteria in most case studies. For example, in [15], the researchers base their selection on volume and complexity, in [3], the authors search for routine, low-cognitive, and rule-based processes, and in [10], the academics analyze along the criteria well-defined, mature, and repetitive.

Table 1 presents an overview on the identified process selection criteria and their importance based on the number of mentions. The findings are in line with other literature reviews on RPA process selection criteria [e.g., 9, 11, 25, 26, 31]. Moreover, they support the selection criteria high execution frequency, long execution time, high degree of standardization, high stability, high failure rate, and low automation rate as introduced in [29]. The proposed criteria are, to our knowledge, one of the first company and industry independent indicators to examine the selection of RPA process candidates. This presents a viable foundation for the coding of our findings. However, as the criteria are not exhaustive and the mathematical descriptions are only applicable for specific log data, we propose refined mathematical definitions and complement the criteria with digital and structured data input (cf. Sect. 4.2).

3.2   Expert Interviews

To include practical insights, we conducted 13 interviews with experts from RPA software providers (eight interviews) and RPA integrators (five interviews). RPA software providers, such as Automation Anywhere, Blueprism, or Uipath, were asked to contribute insights into latest technologies, their requirements for application, and approaches for process selection. RPA integrators, such as FourNxt, Macros Reply, or Roboyo, were selected to contribute an application-driven perspective as well as experiences about implementation challenges. The semi-structured interviews lasted between 30 and 50 min and consisted of three parts. In the beginning, general information about the company, its RPA initiatives and the degree of application were discussed. The main section comprised a detailed elaboration of the identification and selection procedures for major implementation projects, followed by a discussion of resulting benefits, limitations and implementation challenges. The analysis phase consisted of a within-case analysis to identify codes for key motivators and process selection criteria, followed by a cross-case comparison and deduction of generally valid process selection criteria.

The results of the interviews reveal that all software providers and integrators provide structured approaches to identify RPA process candidates as well as to set up internal RPA organizations. Many of the assessed cases suggest the definition of an automation target as a first step of the automation journey. This step can barely be found in existing research but turns out to be an important starting point, since it is critical to define a goal as a basis for the selection of suitable candidate processes. Next, the experts propose the identification of process candidates based on a feasibility analysis. Thereby, potential processes are identified, analyzed, and documented. The analysis serves as a prerequisite for the subsequent assessment along predefined process characteristics, which results in a suitability ranking. The analysis is followed by an economic assessment of promising process candidates based on business cases, a prioritization along economic criteria, and the final selection of processes.

It becomes clear that, even though high-level proceedings are defined, almost all RPA providers and integrators lack objective criteria and assessment models for the selection of process candidates. As a general rule, complexity serves as an approximation to assess the process suitability. However, the operative assessment is, for the most part, not based on measurable criteria, but rather on subjective evaluations. Most experts define low complexity along the criteria high degree of standardization with clearly defined rules and no human judgment, structured data input, high stability of processes and applications, appropriate number of interfaces, and digital data input. Moreover, also high volumes and repetitiveness are critical. The findings confirm the most important process selection criteria as identified in the literature review. In addition, they support the call for an objective process selection model.

4   Development of a Process Suitability Model

4.1   Conceptual Approach for Process Selection

The analyses emphasize that RPA projects call for a structured process to identify and select suitable RPA process candidates as well as for an objective and quantifiable indicator system to identify suitable process candidates [e.g., 3,12,25]. We therefore propose a three-step process selection model to identify and prioritize business processes for the automaton with RPA (cf. Fig. 1).

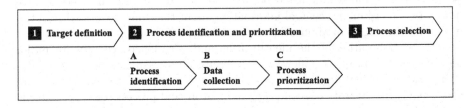

Fig. 1. Approach for process selection in RPA projects.

The proposed approach starts with the definition of the objectives for automation. Strategic decisions about the preferred automation technology in line with company goals and the definition of objectives on an operational level need to be taken into account. Clearly defined objectives are important, because they guide the overall selection process and serve as an appropriate baseline to evaluate the project success [7,14,25]. The most prevalent objectives for the automation with RPA are personnel savings and quality improvements. Moreover, increasing availability and capacity, performing time-critical processes, and improving compliance and security are frequently mentioned.

The second phase consists of process identification (A), data collection (B), and process prioritization (C). First, a high-level preselection of potentially relevant processes is necessary to overcome the large amount of processes within organizations [12,15]. The preselection can be carried out via workshops, suggestions by operational employees, or innovative methodologies such as process mining. Process preselection is followed by data collection to obtain reliable data points as a basis for the process prioritization model. The collection can be carried out based on available user interaction data, system protocols, process walk-throughs, or standardized templates. The next step is process prioritization to detect the most promising process candidates. The process prioritization is based on the mathematical model as introduced in Sect. 4.2 and relies on quantifiable and weighted selection criteria from Sect. 4.3. As a result, all preselected processes are quantified and assessed according to their suitability for automation with RPA.

In the third phase, the selection for implementation follows. The selection addresses the most promising process candidates from phase two and is supplemented by an economic evaluation. The proposed model already includes criteria, which account for economic feasibility such as high volume, standardization, and maturity to reduce implementation and maintenance effort, or error rate to reduce quality costs. In addition, the calculation of business cases based on standardized indicators such as return on investment is recommended to compare the processes from an economic standpoint [e.g., 4, 6, 32]. According to [3], the economic evaluation should be separated from process identification. This is also confirmed by the authors of [32], who argue that the selection of suitable processes should be put into focus first, as a business case follows naturally for almost all suitable RPA processes.

4.2   Prioritization Model for RPA Process Suitability

To ensure an objective selection of RPA process candidates for multiple scenarios, we introduce a mathematical model for quantifying and prioritizing RPA process candidates based on weighted suitability criteria. The model aims to provide a detailed understanding of potential process candidates as well as to prioritize the most suitable processes as a basis for the selection for implementation.

Table 2. Model notation.

Variables	Definition
A_p	Number of activities of process p
S_p	Suitability value of process p
U_p	Number of sub-processes of process p
V_p	Number of process variants of process p
c_1	Constant 1 (s-curve formulation)
c_2	Constant 2 (s-curve formulation)
e_v	Error rate of process variant v
f_{ip}	Fitness value of factor i for process p
n_v	Number of repetitions of process variant v
t_a	Duration of activity a
w_i	Eigenvector of the relative importance or factor i
b_a	=1, if data input for activity a is available with sufficient quality, 0 otherwise
d_a	=1, if data input of activity a is digital, 0 otherwise
m_a	=1, if an activity a is manual, 0 if activity a is automated
s_a	=1, if an activity a is clearly defined and standardized, 0 otherwise
x_{av}	=1, if activity a is required in process variant v, 0 otherwise
y_{au}	=1, if activity a belongs to sub-process u, 0 otherwise
z_a	=1, if an activity a is not expected to change, 0 otherwise

We introduce formal notations for our model (cf. Table 2), whereby a process p consists of V_p process variants v. Each process can be decomposed into U_p

sub-processes u and A_p activities a. Moreover, each process selection criterion is defined by a factor index i. To derive the overall process suitability value S_p of a process, all factors are quantified and normalized to an eigenvector ranging between 0 and 1 and weighted with the derived factor weights from Sect. 4.3. Equation 1 provides the suitability value for each process, which serves as a basis to derive the most suitable process candidates.

$$S_p = \sum_{i=1}^{7}(w_i \cdot f_{ip}) \tag{1}$$

The analysis reveals that a high degree of standardization is the most important selection criterion for RPA process candidates. In the context of RPA, standardization refers to processes that follow a predefined structure, can be decomposed into sub-processes without misinterpretation, and all decisions rely on clearly defined rules without ambiguity [e.g., 3,6,15]. Processes with a high degree of standardization reduce the implementation effort, increase the speed of implementation, and raise the overall probability for project success, which makes them the most promising RPA candidates [6,26]. Hence, standardization reduces the overall cost of RPA, as complexity is reduced and fewer exceptions need to be covered. Particularly in the initial phase, research recommends selecting processes with no need for further standardization or adjustments [10,26]. Equation 2 conceptualizes standardization as the share of sub-processes of a process, where all activities s_a of the sub-process follow clearly defined rules. The equation excludes sub-processes without all activities being standardized in favor of fully standardized sub-processes. Standardization is normalized based on the number of repetitions n_v of activities and their duration t_a.

$$f_{1p} = \frac{\sum_{u}^{U_p}(\sum_{v=1}^{V_p}(\sum_{a=1}^{A_p}(t_a \cdot n_v \cdot y_{au}))) \cdot \left(\min_{a \in \{1,...,A_p | y_{au}=1\}} s_a \right)}{\sum_{a=1}^{A_p} t_a} \tag{2}$$

A high volume of processes in terms of execution frequency and execution time is identified as the second most important process selection criterion. We define volume as the total execution time of a process as a product of the time required for the performance of a process and the frequency of repetitions [e.g., 5,15,21]. Volume is particularly important, since the automation of high-volume processes helps to maximize the benefits of RPA, leverages the potential for cost reduction, and therewith introduces an economic perspective [15,25,26]. Equation 3 operationalizes volume based on the execution time of an activity t_a and the number of repetitions n_v. The equation is based on an s-curve formulation to ensure that low volume processes are valued with lower impact compared to high volume processes. Moreover, as suggested by [15], we introduce a threshold value as target volume for processes. The threshold, as upper limit of the s-curve, can be set individually by modifying the constants c_1 and c_2.

$$f_{2p} = \frac{1}{(1 + e^{-c_1 \cdot (\sum_{v=1}^{V_p}(\sum_{a=1}^{A_p}(t_a \cdot x_{av})) \cdot n_v)})^{c_2}} \tag{3}$$

The analysis results further suggest that the suitability of a process depends on its current automation rate. The authors of [6] argue that processes with a high share of manual activities offer greater and faster economic benefits compared to processes with a high degree of automation. For our model, we define manual effort as the extent to which activities m_a are not yet automated (cf. Eq. 4).

$$f_{3p} = \frac{\sum_{a=1}^{A_p} m_a}{A_p} \tag{4}$$

We further figured out that the maturity of a process is another critical determinant for process selection in RPA projects. [29] consider mature processes as processes with high stability, low probability of exceptions, and predictable outcomes. According to [21], particularly the vulnerability of the involved information systems and interfaces are critical for RPA. By considering disadvantages from potential future changes, the overall risk for adjustments or even the failure of an entire RPA project is mitigated. The automation of stable processes also has a positive impact on the long-term operational costs of RPA. Therefore, we define maturity as stability of a process and the involved systems with low vulnerability to changes and updates. As with manual effort, we measure maturity as the share of activities z_a within a process that are not prone to changes (cf. Eq. 5). Changes can take place within the activity itself, with regards to its position within the sequence of activities resulting in different inputs and outputs, or within the required IT systems and interfaces.

$$f_{4p} = \frac{\sum_{a=1}^{A_p} z_a}{A_p} \tag{5}$$

Our analysis reveals that also the availability of digital data input is critical for RPA process selection. The authors of [10] state that data must be compatible with RPA requirements and need to be available in digital format or at least need to be transferable into digital formats. Therefore, we argue that processes are suitable to RPA if data are available in digital format. This extends the proposed selection criteria from [29]. However, the importance of digital data input is clearly confirmed and therefore needs to be included into the model. We define digital data input as the degree to which the data are available in non-analogue, digital form. Equation 6 provides an operationalization as the share of activities d_a with available digital data input.

$$f_{5p} = \frac{\sum_{a=1}^{A_p} d_a}{A_p} \tag{6}$$

Besides being in digital format, the required data also need to be available in a structured, consistent, and standardized form [10,14]. High input data quality increases the accuracy of performance, prevents errors, and reduces implementation and processing costs. We therefore include input data quality into our model and extend the selection criteria proposed by [29] further. Equation 7 defines quality of input data as the share of activities b_a with sufficient data quality from the total number of activities within a process. The required data for each activity must be unambiguous, with a low probability of exceptions, and usable by RPA without manual or human intervention.

$$f_{6p} = \frac{\sum_{a=1}^{A_p} b_a}{A_p} \tag{7}$$

Finally, processes with a high failure rate are identified as suitable candidates for an automation with RPA and included in the model. Automating processes with high error rates reduces costs of quality as well as potential efforts for rework and therefore increases the overall performance [6]. We operationalize failure rate with Eq. 8 and define it as degree to which a process variant e_v is prone to errors. The calculation should be based on actual historical quality data.

$$f_{7p} = \frac{\sum_{v=1}^{V_p} (n_v \cdot e_v)}{\sum_{v=1}^{V_p} n_v} \tag{8}$$

4.3   Identification of Factor Weights

To derive factor weights for each process selection criterion, we conducted a survey which was sent out to 456 developers, analysts, and sales employees from RPA software developers, 255 consultants and end-users, and six RPA researchers. The survey covered general information of the participants (type of company, position, experience with RPA) and a pairwise comparison of the perceived importance of each criterion when selecting RPA processes as introduced in Sect. 4.2. The selection criteria were compared to each other on a scale ranging from "extremely less important" (1/9), over "equally as important" (1), to "extremely more important" (9) [23]. In total, 134 successfully completed surveys were sent back, of which eight participants with little or no experience with RPA were excluded. To derive the selection criteria's weighted importance, the relative and normalized eigenvectors for each criterion were calculated based on the geometric mean.

The analysis of the results shows that a high degree of standardization constitutes the most important RPA process selection criterion with an eigenvector of 0.23 (cf. Table 3). This is also confirmed by the statistical analysis, which reveals that standardization is significant at a 1% level compared to all other attributes. Standardization is followed by a high volume of transactions with an eigenvector of 0.17. The results are in line with the literature review, where both attributes are detected most [e.g., 5, 7, 15]. The four criteria high maturity of processes and applications, high degree of manual effort, and digital as well as structured data input can be regarded equally important, with eigenvectors ranging between 0.11 and 0.14, which is also confirmed by the conducted statistical analysis. The criterion high failure rate is valued with an eigenvector of 0.10 and is therewith somewhat less important than the before mentioned attributes. To ensure data consistency and reliability, a consistency index and a consistency ratio are applied. For our sample, a consistency index of 0.04 and a consistency ratio of 0.03 result. This underlines that the derived eigenvectors are consistent and non-random [23,24].

Table 3. Process selection criteria and derived factor weights (eigenvectors).

Process selection criteria	Eigenvector
Standardization	$w_1 = 0.23$
Volume	$w_2 = 0.17$
Manual effort	$w_3 = 0.14$
Maturity	$w_4 = 0.13$
Digital data input	$w_5 = 0.12$
Input data quality	$w_6 = 0.11$
Failure rate	$w_7 = 0.10$

5 Application of the Model to a Real Case

To demonstrate and evaluate the developed model, we applied the model to process candidates in the management accounting department of an international technology company [20]. Management accounting seemed promising, because the company faced a high workload for manual and repetitive work at the interface between systems, despite applying an enterprise resource planning system, business intelligence tools, and other applications. Moreover, it suffered from a peak workload during month-end. Therefore, they set the target to free up employee capacities for value-adding tasks by RPA (Step 1).

To identify RPA process candidates (Step 2), we first introduced RPA to all involved employees and invited them to identify process candidates. As a result, we gathered nine processes for which we collected data by measuring execution times and frequencies of each activity, by observing employees while performing processes to obtain assessments of, for example, the rule-based nature of each activity, and by collecting system outputs such as error rates. In total, data points for 102 sub-processes with 792 activities were collected and analyzed. The collection process revealed that the proposed model works particularly well when no log data are available. This holds for processes in management accounting, which leverage multiple systems and applications.

As a next step, we determined the automation potential of each process by computing its suitability value. We discussed the processes with RPA experts to obtain a second opinion based on their experience and internal selection procedures. Summarizing the results in Fig. 2, the model reveals that the automation potential of the company's processes varies significantly. The model provides suitability values ranging from 0.61 to 0.95 and presents guidance for RPA process candidates with values above 0.80. Particularly the two most significant selection

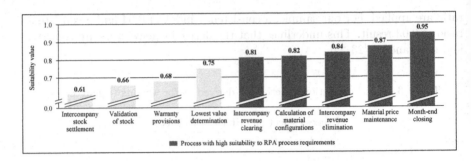

Fig. 2. Examined processes and suitability values.

criteria standardization and volume show high deviations and therefore exert the strongest impact due to their high eigenvectors. For volume, a threshold value of 0.3 full-time equivalents was incorporated according to company requirements. In contrast, the suitability values for manual effort, maturity, digital as well as structured data input, and failure rate were comparable and at a high level. All results were in line with the judgement of the RPA experts.

The technical evaluation showed that the proposed model produced meaningful results and reveals a reasonable basis for process selection. It provided an objective assessment of how well the processes are suitable to RPA and can serve as basis for decision making. The results also supported the subsequent financial analysis as conducted by the company (Step 3). The results confirmed the assumption that it is most important to identify qualified processes according to their suitability value, because the value contains measures that determine the economic viability. Two points of criticism evolved during the assessment. First, data collection appeared to be time consuming. However, as long as the process is not suitable for process mining or no user interaction data are available, data collection will remain cumbersome. Second, a general threshold as indication for process selection was needed. Derived from the case data, 0.8 could serve as first indication as processes below the threshold did not meet RPA requirements in the examined case.

6   Conclusion, Limitations, and Future Research

In this research, we present a systematic and generalizable method to identify and prioritize RPA process candidates based on objective and weighted process selection criteria. To address the research question, we utilize the principles of DSR and identify seven process selection criteria based on a literature review and expert interviews [8,20]. We present a three-step process selection approach, starting with target definition, followed by process identification and prioritization, and completed by process selection to choose the most promising candidates for implementation. To quantify the suitability of processes, we introduce a mathematical model to formalize the criteria and weight their impact based on empirically derived factor weights. The results demonstrate that a high degree of standardization constitutes the most important RPA process selection criterion, followed by a high volume of transactions, a high maturity of processes and applications, a high degree of manual effort, digital as well as high quality data input, and a high failure rate. An evaluation of the model with real-life case data from management accounting confirms its applicability.

To our knowledge, the paper presents the first method to identify RPA process candidates based on weighted factors derived from empirical data as well as based on an objective and formalized description of the degree of alignment between the process and the criteria. The results confirm the criteria proposed by existing research and case studies, which, however, were applied without assessing their importance and lacked structured selection approaches. Moreover, the reference selection criteria as proposed by [29] are confirmed and extended by digital and high quality data input. The paper also yields important practical implications for corporate executives by providing a universal selection approach and reliable indicators. Specifically, the quantification of the process suitability can guide executives to select the most promising process candidates and therewith increases the overall probability for RPA project success.

The model is subject to several limitations. First, the importance of preselected criteria was retrieved without considering application scenarios. Potential differences depending on the use cases and motivation are neglected. Second, the proposed model assesses process candidates based on their status quo and does not account for potential improvements prior to the automation with RPA that could impact the suitability. Third, a broad knowledge about each process and a large amount of input data is required to run the model. If the data are not available in a standardized and structured form, it could be subject to human judgement and lack comparability. The introduced predefined guidelines for all process characteristics and the structured data collection process can help to overcome this. Fourth, the proposed model does not include an explicit economic assessment of the processes, because criteria such as volume or standardization already indicate the economic viability. In addition, the utilization of economic indicators depends on varying implementation scenarios and relies on corporate standards, which is why they are not explicitly incorporated. Fifth, the factors are not independent of each other and can potentially affect one another.

Considering the limitations and the dynamic development of research in the field of RPA, future research opportunities arise. Combining data collection and process identification with innovative approaches and technologies constitutes an interesting field of research. For example, process mining or natural language processing can be used to overcome the need for manual data collection and therewith enable continuous process discovery. Research indicates that RPA is becoming more intelligent [22, 26, 28], which is why we motivate future research to further examine the impact on the importance of process selection criteria and factor weights. Results from our conducted interviews indicate that the need for standardization, maturity, and structured data input could potentially be affected. Moreover, the integration of an economic assessment into the mathematical model depending on the motivation for automation could be of interest.

References

1. van der Aalst, W.M.P., Bichler, M., Heinzl, A.: Robotic process automation. Bus. Inf. Syst. Eng. **60**(4), 269–272 (2018)
2. Aguirre, S., Rodriguez, A.: Automation of a business process using robotic process automation (RPA): a case study. In: Figueroa-García, J.C., López-Santana, E.R., Villa-Ramírez, J.L., Ferro-Escobar, R. (eds.) WEA 2017. CCIS, vol. 742, pp. 65–71. Springer, Cham (2017). https://doi.org/10.1007/978-3-319-66963-2_7
3. Asatiani, A., Penttinen, E.: Turning robotic process automation into commercial success-case OpusCapita. J. Inf. Technol. Teach. Cases **6**(2), 67–74 (2016)
4. Cooper, L.A., Holderness Jr., D.K., Sorensen, T.L., Wood, D.A.: Robotic process automation in public accounting. Account. Horiz. **33**(4), 15–35 (2019)
5. Dias, M., Pan, S.L., Tim, Y.: Knowledge embodiment of human and machine interactions: robotic process automation at the Finland Government. In: 27th European Conference on Information Systems, ECIS 2019, Stockholm-Uppsala, Sweden (2019)
6. Geyer-Klingeberg, J., Nakladal, J., Baldauf, F., Veit, F.: Process mining and robotic process automation: a perfect match. In: International Conference on Business Process Management (2018)
7. Hallikainen, P., Bekkhus, R., Pan, S.L.: How OpusCapita used internal RPA capabilities to offer services to clients. MIS Q. Exec. **17**, 41–52 (2018)
8. Hevner, A.R., March, S.T., Park, J., Ram, S.: Design science in information systems research. MIS Q. Exec. **28**, 75–105 (2004)
9. Hofmann, P., Samp, C., Urbach, N.: Robotic process automation. Electron. Mark. **30**(1), 99–106 (2019). https://doi.org/10.1007/s12525-019-00365-8
10. Huang, F., Vasarhelyi, M.A.: Applying robotic process automation (RPA) in auditing: a framework. Int. J. Account. Inf. Syst. **35**, 100433 (2019)
11. Ivančić, L., Suša Vugec, D., Bosilj Vukšić, V.: Robotic process automation: systematic literature review. In: Di Ciccio, C., et al. (eds.) BPM 2019. LNBIP, vol. 361, pp. 280–295. Springer, Cham (2019). https://doi.org/10.1007/978-3-030-30429-4_19
12. Jimenez-Ramirez, A., Reijers, H.A., Barba, I., Del Valle, C.: A method to improve the early stages of the robotic process automation lifecycle. In: Giorgini, P., Weber, B. (eds.) CAiSE 2019. LNCS, vol. 11483, pp. 446–461. Springer, Cham (2019). https://doi.org/10.1007/978-3-030-21290-2_28
13. Kedziora, D., Kiviranta, H.: Digital business value creation with robotic process automation (RPA) in Northern and Central Europe. Management **13**(2), 161–174 (2018)
14. Kokina, J., Blanchette, S.: Early evidence of digital labor in accounting: innovation with robotic process automation. Int. J. Account. Inf. Syst. **35**, 100431 (2019)
15. Lacity, M.C., Willcocks, L.P.: Robotic process automation at telefónica O2. MIS Q. Exec. **15**(1), 21–35 (2016)
16. Lacity, M.C., Willcocks, L.P.: A new approach to automating services. MIT Sloan Manage. Rev. **58**, 41–49 (2017)
17. Leno, V., Polyvyanyy, A., Dumas, M., La Rosa, M., Maggi, F.M.: Robotic process mining: vision and challenges. Bus. Inf. Syst. Eng., 1–14 (2020). https://doi.org/10.1007/s12599-020-00641-4

18. Mendling, J., Decker, G., Hull, R., Reijers, H.A., Weber, I.: How do machine learning, robotic process automation, and blockchains affect the human factor in business process management? Commun. Assoc. Inf. Syst. **43**(1), 19 (2018)
19. Osmundsen, K., Iden, J., Bygstad, B.: Organizing robotic process automation: balancing loose and tight coupling. In: Proceedings of the 52nd Hawaii International Conference on System Sciences (2019)
20. Peffers, K., Tuunanen, T., Rothenberger, M.A., Chatterjee, S.: A design science research methodology for information systems research. J. Manag. Inf. Syst. **24**(3), 45–77 (2007)
21. Penttinen, E., Kasslin, H., Asatiani, A.: How to choose between robotic process automation and back-end system automation? In: 26th European Conference on Information Systems, ECIS 2018 (2018)
22. Plattfaut, R.: Robotic process automation - process optimization on steroids? In: 40th International Conference on Information Systems, Munich (2019)
23. Saaty, T.L.: How to make a decision: the analytic hierarchy process. Eur. J. Oper. Res. **48**(1), 9–26 (1990)
24. Saaty, T.: The Analytic Hierarchy Process: Planning, Priority Setting. Resource Allocation. Advanced Book Program. McGraw-Hill International Book Company (1980)
25. Santos, F., Pereira, R., Vasconcelos, J.B.: Toward robotic process automation implementation: an end-to-end perspective. Bus. Process. Manag. J. **26**, 405–420 (2019)
26. Syed, R., et al.: Robotic process automation: contemporary themes and challenges. Comput. Ind. **115**, 103162 (2020)
27. Vaidya, O.S., Kumar, S.: Analytic hierarchy process: an overview of applications. Eur. J. Oper. Res. **169**(1), 1–29 (2006)
28. Viehhauser, J.: Is robotic process automation becoming intelligent? early evidence of influences of artificial intelligence on robotic process automation. In: Asatiani, A., et al. (eds.) BPM 2020. LNBIP, vol. 393, pp. 101–115. Springer, Cham (2020). https://doi.org/10.1007/978-3-030-58779-6_7
29. Wanner, J., Hofmann, A., Fischer, M., Imgrund, F., Janiesch, C., Geyer-Klingeberg, J.: Process selection in RPA projects - towards a quantifiable method of decision making. In: 40th International Conference on Information Systems, Munich (2019)
30. Webster, J., Watson, R.T.: Analyzing the past to prepare for the future: writing a literature review. MIS Q. Exec. **26**, xiii–xxiii (2002)
31. Wellmann, C., Stierle, M., Dunzer, S., Matzner, M.: A framework to evaluate the viability of robotic process automation for business process activities. BPM 2020. LNBIP, vol. 393, pp. 200–214. Springer, Cham (2020). https://doi.org/10.1007/978-3-030-58779-6_14
32. Willcocks, L., Lacity, M., Craig, A.: Robotic process automation: strategic transformation lever for global business services? J. Inf. Technol. Teach. Cases **7**(1), 17–28 (2017)

A Rule-Based Recommendation Approach for Business Process Modeling

Diana Sola[1,2(✉)], Christian Meilicke[2], Han van der Aa[2],
and Heiner Stuckenschmidt[2]

[1] Intelligent Robotic Process Automation, SAP SE, Walldorf, Germany
[2] Data and Web Science Group, University of Mannheim, Mannheim, Germany
{diana,christian,han,heiner}@informatik.uni-mannheim.de

Abstract. Business process modeling is a crucial, yet time-consuming and knowledge-intensive task. This is particularly the case when modeling a domain-specific process, which often requires the use of highly specialized terminology in a consistent manner. To alleviate these issues, the process modeling task can be supported by techniques that suggest how a model under development can be expanded. In this work, we provide such suggestions through a rule-based activity recommendation approach, which suggests suitable activities to be included at a user-defined position in a process model. A benefit of our rule-based work over other approaches is that it accompanies recommendations with explanations, providing additional transparency and trustworthiness to users. Furthermore, through comprehensive evaluation experiments on a large set of real-world process models, we show that our rule-based approach outperforms other methods, including an embedding-based one.

Keywords: Process modeling · Activity recommendation · Rule learning

1 Introduction

Business processes structure the operations of organizations. They consist of sets of activities which jointly lead to an outcome that is valuable to an organization or its clients. *Process models* have become the de facto standard to capture information on such processes and are, therefore, present in virtually all facets of the business process management lifecycle. For this reason, documenting business operations using process models has become a quintessential activity for many organizations [9].

Although they are clearly important instruments for the execution, analysis, and improvement of business processes, actually creating process models is a time-consuming task that requires substantial expertise [11,12]. This task is even more challenging when modeling a domain-specific process, which often requires the use of specialized and technical vocabulary in a consistent manner. To mitigate these issues, modeling can be supported through the provision of

© Springer Nature Switzerland AG 2021
M. La Rosa et al. (Eds.): CAiSE 2021, LNCS 12751, pp. 328–343, 2021.
https://doi.org/10.1007/978-3-030-79382-1_20

recommendations that suggest modelers on how they may expand a process model that they are working on [10]. One clear manner in which such support can be provided is through activity recommendation.

Given a business process model under development, *activity recommendation* sets out to suggest suitable activities to extend the model at a user-defined position. A repository of available business process models can serve as a basis for this task. Here, it is crucial that recommendations are provided in a context-aware manner, i.e., they should take the current content and state of a process model into account. To illustrate this, consider Fig. 1, which shows a process model under development where a user has just inserted an unlabeled activity on the model's right-hand side. The activity recommendation task is then to determine a suitable activity for this position, i.e., to find an appropriate label for it. Since the process that has been modeled so far contains activities that are commonly associated with *order-to-cash* processes, a context-aware recommender system will provide recommendations that correspond to activities that occur at a comparable position in similar processes found in a model repository, such as 'Submit purchase order', 'Analyze quotation', and 'Purchase order sent'.

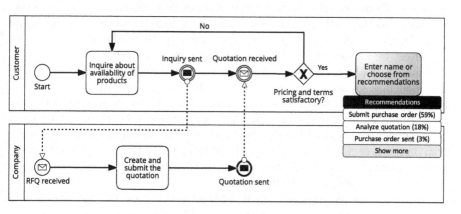

Fig. 1. A business process model under development

In this paper, we propose to tackle the activity recommendation task using a rule-based recommendation approach. Such approaches have their origin in the field of inductive logic programming [4] and have been shown to be competitive for use cases such as knowledge graph completion [17]. An additional benefit is that rule-based approaches offer an explanation for given recommendations, which helps to improve the transparency, trustworthiness, and satisfaction of recommendation systems [23]. Our proposed rule-based approach learns logical rules that describe how activities are used in a given repository of available process models, which we subsequently use to recommend appropriate activities at a given position. Our rule learner is based on the top-down search implemented in association rule mining systems [5,13], which we adapted to support a specific, process-oriented language designed for activity recommendation. An extensive experimental evaluation demonstrates that our rule-based approach outperforms both standard machine learning [14,15] and embedding-based [22] techniques.

In the remainder, we first discuss various other works related to process model recommendation in Sect. 2, before formally defining the activity-recommendation problem in Sect. 3. We present our approach for rule-based activity recommendation in Sect. 4 and discuss our extensive evaluation experiments in Sect. 5. Finally, we conclude the work in Sect. 6.

2   Related Work

There are several activity recommendation approaches that abstract business process models to directed graphs and use graph mining techniques to extract structural patterns from a process repository. The similarity between the extracted patterns and a process model under development can be calculated using different strategies, including common subgraph distance [3] and edit distance [3,6,16]. However, as stated by Wang et al. [22], graph mining methods reach their limits when applied to large complex datasets with thousands of processes. To overcome this, they present an embedding-based activity recommendation method, RLRecommender, which is able to handle large datasets and outperforms the graph-mining-based algorithms in the conducted experiments. Therefore, we include this method in our experimental studies.

Jannach et al. [14,15] propose different recommendation techniques to provide modeling support for users in the specific area of data analysis workflows. The user support consists of recommending additional operations to insert into the machine learning workflow under development and is hence similar to activity recommendation. In this paper, we show that the recommendation strategies from Jannach et al. can also be used to recommend activities for more general process models than data analysis workflows, i.e., business process models, and evaluate them in our experiments.

Since activity recommendation is inherently based on the identification of patterns in a given process repository, the application of *association rule mining* techniques [1] also suggests itself for this purpose. Such techniques consider associations in terms of activity co-occurrence, but ignore the sequence of activities that can best be described with a multi-relational model. Contrary to association rule mining, relational rule mining can distinguish between different relations. One of the early systems is WARMR [5]. More recently, systems as AMIE [13] and AnyBURL [17] have been proposed to learn rules that describe the regularities in a given knowledge base. Before we started to develop our own method, we tried to apply these systems to the given problem. While WARMR can (in principle) learn the types of rules that we are interested in, it does not scale to the large process repositories that we are working with. AMIE and AnyBURL, on the other hand, have a restricted language bias which does not learn the types of rules that are important for recommendations in a process context.

Rule learning is also tightly linked to the field of Inductive Logic Programming (ILP). Prominent ILP approaches are, for example, FOIL [19] and Tilde [2].

While WARMR can also be regarded as an ILP approach, ILP techniques are usually based on a covering approach instead of mining all possibly relevant rules. However, in a prediction scenario we might often encounter situations where the prediction must be based on a rather weak rule that covers only few examples and would be redundant in the set of all rules. Another difference is the need for explicitly given negative examples, which are not available in the scenario we address. For these reasons we abstained from using ILP systems for the activity-recommendation problem.

Finally, our work itself represents a considerable extension and operationalization of ideas originally proposed in a doctoral consortium [21]. There, we conducted initial experiments using one simple rule type and only targeted a simple, context-agnostic recommendation setting.

3   Problem Definition

In this section, we discuss the transformation of business process models into business process graphs and formalize the activity-recommendation problem.

Business Process Graphs. Various modeling notations, such as Petri nets and BPMN, are available to capture business processes. Since we do not want to limit our approach to any specific notation, we extend the abstract view from Dijkman et al. [7], in which a process model is represented as a directed attributed graph:

Definition 1 (Business process graph). *Let $\mathcal{L}$ be a set of labels and $\mathcal{R}$ a set of behavioral relation types. Let $\mathcal{P}(\mathcal{R})$ denote the power set of $\mathcal{R}$. A business process graph is a tuple (N, E, λ, τ), where N is a set of nodes, $E \subseteq N \times N$ is a set of directed edges, $\lambda : N \to \mathcal{L}$ is a function that maps a node to a label, and $\tau : E \to \mathcal{P}(\mathcal{R})$ is a function that maps an edge to a set of relation types.*

In order to treat a business process model as a business process graph, we map the model's contents to the graph representation using an abstraction procedure. This procedure has several degrees of freedom: We might, for example, drop (or keep) certain types of nodes and have to select the types of behavioral relations that we use and assign to edges (e.g., *directly follows*). In the following, we focus on the abstraction of Petri nets. For other modeling notations it is possible to develop similar abstraction procedures. For instance, BPMN models can first be translated into Petri nets [8] before applying the abstraction approach.

From Petri Net to Business Process Graph. Given a Petri net, we consider transitions, which correspond to activities, as nodes in a business process graph, while omitting its places. Then, for any pair of nodes m and n, we have to decide if we create a directed edge $e = (m, n) \in E$ and which relation types from a set $\mathcal{R}$ to assign to this directed edge. For this procedure, we follow Wang et al. [22], who propose three abstraction strategies, based on different sets of behavioral relations. We refer to [22] for details and here stick to an intuitive explanation.

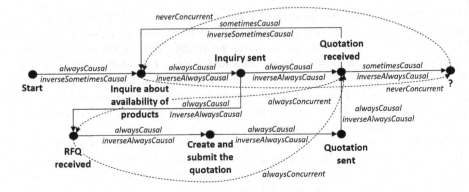

Fig. 2. A business process graph corresponding to the process model in Fig. 1 using the relation types $\mathcal{R}^{causal+concurrent}$

- **Directly-follows abstraction:** This abstraction strategy only considers which activities may follow each other during process execution, captured in the *followedBy* relation. Formally, if a node m can be directly followed by a node n, we add an edge $e = (m, n)$ with $\tau(e) = \{followedBy\}$. Naturally, this strategy loses part of the semantics expressed in the original Petri net. For instance, it does not distinguish between transitions that exclude each other (XOR split) and those that can be executed concurrently (AND split).
- **Causal abstraction:** The second strategy reduces the abstraction loss by distinguishing between *alwaysCausal* and *sometimesCausal* relations, and their inverse counterparts. A pair of activities (m, n) is in the *alwaysCausal* relation if any occurrence of m is always followed by an occurrence of n, whereas the *sometimesCausal* relation applies if this is sometimes the case (due to an XOR-split in the process). Conversely, m and n are in the *inverseAlwaysCausal* relation if any occurrence of n is always preceded by an occurence of m, while the *inverseSometimesCausal* relation holds if this is sometimes the case (due to an XOR-join in the process). Since this distinction is asymetric, e.g., an *alwaysCausal* relation does not guarantee an *inverseAlwaysCausal* relation between two activities, we assign the forward and the inverse relation between m and n to the edge $e = (m, n)$, e.g., $\tau(e) = \{alwaysCausal, inverseSometimesCausal\}$.
- **Causal and concurrent abstraction:** Finally, the third strategy introduces additional relations that can be used to describe types of concurrency between activities, on top of the aforementioned *causal* ones. These relations are called *alwaysConcurrent*, *sometimesConcurrent*, and *neverConcurrent*, reflecting whether two activities can, must, or must not occur concurrently.

In the remainder, we use $\mathcal{R}^X$ to denote a set of relation types that has been used in an abstraction strategy X. For instance, Fig. 2 shows the business process graph obtained for the running example of Fig. 1, based on $\mathcal{R}^{causal+concurrent}$.

Although the graph abstracts from some details, the overall structure and sequence of activities is preserved. Note that a $\mathcal{R}^{causal}$-graph can be obtained by omitting all dashed lines, while a $\mathcal{R}^{followedBy}$-graph corresponds to the $\mathcal{R}^{causal}$-graph in which all relation types are replaced by *followedBy*.

The Activity-Recommendation Problem. With the concept of the abstraction of a business process model to a business process graph at hand, we can now proceed to the definition of the activity-recommendation problem. Given the current status of the process model under development, the activity-recommendation problem is concerned with recommending suitable activities to extend the model at a user-defined position. Since the position of the activity that has to be recommended is given by the user (as the activity being added to a model), the activity-recommendation problem breaks down to finding a suitable label for the so far unlabeled activity node $\hat{n}$.

Definition 2 (Activity-recommendation problem). *Let $\mathcal{B}$ be a set of business process graphs and $\mathcal{L}_\mathcal{B}$ the set of activity labels that are used in $\mathcal{B}$. Let $B = (N, E, \lambda, \tau)$ be a given business process graph under development, where each node $n \in N$ except one node $\hat{n}$ is labeled, i.e., $\lambda(n)$ is given for all $n \in N \setminus \{\hat{n}\}$. The activity-recommendation problem is to find a suitable label $\lambda(\hat{n}) \in \mathcal{L}_\mathcal{B}$ for $\hat{n}$.*

In the next section, we propose our rule-based recommendation approach to address the activity-recommendation problem.

4   A Rule-Based Approach

Our rule-based recommendation approach consists of two main phases. First, *rule learning* derives rules that capture activity inter-relations from the process graphs in a repository. Second, *rule application* employs the learned rules to recommend the most suitable label for a target node in a process model under development, i.e., the recommended activity.

4.1   Rule Learning

Given a repository of business process graphs $\mathcal{B}$, we want to learn rules which capture regularities that appear in the use of labels within $\mathcal{B}$. For that purpose, we first need to determine the constants and predicates to be used to describe $\mathcal{B}$ in terms of logical formulas. We translate each $B = (N, E, \lambda, \tau) \in \mathcal{B}$ as follows.

1. For each edge $e = (m, n) \in E$ and each relation type $r \in \tau(e)$ we add a formula $r(m, n)$ that captures the type of relation between m and n, e.g., *followedBy*(m, n) or *alwaysCausal*(m, n).
2. For each node $n \in N$ we use a predicate λ_n that corresponds to the label $\lambda(n)$ of n and add a formula $\lambda_n(n)$, e.g., *quotationReceived*(n).
3. For each pair of nodes $m \neq n \in N$ we add the formulas *inSameProcess*(m, n) and *inSameProcess*(n, m) to express that m and n appear in the same graph.

Given a set of $\mathcal{R}^X$, this means that we use $|\mathcal{R}^X| + 1$ binary predicates ($+1$ for *inSameProcess*) and $|\mathcal{L}_\mathcal{B}|$ unary predicates to describe the structure of the process graphs in the repository $\mathcal{B}$. Since a label can occur in multiple models, certain unary predicates will be used to describe the labels of nodes that appear in different process models, while the underlying nodes themselves always belong to exactly one model. Given these predicates, we next define *rule templates* and use them to capture activity regularities.

Rule Templates. In the following we use h, j, k and l to refer to placeholders for unary predicates that correspond to the label of an activity, e.g., $l = submit\text{-}PurchaseOrder$. In this work we are interested in a special form of *horn rules*. Particularly, we are interested in rules that have the form $l(Z) \leftarrow \ldots$, which are rules that capture the regularities of activity Z being labeled with l.

To find such rules, our approach employs a set of rule patterns, i.e., templates, for which we generate all possible instantiations that hold in the repository $\mathcal{B}$. In particular, we define the following rule templates for a setting using directly-follows abstraction, i.e., with *followedBy* as the only relation type in $\mathcal{R}^{followedBy}$:

$$l(Z) \leftarrow inSameProcess(Y, Z), k(Y) \tag{1}$$

$$l(Z) \leftarrow followedBy(Y, Z), k(Y) \tag{2}$$

$$l(Z) \leftarrow inSameProcess(X, Y), inSameProcess(Y, Z), j(X), k(Y) \tag{3}$$

$$l(Z) \leftarrow inSameProcess(X, Y), followedBy(Y, Z), j(X), k(Y) \tag{4}$$

$$l(Z) \leftarrow followedBy(X, Y), followedBy(Y, Z), j(X), k(Y) \tag{5}$$

$$l(Z) \leftarrow followedBy(W, X), followedBy(X, Y), followedBy(Y, Z), h(W), j(X), k(Y) \tag{6}$$

To operationalize the templates for the $\mathcal{R}^{causal}$ setting, we replace each occurrence of *followedBy* in templates (2), (4), (5) and (6) by each of the four types of causal relations in $\mathcal{R}^{causal}$. This results in various combinations, due to repeated occurrences of *followedBy* in certain templates. Specifically, we require 90 templates for the $\mathcal{R}^{causal}$ setting, primarily due to $4 \times 4 = 16$ different versions of (5) and $4 \times 4 \times 4 = 64$ of template (6). For brevity, we shall refer to the versions derived from one of the templates (1)–(6) as a *template group* in the remainder. To additionally incorporate the 3 types of concurrent relations in the $\mathcal{R}^{causal+concurrent}$ setting, we introduce a further template group (7), which contains three templates that are similar to template (2), but in which the *followedBy* relation in (2) is replaced by one of the 3 *concurrent* relations.

Note that our approach is extendable, since the rule templates can be modified or complemented with additional ones. However, in light of the aforementioned combinatorial increase, it should be taken into account that longer rule templates and a higher number of templates greatly expand the search space, which may limit the applicability of the approach on large datasets.

When instantiating the rule templates, we replace h, j, k, and l by all possible label predicates created from $\mathcal{L}_\mathcal{B}$. This means that we, for example, have $|\mathcal{L}_\mathcal{B}| * (|\mathcal{L}_\mathcal{B}| - 1) \approx |\mathcal{L}_\mathcal{B}|^2$ different instantiations of templates (1) and (2).

Rule Interpretation. Each of the defined templates captures a certain type of probabilistic regularity about activity inter-relations in process models. The probability of a rule that instantiates template (1) expresses how likely it is that, if an activity (label) k is used in a process, activity l appears in that process as well, whereas the probability of a (2)-rule tells us how probable it is that an activity k is directly followed by an activity l.

Here, it is important to consider that certain rules inherently relate to each other. For instance, any instantiation of a (2)-rule, always results in a corresponding (1)-rule as well. This is the case, because $inSameProcess(X,Y) \leftarrow followedBy(X,Y)$ is always true, i.e., if X can be followed by Y, then X and Y are naturally also part of the same process model. Since the inverse is not true, i.e., $followedBy(X,Y) \leftarrow inSameProcess(X,Y)$ does not have to hold, we say that a (2)-rule is more *special* than a (1)-rule. Similar inter-relations also exist for the other rule templates. Whenever a rule r is more special than a rule r', rule r tends to make fewer and more specific predictions compared to rule r', which will be reflected in the ablation study in Sect. 5.

Rule Confidence. For each *concrete rule*, i.e., an instantiation of one of the rule templates, we compute its *confidence* as a measure of its quality. For this, we follow the definition given in [13]. According to this definition, the *support* of a horn rule $head \leftarrow body$ shall be computed by counting all groundings for which both the head and body of the rule are true. Then, to compute a rule's confidence, we divide its support by the number of those groundings that make the body true. Thus, the confidence of the rule can be understood as the probability that the rule makes a correct prediction within the given repository of business process graphs $\mathcal{B}$. For instance, our employed dataset leads to two rules with the same body related to activities that succeed a 'Quotation received' activity:

$$r_1 = submitPurchaseOrder(Z) \leftarrow inverseAlwaysCausal(Y,Z), quotationReceived(Y)$$
$$r_2 = \quad analyzeQuotation(Z) \quad \leftarrow inverseAlwaysCausal(Y,Z), quotationReceived(Y)$$

The body of both rules is the same and it holds 15 times over $\mathcal{B}$. This means that the pattern described by the body appears in 15 process models from $\mathcal{B}$. Considering that the head is additionally true, these numbers go down to 10 and 5, respectively. Thus, we have $support(r_1) = 10$, $support(r_2) = 5$, $confidence(r_1) = 10/15 = 0.667$, and $confidence(r_2) = 5/15 = 0.333$.

4.2 Rule Application

Given an unfinished business process graph B with its unlabeled node $\hat{n}$, we use the rules learned from $\mathcal{B}$ and apply them on $\hat{n}$, while taking the current state of the process graph B into account. To do this, we set $Z = \hat{n}$ for all rules that we have learned and check if the resulting body is true. An example for a specific rule that instantiates template (4) in the $\mathcal{R}^{causal}$ setting is given by (∗). It is also a rule that leads to the top-ranked recommendation of the running example shown in Fig. 1, where $\hat{n}$ is the rightmost node.

$$submitPurchaseOrder(\hat{n}) \leftarrow inSameProcess(X,Y), inverseAlwaysCausal(Y,\hat{n}), \quad (*)$$
$$createAndSubmitTheQuotation(X), quotationReceived(Y)$$

If we compare the rule to Fig. 1, we can see that the body of this partially instantiated rule is indeed true, as we can map X and Y to nodes that have the respective labels. Thus, the rule recommends *submitPurchaseOrder* as label for $\hat{n}$. This recommendation is weighted via the confidence of the rule, which is $9/9 = 1$ with respect to the dataset used in our experiments. We do the same with all rules and collect the recommendations of the rules where the body was true with respect to the given unfinished model B.

Confidence Aggregation. If several rules lead to the same recommendation, i.e., predict the same label, we aggregate their confidence scores, such that we can assign the recommendation a single score and rank it accordingly. For this, we consider two aggregation methods, which we will compare in our experiments. With the *max*-aggregation method, we assign the maximum confidence of the applicable rules to the recommendation, while the *noisy-or* method multiplies the complement to 1 of all confidence scores and assigns the complement to 1 of this product to the recommendation. This method is based on the noisy-or distribution, which represents a simplification of dependency relations in Bayesian networks [20]. After applying an aggregation method, we obtain a set of recommendations, each with a confidence score.

Then, we remove all recommendations from the set that refer to a label that is already used in B, since it is generally undesirable to have multiple activities with the same label in a single model. Since at most one of the recommendations in the set of recommended activities will be chosen, we normalize the confidence scores of the recommendations such that their sum equals 1. This changes the score for the label *submitPurchaseOrder* from 1 to 0.59.

Result Explanation. One of the advantages of our approach is that the rules that serve as a basis for recommendations can also be used to explain provided recommendations. With respect to the given top recommendation, such an explanation can be phrased like: *Since the previous activity is 'Quotation received' and the process also includes a 'Create and submit the quotation' activity, there is a rather strong indication (normalized score of 0.59) that the activity should be labeled 'Submit purchase order'.* Such an explanation might raise the confidence of the user in the given recommendation and might make it easier for her to make a choice between the presented alternatives. In addition, the recommender system could also provide links to the business process models in the repository that supported this recommendation. Hence, the user can have a look at similar processes, which might further help her with the current modeling task.

5   Experimental Evaluation

In this section we report about our experimental studies[1] in which we assess the quality of the recommendations provided by our rule-based approach and

---

[1] For proprietary reasons, requests for the source code of the employed implementation should be submitted to `diana.sola@sap.com`.

compare our work against learning-based approaches [14,15] and the embedding-based RLRecommender technique [22]. Additionally, we present an ablation study that provides insights into the types of rules that are most important for our recommendation approach.

5.1 Dataset

To conduct the experiments, we employ the model collection of the Business Process Management Academic Initiative [18], which has also been used in the evaluation of RLRecommender [22]. The collection contains almost 30,000 process models in different process modeling languages. The models of the collection are available in different revisions, which is useful for our purposes, since we consider each revision as a separate process model and thus ensure that most of the activities appear repeatedly across different processes in the repository.[2]

For our evaluation, we used all BPMN 2.0 models of the collection with 3 to 50 activities described by English labels. The resulting dataset comprises 15,365 process models and 27,235 unique activity labels. Note that these process models result from 3,688 processes and their revisions. On average, the process models involve 15.7 activities while half of the processes comprise 14 activities or less (median). The standard deviation is 9.2.

5.2 Evaluation Setup

We conducted our evaluation using 10-fold cross validation, i.e., training an approach on 90% of the dataset and evaluating it on the remainder. We report the mean results obtained over 10 runs (i.e., repetitions) of this cross validation.

Evaluation Scenarios. We create one recommendation task for every business process graph in the evaluation set by following different strategies, which vary in terms of the amount of information that is available for the recommendation method, i.e., different ways to simulate the current status of a business process model under development. The basic idea is to remove some of the nodes and all edges connected to these nodes from a given process model. The remaining graph is treated as the intermediate result of a construction process. We choose a node from this graph as the one that has to be predicted and hide its label.

- **given-k.** In the given-k scenario, we pick a path of length $k + 1$ which is a longest path from a source node (node with no incoming edges) to the activity at position $k + 1$ and aim to predict the label of this activity. Especially for low values of k, the given-k evaluation method allows us to compare different methods in the 'cold-start' setting, in which only little information is given. Important here is that this setting only provides a single sequence of activities as information to a recommendation approach.

---

[2] Note that with the decision to keep these different revisions, we follow the setup used to evaluate RLRecommender.

- **hide-last-two.** The opposite to this is the 'hide-last-two' evaluation method, which maintains a near complete process model. Particularly, one sink node n_s (node with no outgoing edges) is randomly chosen and hidden. Then, we randomly select a node that precedes n_s as the node for which a label shall be predicted, while taking all other (non-hidden) activities into account.
- **breadth-first search (BFS).** Finally we have implemented a BFS-based evaluation method, where one activity, which is neither a source nor sink node, is randomly chosen as the one to be predicted. Then, using s to denote the shortest path from a source node to the selected activity, activities that are on a path of length s, starting from a source node are used as a context for the prediction, while all other activities are hidden.

Evaluation Metrics. We quantify the relevance of provided recommendations using two metrics. First, we report on the *hit rate* H@10, which captures the fraction of *hits* in the top 10 recommendations, i.e., the fraction of cases where the activity that was actually used in a process model is among the 10 recommendations with the highest confidence score. Second, we report on the Mean Reciprocal Rank (MRR), which also takes the position of a hit in the recommendation list into account. For a given recommendation, the MRR has the value 0 if the actually chosen activity is not in the list and $1/p$ otherwise, where p denotes the position of the hit in the list. More precisely, we also consider a recommendation list of length 10 to compute MRR, which is a close approximation of the MRR that is based on the full ranking. However, this is more realistic, as the list of recommendations shown to the user has to be limited as well. In the ablation study we additionally report the average number of generated recommendations (i.e., the length of the recommendation list) per recommendation task as $\varnothing|\text{Rec}|$.

Approach Configurations. We evaluate different configurations of our rule-based recommendation approach by varying two aspects. First, we vary the behavioral relations taken into accounts, i.e., we consider configurations that use the *followedBy*, *causal*, and *causal plus concurrent* relations. Second, we vary the aggregation method over the *max* and *noisy-or* methods described in Sect. 4.2. Combining these two aspects results in six different configurations, which we denote, for example, as RULES *followedBy^{max}*.

Baselines and Other Approaches. We compare the performance of our rule-based approach against different baseline techniques and alternative approaches, derived from various existing works:

- CoOccur [14]: This technique is based on the conditional probabilities of the simultaneous occurrence of two activities in a process. Hence, this strategy recommends activities that co-occurred most often with the so far inserted activities of the unfinished process.
- kNN [14]: kNN is a weighted k-nearest-neighbors-based technique. It represents each process model as a vector, capturing whether or not an activity is present in a model. Then, kNN recommends activities that have not yet been included in a model, but appear in similar models in the repository.

- LINK-CTX [15]: Unlike the prior techniques, the link-based LINK-CTX technique takes the order of activities in process models into account. Specially, it considers which activities frequently occur directly after each other.
- CHAIN-CTX [15]: The chain-based CHAIN-CTX method generalizes LINK-CTX by considering longer chains of activities, i.e., it also considers recurring patterns consisting of three or more activities in order to provide recommendations that take a larger amount of contextual information into account.
- HYBRID-CTX [15]: The HYBRID-CTX technique combines a contextualized kNN strategy, kNN-CTX, with LINK-CTX. Compared to kNN, kNN-CTX increases the weight of the neighbour processes that contain activities, which are also included in the context of the process under development. HYBRID-CTX is a weighting strategy which gives more weight to the kNN-CTX technique for larger processes under development, while LINK-CTX receives a higher weight for smaller ones.
- RLREC [22]: The RLRecommender approach embeds activities and behavioral relations into a continuous low-dimensional space. The embedded vectors and their distances are then used to provide activity recommendations.

The first two methods CoOCCUR and kNN can be understood as simple baselines. The other methods are more sophisticated techniques that have especially been designed to perform well in the given (or a highly similar) activity recommendation scenario. Similar to the configurations of our approach, we assess the performance of RLREC for configurations that consider different behavioral relations, i.e., RLREC *followedBy*, RLREC *causal*, and RLREC *causal+conc*. The other approaches cannot distinguish between different relations, which means that we apply them in the $\mathcal{R}^{followedBy}$ setting only.

Note that, since the given-k evaluation scenario always captures the current status of the process under development as a sequence of successive activities, it is pointless to consider different causal or concurrent relations for this setting. Therefore, we only consider the $\mathcal{R}^{followedBy}$ setting for the given-k scenario.

5.3 Evaluation Results

The results of our experiments are shown in Table 1. With exception of the specific 'cold-start' evaluation scenario given-1 our rule-based activity recommendation approach outperforms all other methods.

The CoOCCUR baseline performs comparably poor, while recommendation strategies such as LINK-CTX, which also take structural process patterns into account, achieve better results. This is because they avoid recommending activities that have high co-occurrence statistics, but are not relevant at the current model position. The simple kNN technique performs surprisingly well in cases where more information is given. RLREC *causal* and RLREC *causal+conc* achieve equal results because RLRecommender bases its recommendations on one edge $(m, \hat{n})$ between the activity $\hat{n}$ that has to be labeled and another activity m in the given unfinished process only. In other words, the method does not collect and aggregate the predictions from all edges that are connected with $\hat{n}$. This also leads to the comparably low H@10 and MRR numbers.

Table 1. Experimental results of the methods in different evaluation scenarios

Method	Given-1		Given-3		Given-5		BFS		Hide-last-two	
	H@10	MRR	H@10	MRR	H@10	MRR	H@10	MRR	H@10	MRR
CoOccur	0.290	0.099	0.333	0.105	0.302	0.081	0.215	0.058	0.207	0.049
kNN	0.296	0.121	0.721	0.321	0.749	0.313	0.804	0.434	0.914	0.658
Link-Ctx	0.495	0.389	0.864	0.672	0.875	0.671	0.777	0.577	0.812	0.615
Chain-Ctx	0.495	0.389	0.928	0.781	0.929	0.765	0.816	0.644	0.855	0.697
Hybrid-Ctx	0.495	0.389	0.889	0.721	0.909	0.728	0.857	0.731	0.732	0.646
RLRec $followedBy$	0.470	0.344	0.830	0.590	0.838	0.602	0.738	0.504	0.776	0.524
RLRec $causal$							0.742	0.528	0.786	0.561
RLRec $causal+conc$							0.742	0.528	0.786	0.561
Rules $followedBy^{max}$	0.482	0.380	0.930	0.793	0.941	0.797	0.886	0.833	0.929	0.878
Rules $followedBy^{noisy\text{-}or}$	0.483	0.377	0.930	0.792	0.935	0.791	0.883	0.832	0.928	0.873
Rules $causal^{max}$							0.890	0.837	0.929	0.886
Rules $causal^{noisy\text{-}or}$							0.890	0.841	0.930	0.880
Rules $causal+conc.^{max}$							0.891	0.840	0.931	0.888
Rules $causal+conc.^{noisy\text{-}or}$							0.892	0.845	0.931	0.882

Our rule-based approach can best exploit its potential when more details are given for the recommendation, i.e., if the given process under development already contains several activities and when applying the more precise relation extraction strategies $\mathcal{R}^{causal}$ and $\mathcal{R}^{causal+concurrent}$. The use of the max aggregation in general leads to better overall results, only in the BFS scenario is the $noisy$-or aggregation the better choice. Nevertheless, the differences between our configurations are relatively small in comparison with the differences between our approach and the other methods. This is in particular true when considering the BFS and the hide-last-two evaluation scenarios. In the latter scenario, for example, our method is almost 20% better in terms of MRR. This illustrates that our method is much more capable of leveraging contextual information, while the other methods only benefit from the additional information to a limited degree.

The average time required to provide a recommendation is generally below 0.65 s when running on an Intel® Xeon® E5-2623 v3@16 × 3.00 GHz CPU computer with 256 GB RAM. The LOO scenario using max-aggregation is an exception to this, which may require 1.1 s on average to provide recommendations.

5.4   Ablation Study

We investigate the importance of the individual rule templates (and groups) through an ablation study.[3] In particular, we evaluate the performance of our method when only learning and applying rules from one template group, e.g., a configuration R-(1) only considers rules related to the *inSameProcess* predicate used in template (1). Note that we apply the $\mathcal{R}^{followedBy}$ setting for the given-5 evaluation scenario while we adopt the $\mathcal{R}^{causal+concurrent}$ setting for the BFS and hide-last-two scenarios. Further, we employ the max aggregation for all settings.

---

[3] For brevity, we use *template* and *template group* interchangeably in this section.

Table 2. Results of the ablation study

Rule templates	Given-5			BFS			Hide-last-two		
	H@10	MRR	∅|Rec|	H@10	MRR	∅|Rec|	H@10	MRR	∅|Rec|
R-(1)	0.739	0.298	7280.5	0.773	0.428	10455.1	0.877	0.609	10888.6
R-(2)	0.865	0.676	40.0	0.784	0.673	227.5	0.828	0.723	140.1
R-(3)	0.761	0.310	428.6	0.764	0.432	2616.4	0.881	0.627	2849.4
R-(4)	0.928	0.791	24.2	0.843	0.802	28.6	0.909	0.874	58.7
R-(5)	0.901	0.759	5.5	0.687	0.643	3.6	0.776	0.736	4.3
R-(6)	0.898	0.767	2.1	0.508	0.487	1.2	0.654	0.632	1.3
R-(7)				0.399	0.355	20.1	0.394	0.349	13.6
RULES	0.941	0.797	7280.5	0.891	0.840	10455.1	0.931	0.888	10888.6

The results in Table 2 reveal that the templates that include at least one *followedBy* relation, i.e., R-(2), R-(4), R-(5) and R-(6), achieve good results in the given-5 case, in which the least information is given for the recommendation. The more information is given, the better the performance of rule templates R-(1) and R-(3), which consider co-occurrence (*inSameProcess* relations). When using rule template R-(4) exclusively, we achieve the best results, which reflects the importance of rule templates that consider structural and co-occurrence patterns simultaneously. It is not surprising that considering *concurrent* relations in isolation, as done in R-(7), does not work well.

The results also reflect that certain rule templates are more specific than others. For example, template (2) is more specific than (1), thus, it leads to fewer, but more targeted predictions with a higher confidence, which yield a higher recommendation accuracy. However, templates (5) and (6) are so specific that exclusive use of them cannot fill a recommendation list of length 10, resulting in comparably lower performance. Given this trend, considering longer rule templates, e.g., that depend on longer activity sequences, is likely unfruitful.

Finally, it is interesting to recognize that the combined configuration, RULES, achieves better results than R-(1) to R-(7) in every scenario. Furthermore, we also conducted inverted experiments, where we used all but one rule template. While some combinations yielded slightly better results than achieved by combining all rules, this improvement was never consistent across all evaluation scenarios. This shows that all rule templates make valuable contributions in certain situations, which is why the full approach yields a recommendation quality that is overall higher than the quality achieved by partial configurations.

6   Conclusion

In this paper, we presented a rule-based approach for activity recommendation in process models. We demonstrated different configurations of our approach, highlighting its extendable nature. Our extensive experiments showed that it outperforms a variety of other approaches [14,15] including an embedding-based method [22]. In contrast to these approaches, our rule-based method is, furthermore, able to provide explanations alongside the given recommendations.

In future work, we aim to refine our rule-based method such that it is able to learn and apply rules to variations of previously seen labels or even to completely unseen labels. This requires other types of rule templates and the use of matching techniques that allow us to compare unseen labels with ones in the repository.

Acknowledgement. We would like to thank Dietmar Jannach and Michael Jugovac for providing their code and kind help.

References

1. Agrawal, R., Imieliński, T., Swami, A.: Mining association rules between sets of items in large databases. In: SIGMOD, pp. 207–216. ACM (1993)
2. Blockeel, H., De Raedt, L.: Top-down induction of first-order logical decision trees. Artif. Intell. **101**(1–2), 285–297 (1998)
3. Cao, B., Yin, J., Deng, S., Wang, D., Wu, Z.: Graph-based workflow recommendation: on improving business process modeling. In: CIKM, pp. 1527–1531. ACM (2012)
4. De Raedt, L.: Logical and Relational Learning. Springer, Heidelberg (2008). https://doi.org/10.1007/978-3-540-68856-3
5. Dehaspe, L., De Raedt, L.: Mining association rules in multiple relations. In: Lavrač, N., Džeroski, S. (eds.) ILP 1997. LNCS, vol. 1297, pp. 125–132. Springer, Heidelberg (1997). https://doi.org/10.1007/3540635149_40
6. Deng, S., et al.: A recommendation system to facilitate business process modeling. IEEE Trans. Cybern. **47**(6), 1380–1394 (2017)
7. Dijkman, R., Dumas, M., García-Bañuelos, L.: Graph matching algorithms for business process model similarity search. In: Dayal, U., Eder, J., Koehler, J., Reijers, H.A. (eds.) BPM 2009. LNCS, vol. 5701, pp. 48–63. Springer, Heidelberg (2009). https://doi.org/10.1007/978-3-642-03848-8_5
8. Dijkman, R.M., Dumas, M., Ouyang, C.: Semantics and analysis of business process models in BPMN. Inf. Softw. Technol. **50**(12), 1281–1294 (2008)
9. Dumas, M., La Rosa, M., Mendling, J., Reijers, H.A.: Fundamentals of Business Process Management. Springer, Berlin (2013). https://doi.org/10.1007/978-3-642-33143-5
10. Fellmann, M., Zarvic, N., Metzger, D., Koschmider, A.: Requirements catalog for business process modeling recommender systems. In: WI, pp. 393–407 (2015)
11. Frederiks, P.J., Van der Weide, T.P.: Information modeling: the process and the required competencies of its participants. Data Knowl. Eng. **58**(1), 4–20 (2006)
12. Friedrich, F., Mendling, J., Puhlmann, F.: Process model generation from natural language text. In: Mouratidis, H., Rolland, C. (eds.) CAiSE 2011. LNCS, vol. 6741, pp. 482–496. Springer, Heidelberg (2011). https://doi.org/10.1007/978-3-642-21640-4_36
13. Galárraga, L.A., Teflioudi, C., Hose, K., Suchanek, F.: AMIE: association rule mining under incomplete evidence in ontological knowledge bases. In: WWW, pp. 413–422 (2013)
14. Jannach, D., Fischer, S.: Recommendation-based modeling support for data mining processes. In: RecSys, pp. 337–340 (2014)

15. Jannach, D., Jugovac, M., Lerche, L.: Supporting the design of machine learning workflows with a recommendation system. ACM Trans. Interact. Intell. Syst. **6**(1), 1–35 (2016)
16. Li, Y., et al.: An efficient recommendation method for improving business process modeling. IEEE Trans. Ind. Inf. **10**(1), 502–513 (2014)
17. Meilicke, C., Chekol, M.W., Ruffinelli, D., Stuckenschmidt, H.: Anytime bottom-up rule learning for knowledge graph completion. In: IJCAI, pp. 3137–3143. AAAI Press (2019)
18. Model collection of the Business Process Management Academic Initiative. http://bpmai.org/
19. Quinlan, J.R.: Learning logical definitions from relations. Mach. Learn. **5**(3), 239–266 (1990)
20. Russell, S., Norvig, P.: Artificial Intelligence: A Modern Approach, 3 edn. Prentice Hall (2010)
21. Sola, D.: Towards a rule-based recommendation approach for business process modeling. In: Hacid, H., et al. (eds.) Service-Oriented Computing – ICSOC 2020 Workshops, ICSOC 2020. Lecture Notes in Computer Science, vol. 12632. Springer, Cham (2021). https://doi.org/10.1007/978-3-030-76352-7_4
22. Wang, H., Wen, L., Lin, L., Wang, J.: RLRecommender: a representation-learning-based recommendation method for business process modeling. In: Pahl, C., Vukovic, M., Yin, J., Yu, Q. (eds.) ICSOC 2018. LNCS, vol. 11236, pp. 478–486. Springer, Cham (2018). https://doi.org/10.1007/978-3-030-03596-9_34
23. Zhang, Y., Chen, X.: Explainable recommendation: a survey and new perspectives. arXiv preprint arXiv:1804.11192 (2018)

Sketch2BPMN: Automatic Recognition of Hand-Drawn BPMN Models

Bernhard Schäfer[1,2]([✉]) [ID], Han van der Aa[2] [ID], Henrik Leopold[3,4] [ID],
and Heiner Stuckenschmidt[2] [ID]

[1] Intelligent Robotic Process Automation, SAP SE, Walldorf, Germany
[2] Data and Web Science Group, University of Mannheim, Mannheim, Germany
{bernhard,han,heiner}@informatik.uni-mannheim.de
[3] Kühne Logistics University, Hamburg, Germany
henrik.leopold@the-klu.org
[4] Hasso Plattner Institute, University of Potsdam, Potsdam, Germany

Abstract. Despite the widespread availability of process modeling tools, the first version of a process model is often drawn by hand on a piece of paper or whiteboard, especially when several people are involved in its elicitation. Though this has been found to be beneficial for the modeling task itself, it also creates the need to manually convert hand-drawn models afterward, such that they can be further used in a modeling tool. This manual transformation is associated with considerable time and effort and, furthermore, creates undesirable friction in the modeling workflow. In this paper, we alleviate this problem by presenting a technique that can automatically recognize and convert a sketch process model into a digital BPMN model. A key driver and contribution of our work is the creation of a publicly available dataset consisting of 502 manually annotated, hand-drawn BPMN models, covering 25 different BPMN elements. Based on this data set, we have established a neural network-based recognition technique that can reliably recognize and transform hand-drawn BPMN models. Our evaluation shows that our technique considerably outperforms available baselines and, therefore, provides a valuable basis to smoothen the modeling process.

Keywords: Process modeling · Sketch recognition · Hand-drawn process models

1 Introduction

In many organizations, business process modeling has become an integral activity to document and analyze business processes, as well as to collect requirements in software development projects [1,2]. This importance has led to the availability of a large number of specialized process modeling tools, which support modelers while creating, checking, and maintaining business process models and even entire collections thereof. Although these tools can generally be considered indispensable, it is important to note that the development of most process models

© Springer Nature Switzerland AG 2021
M. La Rosa et al. (Eds.): CAiSE 2021, LNCS 12751, pp. 344–360, 2021.
https://doi.org/10.1007/978-3-030-79382-1_21

does not start with software. For example, pen and paper is a suitable approach for an initial sketch [12, p. 85]. In collaborative settings, process models are typically drawn on whiteboard or brown paper, which stimulates the engagement of process stakeholders [9,12].

However, starting with a hand-drawn model also introduces the need to subsequently convert it into a digital counterpart using a modeling tool [4]. Since this task currently needs to be performed manually, this transformation step is associated with considerable time and effort and, furthermore, creates undesirable interruptions and friction in the modeling process. Some existing methods for collaborative modeling have tried to circumvent this transformation problem by providing tool support for collaborative modeling [3,7]. Nonetheless, these tools do not allow users to freely sketch processes, but require them to stick to predefined constructs and functionality, which actually mitigates the benefits associated with the use of hand-drawn models.

Therefore, recognizing the importance and benefits of hand-drawn process models, as well as the effort involved in their manual transformation, we use this paper to propose an approach that automates this step by transforming sketch process models into digital BPMN models. By expanding state-of-the-art work from the area of diagram recognition [20], our neural network-based approach, Sketch2BPMN, takes a hand-drawn BPMN (Business Process Model and Notation) model as input and produces a respective BPMN XML file, suitable for process modeling tools. Aside from this, a core contribution of our work is the introduction of the publicly available hdBPMN dataset, consisting of 502 manually annotated, hand-drawn BPMN models, covering 25 kinds of BPMN elements and varying considerably in their characteristics. Our experiments conducted on this dataset demonstrate the high accuracy achieved by our approach.

In the remainder, Sect. 2 illustrates the challenges that come with the recognition of hand-drawn BPMN models. Section 3 describes the Sketch2BPMN approach. Section 4 introduces our hdBPMN dataset and Sect. 5 the evaluation in which it is used. Finally, Sect. 6 reflects on related work before Sect. 7 concludes the paper.

2 Problem Illustration

To motivate the importance of our work, we illustrate the challenges associated with the automated recognition of hand-drawn process models using a real-world example from our hdBPMN dataset. Figure 1 depicts a BPMN model concerned with a claims-handling process. Although the depicted model is syntactically sound and correct, the figure illustrates several challenges that must be overcome by an automated recognition approach. Issue (1) shows that model elements may be drawn *incompletely*, such as the *Costumer* (sic) pool. Issue (2) points to one of the many instances where an edge is *not properly connected* to its source and/or target shapes. Other issues relate to overlaps between model components, such as *text that interrupts a line* (3) or lines that *cross each other* (4). We also observe remains of corrected mistakes, i.e., *crossed out parts* (5) and the use of *curved rather than straight lines* (6).

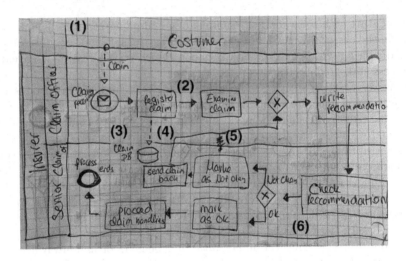

Fig. 1. Example of a hand-drawn BPMN model with highlighted issues

Aside from the drawing itself, additional difficulties can be attributed to the paper that has been used and the way it was digitized. First, the use of *grid paper* adds numerous additional lines to the image that may obscure the distinction between lines of the paper and those drawn as part of a model element (e.g., a *resource pool* or *lane*). Second, the fact that the image has been captured with a camera instead of a scanner introduces additional quality issues, such as curved paper, blur, and perspective distortion.

In summary, these issues make it harder for an automated approach to properly interpret a hand-drawn BPMN model. Although the above only relates to a single example, the spectrum of hand-drawn BPMN models is even more complex, due to the combination of various drawing styles, paper types, pens, and digitization methods. As a result, the dataset we introduce in this paper contains a remarkably high degree of diversity, which a successful BPMN-recognition approach must be able to deal with.

3   Approach

This section introduces Sketch2BPMN, our automated approach for recognizing a hand-drawn BPMN model from an image. As visualized in Fig. 2, Sketch2BPMN

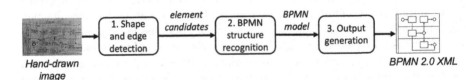

Fig. 2. Sketch2BPMN: overview of the main steps

consists of three main steps: 1) shape and edge detection, 2) BPMN structure recognition, and 3) output generation. Below we introduce each step in detail.

3.1 Shape and Edge Detection

This step of our approach generates sets of candidate BPMN shapes S_C and edges E_C for a provided hand-drawn image. Each candidate shape $s \in S_C$ is formalized as a tuple $s = (b, c, l)$, where b refers to the coordinates of a *bounding box*, i.e., a rectangle encompassing the predicted area of a drawn element, c the predicted BPMN element category, and l the likelihood that the shape s corresponds to category c. Furthermore, each candidate edge $e \in E_C$ is a tuple $e = (b, c, l, src, tgt)$, where b, c, and l are the respective shape counterparts, and src and tgt correspond to the *keypoint* coordinates of the edge, reflecting the points at which e is predicted to connect to shapes in S_C. Figure 3 visualizes such predicted candidates for the running example, showing, for example, that the upper bounding box is determined to have a 99.2% likelihood of being a *pool*.

To predict S_C and E_C, we build on *Arrow R-CNN* [20], an approach we established in earlier work for the recognition of hand-drawn diagrams, and adapt it to the specific characteristics of hand-drawn BPMN models. Particularly, we expand upon existing work through *improved keypoint detection* and *extended data augmentation*.

Arrow R-CNN. Arrow R-CNN [20] is a method we previously defined to recognize flowcharts. At its core, Arrow R-CNN builds on Faster R-CNN [19], a popular deep neural network approach for object detection. Arrow R-CNN detects

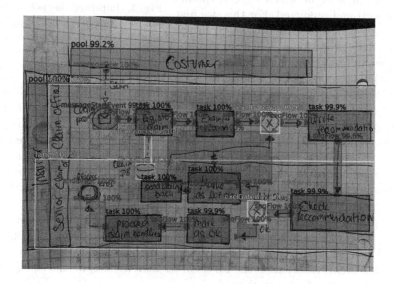

Fig. 3. *Step 1*: Candidate shapes and edges have been classified and localized through bounding boxes, in addition edges have predicted arrow head (▷) and tail (○) keypoints.

objects in an image through the aforementioned bounding boxes, depicted in Fig. 3. For each bounding box, Arrow R-CNN assigns a predicted class (from a set of predefined classes) and a likelihood between 0 and 1. While such bounding-box detection is suitable for shapes, the proper detection of edges is more complex. Specifically, standard object detection, such as provided by Faster R-CNN, cannot be used to identify the source and target shapes of an edge. Therefore, Arrow R-CNN extends Faster R-CNN with an arrow keypoint detection network that predicts the arrowhead and tail of an edge. This means that for edges, Arrow R-CNN provides a (predicted) start and end point along with the bounding box. During training, the keypoint detector loss is averaged over a sample of edges and then integrated into the joint Faster R-CNN loss term. This allows Arrow R-CNN to train all components simultaneously, and it also reduces the risk of overfitting on small datasets, which makes Arrow R-CNN especially suited for small datasets. Given its general applicability for the recognition of arrow-connected diagrams, we train Arrow R-CNN on the 21 different BPMN shape and three edge classes we consider in this work. However, we do this while also incorporating the following two key adaptations that support improved identification of BPMN models in our scenario.

Improved Keypoint Detection. A key challenge when dealing with hand-drawn BPMN models is the correct recognition of edges that are not properly connected to their respective source and target shapes (see issue 2 in Fig. 1). To account for this issue, we adapt the manner in which edge keypoints are encoded and predicted. For this, we first change the way edges are annotated in the training data. In particular, instead of using the drawn tail and head of the edge, we annotate the points where the edge intersects with

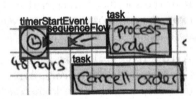

Fig. 4. Improved keypoint detection due to annotating edge intersection (blue ▷) instead of drawn arrow head (green ▷). (Color figure online)

its source and target, as illustrated in Fig. 4. Then, the Arrow R-CNN model trained on these annotations will strive to predict where an edge *should* have ended (or started) if it had been drawn properly, rather than predicting the point where the edge ends (or starts) in the drawing. While this adapted method requires the keypoint predictor to perform reasoning beyond the recognition of a drawn arrowhead, this additional burden on the prediction model improves the accuracy of our approach. In particular, since this improved method considers the direction of a drawn edge when making predictions, it enables the approach to even properly recognize a shape to which an edge should connect, even when it is not the shape that is closest to the end of a drawn edge. For the example in Fig. 4, our approach then correctly recognizes that the edge should connect to the *48* h event, rather than the *cancel order* activity, despite the latter shape being closer to the drawn arrowhead.

Extended Data Augmentation. Aside from BPMN specifics, we also have to account for a second particularity of the hdBPMN dataset, namely its diversity in terms of the means used to create and digitize the hand-drawn models, such as the type of paper and drawing implement (see also Sect. 4.3). Since Arrow R-CNN was designed to deal with much more uniform input (e.g., black drawing on white background), we need to adapt the training approach to the more difficult characteristics of our setting. To do this, we develop an image augmentation pipeline tailored to camera-based hand-drawn diagrams with varying backgrounds. Such augmentations have become a common regularization technique to combat overfitting in deep learning models for various image recognition scenarios [8]. They have been shown to be particularly valuable when training an approach on a dataset with only a few hundred images [20], such as in our case. Therefore, we add augmentation methods to simulate the varying properties of camera-based documents. Specifically, we randomly add gaussian noise, change the brightness and contrast of the image, and shift the hue, saturation, and value (HSV) color scale.

3.2 BPMN Structure Recognition

In the structure recognition step, Sketch2BPMN turns the sets of candidates S_C and E_C into filtered sets $S \subseteq S_C$ and $E \subseteq E_C$. In addition, each edge $e \in E$ is extended to a tuple $e' = (b, c, l, src, tgt, s_{src}, s_{tgt})$, where s_{src} specifies the source shape that e connects, and s_{tgt} the target shape. The resulting BPMN model obtained over S and E is connected and resembles the drawn model as closely as possible. We achieve this through shape disambiguation and edge post-processing.

Shape Disambiguation. To turn a set of candidate shapes S_C into a set of predicted shapes S, we primarily need to disambiguate cases in which multiple candidates in S_C relate to the same drawn shape, i.e., duplicate detection and resolution. Although Faster R-CNN inherently resolves these issues for bounding boxes with the same predicted category, this is not the case when it comes to boxes with different categories. As a result, it may generate two candidate shapes, with different classes, for the same object in an image, as shown in Fig. 5 for two categories of timer events.

However, determining that two candidates $s_1, s_2 \in S_C$ truly relate to the same drawn object is not trivial, especially in the context of BPMN models, whose hierarchical structure naturally leads to overlap between resource shapes (i.e., pools and lanes) and other shapes, such as activities and events. Therefore, we employ so-called *non-maximum suppression* (NMS) over all shape categories. NMS first determines if the bounding boxes of s_1 and s_2 have an overlap of at least 80%. We quantify this as the *Intersection over Union* (IoU), i.e., the ratio between the intersection area and the union area of $s_1.b$ and $s_2.b$. If this ratio exceeds 80%, NMS suppresses the shape with the lower classification score, i.e., it keeps the

Fig. 5. Duplicate shape candidates

candidate that is predicted to be most suitable. In the case of Fig. 5, the two candidates clearly have such significant overlap, which is why after employing NMS, we retain the blue shape corresponding to the more likely *timerStartEvent*, while omitting the other candidate from S.

Edge Post-Processing. To finalize the set of edges E to be included in a BPMN model we use a two-stage approach. First, we associate each edge candidate $e \in E_C$ with a source $s_{src} \in S$ and a target $s_{tgt} \in S$, which are the shapes that are closest to the edge's predicted keypoints, $e.src$ and $e.tgt$, and also correspond to a valid category with respect to the given edge. For instance, if $e.c = sequenceFlow$, edge e will only be connected to shapes that are predicted to be *activities*, *events*, or *gateways*. To determine the closest shape, we compute the minimum Euclidean distance between a keypoint and all sides of a shape's bounding box. After identifying the closest, valid shapes, we turn a candidate edge $e \in E_C$ into a connected edge $e' = (b, t, l, src, tgt, s_{src}, s_{tgt})$.

Once each edge candidate is connected to source and target shapes, we omit all connected edges that correspond to highly unlikely or invalid constructs, such as *self-loops* ($e.s_{src} = e.s_{tgt}$) and invalid data associations (neither $e.s_{src}$ nor $e.s_{tgt}$ is a data store or pool). Finally, we also apply the same approach employed for shape disambiguation to detect and remove duplicate edge candidates.

Note that it is important to consider that this post-processing phase is intended to omit faulty predictions from our generated BPMN model, rather than to correct syntactic mistakes from the hand-drawn image. As such, the employed post-processing rules do not reflect cases that are observed in our training data, but represent a design choice to improve the output of our approach. Figure 6 depicts the outcome of this step for the running example, highlighting

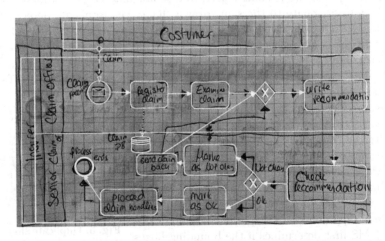

Fig. 6. *Recognized BPMN Model*: the recognized BPMN model has been converted to an image and overlaid over the hand-drawn sketch. The entire process from the input image to the final BPMN model is automated.

that each drawn shape is associated with a single predicted shape in S and that each edge in E properly connects a valid source and target.

3.3 Output Generation

The last step in our approach takes the final shapes and edges after structure recognition to create a BPMN process model in the BPMN 2.0 XML format. The XML consists of two main schemata: the actual process model and the BPMN DI schema, which defines the shape bounding boxes and the waypoints of edges.

Given the output from the previous step, the creation of the XML format is mostly trivial. For each predicted shape $s \in S$, we create a respective element in the XML file. When creating a BPMN DI edge element for each $e \in E$, we follow the typical convention and define the first and last waypoint as the points that intersect with the edge's source ($e.s_{src}$) and target ($e.s_{tgt}$) shapes, respectively. To that end, we shift each predicted keypoint (i.e., $e.src$ and $e.tgt$) to the nearest point on the bounding box boundary of the connecting shapes, except for gateways, where we shift the keypoint to the closest of the four diamond corner points.

4 Dataset

This section discusses the collection, annotation, characteristics, and splits of hdBPMN, the dataset we established for our work. The original and annotated images are publicly available at: https://github.com/dwslab/hdBPMN.

4.1 Collection Procedure

We collected 502 images of hand-drawn BPMN models from 107 participants, all students at the University of Mannheim. Each image corresponds to a solution that was submitted by a student for a graded assignment in an exercise sheet or exam. The obtained models stem from 10 modeling tasks, 9 of which involved the establishment of a BPMN model on the basis of a textual process description, while the other involved the conversion of a Petri net into a BPMN model. Students were asked to hand-draw their models on paper and afterwards embed the scan or photo of their drawing in the submitted exercise sheet or exam PDF, with the only constraint that the models should be readable.[1]

For each received submission, we used the pdfimages command-line utility to extract the images from the PDFs. We split images manually into multiples ones when they spanned different modeling tasks. Note that we deliberately did not further crop images, occasionally resulting in the inclusion of background objects. Finally, we used image editing software to conceal any personal details (e.g., names and student IDs). The resulting images were assigned filenames that follow a taskID_participantID convention, allowing one to identify images contributed by the same participant.

---

[1] See also the public repository for the modeling tasks and provided instructions.

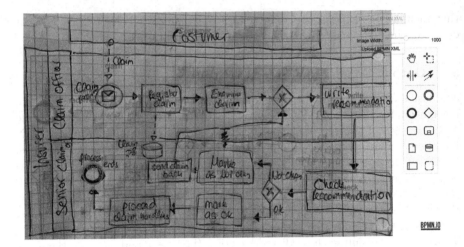

Fig. 7. Example of an annotated hand-drawn model in the *BPMN image annotator*.
Shapes are sized and positioned to match their hand-drawn counterparts, while edges
are modeled using waypoints to resemble the handwritten arrows as much as possible.

4.2   Annotation

To train and evaluate our BPMN recognition approach, we annotated the hand-
drawn shapes and edges in each image. To this end, we developed a BPMN image
annotation tool based on the open-source `bpmn-js`[2] BPMN viewer and editor,
which we have made publicly available.[3] Figure 7 depicts the annotation tool
in action. Note that in order to allow us to also annotate images that contain
modeling errors, we allow our annotation tool to violate certain correctness rules
enforced by `bpmn-js`, e.g., an *end event* with an outgoing *sequence flow*. Upon
completion, the annotation is exported as a *BPMN 2.0 XML* file. Since the image
resolution during annotation is exported as a comment into this file, the location
and size of each shape and edge in the BPMN model can be linked back to the
location and size in the image.

4.3   Dataset Characteristics

The 502 annotated images contain more than 20,000 annotated elements. As
shown in Fig. 1, the models in the dataset are highly expressive, spanning 25
types of BPMN elements, including 4 types of activity shapes, 9 types of events,
4 types of gateways, and 4 types of edges. Largely owing to the different modeling
tasks from which they stem, the individual BPMN models differ in terms of their
size, complexity, and expressiveness (i.e., number of types covered). The models
resulting from the ten different modeling tasks have up to 15 activities and 13
events, and between 0 and 8 gateways, 0 and 8 resources, and 0 and 11 data

---

[2] https://github.com/bpmn-io/bpmn-js.
[3] https://github.com/dwslab/bpmn-image-annotator.

elements. Some tasks result in simpler models (e.g., task1: 11.0 shapes and 11.9 edges on average) and others in more complex ones (e.g., task3: 26.7 shapes and 28.2 edges). Note that the running example depicted in, e.g., Fig. 1, represents a task of intermediate complexity.

Table 1. BPMN elements included in the 502 annotated images

Type Group		Elements and their frequencies
Shape	Activities	task (2,906), subprocess (collapsed) (88), subprocess (expanded) (4), call activity (10)
	Events	start (373), intermediate throw (16), end (587), message start (248), message intermediate catch (220), message intermediate throw (139), message end (52), timer start (71), timer intermediate catch (72)
	Gateways	exclusive (822), parallel (651) inclusive (1), event-based (67)
	Resources	pool (657), lane (523)
	Data elements	data object (707), data store (141)
Edge	Flow elements	sequence flow (6,456), message flow (852), data association (1,395), annotation association (65)
Text	Annotations	text annotation (69)
	Element labels	label (2,971)

Aside from the complexity of a particular process, the recognition difficulty of individual images is affected by various other aspects:

– *Paper type.* The type of paper on which a model is drawn influences the amount of noise that is present in an image, since, e.g., lined or squared paper introduces additional lines that may be hard to distinguish from model-related content in an image. The vast majority of images in our dataset is drawn on squared (about 330) and blank paper (about 140), whereas the remaining used lined or dotted paper.
– *Drawing implement.* The type of drawing implement employed affects the thickness, clarity, and consistency of lines in a drawing. Our dataset primarily contains models drawn by pen (about 430), whereas the remainder were drawn using pencils, fineliners, or a mixture (e.g., pencil to draw shapes and pen for text).
– *Model quality issues.* The hand-drawn models have various kinds and degrees of quality issues, in line with those discussed in Sect. 2, such as models with incomplete, crossing, and curved lines, or with crossed-out elements. Furthermore, the models differ greatly in the spacing that is used between shapes, e.g., some models are spacious, whereas others pack various shapes into a small area.

- *Image capturing issues.* Camera-based image capturing introduces a series of quality issues [11]. This includes images that are rotated or blurry, as well as those that include content beyond the paper or actually cut part of it off (e.g., Fig. 1).

Overall, the 502 images in the publicly-available hdBPMN dataset thus depict BPMN models that span a broad range of BPMN elements and have a high degree of diversity, caused by variation in terms of the employed paper, drawing implement, and image capturing method. Figure 8 visualizes this diversity by showcasing some of the different manners in which various kinds of shapes were drawn.

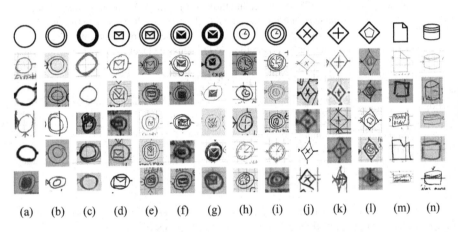

(a)   (b)   (c)   (d)   (e)   (f)   (g)   (h)   (i)   (j)   (k)   (l)   (m)   (n)

Fig. 8. Examples of hand-drawn *events* (start a, intermediate b, end c, message start d, message intermediate catch e, message intermediate throw f, message end g, timer start h, timer intermediate i), *gateways* (exclusive j, parallel k, event-based l) and *data elements* (data object m, data store n).

4.4   Dataset Splits

Following related hand-drawn diagram datasets [6,14], we split up the dataset into publicly available training, validation, and test parts. Each participant in the dataset contributed between one and nine diagrams. While the variability of factors such as writing style, writing medium and image capturing method is high between participants, there are substantial similarities between the diagrams of one participant. Therefore, we split the dataset by participants, such that the participants in the training, validation, and test set are disjoint. Specifically, we created a random 60%/20%/20% split over the participants, and assigned each diagram to the respective part. The resulting training/validation/test set contain 308/102/92 diagrams from 65/21/21 participants, respectively.

5   Evaluation

To demonstrate the capability of our approach, we trained and optimized it using the training and validation set of **hdBPMN**, and conducted an evaluation using its test set. The evaluation results clearly demonstrate that our approach can reliably recognize hand-drawn BPMN models from images and, hence, remove undesirable friction in the modeling workflow.

5.1   Evaluation Setup

Below we elaborate on the details of our employed implementation, as well as the metrics, baselines, and configurations used to evaluate our approach.

Implementation. Our neural network implementation of the shape and edge recognition system Arrow R-CNN (Step 1 of our approach) is based on the *Detectron2* [23] object detection framework. To operationalize our extended augmentations, we use the *Albumentations* library [8]. For training, we use stochastic gradient descent with a batch size of 4 and a learning rate of 0.002. As the CNN backbone, we use ResNet-50 with FPN. We keep the remaining configurations originally used to train Arrow R-CNN [20].

Metrics. To evaluate our approach, we compare the sets of shapes and edges extracted by our approach to those in the manually annotated image (see Sect. 4.2), referred to as the *ground truth*. To quantify the performance, we follow related work in diagram recognition [5,6,22] and use different metrics to assess *shape* and *edge* recognition.

A detected *shape* is considered a true positive if it is assigned the correct class and its bounding box overlaps sufficiently with its counterpart in the ground truth. Particularly, following [22], we consider this overlap sufficient if the bounding boxes have an overlap that exceeds an IoU threshold of 50%, which accounts for annotation inaccuracies in the bounding boxes of the ground truth. To quantify shape-recognition performance, we then use this notion of true positives to match the ground truth to the predicted shapes and compute the standard *precision*, *recall*, and F_1 scores.

For *edge recognition*, a true positive requires that, as for shapes, the predicted class is correct and that its bounding box exceeds a 50% IoU threshold. However, we also require that a detected edge is associated with the correct source and target shapes, s_{src} and s_{tgt}. This means that edge recognition is indirectly affected by the shape-recognition quality: if a shape was not properly detected, all edges that connect to that shape result in false positives as well.[4]

Baselines and Configurations. To demonstrate the efficacy of our approach, we compare its performance to two baselines: Baseline BL1 uses the Faster R-CNN object detector with the standard image augmentations coming with *Detectron2*. Since a standard object detector cannot recognize edges and their

---

[4] Note that an edge is still considered correct if its associated shapes are incorrectly classified.

keypoints, BL2 corresponds to the original Arrow R-CNN system with its default image augmentation methods.

To highlight the relevance of its individual components, we evaluate two configurations of our approach: Configuration C1 corresponds to the Arrow R-CNN system, enhanced with the extended augmentation (EA) of Sect. 3.1. Configuration C2 reflects our full-fledged approach, including the proposed BPMN-specific processing components. Note that we employ the same shape-disambiguation procedure (proposed in Sect. 3.2) for all four systems, in order to ensure a fair comparison in terms of recall.

5.2   Results

This section presents the results of our evaluation for the hdBPMN test set, first in terms of overall results, before taking a detailed look at the results per BPMN element class.

Overall Results. The overall results presented in Table 2 reveal that the two configurations of Sketch2BPMN both outperform the baselines, achieving a micro F_1 score of 95.7 for shape recognition and 91.8 for edge recognition. Note that micro and macro measures differ, because certain classes (e.g., *Tasks*) are much more common than others (e.g., specific events). However, the overall trends are consistent across the two.

Table 2. Overall approach results

Configuration		Shape		Edge	
		Micro F_1	Macro F_1	Micro F_1	Macro F_1
BL1	Faster R-CNN [19]	92.7	77.5	—	—
BL2	Arrow R-CNN [20]	93.2	80.8	85.5	76.0
C1	Arrow R-CNN + Extended Augm. (EA)	**95.7**	**86.2**	90.0	84.8
C2	Arrow R-CNN + EA + BPMN processing	**95.7**	**86.2**	**91.8**	**87.4**

Since each configuration in the table represents an extension of its predecessor, a closer look at the results reveals that the desired improvements associated with the gradual development from BL1 to C2 are achieved. In particular, we observe that Faster R-CNN (BL1), a general-purpose object detector, already recognizes more than 90% of all shapes, though it is unable to detect edges. The Arrow R-CNN approach (BL2), designed for the recognition of hand-drawn flowcharts, improves these results, since it can also detect edges, achieving a macro F_1 of 76.0 for those, while also performing better in terms of shape recognition (80.8 versus 77.5). From BL2 to C1, we observe the improvements achieved by our extended augmentation step, which makes the recognition system more suitable to the diversity in the hdBPMN dataset, boosting the shape recognition from 80.8 to 86.2 and edge recognition from 76.0 to 84.8. Finally, we observe that the additional inclusion of BPMN-specific edge processing in C2 further improves the ability to recognize edges, achieving a macro F_1 of 87.4 and micro F_1 of 91.8.

Shape Recognition. Table 3 provides detailed insights into the performance of our approach (with configuration C2,) by depicting the results obtained per shape and edge class. The table shows that our approach correctly recognizes the vast majority of shapes for most of the classes, achieving an F_1 score of at least 83.9 for the 13 classes that occur more than a dozen times. For other shape types, the number of data points is too low (in both the training and the test set), to sufficiently cover the spectrum of factors such as drawing styles and, therefore, to provide reliable evaluation results.

A post-hoc analysis of the results reveals that the most difficult task for our approach is the correct classification of certain kinds of events. This comes as no surprise, though, the difference between some of the 8 kinds of events may only

Table 3. Shape and edge recognition results per class obtained for the test set

Group	Class	Precision	Recall	F_1	Count
Activity	Task	96.7	99.6	98.2	560
	Subprocess (collapsed)	100.0	72.2	83.9	18
	Subprocess (expanded)	n/a	0.0	n/a	2
	Call Activity	100.0	100.0	100.0	1
Event	Start Event	92.3	95.2	93.8	63
	End Event	94.5	96.3	95.4	107
	Message Start Event	94.2	94.2	94.2	52
	Message Intermediate Catch Event	90.9	93.0	92.0	43
	Message Intermediate Throw Event	78.3	94.7	85.7	19
	Message End Event	87.5	58.3	70.0	12
	Timer Start Event	83.3	83.3	83.3	12
	Timer Intermediate Event	90.0	75.0	81.8	12
Gateway	Exclusive Gateway	98.1	98.1	98.1	156
	Parallel Gateway	93.7	97.5	95.6	122
	Inclusive Gateway	n/a	0.0	n/a	1
	Event-based Gateway	90.0	81.8	85.7	11
Collaboration	Pool	95.3	96.8	96.0	125
	Lane	94.7	93.0	93.9	100
Data element	Data Object	96.3	96.9	96.6	161
	Data Store	95.5	84.0	89.4	25
Edges	Sequence Flow	95.7	94.0	94.9	1216
	Message Flow	86.5	79.7	82.9	177
	Data Association	92.3	77.2	84.1	311
Overall	Macro avg.	92.7	80.9	86.4	3307
	Micro avg.	94.8	92.7	93.7	3307

be due to marginal differences, such as a change in line thickness (start events), as well as different kinds of tiny envelopes (message events) and clocks (timer events). Especially in light of diversity of shapes in our dataset, as highlighted in Fig. 8, identifying such differences in hand-drawn models can already be highly complex for humans, let alone for an automated approach that lacks sufficient training examples for some of the rarer classes.

Edge Recognition. The edge-levels results in Table 3 again demonstrate the overall strong performance of our approach, as well as that *sequence flows* (F_1 of 94.9) are easier to recognize than message flows (82.9) and data associations (84.1). To some extent, this can be attributed to the commonality of sequence flows and the fact that the latter two classes use dashed rather than continuous lines. However, it is only highly interesting to consider the different role of these edges from a process modeling perspective. Particularly, message flows connect (elements in) different pools, which are often placed relatively far from each other. This results in longer edges, which may also cross more nodes, and are, therefore, harder to analyze for an automated approach. For example, we observe that the distance between the head and tail keypoint is more than twice as high for message flows (499 pixels) as for sequence flows (216). For data associations, it is important to consider that elements related to the data perspective are often drawn last [12, p.177], whereas they also often are connected to a numerous shapes, scattered throughout a model. These two factors thus commonly result in data associations that cross other edges or even shapes, which complicates their recognition.

6   Related Work

Our research mainly relates to the area of *hand-drawn diagram recognition*, which has its roots in the graphics recognition area, where several techniques for flowchart [5,16,21,22] and finite automata [6] recognition have been proposed. Most of these are so-called *online* recognition techniques, which depend on data about the order and extent of individual strokes, i.e., the drawing sequence. This means they can only be applied to diagrams drawn on digital devices, like tablets. *Offline* recognition, which we target in this paper, is more complex, because such sequence information is not available and individual strokes cannot be reliably reconstructed from camera-based images of pen and paper drawings. Outside graphics recognition, techniques for hand-drawn diagram detection have been mainly adopted in the area of software engineering [10,15]. More recently, also the first recognition techniques for hand-drawn process models were proposed [17,24]. However, these techniques only target the recognition of shapes, which means that they do not result in complete models.

Our research also relates to work on *collaborative process modeling*, which mainly investigates and supports modeling efforts that involve several people. Works on the former aspect typically use empirical methods to develop a better understanding of how certain factors, such as collaborative tools or participant interaction, affect the modeling outcome [13,18]. Research on the latter aspect provides methods and tools to support collaborative modeling efforts. These include works that enable collaborative process modeling through design storyboards [3] and virtual worlds [7]. Our work also supports collaborative process modeling, since it does not require modelers to follow a particular procedure or use a specific tool to obtain an initial model. Instead, modelers can freely draw a model, which our approach can then transform into a digital counterpart.

7 Conclusion

In this paper, we proposed Sketch2BPMN, a neural network-based approach for automatically recognizing hand-drawn BPMN models from images. Moreover, we introduced hdBPMN, a publicly available dataset consisting of 502 manually annotated, hand-drawn BPMN models, covering 25 different BPMN elements. By using hdBPMN to train, validate, and test our approach, we demonstrated that Sketch2BPMN considerably outperforms available baselines from the area of object and flowchart recognition and, therefore, provides a valuable basis for the automated conversion of hand-drawn BPMN diagrams. We would like to highlight that this paper conceptually targets the recognition of BPMN shapes and edges and, hence, abstracts from recognizing the handwritten textual labels in of BPMN models. However, this can be achieved using off-the-shelf handwriting recognition solutions. In future work, we plan to further improve the practical value of our approach by 1) matching the recognized handwritten textual labels to the respective shapes and edges, and 2) by recognizing the intended rather than the actually drawn model in order to directly fix certain drawing errors.

References

1. Aagesen, G., Krogstie, J.: Analysis and design of business processes using BPMN. In: Handbook on Business Process Management 1, pp. 213–235. Springer (2010). https://doi.org/10.1007/978-3-642-00416-2_10
2. Allweyer, T.: BPMN 2.0: Introduction to the standard for business process modeling. BoD-Books on Demand (2016)
3. Antunes, P., Simões, D., Carriço, L., Pino, J.A.: An end-user approach to business process modeling. J. Netw. Comput. Appl. **36**(6), 1466–1479 (2013)
4. Bartelt, C., Vogel, M., Warnecke, T.: Collaborative creativity: from hand drawn sketches to formal domain specific models and back again. In: MoRoCo@ ECSCW, pp. 25–32 (2013)
5. Bresler, M., Průša, D., Hlaváč, V.: Recognizing off-line flowcharts by reconstructing strokes and using on-line recognition techniques. In: (ICFHR), pp. 48–53 (2016)
6. Bresler, M., Průša, D., Hlaváč, V.: Online recognition of sketched arrow-connected diagrams. Int. J. Doc. Anal. Recogn. (IJDAR) **19**(3), 253–267 (2016). https://doi.org/10.1007/s10032-016-0269-z
7. Brown, R., Recker, J., West, S.: Using virtual worlds for collaborative business process modeling. Bus. Process Manage. J. **17**(3), 546–564 (2011)
8. Buslaev, A., Iglovikov, V.I., Khvedchenya, E., Parinov, A., Druzhinin, M., Kalinin, A.A.: Albumentations: fast and flexible image augmentations. Information **11**(2), 125 (2020)

9. Cherubini, M., Venolia, G., DeLine, R., Ko, A.J.: Let's go to the whiteboard: how and why software developers use drawings. In: SIGCHI, pp. 557–566 (2007)

10. Damm, C.H., Hansen, K.M., Thomsen, M.: Tool support for cooperative object-oriented design: gesture based modelling on an electronic whiteboard. In: SIGCHI, pp. 518–525 (2000)

11. Doermann, D., Liang, J., Li, H.: Progress in camera-based document image analysis. In: ICDAR, vol. 1, pp. 606–616 (2003)

12. Dumas, M., Rosa, M.L., Mendling, J., Reijers, H.A.: Fundamentals of Business Process Management. Springer, 2 edn. (2018). https://doi.org/10.1007/978-3-642-33143-5.pdf

13. Forster, S., Pinggera, J., Weber, B.: Toward an understanding of the collaborative process of process modeling. In: CAiSE Forum, pp. 98–105 (2013)

14. Gervais, P., Deselaers, T., Aksan, E., Hilliges, O.: The DIDI dataset: Digital Ink Diagram data. arXiv:2002.09303 [cs] (2020)

15. Hammond, T., Davis, R.: Tahuti: a geometrical sketch recognition system for UML class diagrams. In: ACM SIGGRAPH 2006 Courses, pp. 25-es (2006)

16. Julca-Aguilar, F., Mouchère, H., Viard-Gaudin, C., Hirata, N.S.T.: A general framework for the recognition of online handwritten graphics. Int. J. Doc. Anal. Recogn. (IJDAR) **23**(2), 143–160 (2020). https://doi.org/10.1007/s10032-019-00349-6

17. Polančič, G., Jagečić, S., Kous, K.: An empirical investigation of the effectiveness of optical recognition of hand-drawn business process elements by applying machine learning. IEEE Access **8**, 206118–206131 (2020)

18. Recker, J., Mendling, J., Hahn, C.: How collaborative technology supports cognitive processes in collaborative process modeling: a capabilities-gains-outcome model. Inf. Syst. **38**(8), 1031–1045 (2013)

19. Ren, S., He, K., Girshick, R., Sun, J.: Faster R-CNN: towards real-time object detection with region proposal networks. In: NeurIPS, pp. 91–99 (2015)

20. Schäfer, B., Keuper, M., Stuckenschmidt, H.: Arrow R-CNN for handwritten diagram recognition. Int. J. Doc. Analy. Recogn. (IJDAR) (2021)

21. Schäfer, B., Stuckenschmidt, H.: Arrow R-CNN for flowchart recognition. In: International Conference on Document Analysis and Recognition Workshops (ICDARW) (2019)

22. Wu, J., Wang, C., Zhang, L., Rui, Y.: Offline sketch parsing via shapeness estimation. In: IJCAI (2015)

23. Wu, Y., Kirillov, A., Massa, F., Lo, W.Y., Girshick, R.: Detectron2. https://github.com/facebookresearch/detectron2 (2019)

24. Zapp, M., Fettke, P., Loos, P.: Towards a Software Prototype Supporting Automatic Recognition of Sketched Business Process Models. Wirtschaftsinformatik 2017 (2017)

Theory Development and Use

Requirements Elicitation via Fit-Gap Analysis: A View Through the Grounded Theory Lens

Tjerk Spijkman[1,2(✉)], Fabiano Dalpiaz[2], and Sjaak Brinkkemper[2]

[1] fizor., Utrecht, The Netherlands
tjerk@fizor.io
[2] Department of Information and Computing Sciences,
Utrecht University, Utrecht, The Netherlands
{f.dalpiaz,s.brinkkemper}@uu.nl

Abstract. While requirements elicitation remains a key success factor for software projects, there is little empirical research on the elicitation methods. We focus on *fit-gap analysis*, a requirements elicitation technique that is common in practice, but hardly studied in requirements engineering research. Fit-gap analysis is a method for matching software products with the needs of customers, with the aim to identify needs that are supported as *fits*, and needs that are not as *gaps*. Through a grounded theory investigation of recording transcripts from fit-gap analysis sessions, we provide empirical knowledge about this elicitation technique. We determine and discuss the different categories of the topics contained in a fit-gap analysis. Additionally, as a first step toward assisting analysts in processing and exploring their analyses, we build and share a set of keywords and phrases that can help automatically identify those categories within the transcripts. We conduct an experiment for early validation, involving both students and practitioners, that determines the relative perceived importance of the identified fit-gap categories. Finally, we derive implications for research in the field that include our perspective on how tooling can assist analysts in fit-gap analysis.

Keywords: Requirements engineering · Fit-gap analysis · Grounded theory · Elicitation techniques · Requirements elicitation

1 Introduction

Requirements engineering (RE) is a crucial phase in software and information systems engineering. Reaching a good understanding of the application domain, of the important stakeholders and of the system goals is one of the key factors of preventing project failure (e.g., over budget, cancelled, etc.) [11]. Requirements *elicitation* is concerned with the activities of seeking, uncovering, acquiring and elaborating requirements [26].

© Springer Nature Switzerland AG 2021
M. La Rosa et al. (Eds.): CAiSE 2021, LNCS 12751, pp. 363–380, 2021.
https://doi.org/10.1007/978-3-030-79382-1_22

Although non-conversational approaches to elicitation exist (e.g., surveys or social media analysis [14]), most requirements elicitation is done through conversational scenarios, such as interviews, workshops, laddering [24,26]. This opens up mostly untapped opportunities for *speech-driven RE*: the analysis of conversation contents aimed at detecting and extracting requirements-relevant information.

Fit-gap analysis is a commonly used elicitation method, especially in a business-to-business setting for enterprise applications such as enterprise resource planning systems [2,8,9,12,13]. Fit-gap analysis (FGA) compares the capabilities of a software product and certain characteristics of the target organization [9]. FGA's outputs include the identification of a need for customization [2] or product evolution as new customer scenarios need to be met. Furthermore, the software vendor gathers information to configure the software. Despite its adoption, fit-gap analysis is largely overlooked by the research community.

In this paper, we conduct an empirical investigation of transcripts of FGA elicitation sessions conducted in the software industry. Our study characterizes, through the grounded theory lens [3,22], the key categories of information we could identify in the FGA transcripts. Based on our study and a survey with practitioners and students, we put forward hypotheses for future research.

We make use of FGA transcripts as they represent a comprehensive report of the verbal discussion between business analysts and customer representatives. Our research is enabled by recent trends in AI, particularly in automated speech recognition: several high-quality, off-the-shelf, inexpensive solutions exist for converting audio recordings into text. Our transcripts are generated automatically using Azure Speech to text. Since this paper is concerned with theory building, we manually analyze the transcripts.

As this research takes a grounded theory approach to investigate the contents of a fit-gap analysis session, without making a-priori hypotheses, we define a set of open-ended research questions [3]. We define a main research question and two sub-questions:

MRQ. How do the contents of a fit-gap analysis transcript assist a business analyst in identifying configuration and customization requirements?

RQ1. How to categorize content segments in a FGA transcript in order to support the identification of configuration and customization requirements?

RQ2. What content segments in a FGA deliver the highest value to an analyst?

Through these research questions, we make initial steps in the under-explored area of speech-driven RE, which emphasizes the identification of requirements-relevant information in conversational settings. For example, in elicitation sessions with stakeholders, and other kinds of workshops. In this paper, we focus specifically on transcripts in FGA sessions, and on the categorization of these conversations.

The foundations we lay are meant to guide future works in the speech-driven RE and to create software tooling that assist analysts in reviewing transcripts by highlighting the most relevant content segments for the fit-gap analysis. Automated processing of fit-gap analysis transcripts is aimed to reduce manual effort (if an analyst would have to manually go through the entire recording), and to improve the FGA process by allowing an analyst to fully focus on the conversation at hand and to minimize note-taking. The automation would also provide assistance in the creation of documentation, for part of the relevant content segments would be identified in the transcript.

Through our research, we make the following contributions to the RE literature:

- We position fit-gap analysis within the landscape of requirements elicitation;
- Through grounded theory, we determine and discuss a categorization of fit-gap analysis, and provide a set of keywords and phrases for identifying such categories;
- We report on an experiment with 7 practitioners and 36 students that assesses the perceived importance of the resulting categories;
- We empirically build a set of hypotheses to guide future research in speech-driven requirements elicitation.

Organization. In Sect. 2, we position fit-gap analysis within requirements engineering. Section 3 presents our research method. In Sect. 4, we discuss the case study and the relevant findings. We report on the validation of the fit-gap categories importance in Sect. 5. We present our implications in Sect. 6, followed by a discussion and outlook in Sect. 7.

2   Fit-Gap in Requirements Engineering

Unlike software that is tailor-made for an organization, software products are developed for a specific market to be sold to many customers [25]. Therefore, there is a need to meet a constant stream of requirements from the market [25]. Software products are in constant evolution, and are in different levels of maintenance. The study by Schach *et al.* [19] revealed that 42.8% were in a state of emergency fixes and routine debugging; 13.8% accommodated changes to the software, 26.8% are actively being improved for user enhancements, and 16.7% did not fall in any of these categories. This indicates that the majority of software products are in a state of change.

Software product vendors need to deal with the heterogeneity in requirements from the market. This often leads to customization of the product, on different levels of granularity. This can impact either a customer-specific version of the software, or the product overall. We use a definition for customization based on the work by Light [13].

Definition 1 (Customization). *Any customer specific change or addition to the functionality available in the standard software product.*

A popular method for managing mass customization is the creation of a product line, a set of products that share similarities and are created from reusable parts [1]. Additionally, many of the products can be tailored to customers through configuration. For this research, we use the following configuration definition from Apel *et al.* [1]:

Definition 2 (Configuration). *Set-up of a software product concerning a pre-defined set of options used to tailor the software to the customer.*

Configuration supports standardization in a software product while enabling customer-specific deployments. A set of alternative options give the customer an opportunity to configure the product. Unfortunately, designing software for reuse is a notoriously difficult and costly endeavor [12], and even then it typically supports a finite set of options. Another common technique for reuse is *clone-and-own* development, which starts from a template of the product that is customized for customer-specific deployment [17]. Cloning goes beyond configuration, facilitates development, and provides software independence. However, cloning is difficult to manage [4] and software developers often don't know the specifics of the instance they have to work on. Similarly to cloning, other customization techniques such as controller change or interface change can be utilized, each with their own set of challenges [10].

Regardless of the scope and implementation of customization, the underlying requirements need to be identified through elicitation from customer organizations. This is often done through a fit-gap analysis, where current product functionality is mapped against the processes and requirements of existing or potential customers.

In the literature, FGA is mostly studied within the ERP domain, as these are complex software products covering many different business processes that might or might not fit those of the customer [2,9,13]. However, the principles are valid for any software product as they aim to support a process that might differ per customer. As the name suggests, the outputs from a fit-gap analysis can be a *fit* between the customer needs and the software product, or a *gap* in the functionality required by the customer. These fits can be out of the box functionality or configuration requirements. Similarly, gaps indicate customization requirements. Figure 1 visualizes the inputs, process and outputs of a FGA. For fit-gap analysis we use the following definition:

Definition 3 (Fit-gap analysis). *A requirements elicitation technique that, based on matching a customer's needs with the functionality of a software product, identifies needs that are supported by the current functionality as fits, and needs that are not as gaps.*

Identified gaps can be dealt with in different ways. They can be developed specifically for a customer, added to the product road-map [8], or ignored. This can depend partly on the market position for a vendor. Tech giants like Google, Microsoft and Netflix have a strong market position which gives their customers few options for tailoring the software to their processes. Additionally, they have so many customers that they tend to use a data-driven approach in determining their road-map.

In a more general sense, consumer apps only support configuration in most cases, while enterprise applications are often configurable and customized [25]. When the customer has a position in which they can, and see the need to demand

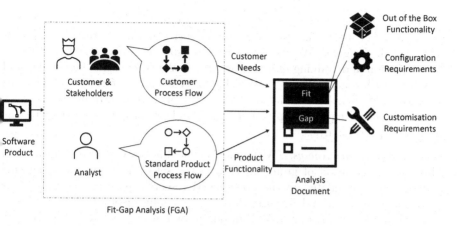

Fig. 1. Fit-gap analysis in the context of requirements elicitation for software products

ustomization, this needs to be scoped. In these cases, vendors with a less domi-ant market position may have to meet their customers needs, or convince them o adapt their process to the software to ensure product sales. Often leading back o a FGA where all gaps are identified, resulting in a document with suggestions or mitigating the gaps (e.g., wait for a next release, or use this workaround) or osts for modifying the software.

In our research, we focus on identifying categories and key content segments 1 these fit-gap analysis. We will discuss these in depth in the following sections.

Research Approach

Ve apply a relatively uncommon research method in information systems engi-eering: grounded theory (GT). In line with the observations by Stol *et al.* [22], ho argue that most articles do not provide enough details about their appli-ation of grounded theory, we provide a detailed view of our approach to make esearch rigor transparent.

While we make no prior hypothesis, as suggested by grounded theory guide-nes, our investigation is guided by our main research question (see Sect. 1), hich aims to analyze how an FGA transcript may contain content segments hat assists an analyst in the identification of configuration and customization equirements.

. *Data Collection.* We conduct an industry case study, whose data was made vailable by having the first author embedded in the case company. This data et our research use case of an industry requirements elicitation with analyst-ustomer dynamics. The data set contained recordings of the complete FGA erformed at the customer. Therefore there was no additional data to gather uring the research for this case study.

2. Transcription of Audio Recordings. While we aim to build a low-effort approach that can assist analysts, the time-intensive nature of transcribing contrasted with our goals. We chose to use Azure speech-to-text system, as it supports creation and training of a custom model. We trained this model using 14 sentences with domain terms that visibly changed the performance, especially, with acronyms. Further training of the model is likely to lead to higher accuracy levels. The resulting transcripts of the case study recordings were used for the grounded theory analysis.

3. Grounded Theory Analysis. We follow the guidelines by Corbin and Strauss [3]. This specific iteration of grounded theory was selected as we have a specific research goal formulated in the open-ended research questions in Sect. 1. As suggested by Corbin and Strauss, these are partially inspired by literature as well as our previous research. Within our prior research, we were inspired by: *i.* a study of requirements-architecture alignment, which revealed the need for customization in software products [20,21], and *ii.* automated documentation in medical consultations, which showed feasibility of automated processing of conversations [15].

4. Coding the Data. Data coding was performed using Nvivo 12 by the first author (the Principal Investigator, PI). While coding the data, notes were taken and documented. The set of categories used for the coding was not predetermined, and if a finding did not meet the existing categories, a new (sub)node was added.

5. Memoing. Memo sorting was performed after each coding session, and used as an input for the collaboration described in the next paragraph. The resulting categories, and memos have been discussed on a weekly basis with the other authors. Pieters and Dornig [18] discuss their experience in collaboration in GT, detailing how their approach helped the principal investigator challenge clarify and support their critical thinking. As they suggest, the PI made the final analytical decisions. These structured discussions on the findings facilitated the continuous comparison of the data and memo's collected during the research They also provided an opportunity for discussing and determining the central category, and validating if the categorization was still valid for the new data Finally, part of the analysis has been coded by an independent business analyst who is not an author, to obtain feedback on the tagging and comparing the coded segments.

4   Fit-Gap Analysis Through the Grounded Theory Lens

We study an on-site FGA that took place over three days, contained in nine separate recordings spanning a total of 12 h with a word-count of 79.938. This analysis was mostly in a one-to-one setting between a business analyst and the process owner at the customer. The FGA focused on the implementation of the software product SCANMAN, an accounts payable automation software. The product is a software solution integrated in the ERP system JD Edwards, and provides automation for invoice processing and approvals. It is offered through customer-specific installations that are configured to match the processes of the customers, and in some cases customized. The installation is often difficult due to existing customizations in the ERP system.

The case chosen for this research is considered unique and challenging by the case company. The customer had unique scenarios, and was in a state of process transformation. We chose to study this specific case because we expect challenging FGAs to result in documentation where the analyst is likely to miss out on some details. These details could however, be found in the interviews transcripts. In the approximately 250 pages of transcript content, 304 segments were tagged in eight categories and nine sub-categories. A set of 207 FGA keywords and phrases detected in the transcripts, the survey used in Sect. 5, survey results split between students and practitioners and tagging statistics can be found in the online appendix[1]. As it contains confidential information, the full transcripts cannot be shared.

4.1   Central Category: Fit-Gap Analysis Topics

In the execution of the grounded theory process, to *determine the central category*, we went over multiple iterations and potential categorizations of the nodes identified in NVIVO. As categories were identified, or existing categories were changed, the central category was revised. Finally, we decided on the central category that matched our scope and was general enough to able contain all but one of the categories we wanted to focus on, *Fit-gap analysis topics*.

Each category that specializes the central category is discussed below, and a summary of the categories and their frequency (both in terms of tagged text and number of tags) is presented in Table 1. We leave out *Uncertainty*, an identified category that does not fit the central category. Uncertainty indicates segments in which the speaker seems to have doubts or be unsure of their statements. While this is left out of the scope of this research, we expect that it could be important in the detection of knowledge gaps, completeness of the information, or importance of a statement. We leave this investigation to future research that could focus on the sentiment perspective of elicitation sessions.

1. Current Process Description or Discussion (As-Is). Within the *as-is situation* we distinguish two sub-categories. The general category is for segments that discuss the current processes of the customer, relevant for the software product. In our case study, these were the current accounts payable processes. The *1a. Customer-specific scenario* sub-category was used for segments that were not common use cases within the domain, and either assumed by the customer to be unique for them, or identified as unique by the analyst. These processes are expected not to be covered in the standard use case of the software, and might lead to customizations or process change. Next to that, we use the sub-category *1b. Example* to indicate a specific instance which is described to illustrate the current situation more specifically. For instance, consider the following quote:

---

[1] Our online appendix can be found at https://zenodo.org/record/4587226.

Table 1. Observed presence of the FGA categories within the case study, and example phrases for the categories (more can be found in the online appendix)

Category	Text tagged	Tags	Example keywords & phrases
1. Current process	31.2%	35.2%	"What we do", "Different for us"
2. Future process	16.8%	18.1%	"Look at", "Our intent is"
3. Explicit requirements	12.0%	8.6%	"We need", "What would be nice is"
4. Questions	4.5%	19.1%	"Could we say", "What happens after"
5. Product functionality	7.2%	12.5%	"Can [product]", "General [product] practice is"
6. Organizational problem	2.1%	4.0%	"Our pain points", "Complicated"
7. Organizational details	0.9%	2.0%	"All of our", "Our company is know for"
8. Product motivation	0.1%	0.7%	"The main reason", "We're looking to"

"The IT department has their own ticketing system for their services, for example repairs that need to be done. This means they have their own purchase orders, which are not within the ERP system."

This fragment has multiple possible implications for the FGA and the documentation. Using the current process, the invoices for IT services do not map to a purchase order (PO) in the ERP, and would have to be configured to go through a non-PO process in the software. Alternatively, the process could be revised to ensure that the PO will be available within the ERP so it can be used in matching scenarios. The current process and its sub-categories were the most occurring segments in the case study, both in frequency (35.2% of tags) and presence (31.2% of text tagged).

2. Future Process Description or Discussion (To-Be). This category is used to denote situations in which the analyst and/or the customer discuss the to-be situation of the customer. This can be due to the use of the software product, or intended and suggested revisions of customers processes. For the to-be process we use a sub-category *2a. Example*, similar to the as-is. Comparing the examples to those of the current process we see that this second category is more conceptual in nature as they denote a hypothetical future. For example, some are introduced with expressions such as *"let's say"*, *"a scenario"*, instead of terms like *"what we do is"*. They can also be differentiated from general to-be process segments due to the use of employee names, or gender pronouns like *"he"* or *"she"* instead of business unit names or *"we"*. A fragment of a to-be process:

> *"We have the opportunity to have some of our big vendors send us EDI (electronic data interchange) files, or invoice files. So we're debating whether we just let these come in as EDI and load them in our ERP, or to come in as invoice files for automatic processing by [product]. But we're leaning towards having everything run through [product], so everything stays in one place."*

In this quote, the customer prompts the analyst on two alternative future scenarios, aiming to assess which of these would be recommended from the software product point of view. In the transcripts, we see similar examples of how the analyst and customer cooperate to determine this to-be scenario. The to-be categories had the second highest presence in the data-set with 18.1% of tags and 16.8% of text tagged.

3. Explicit Discussion of Certain Requirements. In these segments, the customer states a need regarding the software product. Additionally, we identified the sub-category *3a. Negotiation*, in which customer and analyst discuss the priority and necessity for these requirements. Especially those requirements that we related to potential customization led to negotiation, while configuration requirements were mostly stated and accepted. This is logical from the software vendor point of view, for minimizing customizations is the preferred option. These segments were often indicated by keywords like *"we need"* or *"we want"*, with less obvious keywords including *"would be an improvement"*, or *"what would be good"*. The following requirement, for instance, leads to customization:

> *"What will be really good really, really good is in the email if we have. If someone is going to hit reject in the email they can select the different reject reasons so they can click on one of them and hit rejects and it is moved back to the ERP. And so we know exactly why they rejected it."*

From a software point of view, direct rejection through an email is challenging for both design and technical reasons. For instance, allowing an email link to make direct changes to ERP data is a potential security risk. Additionally, emails are generally static, which makes it difficult to also link this to the different rejection reasons. For this use case of approvals outside of the ERP, the software product has the option to use a mobile application that provides these functionalities. This resulted in a longer negotiation where the analyst was trying to find a way in which the existing functionality might meet the customers need. In the end, this requirement led to a potential customization for this customer, which was scoped and priced. Requirements had a presence of 12.0%, of which 6.2% was negotiation in the percentage of text tagged. Requirements made up 8.6% of tags respectively.

4. Questions Made By or to The Analyst. This category groups three different categories of questions. Questions often overlap the other categories, and can indicate the start of a conversation on a new topic, or in-depth discussion of an aspect of the current topic. The first category we discern is *4a. Analyst question or prompt*, in which the analyst asks the customer a question, mostly regarding the current and future process. The second category is straightforward: *4b. Customer questions about the product*. Finally, and perhaps less obvious, we have *4c. Customer questions on own process*. These can arise when the customer questions the rationale behind the current processes, or is asking other stakeholders for their opinions and expertise. We hypothesize questions to be very useful in determining the topics and categories of segments of the transcript. For example, consider the following question made by the analyst:

> *"Could you repeat again why we want to have approval for some vendors but not others?"*

This question concerns a certain requirement for the to-be situation, and indicates that the following segment will discuss this. Similarly:

> *"The question is, can [product] read off of an invoice statement like this?"*

Here, the customer makes a question that leads to a discussion of the product functionalities. While questions had a low presence in text coverage (4.5%), although they represented 19.1% of the tags. This occurred since they are typically short and their role is to give the discussion a different direction.

5. Elaboration on the Existing Functionality of the Product. This category is used to collect segments in which the software product functionalities are discussed. The analyst might bring up configuration (sub-category *5a*), or give an example of certain functionalities (sub-category *5b*). The goals include elaborating on any uncertainties the customer might have, discussing functionalities that need to be configured in one way or another, or managing expectations about those that can be met by the software. An example of expectation management can be seen here in the following fragment:

> <u>Customer</u>: *"I think in the demo it was said you can train the system. E.g., when you see the words tax, freight or whatever, it will automatically add a line."*
> <u>Analyst</u>: *"How it works. It will check the tolerances you set up for voucher match automation. So from there it will check is it within my bounds to automatically accept this and if so process it. If this shipping makes it go above this percentage or total limits that you set, e.g., so say they charge you 600 for shipping while your gap is 300, it will fail to match."*

We see that there are limitations to "automatically" adding a line, based on tolerances to prevent over-billing. Another observation from the customer's comment is that the demo of the application has created certain expectations and assumptions regarding the software product. In this example the analyst manages the expectations by providing further details about the functionality, and discussing its capabilities. These segments made up 7.2% of the tagged text and 12.5% of the tags.

6. Organizational Problem Explanation. In these segments, the (potential) customer explains some root causes for their challenges or problems in their organization. These can impact the implementation of the software, and can for example be due to social factors. For instance, resistance to change due to the impact on jobs. Or it may have to do with the domain and circumstances of the customer, e.g., complex legal requirements. For confidentiality reasons, we provide generalized examples as quotes can be of a sensitive nature. These had a presence of 2.1% of the text, and 4.0% of tags.

7. Organizational Details. This category is used to denote segments in which the customer introduces or talks about their organization, providing context about the setting in which the product will be used. These details include the domain or sector as well as the scale of their operations. For example:

> *"We have offices in multiple European countries, including the Nether-lands, Germany, France and Ireland."*

This can impact the configuration, for instance, because different tax setups are required for the customer. Note that such information can often be found outside of the analysis context, e.g., on the company website. They give the analyst a better view of the customer, and we found them mostly in the early segments of the analysis. This category had an overall presence of 0.9% in text with 2.0% of the tags. While this is true for our case study, we expect that these segments will have relatively higher presence in an analysis with shorter duration.

8. Motivation for Using or Acquiring of Software Product. This category refers to segments in which the customer actively discusses their motivation for acquiring or considering the software product. This might be because it helps them mitigate a problem they face, or because of an advantage compared to other competing products.

> *"The main reason we're looking to [product] is not only to reduce amount of time it takes to enter invoices in the system, but also the approval process."*

These quotes can help during prioritization, and they provide the software vendor with further understanding of the customer's needs. They can also aid an organization in defining their product road-map, and focusing their sales pitches. These segments were not very common in the case study, with less than 1% presence in text and references. However, we did include these as they might play a bigger role in other cases.

5   Validation of the FGA Categories

The eight identified FGA categories were validated through a survey filled out by both industry experts and students. The students took the survey as part of a workshop in a master's level Requirements Engineering course. After a short introduction on the research, fit-gap analysis goals, and context of the software product, the survey participants were asked to conduct two separate tasks:

1. To rate the importance of two textual transcript fragments for each of the eight categories on a four point scale (essential, important, not-important or irrelevant), without being informed of the categories at this stage. A four-point scale was used to minimize desirability bias [7]. In total, the participants rated a total of 16 fragments randomly selected out of a set of 50 fragments.
2. To provide a total order of the importance of the eight categories, based on their perception. Participants could drag the categories in their preferred sequence from high to low importance.

This allows us to conduct triangulation; our findings concerning the importance of the categories are therefore based on three sources: the participants' evaluation of fragments, the participants' ranking of the categories, and our own experience. The survey was filled in by 36 students and 7 industry practitioners who were familiar with the product domain. The average time spent on answering the survey was 16 min.

The box-plot chart in Fig. 2 illustrate the perceived importance of the categories of our 43 respondents from the second survey task. In the x-axis, the value 1 represents the highest rank (the most important category), while the value 8 represents the lowest. The category means clearly show two groups. Of these the current process, future process, and explicitly discussed requirements are consistently ranked as the most important categories.

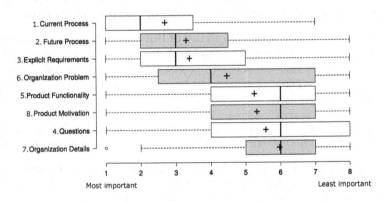

Fig. 2. Box-plot chart showing the perceived importance of the categories, derived from the ranking provided by the participants in survey task 2 (n = 43).

When we look at the rating of the transcript fragments in the first task, shown in Fig. 3, we see similar results to those in the category rankings (Fig. 2). This confirms the importance of the three categories that had the highest rank: current process, future process, and requirements. The "questions" category seems to be an outlier: its fragments are rated as quite important, while it is not highly ranked as a category. We reckon that this may be due to either the selection of the questions, or the formulation of the category name, which was slightly ambiguous for some participants.

Comparing the student answers to those of the practitioners for the importance of the *fragments*, we draw four main observations regarding the FGA categories:

- **Current process:** *Practitioners judged fragments belonging to the current process as more important than the students.* With 86% of the ratings being positive, compared to 68% by the students. Practitioners rated fragments in this category most positively out of all categories, while in the student rankings it comes in 4th place. We hypothesize that this might be because the students lack the domain knowledge to identify the current process in the fragments.
- **Product motivation & customer context:** *Students rate both product motivation and customer context less importantly than practitioners.* Practitioners rated the fragments positively at 43%, and 36% respectively, while students rated these positively at 65% and 49%. The product motivation, also had the highest count of "essential" ratings in the student survey. This discrepancy may arise because practitioners have access to these details via interactions that precede the FGA.
- **Questions:** *The students rated the questions fragments more positively than practitioners.* The questions received 76% positive ratings by the students, making this the second most positive ranking out of all categories. For practitioners, this was 57% positive, leading to a shared fourth ranking out of the categories.
- **Positive answers:** *In general, the students rated more of the fragments as positive than practitioners.* They had an average positive answers over the categories of 64% while the practitioners had 57%. This may be ascribed to the fact that practitioners are more aware of which information can be found from other sources.

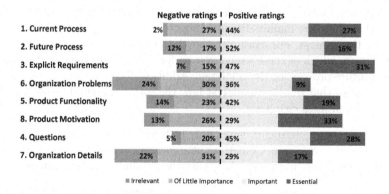

Fig. 3. Diverging stacked bar chart of the transcript fragment ratings in survey task 1

6 Implications for Research and Practice

This research aims to create, in an empirical fashion, the foundations for assisted transcript exploration. Through grounded theory, we provide empirical evidence and minimize assumptions on important content segments within FGA. Based on our observations, we form hypotheses for future work in this research field.

For the FGA categories we identified, the perceived rankings indicated that three of these are more important than the others for an analyst. While the student ratings of the transcript fragments have a discrepancy as questions have the second most positive rating, the remaining categories and practitioner ratings support the following hypothesis:

H1 The most important categories for processing a FGA into documentation are 1) the current process, 2) the future process, and 3) explicitly discussed requirements.

Therefore, these categories should be the focus in generating automated documentation as well as in any tooling that can interactively assist an analyst to explore transcripts.

Only a few requirements were *explicitly* mentioned in the transcripts. The main focus of the analysis instead was on the current situation. Thus, we posit:

H2 The analyst uses bits and pieces of information gathered in the analysis to specify the requirements for the project. Such information compares the *current process* with existing *product functionality* to determine the *future process*.

For future research, it is important to investigate to what extent the resulting requirements in a specification can be traced back to various segments of the transcript, and to identify the sources for requirements not covered in the transcript.

Specifically looking at the configuration requirements in the transcripts, we observe that these are mainly discussed together with the product functionality, driven by the analyst. For example: "So the product can support approvals in multiple ways, which of these would you prefer?". This can then be discussed as part of a future process for the customer. Additionally, there are segments of the current process that inform an analyst how the software should be configured to minimize the process changes.

H3 Configuration requirements can mainly be found in transcript segments within the categories on product functionality, current and future processes. Specifically when discussing processes within the product software domain.

From anecdotal experience, configuration requirements are generally covered in the analyst's notes. However, detecting these in the transcripts can decrease the time spent on digitizing notes and reduce the chance of missing configuration requirements.

In contrast, customization requirements are more often part of future process aims that cannot be met by the software product. Generally, they find their motivation in current processes, as the customer prefers not to change part of the process. Or in processes unique to the customer's domain. These unique processes are likely to result in customization, as rationale for exclusion is less likely. Therefore, we posit:

H4 Customization requirements can be detected from future process discussions that do not match the product functionality. Their justification can often be found in current processes, especially for unique processes.

Detecting customer domain knowledge and information about the product functionality is key in recognition of customization requirements. Also, domain knowledge seems to impact the recognition of current process, as observed in the tagging differences. Therefore, future research should take the role of domain knowledge into account, both to conduct experiments as well as for building automated tools.

7   Discussion and Outlook

Summary. In this grounded theory study, we investigate and position fit-gap analysis as a source of requirements. We performed extensive coding of a real-world data-set and empirically discovered eight categories to categorize the contents of a FGA. We discussed each of these categories through examples, and use the findings to build hypotheses to guide further research in the speech-driven requirements engineering field.

We answer our RQ1 on the categorization in FGA through the eight categories presented in Sect. 4. RQ2 on the most valuable content segments in FGA has been discussed through the experiment in Sect. 5, which indicates current process, future process, and discussed requirements as most valuable.

To support further research in speech-driven requirements engineering and to allow other researchers build on our work, we made publicly available, in a persistent repository, the keywords and noun phrases identified in the categories. Though we acknowledge that this is only an initial set, we expect this can be used to build NLP-powered tools that can recognize the categories. Our dataset also includes frequency and tagging statistics to support replication.

Vision. We answer the MRQ by putting forward our vision. Our findings make us surmise that a fully automated approach is unlikely. Many decisions need to be made while processing a fit-gap analysis into a fit-gap document that guides the rest of the software project. Most of these decisions cannot be traced back to the FGA transcript, as they are essential part of the thinking process of the business analyst during requirements engineering. We see the processing of FGA as an example of a non-algorithmic RE task, using Tjong and Berry's words [23].

We envision an interactive tooling that presents an analyst with relevant content segments, and an overview of the topics that are discussed in the analysis sessions. From there, the analyst can determine which of these are interesting for the document they are working on, and explore relevant segments in the transcripts. This perspective of investigating conversation contents is shared with other domains, prominently healthcare [5,15]. Future research is necessary to determine similarities and differences.

Panichella and Ruiz [16] share a similar, yet different, vision. They argue for the use of machine learning and ontology crawlers for automatic requirements documentation. While we are too interested in the use of automation, our empirical observations indicate that only few requirements are explicitly mentioned. Therefore, at least in the context of fit-gap analysis, automation will have an important yet only partial role.

Validity. Due to the exploratory nature of this research, there is a limitation to *external validity*. Despite its size (12 h of recordings), we conducted a single case study; therefore, it remains to be validated whether the findings can be generalized to different software products, domains and elicitation techniques. For this reason, we only build hypotheses from our findings as opposed to forming conclusions. To prevent *conclusion validity* issues in our results, we have opted to only share observations from the data collected from the survey as opposed to statistical conclusions. Both students and practitioners participated in the validation of our research. Using students as a proxy for practitioners in software engineering is often a point of discussion [6]. While there were similar results in the perceived rankings of category importance, we did see differences in the ratings of the segments. These are expected to be mostly a result of difference in domain knowledge, and to a lesser extent experience. We minimized *construct validity* threats by randomizing the initial category order, giving participants a random subset of fragments and not explicitly showing to which categories the fragments belong.

References

1. Apel S., Batory D., Kästner C., Saake G.: Software product lines. In: Feature-Oriented Software Product Lines, pp. 3–15. Springer, Heidelberg (2013). https://doi.org/10.1007/978-3-642-37521-7_1
2. Blick, G., Gulledge, T., Sommer, R.: Defining business process requirements for large scale public sector ERP implementations: a case study. In: Proceedings of the ECIS, p. 157 (2000)
3. Corbin, J., Strauss, A.: Basics to Qualitative Research, 3 edn. SAGE (2008)
4. Dubinsky, Y., Rubin, J., Berger, T., Duszynski, S., Becker, M., Czarnecki, K.: An exploratory study of cloning in industrial software product lines. In: 17th CSMR, pp. 25–34. IEEE (2013)
5. Epure, E.V., Compagno, D., Salinesi, C., Deneckere, R., Bajec, M., Žitnik, S.: Process models of interrelated speech intentions from online health-related conversations. Artif. Intell. Med. **91**, 23–38 (2018)

6. Falessi, D., et al.: Empirical software engineering experts on the use of students and professionals in experiments. Empir. Softw. Eng. **23**(1), 452–489 (2017). https://doi.org/10.1007/s10664-017-9523-3
7. Garland, R.: The mid-point on a rating scale: is it desirable. Mark. Bull. **2**(1), 66–70 (1991)
8. Grabis, J.: Optimization of gaps resolution strategy in implementation of ERP systems. In: Proceedings of the of ICEIS, pp. 84–92 (2019)
9. Gulledge, T.R.: ERP gap-fit analysis from a business process orientation. Int. J. Serv. Stand. **2**(4), 339–348 (2006)
10. Jansen, S., Houben, G.-J., Brinkkemper, S.: Customization realization in multi-tenant web applications: case studies from the library sector. In: Benatallah, B., Casati, F., Kappel, G., Rossi, G. (eds.) ICWE 2010. LNCS, vol. 6189, pp. 445–459. Springer, Heidelberg (2010). https://doi.org/10.1007/978-3-642-13911-6_30
11. Jones, C.: Software project management practices: failure versus success. J. Defense Softw. Eng. **17**(10), 5–9 (2004)
12. Kuo, T.C.: Mass customization and personalization software development: a case study eco-design product service system. J. Intell. Manuf. **24**(5), 1019–1031 (2013)
13. Light, B.: The maintenance implications of the customization of ERP software. J. Softw. Maint. Evol. **13**(6), 415–429 (2001)
14. Maalej, W., Nayebi, M., Johann, T., Ruhe, G.: Toward data-driven requirements engineering. IEEE Softw. **33**(1), 48–54 (2015)
15. Lepenioti, K., et al.: Machine learning for predictive and prescriptive analytics of operational data in smart manufacturing. In: Dupuy-Chessa, S., Proper, H.A. (eds.) CAiSE 2020. LNBIP, vol. 382, pp. 5–16. Springer, Cham (2020). https://doi.org/10.1007/978-3-030-49165-9_1
16. Panichella, S., Ruiz, M.: Requirements-collector: automating requirements specification from elicitation sessions and user feedback. In: Proceedings of the RE, pp. 404–407. IEEE (2020)
17. Pérez, F., Ballarín, M., Lapeña, R., Cetina, C.: Locating clone-and-own relationships in model-based industrial families of software products to encourage reuse. IEEE Access **6**, 56815–56827 (2018)
18. Pieters, H.C., Dornig, K.: Collaboration in grounded theory analysis: reflections and practical suggestions. Qual. Soc. Work **12**(2), 200–214 (2013)
19. Schach, S.R., Jin, B., Yu, L., Heller, G.Z., Offutt, J.: Determining the distribution of maintenance categories: survey versus measurement. Emp. Softw. Eng. **8**(4), 351–365 (2003)
20. Spijkman, T., Brinkkemper, S., Dalpiaz, F., Hemmer, A.F., van de Bospoort, R.: Specification of requirements and software architecture for the customisation of enterprise software. In: Proceedings of the RE Workshops, pp. 64–73. IEEE (2019)
21. Spijkman, T., Molenaar, S., Dalpiaz, F., Brinkkemper, S.: Alignment and granularity of requirements and architecture in agile development: a functional perspective. Inf. Softw. Technol. **133**, 106535 (2021)
22. Stol, K.J., Ralph, P., Fitzgerald, B.: Grounded theory in software engineering research: a critical review and guidelines. In: Proceedings of the ICSE, pp. 120–131 (2016)
23. Tjong, S.F., Berry, D.M.: The design of SREE – a prototype potential ambiguity finder for requirements specifications and lessons learned. In: Proceedings of the REFSQ, pp. 80–95 (2013)
24. Wagner, S., et al.: Status quo in requirements engineering: a theory and a global family of surveys. ACM Trans. Softw. Eng. Methodol. **28**(2), 1–48 (2019)

25. Xu, L., Brinkkemper, S.: Concepts of product software. EJIS **16**(5), 531–541 (2007)
26. Zowghi, D., Coulin, C.: Requirements elicitation: a survey of techniques, approaches, and tools. In: Aurum, A., Wohlin, C. (eds.) Engineering and Managing Software Requirements. Springer, Heidelberg (2005). https://doi.org/10.1007/3-540-28244-0_2

Lambda+, the Renewal of the Lambda Architecture: Category Theory to the Rescue

Annabelle Gillet[(✉)], Éric Leclercq, and Nadine Cullot

Laboratoire d'Informatique de Bourgogne - EA 7534, University Bourgogne
Franche-Comté, Dijon, France
annabelle.gillet@depinfo.u-bourgogne.fr,
{eric.leclercq,nadine.cullot}@u-bourgogne.fr

Abstract. Designing software architectures for Big Data is a complex task that has to take into consideration multiple parameters, such as the expected functionalities, the properties that are untradeable, or the suitable technologies. Patterns are abstractions that guide the design of architectures to reach the requirements. One of the famous patterns is the Lambda Architecture, which proposes real-time computations with correctness and fault-tolerance guarantees. But the Lambda has also been highly criticized, mostly because of its complexity and because the real-time and correctness properties are each effective in a different layer but not in the overall architecture. Furthermore, its use cases are limited, whereas Big Data need an adaptive and flexible environment to fully reveal the value of data. Nevertheless, it proposes some interesting mechanisms. We present a renewal of the Lambda Architecture: the Lambda+ Architecture, supporting both exploratory and real-time analyzes on data. We propose to study the conservation of properties in composition of components in an architecture using the category theory. We relate a real implementation of our approach to architecture a social network observatory platform.

Keywords: Architecture pattern · Category theory · Lambda Architecture

1 Introduction and Motivations

All information systems have a common point: they need an architectural design before being developed and deployed. The architecture must guarantee some properties and guide the consistency of the overall structure of the information system. In this context, architectural styles and patterns are used to build a system having the expected characteristics for each of its part as well as for its entirety, and to state the requirements of the technologies and programming techniques needed to achieve the goal sought. Thus, global requirements such as scalability, performance, reliability must be clearly identified to select the style of

© Springer Nature Switzerland AG 2021
M. La Rosa et al. (Eds.): CAiSE 2021, LNCS 12751, pp. 381–396, 2021.
https://doi.org/10.1007/978-3-030-79382-1_23

architecture, the different components and the interactions among them [23], and then choose technologies with properties (such as ACID for databases or micro batch capabilities for stream processing) that fit all of the previous choices. The absence of coherence in a definition of an architecture can lead to the dreaded Big Ball of Mud [15], that reduces greatly the maintenance and evolutivity capabilities of the system. To help avoiding this situation, there are two major elements among architectural design artifacts: styles and patterns.

Styles are coarse grained specifications of the organisation of the architecture, that guide the interactions among components [1]. Each style brings naturally some architectural characteristics, while also imposing trade-offs on others. So, there is not a better style than the others, but solely situations where a style would be more suited to fulfill the expected characteristics. Some examples of architecture styles are the layered architecture [28], the microservices architecture [32] and the event-driven architecture [9].

An architecture pattern is a specific abstraction of a fixed architecture style for a particular set of essential characteristics [17]. It helps to identify within a style which combination of components will be more suited for a given context, but still provides enough freedom to adapt the implementation of the pattern to specificities of each situation. The level of detail can vary, as well as the restrictions of the application of the pattern. The Blackboard pattern [11], the Model-View-Controller [12] and the Lambda Architecture [29] are examples of architecture patterns. The Lambda Architecture is well-known in a Big Data context. It was introduced at the beginning of stream processing systems, and thus is oriented to compensate for the flaws of an emerging technology rather that taking advantage of the capabilities of such a technology.

Recent researches in software architecture try to formally define styles and patterns, to anticipate effects of the composition of components, and thus knowing beforehand the result of the evolution of a part of the architecture [6,20]. When architectures evolve and grow, they can combine several smaller parts of architectures developed separately. When building a large scale, complex and distributed architecture, its parts can embed architecture styles on their own. These different cases can result in compositions of smaller architecture parts with their proper styles and patterns, so formalization should be able to express and control these compositions. Category theory [13] is a promising approach for formalization, due to its ease to represent compositions as it considers morphims and functors as first class citizens, and to its already existing proximity to the engineering software world, particularly with functional programming. Moreover, its graphical representation is a visual help to understand the formalization, and leads to a better comprehension of the system [35].

In this article we propose the Lambda+ Architecture pattern, an update of the Lambda Architecture, and a formalization to study the conservation of properties in compositions of components using the category theory. The rest of the article is organized as follows: Sect. 2 describes the original Lambda Architecture pattern, as well as its uses and its flaws; Sect. 3 uses the category theory to prove the loss of properties in the Lambda Architecture; Sect. 4 shows our improved

Lambda+ Architecture pattern; Sect. 5 describes a real applied example of our pattern and; Sect. 6 concludes this article.

2   Lambda Architecture and Related Work

The properties of correctness, low latency and fault-tolerance have always been a major concern when designing architectures. In [23], Lampson sketches some suggestions that are still relevant today, and that can be found, among others, in the Lambda Architecture, introduced by Marz in 2011 [29,30]. The objective is simple: to compute predetermined queries with a very low latency and to ensure the correctness of the processing (Fig. 1). To do so, the Lambda is composed of three layers: the batch layer, the serving layer, and the speed layer.

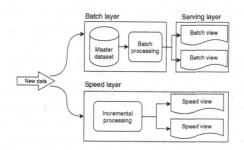

Fig. 1. Overview of the Lambda Architecture

The **batch layer** takes care of storing raw data in the master dataset and of executing the computations on the batch of data. The correctness of the results is the main concern of this layer. With the master dataset, it is possible to recompute the whole set of data if the batch processing appears to be erroneous, or if the needs have evolved. As the batch processing is only computed once in a while, the **speed layer** has to compensate this downside by a low latency capability. The computations are the same as in the batch layer, but the processing has to be incremental. However, this layer lacks the correctness property. The batch processing puts to disposal its results in the **serving layer**, to facilitate their access by users. The serving layer has often a role of indexing and presenting data, to enable a fast access to the views created by the batch layer. To keep results up-to-date, the serving also appends the speed views to the batch views.

With these specifications, the advantages of the Lambda Architecture are a strong fault-tolerance for machine and human faults, a guarantee of a correct result with the batch layer and a low latency with the speed layer. It has inspired many Big Data architectures, such as RADStack [38], which is an open-source plateform used to produce interactive analyzes. They developed Druid to use it as the serving layer, that supports real-time and batch data ingestion. It is also used to allow guided exploratory analyzes concerning pre-determined insights.

In [31], the authors apply the Lambda Architecture to process data of smart grids. They add a querying and an analytics layers, in order to propose more flexibility in the querying capabilities that overcomes the fixed precomputed views of the Lambda. The system developed in [25] uses the Lambda Architecture to develop a recommendation system for restaurants. It alters the original pattern of the Lambda, by having different computations in the batch and in the speed layers. The batch layer is responsible for executing heavy machine learning algorithms, while the speed layer exploits those results to propose recommendations to users. LinkedIn develops Pinot [18], a real-time distributed datastore designed for processing OLAP queries with low latency. They use the Lambda Architecture pattern to provide LinkedIn users with near real-time analytics functionalities, such as who viewed their profile. They compute the speed views in real-time, and when the views are complete (i.e., when they represent a day or a hour depending on the granularity) they become the batch views. The incoming data are then computed in a new speed view.

However, the Lambda has also been criticized a lot, due to its complexity to maintain and to evolve both the speed and the batch layers, that have to perform the same computation, but with different paradigms. It also lacks in flexibility, as its goal is to answer only predetermined queries. Thus, as saw in the examples of implementation of the Lambda Architecture, alternative use cases such as exploratory analyzes require to modify the pattern. Furthermore, by delegating the correctness property only to the batch layer and not to the speed layer, the low latency and the correctness properties cannot be obtained simultaneously. To clarify this statement, the Lambda has to be replaced in the context of its creation. At this time, streaming systems were only at their early stages, and thus did not have all the capabilities that they have today.

2.1   The Evolution of Stream Processing Systems

Streaming systems [4] had begun to emerge approximately at the same time as the conception of the Lambda Architecture. Marz had proposed Apache Storm in 2011 [36], the first stream processing system to encounter success in the industry field. It was born from the ascertainment that to produce a system with a real-time component, it took more time to create workers and queues and to ensure that their interactions are as expected than to develop domain logic. In 2015, Twitter had proposed Apache Heron [22]. They used previously Apache Storm, but needed a system more suited to their needs, with better performance, scaling capabilities and easier to manage. Spark Streaming [39] in 2012 took a different approach and proposes a micro-batch streaming system, relying on the Spark engine dedicated to the batch processing. MillWheel [3] and Apache Flink [8] also joined the world of streaming systems during those years.

The efficiency of streaming systems, on top of the low latency, comes with the guarantee of the processing [4]. There are three main levels of guarantee: 1) *at-most-once*, where elements are never processed more than once, but can be never processed, 2) *at-least-once*, where elements are never processed less than once, but can be processed multiple times, and 3) *exactly-once*, that surpasses the at-most-once and at-least-once guarantees, and thus each element is processed once and only once, allowing to compute correct results. However, the exactly-once guarantee is utopian, and in practice it is closer to effectively-once, where elements can be processed several times, but the effect on the state of the stream is only counted once. This adds a strong constraint: the processing must not have side effects that are not idempotent. It means that in case of the reprocessing of a message, the global result must not be altered. When the Lambda Architecture came out, stream processing systems had mostly only the at-most-once or at-least-once guarantee, and could not offer more. So, the Lambda can be seen as a mean to compensate flaws of an emerging technology, rather than a pattern that fully exploits it.

2.2   Toward the End of the Lambda Architecture

The Kappa Architecture [21] proposes to get rid of the complexity, by keeping only the speed layer, arguing that it is enough to reach the goal of the Lambda. While this is a correct statement regarding the evolution of stream processing systems, it also discards the master dataset and the fault-tolerance property, one of the strengths of the Lambda. Another flaw in the Lambda Architecture is that it is loosely defined. Several interpretations of the serving layer can be found, that include or not the speed views. The aggregation of the speed and the batch views is not clearly defined, especially for unordered streams of data. The lack of precise definition extends to the style of the architecture. Each part is called layer, whereas layered architectures are a stacking of multiple components, where each component can interact with the components directly above or below it [33]. The event-driven architecture would be a more suited style. This leads to a need of a stricter definition of the architecture, as well as an adaptation of the role of its components, updated following the gain in maturity of the stream processing systems.

3   Using the Category Theory to Study Conservation of Properties

In the research field of software engineering for architecture design, the need for proper theory and formalization has raised importance in the last decade [6,20]. Designing, specifying and implementing software architectures are complex tasks, that require careful specifications to link and preserve characteristics through all the steps of creation. The development of theory in this field requests both practical and theoretical skills, in order to propose a model suited to the expectations, that takes into consideration the imperfections of the real-world of engineering.

ADLs [10] (Architectural Description Language) have an important role to formalize architectures. Boxes and lines ADL as well as ADL based on UML [7] cannot easily verify properties, due to their weak formalization. We focus on those ADL having well-established theoretical foundations. In [1], Abowd et al.

provide a formal framework in Z to achieve a description of architectural styles. They argue that diagrams are not sufficient to impose only one meaning to represent an architecture, and that they can lead to misunderstanding. Malkis and Marmsoler in [27,28] work on a formalization of architecture styles. They use the theory of sets and first order logic to build a model with ports and services to represent interactions among components. They apply their proposal on two styles: the layered and the service-oriented architecture. In [24], Le Métayer uses the graph theory to propose a formalization of architectures. Nodes are entities of an architecture (client, server, or object entity depending on the level of abstraction), and links are communications between those entities. Mabrok in [26] tries a different approach, and uses the category theory to formalize the requirements and the attributes of an architecture. Ologs, a particular application of category theory thought to represent the study of the ontology of a subject, is used to organize the architecture.

Existing ADLs are based on set theory, graph theory and use first or high order logic to check properties or consistency of architectures. However, they do not study the conservation of those properties in compositions of components. To fill this need, category theory [13] is a promising approach: it allows to switch from a model to another or to navigate among abstraction levels, and thus to express various problems from different science fields, such as mathematics, physics or computer science [35]. By focusing on relations (the morphisms) and compositions, it proposes powerful mechanisms that can be applied to architectures. In this paper, **we focus on studying the conservation or the discarding of properties in compositions of components, by relying on the behaviour of functors combined to preorders**. This section only introduces some notions of category theory useful to understand this formalization, and cannot relate all the subtleties and the depth of it. We refer the reader to [35] for a more complete explanation of the category theory, and to the supplementary material available[1].

A **category** C is composed of four basic elements: 1) $\mathrm{Ob}(C)$, a collection of objects; 2) for each pair $x, y \in \mathrm{Ob}(C)$, a set $\mathrm{Hom}_C(x, y)$ representing **morphisms** from x to y, namely a mean to get an object y (the codomain) from an object x (the domain). A morphism f from x to y is noted $f : x \to y$; 3) for each $x \in \mathrm{Ob}(C)$, a particular morphism id_x known as the identity morphism on x; 4) for each triplet $x, y, z \in \mathrm{Ob}(C)$, a **composition** $\circ : \mathrm{Hom}_C(y, z) \times \mathrm{Hom}_C(x, y) \to \mathrm{Hom}_C(x, z)$. For two morphisms $f : x \to y$ and $g : y \to z$, the composition is noted $g \circ f : x \to z$. And of two laws: 1) for a morphism $f : x \to y$ with $x, y \in \mathrm{Ob}(C)$, we have $f \circ \mathrm{id}_x = f$ and $\mathrm{id}_y \circ f = f$; 2) for $f : w \to x, g : x \to y$ and $h : y \to z$ with $w, x, y, z \in \mathrm{Ob}(C)$, we have $(h \circ g) \circ f = h \circ (g \circ f) \in \mathrm{Hom}_C(w, z)$.

A **product** of two categories $C1$ and $C2$ produces a new category which objects are all the possible pairs (x, y) with $x \in \mathrm{Ob}(C1)$ and $y \in \mathrm{Ob}(C2)$ and morphisms $(x, y) \to (x', y')$ are pairs (f, g) where $f : x \to x' \in \mathrm{Hom}_{C1}(x, x')$ and $g : y \to y' \in \mathrm{Hom}_{C2}(y, y')$.

---

[1] https://github.com/AnnabelleGillet/CategoryTheoryForArchitectures.

Two particular cases of categories are of special interest to formalize architectures. The **preorders**, in which between each pair $x, y \in \text{Ob}(C)$, there exists a unique morphism $f : x \to y$. If there exist $f : x \to y$ and $g : x \to y$, then $f = g$. The **power sets**, that are sets which contain all the subsets of a given set. In a category, power sets can be organized as preorder, where morphisms link two subsets if the first subset is integrally included in the second.

To formalize architectures, we define three core categories: 1) the *Components*-category, in which objects are all the components of the architecture, without any morphisms; 2) the *Architecture*-category which contains all the components and with morphisms representing the interactions between components, $f : x \to y$ means that the component x sends data to the component y; 3) the *ComponentsPS*-category containing all the objects of the power set of the components, that will be used to connect the components to properties. To link those categories, we use functors.

A **functor** F maps a category C to a category C'. It is noted $F : C \to C'$, and affects both objects ($F : \text{Ob}(C) \to \text{Ob}(C')$) and morphisms (for each pair $x, y \in \text{Ob}(C)$, we have $F : \text{Hom}_C(x, y) \to \text{Hom}_{C'}(F(x), F(y))$). To be valid, a functor must observe two laws: 1) the preservation of identities: $\forall x \in \text{Ob}(C)$, $F(\text{id}_x) = \text{id}_{F(x)}$; 2) the preservation of composition: for any triplet $x, y, z \in \text{Ob}(C)$ with morphisms $g : x \to y$, $h : y \to z$, we have $F(h \circ g) = F(h) \circ F(g)$.

To link the categories we have previously defined, we use functors: 1) $CA: Components \to Architecture$ to integrate components in the architecture; and 2) $CCPS: Components \to ComponentsPS$ to study the behaviour of components in a set of different components.

Properties are represented with preorders, and each value of a property is an object. Morphisms go from the most satisfying value of the property to the least satisfying value. The symbol $\top$ is used as the top value to neutralize a component when it is not concerned by the property. Properties can be simple (only with *true* and *false* objects), multivalued, or more complex, and resulting of the composition of several other properties: in this case, properties are associated with a product of categories, and this product is linked to the next property with a functor that maps each combination to its signification in the next level property. The category *ComponentsPS* is connected to every property of level one (those than are not the result of a product of categories).

This formalization is applied on the Lambda Architecture, to formally prove its weaknesses. A composition exists with the batch, the serving and the speed layers because the serving layer merges the batch and the speed views to provide users with results. Using the category theory, we can extract some high-level knowledge from the known facts, given below (Fig. 2). The morphisms inside categories *ComponentsPS* and *Correctness* are defined as follows (with the notation $B = $ Batch, $Se = $ Serving and $Sp = $ Speed):

$$\begin{array}{c|l}CPS&\text{morphisms with } \emptyset \text{ as domain are omitted}\\(ComponentsPS)&B - BSe : B \rightarrow BSe\\&Se - BSe : Se \rightarrow BSe\\&BSe - BSeSp : BSe \rightarrow BSeSp\\&Sp - BSeSp : Sp \rightarrow BSeSp\end{array} \qquad \begin{array}{c|l}C&\top - t : \top \rightarrow True\\(Correctness)&t - f : True \rightarrow False\\&id_\top : \top \rightarrow \top\\&id_t : True \rightarrow True\\&id_f : False \rightarrow False\end{array}$$

The morphisms inside the category $Real - time$ are the same as those of the $Correctness$-category. The effect on the objects of functors that link the $ComponentsPS$-category to the categories of the properties are given below:

$$\begin{array}{c|l}CPS - C&B \rightarrow True\\(Correctness)&Se \rightarrow \top\\&Sp \rightarrow False\end{array} \qquad \begin{array}{c|l}CPS - RT&B \rightarrow False\\(Real - time)&Se \rightarrow \top\\&Sp \rightarrow True\end{array}$$

From these given facts, we want to deduce the value taken by the first composition of components $\{Batch, Serving\}$ for the correctness property. For this, we have to resolve the effect of the functor $CPS - C$ on the morphisms:

$$CPS - C : \underline{\mathrm{Hom}_{CPS}(B, BSe)} \rightarrow \mathrm{Hom}_C(\underline{CPS - C(B), CPS - C(BSe)})$$

$$CPS - C : \underline{\mathrm{Hom}_{CPS}(Se, BSe)} \rightarrow \mathrm{Hom}_C(\underline{CPS - C(Se), CPS - C(BSe)})$$

where the underlined elements are known. To establish the value of $CPS - C(BSe)$, we have to find two morphisms in the category C that would have the same codomain: one with the domain $True$ ($CPS - C(B)$), the other with the domain $\top$ ($CPS - C(Se)$). Only the pair $(\top - t, id_t)$ satisfies the requirements. As the codomain is $True$, it allows us to deduce that $CPS - C : BSe \rightarrow True$. Thus, the composition $\{Batch, Serving\}$ yields $True$ for the correctness property.

We use the same mechanism to deduce the value taken by the overall architecture for the same property:

$$CPS - C : \underline{\mathrm{Hom}_{CPS}(Sp, BSeSp)} \rightarrow \mathrm{Hom}_C(\underline{CPS - C(Sp), CPS - C(BSeSp)})$$

$$CPS - C : \underline{\mathrm{Hom}_{CPS}(BSe, BSeSp)} \rightarrow \mathrm{Hom}_C(\underline{CPS - C(BSe), CPS - C(BSeSp)})$$

This time, the pair of morphisms that meets the requirements is $(t - f, id_f)$. As the common codomain is $False$, it allows us to deduce that the overall architecture yields $False$ for the correctness property.

The same reasoning can be applied for the real-time property, that yields $False$ for the overall architecture. With the category theory, we proved that the real-time and correctness properties are effective in a different layer, but that they do not hold in the whole Lambda Architecture. We can conclude with a fact about compositions of components in architectures: **if an individual component does not support a property, it will cause its loss in a composition of components.**

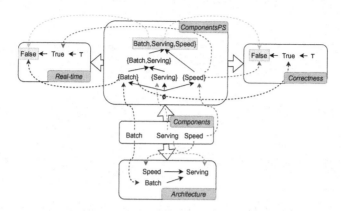

Fig. 2. Study of the preservation of properties in the Lambda Architecture(To simplify the schema, the *ComponentsPS*-category has only individual components, as well as possible compositions of the architecture, and only the links from components to properties that does not lead to ⊤ are represented.)

4   The Lambda+ Architecture Pattern

To improve the Lambda Architecture, the correctness property should hold for all the components. Furthermore, the fault-tolerance should be kept, but as the reprocessing of data in a batch fashion is often incompatible with the real-time property, it should be integrated as an alternative running composition, activated only in case of a technical failure or to satisfy new needs. Use cases should also gain in flexibility, and the complexity induced by the development of the same process with different paradigms in the speed and in the batch layers should be avoided.

The Lambda+ Architecture is meant to be a renewal of the Lambda Architecture, by improving the support of the correctness property and by leveraging two main functionalities: 1) storing data for allowing flexible and exploratory data analyzes, and 2) computing in real-time predefined queries on data streams in order to have insights on well-known and identified needs. The duality between exploratory analyzes and predefined queries is of primary importance in a Big Data context, where the combination of volume and variety of data overcomes the capability of finding all the insights hidden in data. The fault-tolerance mechanism of the Lambda is kept, but is only activated when needed.

The adopted layer model of the Lambda Architecture, as stated in Sect. 2, does not match the style of the architecture. Instead, the Lambda+ is composed of a set of components interacting together asynchronously with messages. This pattern borrows its principles from the Event-Driven Architecture style, which is well-suited for achieving performance, scalability and evolutivity. The trade-offs of this architecture style is a lack of simplicity and the difficulty of testing the whole architecture, due to the dynamic nature of the messaging workflow and the chaining of various processing components. Figure 3 shows an overview of the Lambda+ Architecture which includes five main components.

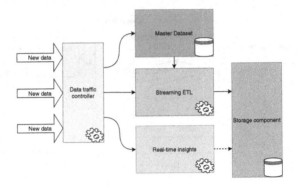

Fig. 3. Overview of the Lambda+ Architecture

The **data traffic controller component** is the entry point of the Lambda+ pattern. Data sources can have very different natures, such as an extraction from an existing store or a connection to an endpoint API that provides data. This diversity requires a structuring of the stream of data, that can be achieved in different ways depending of the functional needs behind the architecture. The data traffic controller organizes data into streams. The filter and pipe architecture style is a suitable fit for this component: only lightweight processing are applied, such as removing duplicates or adding a timestamp, before sending data in a communication system that allows other components to have access to them. This mechanism yields a great independence among components, and is the basement for the fault-tolerance characteristic.

The batch layer has no reason to be anymore, and it can be replaced by a component more suited to the situation: the **streaming ETL component**. ETL processes have been part of analytics since a long time, mainly used to populate a data warehouse. However, these last years the need for more freshness in data has become a major preoccupation, and the batch behaviour of ETL—often run once per day at night—cannot fulfill this need. So, several works focus on executing ETL in real-time in order to perform low latency analysis [14,37]. Streaming ETL transforms data continuously, rather than periodically as it is the case in classic batch ETLs. Stream processing systems are often used to achieve this goal. The role of the streaming ETL component is to populate the storage component, and to transform data if needed for doing so. It works in real-time when data arrive from the data traffic controller, and also in deferred time when data arrive from the master dataset. Data are extracted from the master dataset for example when a schema modification occurs in the storage component.

The aim of the **master dataset component** is the same as in the Lambda Architecture. It stores all the raw data, in case of an evolution of the streaming ETL component or of a failure that requires the re-processing of the data. This component contributes to the fault-tolerance property. To avoid the complexity blamed on the Lambda Architecture with the duplication of processing in the batch and speed layers, data are not directly processed in this component, but rather only extracted from the master dataset, to then be sent to the streaming ETL component. Thus, to maintain or evolve the architecture, only processes in the streaming ETL component have to be modified, avoiding at the same time one of the most criticized pitfall of the Lambda Architecture.

The **real-time insights component** is dedicated to compute predetermined queries or algorithms directly on the stream of data, in real-time, essentially using stream processing systems. The latency and the correctness are critical, but the technical advances of stream processing systems can handle these requirements. Computations can be simple, such as an aggregation (count or sum), or more complex, such as anomaly detection in time series [2]. Operations in this component are well identified and defined, and procure useful insights about data being processed. The storage component can be used to explore data and to find the value they can offer. This knowledge can then be exploited to automate the extraction of value in the real-time insights component. The result of these processing can be stored in the storage component, but due to the behaviour of stream processing systems detailed in Sect. 2, this storage step has to be idempotent.

The **storage component** can be of different nature following the needs. It can be a standard data warehouse, a polystore or a data lake. This storage system is fed with data from the streaming ETL component and eventually by the real-time insights component. It puts to disposal processed data in a more suitable format, used for offline and exploratory analyzes. *Data warehouses* are a mature technology, that have been around before the era of Big Data [19]. They often gather data from different sources among an organisation with the help of ETL processes, in order to format and clean data for a business intelligence use. Data warehouses are built to help business analysts by structuring data according to a static schema for a given subject. By doing so, the analyst must only know the schema of his subject to extract value from data. However, this structuring induces a lack of flexibility. A *polystore* refers to a system that integrates heterogeneous database engines, storage systems and multiple data manipulation or programming languages using different paradigms [16]. The use of polystore brings several advantages: it allows to organize data according to particular use cases (e.g. graph DBMS well support linked data and graph traversal or path queries) and it enables parallel processing among several datastores according to the specificities of each kind of system in the polystore [5]. *Data lakes* are less well-defined than data warehouses or polystores [34]. They are often a solution when all data available are harvested, but their use from an analytical point of view is not yet defined. They have emerged to compensate the lack of flexibility of data warehouses. In these lakes, all data are gathered without a common schema, often in a unstructured or semi-structured form. Yet, with this freedom comes a high heterogeneity among data of the lake (in their source, their format, their content, their veracity, etc.), which can turn the data lake into a data swamp if it is not correctly organized.

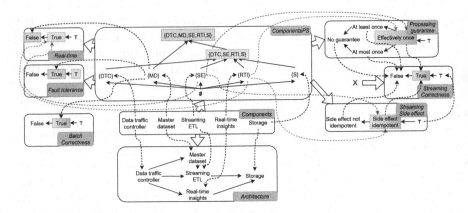

Fig. 4. The formalization of the Lambda+ Architecture pattern

The application of the formalization on the Lambda+ Architecture pattern (Fig. 4) is straightforward and follows the same mechanism that the one explained in Sect. 3. A more detailed proof is given in the supplementary material, including the one for products of categories. Two running compositions of components are possible: with or without the master dataset, as it is only linked to the streaming ETL when data have to be reprocessed. **There is no component that invalidates the correctness property, so it cannot be lost in a composition, and, contrary to the Lambda Architecture, this property holds for the overall architecture.** Concerning the real-time property, only the master dataset induces its loss, but in exchange the Lambda+ activates the fault-tolerance property. It is an acceptable trade-off, as the master dataset is only used in emergency cases, to reprocess data after a failure or when the needs change.

5   An Example: Hydre

We have applied the Lambda+ pattern in an interdisciplinary research project (Cocktail) which aims at studying the discourses in the domains of health and food, as well as identifying weak signals in real time using social network data. We needed an architecture able of supporting a continuous gathering of data, while allowing real-time and flexible off-line analytics. It should also have a strong fault-tolerance property, as the use of data could change depending on the results of our researches. It resulted in the Hydre architecture (Fig. 5), that has been in production since April 2019, to harvest data from Twitter, compute real-time insights and store data for exploratory analyzes. It uses a 20 nodes Hadoop cluster, a 5 nodes Kafka cluster and 4 other servers to host a polystore and applications for exploratory analyzes, including Jupyter notebooks and Spark/Scala analytics processes. The major components of the Lambda+ Architecture are implemented as follows.

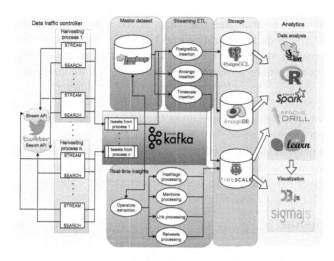

Fig. 5. The Hydre architecture

The **data traffic controller** is composed of harvesting sub-components, that use Twitter Search and Stream API with specific criteria (hashtags, accounts, etc.) in order to gather tweets in JSON format about a chosen subject. We have only one datasource in this case. The harvesting sub-components add only lightweight information such as the timestamp of the harvesting. They are developed following the actor model with Akka, and send data to Kafka topics, the backbone of the architecture, that allows loosely coupled communications with the other components. The **master dataset** is implemented with Hadoop HDFS. Raw tweets are stored as lines of files, and the re-processing of data can be done by reading these files and sending each line as is, in another Kafka topic. The **streaming ETL** uses Kafka consumers to insert data in micro batch. The streaming ETL applies some transformations, and then stores tweets in the **storage** component, a polystore in our case. The polystore includes a relational, a graph, and a time series DBMSs. These databases are used for exploratory analyzes, mainly performed with Jupyter notebooks. Alongside, the **real-time insights** component extracts and aggregates several information about the harvesting, such as popular hashtags or users, using Kafka Streams. It stores the results in the time series database of the polystore. Although this insertion is a side-effect of the stream processing, it is an idempotent action, because the count of the elements will always yield the same result with an effectively once guarantee, and this result is stored for each element, replacing the old value if it already exists.

We have three main harvests continuously running, two global on food and health, and one more specific on COVID-19 vaccines. With the architecture active for 20 months in production, we have gathered 8.3To of raw data. We have already leveraged the fault-tolerance property of the master dataset several times, to apply a new processing as the needs had changed. It was done without impacting the real-time insertions of the streaming ETL. We have also realized some maintenance operations on the streaming ETL without having to stop the harvesting thanks to the message retention of Kafka, and by resuming the processing where it was paused once the maintenance was over. From a user point of view, the polystore is used to cover different needs: 1) to help social science researchers to find new keywords by displaying some query results and macroscopique indicators computed by the real-time insights component on an application server and on Jupyter notebooks; 2) during research meetings, exploratory analyzes are done in live to guide the formulation of a social hypothesis based on available data; and 3) once the hypothesis is well-defined, to extract a specific corpus fixed in time to perform more deeper analyzes.

6   Conclusion

We showed the obsolescence of the Lambda Architecture, mainly due to its limited use cases and to the evolution of stream processing systems. We proposed the Lambda+ Architecture pattern, the successor of the Lambda Architecture, that gets rid of its flaws. The Lambda+ defines a more flexible architecture, capable of handling both exploratory and real-time analyzes, and that fits more various use cases than the Lambda Architecture. We uses the category theory to study the conservation of properties in compositions of components, and applied it on the Lambda and on the Lambda+ Architecture.

For future work, we plan to develop our formalization to study more various aspects of architectures: 1) to navigate among abstraction levels (i.e., the level of detail of the representation of the architecture); 2) to verify if an architecture follows a given style or pattern by using full functors (i.e., surjective functors); and 3) to extend the property description, including numerical values (e.g., to measure the execution time and deduce if it can be considered as real-time).

Acknowledgment. This work is supported by ISITE-BFC (ANR-15-IDEX-0003) coordinated by G. Brachotte, CIMEOS Laboratory (EA 4177), University of Burgundy.

References

1. Abowd, G.D., Allen, R., Garlan, D.: Formalizing style to understand descriptions of software architecture. ACM Trans. Softw. Eng. Methodol. (TOSEM) **4**(4), 319–364 (1995)
2. Ahmad, S., Lavin, A., Purdy, S., Agha, Z.: Unsupervised real-time anomaly detection for streaming data. Neurocomputing **262**, 134–147 (2017)
3. Akidau, T., et al.: MillWheel: fault-tolerant stream processing at internet scale. VLDB Endow. **6**(11), 1033–1044 (2013)
4. Akidau, T., Chernyak, S., Lax, R.: Streaming Systems: The What, Where, When, and how of Large-scale Data Processing. O'Reilly Media Inc., Newton (2018)
5. Alotaibi, R., Bursztyn, D., Deutsch, A., Manolescu, I., Zampetakis, S.: Towards scalable hybrid stores: constraint-based rewriting to the rescue. In: Proceedings of the 2019 International Conference on Management of Data, pp. 1660–1677 (2019)

6. Broy, M.: Can practitioners neglect theory and theoreticians neglect practice? Computer **44**(10), 19–24 (2011)
7. Broy, M., Cengarle, M.V.: UML formal semantics: lessons learned. Softw. Syst. Model. **10**(4), 441–446 (2011). https://doi.org/10.1007/s10270-011-0207-y
8. Carbone, P., Katsifodimos, A., Ewen, S., Markl, V., Haridi, S., Tzoumas, K.: Apache flink: stream and batch processing in a single engine. Bull. IEEE Comput. Soc. Tech. Comm. Data Eng. **36**(4), 28–38 (2015)
9. Clark, T., Barn, B.S.: Event driven architecture modelling and simulation. In: International Symposium on Service Oriented System, pp. 43–54. IEEE (2011)
10. Clements, P.C.: A survey of architecture description languages. In: International Workshop on Software Specification and Design, pp. 16–25. IEEE (1996)
11. Craig, I.D.: Blackboard systems. Artif. Intell. Rev. **2**(2), 103–118 (1988). https://doi.org/10.1007/BF00140399
12. Deacon, J.: Model-view-controller (MVC) architecture (2009)
13. Eilenberg, S., MacLane, S.: General theory of natural equivalences. Trans. Am. Math. Soc. **58**(2), 231–294 (1945)
14. Fernandez, R.C., et al.: Liquid: unifying nearline and offline big data integration. In: Conference on Innovative Data System Research (CIDR 2015) (2015)
15. Foote, B., Yoder, J.: Big ball of mud. Pattern Lang. Program Des. **4**, 654–692 (1997)
16. Gadepally, V., et al.: The BigDAWG polystore system and architecture. In: High Performance Extreme Computing Conference, pp. 1–6. IEEE (2016)
17. Morrison, R., Balasubramaniam, D., Oquendo, F., Warboys, B., Greenwood, R.M.: An active architecture approach to dynamic systems co-evolution. In: Oquendo, F. (ed.) ECSA 2007. LNCS, vol. 4758, pp. 2–10. Springer, Heidelberg (2007). https://doi.org/10.1007/978-3-540-75132-8_2
18. Im, J.F., et al.: Pinot: realtime OLAP for 530 million users. In: ACM SIGMOD, pp. 583–594 (2018)
19. Inmon, W.H.: Building the Data Warehouse. Wiley, New York (2005)
20. Johnson, P., Ekstedt, M., Jacobson, I.: Where's the theory for software engineering? IEEE Softw. **29**(5), 96 (2012)
21. Kreps, J.: Questioning the Lambda Architecture. O'Reilly RADAR, online article, July 2014. https://www.oreilly.com/ideas/questioning-the-lambda-architecture
22. Kulkarni, S., et al.: Twitter heron: stream processing at scale. In: ACM SIGMOD, pp. 239–250 (2015)
23. Lampson, B.W.: Hints for computer system design. In: Proceedings of the Ninth ACM Symposium on Operating Systems Principles, pp. 33–48 (1983)
24. Le. Métayer, D.: Describing software architecture styles using graph grammars. IEEE Trans. Softw. Eng. **24**(7), 521–533 (1998)
25. Lee, C.H., Lin, C.Y.: Implementation of lambda architecture: a restaurant recommender system over apache mesos. In: International Conference on Advanced Information Networking and Applications (AINA), pp. 979–985. IEEE (2017)
26. Mabrok, M.A., Ryan, M.J.: Category theory as a formal mathematical foundation for model-based systems engineering. Appl. Math. Inf. Sci. **11**, 43–51 (2017)
27. Malkis, A., Marmsoler, D.: A model of service-oriented architectures. In: Brazilian Symposium on Components, Architectures and Reuse Software, pp. 110–119. IEEE (2015)
28. Marmsoler, D., Malkis, A., Eckhardt, J.: A model of layered architectures, vol. 178, pp. 47–61. arXiv preprint arXiv:1503.04916 (2015)
29. Marz, N.: How to beat the cap theorem (2011). http://nathanmarz.com/blog/how-to-beat-the-cap-theorem.html

30. Marz, N., Warren, J.: Big Data: Principles and best practices of scalable real-time data systems. Manning (2015)
31. Munshi, A.A., Mohamed, Y.A.R.I.: Data lake lambda architecture for smart grids big data analytics. IEEE Access **6**, 40463–40471 (2018)
32. Namiot, D., Sneps-Sneppe, M.: On micro-services architecture. Int. J. Open Inf. Technol. **2**(9), 24–27 (2014)
33. Richards, M., Ford, N.: Fundamentals of Software Architecture. O'Reilly, Newton (2020)
34. Sawadogo, P., Darmont, J.: On data lake architectures and metadata management. J. Intell. Inf. Syst. **56**(1), 97–120 (2020). https://doi.org/10.1007/s10844-020-00608-7
35. Spivak, D.I.: Category Theory for the Sciences. MIT Press, Cambridge (2014)
36. Toshniwal, A., et al.: Storm@ twitter. In: ACM SIGMOD, pp. 147–156 (2014)
37. Vassiliadis, P., Simitsis, A.: Near real time ETL. In: Kozielski, S., Wrembel, R. (eds.) New Trends in Data Warehousing and Data Analysis. Springer, Boston (2009). https://doi.org/10.1007/978-0-387-87431-9_2
38. Yang, F., Merlino, G., Ray, N., Léauté, X., Gupta, H., Tschetter, E.: The RAD-Stack: Open source lambda architecture for interactive analytics. In: Proceedings of the 50th Hawaii International Conference on System Sciences (2017)
39. Zaharia, M., Das, T., Li, H., Shenker, S., Stoica, I.: Discretized streams: an efficient and fault-tolerant model for stream processing on large clusters. In: USENIX Hot Topics in Cloud Computing (2012)

Category Theory Framework for Variability Models with Non-functional Requirements

Daniel-Jesus Munoz[1,2($\boxtimes$)], Dilian Gurov[3], Monica Pinto[1,2],
and Lidia Fuentes[1,2]

[1] ITIS Software, Universidad de Málaga, Málaga, Spain
[2] CAOSD, Departamento LCC, Universidad de Málaga,
Andalucía Tech, Málaga, Spain
{danimg,pinto,lff}@lcc.uma.es
[3] KTH Royal Institute of Technology, Stockholm, Sweden
dilian@kth.se

Abstract. In *Software Product Line* (SPL) engineering one uses *Variability Models* (VMs) as input to automated reasoners to generate optimal products according to certain *Quality Attributes* (QAs). Variability models, however, and more specifically those including numerical features (i.e., NVMs), do not natively support QAs, and consequently, neither do automated reasoners commonly used for variability resolution. However, those satisfiability and optimisation problems have been covered and refined in other relational models such as databases.

Category Theory (CT) is an abstract mathematical theory typically used to capture the common aspects of seemingly dissimilar algebraic structures. We propose a unified relational modelling framework subsuming the structured objects of VMs and QAs and their relationships into algebraic categories. This abstraction allows a combination of automated reasoners over different domains to analyse SPLs. The solutions' optimisation can now be natively performed by a combination of automated theorem proving, hashing, balanced-trees and chasing algorithms. We validate this approach by means of the edge computing SPL tool HADAS.

Keywords: Numerical variability model · Feature · Non-functional requirement · Quality attribute · Category theory

1 Introduction

Variability Models [24] (VMs) are used for the design of highly configurable systems to represent their common and variable features, typically by means of a rooted tree graph with a set of constraints. These models employ two types of constraints: hierarchical (or tree) constraints, and cross-tree constraints, where the absence or value of some features instantiates or precludes other features

© Springer Nature Switzerland AG 2021
M. La Rosa et al. (Eds.): CAiSE 2021, LNCS 12751, pp. 397–413, 2021.
https://doi.org/10.1007/978-3-030-79382-1_24

(e.g., $feature_A$ implies/excludes $feature_B$). Variability models are the key asset in *Software Product Lines* (SPLs) [33], where valid configurations (i.e., solutions) are generated by reasoners called *solvers*, such as Choco [23] and Z3 [12], that take into account some external requirements. The most popular VMs are the *Feature Models* (FMs), but our problem formulation is agnostic of the VM type, so we will just refer generically to VMs throughout the rest of the paper.

One of the most valuable uses of VMs is the generation of optimal solutions [9] based on *Quality Attributes* (QAs) or *Non-Functional Requirements* (NFRs), e.g., to maximise performance or minimise energy consumption [29]. This becomes a difficult issue when tackling some emergent domains characterised by intensive variability such as *Internet of Things* (IoT) or *Edge Computing* (EC) systems [34], with variations at the hardware (e.g. sensors and edge devices), communication network (e.g. WiFi, BLE), application (e.g. filtering, mixing, collecting tasks) and infrastructure (e.g. virtualization) dimensions. Regarding these application domains, one possible approach is to use VMs to specify the variability dimensions and use a solver to generate optimal application deployments in certain IoT/EC environments considering certain NFRs, such as latency or energy consumption. However, the standard VMs do not natively support non-functional properties, especially needed when one wants to express a relationship between one product and a NFR measured with a quality metric represented as a *measurement function* [18]. For example, the feature 'WiFi' of an IoT device consumes more or less energy, depending on the feature 'distance' to the Edge or Cloud device. The same concerns the automated reasoners for VMs that neither consider NFRs nor quality metrics as a built-in characteristic.

This problem has been tackled in different ways in recent years. For instance, *Extended VMs* [5] proposed to extend features with attached attributes, and they are used to indicate a QA value (e.g. energy_consumption, latency) of that specific feature. For example, one can express that the 'WiFi' feature consumes 'x' Joules or has a latency of 'y' Seconds, where Joules and Seconds are attributes. Extended VMs cannot represent that a certain QA is measured as a function of several features. But, QAs usually depend on several features representing a complete running product [32]. Another approach is to have independent VMs extended with a set of variables representing QA measurements and cross-model constraints as part of a constraint satisfaction problem [22], but not as part of the VM itself. This results in improper semantics, and variables and constraints overloading. A hybrid model that rudimentary links a VM with a QAs database is our previous work HADAS [31]. But again, the management of two different and interconnected models as well as two independent reasoners (i.e., Choco/database) is complex and computationally overloading.

Our goal is to extend the core definition of VMs with NFRs associated with product solutions, so that we can reason and generate optimal solutions that fit certain QAs. We propose *Category Theory* (CT) as a means to abstract and unify dissimilar relational models. We present a CT framework aiming to represent that: "each SPL product, defined as a set of 'n' features, is related to a set of QAs with concrete values that fulfil certain NFRs". In our CT framework, relational models are specified as objects and their relationships. As a result, we unify as a category: VMs, NFRs and QA metrics as measurement functions.

In the IoT/EC, it is common that some features (e.g. different message sizes) are *numerical features*; different numerical values can influence the energy consumption or the computation time NFRs. Therefore, our CT proposal considers to effortlessly represent and reason about *Numerical VMs* (NVMs), which is not straightforward with traditional VMs [30]. This can be achieved only if they are part of the variability tree hierarchy when generating valid products. Contrarily to many of the existing Boolean VMs (e.g., FeatureIDE, Glencoe, and UVL), NVMs (e.g., Clafer [2] and Z3 [12]) additionally support numerical features and the relationships between them (i.e., variables and equations). However, the limitations of NVM solvers have prevented software developers from actively considering modelling numerical features [30]. Our contributions are:

1. A unified CT framework to model NVMs and QAs with NFRs and their relationships, and generate products as solutions with a sufficient quality.
2. As a proof of concept, we transform HADAS [31], a SPL to reason about energy consumption of IoT/Edge applications, into a category. We perform optimisation analyses with a combination of different reasoners, including a theorem prover and relational search algorithms, each one being able to reason at the same time about both VMs and quality metrics.

The paper is organised as follows. Section 2 describes VMs and QAs, while Sect. 3 defines CT and presents the framework to subsume VMs and QAs into categories. In Sect. 4 we test our approach by transforming an SPL tool into a category, and by reasoning about an EC case study. Section 5 reviews and discusses the pertinent related work, while Sect. 6 concludes with a summary highlighting the contributions and next steps of this research.

2   Motivation

Our goal is to use CT to define a joint model encompassing variability and NFRs modelling to reason about solutions that satisfy certain quality attributes. In this section, we discuss some background on both variability and NFR modelling. The third part of our proposal, the CT, is explained in detail in Sect. 3.

2.1   Variability Modelling

Feature-oriented Domain Analysis (FODA) was the first formalisation of variability modelling and reasoning [24] as FMs. FMs are used to model the commonality and variability, and external solvers are used mainly to automatically generate the product variants. FMs are represented as a rooted tree graph – one parent, many children, composed of features as Boolean variables, and relationships (see Fig. 1). Relationships among features are specified as propositional logic, including tree (e.g., And, Or) and cross-tree constraints. Consequently, it is possible to reason about FMs as a Boolean *satisfiability* (SAT) problem [7].

Several application domains, such as our IoT/EC illustrative example, require additional constructs that traditional feature models do not include. More than 45 extensions have been proposed for different needs [8], being the NVM [30] one of the most relevant for intensive variability domains. NVMs represent systems that also contain numerical features along with arithmetic cross-tree relationships (e.g., automated reasoner GreenScaler [10]).

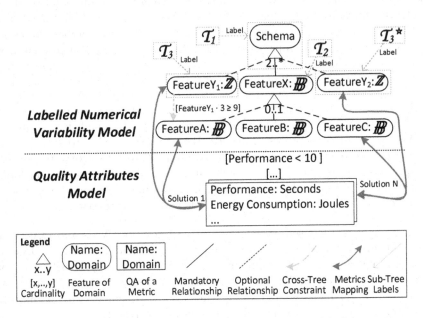

Fig. 1. Example: relationship of NVM solutions with QAs

NVMs consider both Boolean ($\mathbb{B}$) and discrete numerical domains such as *Integers* ($\mathbb{Z}$)[1]. As depicts in the rooted tree graph of top-Figure 1, an NVM supports the variables **and** operations of those domains together, allowing mixing $\mathbb{B}$ conditions and arithmetic (e.g., $Feature_{\mathbb{Z}}Y_1 * 3 \geq 9 \rightarrow FeatureA_{\mathbb{B}}$). Another extension to FODA that we also consider in this work (see Fig. 1) is the specification of the exact number of children features (i.e. feature cardinality [11]). One more extension required by variability intensive systems is the sub-tree labelling presented in top-Figure 1, which allows: (1) variability tree composition of layered NVMs [31], (2) partial instances [2], (3) cloneables like $\mathbb{T}_3$ [16], and (4) the intrinsic hierarchy between trees [19]. In summary, VMs cover the functional requirements – the actions that a system must be capable of doing. However, optimisation analyses of SPLs require NFRs - the non-behavioural aspects under

---

[1] *Real* ($\mathbb{R}$), and other continuous domains, are not completely supported by SPL automated reasoners because they generate unlimited solutions.

which the system must operate [17] and, as previously stated in the introduction, this is not natively included as part of VMs.

2.2 Non-functional Requirements Modelling

For this work, we define a *QA model* (QAM) as any model that specifies and hosts QAs being name-domain-metric with NFRs. Quality models [1] are a broader type of models not used in this work. QAs whose values can be quantified, such as *Performance* and *EnergyConsumption* of bottom-Figure 1, can be modelled as a set of measurements. To reason about the quality of a certain VM solution, these measurements need to be somehow linked to the variability model. In bottom-Figure 1 there is an example of a user NFR *"Performance < 10 s"* for the defined QA (e.g., performance measured as execution time). To clarify, the QAM in the example potentially encodes the total performance and energy consumption of each possible valid solution (i.e., product).

There is no consensus on how QAs measurements should be linked to features in a VM, existing two main approaches. One in which measurements are linked to individual features (i.e., each feature contributes individually to the system QA). Another, which is in line with our approach, considers that the set of measurements of a QAM should be univocally linked to a VM valid solution.

The first specific SPL solution for QAs is *Extended Variability Model* [5] already cited in Sect. 1, where the concept of feature in FODA is extended with attributes. Attributes have a name and a domain, and they are linked to individual features. This is useful if we consider that a feature can be assessed by a single quality measurement (e.g., an encryption code consumes 1.3 J). But, the quality of certain features usually cannot be assessed using a single feature. For example, to adequately assess the energy consumption of an encryption code, we need to specify several features, modelling the different key sizes, modes and paddings [27]. Therefore, we cannot model the energy consumption of an encryption code with an attribute, we need a way to link a complete solution, for example, composed by the features: AES algorithm, Mode_CBC, NoPadding, key_size = 256, to an energy measurement. Another argument is that with this approach, we can only assess the overall quality of the system as a simple direct addition of individual QAs; first, not even linear equations adjust real-world QA metrics, and second, the process of adjusting a function to a set of measurements is computationally costly, mutable, and inaccurate in average [35].

Another common approach to model QAs in SPLs is a balanced tree graph alike hierarchical activity/data models describing metrics in a top-down approach [17]. However, hierarchical trees cause extreme repetition, as each solution must be intrinsically modelled in order to connect them to their NFRs [19]. To overcome this limitation, multi-NVMs interconnected with a bunch of cross-model constraints have been proposed [22]. However: (1) hierarchical trees are useless to optimisation-type metrics (e.g., energy consumption constraining runtime metrics), and (2) so many cross-model constraints complicate the model while decreasing reasoning performance. Nonetheless, most of these solutions are not directly compatible with automated reasoners.

We use the HADAS tool [31] as a running example, where an NVM defines systems components, and an entity-relationship schema defines the QAM. Clafer [2] and the database reasoners are embedded as **Solution-to-QAs** mapping procedures, allowing hybrid automatic reasoning. Databases functionality, as querying in batches or random sampling, offers potential advantages for SPL analyses. However, the drawback of maintaining two individual but different models, the computational overhead of two co-existing reasoners, and their in-between resulting models transformations, diminish the scabalibty for very large NVMs [29]. Hence, SPL reasoning lack of a unified model that appropriately supports Boolean and numerical variability with non-functional metrics.

Every alternative contains a high degree of interlocking relationships – we are dealing with relational models. While originally, they dealt with different problems developing different methods, there are overlaps – different methods to solve the same problem. But yet, there are specific limitations of each alternative [21]. Contrarily to these approaches, we propose to abstract SPLs systems into a single relational modelling framework, where a unified semantics can jointly define seemingly dissimilar structures and the connections between them.

3   Category Theory for Software Product Lines

In this section, we give a light-weight description of Category Theory (CT) and the way we use it as a unifying modelling and reasoning framework. For a deeper introduction to CT, we refer the interested reader to, e.g., [3].

Category Theory is a general mathematical theory of algebraic structures that allows the common aspects of different structures to be captured and related, while abstracting from their individual specifics. Informally speaking, a category $\mathcal{C}$ is any collection of *objects* representing spaces that can be related to each other via *arrows* (i.e., *morphisms*). Two standard examples are the categories $\mathcal{V}ec$ where the objects are vector spaces and the arrows are linear maps, and $\mathcal{S}et$ where objects are sets and arrows are functions from one set to another.

Category Theory is built from the following main concepts:

- **Object**: a structured class $X \in Ob(\mathcal{C})$, graphically depicted as a node $\bullet^X$.
- **Arrow**: a structure-preserving function $a \in Arr(\mathcal{C})$ with source and target objects $X = src(a)$ and $Y = tgt(a)$, respectively, depicted $\overset{X}{\bullet} \overset{a}{\to} \overset{Y}{\bullet}$.
  - **Identity**: for all $X \in Ob(\mathcal{C})$, we have $\overset{X}{\bullet} \xrightarrow{identity} \overset{X}{\bullet}$.
  - **Composition**: if $\overset{X}{\bullet} \overset{a_1}{\to} \overset{Y}{\bullet}$ and $\overset{Y}{\bullet} \overset{a_2}{\to} \overset{Z}{\bullet}$, then $\overset{X}{\bullet} \xrightarrow{a_1 \circ a_2} \overset{Z}{\bullet}$.
    It is associative, i.e., $a_1 \circ (a_2 \circ a_3) = (a_1 \circ a_2) \circ a_3$.
- **Category**: consists of $Ob(\mathcal{C})$ and $Arr(\mathcal{C})$. It is depicted as a directed graph.
- **Functor**: a mapping F between categories $C = src(F)$ and $D = tgt(F)$, depicted $\overset{C}{\bullet} \overset{F}{\to} \overset{D}{\bullet}$, which preserves identity and function composition.

In addition, we shall need the following concepts and terminology, borrowed from a CT framework for algebraic data integration [6]:

- **Path**: a concrete sequence of composed arrows: $\overset{X_0}{\bullet} \xrightarrow{a_1} \overset{X_1}{\bullet} \ldots \overset{X_{n-1}}{\bullet} \xrightarrow{a_n} \overset{X_n}{\bullet}$.
- **Generalised Element**: for $X \in \mathrm{Ob}(\mathcal{C})$, a *generalised element* of X is a morphism $\overset{U}{\bullet} \xrightarrow{element} \overset{X}{\bullet}$, where U is a select "unit" object.
- **Instance**: a set-valued functor that assigns values to elements.

In the following subsections, we illustrate intuitive examples of how to represent NVMs and QAMs as related categories. In summary, each model will be represented as a category with objects variability trees (for NVMs) and metrics sets (for QAMs), and relationships will be represented as arrows. This will allow us to generate *joint solution spaces* (i.e., SPL products with their QAs) with any automated reasoner for any type of model.

3.1   Category of Numerical Variability Models ($\mathcal{NVM}$)

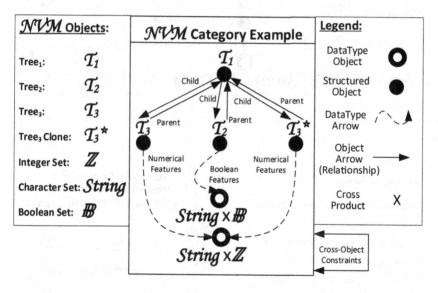

Fig. 2. $\mathcal{NVM}$ category: 4 composing variability trees (T_3 cloned), and 2 domains

The NVM from Fig. 1 is transformed into the category $\mathcal{NVM}$, depicted in Fig. 2. Since the NVM is a composition of trees, $\mathrm{Ob}(\mathcal{NVM})$ is a set of four variability trees: T_1 and T_2 having numerical features, and T_3 and its clone T_3* having Boolean features. $\mathrm{Arr}(\mathcal{NVM})$ is the set of relationships in NVMs: hierarchy (i.e., Parent/Child), cardinality, and Boolean and arithmetic cross-tree constraints. A tree trace is an $\mathcal{NVM}$ path, and an instance is populating $\mathcal{NVM}$-features with values. The basic datatype objects are programming languages library types. Here, arrow composition allows, for example, to access the Boolean value of an element (i.e., arrow) in T_1, which was required by a parent relationship (i.e., arrow) in $\mathcal{T}_3$. These two arrows are of a different nature in NVMs, but not in $\mathcal{NVM}$. In summary, the $\mathcal{NVM}$ category is $\mathrm{Ob}(\mathcal{NVM}) \cup \mathrm{Arr}(\mathcal{NVM})$. While the example objects are mono-type, multi-type is also supported.

3.2 Category of Quality Attributes Model ($\mathcal{QAM}$)

The QAM from Fig. 1 is transformed into the category $\mathcal{QAM}$ depicted in Fig. 3. As QAM is a set of valued-QAs and NFRs, $\mathrm{Ob}(\mathcal{QAM})$ consists of the *Measured QAs* ($\mathcal{M_S}$) and datatype objects. Consequently, $\mathrm{Arr}(\mathcal{QAM})$ consists of NFRs and datatype arrows. Elements as *measurement* $\in \mathcal{M_S}$ are of *name-domain-metric*, where the arrow is *measurement* $\xrightarrow{metric} String \times \mathbb{Z} \times String$.

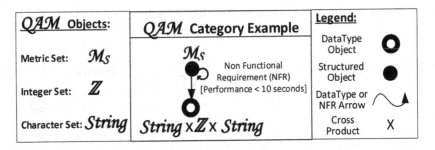

Fig. 3. $\mathcal{QAM}$ category: a metrics set object ($\mathcal{M_S}$) with a structured domain element

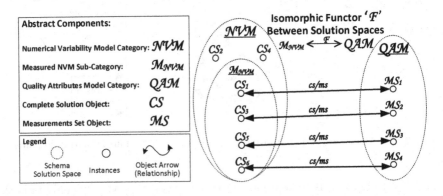

Fig. 4. Measured $\mathcal{NVM}$ and $\mathcal{QAM}$ solution space isomorphism

3.3 Solution Space Categories Isomorphism

Now that we have unified the models, we shall describe how to connect a specific set of features with its specific set of QAs and values. $\mathcal{NVM}$ and $\mathcal{QAM}$ are solution-space related categories as illustrated in Fig. 4. Each solution space structure is defined as a *results* object, similarly to the resulting table of a database query. In the case of $\mathcal{NVM}$, the *Complete Solution* object $\mathcal{CS}$ comprises *Sets* of elements $(\mathcal{CS}_x)$ forming a unique solution according to Arr($\mathcal{NVM}$) – i.e., the satisfiable products of the SPL. Similarly, in $\mathcal{QAM}$ the object $\mathcal{MS}$ comprises the QA *Measurements Sets* $\mathcal{MS}_x$ according to Arr($\mathcal{QAM}$). The basic automated reasoners for categories are mathematical theorem provers; however, they are typically supported by other optimisation engines for specific tasks (e.g., Knuth-Bendix completion prover with a Chase searching algorithm [6]).

Some $\mathcal{CS}_x$ solutions do not correspond to $\mathcal{MS}_x$ measurements (Fig. 4). The reason is that we need to consider that not every system has been measured. Hence, $\mathcal{M}_{\mathcal{NVM}}$ is the sub-category of measured $\mathcal{NVM}$, where the $\mathcal{CS}$ object has a bijective (i.e., one-to-one) arrow cs/ml to the $\mathcal{ML}$ object of $\mathcal{QAM}$. Consequently, there is an isomorphic functor[2] [20] between $\mathcal{M}_{\mathcal{NVM}}$ and $\mathcal{QAM}$.

4 Validation and Discussion

To validate our framework, we deploy a CT prototype of a running SPL tool[3] – the NVM and QAM optimisation assistant for Edge Computing HADAS [31]. Edge devices were defined in a composed Clafer NVM (left-side Fig. 5), with two main trees: Hardware and Software. The last is composed of four trees: *Operating System* (OS), *Programming Language* (PL), *Operation* and *Context*. Again, the latter is composed of *Libraries* and *Numerical Parameters* trees. All the trees have Boolean features, besides *Numerical Parameters*, which only contains Integer features (e.g., Encryption_Key: 64 bytes [29]). HADAS QAM is a relational database that links NVM solution-tree leaves with QAM dynamic identifiers.

---

[2] A categories isomorphism is a one-to-one mapping between their sets of objects.
[3] HADAS web-services: https://hadas.caosd.lcc.uma.es/.

4.1 $\mathcal{HADAS}$ Category

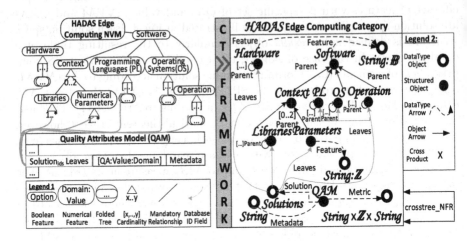

Fig. 5. Transformation of HADAS NVM and QAM in a single $\mathcal{NVM}$ category

In Fig. 5 we can see on the left the HADAS base NVM and QAM structures, and on the right its unified category $\mathcal{HADAS}$ by means of the framework presented in Sect. 3. Our framework is as flexible as CT; existing models can be transformed into categories differently and yet perform equally. For example, an object could be modelled as a category with a single object and vice-versa. Our philosophy in this proof-of-concept is to keep the category simple; hence, we applied this example combining $\mathcal{NVM}$ and the single object category $\mathcal{QAM}$ into $\mathcal{HADAS}$, where the technical implication is switching the categories functor by an objects arrow. In summary, data-types, NVM trees and QAM are 12 $\mathcal{HADAS}$ objects, and variability trees relationships, cross-tree constraints and NFRs are a minimum of 6 arrows. $\mathcal{HADAS}$ consists of the following components:

- Ob($\mathcal{HADAS}$) $\ni$ $String$, $String \times \mathbb{B}$, $String \times \mathbb{Z} \times String$, $Hardware$, $Software$, $\mathcal{PL}$, $\mathcal{OS}$, $Operation$, $Context$, $Libraries$, $Parameters$, $Solutions$.
- Arr($\mathcal{HADAS}$) $\ni$ $feature$, $metric$, $parent$, $cardinality$ (e.g., [0..2]), $metadata$, $crosstree\_NFR$, $solution$, $leaves$. In occasions $parent$ is the $identity$ (Fig. 5).
- Elements: based on Arr($\mathcal{HADAS}$), there are Boolean and integer $features$, QA $metrics$ with format $name\text{-}domain\text{-}metric$, QA $metadata$, and $solution$ the set of object features leaves to QAs (i.e., $\mathcal{HADAS}$ solution space).

4.2 Optimal Deployment

The next step in this proof-of-concept is to instantiate (i.e., populate) $\mathcal{HADAS}$, to later generate the solution space (e.g. IoT/EC deployments), and optimise its QAs. EC and IoT systems require fast real-time processing of random amounts of data and have relatively strict NFRs on the performance and energy consumption [34]. Hence, we propose to turn into a category the model shown in Fig. 6 on the left, aiming to gain insights into which features and solutions are affecting those QAs in transmitting and/or compressing operations. The NVM contains 28 Boolean features and two numerical features, while the QAM contains two QAs – performance in Seconds and energy rate in milliWatts. Operations are partial configurable benchmarks of the Phoronix Test Suite[4].

Having a clear picture of the category base model in Fig. 5, we need to program and deploy it. While there are libraries aiming to add CT support to SPL reasoners (e.g., Conal Elliot libraries for Z3 [14]), the only production-ready *Integrated Development Environment* (IDE) is the *Categorical Query Language* (CQL) IDE: an open-source software, commercialised by Conexus AI[5]. It is a canonical functional IDE that generates CT graphs as the presented figures.

On the right of Fig. 6, there is a partial code-snapshot; the CQL model can be downloaded from the HADAS server[6]. There one can find the 30 NVM features and the 2 QAs distributed in the $\mathcal{HADAS}$ objects shown on the right side of Fig. 6. We did not include cross-tree constraints in the graph due to extension limitations; however, they are arrows in $\mathcal{HADAS}$.

4.3   Results and Discussion

CQL IDE reasoning is automatically performed with a combination of different algorithms – the key of our performance. We used them as such: automated theorem prover with Knuth-Bendix completion [28] for logic and equations, and hashing, balanced trees and chasing for data-type and cross-object arrows.

We have obtained 162 valid solutions with their respective 324 measurements in 0.1 s. If we reduce the category, the runtime is still 0.1 s. Extending the category as a supra-category formed by a self-cross-product 3 times results in 0.2 s. Running CQL IDE on another computer did not change the runtimes. This suggests that CQL IDE scales linearly, and that the minimum runtime is 0.1 s independently of the computer, probably due to being a Java application running on a Java virtual machine.

Optimisation arrows are a step further from the solution space. Maximising performance or minimising energy rate increases the reasoning runtime by 0.1 s, independently of the solution space size. However, we expect linear increments for larger models (i.e., linear scalability). Regarding the interaction of features with regards to the QAs in our EC case study, the main insights are:

---

[4] Phoronix Test Suite details: https://openbenchmarking.org/tests/pts.

[5] CQL IDE main website: https://www.categoricaldata.net/.

[6] HADAS CQL CT model: https://hadas.caosd.lcc.uma.es/ctprototype.cql.

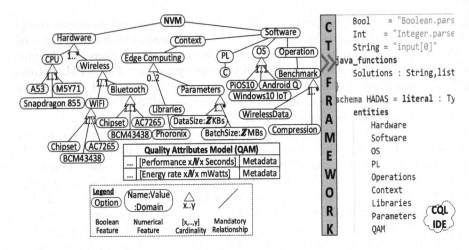

Fig. 6. Transformation of HADAS for Edge Computing in CQL IDE $\mathcal{HADAS}$ category

- Compressing/uncompressing while sending/receiving data improves the run-times for large batches of data, but for small ones, it is the opposite independently of the original data size. In any case, compressing increased the energy rate – more Joules per Second.
- The more powerful the CPU is, the lesser is the compressing time, and the higher the energy rate; the maximum energy rate of *Snapdragon 855* was 3.4 W, of *A53* was 3.7 W, and of *M5Y71* was 11.8 W. In the case of communication without compression, CPUs barely affected QAs.
- Communication peripherals affected equally the QAs. WiFi and Bluetooth channels performed equally for small batches of data. WiFi has tends to be faster above 300 MB, while the Bluetooth energy-rate is substantially lower (with an average of 0.5 W) than these 300 MB.

As **internal validity**, we tested our proposal by first transforming an SPL tool into a category, and second, by modelling an EC case study in a category. Additionally, we implemented that category in CQL IDE, performing reasoning to generate the solution space, and also performing an optimal search to obtain quality insights from the EC category. To mitigate scalability assumptions, we ran CQL IDE with different solution spaces in different computers.

As **external validity**, we identified two threats. First, we have not tested our approach on large models with other IDEs, since our aim was a proof-of-concept. Second, as it is the first CT NVM/QAM framework to the best of our knowledge, we cannot compare it with other CT alternatives.

5 Related Work

Table 1. Characteristics of abstraction alternatives for a unified NVM/QAM

→Model ↓Entity	NVM	Category Theory	Set Theory	FODA	Codd Algebra	HOL	Arith-metic
Structured Model	Labelled NVM	Category	Finite Set	Labelled FM	Data Schema	Logic Formula	Plane
Entities	Sub-tree, Feature, Solution	Sub-Category, Object, Instance	Sub-Set, Element	Sub-tree, Feature, Configu-ration	*Table, Cell*	Partial Formula, Variable	Sub-System, Equation, Variable
Boolean Type	$\mathbb{B}$ Feature	$\mathbb{B}$	$\mathbb{B}$	Feature	$\mathbb{B}$	$\mathbb{B}$	*Pseudo-$\mathbb{B}$: [0,1]*
Numerical Type	$\mathbb{N}, \mathbb{Z}, \mathbb{R}$ Feature	$\mathbb{N}, \mathbb{Z}, \mathbb{R}$	*$\mathbb{N}, \mathbb{Z}$ Finite Sets*	*Un-supported*	$\mathbb{N}, \mathbb{Z}, \mathbb{R}$	*Un-supported*	$\mathbb{N}, \mathbb{Z}, \mathbb{R}$
Requirements	Cross-tree Equation	Categories Functor	Predicate	Cross-tree Constraint	σ Constraint	Formula	Equation
Selection	Assert	Δ	$\in$	Require	$\pi_{[\text{Column}]}$	True	$=$
Exclusion	Not	$-\Delta$	$\nsubseteq$	Exclude	$-\pi_{[\text{Column}]}$	False	$\neq$
Connectives	$\&\&, \|\|\|,$ $[\text{x..y}],$ $\Rightarrow, \equiv$	$\sum_{[\text{Functor}]}$ $\prod_{[\text{Functor}]}$, X	$\wedge, \vee, \oplus,$ If, $\Rightarrow, \equiv$	And, Or, xOR, $\Rightarrow$, $\equiv$	Foreign Key, $\cap$, $\cup, \uplus,$ Joins$_{[X]}$	$\wedge, \vee, \oplus,$ If, $\Rightarrow, \equiv$ $\forall, \exists, !$	Equation Systems
Equalities	$=, \neq, >,$ $\geq, <, \leq$	$=, \neq, >,$ $\geq, <, \leq$	$=, \neq$	$=, \neq$	$=, \neq, >,$ $\geq, <, \leq$	$=, \neq$	$=, \neq, >,$ $\geq, <, \leq$
Mathematics	$+, -, *,$ $\div, \%\ldots$	$+, -, *,$ $\div, \%\ldots$	*Pre/Suc-cessor*	*Un-supported*	*Un-supported*	*Un-supported*	$+, -, *,$ $\div, \%\ldots$

Having already presented the relevant publications for the foundations of this paper, we now discuss further related work. Firstly, while we have discussed the advantages of CT, one could argue that more simple structures could be used instead to unify NVMs with QAMs. In Table 1 there is a summary of the alternatives, where we highlight first the needs of NVMs, and second what CT provided as a reference. Whether we are talking about NVMs with or without QAMs, we need a complete Boolean and numerical domain. *FODA*, the first VM formalisation [24], has already been discussed and discarded due to its lack of support for numerical features and constraints necessary in EC analyses. In fact, as identified in Table 1, most of the alternatives lack numerical support. One of them is *Set Theory* (ST), which, similarly to CT, is a branch of mathematical logic that studies sets, which informally are collections of objects [15]. ST lacks support for numerical equations, inequalities, and infinite data-types. Similarly, *Higher-Order Logic* (HOL) deals just with declarative propositions, predicates and quantification (e.g., $\forall x$) [26]. *Codd Theory* is the first and only formalisation of relational algebra, which uses algebraic structures with well-founded semantics for modelling data and defining queries on it. While databases support a wide range of numerical components as datatypes, counting, grouping, arithmetic, etc., they are programming workarounds outside of Codd Theory. In other words, it is not yet clear that Codd relational algebra should be extended above a pure Boolean domain [25]. Pseudo-Boolean (i.e. [0,1]) reasoners are based on *Arithmetic* [25] – the study of numbers and their operations. While they are promising, if not considering the complexity and overload of model-transforming HOL, their performance in current SAT competitions is often quite poor [13]. It should be pointed out that all of the above-mentioned theories (ST, HOL, Codd Algebra) are well-formalised categories in CT.

A computational design framework based solely on objects and arrows is proposed in [4], where Model Driven Engineering meets (Boolean) SPLs. This approach was extended with explicit use of CT in [36], where VMs and Domain Models are unified. In Clafer SPL suite, VMs are modelled as abstract classes, literally an idea borrowed from CT [2]. A generic CT approach for different data domains integration is formalised in [6], where as a case study entity-relational models (i.e., database models) are transformed into a category in which tables are objects, columns are elements, and foreign keys are arrows.

6   Conclusions and Future Work

In this paper, we identify the lack of automated tools to model and optimise SPLs defined as an NVM related to sets of QAs with values. To address this, we define a unified model supporting: (1) Boolean and numerical domains in the form of features and their relationships, and (2) a map between the solution spaces of NVMs and QAMs. For that, we propose a CT framework with two categories. The first one is $\mathcal{NVM}$ where variability trees and data-types are objects, and hierarchical and cross-tree constraints are arrows. The second one is $\mathcal{QAM}$ where the sets of QAs and their data-types are objects, and NFRs are arrows. Finally, we establish a functorial relationship between measured products of $\mathcal{NVM}$ with QAs sets of $\mathcal{QAM}$. As a proof-of-concept, we transformed the SPL HADAS into the category $\mathcal{HADAS}$. Then, we have implemented and deployed it in the CQL IDE and performed a brief EC case study using a combination of theorem provers and database algorithms as automated reasoners. As future work, we plan to improve the framework to support other proposed extended functionalities of NVMs, as well as integrate quality models. Currently, we are in the process of evaluating this approach with large SPLs.

Acknowledgements. Munoz, Pinto and Fuentes work is supported by the European Union's H2020 research and innovation programme under grant agreement DAEMON 101017109, by the projects co-financed by FEDER funds LEIA UMA18-FEDERJA-15, MEDEA RTI2018-099213-B-I00 and Rhea P18-FR-1081 and the PRE2019-087496 grant from the Ministerio de Ciencia e Innovación.

References

1. Al-Qutaish, R.E.: Quality models in software engineering literature: an analytical and comparative study. J. Am. Sci. **6**(3), 166–175 (2010)
2. Bąk, K., Diskin, Z., Antkiewicz, M., Czarnecki, K., Wąsowski, A.: Clafer: unifying class and feature modeling. Softw. Syst. Model. **15**(3), 811–845 (2014). https://doi.org/10.1007/s10270-014-0441-1
3. Barr, M., Wells, C.: Category Theory for Computing Science. Prentice Hall, New York (1990)
4. Batory, D., Azanza, M., Saraiva, J.: The objects and arrows of computational design. In: Czarnecki, K., Ober, I., Bruel, J.-M., Uhl, A., Völter, M. (eds.) MOD-ELS 2008. LNCS, vol. 5301, pp. 1–20. Springer, Heidelberg (2008). https://doi.org/10.1007/978-3-540-87875-9_1
5. Benavides, D., Trinidad, P., Ruiz-Cortés, A.: Automated reasoning on feature models. In: Pastor, O., Falcão e Cunha, J. (eds.) CAiSE 2005. LNCS, vol. 3520, pp. 491–503. Springer, Heidelberg (2005). https://doi.org/10.1007/11431855_34
6. Brown, K.S., Spivak, D.I., Wisnesky, R.: Categorical data integration for computational science. Comput. Mater. Sci. **164**, 127–132 (2019)
7. Budiardjo, E.K., Zamzami, E.M., et al.: Feature modeling and variability modeling syntactic notation comparison and mapping. Comput. Commun. **2**, 101–108 (2014)
8. Chen, L., Ali Babar, M., Ali, N.: Variability management in software product lines: a systematic review. In: Proceedings of the 13th International Software Product Line Conference, SPLC 2009, pp. 81–90. Carnegie Mellon University, USA (2009)
9. Chohan, A.Z., Bibi, A., Motla, Y.H.: Optimized software product line architecture and feature modeling in improvement of SPL. In: 2017 International Conference on Frontiers of Information Technology (FIT), pp. 167–172. IEEE (2017)
10. Chowdhury, S., Borle, S., Romansky, S., Hindle, A.: Greenscaler: training software energy models with automatic test generation. Empir. Softw. Eng. **24**(4), 1649–1692 (2019). https://doi.org/10.1007/s10664-018-9640-7
11. Czarnecki, K., Helsen, S., Eisenecker, U.: Formalizing cardinality-based feature models and their specialization. Softw. Process **10**(1), 7–29 (2005)
12. de Moura, L., Bjørner, N.: Z3: an efficient SMT solver. In: Ramakrishnan, C.R., Rehof, J. (eds.) TACAS 2008. LNCS, vol. 4963, pp. 337–340. Springer, Heidelberg (2008). https://doi.org/10.1007/978-3-540-78800-3_24
13. Elffers, J., Giráldez-Cru, J., Nordström, J., Vinyals, M.: Using combinatorial benchmarks to probe the reasoning power of pseudo-Boolean solvers. In: Beyersdorff, O., Wintersteiger, C.M. (eds.) SAT 2018. LNCS, vol. 10929, pp. 75–93. Springer, Cham (2018). https://doi.org/10.1007/978-3-319-94144-8_5
14. Elliott, C.: Compiling to categories. In: Proceedings of the ACM on Programming Languages, vol. 1, issue number (ICFP), pp. 1–27 (2017)
15. Fraenkel, A.A., Bar-Hillel, Y., Levy, A.: Foundations of Set Theory. Elsevier, Burlington (1973)
16. Gamez, N., Fuentes, L.: Software product line evolution with cardinality-based feature models. In: Schmid, K. (ed.) ICSR 2011. LNCS, vol. 6727, pp. 102–118. Springer, Heidelberg (2011). https://doi.org/10.1007/978-3-642-21347-2_9
17. Glinz, M.: On non-functional requirements. In: 15th IEEE International Requirements Engineering Conference (RE 2007), pp. 21–26. IEEE (2007)
18. González-Huerta, J., Insfran, E., Abrahão, S., McGregor, J.D.: Non-functional requirements in model-driven software product line engineering. In: Proceedings of the Fourth International Workshop on Nonfunctional System Properties in Domain Specific Modeling Languages, NFPinDSML 2012, NY, USA (2012)

19. Gurov, D., Østvold, B.M., Schaefer, I.: A hierarchical variability model for software product lines. In: Hähnle, R., Knoop, J., Margaria, T., Schreiner, D., Steffen, B. (eds.) ISoLA 2011. CCIS, pp. 181–199. Springer, Heidelberg (2012). https://doi.org/10.1007/978-3-642-34781-8_15

20. Gurrola-Ramos, L., Macías, S., Macías-Díaz, J.: On the isomorphism of injective objects in Grothendieck categories. Quaest. Math. **40**(5), 617–622 (2017)

21. Hellendoorn, V.J., Sutton, C., Singh, R., Maniatis, P., Bieber, D.: Global relational models of source code. In: International Conference on Learning Representations (2019)

22. Horcas, J.M., Pinto, M., Fuentes, L.: An automatic process for weaving functional quality attributes using a software product line approach. J. Syst. Softw. **112**, 78–95 (2016)

23. Jussien, N., Rochart, G., Lorca, X.: Choco: an open source java constraint programming library. In: HAL Archives Ouvertes (2008)

24. Kang, K.C., Cohen, S.G., Hess, J.A., Novak, W.E., Peterson, A.S.: Feature-oriented domain analysis (foda) feasibility study. Carnegie-Mellon University Pittsburgh Pa Software Engineering Institute, Technical report (1990)

25. Kızıltoprak, A., Köse, N.Y.: Relational thinking: the bridge between arithmetic and algebra. Int. J. Elem. Educ. **10**(1), 131–145 (2017)

26. Lambek, J., Scott, P.J.: Introduction to Higher-Order Categorical Logic, vol. 7. Cambridge University Press, Cambridge (1988)

27. Montenegro, J.A., Pinto, M., Fuentes, L.: What do software developers need to know to build secure energy-efficient android applications? IEEE Access **6**, 1428–1450 (2018)

28. Mueller, J.: Theopogles–a theorem prover based on first-order polynomials and a special Knuth-Bendix procedure. GWAI-87 11th German Workshop on Artifical Intelligence. Informatik-Fachberichte (Subreihe Küstliche Intelligenz), vol. 152. Springer, Heidelberg (1987). https://doi.org/10.1007/978-3-642-73005-4_26

29. Munoz, D.J., Montenegro, J.A., Pinto, M., Fuentes, L.: Energy-aware environments for the development of green applications for cyber-physical systems. Future Gener. Compu. Syst. **91**, 536–554 (2019)

30. Munoz, D.J., Oh, J., Pinto, M., Fuentes, L., Batory, D.: Uniform random sampling product configurations of feature models that have numerical features. In: Proceedings of the 23rd International Systems and Software Product Line Conference - Volume A, pp. 289–301. Association for Computing Machinery, NY, USA (2019)

31. Munoz, D.J., Pinto, M., Fuentes, L.: Hadas: analysing quality attributes of software configurations. In: Proceedings of the 23rd International Systems and Software Product Line Conference-Volume B, pp. 13–16 (2019)

32. Olaechea, R., Stewart, S., Czarnecki, K., Rayside, D.: Modelling and multi-objective optimization of quality attributes in variability-rich software. In: Proceedings of the Fourth International Workshop on Nonfunctional System Properties in Domain Specific Modeling Languages, pp. 1–6 (2012)

33. Pohl, K., Böckle, G., van Der Linden, F.J.: Software Product Line Engineering: Foundations, Principles and Techniques. Springer Science & Business Media, Heidelberg (2005). https://doi.org/10.1007/3-540-28901-1

34. Ren, J., Wang, H., Hou, T., Zheng, S., Tang, C.: Federated learning-based computation offloading optimization in edge computing-supported internet of things. IEEE Access **7**, 69194–69201 (2019)

35. Siegmund, N., Rosenmüller, M., Kuhlemann, M., Kästner, C., Apel, S., Saake, G.: SPL conqueror: toward optimization of non-functional properties in software product lines. Softw. Qual. J. **20**(3–4), 487–517 (2012). https://doi.org/10.1007/s11219-011-9152-9

36. Taentzer, G., Salay, R., Strüber, D., Chechik, M.: Transformations of software product lines: a generalizing framework based on category theory. In: 20th International Conference on Model Driven Engineering Languages and Systems (MODELS) (2017)

Platforms and Architectures

Comparing Digital Platform Types
in the Platform Economy

Thomas Derave[1]([⊠]) [iD], Tiago Prince Sales[2] [iD], Frederik Gailly[1] [iD], and Geert Poels[1] [iD]

[1] Department of Business Informatics and Operations Management, Ghent University,
Tweekerkenstraat 2, 9000 Ghent, Belgium
{thomas.derave,frederik.gailly,geert.poels}@UGent.be
[2] Faculty of Computer Science, Free University of Bozen-Bolzano, Bolzano, Italy
tiago.princesales@unibz.it

Abstract. In the domain of the platform economy we identified two gaps in the current literature. First the lack of a shared conceptualization of digital platform types. We solve this issue with a taxonomy giving an overview of digital platform attributes, with attribute values expressing the possible variations between platforms depending on their type. These attributes and attribute values are then used in the typology giving a clear overview of all the digital platform types and how they are related to each other. The second gap is the lack of knowledge concerning the software functionalities of digital platforms. We contribute to this with a proposal of a reference ontology allowing for a better communication between developers and other stakeholders. Our envisioned ontology can be used as a common language that all platform stakeholders can understand to facilitate future research and support ontology-driven development of digital platforms.

Keywords: Digital platform · Ontology model · UFO · Taxonomy

1 Introduction

The platform economy is a broad term that encompasses a growing number of digitally enabled activities in business, politics, and social interaction facilitated by digital platforms [1]. This platform economy, including platforms like Airbnb, eBay, Etsy, Ticketswap, Tinder, Dropbox and Uber, is defined very broadly and overlaps with other phenomena; 'sharing economy', 'collaborative economy', 'gig economy', 'on-demand economy', 'collaborative commons', 'peer-to peer economy', 'access economy', 'the mesh', ... [2]. On these markets a wide range of services are exchanged by both human and organizational actors, in sectors such as travel, car rental, finance, staffing, information, music and video streaming, that were previously provided uniquely by firms [3, 4]. Problematic for academic studies is that the types of digital platform used in these markets, including 'sharing economy platform', 'digital marketplace', 'on-demand platform' and 'multi-sided platform', are umbrella concepts or 'buzz words' getting a lot of attention in both academic and professional communities but without consensus on what they comprise [3, 5–10]. These platform types have a lot in common, but also have

M. La Rosa et al. (Eds.): CAiSE 2021, LNCS 12751, pp. 417–431, 2021.
https://doi.org/10.1007/978-3-030-79382-1_25

substantial differences in functionalities offered and the type of business model that is supported, resulting in different information system structures.

This lack of agreement has made it difficult for scholars to determine the impact that the digital platforms have for the economy as well as for society at large. It remains difficult to compare different studies and their results since each of them conceptualizes the markets and their platforms differently [11]. Clearer definitions of the used digital platform types can improve communication, guide future research and produce useful contributions and recommendations for practitioners who are keen on learning more about the opportunities that digitalization brings for fostering the sharing economy [11, 12].

Furthermore, the literature of these digital platform types offers a very partial view with a relatively small number of papers focusing on the functionality of the software enabling digital platforms of different types. It is observed "that perspectives on technology are currently lacking in the research on the sharing economy" [7] as "few research works have been done from the perspective of information technologies" [13]. Although there has been some interest in the discipline of Information Systems to create a knowledge base for developing platforms that realize goods and service access for sharing [13], there is a lack of knowledge regarding the requirements and design of the different types of digital platforms. Providing an overview of the various distinctions in the digital platform types is not only important from an academic perspective but also for regulation and policy, as a 'one size fits all' policy and regulatory approach is inappropriate [14].

This paper contributes to filling both gaps regarding the state-of-the-art in the research on digital platforms. We do so by creating two artefacts and proposing a third one. First, we contribute to the lack of shared conceptualization by creating a taxonomy and a typology for digital platforms. The taxonomy gives an overview of digital platform attributes, with attribute values expressing the possible variations between digital platforms depending on their type. These attributes and attribute values are then used in the typology giving a clear overview of all the digital platform types and how these types are related. Second, the lack of knowledge concerning the software functionalities of each type is tackled with both the taxonomy and a first module of a reference ontology. The envisioned reference ontology describes the general functionality of any digital platform and the more specific functionality of each digital platform type in relation to its attribute values as defined in the taxonomy. The reference ontology thus describes the functionality of the distinct digital platform types by referring to typical digital platform concepts including 'listing', 'transaction', 'subscription', 'peer', 'matching' and 'access-based', allowing for a better communication between developers and other stakeholders. Further, a digital platform reference ontology can support ontology-driven development of platforms, hence capitalizing on a design knowledge base of the software functionalities for different types of platforms. Summarizing, the reference ontology is envisioned as a common language that all platform stakeholders (including software engineers, entrepreneurs, managers, economists, governments and social scientists) can use to facilitate future research and development of digital platforms.

This paper is structured as follows; In Sect. 2 we explain our methodology. In Sect. 3 we present our taxonomy. In Sect. 4 we propose the typology. In Sect. 5 we discuss the first module of the ontology and provide a link to the other modules which are work in progress. In Sect. 6 we discuss these artifacts and in Sect. 7 we present our conclusion.

2 Methodology

We develop three related artefacts that contribute to addressing the previously observed gaps in digital platform research:

1. A taxonomy including a set of digital platform attributes and their possible values to differentiate between the main digital platform types;
2. A typology to have a compete overview of the digital platform types and how they are related to each other depending on their attribute values;
3. A reference ontology describing the required software functionality of the digital platform types in relation to their attribute values defined in the taxonomy.

Our research methodology for building and evaluating these artefacts is shown in Fig. 1 and explained below.

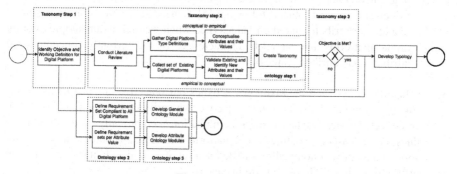

Fig. 1. Methodology

First, to create the digital platform taxonomy, we use the method for taxonomy development and its application in Information Systems research of [15]. This method was used by [16] to create a taxonomy for P2P sharing and collaborative consumption and by [17] to create a Crowdfunding taxonomy. Compared to these taxonomies, our taxonomy has a broader scope by including a wider range of digital platform types. The method of [15] includes three steps:

1. Identify the objective: As stated in the introduction, our digital platform taxonomy should be able to differentiate between the main digital platform types in our scope. To define the scope of our research we construct a working definition for digital platform.
2. Taxonomy development: The taxonomy development step is done in an iterative manner for which we alternatingly use the 'conceptual to empirical' and 'empirical to conceptual' approach, starting in the first iteration with the former.

a. For the 'conceptual to empirical' approach, we gather digital platform types in line with our working definition. This is done by a literature search of secondary sources (literature reviews) on digital platform type. As these literature reviews include a lot of contradictive definitions for these types, we use convenience sampling to gather platform types and their definitions that are most used and widely accepted by the academic community, but are still easy to understand and compare. When the digital platform types are gathered, we compare their definitions to conceptualize the attributes and their values that enables us to differentiate between them.

b. For the 'empirical to conceptual' approach, we collect a set of existing digital platforms used in the primary sources of the literature reviews found using the previous approach. This way the objects of this set can be directly linked to their digital platform types. As these primary sources mention and use a very large number of objects, we compose the set using a purposive sampling method called Maximum Variation Sampling [18] to eventually collect a rather small but diverse enough sample that covers all types discussed in the selected literature reviews. The attributes and attribute values that were conceptualized in the 'conceptual to empirical' approach, are then validated using the composed set of existing digital platforms. Doing so, the emergent taxonomy is compared systematically with evidence from each object, following [5]. If needed, a new iteration is started to add new attributes and their values (i.e., when we find in our sample existing digital platforms that cannot be characterised by the currently conceptualized attributes and attribute values).

3. Evaluation: Only when the taxonomy satisfies our objective, the taxonomy development is terminated. To reach our objective, we verify that every digital platform type collected in step two had a unique combination of empirically validated attribute values (i.e., at least one existing digital platform with those attribute values is found), implying that the taxonomy allows to define a set of unique and inter-related digital platform types that all have real-life instances.

A second artefact is the typology. A typology is an organized system of types that can be used for forming concepts and sorting cases [14]. To create the typology we follow the multi-level modelling theory of [19] and use UML as a notation to describe the types as super and subclasses of each other. Every digital platform type captures the common features of existing digital platforms that are instances of the type. For example, both Airbnb and Uber intermediate P2P services between their users. The attributes and attribute values are then used to highlight the differences between the types. As each type has a unique combination of attribute values, we can differentiate between each type in our typology. To conclude, the typology provides a complete overview of how the digital platform types, including sharing economy platform, digital marketplace and on-demand platform, are related to each other in relation to their attribute values.

The third artefact is the creation of a digital platform reference ontology. Ontology modelling is a special type of conceptual modelling [20] that is used as a basis for the engineering and evaluation of information systems [19]. Ontology modelling also helps in the common understanding of a domain by making the domain assumptions explicit

[21] and by providing a clear account of domain concepts to foster communication, consensus and alignment [22]. Our approach to ontology modelling follows the patterns of the Unified Foundational Ontology (UFO), a high-level ontology that provides us with basic concepts for objects, events, social elements and relations [20]. We create the digital platform reference ontology by combining the reference ontology engineering approaches proposed by [23, 24] consisting of three steps. In step one, we split the digital platform domain into modules. This step is already accomplished during the taxonomy creation, when we conceptualized distinctive digital platform attributes and attribute values. In step two, we define the requirements for the platform software to provide the features that are expressed by the attribute values that are conceptualized in the taxonomy. We also define a set of general requirements relevant to all digital platforms, based on the working definition of a digital platform that is developed in the first step of the taxonomy development. These general requirements are independent of the type of digital platform. A digital platform that is an instance of a certain digital platform type, has to fulfill the set of general requirements and the sets of specific requirements for the attribute values that define the type. Elaborating on the design of the requirements per attribute value doesn't fit the scope of this paper, hence we provide a link towards work in progress on these requirements, and focus instead in this paper on the general requirements. Finally, in a third step, the ontology is described using OntoUML [25], a UFO-based ontology-driven conceptual modelling language capable of representing objects, events and social entities. In this paper, given the focus on the general requirements, one general ontology module is presented that holds for all digital platforms, regardless their type. The link also guides the reader to work in progress where ontology modules are defined for the specific requirements that cover the unique attribute values. The ontology of a certain digital platform is thus composed of the general ontology module and of all ontology modules for the attribute values that characterize the type of the digital platform.

3 Taxonomy

Due to the dispersal of digital platform research across a number of fields, there is a miscellany of perspectives concerning a digital platform. To reach our objective, a clear working definition of a digital platform independent of their type is needed. For example the term 'sharing economy platform' or 'digital marketplace' is used alternately as the algorithm, the abstract term 'platform', the technology [7], the company owning the algorithm [26], a business model [27] or (part of) an intermediary service [28, 29]. This conceptual confusion makes academic decision-making difficult, and makes decisions difficult to communicate [12]. As we wish to cover a wide range of digital platform types, we relate a platform to the broader concept of service economy, and therefore follow [1, 10, 28, 29] in defining a digital platform as 'a service offering by the digital platform management to the users. The primary action offered are interactions between users and these interactions are enabled by a software'. This definition is very broad, as these interactions can consist solely of information transfer (e.g., WhatsApp, Tinder) but can also include offerings of products (e.g., eBay) and/or services (e.g., Airbnb). It is required that the interactions are the primary actions offered by the platform, and not secondary actions such as product reviews on regular B2C e-commerce sites and apps.

Now that the working definition is formulated, we start the digital platform taxonomy development. After numerous runs of the 'conceptual to empirical' approach, we ended up with six literature reviews [2, 3, 7, 8, 14, 30]. Out of these literature reviews and their primary sources, eventually nine digital platform types where collected: Multi-Sided (including two-sided) platform by Hagiu and Wright [6]; transaction platform by Acquier et al. [9]; investment platform by Evans and Gawer [10]; crowdfunding platform by Haas et al. [17]; digital marketplace by Täuscher and Laudien [27]; Peer-to-Peer (P2P) sharing and collaborative consumption platform by Chasin et al. [16]; sharing economy platform by Frenken and Schor [31]; on-demand platform by Mamonova [32]; and second-hand P2P platform by Acquier et al. [9]. The definitions of these nine types were compared to each other and their differences were conceptualized by defining digital platform attributes and their values.

During the 'empirical to conceptual' approach iterations, we collected information on existing digital platforms for the types identified by the previous 'conceptual to empirical' approach iterations. For each digital platform that was selected, we collected data based on sources such as the official website, blogs and industry magazines, following the approach of [5]. The attributes and their values for the types that were identified, were validated and if needed adjusted based on the information of the real instances selected for these types. The total sample of digital platforms investigated is given in following link[1].

The taxonomy itself is given in Table 1. Market sides [6] indicates the number of different groups of platform users in the market that are connected. Although it is not allowed by the method of [15], for practical reasons and in alignment with our sample we decided to make the following three attributes inclusive[i], meaning a platform can have more than one attribute value for the same attribute; Affiliation [8] refers to different ways that users (per group) can be connected to the platform. Because this attribute is inclusive, our taxonomy allows users to be connected to the platform by multiple affiliation options. Centralization [7, 33] depends on the way the users can connect to each other. This can be via a decentralized search by the users of one side, or a centralized, automated matching by the platform software. The following two attributes are only applicable if the platform has multiple sides[ms]; Participation [27, 34] indicates if the market that is intermediated by the platform is Business-to-Business (B2B), Business-to-Consumer (B2C), Consumer-to-Consumer (C2C) or Peer-to-Peer (P2P); the latter case holds when platform participants are considered as 'equals', where C2C is a specialization of P2P when users of at least two sides are only allowed to be private persons. The offering orientation [35] differentiates between product selling, result-oriented services or user-oriented when it's a combination of the previous two. The last two attributes are only relevant for user-oriented offerings[uo]. A digital platform offers immediate access [36, 37] if access to the product is possible when the customer needs it. Under-utilized [31] indicates that the product is offered because of excess capacity.

The reason why only these attributes are included in the taxonomy is simply because these attributes are necessary to classify the existing digital platforms (of our sample) to the right type(s) (collected by the literature review). For example, without checking the under-utilization of the product it is not possible to know if rentmydress.com is a

---

[1] http://model-a-platform.com/sample-of-existing-digital-platforms/.

Table 1. Digital platform taxonomy

Attribute	Values			
Market sides	One-sided		Multi-sided	
Affiliation[i]	Registration	Subscription	Transaction	Investment
Centralization[i]	Decentralized		Centralized	
Participation[i,ms]	B2C	B2B	P2P	C2C
Offering orientation[ms]	Product		Result	User
Immediate access[uo]	True		False	
Under-utilized[uo]	True		False	

sharing economy platform by [31] and/or a digital marketplace by [27]. These attributes and attribute values are further explained in relation to the digital platform types in next section. Notice that as future types arise, or new platforms are added to the sample the taxonomy can (and needs to) be modified.

4 Typology

In this section, we provide an overview of the digital platform types that can be distinguished based on the attributes and their values as defined in the taxonomy (Table 2). The typology shows the instantiations of digital platform type as super- and subclasses of each other. This means that every digital platform type captures the common features of the digital platforms that are instances of the type. Our typology, shown in Fig. 2, confirms to the suggestions of [14] as it (i) has descriptive power and is empirically grounded, (ii) reduces complexity, and (iii) identifies similarities and differences between the types. Further on, we explain how the attribute values of our taxonomy are related to the nine types of digital platform that we identified before.

On the top of our typology we have the root superclass 'digital platform', meaning that all instances of our 9 digital platform types are considered digital platforms following our working definition. For all nine digital platform types we found real-life instances, but notice that, in theory, every unique combination of attribute values can be defined as a distinct type. If needed, new types can be included in the typology if instances of such types would appear.

The most popular definition of a Multi-Sided (MS) platform is by [38]; "Including at least two distinct but interdependent sides to have direct and clearly identified interactions with each other with direct and indirect network externalities that they internalize". Because of the complexity of this definition, we used the more convenient and also popular definition of [6]: "A MS market enables direct interactions between multiple sides with each side affiliated with the market".

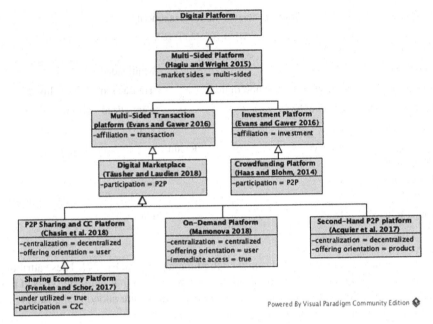

Fig. 2. Digital platform typology

In case the platform allows users to make transactions, the digital platform is a MS transaction platform as defined by [10]. These transactions can be facilitated by the platform in multiple ways, what is referred to in many papers as part of the 'intermediation' by the platform software. This intermediation can be all kinds of software supported functionality including the exchange of the product, service and the transfer of payments between the users [39]. The transactions can involve tangible products (e.g., bags on O My Bag), intangible products (e.g., games on Xbox), services (e.g., teaching on Preply) or a combination of these (e.g., meal delivery on Uber Eats).

In case users of one market side make an investment of financial resources that benefits users of another market side, the platform is an investment platform, as defined by [10]. This type includes online stockbrokers (e.g., Degiro, Keytrade) that intermediate financial instruments between stock exchanges and investors.

When the users of the different market sides are considered as peers, meaning equal participants, also called prosumers alternating in their role as producer (or creator, capital seeker, provider) and consumer [35], the platform operates in a Peer-to-Peer (P2P) market. How to define and agree on what this equality means is one of the reasons why an ontology is needed as it helps to find and communicate a generally accepted definition. When an investment platform has P2P participants, it is a crowdfunding platform, as defined by [17] based on the P2P lending principles of [40]. An example is Kickstarter helping projects to life by connecting creative people with their community [41].

For a digital platform to be a digital marketplace, four conditions need to be fulfilled [27]. The first condition, 'connects independent actors from a demand and supply side and these individual actors can participate on both sides', implies that a digital marketplace needs to be a P2P multi-sided platform, which is confirmed by our sample. The second, third and fourth condition, respectively 'these actors enter direct interactions with each other to initiate and realize commercial transactions', 'the marketplace platform provides an institutional and regulatory frame for transactions' and 'the marketplace does not substantially produce or trade products or services itself', indicates a digital marketplace is a transaction platform. Hence, multi-sided platforms without clear transactions between the users (e.g., YouTube) or intermediating non-P2P markets (e.g., Amazon) are not considered digital marketplaces.

The definition of P2P sharing and collaborative consumption platform by [16] also has four conditions. The first condition 'individuals can assume the role of a peer-provider on the platform' translates to the P2P value for the participation attribute. For the second and third condition, respectively 'peer-providers can offer physical resources on the platform' and 'access to a resource is granted temporarily', we rely on [35] stating that an offering can be placed on a continuous scale between product-oriented and result-oriented. Product-oriented offerings are geared towards sales of products, while in result-oriented offerings the provider is selling a result or competence, by offering a mix of services. In the middle of this continuum are the user-oriented offerings consisting of product leasing, renting, sharing and pooling [42], which is the case for the definition P2P sharing and collaborative consumption platforms by [16]. The last condition, 'Peer-consumers can search for resources offered by peer-providers', means a decentralized market following the frameworks of [7, 33]. In a decentralized market, the platform exercises little control for exchanges beyond matchmaking. The provider sets the price and the customer can search for the right provider. In a centralized market, on the other hand, the platform provides access to a centralized resource pool and has a strong influence on the interactions between users by assigning matches and setting dynamic and time-related prices. To conclude, the P2P sharing and collaborative consumption platform type includes platforms where customers can search and rent physical resources (in combination with other services) from their peers. This type includes platforms such as Airbnb for home renting, BlaBlaCar for carpooling, and Sharedesk to book a working spot.

The basic concept of an on-demand platform, as defined by [32], is 'immediately and effectively access to a product and service' with Uber as main example. Uber is clearly operating in a centralized market, also known as a matchmaker [43], where the platform management acts as a brokering service offering and facilitating transactions between providers and customers [43]. Secondly, an on-demand platform is part of the (immediate) access economy described by [37] as 'offering customers access to a product and service where and when the customer needs it, and this can be straight away'.

A second-hand P2P platform as mentioned by [9] is a decentralized, product-oriented digital marketplace, as it facilitates the searching and sales of used products between peers. An example is Carousell, a platform to resell used goods.

The definition most used for 'sharing economy' is the one by [31]: "Consumers granting each other temporary access to under-utilized physical assets (idle capacity), possibly for money." A typical example of a platform operating in the sharing economy is Couchsurfing, where private persons rent out temporarily vacant accommodation (under-utilized physical good) to other private persons (C2C) for an agreed upon number of days (temporary access). It includes the six affordances of sharing economy by [7] (generating flexibility, matchmaking, extending reach, transaction management, trust, and facilitating collectivity). In this paper we consider a sharing economy platform by [31] as a platform where all transactions operate in the sharing economy. This is equal to the already discussed P2P sharing and collaborative consumption platform of [16], but with under-utilized products offered and consumed by private persons (i.e., C2C specialization of P2P).

5   Reference Ontology

In this paper we only discuss the first module of our ontology. The reference ontology describes the functionality of a general digital platform and of each digital platform type in relation to their attribute values defined in the taxonomy. The entities of our ontology modelled in OntoUML can come from three UFO sub-ontologies: UFO-A, an ontology of objects (indicated in red in Fig. 3), UFO-B, an ontology of events (in yellow) and UFO-C, an ontology of social entities with the power to connect entities built on top of UFO-A and UFO-B (in green). A 'type' entity (indicated in purple) is used to categorize user roles [44], like Airbnb homeseeker, Airbnb homeowner, and Uber Eats rider.

Based on the working definition in Sect. 3, we define general digital platform requirements as a basis for the general ontology module. We recall that a service offering has to implement these requirements in order to be qualified as a digital platform. The general digital platform requirements are partly derived from UFO-S [22], a core ontology grounded in UFO that provides a clear account of services and service-related concepts. Because a digital platform is a service offering to its users, and users can also offer services (and products) through the digital platform, it is convenient to reuse UFO-S concepts and relations to model the ontology patterns of a digital platform. Also, reuse is pointed out as a promising approach for ontology engineering, since it enables speeding up the ontology development process [45]. In UFO-S, a service offer event results in the establishment of a service offering between a service provider and a target customer community [22], from which we derive the following two requirements for a digital platform:

1. A digital platform is a service offering [22]
2. This service offering is offered by a digital platform management towards a certain 'target platform user community' consisting of 'target platform users'.

The following requirements come from the literature and are confirmed by the instances of our sample:

3. This service offering is enabled by software [10]
4. This service offering includes platform supported interaction between the users [1]

Figure 3 shows the general ontology module for our digital platform reference ontology. The detailed rationale for the design of this ontology module out of (specialized)

UFO-S ontology patterns, cannot be explained within the scope of this paper. Instead, we provide a general account of how this ontology model can be read, followed by an example of how it can be used to describe existing digital platforms.

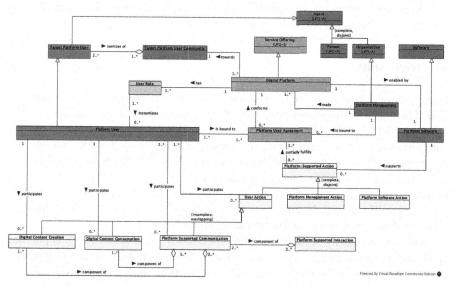

Fig. 3. General digital platform ontology module (Color figure online)

The green part of Fig. 3 shows that a digital platform is a service offering. Moving to the red part, we see that this service offering is made by the company managing the platform (i.e., 'platform management') to a target platform user community. These targeted users can be organisations or private persons. The digital platform is enabled by running platform software that supports different kinds of actions. Moving to the yellow part of Fig. 3, we see that these platform-supported actions are divided into user actions, platform management actions, and platform software actions. In this general digital platform ontology module, the focus is on the user actions as they clarify the functionality that a digital platform offers to platform users. The most basic user actions are digital content creation (e.g., sending a message) and consumption (e.g., receiving a message). When both creation and consumption take place, we talk about a communication action. To fulfil the fourth requirement of a digital platform, the platform software must allow interactions, which is communication of two (or more) users in at least two directions (e.g., sending, receiving, replying, receiving).

A digital platform can have different user roles (in purple) that allow defining distinct user groups, with distinct user actions, but in the most general sense of digital platform, all users have equal participation rights (e.g., WhatsApp). Notice however, that depending on the type and related attribute values of our taxonomy, a digital platform can distinguish between actions allowed for different user groups. For example, depending on the affiliation, a user of a certain type is able to register, subscribe, make transactions and/or invest using the software. The moment a user is affiliated with the digital platform, a platform user agreement that defines the allowed actions (in green, middle of Fig. 3) comes into existence (even if this agreement may be tacit).

The requirements per attribute value and their related ontology modules are work in progress and can be found under following link[2]. The reference ontology has to conceptualize a common understanding of the digital platform domain. As this domain and common understanding evolves, so will the ontology.

6 Discussion

Our typology, based on a taxonomy of attributes and attribute values that characterise digital platforms, distinguishes nine types of digital platform, which contributes towards a better understanding of the platform domain. We acknowledge that this typology is a simplification (or stated more positively, a research abstraction), that does not take into account the full complexity of the digital platform domain. Further, the typology only includes types for which instances exist given the current state of the domain. As this domain is in constant state of change, the typology needs to be corrected and enlarged accordingly. This is exactly why the typology is based on a taxonomy, which provides a more robust structure for defining digital platform types.

Another complexity in the digital platform domain is that different digital platform types are starting to merge, combining providers of different sorts on one platform for a single offering. An example is meal delivery platforms such as Deliveroo and Uber Eats, which include a combination of two digital platform types. First, the meals are offered by the restaurants who can set the price themselves and offer them compliant with a decentralized digital marketplace. Afterwards, a customer orders the meal using the platform, an on-demand platform mechanism comes into place and the meal is delivered by (bike) deliverers at a price/cost set by the platform. Another example is a travel platform as described in [46], where multiple assets, goods and services (including accommodation, car, activities, guide and driver) by different providers can be combined as one offering on the platform. These combinations of platforms are also called hybrid platforms [33] or integrated platforms [10], allowing more than one provider and different platform types for one offering. As shown by these examples, the typology can help to analyse such evolutions by classifying digital platforms according to the distinctive features of the platform types that are included.

Our reference ontology on the other hand can help comprehend the complexity and functionality of each digital platform type (or combination), and support ontology-driven development of platforms. A better understanding of the functionality can help to create such platforms in a fast and efficient way, with clear terminology to improve the communication and decision-making between the stakeholders.

7 Conclusion

In this paper, we contribute to addressing two research gaps in the digital platform domain. The first gap is the lack of shared conceptualization of digital platform types.

---

[2] http://model-a-platform.com/digital-platform-ontology-2/.

Many platform types, including sharing economy platform, on-demand platform and multi-sided platform, are buzz words, used a lot in both academic and professional communities but without consensus on what they comprise. To solve this issue, we created a taxonomy and typology for digital platforms based on both existing literature and an empirical sample. The taxonomy gives an overview of digital platform attributes, with attribute values expressing the possible variations between digital platforms depending on their type. These attributes and attribute values are than used in the typology giving a clear overview of all the digital platform types and how these types are related. With the help of these artefacts, researchers and practitioners can improve their communication and improve the comparability of future studies. This includes the comparability of research using the same digital platform type name but with a different meaning (e.g., sharing economy by [13, 31]). We also discussed our method based on [15] on how to improve these artefacts when new types arise to keep a good overview in this fast-changing and complex domain of digital platforms.

The second gap this paper tackles is the lack of knowledge concerning the software functionalities of digital platforms. The reference ontology proposed in this paper can help with this issue as it describes the general functionality of any digital platform. This reference ontology is based on UFO [20], a high-level ontology that provides us with basic concepts for objects, events, social elements and relations and modelled in OntoUML [25], an ontology-driven conceptual modelling language capable of representing these concepts. At this point the more specific functionality of each digital platform type in relation to its attribute values as defined in the taxonomy is under construction. In future research we plan to fully develop an ontology module for each attribute value in our taxonomy. First, we will verify the syntactic correctness of the ontology representation using the OntoUML plugin for Visual Paradigm[3]. Second, these modules will be validated by ontology experts to make sure our ontology is correctly modelled. And third, we plan to validate the platform domain knowledge in our ontology (modules) by applying the ontology to a selection of existing digital platforms in our sample by combining the modules as building blocks. Eventually, the envisioned reference ontology can improve the common language that all sharing economy stakeholders can use to facilitate future research and development of digital platforms.

References

1. Kenney, M., Zysman, J.: The rise of the platform economy. Issues Sci. Technol. **32**, 61–69 (2016)
2. Ranjbari, M., Morales-Alonso, G., Carrasco-Gallego, R.: Conceptualizing the sharing economy through presenting a comprehensive framework. Sustainability **10**, 2336 (2018)
3. Görög, G.: The definitions of sharing economy: a systematic literature review. Management **13**, 175–189 (2018)
4. Puschmann, T., Alt, R.: Sharing economy. Bus. Inf. Syst. Eng. **58**, 93–99 (2016)
5. Trabucchi, D., Buganza, T.: Fostering digital platform innovation: from two to multi-sided platforms. Creat. Innov. Manage. **1**, 14 (2019)
6. Hagiu, A., Wright, J.: Multi-sided platforms. Int. J. Ind. Organ. **43**, 1–32 (2015)

---

[3] https://github.com/OntoUML/ontouml-vp-plugin.

7. Sutherland, W., Jarrahi, M.H.: The sharing economy and digital platforms: a review and research agenda. Int. J. Inf. Manage. **43**, 328–341 (2018)

8. Sanchez-Cartas, J.M., Leon, G.: Multi-sided platforms and markets: a literature review. SSRN Electron. J., 1–62 (2019)

9. Acquier, A., Daudigeos, T., Pinkse, J.: Promises and paradoxes of the sharing economy: an organizing framework. Technol. Forecast. Soc. Change. **125**, 1–10 (2017)

10. Evans, P.C., Gawer, A.: The rise of the platform enterprise: a global survey (2016)

11. Ertz, M., Durif, F., Arcand, M.: Collaborative consumption: conceptual snapshot at a buzzword. J. Entrep. Educ. **19**, 1–23 (2016)

12. Wieringa, R.: What is a platform. https://www.thevalueengineers.nl/what-is-a-platform/

13. Yin, C., Wang, X., Rong, W., Wang, T., David, B.: A system framework for sharing economy. In: Proceedings 2018 IEEE 22nd International Conference on Computer Supported Cooperative Work in Design, CSCWD 2018, pp. 779–784 (2018)

14. Codagnone, C., Biagi, F., Abadie, F.: The passions and the interests: unpacking the "Sharing Economy" (2016)

15. Nickerson, R.C., Varshney, U., Muntermann, J.: A method for taxonomy development and its application in information systems. Eur. J. Inf. Syst. **22**, 336–359 (2013)

16. Chasin, F., Hoffen, M., Cramer, M., Matzner, M.: Peer-to-peer sharing and collaborative consumption platforms: a taxonomy and a reproducible analysis. Inf. Syst. e-Bus. Manage. **16**(2), 293–325 (2017). https://doi.org/10.1007/s10257-017-0357-8

17. Haas, P., Blohm, I., Leimeister, J.M.: An empirical taxonomy of crowdfunding intermediaries. In: 35th International Conference on Information System "Building a Better World Through Information System", ICIS 2014, pp. 1–18 (2014)

18. Etikan, I.: Comparison of convenience sampling and purposive sampling. Am. J. Theor. Appl. Stat. **5**, 1 (2016)

19. Carvalho, V.A., Almeida, J.P.A.: Toward a well-founded theory for multi-level conceptual modeling. Softw. Syst. Model. **17**(1), 205–231 (2016). https://doi.org/10.1007/s10270-016-0538-9

20. Guizzardi, G.: Ontological foundations for structural conceptual models (2005)

21. OntoText: What are Ontologies? https://www.ontotext.com/knowledgehub/fundamentals/what-are-ontologies/

22. Nardi, J.C., et al.: A commitment-based reference ontology for services. Inf. Syst. **54**, 263–288 (2015)

23. Ruy, F.B., Guizzardi, G., Falbo, R.A., Reginato, C.C., Santos, V.A.: From reference ontologies to ontology patterns and back. Data Knowl. Eng. **109**, 41–69 (2017)

24. de Almeida Falbo, R.: SABiO: systematic approach for building ontologies. In: CEUR Workshop Proceedings, vol. 1301 (2014)

25. Guizzardi, G., Fonseca, C.M., Benevides, A.B., João Paulo, A., Almeida, D.P., Sales, T.P.: Endurant types in ontology-driven conceptual modeling: towards ontoUML 2.0. In: Trujillo, J.C., et al. (ed.) ER 2018. LNCS, vol. 11157, pp. 136–150. Springer, Cham (2018). https://doi.org/10.1007/978-3-030-00847-5_12

26. Oh, S., Moon, J.Y.: Calling for a shared understanding of the "sharing economy", pp. 1–5 (2016)

27. Täuscher, K., Laudien, S.M.: Understanding platform business models: a mixed methods study of marketplaces. Eur. Manage. J. **36**(3), 319–329 (2018). https://doi.org/10.1016/j.emj.2017.06.005

28. Wu, L.: Understanding collaborative consumption business model: case of car sharing systems. DEStech Trans. Mater. Sci. Eng., 403–409 (2017)

29. Apte, U.M., Davis, M.M.: Sharing economy services: business model generation. Calif. Manage. Rev. **61**, 104–131 (2019)

30. Nguyen, S., Llosa, S.: On the difficulty to define the sharing economy and collaborative consumption–literature review and proposing a different approach with the introduction of "collaborative services." Journée la Relat. à la Marque dans un Monde Connect., 19–25 (2018)
31. Frenken, K., Schor, J.: Putting the sharing economy into perspective. Environ. Innov. Soc. Trans. **23**, 3–10 (2017)
32. Mamonova, Y.: Sharing economy vs. on-demand economy: the major differences. https://ikajo.com/blog/sharing-economy-on-demand-economy-differences
33. Acquier, A., Carbone, V., Massé, D.: How to create value(s) in the sharing economy: business models scalability, and sustainability. Technol. Innov. Manag. Rev. **9**(5), 25 (2019)
34. Ehikioya, S.A.: A formal model of peer-to-peer digital product marketplace. Int. J. Netw. Distrib. Comput. **6**, 143–154 (2018)
35. Ritter, M., Schanz, H.: The sharing economy: a comprehensive business model framework. J. Clean. Prod. **213**, 320–331 (2019)
36. Andersson, M., Hjalmarsson, A., Avital, M.: Peer-to-peer service sharing platforms: driving share and share alike on a mass-scale. In: Proceeding of the 34th International Conference on Information Systems, vol. 4, pp. 2964–2978 (2013)
37. Gobble, M.A.M.: Defining the sharing economy. Res. Technol. Manag. **60**, 59–61 (2017)
38. Rochet, J., Tirole, J.: Platform competition in two-sided markets. J. Eur. Econ. Assoc. **1**, 990–1029 (2001)
39. Hepp, M.: GoodRelations: an ontology for describing products and services offers on the web. In: Gangemi, A., Euzenat, J. (eds.) EKAW 2008. LNCS (LNAI), vol. 5268, pp. 329–346. Springer, Heidelberg (2008). https://doi.org/10.1007/978-3-540-87696-0_29
40. Burtch, G., Ghose, A., Wattal, S.: An empirical examination of the antecedents and consequences of attitudes tow. Inf. Syst. Res. **24**, 499–519 (2013)
41. Kickstarter: Our mission is to help bring creative projects to life. https://www.kickstarter.com/about?ref=global-footer
42. Tukker, A.: Eight types of product-service system: eight ways to sustainability? Exp. Suspronet. Bus. Strateg. Environ. **13**, 246–260 (2004)
43. Hafermalz, E., Boell, S.K., Elliot, S., Hovorka, D., Marjanovic, O.: Exploring dimensions of sharing economy business models enabled by IS: an Australian study. In: Australasian Conference on Information Systems, pp. 1–11 (2016)
44. Carvalho, V.A., Almeida, J.P.A., Fonseca, C.M., Guizzardi, G.: Extending the foundations of ontology-based conceptual modeling with a multi-level theory. In: Johannesson, P., Lee, M.L., Liddle, S.W., Opdahl, A.L., López, Ó.P. (eds.) ER 2015. LNCS, vol. 9381, pp. 119–133. Springer, Cham (2015). https://doi.org/10.1007/978-3-319-25264-3_9
45. Ruy, F.B., Reginato, C.C., Santos, V.A., Falbo, R.A., Guizzardi, G.: Ontology engineering by combining ontology patterns. In: Johannesson, P., Lee, M.L., Liddle, S.W., Opdahl, A.L., López, Ó.P. (eds.) ER 2015. LNCS, vol. 9381, pp. 173–186. Springer, Cham (2015). https://doi.org/10.1007/978-3-319-25264-3_13
46. Derave, T.: A reference architecture for customizable marketplaces. In: Guizzardi, G., Gailly, F., Maciel, R.S.P. (eds.) ER 2019. LNCS, vol. 11787, pp. 222–229. Springer, Cham (2019). https://doi.org/10.1007/978-3-030-34146-6_20

Microservice Remodularisation of Monolithic Enterprise Systems for Embedding in Industrial IoT Networks

Adambarage Anuruddha Chathuranga De Alwis[1]([✉]) [ID], Alistair Barros[1] [ID],
Colin Fidge[1] [ID], and Artem Polyvyanyy[2] [ID]

[1] Queensland University of Technology, Brisbane, Australia
{adambarage.dealwis,alistair.barros,c.fidge}@qut.edu.au
[2] The University of Melbourne, Parkville, VIC, Australia
artem.polyvyanyy@unimelb.edu.au

Abstract. This paper addresses the challenge of decoupling "back-office" enterprise system functions in order to integrate them with the Industrial Internet-of-Things (IIoT). IIoT is a widely anticipated strategy, combining IoT technologies managing physical object movements, interactions and contexts, with business contexts. However, enterprise systems, supporting these contexts, are notoriously large and monolithic, and coordinate centralised business processes through software components dedicated to managing business objects (BOs). Such objects and their associated operations are difficult to manually decouple because of the asynchronous and user-driven nature of the business processes and complex BO dependencies, such as many-to-many and aggregation relationships. Here we present a software remodularisation technique for enterprise systems, to support the discovery of fine-grained microservices, which can be extracted and embedded to run on IIoT network nodes. It combines the semantic knowledge of enterprise systems, i.e., the BO structure, with syntactic knowledge of the code, i.e., various dependencies at the level of classes and methods. Using extracted feature sets based on both semantic and syntactic dependencies, K-Means clustering and optimisation is then used to recommend microservices, i.e., redistributions of BO operations through microservices from BO-centric components of enterprise systems. The approach is validated using the Dolibarr open source ERP system, in which we identify processes comprising both "edge" operations and request-response calls to the Cloud-based enterprise system. Through experimentation using Amazon Green-Grass deployments, simulating IIoT nodes, we show that the recommended microservices demonstrate key non-functional characteristics, of high execution efficiency, scalability and availability.

Keywords: Microservice discovery · System remodularisation · Cloud migration

© Springer Nature Switzerland AG 2021
M. La Rosa et al. (Eds.): CAiSE 2021, LNCS 12751, pp. 432–448, 2021.
https://doi.org/10.1007/978-3-030-79382-1_26

1   Introduction

The Industrial Internet of Things (IIoT) is widely expected to transform automation processes of construction, manufacturing, utilities and other asset-intense sectors through the real-time integration of physical environments and enterprise systems. Under the IoT, physical object movements, interactions and contexts are tracked and controlled through sensors and actuators, and data is transceived, via gateways, with Cloud systems providing intelligent analytics. The IIoT extends the scope of coordination to business contexts, where the processes, rules and data of enterprise systems are opened up through IoT devices and contexts. Examples from construction [25] include: real-time tracking of physical construction/assembly work against production schedules and constraints (e.g., time allocation, stock use, wastage and budget impact); automatic re-ordering of products, in-situ, subject to stock threshold levels and supplier contract conditions; and automatic "wayfinding" of new stock to demand points on large sites. Such examples require that software components of enterprise systems be integrated with, and partially embedded to run on, IIoT nodes, to support low-latency, real-time processing. In addition, IoT (and thus IIoT) networks have recently been endowed with distributed computing tiers, through developments in Fog computing. As such, IIoT nodes support processors, designated as the master, worker and edge nodes, each of which can host and run parts of systems. This means, an enterprise system could have its parts simultaneously deployed to run across the nexus of Cloud and IIoT nodes while being connected to other distributed processes [18].

However, major uncertainty exists as to how microservices, compatible with IIoT, can be created by decoupling and reusing parts of existing enterprise systems. This is essential to preserve continuity with, and exploit the large investment in, enterprise systems that have been developed over many years. Such systems [2] manage thousands of inter-dependent BOs, across a multitude of software packages and support asynchronous and unstructured business processes [3–5]. For example, an order-to-cash process in SAP ERP has multiple sales orders, with deliveries shared across many customers, shared containers in transportation carriers, and multiple invoices and payments, processed before or after delivery [6]. This poses challenges for identifying fine-grained, modular tasks, to implement as IIoT-based microservices.

Microservices must exhibit high cohesion, low coupling, object encapsulation and composability, as per basic modularisation principles [7–9]. Applied to enterprise systems, they provide subsets of BO create, read, update and delete operations (corresponding to decomposed business tasks). Microservices should also improve the scalability, availability (resilience) and execution efficiency of the overall system [1]. Therefore, an efficient re-distribution of BO operations is required from existing enterprise systems components, reflecting these properties. Specifically, highly dependent operations of a BO need to be combined into highly scalable, available and efficient microservices, while the business processes, across existing enterprise systems and newly introduced microservices, must still execute correctly.

Software remodularisation techniques have been proposed to scan different aspects of systems, extract relevant structural and behavioural feature sets, and recommend new modules using multi-objective optimisation. They have focussed on a system's code implementation, or syntactic properties, through two areas of coupling and cohesion evaluation. The first is structural coupling and cohesion [7], involving structural relationships between the software classes in the same or in different components. These include structural inheritance relationships between classes and structural interaction relationships resulting when one class creates another class and uses an object reference to invoke its methods. The structural relationships are automatically profiled through Module Dependency Graphs (MDG), capturing classes as nodes and structural relationships as edges [8], and are used to cluster classes using K-means, Hill-climbing, and other clustering algorithms. The second form is structural class similarity [9] based on information retrieval (IR) techniques, for source code comparison of classes. Relevant terms are extracted from the classes and used for latent semantic indexing and cosine comparison to calculate similarity values between them.

Nonetheless, despite many proposals for automated analysis of systems, studies show that the success rate of software remodularisation remains low given the limited insights available from purely syntactic structures [10].

More recently, semantic knowledge available through BOs of enterprise systems has been exploited to improve the feasibility of applications' architectural analysis [13]. Our previous research on MS discovery from enterprise systems for cloud deployments, involving analysis of source code and systems logs, similarly exploits knowledge of BO relationships [14,15]. This was based on class-level feature set extractions for software remodularisation analysis: structural inheritance relationships (class supertypes and subtypes), structural interaction relationships (class level creations and invocations), structural class similarity (intra-class level), and class semantic properties (class and BO dependencies for BOs managed through classes). However, for the highly distributed context of the IIoT, more fine-grained dependency analysis is critical and must be at the level of individual methods (i.e., operations of classes).

Here we present a novel combination of syntactic and semantic remodularisation analysis techniques. It applies both static (source code) and dynamic (event log) analysis to extract crucial dependencies between classes of components, between classes and BOs, and between BOs, and uses these insights to reason more reliably about fine-grained, remodularisation and effective distribution at the level of class methods for IIoT applications. It uses the following feature set extractions: method interactions (intra- and inter-class), method similarity (intra-method level), and method semantic properties (method and BO dependencies for BOs manipulated through SQL statements in methods). Recommended clusters of operations for creating microservices are based on subsets of BO operations.

We validated the technique using an open-source Enterprise Resource Planning system, Dolibarr. Amazon Greengrass was used for testing the recommended microservices for the required non-functional properties of high scalability, availability and execution efficiency. Greengrass nodes were used as IIoT nodes to host and run the test microservices. The microservices then ran business processes involving BO operations and made request-response calls to corresponding BO components in Dolibarr.

The remainder of the paper is structured as follows. Section 2 describes the related works and background on system remodularisation techniques. Section 3 provides a detailed description of our microservice discovery approach while Sect. 4 describes its implementation and evaluation. Section 5 discusses the outcomes and possible future work. The paper concludes with Sect. 6.

2   Background and Motivation

This section provides details of existing software remodularisation and reengineering techniques while comparing their relative strengths and weaknesses. We then give an overview of the architectural context of enterprise systems and their alignments with microservices for the IIoT. This context is assumed in the presentation of our software remodularisation techniques in Sect. 3.

2.1   Related Work and Techniques Used for Software Remodularisation

Software remodularisation techniques have been introduced to analyse different facets of systems, including software structure, behaviour, functional requirements, and non-functional requirements. They focus on the behavioural and structural aspects of software systems. The static analysis applies to code structure and the database schemas of software systems while dynamic analysis involves the mining of systems logs for method invocations occurring at run time. Both of these techniques can be used to provide complementary details in the system remodularisation process.

Traditional static analysis techniques are used to remodularise software systems in order to improve the coupling and cohesion of system modules. These are based on structural interaction relationships between classes and object reference relationships between classes resulting when one class creates another class and uses an object reference to invoke its methods [7]. These relationships are profiled through Module Dependency Graphs (MDG) while capturing classes as nodes and structural relationships as edges [7,8]. They are used to cluster methods using K-means, Hill-climbing, NSGA II and other clustering algorithms. Some other techniques were developed to evaluate class-level relationships by considering their conceptual similarity using information retrieval (IR) techniques [9].

However, given the code's complexity and the semantic complexity of the structural interaction relationships, such analyses are not enough. As such structural method similarity (i.e., *conceptual similarity*) [9] was introduced to capture semantic similarities between methods using information retrieval (IR) techniques. This technique compares methods under the assumption that similarly named variables, object references, etc., infer conceptual similarity of methods. The extracted terms from methods are used for latent semantic indexing and cosine comparison to calculate the similarity values between them.

Despite many proposals for automated analysis of systems, studies show that the success rate of software remodularisation remains low [10]. One of the major reasons for this is the limited insights available from purely structural system analysis which only focuses on the systems' source code. Recent research shows that the semantic insights available through BO relationships provide information regarding the systems' behavioural aspects and these can be exploited to improve the feasibility of applications' architectural analysis. Enterprise systems manage domain-specific information using BOs, through their databases and business processes [4]. Evaluating such BO relationships and deriving useful insights from them to remodularise software systems falls under the category of *semantic structural relationships* analysis. Such semantic relationships are highlighted by Pĕrez-Castillo *et al.*'s experiments [12], in which the transitive closure of strong BO dependencies derived from databases was used to recommend software function hierarchies, and by Lu *et al.*'s experiments [13], in which SAP ERP logs were used to demonstrate process discovery based on BOs. Also, our own previous research on microservice discovery based on BO relationship evaluation [14,15] showed the impact of considering semantic structural relationships in software remodularisation.

However, to date, techniques related to semantic structural relationships have not been integrated with static syntactic techniques at the method level. As a result, currently proposed design recommendation tools provide insufficient insights for software remodularisation targeting IIoT applications.

2.2 Architecture for Enterprise System to Microservice Remodularisation

In this section, we define the importance of considering the different factors detailed in Sect. 2.1 with respect to the architectural configuration of an enterprise system and related microservices in an IIoT network, underpinned by "fog" nodes in which much of the computation is done on "edge" devices. In order to provide a clear understanding of the structural complexity and behavioural implications of combining an enterprise system with an IIoT network, consider Fig. 1, in which the current and future process states are depicted. Current-state processes, typically triggered by user actions, involve interactions through the methods of the enterprise system only. Future-state processes cover both a central enterprise system and its MSs deployed in the IIoT Network.

Figure 1 shows a central administration process for a construction/manufacturing scenario involving Production Management lists for Users (workers) which refer to Products being assembled and Reports for auditing and risk detection. It also includes Orders for faulty parts listed in Order Lines. In the future-state processes, some operations of the Production Management, Product Management and Report Management components are decoupled as microservices and embedded in a physical environment so that real-time and low-latency scheduling, checking, reporting and risk detection is enabled. This use case is inspired by Oswald *et al.*'s business analysis [16].

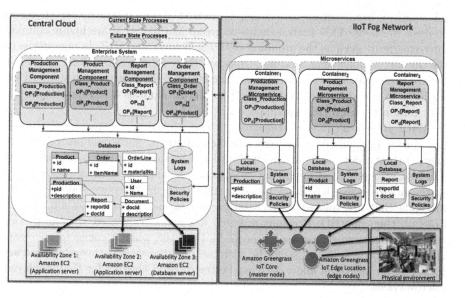

Fig. 1. Overview of an enterprise system extended with extracted microservices.

The internal structure of the enterprise system consists of a set of self-contained modules related to advance manufacturing drawn from different subsystems and is deployed on a "backend". Each module is a combination of software classes that contain methods that manage one or more BOs through create, read, update and delete (CRUD) operations. These methods guide the system's execution through method calls between different classes in the same module or in different modules. For example, operation '$OP_1[Production]$' references an external method '$OP_1[Product]$' of the 'Product Management Module' through an object reference call and '$OP_1[Report]$' references an internal method in the 'Report Management Module' which calls '$OP_m[]$' in the same class. Execution of these methods generates system logs and the security of the modules and the system is governed through the security policies defined.

The microservices each support a subset of methods through classes that are specifically related to individual BOs, as depicted in Fig. 1. This results in high cohesion within microservices and low coupling between the microservices. The microservices communicate with each other and with the enterprise system through API calls. Execution of methods across the enterprise system and microservices is coordinated through business processes, which means that invocations of methods in the enterprise system will trigger methods on microservices by passing parameters required by the microservices' APIs. Data consistency of different microservice databases and the enterprise system's database is achieved via regular synchronisation.

Based on this understanding of the structure of the enterprise system and its microservices, it is apparent why we must consider both semantic and syntactic information for our microservice discovery process. To capture the method call relationships in the enterprise system, we need *structural interaction relationship* analysis methods. This analysis helps to group methods that are highly coupled into one group, such as the grouping of '$OP_1[Report]$' and '$OP_m[]$' operations in the 'Report Management Module'. However, those relationships alone would not help to capture method similarities at the code level. To capture such similarities, we have to use the structural method similarity analysis techniques based on information retrieval (IR) techniques.

With *structural method relationships* and *structural method similarity* we can cluster methods into different modules. However, such modules might not align with the domain relationships until we consider the BO relationships of different methods. It is important to consider *semantic structural relationships* in the microservice derivation process, since each microservice should contain methods that are related to each other and should perform method invocations on the same BO. Previous research has extensively used *structural relationships* in system remodularisation [7–9]. However, when it comes to microservice derivation, combining *semantic structural relationships* with *syntactic structural relationships* will allow deriving better method clusters for IIoT deployed microservices.

3   Clustering Recommendation for Microservice Discovery

In order to derive IIoT-based microservices while considering the factors defined in Sect. 2, we developed a five-step approach, as illustrated in Fig. 2. In Step 1, we derive the BOs by evaluating the SQL queries in the source code structure and also the database schemas and data as described by Nooijen *et al.* [17]. In Step 2, we identify the semantic structural relationships by deriving the method and BO relationships. Steps 3 and 4 are used to discover the syntactic details related to the enterprise system. In Step 3, we measure the structural method similarities between methods in the same class and in different classes, and in Step 4 we capture the structural interaction relationships between different methods. The details obtained through Steps 2 to 4 are used in Step 5 where a K-means clustering algorithm is used to evaluate and recommend effective combinations of methods for IIoT-based microservice deployment. These steps are described further in Sect. 3.1.

3.1   Clustering Discovery Algorithms

As depicted in Fig. 2, we supply a K-means algorithm with three main feature sets to derive a satisfactory clustering of system methods and suggest microservice designs. To derive these sets, we use Algorithm 1, which is composed of eight steps. We use the following formalisation here onwards to describe the algorithm.

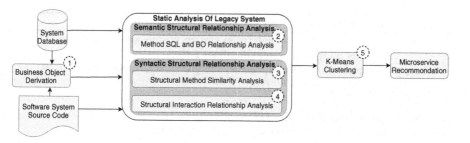

Fig. 2. Overview of our microservice discovery approach.

Let $\mathbb{I}$, $\mathbb{O}$, $\mathbb{OP}$, $\mathbb{B}$, $\mathbb{T}$ and $\mathbb{A}$ be a universe of *input* types, *output* types, *operations*, *BOs*, *database tables* and *attributes* respectively. We characterise a *database table* $t \in \mathbb{T}$ by a collection of attributes, i.e., $t \subseteq \mathbb{A}$, while a *business object* $b \in \mathbb{B}$ is defined as a collection of database tables, i.e., $b \subseteq \mathbb{T}$. An *operation/method* op, either of an enterprise system or microservice system, is given as a triple (I, O, T), where $I \in \mathbb{I}^*$ is a sequence of *input types* the operation expects for input, $O \in \mathbb{O}^*$ is a sequence of *output types* the operation produces as output, and $T \subseteq \mathbb{T}$ is a set of *database tables* the operation accesses, i.e., either reads or augments.[1] Each *class* $cls \in CLS$ is defined as a collection of operations/methods, i.e., $cls \subseteq \mathbb{OP}$.

The *BOS* function in Algorithm 1 is used to derive BOs B from enterprise systems as detailed by Nooijen *et al.* [17] (line 1). In the second step of the algorithm, function *CLSEXT* is used to extract code related to each class $cls \in CLS$ from the system code by searching through its folder and package structure (line 2). The extracted classes CLS are provided to the next step of the algorithm which uses the *MTDEXT* function to extracts the methods related to these classes (line 3). This step extracts the methods and the comments related to each method into separate text files and saves them for further processing.

	Product	Order	Inventory	Purchase	Shipment	Customer	Budget	Tax
Method 1	0	3	0	5	0	0	1	0
Method 2	3	0	0	7	0	0	0	0
Method 3	0	0	0	0	6	0	0	0
Method 4	5	7	0	0	0	0	0	0
Method 5	0	0	6	0	0	7	0	0
Method 6	0	0	0	0	7	0	0	0
Method 7	1	0	0	0	0	0	0	0
Method 8	0	0	0	0	0	0	0	0

Fig. 3. Example word matrix extracted from program code (*mtduwcount* in Algorithm 1).

In the fourth step, we rely on the information required for structural method similarity analysis using information retrieval (IR) techniques. As such, in the

---

[1] A^* denotes application of the Kleene star operation to set A.

Algorithm 1: Discovery of BO and method relationships

Input: System code SC of an enterprise system s, stop words related to
      methods STW and system database DB

Output: Feature set data $borel$, $cosine$, $subtyperel$, $referencerel$ and BOs B

1 $B = \{b_1, \ldots, b_n\} := BOS(SC, DB)$
2 $CLS = \{cls_1, \ldots, cls_m\} := CLSEXT(SC)$
3 $MTD = \{mtd_1, \ldots, mtd_m\} := MTDEXT(CLS)$
4 $UW = \langle uw_1, \ldots, uw_z \rangle := UWORDEXT(MTD, STW)$
5 **for each** $mtd_i \in MTD$ **do**
6   **for each** $b_k \in B$ **do**
7 | $mtdborel[i][k] := BCOUNT(mtd_i, b_k);$
8   **end**
9   **for each** $uw_s \in UW$ **do**
10 | $mtduwcount[i][s] := WCOUNT(uw_s, mtd_i);$
11   **end**
12 **end**
13 **for each** $mtd_i, mtd_k \in MTD$ **do**
14 | $mtdcosine[i][k] := MTDCOSINECAL(mtduwcount[i], mtduwcount[k]);$
15 **end**
16 $mtdrel := MTDRELCAL(MTD);$
17 **return** $CLS, MTD, mtdborel, mtdcosine, mtdrel, B$

---

third step, the algorithm identifies unique words UW related to all the methods using function $UWORDEXT$ (line 3), which requires all the source codes of the methods MTD, and stop words STW, which should be filtered out from the methods. In general, IR techniques analyse documents and filter out the contents that do not provide any valuable information for document analysis, referred to as 'stop words'. In our case, the stop words (STW) contain syntax related to the methods, standard technical terms used in coding in that particular programming language (in our case PHP) and common English words that would not provide any specific insight into a method's purpose. These are specified by the user based on the system's programming language. Function $UWORDEXT$ first filters out the stop words STW from the methods MTD and then identifies the collection of unique words UW in methods MTD as a 'bag of words' [19]. This produces a collection of non-repeating words as depicted by the column names in the example in Fig. 3.

	BO1	BO2	BO3
Mtd 1	1	3	0
Mtd 2	0	3	0
Mtd 3	0	2	0
Mtd 4	1	0	3
Mtd 5	4	0	0

(a) mtdborel

	Mtd 1	Mtd 2	Mtd 3	Mtd 4	Mtd 5
Mtd 1	1	0.75	0.83	0.44	0.05
Mtd 2	0.75	1	0.65	0.51	0.02
Mtd 3	0.83	0.65	1	0.53	0.03
Mtd 4	0.44	0.51	0.53	1	0.12
Mtd 5	0.05	0.02	0.03	0.12	1

(b) mtdcosine

	Mtd 1	Mtd 2	Mtd 3	Mtd 4	Mtd 5
Mtd 1	1	1	0	0	0
Mtd 2	1	1	0	0	0
Mtd 3	1	0	1	1	0
Mtd 4	0	1	1	1	0
Mtd 5	0	0	0	1	1

(c) mtdrel

Fig. 4. Examples of matrices derived from code using Algorithm 1 ($mtdborel$, $mtdcosine$ and $mtdrel$).

In the fifth step, the algorithm evaluates each method $mtd \in MTD$ extracted in the third step and identifies the BOs which are related to each method. For this purpose, the algorithm uses function $BCOUNT$ which processes the SQL statements, comments and method names and counts the number of times tables relating to BOs appear in the methods. This information is stored in matrix $mtdborel$ (lines 5–8). In this matrix, each row represents a method, and each column represents the number of relationships that method has with the corresponding BO, as depicted in Fig. 4(a). This helps capture the semantic structural relationships (i.e., BO relationships), which provides an idea about the "boundedness" of methods to BOs. For example, Method 1 ('Mtd 1') is related to 'BO1' and 'BO2' in Fig. 4(a).

In the sixth step, the algorithm derives another matrix $mtduwcount$, which keeps a count of unique words related to each method using function $WCOUNT$ (lines 9–11). Figure 3 provides an overview idea of a possible matrix that can be generated for $mtduwcount$. Again, in this matrix, rows correspond to methods, and columns correspond to unique words identified in step four of the algorithm that appear in the corresponding methods. The values in $mtduwcount$ are then used in the seventh step to calculate the cosine similarity between the methods using function $COSINECAL$ (lines 12–14).

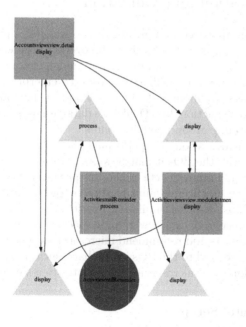

Fig. 5. Mondrian method call graphs (Color figure online)

Next, the algorithm's eighth step extracts the structural interaction relationships (i.e., method call relationships)using function $MTDRELCAL$ (line 16).

In this function, the code is first evaluated using the Mondrian code analysis tool[2], which generates graphs based on method call relationships as depicted in Fig. 5. In Fig. 5 the red circle shows the class, the grey squares show the methods in different classes and the arrow between them shows the method call relationships. Then the graphs are analysed to create matrix *mtdrel* which summarises the method call relationships for further processing (see the example in Fig. 4(c)).

The feature set data in variables *mtdborel*, *mtdcosine*, *mtdrel* and the BOs B obtained from Algorithm 1 are provided as input to the K-Means algorithm to cluster the methods related to BOs based on their syntactic and semantic relationships. We followed a similar approach in our previous work [11], in which we adapted class-level relationships for microservice cluster discovery. However, here we have moved to the next level of system analysis by evaluating method level relationships. As such, in Algorithm 1, each dataset captures different aspects of relationships between the methods in the given system (Fig. 4). Finally, as per our earlier work [11], we configured the K-Means algorithm to produce a set of clusters that group the methods of the analysed enterprise system as recommendations for constructing microservices.

4   Implementation and Validation

To demonstrate our approach's applicability we developed a prototype microservice recommendation system[3] capable of discovering coherent method clusters related to different BOs, which lead to different microservice configurations. The system was tested using the Dolibarr open-source enterprise management system. Dolibarr consists of about 11,000 files and out of them around 1850 classes are related to its core functionality. Dolibarr's database uses MySQL and consists of 250 tables containing around 660 attributes.

Using our implementation, we performed the static analysis of Dolibarr's source code to identify the BOs it manages. As a result, 39 BOs were identified, e.g., Product, Order, Shipment, etc. Then, we performed the static analysis of the system to derive matrices, similar to those depicted in Fig. 4, summarising the BO relationships, method similarity relationships and, method call relationships. All the results obtained were processed by our prototype software to identify method clusters and recommend microservices. The prototype identified 39 method clusters related to the BOs in Dolibarr, such that each cluster groups methods for developing a microservice that relates to a single BO.

4.1   Experimental Setup

In order to evaluate the effectiveness of the microservices suggested by our prototype for potential IIoT deployment, we compared the performance of the enterprise system with and without microservice extensions. Each enterprise system

---

[2] https://github.com/Trismegiste/Mondrian.

[3] https://github.com/AnuruddhaDeAlwis/KMeans.git.

was hosted in an Amazon Web Services cloud by creating two EC2 instances having two virtual CPUs and a total memory of 2 GB, as depicted on the left side of Fig. 6. Amazon Greengrass nodes were then used to simulate IIoT nodes running on Raspberry Pis as shown on the right. The systems' data were stored in a MySQL relational database instance which has one virtual CPU and total storage of 20 GB.

These systems were tested against 200 and 400 executions generated by four machines simultaneously, simulating customer requests. We recorded the total execution time, average CPU consumption, and average network bandwidth consumption for these executions (see the first two rows in Table 1). During the executions we tested the functionality related to operation 'order product'. The simulations were conducted using Selenuim[4] scripts which ran the system in a way similar to a real user.

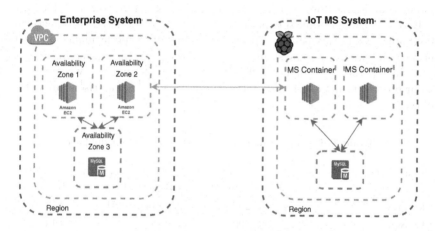

Fig. 6. System implementation using Amazon Web Services and Raspberry Pis.

Next, we introduced the 'purchase order' microservice from the Dolibarr system. As depicted on the right side of Fig. 6, we hosted each microservice on an Amazon Greengrass node run on a Raspberry Pi 4, each containing its own local MySQL database. The tests were also performed on the original enterprise system, again simulating ordering a product. Since the microservices were refactored parts of the enterprise systems in these tests, the enterprise systems used API calls to pass the data to the microservices and the microservices processed and sent back the results. Again, we recorded the total execution time, average CPU consumption, and average network bandwidth consumption for the entire system, i.e., enterprise system and microservice as a whole (see rows 3 and 4 in Table 1).

The scalability, availability and execution efficiency of the systems were calculated based on the measured results. The obtained results are summarised in

---

[4] https://www.seleniumhq.org/.

Table 2 as *ES with MSs (1)* (second row in Table 2). Scalability was calculated according to the resource usage over time, as described by Tsai *et al.* [20]. To determine availability, first we calculated the packet loss for one minute when the system is down and then obtained the difference between the total up time and total time (i.e., up time + down time), as described by Bauer *et al.* [21]. Dividing the total time taken by the legacy system to process all requests by the total time taken by the corresponding enterprise system which has microservices led to the calculation of efficiency gain.

Next, we tested the quality of our system's microservice recommendations by disrupting its suggestions and developed a 'purchase order' microservice, while introducing operations related to the 'user' microservice, also running on an Amazon Greengrass deployment. Again, with this change, we set up the experiment as described earlier and measured the results (rows 5 and 6 in Table 1). Then we calculated the scalability, availability and execution efficiencies of the systems, summarised in Table 2 as *ES with MSs (2)* (third row in Table 2).

Based on these obtained experimental results we evaluated the effectiveness of our approach in two aspects. Firstly, we evaluated the performance differences between the microservice system and the original enterprise system. Secondly, we evaluated the performance differences between the microservices suggested by our prototype and other microservice designs. These comparisons are detailed below.

Table 1. Legacy vs microservice system results for dolibarr.

System type	No of requests	Ex. Time (ms)	Avg CPU EC2	Avg CPU DB
ES only	200	822000	9.54	2.37
ES only	400	1740000	8.81	2.13
ES with MSs (as recommended)	200	816000	5.05	1.67
ES with MSs (as recommended)	400	1728000	5.23	1.55
ES with MSs (when 'disrupted')	200	819000	8.88	1.88
ES with MSs (when 'disrupted')	400	1734000	8.05	2.00

Table 2. Legacy vs microservice system EC2 characteristics comparison for Dolibarr.

System type	Scalability [CPU]	Scalability [DB CPU]	Availability [200]	Availability [400]	Efficiency [200]	Efficiency [400]
ES only	3.458	3.365	99.27	99.31	1.000	1.000
ES with MSs (1)	3.398	3.045	99.27	99.31	1.007	1.007
ES with MSs (2)	3.427	4.031	99.27	99.31	1.003	1.003

Recommended Microservices vs Original Enterprise System. As per Tsai *et al.*'s metric [20], the lower the measured number, the better the scalability. Thus, it is evident that the microservice systems derived based on our clustering algorithm managed to achieve 0.7% improved system execution efficiency and 1.74% scalability improvement (considering CPU scalability), see Table 1. As such, our recommendation system discovers microservices that can achieve improved cloud capabilities such as high scalability, high availability and high execution efficiency. Notably, the integrated ES with MSs system achieved 59% (5.23/8.81) and 72% (1.55/2.13) CPU utilisation at EC2 instances and DB as compared to the original ES.

Recommended Microservices vs Other Microservices. Microservices developed based on the suggestions provided by our recommendation system for Dolibarr managed to achieve: (i) 1.74% calability improvement in EC2 instance CPU utilisation; (ii) 9.51% scalability improvement in database instance CPU utilisation; and (iii) a 0.7% improvement in execution efficiency. However, the "disrupted" microservices that violated the recommendations reduced (i) EC2 instance CPU utilisation to 0.89%; (ii) database instance CPU utilisation to (−)19.79%; and (iii) execution efficiency to 0.3%. As such, it is evident that the microservices developed by following the recommendations of our system provided better cloud characteristics than the microservices developed against these recommendations.

4.2   Limitations

Although this paper presents an algorithm that resolves some of the challenges in discovering IIoT microserviceable components from enterprise systems, there remain several limitations that should be addressed in future research.

Limitation of BO Derivation: To derive the BOs related to the given enterprise systems, we used Nooijen *et al.*'s method [17]. However, as Lu *et al.* explain [13], such methods cannot always derive BOs accurately without some domain knowledge from the system's developers. We tried to avoid errors by manually evaluating the results obtained for the BOs by referring to the system's manuals and documentation. Still, such an approach remains complex and error prone.

Limitation of Structural Method Similarity Analysis: The structural method similarity analysis obtained a 'bag of words' term frequency and, finally, calculated the cosine similarity between the documents. The first limitation of this method is the potential filtering out of valuable information in the data preprocessing stage. We mitigated this by manually evaluating the stop words used in the text preprocessing step. In addition, the cosine values might not provide an accurate idea about structural method similarity since it may also depend on the terms used in the definitions of the method names and descriptions given in the comments. We mitigated this to a certain extent by evaluating the code structure of the software systems and verifying that the method names and comments provide valuable insights into the logic behind the methods that implement the system, but again it is easy to make mistakes during such a manual process.

5   Discussion

This paper we showed how to identify the components in enterprise systems that can be developed as IIoT deployable microservices. However, through the introduction of microservices, new behaviours can arise in relation to current state enterprise systems, given increased flexibility of execution, resulting from asynchronous and branching actions and new extension points introduced by microservice architectures. In order to evaluate the behavioural changes caused by the introduction of IIoT components to enterprise systems, testing should be conducted using methods such as conformance checking.

Similarly, distributing enterprise systems in "fog" networks, where significant parts of the computation occur on edge devices, opens up significant security vulnerabilities. Under a central system, the users' and systems' interactions are subject to local access control, constraining data access via permissions and security modes. However, the distributed architecture of IIoT and fog computing poses new threats to authentication and trust, secure communications, and end-user privacy [22]. In particular, a fog network makes it difficult to authenticate the identity of nodes as they enter and leave the network [23], is vulnerable to data breaches caused by malicious or malfunctioning nodes, risks end-user privacy due to the large amount of user-specific data generated by nodes, and inhibits anomaly detection due to the difficulty of monitoring large numbers of nodes [24]. Developing new security technologies and verification methods for IIoT applications would be another interesting future research area.

6   Conclusion

Here we presented a novel technique for automated analysis and remodularisation of enterprise systems as IIoT deployable microservices by combining techniques that consider semantic knowledge and syntactic knowledge about the system's code. A prototype recommendation system was developed and validated by implementing the microservices recommended by the prototype for Dolibarr which is an open-source ERP system. The experiment showed that our approach could derive method clusters that produced IIoT deployable microservices with desired Cloud characteristics, such as high scalability, high availability, and processing efficiency.

References

1. Newman, S.: Building Microservices. O'Reilly Media Inc, Beijing (2015)
2. Barros, A., Duddy, K., Lawley, M., Milosevic, Z., Raymond, K., Wood, A.: Processes, roles, and events: UML concepts for enterprise architecture. In: Evans, A., Kent, S., Selic, B. (eds.) UML 2000. LNCS, vol. 1939, pp. 62–77. Springer, Heidelberg (2000). https://doi.org/10.1007/3-540-40011-7_5

3. Schneider, T.: SAP Business ByDesign Studio: Application Development, pp. 24–28. Galileo Press, Boston (2012)

4. Decker, G., Barros, A., Kraft, F.M., Lohmann, N.: Non-desynchronizable service choreographies. In: Bouguettaya, A., Krueger, I., Margaria, T. (eds.) Non-desynchronizable service choreographies. In International Conference on Service-Oriented Computing (pp. 331–346). Springer, Berlin, Heidelberg. LNCS, vol. 5364, pp. 331–346. Springer, Heidelberg (2008). https://doi.org/10.1007/978-3-540-89652-4_26

5. Barros, A., Decker, G., Dumas, M.: Multi-staged and multi-viewpoint service choreography modelling. In Proceedings of the Workshop on Software Engineering Methods for Service Oriented Architecture (SEMSOA), Hannover, Germany. CEUR Workshop Proceedings, vol. 244 (May 2007)

6. Barros, A., Decker, G., Dumas, M., Weber, F.: Correlation patterns in service-oriented architectures. In: Dwyer, M.B., Lopes, A. (eds.) FASE 2007. LNCS, vol. 4422, pp. 245–259. Springer, Heidelberg (2007). https://doi.org/10.1007/978-3-540-71289-3_20

7. Praditwong, K., Harman, M., Yao, X.: Software module clustering as a multi-objective search problem. IEEE Trans. Soft. Eng. **37**(2), 264–282 (2010)

8. Mitchell, B.S., Mancoridis, S.: On the automatic modularization of software systems using the bunch tool. IEEE Trans. Software Eng. **32**(3), 193–208 (2006)

9. Poshyvanyk, D., Marcus, A.: The conceptual coupling metrics for object-oriented systems. In: 22nd IEEE International Conference on Software Maintenance, pp. 469–478. IEEE (September 2006)

10. Candela, I., Bavota, G., Russo, B., Oliveto, R.: Using cohesion and coupling for software remodularization: is it enough? ACM Trans. Softw. Eng. Methodol. (TOSEM) **25**(3), 24 (2016)

11. De. Alwis, A.A.C., Barros, A., Fidge, C., Polyvyanyy, A.: Remodularization analysis for microservice discovery using syntactic and semantic clustering. In: Dustdar, S., Yu, E., Salinesi, C., Rieu, D., Pant, V. (eds.) CAiSE 2020. LNCS, vol. 12127, pp. 3–19. Springer, Cham (2020). https://doi.org/10.1007/978-3-030-49435-3_1

12. Pérez-Castillo, R., García-Rodríguez de Guzmán, I., Caballero, I., Piattini, M.: Software modernization by recovering web services from legacy databases. J. Softw. Evol. Process **25**(5), 507–533 (2013)

13. Lu, X., Nagelkerke, M., van de Wiel, D., Fahland, D.: Discovering interacting artifacts from ERP systems. IEEE Trans. Serv. Comput. **8**(6), 861–873 (2015)

14. De. Alwis, A.A.C., Barros, A., Fidge, C., Polyvyanyy, A.: Business object centric microservices patterns. In: Panetto, H., Debruyne, C., Hepp, M., Lewis, D., Ardagna, C.A., Meersman, R. (eds.) OTM 2019. LNCS, vol. 11877, pp. 476–495. Springer, Cham (2019). https://doi.org/10.1007/978-3-030-33246-4_30

15. De. Alwis, A.A.C., Barros, A., Polyvyanyy, A., Fidge, C.: Function-splitting heuristics for discovery of microservices in enterprise systems. In: Pahl, C., Vukovic, M., Yin, J., Yu, Q. (eds.) ICSOC 2018. LNCS, vol. 11236, pp. 37–53. Springer, Cham (2018). https://doi.org/10.1007/978-3-030-03596-9_3

16. Oswald, D., Zhang, R.P., Lingard, H., Pirzadeh, P., Le, T.: The use and abuse of safety indicators in construction. Engineering, construction and architectural management (2018)

17. Nooijen, E.H.J., van Dongen, B.F., Fahland, D.: Automatic discovery of data-centric and artifact-centric processes. In: La. Rosa, M., Soffer, P. (eds.) BPM 2012. LNBIP, vol. 132, pp. 316–327. Springer, Heidelberg (2013). https://doi.org/10.1007/978-3-642-36285-9_36

18. Zhang, H., Xiao, Y., Bu, S., Niyato, D., Yu, F.R., Han, Z.: Computing resource allocation in three-tier IoT fog networks: a joint optimization approach combining Stackelberg game and matching. IEEE Internet Things J. **4**(5), 1204–1215 (2017)

19. Lebanon, G., Mao, Y., Dillon, J.: The locally weighted bag of words framework for document representation. J. Mach. Learn. Res. **8**, 2405–2441 (2007)

20. Tsai, W.T., Huang, Y., Shao, Q.: Testing the scalability of SaaS applications. In: 2011 IEEE International Conference on Service-Oriented Computing and Applications (SOCA), pp. 1–4. IEEE (December 2011)

21. Bauer, E., Adams, R.: Reliability and Availability of Cloud Computing. Wiley, Piscataway (2012)

22. Mukherjee, M., et al.: Security and privacy in fog computing: challenges. IEEE Access **5**, 19293–19304 (2017)

23. Zhang, Z.-K., et al.: IoT security: ongoing challenges and research opportunities. In: Proceedings of the 7th International Conference on Service-Oriented Computing and Applications, pp. 230–234. IEEE (2014)

24. Khan, S., Parkinson, S., Qin, Y.: Fog computing security: a review of current applications and security solutions. J. Cloud Comput. Adv. Syst. Appl. **6**(19), 1–22 (2017)

25. Woodhead, R., Stephenson, P., Morrey, D.: Digital construction: from point solutions to an IoT ecosystem. J. Autom. Constr. **93**, 35–46 (2018)

Data and Cloud Polymorphic Application Modelling in Multi-clouds and Fog Environments

Yiannis Verginadis[1,2(✉)], Kyriakos Kritikos[3,4(✉)], and Ioannis Patiniotakis[1(✉)]

[1] Institute of Communications and Computer Systems, Athens, Greece
{jverg,ipatini}@mail.ntua.gr
[2] Athens University of Economics and Business, Athens, Greece
[3] FORTH-ICS, Heraklion, Crete, Greece
kritikos@ics.forth.gr
[4] Aegean University, Karlovassi, Samos, Greece

Abstract. Multi-cloud management prevents vendor lock-in as well as improves the provisioning of cloud applications. However, the optimal deployment of such applications is still impossible, not only due to the dynamicity of the cloud and hybrid environments that host these applications but also due to the use of potentially unsuitable forms or configurations of application components. As such, the real cloud application optimisation can only be achieved by considering all possible component forms and selecting the best one, based on both application requirements and the current context. This gives rise to the era of polymorphic applications which can change form at runtime based on their context. A major pre-requisite for the management of such applications is their proper modelling. Therefore, this paper presents extensions on two well-integrated cloud modelling solutions to support the complete specification of polymorphic applications and it presents an illustrative example of their use.

Keywords: Polymorphic · Application · Multi-cloud · Modelling · Language

1 Introduction

Nowadays, an abundance of cloud service offerings is obtainable and rapidly adopted by enterprises based on their preeminence to traditional computing models [1]. However, at the same time, the computing requirements of modern cloud applications have been exponentially increased due to available big data that require processing [2, 3]. The emergence of data-intensive applications necessitated the wide adoption of multi-cloud deployment models, to vest on all cloud computing advantages without any restriction on who is the cloud service provider [3]. Considering different application forms, based on current needs or available infrastructural offers near the data sources, is also a significant challenge for multi-cloud management platforms (MCMPs).

We refer to polymorphic applications, i.e., applications that can have alternative architecture variants, derived from the different application components forms (e.g.,

M. La Rosa et al. (Eds.): CAiSE 2021, LNCS 12751, pp. 449–464, 2021.
https://doi.org/10.1007/978-3-030-79382-1_27

function or micro-service) or configuration styles (VM, serverless). As such, each architecture variant maps to selecting one form of each component from those possible. Thus, depending on the application requirements, one architecture variant can be selected and deployed in a single cloud or across multiple ones or even fog environments. So, the main research issues involved are: (a) how to automatically select and deploy the right architecture variant; (b) how to adapt both the application architecture variant and its configuration, based on current application requirements and context. The benefits of addressing these research issues are considerable since the application deployment always optimally satisfies the current requirements and context, leading to a reliable service level delivery, the increase of application and its provider reputation and the subsequent increase of provider's net gain. So, polymorphic applications tend to change the research map of multi-cloud application management [1].

A major pre-requisite to support polymorphic application management in multi-clouds is polymorphic application modelling. Without the proper modelling of polymorphic applications, their optimal deployment and reconfiguration cannot be supported by any MCMP. Thus, this modelling kind not only needs to be rich enough but should deeply cover all necessary management domains, including deployment, requirements and monitoring. To the best of our knowledge, no other related approach can supply such a support. We elaborate more on this in Sect. 2 to argue that currently no cloud modelling language can satisfy all the aspects of polymorphic application modelling. This shortcoming is also affirmed by the fact that currently there are not any MCMPs that can automatically support application polymorphism at runtime. This is true both for research platforms in the cloud domain but also well-established tools (e.g., Kubernetes). As such, in this work, we discuss extensions over our previous work on application modelling for multi-clouds, using the Cloud Application Modelling and Execution Language (CAMEL) [2] and the Metadata Schema (MDS) [3] so as to sufficiently support the modelling of polymorphic applications.

CAMEL is a rich modelling language covering all necessary domains for multi-cloud application management. However, it currently lacks the necessary conceptual capabilities to support polymorphic application specification as it is not able to model all possible application component forms and configurations. Further, it misses other heterogeneous resources (e.g., accelerators, edge resources) and network-related concepts. As such, this work discusses the extensions conducted in CAMEL to deliver the missing polymorphic application modelling capabilities.

MDS is also a rich metadata schema covering concepts and their relations across the application deployment, big data management and contextual security domains. It includes concepts and properties related to where (big data) applications should be placed, how big data can be actually managed and how access to both data and resources (including application components) can be restricted. Such a schema is quite handy in the context of extending CAMEL at the model level plus supplying suitable annotations for CAMEL elements at the same level. As such, CAMEL is enhanced to describe additional features or domains (e.g., requirements for resources like Virtual Machines (VMs) and Graphical Processing Units (GPUs)) without the need to extend it at the conceptual level. However, after carefully examining the application deployment domain, MDS was found to lack some important concepts related to specific resource kinds (e.g.,

High-Performance Computing (HPC), hardware-accelerated ones), platform kinds (e.g., serverless) and network elements. Further, some small gaps (e.g., missing trusted execution environment concepts) were also identified in terms of the other two domains (i.e., big data management and contextual security). Thus, in the context of supporting polymorphic application modelling and annotation, MDS has been also extended to cover all missing conceptual elements.

The rest of this paper is structured as follows. Section 2 discusses relevant work on cloud application modelling. Section 3 presents CAMEL and its extensions towards polymorphic application modelling, while it also discusses its enhancement via MDS. Section 4 focuses on the new aspects that were appended to MDS so as to offer a complete and formal vocabulary of concepts and properties for describing cloud service offerings. Section 5 showcases the capabilities of this application modelling approach in a real 5G cloud-RAN application. The last section finally concludes this work and discusses future directions with respect to cloud application modelling.

2   Related Work

2.1   Cloud Application Modelling Languages

This section assesses whether the cloud (application) modelling languages (CMLs) support both multi-cloud and polymorphic application modelling. To assess all relevant cloud application and service modelling languages, we rely on the criteria framework in [2] that we extend to cover the polymorphic modelling aspect. This framework includes the following evaluation criteria: i) *domain coverage*: which domains relevant to the application lifecycle are covered; ii) *integration level*: what is the level of integration [2] between the different domains/sub-languages covered/utilized; iii) *delivery model support*: which kinds of cloud services are supported; iv) *models@runtime*: for which domains is models@runtime paradigm [4] adopted.

A CML supports polymorphic modelling when it satisfies the following criteria: i) *application architecture variability*: a CML can capture different forms of application components and thus cover the different variations of an application architecture. This criterion is evaluated as "low" when the CML does not support modelling component forms, "medium" when it indirectly supports this, or "high", otherwise. ii) *component configuration variability*: the CML can capture any kind of component configuration, such as script, container, serverless and accelerated resource configurations. Thus, the higher is the number of different configuration kinds captured, the better is the CML. This criterion is evaluated as "low" when the CML supports one or two configuration kinds, "medium" when it supports three to four kinds, or "high" otherwise. iii) *component complexity*: application components in one form can be standalone and composite in another. Thus, a CML should support the modelling of both component kinds. This criterion is evaluated as "low" when a CML does not make explicit the distinction of single and complex components, "medium" when it makes this distinction but not properly models complex components, or "high" otherwise.

Based on the enhanced criteria framework, we have analysed 13 provider-independent CMLs (see Table 1), including CAMEL, as provider-independence is a crucial feature to support cross- and multi-cloud application deployments. As can be seen, CAMEL 2.0 was already above competition due to its domain coverage, integration level, cloud service type coverage and models@runtime support for the deployment, monitoring and data domains. CAMEL 3.0 builds on CAMEL 2.0 so as to enhance it with polymorphic modelling capabilities. Thus, CAMEL 3.0 advances the state-of-the-art in both multi-cloud and polymorphic application modelling.

From the rest of the CMLs, we can distinguish three languages, which exhibit better performance in different criteria clusters. TOSCA is a standard widely used in research able to cover two kinds of cloud services while its ongoing extension will support the models@runtime paradigm for the deployment domain. However, in terms of domain coverage, this CML seems to focus mainly on the deployment domain and slightly on the requirement one. TOSCA has a medium component configuration variability due to its ability to support some but not all configuration kinds. However, the latter support is not exactly implanted in TOSCA syntax as in CAMEL.

ModaCloudML can be discerned due to its polymorphic modelling support which is close but not equal to that of CAMEL 2.0. In particular, this CML seems to support some of the possible component configuration kinds while it caters for component complexity: it allows specifying composite components through their constituent components but does not fully explicate their internal deployment model.

StratusML can be distinguished from ModaCloudML & TOSCA based on its domain coverage and integration level, where the latter is due to its homogenous way to model

Table 1. Evaluation of cloud application modelling languages.

DSL	Dom. Cover.	Integr. Level	Deliv. Model Supp.	models@ runtime	App. Arch. Var.	Comp. Conf. Var.	Comp. Compl.
Vamp [5]	Low	N/A	IaaS	N/A	Low	Low	Low
4CaaSt Template [6]	Low	N/A	IaaS, PaaS	N/A	Low	Low	Low
TOSCA [7]	Medium	Medium	IaaS, PaaS	Deployment	Low	Medium	Low
GENTL [8]	Low	N/A	IaaS	N/A	Low	Low	Low
ModaCloudML [9]	Medium	Low	IaaS, PaaS	Deployment	Low	Medium	Medium
CAML [10]	Medium	Medium	IaaS	N/A	Low	Low	Low
StratusML [11]	Medium	High	IaaS	Deployment	Low	Low	Low
CAMEL 2.0	High	High	IaaS, PaaS, SaaS	Deployment, metric, data	Medium	Medium	Medium
CAMEL 3.0	High	High	IaaS, PaaS, SaaS	Deployment, metric, data	Medium	High	High

different domains. However, the domain coverage is not as extensive and deep as in CAMEL. Further, no polymorphic modelling capabilities exist in that language.

2.2 Ontologies and Metadata for Cloud Application and Services Description

Next, we highlight all approaches consulted to extend MDS so as to completely cover all possible resource and platform kinds. As MDS already covers well the big data domain and supplies adequate support for common resource types and services [3], the analysis focuses on the network and hardware-accelerator domains, i.e., the two most significant MDS extensions.

Network Domain. In [12] a meta-model for cyber-physical systems is suggested, mainly focusing on their communication. [13] proposes a network description language specialised in describing network topologies for hybrid networks. The ToCo ontology [14] can specify the physical infrastructure as well as the quality of channel, services and users in heterogeneous, multi-domain telecommunication networks. The ontology in [15] enables to specify telecommunication services, to easily discover them plus address the semantic interoperability problem.

Hardware Accelerator Domain. [16] suggests a modular and extensible XML-based platform language able to specify heterogeneous multicore systems and clusters at both the hardware and software level. OMG's MARTE [17] enables specifying hardware architectures. It includes the GRM meta-model, able to describe various resource types like storage, communication, computing and device, as well as the HRM meta-model spanning two views: logical that classifies each hardware resource based on its functional properties while covering various concrete resources of multiple resource types and the physical view focusing on the resources' physical properties. The CloudLightning ontology [18] facilitates the incorporation of heterogeneous resources and HPC environments in the Cloud. It provides support for resource management by modelling hardware accelerators as well as different resource abstraction methods and intelligently matching service requests to heterogeneous infrastructures.

3 CAMEL

3.1 Introduction to CAMEL

CAMEL is a multi-domain-specific language (multi-DSL) enabling to specify provider-independent, multi-cloud applications. CAMEL covers well all relevant domains in the application lifecycle via its respective DSLs. These DSLs have been developed to map to the same level of expressiveness while they have been properly integrated to avoid various modelling discrepancies, like the duplication of information [2]. Further, these DSLs are assorted with rules which cover the semantic and syntactic validation of models conforming to them within and across domains. CAMEL conforms to the models@runtime paradigm. In particular, devops users specify domain (e.g., deployment) models at the type-level which are then exploited by the MCMP to drive the deployment and management of the respective application. During such exploitation, the MCMP produces and maintains domain models at the instance level which reflect the current application state in the respective domains. The production of the sub-models of an application's CAMEL model is facilitated by the use of a textual-based CAMEL editor, generated via Eclipse Xtext[1]. This editor enables the rapid, user-intuitive editing of CAMEL models as it exhibits various features, such as error and syntax highlighting, syntax completion and hove-over documentation-based assistance. Complementary, the devops can consult the online CAMEL documentation[2] for further assistance.

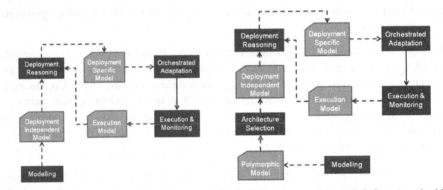

Fig. 1. The cloud application management process and CAMEL without (left figure) and with polymorphic capabilities (right figure)

Figure 1 (left part) depicts the way CAMEL models are exploited and evolved by a MCMP. Initially, the DevOps supplies a *provided-independent model* of her application. The MCMP then via deployment reasoning produces a *provider-specific model*. Next, this model is exploited to orchestrate the application deployment. Finally, while the application executes, relevant execution facts are fed into the application's execution sub-model, giving rise to a CAMEL *execution model*. Such facts are exploited to optimally reconfigure the application to close the application's optimisation loop.

3.2 Enhancing CAMEL Through MDS

The application placement domain includes other domains like the resource and platform ones. Such domains are in constant change due to the introduction of new technologies resulting in new resource and platform kinds. This creates the need to extend existing CMLs at the language level to enable the modelling of elements or models relevant to these new kinds. However, such an extension is conducted by either enhancing existing meta-models or modelling and incorporating new ones with the same formalism. This increases the modelling effort, introduces unnecessary restrictions in modelling such domains while makes CMLs quite complex. Thus, this increases their learning curve and decreases their usability. Another alternative is to allow for a generic description of any domain such that each domain can be extended at will. This, however, means that

---

[1] https://www.eclipse.org/Xtext/.

[2] http://camel-dsl.org/documentation/.

the semantics of each domain is not precisely captured. As a result, the respective CML becomes hard to comprehend and use.

To this end, it was decided to follow a solution that lies in between the two extremes. This relies on the fact that CAMEL 2.0 captures well the core of all domains while an arbitrary structure can be followed for extensions of these domains or their sub-domains. To achieve this, a novel and lightweight mechanism has been introduced in CAMEL 2.0 that plays a dual role: (a) it enables semantically annotating almost any CAMEL element kind to supply precise semantics for them. This can facilitate, e.g., raising the automation in application management; (b) it enables arbitrarily extending CAMEL models. In particular, CAMEL elements can include sub-features and attributes that could enable, e.g., to specify constraints on various kinds of resources or platforms. In this sense, CAMEL does not need to be extended at all at the language level to cover new resource/platform sub-domains.

The mechanism was realised via 2 main extensions while transiting from CAMEL 1.0 to 2.0. First, the introduction of new CAMEL super-concepts, inherited by most of the others. Such super-concepts enable to semantically annotate CAMEL model elements through references to MDS elements as well as to enable an arbitrary structure on a CAMEL element via its potential expansion with feature hierarchies. Second, the introduction of the metadata domain. This enables to codify in CAMEL any conceptual schema (in any kind of form like an ontology or taxonomy), including the MDS.

The benefits from introducing the above mechanism are numerous. First, CAMEL can be re-used in different MCMPs, if such MCMPs have already decided to rely on a certain schema. Second, CAMEL can be extended at the model level to cover new resource and platform sub-domains. As such, CAMEL model specifications can be quite rich, incorporating constraints on, e.g., various kinds of hardware-accelerated resources like GPUs and FPGAs. An example of how MDS is used in CAMEL is provided in Sect. 5 code excerpts where certain modelling artefacts are annotated with a prefix following the pattern "*MetaDataModel.MELODICMetadataSchema*".

3.3 CAMEL v3.0

CAMEL 3.0 was designed based on specific requirements, which relate to CAMEL's improvement feedback collected from past European projects [2], the realisation of the polymorphic modelling capability and some generic requirements from real use-cases. These requirements can be summarised as follows (where *PM* means polymorphic-related, *IR* improvement related, and *UC* use-case related): i) *PM1*: New configurations for components have to be covered, especially those related to hardware-acceleration-use scenarios; ii) *PM2*: Each component configuration may come with its own requirement set with respect to, e.g., the resources or the environment on top of them; iii) *PM3*: Components, depending on their form, can be either standalone or complex. For example, a component managing users could be either offered as a micro-service or as a composite component comprising a set of serverless functions; iv) *IR1*: Components should be re-used in the context of different applications to reduce both the application modelling and development time; v) *UC1*: Communication requirements must be expressed as constraints on the quality of the communication (e.g., latency) between two application components. Such constraints deliver flexibility in the deployment of the component pair.

All these requirements led to extending existing CAMEL domains with some missing concepts and relations. The main rationale for such an extension was that the communication aspect was neglected in CAMEL 2.0 while the polymorphic modelling support had to be improved mainly on the deployment domain. The communication-related changes (UC1) led to introducing *CommunicationRequirement*, a feature-based kind of requirement over the quality of communication between components, *CommunicationMeasurement*, a measurement related to communication quality, as well as updating monitoring related concepts like *ObjectContext* (such that the object being measured can be also a communication). The latter change enables to specify communication related metrics and SLOs which can then be evaluated and possibly lead to the application reconfiguration at runtime.

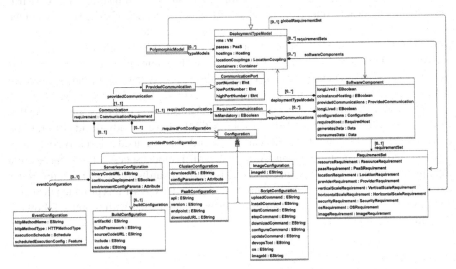

Fig. 2. The deployment domain in CAMEL

Concerning the deployment domain, new component configuration kinds were introduced (PM1), covering hardware-accelerated scenarios, while each configuration is now associated with its own requirement set (PM2). Further, a new concept was incorporated called *PolymorphicModel*, representing a provider-independent polymorphic application deployment architecture that covers all deployment architecture variants, which can be produced by selecting one from all possible configurations per each component (and be modelled via a *DeploymentTypeModel*). Finally, component complexity was catered by associating a composite component with its own internal polymorphic model (PM3). This enables component re-use in the sense that composite components can be regarded as individual applications on their own or can be exploited to build more complex applications (IR1). In Fig. 2 we depict a UML class diagram that covers the modelling in this domain.

Apart from evolving CAMEL, the polymorphic application modelling has extended the deployment reasoning activity (see Fig. 1 - right part). As first, the right application architecture variant needs to be selected and then the right cloud providers and resources need to be selected to provide support to the selected component configurations. The input to the first reasoning activity is named as *polymorphic model* while its result is the *provider-independent model* (see *DeploymentModelType* class), i.e., the input to the original deployment reasoning activity, now second in order.

4   Metadata Schema

4.1   Overview of MDS

This section introduces an extensive update of the vocabulary entitled *Metadata Schema* (MDS) [3] which aggregates a number of concepts and properties to support describing requirements, constraints and offerings' characteristics in multi-cloud placement decisions. The structured description of these characteristics constitutes the formal means for extending CAMEL with appropriate concepts related to big data management, application component placement and access control in multi-cloud environments. In this respect, MDS comprises the *Application Placement*, *Big Data* and *Context Aware Security* models that group a number of classes and properties as it is depicted in Fig. 3 which unveils MDS top-level classes.

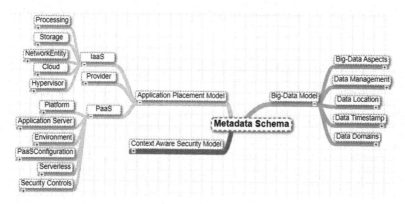

Fig. 3. Metadata Schema overview.

In this work, MDS is enhanced to cover the desired abstraction constructs, which will be used in CAMEL to model polymorphic applications, regarding the areas of data management, polymorphic application design plus the use of heterogeneous resources (including HPC resources, accelerators) and platforms (including serverless). Besides the above aspects, the extensions involve network related aspects that should drive or affect the cloud application deployment. Due to space limitations, we now supply for each MDS extension a short description along with a fine-grained depiction of its UML class diagram, which also shows the value types of object and data properties. A complete view in the form of a high-resolution image of the complete MDS taxonomy can be found here[3].

4.2 MDS Extensions

In the first version of MDS, the *Processing* class (a subclass of *Application Placement Model/IaaS*) involved only the *RAM*, *CPU* and *GPU* subclasses. Figure 4 supplies a fine-grained view of MDS updates, regarding the *Processing* class, involving any infrastructural feature bound to the processing capability of virtualised resources. Classes *Processing, CPU* and *Memory* were enriched with extra properties (e.g., *hasCacheType, hasBlockSize* regarding *CacheStructure, hasReplicationPolicy* etc.), while new classes were added (e.g., *HPC, ASIC, VPU* etc.) as it is explained below.

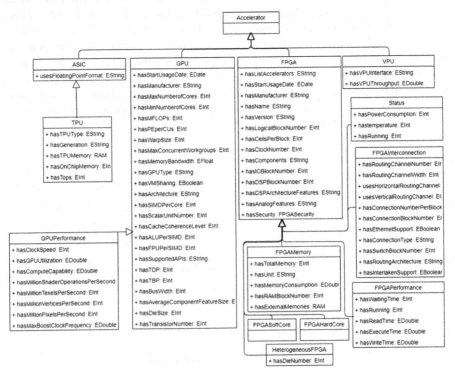

Fig. 4. Part of the UML class diagram for the processing domain

Specifically, *HPC* and *Accelerator* classes were introduced. *HPC* refers to the high performance features provided by the computing platform which can boost the overall application performance. The *Accelerator* class refers to application-specific hardware designed or programmed to compute operations faster than a general-purpose computer processor. It involves the following main subclasses: i) *GPU* which refers to IaaS

---

[3] https://melodic.cloud/UuTf-KRW.png.

resources that use graphics processing units (GPUs), i.e., specialized electronic circuits initially designed to rapidly manipulate memory to accelerate the creation of images in a frame buffer; ii) ASIC referring to application-specific integrated circuits (ASICs), an accelerator category that employs strategies like optimised memory and use of lower precision arithmetic, to accelerate calculation and increase computation throughput; iii) *VPU* which refers to the vision processing unit (VPU), a category of microprocessors intended to accelerate machine vision algorithms and tasks; iv) *FPGA*: refers to IaaS resources that use field programmable gate arrays (FPGAs), as integrated circuits made to be configured by the user after manufacturing.

Another important IaaS subclass introduced is the *NetworkEntity* representing any kind of network entity that could be included in a Cloud. Several properties and subclasses have been added to cover all the network-related elements that can be considered for managing applications hosted over multi-clouds and fog computing environments. The main subclasses of the *NetworkEntity* class are the following: i) *Network* which refers to the network related aspects that bind the operation and communication capabilities of an offered or a requested (Fog) IaaS resource; ii) *NetworkQoS* that represents the main aspects of the network quality of service; iii) *SoftwareNetworkEntity* that represents a software-based network entity; iv) *HardwareNetworkEntity*: refers to all aspects of hardware-based network entities that may constitute network nodes serving the cloud application components.

The *PaaS class* encapsulates all attributes related to platform level cloud resources required and offered for deploying multi-cloud applications. The main addition is its new *Serverless* subclass that represents all serverless platform-as-a-service (PaaS) aspects that enable the deployment of functions/serverless components in the cloud. The main subclasses of the *Serverless* class (see also Fig. 5) are the following: i) *Composition*: represents the technology used to support function composition; ii) *Cost:* represents the cost model of a serverless PaaS; iii) *FreeQuota*: concerns the free quota per month for a serverless PaaS account; iv) *Limits*: represents the set of limitations that are associated with a serverless PaaS.

The platform level also involved extensions in the *Security Controls* class. Specifically, the subclasses *SecurityConfiguration* and *HardwareBasedSecurity* were introduced. The first refers to all configuration aspects over a network entity, specified via a network access rule set (defined as a separate subclass called *NetworkAccessRule*). The latter aggregates all security capabilities offered as a service by dedicated hardware components. The *HardwareBasedSecurity* subclasses are: i) *FPGASecurity*: refers to security capabilities implanted in a FPGA hardware; ii) *SecureEnclave* which refers to the capability of a trusted execution environment based on dedicated microkernels that support isolation and encryption.

Also, a number of important extensions were introduced in MDS Big-Data Model. For example, the *Data Management* class of the *Big-Data Model* was extended. It encapsulates all relevant concepts enabling to describe major technological choices with respect to how big data is acquired, stored, processed, transferred or replicated for redundancy reasons. The extensions involve both new subclasses and properties.

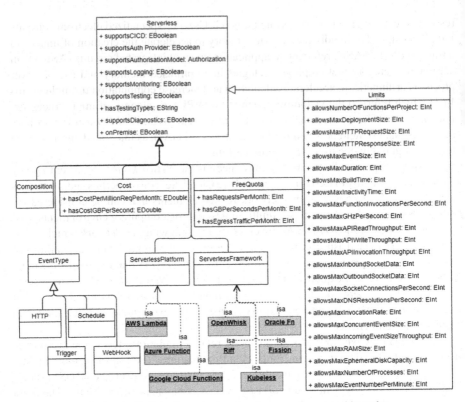

Fig. 5. UML class diagram showing the serverless class hierarchy.

5   Modelling a 5G Cloud-RAN Application

This section involves the modelling of a real application in the 5G Software-defined Radio Access Networks (RAN) domain mapping to a use-case of the Morphemic project (www.morphemic.cloud) provided by use-case partner IS-Wireless (www.is-wireless.com). Such a modelling, covering CAMEL 3.0 & MDS extensions, relates to the basic use-case scenario of cloud deployment with one optimisation objective, specific communication requirements and components with multiple configurations.

A RAN system comprises various protocols like radio-frequency (RF) and the physical one. Many such protocols can be virtualised and grouped in the form of components: the Distributed Unit (DU) one comprising intermediate-level protocols and the Central Unit (CU) one comprising high-level protocols. The CU unit can be also separated into the control (CP) and user plane (UP) such that the respective parts, i.e., CU-CP and CU-UP, can be independently deployed.

For the static deployment scenario, various kinds of requirements have been considered. The generic requirements are the following: i) the location of all components should be in Poland; ii) each component must have at least 2 GBs of RAM; iii) script-based configurations for components require at least 5 number of cores; iv) the application average availability should be at least 99.999%; v) the overall average response time should be minimised. The communication-specific requirements are the following: i) DU ↔ CU-CP: 5 ms latency and 0.4 Gbps throughput; ii) DU ↔ CU-UP: 1 ms latency and 4 Gbps throughput. Finally, FPGA-specific requirements are given for the CU-CP component: i) Total memory should be at least 2430 Kb; ii) Number of logic elements should be at least 145000.

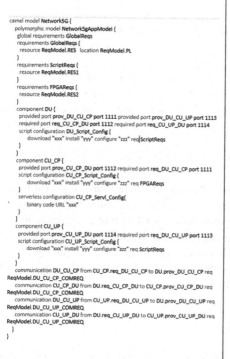

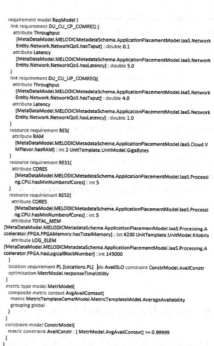

Fig. 6. The 5G RAN use case polymorphic model

Fig. 7. Requirement, constraint, and metric models

The first snippet of RAN application's CAMEL 3.0 model (see Fig. 6) focuses on the polymorphic model, which involves the specification of the aforementioned components. This model includes the definition of a global set of requirements related to the components' location and the demanded number of resources. Further, four communications with their quality requirements are described while CU-CP has two configurations (a script-based with FPGA requirements and a serverless).

The next snippet (see Fig. 7) shows the requirement, metric type and constraint sub-models. The requirement model includes two requirements covering the quality of communication between DU and CU-CP as well as between DU and CU-UP. Each requirement specifies 2 attributes defining constraints on communication latency and throughput, annotated using MDS to point to the right network QoS data properties.

The requirement model also involves one resource requirement applied to all application components imposing a lower bound on RAM size. There is another resource requirement for all script-based component configurations imposing a lower bound on the number of cores. Another resource requirement covers lower bounds on logical element number and total memory for the required FPGA. All resource requirements are annotated with MDS elements. Finally, the requirement model specifies a requirement demanding that all application components are located in Poland, an SLO related to a constraint on average application availability (described in the constraint sub-model) plus an optimization requirement over average response time.

The metric type model (not completely shown due to page number restrictions) re-uses availability-based metrics from a metric (template) model. Thus, it only specifies a composite metric context explicating the metric to be computed (average application availability) and the way measurements of the downstream metric (raw application availability) can be aggregated to compute it.

The above modelling clearly indicates that the combination of MDS and CAMEL enables to flexibly specify various requirement kinds over various attributes of related concepts like FPGAs, communication quality and CPUs. These concepts are not covered at the language level by CAMEL but only MDS. However, CAMEL has the flexibility to introduce requirements on those concepts at the model level.

The ability to select different deployment models from the polymorphic ones featured by the Morphemic platform and powered by CAMEL must be highlighted. Currently, the optimization objective is to minimize application's response time. Through a utility-based optimization approach, Morphemic will select a provider-agnostic deployment architecture with the script-based configuration for CU-CP that enables to utilize FPGAs. However, if the objective was to maximise the overall throughput, then the serverless configuration for CU-CP would have been selected. Thus, different optimization requirements lead to selecting different deployment architectures while the overall variability is covered and enabled by CAMEL.

6   Conclusions and Future Work

This work introduced novel modelling artefacts to support the complete modelling of polymorphic applications. Specifically, enhancements over two related modelling frameworks were discussed, CAMEL and MDS. A new CAMEL version was presented with additional artefacts that enable the complete specification of multi-cloud polymorphic applications, which can be deployed via MCMPs. The MDS schema, initially introduced as a formal vocabulary that properly covers the basic cloud resource and service types as well as multiple data management aspects, it was significantly extended to cover a richer set of resources. Now it includes HPC, edge and hardware-accelerated resources, plus network domain aspects. Last, a walkthrough of how application modelling works in a real 5G cloud-RAN application was provided.

The next steps of this work will involve a further evaluation and potential evolution of both the CAMEL language and its MDS vocabulary, through the validation of the extended modelling capabilities in terms of advanced, polymorphic-enabled scenarios, such as an e-BrainScience application for AI-driven analysis of clinical data and a computational fluid dynamics simulation deployed over HPC resources.

Acknowledgments. The research leading to these results has received funding from the EU's Horizon 2020 research and innovation programme under grant agreement No. 871643 MORPHEMIC project.

References

1. Kritikos, K., Skrzypek, P., Zahid, F.: Are cloud platforms ready for multi-cloud? In: Brogi, A., Zimmermann, W., Kritikos, K. (eds.) ESOCC 2020. LNCS, vol. 12054, pp. 56–73. Springer, Cham (2020). https://doi.org/10.1007/978-3-030-44769-4_5
2. Achilleos, A.P., et al.: The cloud application modelling and execution language. J. Cloud. Comput. **8**(1), 20 (2019)
3. Verginadis, Y., Patiniotakis, I., Mentzas, G.: Metadata schema for data-aware multi-cloud computing. In: INISTA, Thessaloniki, pp. 1–9 (2018)
4. Morin, B., Barais, O., Jézéquel, J.M., Fleurey, F., Solberg, A.: Models@run.time to support dynamic adaptation. Computer **42**(10), 44–51 (2009)
5. Etchevers, X., Coupaye, T., Boyer, F., Palma, N.: Self-configuration of distributed applications in the cloud. In: CLOUD, Washington, USA, pp. 668–675 (2011)
6. Nguyen, D.K., Lelli, F., Papazoglou, M.P., van den Heuvel, W.-J.: Blueprinting approach in support of cloud computing. Future Internet **4**(1), 322–346 (2012)
7. Palma D., Spatzier, T.: Topology and orchestration specification for cloud applications (TOSCA). Organization for the Advancement of Structured Information Standards (OASIS) (2013). https://bit.ly/3cd8AGJ. Accessed June 2013
8. Andrikopoulos, V., Reuter, A., Gómez Sáez, S., Leymann, F.: A GENTL approach for cloud application topologies. In: Villari, M., Zimmermann, W., Lau, K.-K. (eds.) ESOCC 2014. LNCS, vol. 8745, pp. 148–159. Springer, Heidelberg (2014). https://doi.org/10.1007/978-3-662-44879-3_11
9. Ardagna, D., et al.: MODACLOUDS, a model-driven approach for the design and execution of applications on multiple clouds. In: ICSE MiSE, Zurich, Switzerland, pp. 50–56 (2012)
10. Bergmayr, A., Breitenbücher, U., Kopp, O., Wimmer, M., Kappel, G., Leymann, F.: From architecture modeling to application provisioning for the cloud by combining UML and TOSCA. In: CLOSER, Rome, Italy, pp. 97–108 (2016)
11. Hamdaqa, M., Tahvildari, L.: Stratus ML: a layered cloud modeling framework. In: IEEE International Conference on Cloud Engineering, Tempe, USA, pp. 96–105 (2015)
12. Fitz, T., Theiler, M., Smarsly, K.: A metamodel for cyber-physical systems. Adv. Eng. Inform. **41**, 100930 (2019)
13. van der Ham, J.J.: A semantic model for complex computer networks: the network description language. Ph.D thesis (2010). https://hdl.handle.net/11245/1.318784
14. Zhou, Q., Gray, A.J.G., McLaughlin, S.: ToCo: an ontology for representing hybrid telecommunication networks. In: Hitzler, P., Fernández, M., Janowicz, K., Zaveri, A., Gray, A.J.G., Lopez, V., Haller, A., Hammar, K. (eds.) ESWC 2019. LNCS, vol. 11503, pp. 507–522. Springer, Cham (2019). https://doi.org/10.1007/978-3-030-21348-0_33
15. Qiao, X., Li, X., Che, J.: Telecommunications service domain ontology: semantic interoperation foundation of intelligent integrated services. In: Ortiz, J. (ed.) Telecommunications Networks—Current Status and Future Trends. InTech (2012)
16. Kessler, C., Li, L., Atalar, A., Dobre, A.: XPDL: extensible platform description language to support energy modeling and optimization. In: 44th International Conference on Parallel Processing Workshops. Beijing, China, pp. 51–60 (2015)

17. Object Management Group: UML Profile for MARTE: Modeling and Analysis of Real-Time Embedded Systems. Object Management Group (OMG), OMG Document formal/2009-11-02 (2009). https://www.omg.org/spec/MARTE/1.0/PDF. Accessed 11 Feb 2009
18. Castañé, G.G., Xiong, H., Dong, D., Morrison, J.P.: An ontology for heterogeneous resources management interoperability and HPC in the cloud. Future Gener. Comput. Syst. **88**, 373–384 (2018)

Models, Methods and Tools

A Multi-label Propagation Community Detection Algorithm for Dynamic Complex Networks

Hanning Zhang[1]⊙, Bo Dong[2,3](✉)⊙, Haiyu Wu[4]⊙, and Boqin Feng[1]⊙

[1] School of Computer Science and Technology, Xi'an Jiaotong University,
Xi'an 710049, China
zhanghn@stu.xjtu.edu.cn
[2] School of Continuing Education, Xi'an Jiaotong University, Xi'an 710049, China
dong.bo@xjtu.edu.cn
[3] National Engineering Lab for Big Data Analytics, Xi'an Jiaotong University,
Xi'an 710049, China
[4] Xi'an Network Computing Data Technology Co., Ltd., Xi'an 710049, China

Abstract. With the rapid development of the Internet, the complex network data presents an explosive growth. However, most of the complex networks in the real world are dynamic, How to effectively detect communities in dynamic complex networks has become a hot issue in current research. Therefore, we propose a dynamic network oriented multi-label propagation algorithm. Firstly, in order to reduce the running time, the SLPA algorithm of multi-label propagation class is selected as the basic algorithm; secondly, the SLPA algorithm is improved by using the history label to initialize the labels, and then the DSLPA (Speaker-listener Label Propagation Algorithm for Dynamic network) algorithm is designed and implemented. The experimental results showed that the proposed algorithm has high modularity and greatly reduces the running time.

Keywords: Multi-label propagation · Complex network · Dynamic network · Community detection

1 Introduction

With the rapid development of the Internet, complex network data presents an explosive growth. [1–6] have gotten a tremendous improvement on static community detection. However, most of the complex networks in the real world are dynamic, such as the addition of new users, the formation of new social relationships, and the emergence of new transactions in trading networks. With the dynamic change of network data, the community structure is also changing dynamically. Overlapping community detection [7–12] in dynamic networks has become a hot spot in the field of community detection. When the network changes dynamically with time, we can select the network at a certain time and use the static community detection algorithm to partition the community.

© Springer Nature Switzerland AG 2021
M. La Rosa et al. (Eds.): CAiSE 2021, LNCS 12751, pp. 467–482, 2021.
https://doi.org/10.1007/978-3-030-79382-1_28

A series of community structures at a specific time can reflect the change of network community structure with time to a certain extent, but there still are some disadvantages in this truncation method. Because the static community partition based on the network structure at a certain time does not consider the community structure information of the previous moments, which will destroy the dynamic evolution process of community structure. Based on the SLPA algorithm, this paper proposes a DSLPA algorithm using historical community information. In this process, we mainly encountered the following difficulties.

First of all, our algorithm needs to be able to quickly partition communities on dynamic complex networks. Because of the timeliness of the community structure of the dynamic network, if the community structure cannot be given in time when the current time is needed, it will be useless to get the community structure at this moment after the network has changed greatly. Therefore, this paper selected the low time complexity SLPA algorithm to do the optimization.

Secondly, our algorithm needs to ensure the dynamic structure of the community. If the community structure of a dynamic network is analyzed in a truncated way, the community structure at the previous moment of the network is meaningless. Therefore, there must be some relationships between the current community structure and the previous one. Although it cannot be accurately expressed at present, it must be taken into account in the division of the community. Therefore, in this paper, the community structure information of $t - 1$ time is taken into account in the community detection at time t, which ensures the dynamic of community structure.

After solving the above problems, this paper designed and implemented a dynamic complex network oriented overlapping community detection algorithm - DSLPA.

2   Related Work

Community detection algorithms for static complex networks are collectively referred to as static community detection algorithms. Accordingly, community detection algorithms for dynamic complex networks are collectively referred to as dynamic community detection algorithms. [13] divided dynamic community detection algorithms into two categories, one is real-time, the other is to know network changes in advance, which is equivalent to offline. [14] formulated the three cost functions i-cost, g-cost, and c-cost to transform the community detection problem in dynamic networks into an optimization problem, and proposed an algorithm framework based on the coloring method to analyze community evolution. FacetNet proposed by [15] is a framework to study the dynamic evolution of communities. When detecting communities, it not only depends on the current network data but also considers the network information before the evolution. [13] used greedy aggregation technology, and the extended method can be used for community detection in dynamic networks. [1] improved the Louvain algorithm by introducing the concept of dynamics. The key point of their algorithm is to use the community structure at time $t - 1$ to detect communities at time t. [16] tried to find non-overlapping communities in dynamic networks, and proposed a modular QCA (Quick Community Adaptation) method. QCA can track the evolution of communities online. [17] proposed two improved spectral clustering frameworks PCQ (Preserving Cluster Quality) and PCM (Preserving Cluster Membership). These two frameworks combine community detection and community evolution, so as to detect the change of the number of nodes in the dynamic changes of communities. [18] proposed a two-stage clustering algorithm called CHRONICLE. In the first stage and the second stage, cosine similarity and general similarity are used to measure the similarity, respectively. It is a combination of structural affinity and weight affinity.

3   Dynamic Complex Network

3.1   Representation of Dynamic Complex Network

The dynamic property of a dynamic complex network is mainly manifested in the dynamic change of nodes and edges with time, which can be expressed by formula 1 as follows:

$$G_d(t) = (V(t), E(t)) \tag{1}$$

Where $G_d(t)$ is the dynamic complex network G_d changes with time t; $V(t)$ is the node set V changing with time t; and $E(t)$ is the change of edge set E with time t. If $t = t_0$, then the node set and edge set of dynamic network $G_d(t)$ at t_0 are $V(t_0)$ and $E(t_0)$.

The change of node-set and edge set in a dynamic network can be divided into an increase and decrease. For instance, in the social network formed by microblog, the addition of new users and the cancellation of old users are represented by the generation of new nodes and the deletion of old nodes, while the subscribing behavior and the unsubscribing behavior between users are represented by the generation of new edges and the deletion of old edges.

3.2   Dynamic Community Evolution

As one of the important characteristics of complex networks, community structure also exists in dynamic complex networks. With the dynamic change of the network, its internal community structure is also changing dynamically. As shown in Fig. 1, the evolution process of community is mainly composed of six change modes, namely, the growth and contraction of a single community, the merger of multiple communities, the splitting of a single community, the birth of new communities and the death of old communities. Communities in dynamic complex networks will evolve dynamically with time, so it is very meaningful to mine the evolution rules. For example, in the social network formed by microblog, those influencers often play the role of core nodes in the community, and these core nodes are related to the life cycle of the whole social circle. Therefore, projecting the core nodes in the social network helps to maintain the stability of the social circle.

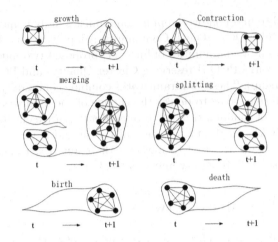

Fig. 1. Dynamic community evolution diagram

3.3   The Community Detection in Online Trading Network

The online trading network is a typical complex network. We can use user's registration information, user's label, user's pre-selection preferences, goods, goods category relationship, goods label relationship, trading data, and trading evaluation, to quickly build a complex network. In the online trading network, different users may need to buy different products in different periods. If the user groups in the current period can be found in time, more accurate commodity recommendations can be made, and the transaction of success probability can be improved. Therefore, it is necessary to use a community detection algorithm to discover consumers' communities and then recommend corresponding goods.

The construction of a complex network of the online trading platform includes four aspects: network topology, network node weight, network selection orientation, and network time adjustment. We take the users and goods as the node, the trading relationship as the edge, and the number of trading and the user's trading evaluation as the weight of the edge. According to the time relativity of the trading, we construct a complex network on the dynamic trading set of time changes. In this network, the dynamic community detection algorithm is used to detect the community, divide the community, and recommend products based on the results. The structure of a community discovery application system in a typical online trading network is shown in Fig. 2.

The system is mainly divided into three sub-modules: 1) Data acquisition, extraction, and storage module. The data includes user registration information, user's tag information, user's pre-selection preferences information, goods, goods category, goods tag, dynamic trading data. The storage system can use a relational database such as MySQL, a cloud database such as HBase, or a graph database such as neo4j. These can support user scale of more than one million, goods scale of more than ten million, and trading number scale of more than one million daily average. 2) Complex network community construction

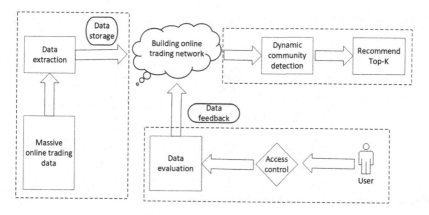

Fig. 2. The architecture of community detection in online trading network

community detection, and recommendation module. The construction of the complex network and community detection are the basis of commodity recommendation, while the data update of the online trading network is faster, so we need to use a more efficient dynamic community detection algorithm to ensure that the iterative update of complex network and the time of community detection are at the minute level. 3) User privacy, access control, and data evaluation feedback module. The core value of this module is to dynamically influence the network structure by collecting users' evaluation feedback and then influence the goods recommendation ranking. Through the above architecture, the community detection algorithm can be applied to the online trading platform quickly and effectively for goods recommendation.

3.4 Overview of SLPA Algorithm

SLPA [19] (Speaker-listener Label Propagation Algorithm) algorithm is extended from LPA [20] (Label Propagation Algorithm) algorithm. Because each node has only one community label in the LPA algorithm, each node only belongs to one community after partition, so the LPA algorithm can only detect non-overlapping communities. [19] extended the LPA algorithm and introduced a multi-label and labeled filtering mechanisms to improve the SLPA algorithm. The main steps of the SLPA algorithm are as follows:

Step 1 Initialize the community label and add a unique community label to the label list of all nodes.

Step 2 Sequentially select all nodes as listeners and their neighbors as speakers to propagate community labels.

Step 3 If the preset number of iterations is reached, the algorithm stops; otherwise, step 2 will continue.

Step 4 The community labels are filtered to remove the community labels which are less than the filtering threshold.

The label propagation process of the SLPA algorithm can be shown in Fig. 3 as follows:

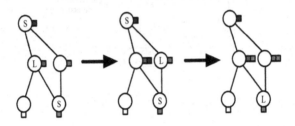

Fig. 3. Schematic diagram of SLPA label propagation process (Color figure online)

In Fig. 3, the square color block attached to the node represents the community label. In the first step, the red label node is selected as the listener, and its neighboring nodes, purple and blue label nodes, are selected as speakers, from which the purple label is randomly selected to be added to its label list as the community label of this propagation process; in the second step, the green label node is selected as the listener, and the purple and blue label nodes of its neighbor nodes are selected as the speaker, from which the blue label is randomly selected to be added to its label list as the community label of this communication process. Other labels are propagated in the same way.

When the preset number of iterations is reached, the label propagation iteration process is stopped. In the label filtering stage, the community labels whose frequency is less than the filtering threshold can be removed.

In the research of dynamic community detection algorithms, some researchers [15] adopted a two-stage research method. In the first stage, the dynamic network is sliced, and the community structure of each time slice network is divided by the static community detection algorithm; in the second stage, the community structures of each time slice in the first stage are connected in series to form a complete evolution process of community structure. Although this method can excavate the dynamic community structure of the network to a certain extent, it separates the dynamic nature of the community structure. When partitioning the community structure of the current time, the historical community information of the network in the previous moment is not considered, so the community structure of the network is likely to transfer unexpectedly. In this paper, based on the SLPA algorithm, we use the community label of the previous time to initialize the label, so that the improved DSLPA algorithm can avoid the above problems.

4   DSLPA Algorithm

4.1   Improvement of SLPA Algorithm

As mentioned above, the two-stage dynamic community detection algorithm will split the dynamics of community structure. Therefore, the improvement of the

SLPA algorithm mainly focuses on two points: generation and absorption of historical community information.

The Generation of Historical Community Information: Historical community information refers to the community information of the network at the previous moment. In the SLPA algorithm, the final generation is a set of nodes, each node set represents a community. Because the SLPA algorithm is overlapping community detection, the same node will appear in different node sets, which means that the node belongs to multiple communities at the same time. The community composed of such a set of nodes in the community structure was obtained in the process of community partition. However, such a community structure is too large, so this paper will simplify it.

After the SLPA algorithm completes the label propagation process, the community label list of each node has been fixed. If the community label with the largest frequency in node i is marked as C_i^{max} (if there are more than one, one of them is randomly selected), then each node and its corresponding C_i^{max} are called historical community information. In the output phase of the algorithm, a historical community information file composed of the node number and its C_i^{max} is generated.

The Absorption of Historical Community Information: The absorption of historical community information is the utilization of historical community information files. In the label initialization stage, if the node appears in the historical community information file, its label will be initialized to the corresponding C_i^{max}; if the node does not appear in the historical community information file, a new community label will be initialized. The historical community structure of the network is transmitted through the nodes that have not changed in the dynamic network, so as to ensure the integrity of the dynamic change of the community structure to a certain extent.

The generation of historical community information is the preparation for its absorption in the next community detection process. Through the transmission of historical community information, the community structure at different times can be smoothly evolved to avoid the unexpected transfer of community structure.

4.2 Description of DSLPA Algorithm

In the previous section, we have introduced the improvement of the SLPA algorithm. The following are the specific steps of the DSLPA algorithm.

Step 1 Initialize the community label of the node according to the historical community information file: if the node appears in the historical community information file, initialize its community label as the corresponding label; if the node does not appear in the historical community information file, initialize a new community label for it.

Step 2 Perform the following procedures for all nodes sequentially.
    Step 2.1 Select the current node as the listener.

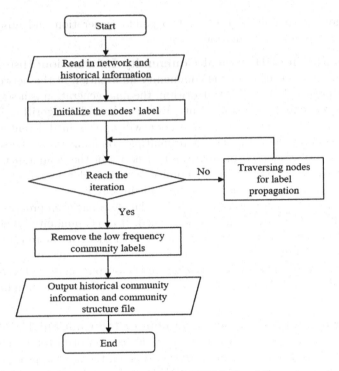

Fig. 4. The flowchart of DSLPA algorithm

Step 2.2 All nodes that can reach the listener are regarded as speakers. Each speaker nodes passes a community label to the listener nodes according to the speaking rule.

Step 2.3 The listener node selects one of the labels from the speaker node according to the listening rule and puts it into the community label list.

Step 3 If the preset number of iterations is reached, step 4 is executed; otherwise, step 2 is executed.

Step 4 According to the preset label filtering threshold, the community labels with low frequency are eliminated

Step 5 Generate community structure files and historical community information files.

In this algorithm, the speaking rule in step 2 is to select the label with the highest frequency in the community label list. If there is more than one label, one label will be randomly selected; the listening rule is to select the label with the most frequent occurrence from the speakers, and if there is more than one, randomly select one. When there is no historical community information file, the DSLPA algorithm will degenerate to the SLPA algorithm. The flowchart of the DSLPA algorithm is shown in Fig. 4 and the algorithm is shown in Algorithm 1.

Algorithm1. DSLPA Algorithm

1: **Input:** $G_t = (V_t, E_t)$: dynamic network G when t;
C_{t-1}: history community information of G_{t-1};
T_p: the iteration number of propagation;
α: label filtering threshold

2: **Begin**

3: $[n, Nodes] = loadnetwork();$

4: Stage 1: initialization

5: **for** $i = 1 : n$ **do**

6:      **if** $C_{t-1}.find(i) == true$ **then**

7:          $Nodes(i).Mem = C_{t-1}^i;$

8:      **else**

9:          $Nodes(i).Mem = i;$

10:      **end if**

11: **end for**

12: Stage 2: evolution

13: **for** $T = 1 : T_p$ **do**

14:      $Nodes.ShuffleOrder();$

15:      **for** $i = 1 : n$ **do**

16:          $Listener = Nodes(i);$

17:          $Speakers = Nodes(i).getNbs();$

18:          **for** $j = 1 : Speakers.len$ **do**

19:              $LabelList(j) = Speakers(j).speakerRule();$

20:          **end for**

21:          $w = Listener.listenerRule(LabelList);$

22:          $Listener.Mem.add(w);$

23:      **end for**

24: **end for**

25: Stage 3: post-processing

26: **for** $i = 1 : n$ **do**

27:      remove $Nodes(i)$ labels seen with probability $< \alpha$;

28: **end for**

29: Stage 4: writing history community information

30: **for** $i = 1 : n$ **do**

31:      $m = Nodes(i).Mem.max();$

32:      write $pair(i, m)$ into history community information file C_t;

33: **end for**

34: **End**

35: **Output:** $Nodes.labels$: community structure of G_t; C_t: history community information of G_t;

4.3 Complexity Analysis

Spatial Complexity Analysis: The main space of the DSLPA algorithm is used to store community labels of storage nodes. Its storage structure is shown in Fig. 5. The length of the label list of each node is the same as the iteration number T_p. Therefore, the space complexity of the DSLPA algorithm is $O(nT_p)$, and n represents the total number of nodes.

Time Complexity Analysis: The time complexity of the label initialization stage is $O(n)$; in the label propagation phase, the outer loop is controlled by the iteration number parameter T_p, which is a small constant; the inner loop is controlled by the number of nodes n, and the time complexity of each speaking process is $O(1)$. Each listening process needs to check the labels of all adjacent nodes, and its time complexity is $O(d)$, where d represents the average degree of nodes. Therefore, the time complexity of the label propagation stage is $O(nT_p)$; in the label filtering stage, each label on each node needs to be judged, so the time complexity is $O(nT_p)$; in the historical community information output stage, the time complexity is $O(n)$. The time complexity of DSLPA is $O(nT_p)$.

5   Experimental Analysis

5.1   Dataset and Experimental Platform

In this experiment, two real-world dynamic network datasets are used, which are mobile communication network [21] and the Enron email network. The experimental platform is a Windows 10 operating system with an Intel Core i5-2400 3.10 GHz CPU, an 8 GB Memory, a 2 TB hard drive and Matlab framework.

Mobile Communication Network: Mobile communication network records the 10-day communication information between mobile phones in a certain area in June 2006. Each node is associated with a unique mobile phone number. The edge between nodes indicates that there is a call between the two mobile phones, and the weight on the edge represents the number of calls between the two mobile phones. In this dataset, there are 400 mobile phones in total. If any mobile phone has not made a call on the same day, it will not appear in the communication network of that day. 10 days of mobile phone communication information can form 10 networks, and the specific information is shown in Table 1. These 10 networks can be regarded as 10 moments of a dynamic network.

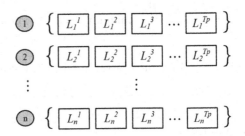

Fig. 5. Label storage structure of DSLPA algorithm

Table 1. Mobile communication network dataset

Time step	Type	#Node	#Edge	Average degree	Clustering coefficient
1	Directed, Weighted	370	987	2.6250	0.0328
2	Directed, Weighted	373	964	2.4950	0.0192
3	Directed, Weighted	374	953	2.5450	0.0137
4	Directed, Weighted	374	1013	2.5700	0.0179
5	Directed, Weighted	373	991	2.5400	0.0160
6	Directed, Weighted	373	963	2.5600	0.0207
7	Directed, Weighted	367	936	2.4900	0.0118
8	Directed, Weighted	365	1005	2.5550	0.0203
9	Directed, Weighted	374	982	2.5900	0.0290
10	Directed, Weighted	384	1040	2.6500	0.0095

Enron Email Network: Enron mail 3 is a three-year potentially dangerous e-mail collected by an American enterprise. The original dataset includes 517431 emails sent by 151 users, the specific information is shown in Table 2.

5.2 Comparative Experiment and Parameter Setting

For the DSLPA algorithm, this paper selects FacetNet [15] and DYNAMO [21] two algorithms to do comparative experiments. The facetNet algorithm is based on the SNFM static community detection algorithm. It integrates community

Table 2. Enron email network dataset

Time step	Type	#Node	#Edge	Average degree	Clustering coefficient
1	Directed, Weighted	96	1070	2.3841	0.4415
2	Directed, Weighted	93	1559	2.7020	0.5406
3	Directed, Weighted	97	1844	2.8874	0.4646
4	Directed, Weighted	108	1869	3.4040	0.4430
5	Directed, Weighted	125	1919	3.8675	0.4993
6	Directed, Weighted	120	1001	3.0596	0.3959
7	Directed, Weighted	109	1325	3.3377	0.4882
8	Directed, Weighted	131	2270	5.2450	0.4783
9	Directed, Weighted	128	3152	4.7815	0.4950
10	Directed, Weighted	135	8693	7.6159	0.4957
11	Directed, Weighted	127	6276	6.2119	0.5062
12	Directed, Weighted	113	2146	4.3046	0.4519

detection and evolution analysis by minimizing a cost function, and supports overlapping community detection. In order to avoid the noise generated by evolution, the FacetNet algorithm not only depends on the current network structure, but also takes into account the past network characteristics. DYNAMO (DYNamic MultiObjective Genetic Algorithms) is based on a genetic algorithm, and its method of smooth community detection can be expressed as a multiobjective optimization problem. The first is to maximize the modularity of the current network, and then to minimize the distance between the current network community structure and the previous community structure. In the DYNAMO algorithm, the parameter α is used to represent the weight of modularity in the objective function, and $1 - \alpha$ is used to represent the weight of the similarity function. When $\alpha = 1$ or 0, the objective function degenerates to a single objective optimization function.

Because the different parameter values in the experiment have great influence on the experimental results, this paper sets the parameters in each algorithm according to the relevant literature [15,19,21], and the specific parameter values are shown in Table 3.

Table 3. Parameter settings of experimental algorithm

Algorithm	Parameter	Value
FacetNet	α	0.80
DYNAMO	Population size	100
	Number of generations	100
DSLPA	Iteration number	30
	Label filter parameter	0.3

5.3 Experimental Results and Analysis

Because there is no community label in both datasets, the NMI value between the partition result and the real community structure cannot be calculated. The experimental results are as follows.

Modularity: The modularity of the community structure divided by the three algorithms at each time of the two datasets is calculated, and the experimental results are shown in Fig. 6. According to the experimental results and Fig. 6 (a) and Fig. 6 (b), the modularity obtained by DSLPA is higher than that obtained by FacetNet algorithm and DYNAMO algorithm on mobile communication network dataset and Enron e-mail network dataset.

Running Time: In the mobile communication network and Enron e-mail network, the running time of the three algorithms is shown in Table 4 and Table 5 respectively. As can be seen from Table 4 and Table 5, the running time of the DSLPA algorithm on the mobile communication network dataset and Enron e-mail network dataset is less than FacetNet algorithm and DYNAMO algorithm.

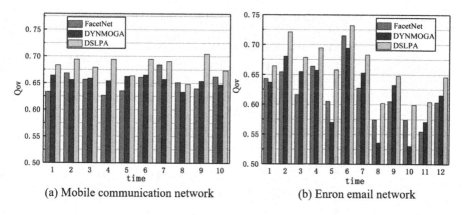

(a) Mobile communication network   (b) Enron email network

Fig. 6. The experimental results comparison of modularity

It can be seen that in larger networks, the advantages of the DSLPA algorithm will be more prominent.

Table 4. Running time on mobile communication network (s)

Time step	FacetNet	DYNAMO	DSLPA
1	7.0	4.8	3.3
2	7.1	5.1	3.4
3	6.8	5.1	3.4
4	7.0	5.0	3.3
5	7.1	5.2	3.2
6	6.7	5.0	3.1
7	6.9	5.1	3.5
8	7.0	5.3	3.3
9	7.2	5.6	3.4
10	7.1	6.0	3.3

In summary, the DSLPA algorithm is better than other algorithms in modularity. In terms of running time, the DSLPA algorithm has greater advantages and can complete dynamic overlapping community detection in a short time.

Table 5. Running time on Enron email network (s)

Time step	FacetNet	DYNAMO	DSLPA
1	3.1	2.5	1.8
2	3.1	2.6	1.9
3	3.0	2.5	1.8
4	3.2	2.7	1.8
5	3.1	2.6	1.9
6	3.0	2.4	1.8
7	3.3	2.7	1.9
8	3.2	3.1	2.0
9	4.0	3.4	1.9
10	4.1	3.6	2.1
11	3.8	2.7	2.0
12	3.7	2.6	1.9

6   Conclusions

To solve the problem of overlapping community detection in the dynamic complex network, this paper proposes a DSLPA algorithm. Through the research of the evolution of a dynamic community and the SLPA algorithm, we improve the SLPA algorithm to adapt to the dynamic complex network. The experimental results show the effectiveness and efficiency of the DSLPA algorithm in dynamic complex networks. In addition, we take the online trading network as an example to introduce how the dynamic community detection algorithm is applied in the system. In the future, we will study the parallel of the DSLPA algorithm in the distributed system and the performance optimization based on the graph database, so as to make it better meet the application in the larger-scale dynamic complex network.

Acknowledgement. This research was partially supported by "The Fundamental Theory and Applications of Big Data with Knowledge Engineering" under the National Key Research and Development Program of China with Grant No. 2018YFB1004500, the National Science Foundation of China under Grant Nos. 62037001, 61721002, 62050194 and 62002282, the MOE Innovation Research Team No. IRT_17R86, and Project of XJTU-SERVYOU Joint Tax-AI Lab.

References

1. He, J., Chen, D.: A fast algorithm for community detection in temporal network. Phys. A Stat. Mech. Appl. **429**, 87–94 (2015)
2. Wang, Z., Zhang, D., Zhou, X., Yang, D., Yu, Z., Yu, Z.: Discovering and profiling overlapping communities in location-based social networks. IEEE Trans. Syst. Man Cybern. Syst. **44**(4), 499–509 (2013)

3. Rhouma, D., Ben Romdhane, L.: An efficient multilevel scheme for coarsening large scale social networks. Appl. Intell. **48**(10), 3557–3576 (2018)
4. LaSalle, D., Karypis, G.: Multi-threaded modularity based graph clustering using the multilevel paradigm. J. Parallel Distrib. Comput. **76**, 66–80 (2015)
5. Li, Z., Liu, J., Kai, W.: A multiobjective evolutionary algorithm based on structural and attribute similarities for community detection in attributed networks. IEEE Trans. Cybern. **48**(7), 1963–1976 (2017)
6. Zhang, H., Dong, B., Feng, B., Wu, H.: An overlapping community detection algorithm based on triangle reduction weighted for large-scale complex network. In: Qiu, M. (ed.) ICA3PP 2020. LNCS, vol. 12452, pp. 627–644. Springer, Cham (2020). https://doi.org/10.1007/978-3-030-60245-1_43
7. Cordeiro, M., Sarmento, R.P., Gama, J.: Dynamic community detection in evolving networks using locality modularity optimization. Social Netw. Anal. Min. **6**(1), 1–20 (2016). https://doi.org/10.1007/s13278-016-0325-1
8. Clementi, A., Di. Ianni, M., Gambosi, G., Natale, E., Silvestri, R.: Distributed community detection in dynamic graphs. Theor. Comput. Sci. **584**, 19–41 (2015)
9. Zhan, B., Zhiang, W., Cao, J., Jiang, Y.: Local community mining on distributed and dynamic networks from a multiagent perspective. IEEE Trans. Cybern. **46**(4), 986–999 (2015)
10. Samie, M.E., Hamzeh, A.: Change-aware community detection approach for dynamic social networks. Appl. Intell. **48**(1), 78–96 (2017). https://doi.org/10.1007/s10489-017-0934-z
11. Chen, N., Bo, H., Rui, Y.: Dynamic network community detection with coherent neighborhood propinquity. IEEE Access **8**, 27915–27926 (2020)
12. Zeng, X., Wang, W., Chen, C., Yen, G.G.: A consensus community-based particle swarm optimization for dynamic community detection. IEEE Trans. Cybern. **50**(6), 2502–2513 (2019)
13. Bansal, S., Bhowmick, S., Paymal, P.: Fast community detection for dynamic complex networks. In: da F. Costa, L., Evsukoff, A., Mangioni, G., Menezes, R. (eds.) CompleNet 2010. CCIS, vol. 116, pp. 196–207. Springer, Heidelberg (2011). https://doi.org/10.1007/978-3-642-25501-4_20
14. Chayant, T., Tanya, B., David, K.: A framework for community identification in dynamic social networks. In: Proceedings of the 13th ACM SIGKDD International Conference on Knowledge Discovery and Data Mining, pp. 717–726 (2007)
15. Lin, Y.R., Chi, Y., Zhu, S., Sundaram, H., Tseng, B.L.: FacetNet: a framework for analyzing communities and their evolutions in dynamic networks. In: Proceedings of the 17th International Conference on World Wide Web, pp. 685–694 (2008)
16. Nguyen, N.P., Dinh, T.N., Shen, Y., Thai, M.T.: Dynamic social community detection and its applications. PloS One **9**(4), e91431 (2014)
17. Chi, Y., Song, X., Zhou, D., Hino, K., Tseng, B.L.: On evolutionary spectral clustering. ACM Trans. Knowl. Disc. Data (TKDD) **3**(4), 1–30 (2009)
18. Kim, M.-S., Han, J.: CHRONICLE: a two-stage density-based clustering algorithm for dynamic networks. In: Gama, J., Costa, V.S., Jorge, A.M., Brazdil, P.B. (eds.) DS 2009. LNCS (LNAI), vol. 5808, pp. 152–167. Springer, Heidelberg (2009). https://doi.org/10.1007/978-3-642-04747-3_14
19. Xie, J., Szymanski, B.K., Liu, X.: SLPA: uncovering overlapping communities in social networks via a speaker-listener interaction dynamic process. In: 2011 IEEE 11th International Conference on Data Mining Workshops, pp. 344–349. IEEE (2011)

20. Raghavan, U.N., Albert, R., Kumara, S.: Near linear time algorithm to detect community structures in large-scale networks. Phys. Rev. E **76**(3), 036106 (2007)
21. Folino, F., Pizzuti, C.: An evolutionary multiobjective approach for community discovery in dynamic networks. IEEE Trans. Knowl. Data Eng. **26**(8), 1838–1852 (2014)

Comparing UML-Based and DSL-Based Modeling from Subjective and Objective Perspectives

África Domingo[1]([✉]), Jorge Echeverría[1]([✉]), Óscar Pastor[2]([✉]),
and Carlos Cetina[1]([✉])

[1] SVIT Research Group, Universidad San Jorge, Zaragoza, Spain
{adomingo,jecheverria,ccetina}@usj.es
[2] PROS Research Center, Universidad Politecnica de Valencia, Valencia, Spain
opastor@dsic.upv.es

Abstract. In the last two decades, researchers have conducted several empirical evaluations, involving thousands of subjects, to understand the use of models in software development. The results of these evaluations show that most of the subjects make informal use of the models, which is known as 'modeling as sketch'. In this paper, we present an experiment that compares UML-based and DSL-based modeling when subjects model a part of a commercial video game. In the comparison, we have used objective and subjective measures, in contrast to other works that focus either on objective measures to evaluate modeling performance or on subjective measures to analyze modeling styles. Our results reveal that subjects underestimate the potential of their own models. Our finding is relevant for the design of future evaluations and for the teaching and adoption of modeling. If users correctly assess their models, they might leverage their potential as programs.

Keywords: Empirical comparison · Modeling languages · UML · DSL

1 Introduction

The software engineering process goes from the initial idea for building a particular software (problem space) to the code that implements the software (solution space) through different transformations. The idea is first conceptualized through models, and then the models are transformed into fully functional code. To understand the use of modeling languages in software development, in the last two decades, researchers have conducted surveys [1,2,8,13,16,17,20,27], case studies [4,8,26], experiments [5,8,11,23,25,31], and interviews [8] involving more than 5,355 subjects. The researchers classified the styles of modeling into three categories: *sketch* (informal models to aid in communication, see Fig. 1.a), *blueprint* (models as the basis for programmers to create code, see Fig. 1.b), and

Partially supported by MINECO under the Project ALPS (RTI2018-096411-B-I00).

M. La Rosa et al. (Eds.): CAiSE 2021, LNCS 12751, pp. 483–498, 2021.
https://doi.org/10.1007/978-3-030-79382-1_29

programs (models that include all of the details needed to generate code, see Fig. 1.c). All of the works that evaluated the style of modeling [2,8,16,17,27] concur that most of the subjects make an informal use of the models, which is known as 'modeling as sketch'. Despite the benefits of using models as programs [14], models are still mainly used as sketch.

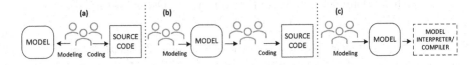

Fig. 1. (a) Models as sketch, (b) Models as blueprint, (c) Models as programs

The Unified Modeling Language (UML) is a general-purpose modeling language that has become the 'de facto' standard for modeling software systems [7,8,17]. Despite the available evidence about the efficiency of UML modeling, UML shortcomings have been identified by several authors [1,4,7,8,13,17,26]. In addition, to reduce the complexity of software development, the use of domain-specific languages (DSLs), languages closer to the problem domain, has proven to outperform the use of general-purpose programming languages [19]. We can also find empirical works that indicate that the use of a DSL can reduce the effort of developers when working in modeling performance testing tasks [5].

In empirical research, comparing UML against DSL is an open problem towards understanding software modeling [7,22]. Previous works [5,19] suggest that the usage of DSLs outperforms the usage of other software artifacts. Our own previous work in the field [14] points in the same direction. Thus far, works that have compared UML against other modeling languages [5,11,23,25,31] have focused solely on objective measures. In this work, we combine objective measures (correctness and efficiency) with the subjective assessment of subjects (model style classification and satisfaction) through a crossover experiment that compares UML vs DSL when subjects model an element of a commercial video game. Game software engineering has been identified as a knowledge area that needs more fundamental research [3]. Moreover, despite video-game development being one of the fastest growing industries, there are few works in the field, which makes it an original domain for exploring modeling adoption.

Building upon previous work we hypothesize that the usage of a DSL will outperform the usage of UML models in the video-games domain. The findings of this empirical study not only confirm this hypothesis, but in addition, reveal a problem that was not found in evaluations performed by other authors: no matter how correct the models are, and their ability to actually generate software, the subjects think of them more as sketches than as programs. Our results are useful for teaching modeling and model adoption because they put the focus on the problem of subjects underestimating the potential of their own models.

The rest of the paper is organized as follows: Sect. 2 reviews the related work. Section 3 describes our experiment, and Sect. 4 shows the results. Section 5 describes the threats to validity. Finally, Sect. 6 concludes the paper.

2   Related Work

Modeling languages have been identified as a key challenge to increase the adoption of models as programs [22], and the use of DSLs has been identified as more effective and efficient than general-purpose programming languages [19]. However, it is difficult to find empirical works that compare UML with an alternative modeling language. Budgen [7] explained in 2011 that this was because of the underlying assumption that UML did not require testing because it was a de facto standard. The oldest comparison work we have found dates from 2001. Zendler et al. [31] compared three object-oriented approaches (UML, Open modeling language [OML], and taxonomic object system [TOS]) in two different application systems with respect to coarse-grained modeling concepts. They conclude that the coarse-grained concepts of the object-oriented approaches OML and TOS were superior to those of UML when modeling a database-oriented application.

In 2004, Otero and Dolado [23] presented the results of a controlled experiment comparing the comprehension of UML and OML diagrams in the design of a real-time embedded system. They found that the specification of dynamic data is faster and easier to comprehend in OML than in UML. A year later, Iris Reinhartz-Berger and Dov Dori [25] compared UML with Object-Process Methodology (OPM) with respect to the level of comprehension and the quality of Web application models. The results of their experiment suggest that OPM is better than UML when modeling web applications, especially in the dynamics aspects and in the quality of the models.

In 2010, De Lucia et al.[11] presented the results of three sets of controlled experiments comparing UML class diagrams and Entity-Relationship (ER) diagrams with respect to the comprehension and the interpretation of data models during maintenance activities. The results demonstrated that the two notations gave the same support, except during verification activities when UML class diagrams provided better support than ER diagrams. In 2016, Bernardino et al. [5] presented the results of an experiment about the benefits and drawbacks when using UML or a DSL for modeling performance testing in an IT company. Their results indicate that the effort using a DSL was lower than using UML.

Table 1 shows the works on adopting models in the industrial context. Modeling as sketch (also known as informal modeling) is the second problem that has been identified most frequently in the literature [2,8,16,17,27] (see P1 in Table 1). Other studies have identified other problems such as the lack of understanding [1,13,17] (see P2) or training [1,2,4,13] (see P3), or the lack of integration between modeling tools [1,2,4,8,20,26] (see P4 in Table 1).

Through a survey, Grossman et al. [17] investigated if individuals who use UML perceive it to be beneficial and which characteristics affect the use of UML. They used the Task Technology Fit index to evaluate the respondents' perceptions. They affirmed that most of the respondents of the survey were using what

Table 1. Empirical studies on modeling adoption

Work Year	Empirical strategy	Sample size	Context	Modeling language	Main problems identified
Grossman et al. [17] 2004	Survey	131 UML users	Industry	UML	UML as sketch is the most used style of UML modeling (P1) Lack of adequate UML understanding (P2)
Anda et al. [4] 2006	Case Study	16 System developers and project manager	Industry	UML	Inadequate level of UML training (P3) Inadequate modeling tools (P4)
Dobing and Parson [13] 2006	Survey	171 annalist using UML	Industry	UML	Lack of adequate UML understanding (P2) Inadequate offer of UML training (P3)
Staron [26] 2006	Case Study	8 Professionals	Industry	UML	Lack of well-integrated tools (P4)
Chaudron et al. [8] 2012	1 Experiment, 1 Case Study, 2 Surveys, 20+ Interviews	200+ Professionals and students	Industry Academia	UML	Modeling as sketch and for communication are the most used styles of modeling (P1) Lack of well-integrated tools (P4)
Agner et al. [1] 2013	Survey	209 Embedded-industry developers	Industry	UML	Lack of adequate UML understanding (P2) Lack of specialized professionals (P3) Inappropriate tool support (P4)
Gorschek et al. [16] 2014	Survey	3785 Developers	Industry	All	Models are used primarily in communication and collaboration (P1) Inadequate modeling tools (P4)
Marko et al. [20] 2014	Survey	112 Embedded-industry developers	Industry	All	Lack of well-integrated tools (P4)
Strrle [27] 2017	Survey	96 Professionals	Industry	All	Modeling as sketch is the most used style of modeling (P1) Cultural differences in modeling usage (P6)
Akdur et al. [2] 2018	Survey	627 Embedded-industry developers	Industry	All	Modeling as sketch is the most used style of modeling (P1) Lack of modeling expertise(P3) Inappropriate tool support (P4)

Fowler [15] calls 'UML by sketch', an informal approach to modeling and the values of TTF index indicated a slightly positive perception of UML. Chaudron et al. [8] synthesized a selection of empirical evidence (one experiment, one Case Study, two Surveys, and more than 20 Interviews) about the efficiency of UML modeling in software development. They concluded that especially for larger and distributed projects, UML is used to understand a problem at an abstract level and to share information with other team members. In these cases, UML was used without rigor and specialized tools were not used for the modeling.

Gorschek et al. [16] presented the results of a survey summarizing the answers of 3785 developers to a simple question: Which design models are used before coding? The answer was that design models were not used very extensively in industry and that when they were used, their use was informal and without tool support, and the notation was often not UML. Again, they found that models were used primarily as a communication and collaboration mechanism, where there is a need to solve problems or to obtain a joint understanding of the overall design by a team. Störrle [27] presented the results of an online survey, with 96 industry participants from all over the world. The questions in this case were

'How and what are the models used for?' He found that models were widely used in industry and that UML was indeed the leading language. This directly contradicts the results of Gorschek et al. [16]. He reported three distinct usage modes of models, the most frequent of which was informal usage for communication and understanding, and program-style [24] usage was rare. A year later, in 2018, Akdur et al. [2] conducted another online survey with opinions of 627 practicing embedded software engineers from 27 different countries. The survey addressed the state of software modeling and MDE practices in the worldwide embedded software industry. Their results match those of H. Störrle [27]: the majority of participants were using UML, and its use was informal. Our work includes a quantitative perspective to discuss the differences in performance of the modeling languages, but we also take into account the modeling style in the analysis to reach a more complete understanding of modeling usage. Furthermore, the classification of models in previous works [2,8,16,17,27] is taxonomic; the use that subjects made of models is classified into one style or another in accordance with their responses to certain questions in surveys or interviews. In our experiment, the subjects evaluate their models according to the usefulness of the model for each one of the modeling styles (sketch, blueprint or programs). This offers more complete information on the perception that the subjects have of the usefulness of their models.

3 Experiment Design

3.1 Objectives

According to the guidelines for reporting software engineering experiments [30], we have organized our research objectives using the Goal Question Metric template for goal definition. Our goal is to **analyze** modeling languages and their perceived usefulness, **for the purpose of** comparison, **with respect to** correctness of the models constructed, efficiency, and user satisfaction, **from the point of view of** novice and professional developers, **in the context of** modeling for a video-game company.

3.2 Variables

In this study, the factor under investigation is the *Modeling Language*. There are two alternatives, UML and DSL, which are the modeling languages used by subjects to model an enemy of a commercial video game.

Since the goal of this experiment is to evaluate the effects of the use of different modeling languages, we selected *Correctness* and *Efficiency* as the objective response variables, which are related to modeling performance. We measured *Correctness* using a correction template, which was applied to the models developed by the subjects after the experiment. To calculate *Efficiency*, we measured the time employed by each subject to finish the task, using the start and end time of each task. *Efficiency* is the ratio of *Correctness* to time spent (in minutes) to perform a task.

We also compared UML and the DSL with respect to *Satisfaction* using a 5-point Likert-scale questionnaire based on the Technology Acceptance Model (TAM) [21].

We decompose *Satisfaction* into three subjective response variables as follows: *Perceived Ease of Use* (PEOU), the degree to which a person believes that learning and using a particular language would require less effort. *Perceived Usefulness* (PU), the degree to which a person believes that using a particular language will increase performance, and *Intention to Use* (ITU), the degree to which a person intends to use a modeling language. Each of these variables corresponds to specific items in the TAM questionnaire. We average the scores obtained for these items to obtain the value for each variable.

To analyze the subjective perception of the models, the subjects evaluated the usefulness of their models using a 5-point Likert-scale for each style of modeling: to understand and communicate (sketch), for developers to create code (blueprint) and to automatically generate code (programs).

3.3   Design

We chose a factorial crossover design with two periods using two different tasks, T1 and T2, one for each period. All of the subjects used the two modeling languages, each one of which was used in a different task. The subjects had been randomly divided into two groups (G1 and G2). In the first period of the experiment, all of the subjects solved T1 with G1 using UML and G2 using DSL. Afterwards, all of the subjects solved T2, G1 using DSL and G2 using UML.

This repeated measures design increases the sensitivity of the experiment [28]: the observation of the same subject using the two alternatives controls between-subject differences, improving experiment robustness regarding variation among subjects. By using two different sequences for each group (G1 used UML first and DSL afterwards, and G2 used DSL first and UML afterwards) and different tasks, the design counterbalances some of the effects caused by using the alternatives of the factor in a specific order (i.e., learning effect, fatigue). To verify the experiment design, we conducted a pilot study with two subjects. The subjects in the pilot study did not participate in the experiment.

3.4   Research Questions and Hypotheses

The research questions and null hypotheses are formulated as follows:

RQ1. Does the modeling language used for modeling software impact the *Correctness* of the models? The corresponding null hypothesis is $H_{0,C}$: The modeling language does not have an effect on *Correctness*.

RQ2. Does the modeling language used for modeling software impact the *Efficiency* of developers to model? The null hypothesis for *Efficiency* is $H_{0,E}$: The modeling language does not have an effect on *Efficiency*.

RQ3. Is the user satisfaction different when developers use different modeling languages? To answer this question, we formulated three hypotheses based on the variables *Perceived Ease of Use*, *Perceived Usefulness*, and *Intention to Use*, with their corresponding null hypotheses. These are: $H_{0,PEOU}$, The modeling language does not have an effect on *Perceived Ease of Use*; $H_{0,PU}$, The modeling language does not have an effect on *Perceived Usefulness*; $H_{0,ITU}$, The modeling language does not have an effect on *Intention to Use*.

The hypotheses are formulated as two-tailed hypotheses.

3.5 Participants

The subjects were selected using convenience sampling [30]. We invited 26 third-year undergraduate students (novices) from a technology program who had passed previous courses where UML modeling was analyzed and used. Of these subjects, 25 decided to participate and 22 completed the tasks and forms. We also invite 17 professionals who are linked to modeling or video-game development to participate in the experiment. Nine of them decided to participate and completed the experiment. A total of 31 subjects with different knowledge about modeling performed the experiment.

The subjects filled out a demographic questionnaire that was used for characterizing the sample. Table 2 shows the mean and standard deviation of age, hours per day developing software (Developing time), and hours per day working with models (Modeling time). We used a 5-point Likert-scale to measure the subjects' knowledge of programming languages (Programming knowledge), modeling languages (Modeling Knowledge) and domain-specific languages (DSL knowledge). The mean and standard deviation of their answers are also shown in Table 2. The subjects recognized having a medium-high knowledge about software modeling or specific domain languages. All of them spent more time coding than modeling and evaluated their programming language knowledge or their ability with models higher than their knowledge about domain-specific languages.

Table 2. Results of the demographic questionnaire

	Age $\mu \pm \sigma$	Developing time$\pm \sigma$	Modeling time$\pm \sigma$	Programming known$\pm \sigma$	Modeling known$\pm \sigma$	DSL known$\pm \sigma$
All subjects	23.1±4.5	2.5±2.4	0.9±1.1	3.8±0.9	3.0±1.1	2.6±1.1
Novices	21.1±1.8	1.6±1.7	0.7±0.8	3.5±0.9	2.5±0.8	2.2±0.9
Professionals	27,9±5.4	4.8±2.2	1.3±1.5	4.4±0.5	4.0±0.8	3.7±0.9

The experiment was conducted by two instructors and one expert in the video-game software domain. The expert provided information about the domain and about the Kromaia DSL. This expert was not the same person who was responsible for designing the tasks. During the experiment, one of the instructors gave the instructions and managed the focus groups. The other instructor clarified doubts about the experiment and took notes during the focus group.

3.6   Experimental Objects and Procedure

The tasks of our experiment were extracted from a real-world software development, Kromaia, which is a commercial video game released on PlayStation 4 and Steam. In Kromaia, the models are interpreted at run-time to create the C++ games' objects [6]. For modeling, the subjects used Shooter Definition Modeling Language, which is the DSL used in Kromaia[1] and UML. A video-game software engineer, involved in the development of Kromaia, designed the two tasks of similar difficulty and prepared the correction template for the DSL task. An expert on modeling prepared the correction template for the UML task. The experimental objects used in this experiment (which includes the training material, the tasks and the forms used for the questionnaires) as well as the results and the statistical analysis are available at http://svit.usj.es/UMLvsDSL-experiment.

The experiment was conducted on-line due to the COVID19 pandemic restrictions. During the experiment, all of the participants joined the same videoconference via Microsoft Teams, and the chat-session was used to clarify doubts or share information. Two forms were prepared on Microsoft Forms for data collection, one for each experimental sequence. The experiment, scheduled for 2 h, was conducted on two different days with different groups. On the first day, it was performed by novices and on the second day it was performed by professionals. The experimental procedure is described as follows:

1. An instructor explained the parts in the session, and he advised to the subjects that it was not a test of their abilities.
2. The subjects attended a tutorial about the video-game enemies to be modeled and about the DSL used in the experiment. The information used in the tutorial and a UML usage guide were available to the subjects during the experiment. The time spent on this tutorial was less than 10 min.
3. The subjects received clear instructions on where to find the links to access the forms for the experiment. They were also told about the structure of these forms and where they could find information about UML and the DSL if they needed to. The subjects were randomly divided into two groups (G1 and G2); the subjects from G1 received the links to access one form and the subjects from G2 received a link to another form.
4. The subjects accessed to the on-line form and read and confirmed having read the information about the experiment, the data treatment of their personal information, and the voluntary nature of their participation before accessing the questionnaires and tasks of the experiment.
5. The subjects completed a demographic questionnaire.
6. The subjects performed the first task. The subjects from G1 had to use DSL to model a video-game enemy, and the subjects from G2 had to use UML to model the same enemy. After submitting their solution, the subjects classified the model they had built according to its usefulness, and they completed a satisfaction questionnaire about the modeling language used.

---

[1] Learn more of Kromaia DSL at: https://youtu.be/Vp3Zt4qXkoY.

7. The subjects performed the second task. The subjects from G1 modeled another video-game enemy using UML, and the subjects from G2 modeled the same enemy using the DSL. Then, the subjects classified the model they had built and completed the satisfaction questionnaire.
8. A focus group interview about the tasks (with average duration of 15 min) was conducted by one instructor while the other instructor took notes.
9. Finally, the tasks were corrected and a researcher analyzed the results.

3.7   Analysis Procedure

We have chosen the Linear Mixed Model (LMM) [29] for the statistical data analysis. LMM handles correlated data resulting from repeated measurements, and it allows us to study the effects of factors that intervene in a crossover design (period, sequence, or subject) and effects of other blocking variables (e.g., in our experiment, professional experience) [28].

In this study, we apply the Type III test of fixed effects with unstructured repeated covariance. The *Modeling Language*(ML) was defined as a fixed-repeated factor to identify the differences between using UML or DSL, and the subjects were defined as random factor $(1|Subject)$ to reflect the repeated measures design. The response variables (RV) for this test were *Correctness* and *Efficiency*, and the three other variables correspond to *Satisfaction*: *Perceived Ease of Use* (PEOU), *Perceived Usefulness* (PU) and *Intention to use* (ITU).

The assumption for applying LMM is normality of the residuals of the response variables. To verify this normality, we used Kolmogorov-Smirnov tests as well as visual inspections of the histogram and normal Q-Q plots.

The starting statistical model (Model 0) to be tested reflects the principal factors used in this experiment and is described as:

$$RV \sim ML + (1|subject) \ (Model \ 0) \tag{1}$$

In order to take into account the potential effects of factors that intervene in a crossover design in determining the main effect of *Modeling Language*, we considered *Period* and *Sequence* to be fixed effects. We also considered fixed factors that are related to the subject's experience in the statistical model in order to explore the potential effects of *Experience* or the effects of the sequence *Modeling Language* and *Experience* $(ML * Experience)$ to determine the variability in the response variables. We tested different statistical models like the ones used in the following formulas in order to find out which factors, in addition to *Modeling Language*, could best explain the changes in the response variables:

$$
\begin{aligned}
RV &\sim ML + Experience + (1|Subject) & (Model \ 1) \\
RV &\sim ML + Experience + ML * Experience + (1|Subject) & (Model \ 2) \\
RV &\sim ML + Experience + Period + (1|Subject) & (Model \ 3)
\end{aligned} \tag{2}
$$

The statistical model fit of the tested models was evaluated based on goodness of fit measures such as Akaike's information criterion (AIC) and Schwarz's Bayesian Information Criterion (BIC). The model with the smallest AIC or BIC is considered to be the best fitting model [18]. To describes the changes in each response variable we selected the statistical model that satisfied the normality of residuals and also obtained the smallest AIC or BIC value.

To quantify the differences in the response variables due to significant fixed factors, we calculated the Cohen d value [9] between the alternatives of these factors. Values of Cohen d between 0.2 and 0.3 indicate a small effect, values around of 0.5 indicate a medium effect, and values greater than 0.8 indicate a large effect. We selected histograms and box plots to graphically describe the data and the results.

4   Results

4.1   Changes in the Response Variables

There were differences in the means of all of the response variables depending on which *Modeling Language* was used to model a video-game enemy. Table 3 shows the values for the mean and standard deviation of the dependent variables *Correction, Efficiency, Perceived Ease of Use* (PEOU), *Perceived Usefulness* (PU), and *Intention to use* (ITU) for each one of the *Modeling Languages* compared: UML and DSL.

Table 3. Values for the mean and standard deviation of the response variables

	Correctness $\mu\% \pm \sigma$	Effectiveness $\mu\%/min \pm \sigma$	Satisfaction $\mu \pm \sigma$		
			PEOU	PU	ITU
DSL	90.32% $\pm$ 12.36	6.16%/min $\pm$ 2.91	4.27 $\pm$ 0.61	4.11 $\pm$ 0.63	3.9 $\pm$ 0.99
UML	71.87% $\pm$ 25.16	4.10%/min $\pm$ 3.51	2.85 $\pm$ 0.95	2.83 $\pm$ 1.02	2.45 $\pm$ 1.23

According to the Cohen d values of the response variables, we can affirm that the effect of the *Modeling Language* on *Correctness* is large, with a Cohen d value of 0.930 and that the effect on *Efficiency* is medium-large, with a Cohen d value of 0.639. The effect size for *Satisfaction* is very large, with Cohen d values of 1.786, 1.515, and 1.327 for *Perceived Ease of Use, Perceived Usefulness*, and *Intention to use*, respectively. These values are related to the percentage of non-overlap between the distributions of the response variables for each modeling language. Higher values correspond with greater percentages of non-overlap and larger differences. The histograms of Fig. 2 illustrate the differences in the response variables. In the histograms, the non-overlapping parts have a single pattern (either dots or shaded), while the overlapping parts have both patterns (dots and shaded).

For all of the variables, the factor *Modeling Language* obtained p-values of less than 0.05, regardless of the statistical model used for its calculation. Therefore, all of the null hypotheses are rejected. Thus, the answers to the research

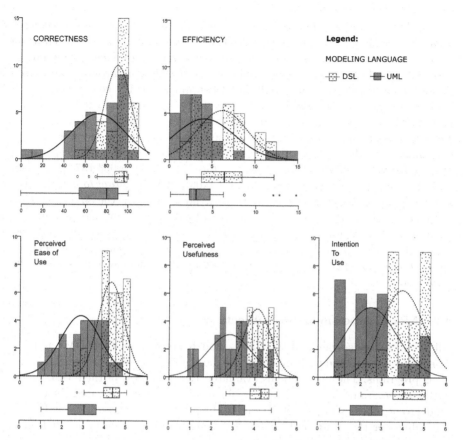

Fig. 2. Histograms with normal distributions and box plots for the response variables

questions **RQ1**, **RQ2**, and **RQ3** are affirmative. The Modeling Language used for developing software has a significant impact on the correctness of the model, efficiency, and the satisfaction of software developers.

For *Correctness*, the chosen statistical model was Model 1 (See formula (2)), which was the best fitting model that satisfied normality in the residuals of the response variable. The fixed factors, *Modeling Language* (F = 15.156, p = 0.001) and *Experience* (F = 4.393, p = 0.045), were considered to be statistically significant to explain the changes in correctness. The Cohen d value of -0.654 calculated with the standardized difference between the means of *Correctness* for novices and professionals indicates a medium-large effect in favour of the professionals. The models made by professionals are more correct than the ones made by novices.

For *Efficiency* the chosen statistical model was Model 3 (See formula (2)). The fixed factors *Modeling Language* (F = 12.337, p = 0.001), *Experience* (F = 5.275, p = 0.029), and *Period* (F = 16.451, p = 0.000) were considered to be statistically significant to explain the changes in correctness. The Cohen d value of -0.592 for *Efficiency* between novices and professionals indicates a medium-large effect in favour of the professionals. The professionals are more efficient than novices when modeling. The Cohen d value of -0.788 for *Efficiency* between the first period and the second period, indicates a large effect in favour of the second period. The subjects were more efficient when modeling the second task.

For *Satisfaction* the *Modeling Language* factor was the one fixed factor that was found to be significant for all the statistical models tested. For *Perceived Ease of Use* and *Perceived Usefulness*, the chosen model was the starting statistical model, Model 0 (See formula (1)) and the *Modeling Language* factor obtained p-values of 0.000 for *Perceived Ease of Use* ($F = 963.137$, $p = 0.000$) and *Perceived Usefulness* ($F = 892.660$, $p = 0.000$). For *Intention to use*, the chosen model was Model 2 (See formula (2)); however, only the *Modeling Language* factor ($F = 13.846$, $p = 0.001$) was statistically significant in explaining the changes in this response variable. The changes in *Intention to use* due to *Experience* ($F = 0.604$, $p = 0.443$) or the sequence *Modeling Language* and *Experience* ($ML * Experience$) ($F = 0.115$, $p = 0.737$) were not considered to be statistically significant.

4.2   Model Assessment by Subjects

All of the subjects evaluated their DSL models better than their UML models. The novices considered their models to be more useful as sketch than as blueprint or as programs. The professionals evaluated the usefulness of their DSL model better as programs than as sketch or blueprint, and they evaluated their UML model to be more useful as sketch than as blueprint or as programs. Table 4 shows the values for the mean and standard deviation of the subjects' evaluation of their own models for each modeling style.

Table 4. Values for the mean and standard deviation for models usefulness

		As sketch $\mu \pm \sigma$	As blueprint $\mu \pm \sigma$	As a program $\mu \pm \sigma$
DSL	Novices	4.1 ± 1.0	3.9 ± 1.1	3.5 ± 1.4
	Professionals	4.2 ± 0.8	3.7 ± 0.8	4.3 ± 0.5
UML	Novices	3.0 ± 1.0	3.3 ± 0.8	2.6 ± 1.1
	Professionals	3.8 ± 1.0	3.0 ± 1.1	2.9 ± 1.2

During the focus group, the novices declared that they found the DSL to be useful for communication, but they believed that UML would be necessary to generate a video-game enemy with all of its characteristics. The professionals (especially those linked to video games) said that UML could be useful to define a video-game enemy in general, at the beginning of the development, but that they would choose a DSL to define a specific video-game enemy.

4.3   Interpretation of the Results

During the training of the experiment, the subjects were introduced to Kromaia, and the use of models made in Kromaia was explained to them. In Kromaia, models are used as programs (see Fig. 1.c). It is very striking that, despite the fact that a successful case of models as programs was used and that the subjects were explicitly told that Kromaia developers use models as programs, most of the subjects continue to view their models as sketch rather than as programs.

Furthermore, the results also show that models are not far from scoring a value of 100% correct. On average, only 28% would have to be corrected in UML models and 10% in DSL models to be used as programs. Actually, more than five subjects produced models with a value of 100% correct. These models can be run on top of the Kromaia model interpreter. Nevertheless, they did not give a higher score to programs than to sketch. This is a problem that was not covered in evaluations by others authors: no matter how correct the models are, the subjects value them more as sketches than as programs. We suggest that this is a major problem: it is not that the models are not ready to be used as programs because we must improve tools and teaching, it is that subjects think of models more as sketches than as programs.

5   Threats to Validity

To describe the threats to validity of our work, we use the classification of [30]:

Conclusion validity. The *low statistical power* threat was minimized because the confidence interval is 95%. The *fishing and the error rate* threat was minimized using tasks and fixes designed by a video-game software engineer. The *Reliability of measures* threat was mitigated because the objective measurements were obtained from the digital artifacts generated by the subjects when they performed the tasks. The *reliability of treatment implementation* threat was alleviated because the procedure was identical in the two sessions. Also, the tasks were designed with similar difficulty.

Internal validity. The *compensatory rivalry* threat affected the experiment; the subjects may have been motivated to perform the task with a higher level of quality by using the modeling language that was the most familiar to them. The *interactions with selection* threat affected the experiment because of the voluntary nature of participation. To avoid student demotivation, we selected students of a course whose contents fit the design of the experiment. In addition, the subjects had different levels of modeling language knowledge and different levels of knowledge of the video-game domain. To mitigate this threat, the treatment was applied randomly. However, we found two outliers during the analysis of correctness and efficiency. The extreme values that were found correspond to subjects with scores of less than 25% in correctness in the UML task. Following the recommendations of Dean et al. [12], we repeated the statistical analysis by excluding the data of these two subjects, and we found that the language factor remained statistically significant to explain the changes in all of the response variables for all of the models tested. Hence, our conclusions were not sensitive to the responses of subjects with low scores in correctness. Even though the tasks were designed with similar complexity, the effect of the task (period) was significant for efficiency. The effect of the language being the same for both tasks suggests a learning effect; the subjects spent less time performing the second task. We minimized this *maturation* threat by using a crossover design.

Construct validity. All of the measurements were affected by *Mono-method bias*. To mitigate this threat for the correctness and efficiency measurements, we mechanized these measurements as much as possible by means of correction templates. We mitigated the threat to satisfaction by using a widely applied model (TAM) [10]. The *hypothesis guessing* threat was mitigated because we did not explain the research questions to the subjects. To weaken the *evaluation apprehension* threat, at the beginning of the experiment, the instructor told the subjects that the experiment was not a test of their abilities. To mitigate the *Author bias* threat, the tasks were extracted from a commercial video game and designed with similar difficulty. Finally, the experiment was affected by the *mono-operation bias* threat because we worked with a single treatment.

External validity. The *domain* threat occurs because the experiment has been conducted in a specific domain, i.e., video-game development. We think that the generalizability of the findings should be undertaken with caution. Other experiments in different domains should be performed to validate our findings.

6   Conclusion

In this work, we present an experiment that compares UML and a DSL when subjects model in the video-game domain. To that extent, we combined objective measures and subjective measures. Our results reveal that the subjects underestimate the potential of their own models. This problem was not discovered by previous works that focus either on objective measures to evaluate modeling performance or on subjective measures to classify modeling styles. Our findings suggest that future evaluations should take into account both objective and subjective measures to better understand modeling languages. Our results are also relevant for teaching modeling and model adoption. If users were able to assess their models correctly, they might leverage their latent potential as programs.

References

1. Agner, L.T.W., Soares, I.W., Stadzisz, P.C., SimãO, J.M.: A Brazilian survey on UML and model-driven practices for embedded software development. J. Syst. Softw. **86**(4), 997–1005 (2013)
2. Akdur, D., Garousi, V., Demirörs, O.: A survey on modeling and model-driven engineering practices in the embedded software industry. J. Syst. Archit. **91**, 62–82 (2018)
3. Ampatzoglou, A., Stamelos, I.: Software engineering research for computer games: a systematic review. Inf. Softw. Technol. **52**(9), 888–901 (2010)

4. Anda, B., Hansen, K., Gullesen, I., Thorsen, H.K.: Experiences from introducing UML-based development in a large safety-critical project. Empirical Softw. Eng. **11**(4), 555–581 (2006)
5. Bernardino, M., Rodrigues, E.M., Zorzo, A.F.: Performance testing modeling: an empirical evaluation of DSL and UML-based approaches. In: Proceedings of the 31st Annual ACM Symposium on Applied Computing, pp. 1660–1665 (2016)
6. Blasco, D., Font, J., Zamorano, M., Cetina, C.: An evolutionary approach for generating software models: the case of Kromaia in game software engineering. J. Syst. Softw. **171**, 110804 (2021)
7. Budgen, D., Burn, A.J., Brereton, O.P., Kitchenham, B.A., Pretorius, R.: Empirical evidence about the UML: a systematic literature review. Softw. Pract. Exp. **41**(4), 363–392 (2011)
8. Chaudron, M.R., Heijstek, W., Nugroho, A.: How effective is UML modeling? Softw. Syst. Model. **11**(4), 571–580 (2012)
9. Cohen, J.: Statistical Power for the Social Sciences. Lawrence Erlbaum and Associates, Hillsdale (1988)
10. Davis, F.D.: Perceived usefulness, perceived ease of use, and user acceptance of information technology. MIS Q. **13**(3), 319–340 (1989)
11. De Lucia, A., Gravino, C., Oliveto, R., Tortora, G.: An experimental comparison of ER and UML class diagrams for data modelling. Empirical Softw. Engi. **15**(5), 455–492 (2010)
12. Dean, A., Voss, D., Draguljić, D., et al.: Design and Analysis of Experiments, vol. 1. Springer, New York (1999). https://doi.org/10.1007/b97673
13. Dobing, B., Parsons, J.: How UML is used. Commun. ACM **49**(5), 109–113 (2006)
14. Domingo, Á., Echeverría, J., Pastor, Ó., Cetina, C.: Evaluating the benefits of model-driven development. In: Dustdar, S., Yu, E., Salinesi, C., Rieu, D., Pant, V. (eds.) CAiSE 2020. LNCS, vol. 12127, pp. 353–367. Springer, Cham (2020). https://doi.org/10.1007/978-3-030-49435-3_22
15. Fowler, M.: UML Distilled: A Brief Guide to the Standard Object Modeling Language. Addison-Wesley Professional, Boston (2004)
16. Gorschek, T., Tempero, E., Angelis, L.: On the use of software design models in software development practice: an empirical investigation. J. Syst. Softw. **95**, 176–193 (2014)
17. Grossman, M., Aronson, J.E., McCarthy, R.V.: Does UML make the grade? insights from the software development community. Inf. Softw. Technol. **47**(6), 383–397 (2005)
18. Karac, E.I., Turhan, B., Juristo, N.: A Controlled Experiment with Novice Developers on the impact of task description granularity on software quality in test-driven development. IEEE Trans. Softw. Eng. (2019). https://doi.org/10.1109/TSE.2019.2920377
19. Kosar, T., Gaberc, S., Carver, J.C., Mernik, M.: Program comprehension of domain-specific and general-purpose languages: replication of a family of experiments using integrated development environments. Empirical Softw. Eng. **23**(5), 2734–2763 (2018)
20. Marko, N.C., et al.: Model-based engineering for embedded systems in practice. In: Research Reports in Software Engineering and Management, pp. 1–48 (2014)
21. Moody, D.L.: The method evaluation model: a theoretical model for validating information systems design methods. In: ECIS 2003 Proceedings, p. 79 (2003)

22. Mussbacher, G., et al.: The relevance of model-driven engineering thirty years from now. In: Dingel, J., Schulte, W., Ramos, I., Abrahão, S., Insfran, E. (eds.) MODELS 2014. LNCS, vol. 8767, pp. 183–200. Springer, Cham (2014). https://doi.org/10.1007/978-3-319-11653-2_12

23. Otero, M.C., Dolado, J.J.: Evaluation of the comprehension of the dynamic modeling in UML. Inf. Softw. Technol. 46(1), 35–53 (2004)

24. Pastor, O., Molina, J.C.: Model-Driven Architecture in Practice: A Software Production Environment Based on Conceptual Modeling. Springer Science & Business Media, Berlin (2007). https://doi.org/10.1007/978-3-540-71868-0

25. Reinhartz-Berger, I., Dori, D.: OPM vs. UML-experimenting with comprehension and construction of web application models. Empirical Softw. Eng. 10(1), 57–80 (2005)

26. Staron, M.: Adopting model driven software development in industry – a case study at two companies. In: Nierstrasz, O., Whittle, J., Harel, D., Reggio, G. (eds.) MODELS 2006. LNCS, vol. 4199, pp. 57–72. Springer, Heidelberg (2006). https://doi.org/10.1007/11880240_5

27. Störrle, H.: How are conceptual models used in industrial software development? a descriptive survey. In: Proceedings of the 21st International Conference on Evaluation and Assessment in Software Engineering, pp. 160–169 (2017)

28. Vegas, S., Apa, C., Juristo, N.: Crossover designs in software engineering experiments: benefits and perils. IEEE Trans. Softw. Eng. 42(2), 120–135 (2015)

29. West, B.T., Welch, K.B., Galecki, A.T.: Linear Mixed Models: A Practical Guide Using Statistical Software. Chapman and Hall/CRC, Boca Raton (2014)

30. Wohlin, C., Runeson, P., Höst, M., Ohlsson, M.C., Regnell, B., Wesslén, A.: Experimentation in Software Engineering. Springer Science & Business Media, Berlin (2012). https://doi.org/10.1007/978-3-642-29044-2

31. Zendler, A., Pfeiffer, T., Eicks, M., Lehner, F.: Experimental comparison of coarse-grained concepts in UML, OML, and TOS. J. Syst. Softw. 57(1), 21–30 (2001)

On the Development of Enterprise-Grade Tool Support for the DEMO Method

Mark A. T. Mulder[1,2]($\boxtimes$) (ID) and Henderik A. Proper[3,4] (ID)

[1] TEEC2, Hoevelaken, The Netherlands
markmulder@teec2.nl
[2] Radboud University, Nijmegen, The Netherlands
[3] Luxembourg Institute of Science and Technology (LIST), Belval, Luxembourg
e.proper@acm.org
[4] University of Luxembourg, Esch-sur-Alzette, Luxembourg

Abstract. The Design and Engineering Methodology for Organisations (DEMO) is a core method within the discipline of Enterprise Engineering (EE). It enables the creation of so-called *essential* models of organisations. Such models are enterprise models that focus on the organisational essence of an organisation. They do so primarily in terms of the actor roles involved, and the business transactions between them. The DEMO method has a firm theoretical foundation. At the same time, there is increasing uptake of DEMO in practice. This uptake also results in a need for enterprise-grade tool support for the use of the method. In this experience paper, we report on experiences in the development of enterprise-grade tool support for the practical use of DEMO.

Keywords: Enterprise engineering · DEMO · Modelling tools

1 Introduction

This *experience paper* reports on experiences in the development of enterprise-grade tool support for the Design and Engineering Methodology for Organisations (DEMO) method. DEMO [6] is a key method within the discipline of Enterprise Engineering (EE) [7]. It focuses on the creation of *essential* models of organisations in terms of the actor roles involved, as well as the business transactions between these actor roles.

DEMO has strong methodological, and theoretical, roots [6,7]. At the same time, there is increasing uptake of DEMO in practice. The latter is illustrated by the active usage (and certification) community[1], reported cases concerning the use of DEMO [2,8], as well as the integration with other mainstream enterprise modelling approaches such as ArchiMate [15,31] and BPMN [12,19].

The increased uptake of DEMO has also triggered the need for enterprise-grade tool support. Due to its academic roots, there was not much attention

---

[1] http://www.ee-institute.org/en
https://www.linkedin.com/company/enterprise-engineering-institute.

© Springer Nature Switzerland AG 2021
M. La Rosa et al. (Eds.): CAiSE 2021, LNCS 12751, pp. 499–515, 2021.
https://doi.org/10.1007/978-3-030-79382-1_30

for the development of enterprise-grade tool support (we will discuss the notion of enterprise-grade in more detail in Sect. 2) so far. Tools supporting DEMO have indeed been developed. However, these generally involve either (advanced) academic prototypes, or are provided by smaller "boutique" tool vendors. These tools, regretfully, do not classify as enterprise-grade tooling (see [23] for more details). Meanwhile, however, the lack of such tool support is now also seen as hampering the further uptake of DEMO by larger organisations.

The focus of this (empirical) paper is on our experience in the development of such enterprise-grade tool support for the DEMO method on top of the Sparx Enterprise Architect (SEA) platform. The development of tool support for DEMO also provided interesting insights into limitations of DEMO Specification Language (DEMOSL), the specification language that accompanies the DEMO method. These insights include: (1) the need to elaborate the meta-model of the method, e.g. enable verification and analysis, (2) the need to complement the core meta-model of the method with a visualisation oriented meta-model dealing, and (3) the need to be able to exchange the models between tools, resulting in an exchange oriented meta-model. Each of these experiences will be illustrated in terms of the needed landscape of meta-model(s), as well as some fragments of the actual meta-models.

The work, as reported on in this paper, is part of a larger design science effort [25] to evolve two artefacts: (1) DEMOSL and (2) its associated tool support, towards a more enterprise-grade level. Design science, according to Wieringa [34], is the design and investigation of artefacts within a context that are designed to interact with this context and should improve something in that context. A (design science) artefact is an object that solves a problem by interaction with the context of that artefact. In our case, the involved artefacts are the DEMOSL and the associated tool support.

The remainder of this paper is structured as follows. Section 2 provides background on what we mean by "enterprise-grade" tool support. In Sect. 3, we then provide background to the DEMO method, also illustrating its theoretical foundations, and its uptake in practice. We then continue in Sect. 4 with the need to extend, and even improve, the original meta-model to e.g. enable model verification. Section 5 then takes us to the need to be able to visualise models; both in order to create/edit models as well as to communicate them. Before concluding, Sect. 6 discusses the consequences of the need to be able to exchange models between tools.

2   Enterprise-Grade Tool Support

The term "enterprise-grade" does not originate from science[2], but is a term commonly used in practice. As reported by practitioners, the term is used to differentiate consumer products from enterprise products [29]. In [10], Gartner

---

[2] Even though we can not claim to have conducted an in-depth literature survey on the term "enterprise-grade", the papers we did find (through a basic google scholar search) left the definition implicit.

defines it as: *"Enterprise-grade describes products that integrate into an infrastructure with a minimum of complexity and offer transparent proxy support."* In line with this, enterprise-grade (in the context of software applications in general) is associated by practitioners [14,29,32] to characteristics such as *productivity, security* (including e.g. encryption of data, data security, granular levels of user access, protection of data, compliance), *integration, administration, support,* and *scalability.*

For a modelling tool to be enterprise-grade, it also implies that there must be a solid and secure repository (to store the models). Essential qualities for such repositories include *extensibility, maintainability, interoperability,* and *portability* [26]. Since enterprise engineering and architecting efforts typically involve many different aspects, as well as many different stakeholders [28,33], it is important for modelling tools to provide different visualisations. Even more, these visualisations should be in a format that can be easily integrated into standard presentation and text editing software.

The above considerations provided the motivations (as reported in [23]) to develop support for DEMO on top of the Sparx Enterprise Architect (SEA) platform. The SEA platform is widely used in the industry for enterprise modelling, supports multiple models, has a repository, can apply consistency rules to the stored models, and is extendable. In line with this, the remainder of the paper focuses on the experiences in realising DEMO support on top of the SEA platform.

3 DEMO Background

As mentioned before, DEMO [6] is a core method within the discipline of EE [7]. The method has strong theoretical roots [4–7,30], and focuses on the creation of so-called *essential models* of organisations. Such essential models aim to capture the organisational essence of an organisation, primarily in terms of the (human) actor roles involved, the business transactions [4,30] between these actor roles, as well as the processes needed in their realisation. From a theoretical perspective [4,30], the business transactions are based on speech acts [13] between the actors who enact these roles. DEMO supports the modelling of the overall, as well as the more detailed, processes in an organisation, and the underlying information processing. Its strong focus on identifying the business transactions between (human) actor roles in order to capture the organisational essence, is what makes DEMO complementary to main stream enterprise modelling standards such as BPMN [27] and ArchiMate [3,17]. This complementarity has also been the subject of publications reporting on the combination of DEMO and e.g. BPMN [12,19], ArchiMate [15,31], or e3Value [16].

DEMO is model-driven in the sense that models are used as its mainstream of deliverables. As such, it also fits well in the context of Model-Driven Engineering. More specifically, the earlier mentioned essential models comprise of four (integrated) aspect models: the Construction Model (CM), the Action Model

(AM), the Process Model (PM) and the Fact Model (FM). Each of these models is expressed in one or more diagrams and one or more cross-model tables providing viewpoints on the complete model.

The aspect models overlap in elements; specifically, the concept of *transaction kind* appears in all aspect models; therefore, being the de-facto integration point of the model as a whole. A complete DEMO model covers the product, process, and information view on the essential organisations. These views are linked by the action rules that, in organisations, are often called business rules.

DEMO is built on a set of theories, where the Performance in Social Interaction theory (PSI-theory) constitute the foundation of Enterprise Ontology (EO) from a construction perspective. The PSI-theory divides an organisation into three worlds of acts and facts that reach commitments and agreements in predictable phases. One composes these agreements in a logical order that demands the right responsibilities of the right subjects. Finally, the subjects' capabilities are appointed into three categories to make distinctions in decisions and other actions. This standard pattern and production can be used anywhere in the organisation to enhance communication between subjects.

The PSI-theory divides the world into three worlds: actors and actor roles (a-world), communication (c-world) and products (p-world). Each of the c- and p-worlds may perform acts and produce facts. The communication acts, performed by actor-roles, produce communication facts. The same rule holds for the p-world. In short, actors perform communication and production acts, thereby creating communication facts about the creation of production facts. Furthermore, the PSI-theory defines the communication pattern between two actor roles. Every commitment to reach a production result follows this universal pattern, again expressed in the transaction kind.

Construction Model – The CM is the first and most comprehensive model to produce when modelling an organisation in DEMO, applying the Organisational Essence Revealing (OER) method. A CM is a model that represents the construction of an organisation. This model consists of the identified transaction kinds and the actor roles that are either executor or initiator of these transaction kinds. The resulting 'network' of transaction kinds and actor roles is always a set of tree structures, which arise from the inherent property that every transaction kind has exactly one elementary actor role as its executor (and vice versa) and that every actor role may be the initiator of no, one or more transaction kinds. The Construction Model (CM) involves the Construction Diagram (OCD) showing the Transaction Kind (TK), Aggregate Transaction Kind (ATK), Elementary Actor Role (EAR), Composite Actor Role (CAR) within a Scope of Interest (SoI). These diagrams show the dependencies between roles in execution and information. The high abstraction level makes this a compact diagram in relation to the implementation of the organisation.

The Product Table (TPT) shows the TK identification and description together with the product identification and description. This table is used to get insight into the products that are being created in the organisation.

Finally, the Bank Contents Table (BCT) shows the contents of the ATK. This contains the identification and name of the ATK and the Entity Type (ET) and attributes of those ETs that are present. This is used to show the extend of (external) data.

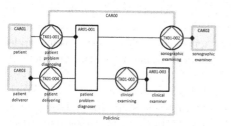

Fig. 1. Poligyn OCD modelled in the tool

Name	Alias	Product Kind Formulation
TK01-004	patient delivering	the patient of [patient problem] is delivered
TK01-003	clinical examining	[clinical examination] is performed
TK01-002	sonographic examining	[sonographic examination] is completed
TK01-001	patient problem diagnosing	[patient problem] is diagnosed

Fig. 2. Poligyn TPT modelled in the tool

Process Model – The PM bridges its CM and the coordination part of its AM. To this end, it specifies how the transaction kinds in a tree are related to each other. More precisely, it specifies which transaction steps in an enclosed transaction kind are connected to which steps in the enclosing transaction kind, and by which kind of link (response-link or wait-link).

The PM involves a single diagram kind, the Process Structure Diagram (PSD), which shows the relations between the process steps of interrelated transactions. This is used to explain the order and dependencies between transactions. Business rules are partially covered as well.

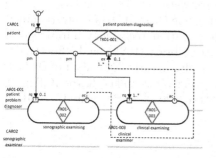

Fig. 3. Poligyn PSD modelled in the tool

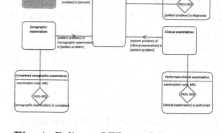

Fig. 4. Poligyn OFD modelled in the tool

Fact Model – The FM of a Scope of Interest bridges its CM and the production part of its AM. It specifies the various entity types, property types, attribute types, and entity types, as well as their mutual relationships. The FM also involves a single diagram kind, the Object Fact Diagram (OFD), which shows ETs and Product Kinds (PKs), and the Information Use Table (IUT). This model is often called the data model, although it shows much more information.

Action Model – The AM comprises the guidelines that guide actors in doing their work, i.e. performing their coordination acts and their production acts. Action rules, which are actually (imperative) business rules, guide actors in responding to the coordination events they have to deal with. A semi-structured English-like language is used to express the action rules. Work instructions guide actors in performing the production acts, i.e. in bringing about the products of transactions.

This last aspect model contains Action Rules Specification (ARS) and Work Instruction Specification (WIS). Per non-trivial process step minimal one specification shows the input and conditions to proceed in the transaction pattern or advance to other transactions. This specification is used to model all details of the (to-be) organisation.

Different aspect models contain overlapping elements; therefore, the DEMO *essential model* is the result of the combination of all aspect models.

We modelled the example case of [8, chapter 17], named Poligyn using the tool. In Fig. 1 we see the four TK of the CM with its initiating and executing actor roles within the modelled organisation. These TKs can also be shown in a table as the TPT in Fig. 2. One step further in the analysis, we get to the process dependencies depicted in Fig. 3. Finally, in Fig. 4 the FM shows the internal references between ETs and the relations between ET and TK.

As discussed in the introduction, there has been an increasing uptake in practice of DEMO. This can be partially attributed to the complementary perspective that DEMO offers next to mainstream enterprise modelling languages such as ArchiMate and BPMN. Meanwhile, DEMO has a proven track record in process (re)design and reorganisation, software specifications based on the organisation, modelling business rules and proving General Data Protection Regulation (GDPR) [11] and other business Information Technology Infrastructure Library (ITIL), Business information Services Library (BiSL), and NEderlandse Norm (NEN) norm compliance [24]. Additionally, an early descendant of DEMO, called 'Voorwaarden scheppen voor de Invoering van Standaardisatie ICT in de bouw' (VISI), has evolved into the ISO 29481-2:2012[3] (BIM related) standard for the construction sector.

4   Meta-model Extensions

A first issue we encountered in the development of tool support for DEMO was that, even though it has a thorough theoretical basis, the original meta-model of DEMO was not specific and detailed enough to enable an immediate implementation. The latter can be explained by the fact that the book defining the DEMO method [6] was primarily written to teach learners (students and

---

[3] https://www.iso.org/obp/ui/#iso:std:iso:29481:-2:ed-1:v1:en.

practitioners) to create DEMO models in accordance with the DEMO way of thinking, and draw (human to human) communicable DEMO models to reason about the organisation. As such, the book puts the priority on "doing", when introducing the different DEMO aspect model kinds. There was no need for a strict meta-model. In line with this, the formalisation(s) provided in the original DEMO book [6] aimed to support didactic goals rather than the development of automated modelling tools. As such, it was never meant to provide formal meta-models that would enable the development of, and automated support for, the methodology.

While a good theory should help professionals to do their job, more professionals are raised using automation as their main tooling. Where pencils were used, tablets have taken their place, and people see automation as their starting point. Tooling fulfils a lever function in broadening the use of the methodology. As a result, to enable tool development, a more complete and detailed formalisation and meta-model were needed. This resulted in the development, and evolution, of the DEMOSL [9], the specification language for DEMO. A first validation of the meta-model of this specification language was reported in [21]. As part of the (partial) validation [21], all existing DEMO (example) aspect models (taken from the official course material and practical cases) were positioned within the specification language to see if they fitted.

Beyond the ability to "capture" actual DEMO models in the specification language, more extensions of the meta-model were needed to enable verification of the models, and the operational use of the method in practice [22]. In the remainder of this section, we discuss some examples of changes/refinements that were made in relation to the original meta-model, the results of which are summarised in Fig. 6.

For instance, when modelling an organisation, the functional components like departments are needed for stakeholders to understand the structures of the organisation. Given DEMO's focus on the ontological essence of organisations, it does not provide functional concepts like departments. It does, however, provide the constructional concept of Composite Actor Role (CAR; see the previous section). CARs are now allowed to be used to represent functional concepts such as departments, enabling modellers to model departments (or other organisational units) as organisations within organisations. This hierarchical relation has been added to the meta-model.

It also turned out that, for practical purposes, some concepts could actually be removed from the meta-model. For instance, according to the theory, each Organisation Construction Diagram (OCD) corresponds to an explicitly defined Scope of Interest (SoI). In practice, however, the SoI always corresponds directly to a Composite Actor Role (CAR). As a consequence, in practice, the SoI concept is redundant, and, therefore, does not have to be included in the meta-model explicitly.

A further issue pertained to the fact that the DEMO method allows modellers to start from any of the four aspect models. When learning the method, one generally starts with a Construction Model (CM) and gradually works down to the Action Model (AM; see Fig. 5). However, in practice, when interviewing domain experts in an organisation, these experts usually talk about the existing process and associated rules. In other words, starting with AM related information first. Additionally, the Fact Model (FM) information about entity types and attribute type is also provided relatively early when interviewing the domain experts.

The original DEMO meta-model did not allow for models to "grow" from the different aspect models, in the sense that the consistency rules would require the model to always be complete as a whole (so, including all aspect models). Therefore adjustments to the meta-model needed to be made to allow for such flexibility, while still enforcing (at the end of the modelling process) the overall consistency.

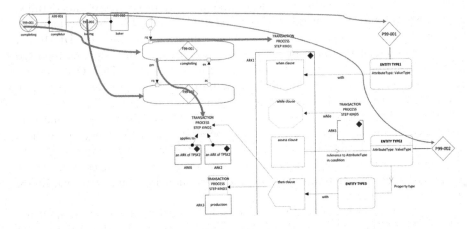

Fig. 5. CM-AM flow

In practice, organisation models that resulted from the OER analysis often raised questions regarding the *origins* of the included transaction kinds. More specifically, a cross-reference from the elements in the organisation model to the original OER analysis was missing. To support this kind of cross-reference, we have added the interview and interview-line concept into the meta-model. By registering every aspect of the OER analysis as a connection from the interview-line to the elements modelled from that line information we have created a cross-reference from the source to the final model.

Another finding is that in practice, there was a need for DEMO models to be related to their existing/planned implementation. For instance, a "serving" connector was introduced that can be used to connect e.g. DEMO model elements to e.g. application components in the ArchiMate's Application layer. With this connector, one can, for instance, point to application components that implement the transaction kind or Transaction Process Step Kind (TPSK). Another example of the need to be able to include more of the implementation context involves the introduction of an actor (type) that aggregate actor roles. Such actors types correspond to job functions and, therefore, combine all competences of the actor roles that are aggregated. This can be used for HR implementation information.

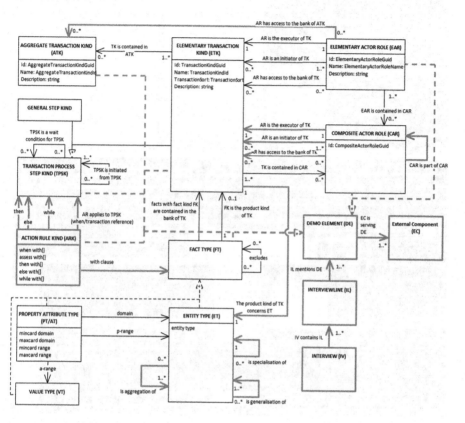

Fig. 6. Extension of DEMO meta-model (red bold lines are new) (Color figure online)

Finally, the action rule specification, as described in the DEMO method and associated specification language, consists of a semi formalised way to describe the communication actions that result in a decision on either actor role. To start using the Action Rules Specification (ARS) in a more formal way, a more elaborate definition was needed. Therefore, based on earlier work [1], a grammar to represent action rules was created.

Figure 6 summarises the (discussed) extensions of DEMOs original meta-model, while Fig. 7 shows both the tool "in action", as well as some details of the tool's *implementation* on the Sparx Enterprise Architect (SEA) platform. In the latter, we see (numbers referring to the respective windows as displayed in the figure) how SEA provides a set of base classes (1) for elements, connectors, diagrams, and toolboxes. Each DEMO model element involves an extension of

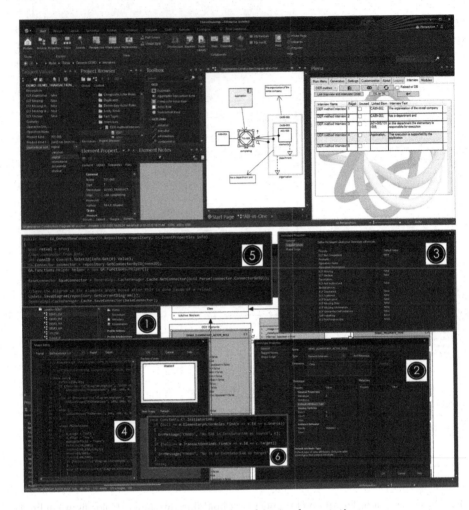

Fig. 7. Tool in action, and its implementation

one of the base classes of SEA (2), while also having custom properties based on the DEMO meta-model (3). To enable different visualisations, SEA provides simple scripts that enable the drawing of shapes (4). SEA provides interface "hooks", that are triggered when editing models in the graphical user interface, that can be used by add-on applications to provide functionality that is not available in SEA (5). The verification of DEMO models has been implemented in C# using these "hooks" (6).

The meta-models have been updated according to Fig. 6. These models are created for tool developers and the users have no meddling in these meta-models. The models improve the usability of the methodology through tool usage and the methodology, therefore, becomes even more powerful in performance than without tooling.

5 Visualisation

Since the DEMOSL [9] primarily focuses on consistency and completeness of DEMO models from a "content" perspective, it does not include any specifics about the actual representation of these models in terms of diagrams, tables and other possible visualisations. As such, the DEMOSL does not provide guidelines regarding the concrete syntax of models in terms of e.g. shapes and icons to be used. When examining a corpus of models produced across different cases, we found various variations in drawings of elements that each could be interpreted as the convention of those elements. In moving towards (standardised) tool support, this had to be remedied in terms of an explicit meta-model of the allowed visualisations.

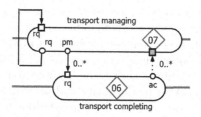

Fig. 8. PSD specification example

As an example, consider the diagram provided in Fig. 8. In an OCD, the shape is normally drawn as a circle enclosing a diamond and this circle is stretched in the PSD with the diamond displayed at a seemingly random position within this "stretched circle". In Fig. 8, the name of the transaction appears below or above or at the side-top of the transaction Fig. 8, the diamond is at a certain percentage from the left side, the stretching is a random length, while the swim lane usage is not consistent (i.e. 07 has the same initiator and executor but is visualised on top of two swim lanes).

Furthermore, the examples of the same case are different between different DEMO versions without explaining why this is the case, making it impossible to give guidance to readers that were trained in a different version to interpret the visualisation, and also making it impossible for a tool to comply to the specifications.

Due to the complexity reduction of the CM the resulting aspect model visualisation is not readable for stakeholders that expect a flow. This flow is only available when modellers have finished the analysis from CM through PM to AM. The DEMO specification has a language for the AM that is semi-formalised and we tried to create a formalised form for that model (see Fig. 9). This specification, though formally more correct, is still not readable for many stakeholders. Visualising the final aspect model AM in a recognisable form has positive effects on the comprehension with stakeholders of the modelling of DEMO.

```
sincerity: <no specific condition>            truth:
truth:                                            for each Order Item in {the contents of
    for each Order Item in the contents of            Order} {
        Order:                                        the availability of pizza kind of
        the pizza kind of Order Item is                   Order Item is equal to
            available                                     true;

        the amount of Order Item is               the [producebility of amount] of
            producible                                Order Item is equal to true;
    the requested production time of              the requested production time of
        Order is greater than Now plus 10             Order is greater than the [Now
        minutes                                       plus10 minutes] of Time;

                                                  }
```

Fig. 9. ARS grammar upgrade example

When visualising an (aspect) model the visualisation is a representation of the model. On a meta-level one needs to define the elements that are visualised and the components of those elements of the meta-model that are used in this visualisation. The omission of this component visualisation definition makes the visualisation arbitrary. Defining these visualisations requires a mapping specification of every visualisation to the entity and attribute of the meta-model it is representing. These mappings also need translations from available values to required visualisations. For example, the transaction sort of a Elementary Transaction Kind (ETK) is defined as original, informational or documental and can be visualised as a red, green or blue diamond, respectively. While creating the models and tooling and trying to visualise the model for various stakeholders this omission of the mapping became apparent, whereas this never happens with the toy examples from the educational material.

The mapping of the visualisation is the definition of viewpoints of DEMO modelling. At this moment just a few viewpoints have been defined in Table 1, but more exist and can be defined for specific stakeholders. Viewpoints that cover multiple notations have to be defined to cover the representation combinations of DEMO and other notations (e.g. ArchiMate).

Each viewpoint needs, next to the definition and mapping, the semantic explanation of the information represented. Not only does every element and connection needs an explanation, also the whole viewpoint needs an explanation, and even a definition. The current viewpoints (e.g. diagrams and tables) do not have a definition or explanation of what they represent. The OFD does show the entity types, attribute types, property types and product types (the product type is another viewpoint of the ETK) but it is not defined what is represented. It has been interpreted as the data model, the creation of data due to transaction acts, the relational model, the possible-state model and the authorisation model. Each interpretation of the OFD is possible and, therefore, it is likely that the OFD contains too much information. Our experience tells us that the richness of each of the DEMO diagrams and tables is too much for the average stakeholder to grasp.

Table 1. Elements and diagrams

Diagram → Entity types ↓	OCD	PSD	TPD	OFD	ARD	RHD	AFD	..
ETK	X	X	X	X	–	–	–	–
ATK	X	–	–	–	–	–	–	–
EAR	X	X	–	–	–	X	X	–
CAR	X	X	–	–	–	X	–	–
ET	–	–	–	X	–	–	–	–
CET	–	–	–	X	–	–	–	–
TPSK	–	X	X	–	X	–	–	–
ARS	–	–	–	–	X	–	–	–

At the moment of writing this paper, a list of viewpoints of a DEMO model exists in the tool. For example (see Table 1): OCD, PSD, Transaction Pattern Diagram (TPD), OFD, Action Rules Diagram (ARD), Role Hierarchy Diagram (RHD), and Actor role Function Diagram (AFD) These diagrams contain various elements of the DEMO model: ETK, ATK, EAR, CAR, ET, Composite Entity Type (CET), TPSK, and ARS.

As mentioned before in our discussion regarding the meaning of enterprise-grade in Sect. 2, since enterprise engineering typically involves many different aspects, as well as many different stakeholders [18,28,33], it is important for modelling tools to provide different visualisations. For instance, the OCD does not work for C-level stakeholders [22] C-level prefers high-level blocks and arrow representations of processes, such as provided by the ARS level diagrams. Similarly, towards C-level management, the PSD also do not work well when dealing with complex processes. Finally, the OFD, when completely drawn, is also uneasy to read for a lot of people. Dividing it into several partial models helps to make partial models clear to stakeholders.

As such, in line with [18], it is necessary to distinguish between different visualisation strategies for different stakeholder groups and different purposes. For instance, visualisation can also involve the creation of animation of a process, or even gamification. Enabling stakeholders to simulate, or even "play", their processes allows them to see the modelled processes as they are running. It also combines the view on processes with the production facts that are created in a transaction.

Our first attempt with gamification of DEMO models (see Fig. 10) visualises the OCD in a 3D setting where the actor roles are visualised as people doing tasks behind their desks. This visualisation is supported by a multi-user environment that can play one or more roles in the gamification scope. The setting allows for multiple roles played by a single player, therefore, restricting the execution of multiple roles with only one actor to fulfil all labour.

Fig. 10. Simulation of a DEMO model

These experiences require new visualisations to be created, evaluated and improved. When new insights appear, first, the meta-model needs to be extended with all new concepts that emerge in the visualisation and implementation activities. Furthermore, viewpoints can be defined and reference the existing and new concepts in the meta-model. Next, new diagrams and toolboxes with elements and connectors can be added to the tool where the basics functionality of SEA allows for. Finally, the functionality that cannot be solved by configuration will be implemented in the add-on.

6   Model Exchange

As reported in earlier work [23], a number of tools[4] can model (partial) DEMO models, while some of these even have a build-in engine to execute the actual models. It would be beneficial to be able to export and import DEMO models across tools because specific tools can have specific benefits when used in a certain organisational environment.

In addition, given the complementarity between e.g. BPMN, ArchiMate, e3Value, and DEMO, it would be beneficial to also bridge between the respective models. Experimental results regarding the potential benefits of this have been reported in e.g. [12,15,16,19,31]. This requires DEMO modelling tools to be able to export (and import) DEMO models. To this end, an exchange meta-model has been created that enables the exchange of both the actual model, including the different aspect models, as well as their visualisations. The exchange meta-model enables translation and connection to various other languages and includes model extensions to store models in other modelling languages such as ArchiMate and Business Process Model and Notation (BPMN). The exchange meta-model is based on XML Schema Definition (XSD), due to its common availability in modern-day development environments [20].

The SEA based modelling tool has been extended with this export capability. Both as a way to validate the exchange meta-model, and to experiment with the export of DEMO models towards a gamification application (as illustrated in Fig. 10).

A specific class of model exchanges needed in practice is the exchange between DEMO and VISI. As mentioned in Sect. 3, VISI is an early descendant of DEMO

---

[4] Created by e.g. Bakker&Spees, Technia, Future Insight, and Formetis.

which has now evolved into the ISO 29481-2:2012 (see Footnote 3) (BIM-related) standard for the construction sector. The exchange model between DEMO and VISI has been defined in the standard ISO 29481-2:2012.

7 Conclusions and Future Research

In this experience paper, we reported on some of the experiences in the development of enterprise-grade tool support for the practical use of DEMO. The chosen platform to realise this was the SEA platform. Some of the lessons learned from this research effort, that might be applicable to the development of modelling tools for other modelling languages as well, are:

1. There is a considerable difference between the meta-model used for educational (and theory development) purposes compared to the meta-model needed for actual tool development. Especially when also taking the experiences from practitioners using the modelling language in real-world projects into account
2. The core meta-model of the modelling language also needed to be extended with a visualisation meta-model to accommodate for different visualisations (of the same models).
3. Usage of a generic enterprise-grade tool platform, such as SEA provides a quick path towards enterprise-grade tool support. From a development perspective, the development of a bespoke solution may provide more flexibility. However, the usage of an existing tool (enterprise-grade) platform increases the initial acceptance.

In future research, we expect more feedback from practitioners based on the day-to-day use of DEMO. We also expect this to result in the need for new visualisations (including simulation and gamification) catering to the needs of different stakeholders. New research efforts have already been started to get more insight into the relation between the complexity of the information and the way we try to communicate this information.

In addition, we expect that further extensions to the core meta-model will be needed to enable sensible connections to complementary modelling languages and methods.

References

1. Andrade, M., Aveiro, D., Pinto, D.: Bridging ontology and implementation with a new DEMO action meta-model and engine. In: Aveiro, D., Guizzardi, G., Borbinha, J. (eds.) EEWC 2019. LNBIP, vol. 374, pp. 66–82. Springer, Cham (2020). https://doi.org/10.1007/978-3-030-37933-9_5
2. Aveiro, D., D. Pinto, D.: A case study based new DEMO way of working and collaborative tooling. In: 2013 IEEE 15th Conference on Business Informatics, pp. 21–26. IEEE Computer Society Press, Los Alamitos, California (2013)
3. Band, I., et al.: ArchiMate 3.0 Specification. The Open Group, San Francisco (2016)

4. Dietz, J.L.G.: Generic recurrent patterns in business processes. In: van der Aalst, W.M.P., Weske, M. (eds.) BPM 2003. LNCS, vol. 2678, pp. 200–215. Springer, Heidelberg (2003). https://doi.org/10.1007/3-540-44895-0_14

5. Dietz, J.L.G.: A world ontology specification language. In: Meersman, R., Tari, Z., Herrero, P. (eds.) OTM 2005. LNCS, vol. 3762, pp. 688–699. Springer, Heidelberg (2005). https://doi.org/10.1007/11575863_88

6. Dietz, J.L.G.: Enterprise Ontology – Theory and Methodology. Springer, Berlin (2006). https://doi.org/10.1007/3-540-33149-2

7. Dietz, J.L.G., et al.: The discipline of enterprise engineering. Int. J. Organ. Des. Eng. 3(1), 86–114 (2013)

8. Dietz, J.L.G., Mulder, J.B.F.: Enterprise Ontology - A Human-Centric Approach to Understanding the Essence of Organisation. Springer, Berlin (2020). The Enterprise Engineering Series

9. Dietz, J.L.G., Mulder, M.A.T.: Demo specification language 3.7 (2017). https://www.eei-test.nl/mdocs-posts/demo-specification-language-3-7/

10. Gartner: Information technology glossary. Website (Nov 2020). https://www.gartner.com/en/information-technology/glossary/enterprise-grade

11. Gouveia, D., Aveiro, D.: Modeling the system described by the EU general data protection regulation with DEMO. In: Aveiro, D., Guizzardi, G., Guerreiro, S., Guédria, W. (eds.) EEWC 2018. LNBIP, vol. 334, pp. 144–158. Springer, Cham (2019). https://doi.org/10.1007/978-3-030-06097-8_9

12. Gray, T., Bork, D., De. Vries, M.: A new DEMO modelling tool that facilitates model transformations. In: Nurcan, S., Reinhartz-Berger, I., Soffer, P., Zdravkovic, J. (eds.) BPMDS/EMMSAD-2020. LNBIP, vol. 387, pp. 359–374. Springer, Cham (2020). https://doi.org/10.1007/978-3-030-49418-6_25

13. Habermas, J.: The Theory for Communicative Action: Reason and Rationalization of Society, vol. 1. Boston Beacon Press, Boston (1984)

14. Kepes, B.: What does enterprise gradereally mean? website. https://www.forbes.com/sites/benkepes/2013/12/18/what-does-enterprise-grade-really-mean

15. de Kinderen, S., Gaaloul, K., Proper, H.A.E.: On transforming DEMO models to ArchiMate. In: Bider, I., Bider, I., et al. (eds.) BPMDS/EMMSAD -2012. LNBIP, vol. 113, pp. 270–284. Springer, Heidelberg (2012). https://doi.org/10.1007/978-3-642-31072-0_19

16. de Kinderen, S., Gaaloul, K., Proper, H.A.: Bridging value modelling to ArchiMate via transaction modelling. Softw. Syst. Model. 13(3), 1043–1057 (2012). https://doi.org/10.1007/s10270-012-0299-z

17. Lankhorst, M.M., et al.: Enterprise Architecture at Work - Modelling, Communication and Analysis. Springer, Berlin (2005)

18. Lankhorst, M.M., van der Torre, L., Proper, H.A.E., Arbab, F., Hoppenbrouwers, S.J.B.A., Steen, M.W.A.: Viewpoints and visualisation. In: Enterprise Architecture at Work. TEES, pp. 171–214. Springer, Heidelberg (2017). https://doi.org/10.1007/978-3-662-53933-0_8

19. Mráz, O., Náplava, P., Pergl, R., Skotnica, M.: Converting DEMO PSI transaction pattern into BPMN: a complete method. In: Aveiro, D., Pergl, R., Guizzardi, G., Almeida, J.P., Magalhães, R., Lekkerkerk, H. (eds.) EEWC 2017. LNBIP, vol. 284, pp. 85–98. Springer, Cham (2017). https://doi.org/10.1007/978-3-319-57955-9_7

20. Mulder, M.A.T.: Towards a complete metamodel for DEMO CM. In: Debruyne, C., Panetto, H., Guédria, W., Bollen, P., Ciuciu, I., Meersman, R. (eds.) OTM 2018. LNCS, vol. 11231, pp. 97–106. Springer, Cham (2019). https://doi.org/10.1007/978-3-030-11683-5_10

21. Mulder, M.A.T.: Validating the DEMO specification language. In: Aveiro, D., Guizzardi, G., Guerreiro, S., Guédria, W. (eds.) EEWC 2018. LNBIP, vol. 334, pp. 131–143. Springer, Cham (2019). https://doi.org/10.1007/978-3-030-06097-8_8

22. Mulder, M.A.T.: A design evaluation of an extension to the DEMO methodology. In: Aveiro, D., Guizzardi, G., Borbinha, J. (eds.) EEWC 2019. LNBIP, vol. 374, pp. 55–65. Springer, Cham (2020). https://doi.org/10.1007/978-3-030-37933-9_4

23. Mulder, M.A.T., Proper, H.A.: Towards enterprise-grade tool support for DEMO. In: Grabis, J., Bork, D. (eds.) PoEM 2020. LNBIP, vol. 400, pp. 90–105. Springer, Cham (2020). https://doi.org/10.1007/978-3-030-63479-7_7

24. Mulder, M.A.T.: Nen 75xx modelled in demo. Unpublished manuscript (2020)

25. Mulder, M.: Enabling the automatic verification and exchange of DEMO models. Ph.D. thesis, Radboud University, Nijmegen, the Netherlands (Forthcomming)

26. Nunn, R.: What is "enterprise grade software"? website (Nov 2015). http://tractsystems.com/what-is-enterprise-grade-software/

27. OMG: Business Process Modeling Notation, V2.0. Technical report. OMG Document Number: formal/2011-01-03, Object Management Group, Needham, Massachusetts (Jan 2011)

28. Op't Land, M., Proper, H.A., Waage, M., Cloo, J., Steghuis, C.: Enterprise Architecture - Creating Value by Informed Governance. Springer, Berlin (2008). The Enterprise Engineering Series

29. Partridge, T.: What exactly does "enterprise-grade" mean?. https://www.linkedin.com/pulse/what-exactly-does-enterprise-grade-mean-todd-partridge

30. van Reijswoud, V.E., Mulder, J.B.F., Dietz, J.L.G.: Communicative action based business process and information modelling with DEMO. Inf. Syst. J. 9(2), 117–138 (1999)

31. Ettema, R., Dietz, J.L.G.: ArchiMate and DEMO – mates to date? In: Albani, A., Barjis, J., Dietz, J.L.G. (eds.) CIAO!/EOMAS-2009. LNBIP, vol. 34, pp. 172–186. Springer, Heidelberg (2009). https://doi.org/10.1007/978-3-642-01915-9_13

32. Sparks, G.: What does enterprise grade mean? website (Aug 2020). https://www.quora.com/What-does-Enterprise-Grade-mean

33. Wagter, R., Proper, H.A.: Enterprise coherence governance: involving the right stakeholders. In: Architectural Coordination of Enterprise Transformation. TEES, pp. 99–110. Springer, Cham (2017). https://doi.org/10.1007/978-3-319-69584-6_10

34. Wieringa, R.J.: Design Science Methodology for Information Systems and Software Engineering. Springer, Heidelberg (2014). https://doi.org/10.1007/978-3-662-43839-8

Novel Applications

Cut to the Trace! Process-Aware Partitioning of Long-Running Cases in Customer Journey Logs

Gaël Bernard[✉], Arik Senderovich, and Periklis Andritsos

Faculty of Information, University of Toronto, Toronto, Canada
{gael.bernard,arik.senderovich,periklis.andritsos}@utoronto.ca

Abstract. Customer journeys are recordings of customer interactions with organizational information systems. These interactions are often recorded into so-called customer journey logs. Customer journeys often correspond to long-running and flexible traces that may temper the use of process analytics techniques such as process mining. A common method to make long-running traces suitable for process mining algorithms is to partition them at the largest temporal differences between consecutive events. However, these techniques ignores process context that journeys are often influenced by. In this work, we propose a probabilistic framework that generalizes previous techniques and introduces two novel process-aware partitioning approaches. The first method is inspired by the directly-follows relation, a predominant abstraction in process discovery. The second approach leverages LSTMs, a type of Neural Networks that learn long-term dependencies in sequences. We show that both approaches outperform existing time partitioning methods on both synthetic and real-world customer journey data.

Keywords: Customer journey analysis · Process mining · Trace partitioning

1 Introduction

A *customer journey* is an abstract representation of all interactions between a customer and an organization. In the banking industry, a journey involves interactions with tellers, website logins, money withdrawals, etc. Describing and understanding these customer pathways is referred to as customer journey analytics [20]. A recent study reveals that almost half of information technologies and business leaders consider customer journey analysis to be their top priority [11]. Better understanding of customers and deeper insights into their behavior implies improvement in quality-of-service. These insights are expected to increase customer satisfaction which, ultimately, is positively linked with revenue [20]. For these reasons, customer journey management is an essential topic in information systems management.

© Springer Nature Switzerland AG 2021
M. La Rosa et al. (Eds.): CAiSE 2021, LNCS 12751, pp. 519–535, 2021.
https://doi.org/10.1007/978-3-030-79382-1_31

Customer journey logs are sequential databases that contain transactions of customer interactions (aka 'touchpoints') with information systems (e.g., Customer Relationship Management systems). Due to the similarity between customer journey logs and event logs, process mining was shown to be a promising discipline for performing customer journey analysis [4]. By viewing a customer journey as a trace of events, one can immediately apply process mining techniques and gain insights into customer journeys.

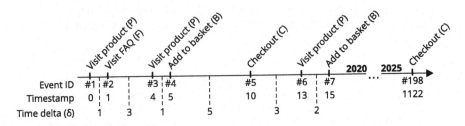

Fig. 1. Illustration of a customer journey composed of 198 events

Figure 1 illustrates a sample of a customer journey produced by a single customer browsing an online retail store. Clearly, after several years of customer interactions, one would expect to have a large number of events per customer (in our case, 198 events in 5 years). On the one hand, the flexibility offered to customers to consume a company's services accommodates their needs. On the other hand, these unique aspects of customer journeys, namely long-running and flexible cases, may result in several challenges for traditional process mining techniques.

Firstly, long-running cases cause process discovery algorithms to produce overly complex (spaghetti-like) process models, since they consider too many process variants [9]. Secondly, process discovery algorithms such as the inductive miner, [19], may overgeneralize and produce models that allow for events to happen in any order (flower models) [26]. In both cases, the resulting process models do not provide useful insights [9,26].

An approach that led its authors to win the 2011 BPI challenge, [13], consists of partitioning long traces into shorter ones by cutting at the largest time differences between events [8]. We shall refer to this approach as time-aware partitioning (TAP). The main limitation of TAP is that it relies solely on the time gap between events and disregards any process context. In our running example, the activity 'Checkout' shortly follows the activity 'Add to Basket'. Occasionally, an unexpected delay may occur between the two activities, e.g., due to customer characteristics. In such cases, TAP would assign the two closely related events to two distinct cases, causing a trace to start with the activity 'Checkout', which does not make sense from a business process standpoint.

In this paper, we use contextual information when cutting long-running traces. Specifically, we propose two novel *process-aware partitioning* approaches that build upon a probabilistic view of the partitioning problem, while taking process context into account. The first method, namely *local context process-aware partitioning* (LCPAP) is based on local dependencies between event labels. Similarly to the directly-follows relation that often stars in process mining algorithms (e.g., [28]), LCPAP employs the fact that pairs of directly following activities will present (on average) shorter temporal gaps. Our second approach, *global-context process-aware partitioning* (GCPAP), leverages the strength of long-short term memory (LSTM) Neural Networks to better account for global context when partitioning customer journeys. The main contribution of the paper is threefold:

1. We formalize the long-running trace partitioning problem.
2. We provide a general probabilistic framework for temporal trace partitioning and show that our framework subsumes existing approaches.
3. We propose two novel process-aware approaches and demonstrate their effectiveness by conducting an extensive empirical evaluation.

The rest of the paper is organized as follows. Section 2 defines the problem of trace partitioning. Subsequently, Sect. 3 formalizes a probabilistic framework for customer journey partitioning and instantiates the framework using two novel approaches. Section 4 evaluates the framework using synthetic journey logs and show the relevance of the approach by demonstrating its application on real-life customer journey data. In Sect. 5, we discuss the limitations of our approach, while Sect. 6 and Sect. 7 present related work and conclude the paper.

2 The Problem of Customer Journey Partitioning

In this section, we pose the problem of customer journey partitioning (CJP). We refer to long-running traces as customer journeys, however, our problem and approaches for solving it are applicable to general event logs. We start by providing a model for customer journey data, proceed by motivating CJP using our running example and conclude the section with the CJP problem statement.

2.1 Customer Journey Data

Let $\mathcal{E}$, $\mathcal{I}$, $\mathcal{A}$, and $\mathcal{T}$ be the universes of customer events, customer identifiers, activities, and timestamps, respectively. We assume that a customer event $e \in \mathcal{E}$ comprises three elements $e = (i, a, t)$ such that,

- $i \in \mathcal{I}$ is a unique customer identifier,
- $a \in \mathcal{A}$ is a customer activity associated with the event,
- $t \in \mathcal{T}$ is a timestamp associated with the event.

A customer journey $\mathcal{J}_i$ is a sequence of events sorted by time and associated with customer i. Formally, let $\mathcal{E}^*$ be the set of all finite sequences over $\mathcal{E}$. Then, a journey $\mathcal{J}_i \in \mathcal{E}^*$ of length n can be written as a sequence of triplets,

$$\mathcal{J}_i = \langle (i, a_1, t_1), \ldots, (i, a_n, t_n) : t_1 \leq, \ldots, \leq t_n \rangle.$$

For convenience, given an event e we let $i(e)$, $a(e)$, and $t(e)$ be the identifier, the activity, and the timestamp associated with event e. A customer journey log $\mathcal{L}_{\mathcal{J}}$ is a set of customer journeys.

2.2 Customer Journey Partitioning

Motivation. We return to the journey log in our running example (Fig. 1). One searches for a way to cut the 198 events to form meaningful cases. Without cutting the log, applying process mining techniques to $\mathcal{L}_{\mathcal{J}}$ would result in a model that represents all customer interactions rather than customer journeys. We demonstrate this issue by running a discovery algorithm on a real-life customer journey log describing customers' interaction with a service desk (dataset used in the evaluation in Sect. 4.3). We observe that the resulting model, depicted in Fig. 2 is a 'spaghetti' model, which is far from useful if we wish to perform cycle time prediction or discover a variant that customers go through when instantiating the process. Motivated by the need for useful models, we arrive at the problem of customer journey partitioning.

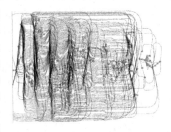

Fig. 2. Heuristic net discovered on real customer journey data.

Problem Formulation. As our first step towards formulating the problem, we define a journey partitioning function, $\chi : \mathcal{E}^* \to \mathbb{N}^{+*}$ to be a mapping that takes customer journeys and returns finite tuples of indices $\chi(\mathcal{J}_i)$ with each index corresponding to the end event of a case in journey i. The order between the elements of the tuple respects the temporal order within the journey, i.e., given a partition $\chi(\mathcal{J}_i) = (i_1, \ldots, i_k)$, we get that $t_{i_{k-1}} \leq t_{i_k}$. Thus, given a journey $\mathcal{J}_i = \langle (i, a_1, t_1), \ldots, (i, a_n, t_n) : t_1 \leq, \ldots, \leq t_n \rangle$ and a partition $\chi(\mathcal{J}_i) = (i_1, \ldots, i_k)$ we can derive k cases,

$$\sigma_1 = \langle (i, a_1, t_1), \ldots, (i, a_{i_1}, t_{i_1}) \rangle$$
$$\sigma_2 = \langle (i, a_{i_1+1}, t_{i_1+1}), \ldots, (i, a_{i_2}, t_{i_2}) \rangle,$$
$$\ldots$$
$$\sigma_k = \langle (i, a_{i_{k-1}+1}, t_{i_{k-1}+1}), \ldots, (i, a_{i_k}, t_{i_k}) \rangle. \tag{1}$$

For example, the partition $\chi(\mathcal{J}_1) = (4, 198)$ transforms the journey from Fig. 1, $\mathcal{J}_1 = [(P, 0), (F, 1), (P, 4), (B, 5), (C, 10), ...]$, into two cases: $\sigma_1 = [(P, 0), (F, 1), (P, 4), (B, 5)]$ and $\sigma_2 = [(C, 10), ...]$. We denote $\mathcal{L}_{\chi(\mathcal{J}_i)}$ the set of cases $\{\sigma_1, \ldots, \sigma_k\}$ that results from applying χ to $\mathcal{J}_i$. We assume the existence of a *true* partitioning of the journey log, which we are aiming to reconstruct. Different instances of χ can be viewed as approximations of the true partitioning.

Next, we let $\Pi(\mathcal{L}_{\chi(\mathcal{J}_i)})$ denote the loss associated with wrong case reconstruction from customer journey i. The customer journey partitioning (CJP) problem is to minimize the total loss given χ and a journey log $\mathcal{L}_{\mathcal{J}}$ defined as,

$$\Pi_\chi(\mathcal{L}_{\mathcal{J}}) = \sum_{i=1}^{n} \Pi(\mathcal{L}_{\chi(\mathcal{J}_i)}). \tag{2}$$

There are various options for measuring the loss between partitions. We shall provide some of those distance functions when instantiating our approach in Sect. 4.1.

3   Probabilistic Customer Journey Partitioning

Solving CJP directly by minimizing $\Pi_\chi(\mathcal{L}_{\mathcal{J}})$ would require case labeling of the journey events, which is unrealistic to obtain in many practical scenarios. In this paper, we circumvent this challenge by introducing a probabilistic framework for CJP that would allow us to approximate the solution to the partitioning problem. The key in our solution is the ability to accurately identify that a case ends after a given event.

Formally, given an event $e \in \mathcal{E}$, let $E(e)$ be an indicator that equals 1 if e is a case-ending event, and 0 otherwise. Thus, we define $p(e) = P(E(e) = 1)$ as the probability that e is a case ending event. The foundation of our approach lies in the ordering of the probabilities for events to be case ending events and choosing the top K events[1] to set the cuts. Below, we provide three approaches that instantiate the above.

3.1   Time-Aware Partitioning (TAP)

Time-aware partitioning (TAP) assumes that journey cuts correspond to longer inter-event durations. TAP is used as the standard state-of-the-art way to partition long traces when preprocessing event logs (see [8]). A time partitioning algorithm cuts journeys at the longest time differences between events. To quote [8]:

"One can use a parameter, say δ days, to demarcate the boundaries between process instances. Two events or event sequences with a time period between them greater than δ fall under two process instances."

We will formalize the above using our probabilistic framework by defining the dependence between $E(e)$ and observed inter-event times.

For a given journey of customer i, $\mathcal{J}_i$, let $\lambda_i = (\lambda_{i,1}, \ldots, \lambda_{i,n_i})$ be the sequence of inter-event times with n_i being the number of events in the journey, i.e., $\lambda_{i,1} = t_2 - t_1, \lambda_{i,2} = t_3 - t_2, \ldots$ and so on. For example, if our journey log has one journey, $\mathcal{J}_1 = [(P,0), (F,1), (P,4), (B,5), (C,10), \ldots]$, the sequence λ_i is $[1, 3, 1, 5, \ldots]$. When we refer to some event e in the log, we denote λ_e the inter-event time between e and the next observed event in the same journey. If e is

---

[1] K is a hyper-parameter that controls for the number of cases in the journey log.

the last event in the journey, we set $\lambda_e = \infty$ to denote that the next event will not be occurring (as e is last); note that we only consider completed journeys.

Further, we assume that the inter-event time Λ_e (which is realized by λ_e) is a random variable that comprises a baseline inter-event time Λ_0 and a random gap Δ that exists only if the case ends after e,

$$
\Lambda_e = \begin{cases} \Lambda_0, & \text{for } E(e) = 0 \\ \Lambda_0 + \Delta, & \text{for } E(e) = 1 \end{cases}
$$

Let δ be the expected value of Δ, i.e., $\mathbb{E}\Delta = \delta$ and let $p(e) = P(E(e) = 1)$. From the law of total expectation we get that

$$
\begin{aligned}
\mathbb{E}\Lambda_e &= p(e)(\mathbb{E}(\Lambda_0 + \Delta)) + (1 - p(e))\mathbb{E}\Lambda_0 \\
&= p(e)(\mathbb{E}\Lambda_0 + \mathbb{E}\Delta) + (1 - p(e))\mathbb{E}\Lambda_0 = \mathbb{E}\Lambda_0 + p(e)\delta.
\end{aligned} \tag{3}
$$

Therefore, we get that

$$
p(e) = \frac{\mathbb{E}\Lambda_e - \lambda_0}{\delta}, \tag{4}
$$

with $\lambda_0 = \mathbb{E}\Lambda_0 > 0$ being a positive constant. This result allows us to compare two observed events e, e' and decide which one has the higher likelihood to end a case.

Consider two events in the journey log, e and e', such that the gap of the former is greater than the gap of the latter, namely $\lambda_e > \lambda'_e$. Since every event e corresponds to a single random variable Λ_e and a single observation λ_e, our best estimate of $\mathbb{E}\Lambda_e$ is $\widehat{\mathbb{E}\Lambda_e} = \lambda_e$. Therefore, we get that

$$
\frac{\widehat{p(e)}}{\widehat{p(e')}} = \frac{\lambda_e - \lambda_0}{\lambda_{e'} - \lambda_0} > 1, \tag{5}
$$

since $\lambda_0 > 0$ and $\lambda_e > \lambda_{e'} > 0$. Therefore, ordering the events according to their corresponding inter-event times (including ∞ for journey ending events) and cutting after the top K events on the list, guarantees that we are selecting the events with highest (estimated) chances of being case ending events.

One of the main drawbacks of TAP is that it does not take into account any contextual information. Returning to our example, although the activity 'Checkout' cannot happen before the activity 'Add to basket', TAP might insert a cut. In fact, TAP is sensitive to extreme values drawn from Λ_0, e.g., if the time between two consecutive events that belong to the same case is unexpectedly long, the two events might end up in two separate cases according to TAP.

In Fig. 3, we provide an illustrative customer journey that we use to apply the partitioning techniques. Taking this figure, TAP would partition at: ∞ (#10, journey ending events), 10 (#4), 5 (#7), and 4 (#5); respectively producing the cuts TAP4, TAP1, TAP3, and TAP2. Figure 3 illustrates that we cannot retrieve any of the ground truth by cutting based on the inter-event times. In the next part, we provide two approaches that take contextual information into account when cutting long-running traces.

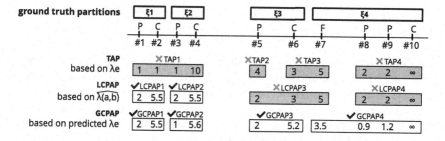

Fig. 3. Illustration of the three CJP techniques.

3.2   Local Context Process-Aware Partitioning (LCPAP)

Unlike TAP that only observes temporal differences, our second solution, namely LCPAP, employs the directly-follows relation between pairs of activities, and their inter-event times to decide on the cut. For LCPAP, we refine the definition of a case ending event by letting it depend on the pair of activities that corresponds to an event e and to its direct follower e' (both events are part of the same journey).

Let $d(e) \in \mathcal{A} \times (\mathcal{A} \cup \{\bot\})$ be the directly follows relation such that $d(e) = (a, b)$ with $a = a(e)$ and $b = a(e')$ and e' directly follows e. Note that $b = \bot$ implies that e is a journey ending event. We assume that the inter-event time, Λ_e, depends not on the event itself, but on the pair (a, b). Formally, we write it as,

$$\Lambda_e^{(a,b)} = \begin{cases} \Lambda_0^{(a,b)}, & \text{for } E(e) = 0, d(e) = (a, b) \\ \Lambda_0^{(a,b)} + \Delta, & \text{for } E(e) = 1, d(e) = (a, b) \end{cases} \quad (6)$$

This implies that the end of a case is dictated by Δ, as before, but its standard duration Λ_0 is a function of the activity pair, (a, b). Repeating a similar derivation as in Sect. 3.1, we get that

$$p_{a,b}(e) = P(E(e) = 1, d(e) = (a, b)) = \frac{\mathbb{E}\Lambda_e^{(a,b)} - \lambda_0^{a,b}}{\delta}. \quad (7)$$

Note that in the equation above, we added contextual information regarding the directly follows relation associated with event e, which was not used by TAP.

We estimate $p_{a,b}(e)$ by assuming that all baseline durations $\lambda_0^{(a,b)}$ are identical and equal to some λ_0. Therefore, it is enough to estimate $\mathbb{E}\Lambda_e^{(a,b)}$ by simply averaging the inter-event times, namely $\{\lambda_{i,j} \mid a_j = a, a_{j+1} = b\}$. We denote this average by $\bar{\lambda}_{(a,b)}$ and for any pair of events e, e' we write,

$$\frac{\widehat{p_{a,b}(e)}}{\widehat{p_{a,b}(e')}} = \frac{\bar{\lambda}_{(a,b)} - \lambda_0}{\bar{\lambda}_{(c,d)} - \lambda_0}, \quad (8)$$

with (a, b) and (c, d) being arbitrary pairs of activity labels of e and e', respectively. Hence, given a pair of events, it is enough to observe the average durations of their activity labels $\bar{\lambda}_{(a,b)}$ to determine their ordering. Note that for $b =\perp$, we define $\bar{\lambda}_{(a,b)} = \infty$ and thus we shall always have a cut after a journey ending event.

Subsequently, we perform a cut after the top K observed average durations of the pairs that correspond to the events. For instance, in Fig. 3, we get the $\lambda_{P,C} = [1, 1, 4, 2]$ (event IDs #1, #3, #5, and #9). Thus, we get that $\bar{\lambda}_{(P,C)} = 2$. The four largest values are: ∞ (#10, journey ending events), 5.5 (#2, $\bar{\lambda}_{(C,P)}$), 5.5 (#4, $\bar{\lambda}_{(C,P)}$), and 5 (#5, $\bar{\lambda}_{(F,P)}$); respectively producing the cuts LCPAP4, LCPAP1, LCPAP2, and LCPAP3 visible in Fig. 3. Two out of the four cuts are correct with respect to ground truth.

3.3   Global Context Process Aware Partitioning (GCPAP)

Local context PAP considers the directly follows relation between a pair of events. As the name suggests, GCPAP generalizes the notion of context by adding: (1) w activities preceding the current event e, (2) w time inter-event times preceding event e, (3) activity $a(e)$ that is associated with e, (4) w activities following e, and (5) w inter-event times following e. If there are less than w events that precede or follow e, we take the actual number of preceding or following events. Formally, let $\kappa(e, w)$ be the concatenation of the five context elements of event e, hyper-parametrized by $w > 0$. Then, similarly to the definition of Λ_e in Eq. (9), we write,

$$\Lambda_e^{\kappa(e,w)} = \begin{cases} \Lambda_0^{\kappa(e,w)}, & \text{for } E(e) = 0, \kappa(e, w) \\ \Lambda_0^{\kappa(e,w)} + \Delta, & \text{for } E(e) = 1.\kappa(e, w) \end{cases} \quad (9)$$

Let $p_\kappa(e) = P(E(e) = 1), \kappa(e, w))$ be the probability of event e being a case ending event. By similar assumptions as in LCPAP derive that for any pair of events e, e':

$$\frac{\widehat{p_\kappa(e)}}{\widehat{p_\kappa(e')}} = \frac{\hat{\lambda}_{\kappa(e,w)} - \lambda_0}{\hat{\lambda}_{\kappa(e',w)} - \lambda_0}. \quad (10)$$

In this case, $\hat{\lambda}_{\kappa(e,w)}$ is the mean value of the random variable $\Lambda_e^{\kappa(e,w)}$. However, since it comprises a complex context conditioned on the 5 elements mentioned above, we do not simply estimate it using a simple mean over the different context levels, but regress the inter-event time on the context elements (treating them as features). Therefore, estimating $\hat{\lambda}_{\kappa(e,w)}$ (and $\hat{\lambda}_{\kappa(e',w)}$) turns into a regression problem that we solve using deep-learning.

Concretely, we propose the Neural Network (NN) architecture presented in Fig. 4. It comprise LSTM, which is a special type of Recurrent Neural Network (RNN) introduced in [17]. LSTM possesses an advanced memory cell that gives it powerful modeling capabilities for long-term dependencies [27]. The advantage of LSTM is that it can work with sequence tensor possessing more than two dimensions, which is unconventional for machine-learning algorithms [29]. Ultimately, it means that we can use the sequence of activities "as-is" [29] without retreating

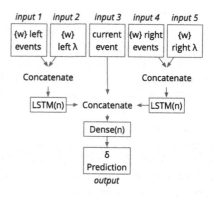

Fig. 4. NN architecture for the GCPAP.

to simplifications such as the directly-follows relation. The five inputs visible in Fig. 4 reflect the 5 aforementioned pieces of contextual data. The NN is composed of two separate LSTM layers made, followed by a Dense layer. It is a design choice since various alternative architectures are possible. The output is the expected time gap before the next event that we will use to cut the traces. Figure 3 provides an example of how this approach may outperform TAP and LCPAP. In fact, the four largest predicted time gaps are: ∞ (#10, journey ending events), 5.6 (#4), 5.5 (#2), and 5.2 (#6); respectively producing the cuts GCPAP4, GCPAP2, GCPAP1, and GCPAP3 visible in Fig. 3. We conveniently set the predicted values to time gaps that allow GCPAP to find the true partitions. It was done for demonstration purposes as more than 10 events are typically needed to get predicted time gaps that allows to retrieve ground truth cuts.

4 Evaluation

The goal of the experimental evaluation is to benchmark the three methods for customer journey partitioning presented in Sect. 3. Our experiments show that:

1. The best performing CJP is GCPAP, followed by LCPAP for both synthetic and real customer journey data, while TAP comes last.
2. The synthetic dataset highlights the value of LCPAP, especially when the customer journey data is complex; i.e., when the time gaps are not very informative.
3. We show in the real dataset the existence of outlier time gaps that TAP cannot handle well.

The implementation of the three methods, as well as the results of the experiments and the instructions to reconstruct the experiments are available online[2].

---

[2] https://github.com/gaelbernard/cjp.

For the GCPAP, we set w to 10, the number of unit to 64 (LSTM and dense layers) and the number of epochs to 20.

In the remainder of the section, we first introduce the loss function, Π, used for the evaluation. Then, we present the first set of experiments performed on a synthetic customer journey dataset. We report a more extensive experiment containing 10 customer journey logs, and a scalability analysis in a separate technical report [7].

Lastly, we demonstrate the applicability of our approach by presenting a second set of experiments performed on a real-world dataset, which contains customer interactions with a service desk of a large municipality. Note that the real-world data experiment does not aim at an exhaustive application of the approach to numerous datasets, but rather exemplifies how one would use the method in similar realistic settings.

4.1   The Loss Function

Customer journey partitioning can be viewed as a series of binary classification problems: we either correctly identify the true case, or make an error identifying that a sequence corresponds to a case. Our classification may hence fall into one of the following categories: (1) True Positive (TP): Partition correctly found, (2) False Positive (FP): Case wrongly cut, (3) True Negative (TN): Case correctly not cut, and (4) False Negative (FN): Partition not found. The True Positive Rate (TPR), calculated as $\frac{TP}{TP+FN}$, provides the fraction of partitions we are able to retrieve. Conversely, the False Positive Rate (FPR), $\frac{FP}{FP+TN}$, measures the fraction of cases that are wrongly cut. The number of cases, K, is not known in advance and hence we can reach a perfect TPR by classifying all the events as cuts ($K = |\mathcal{L}_\mathcal{J}|$). The other extreme would be to get a perfect FPR by not partitioning the event logs ($K = 0$).

ROC curve analysis offers a suitable tool to evaluate the trade-off between TPR and FPR for various values of K. The diagonal represents a random guess (dashed lines in Fig. 7), while the coordinate (0,1) is a perfect classifier. Moreover, we use the *area under the curve* (AUC) as a loss function, since it allows summarizing the ROC curve using a single metric [10].

4.2   Evaluation Using Synthetic Customer Journey Data

The Dataset. We define a process model depicted in Fig. 5. Then, we produce 1,000 traces from this process model using the plugin "Simple simulation of a (stochastic) Petri net" in ProM 6.7. Next, we randomly assign each of the traces to 10 customers in order to form 10 customer journeys. Eventually, this means that these 10 customer journeys are composed, on average, of 100 stacked traces

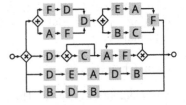

Fig. 5. Process Model used for the experiment.

that we wish to retrieve by leveraging one of the three partitioning techniques. The inter-event time is a key parameter to control for the complexity of the experiment. To simulate the time difference, we assume that the inter-event time corresponds to an exponential distribution, which implies that events arrive according to a Poisson process. Formally, we set

$$timeDiff(\lambda, r) = \frac{-ln(r)}{(1/\lambda)} \begin{cases} +d, & \text{if new variant} \\ +0 & \text{otherwise} \end{cases}$$

where:

λ is the rate of the Poisson Process that we set to 1
r random value uniformly distributed between 0 and 1
d is a constant (delay) which is added if the next event belongs to a new journey

By adding a delay (d) when the next event belongs to a new case, we control the difficulty to retrieve the optimal partitions. The larger the d is, the easier it is to retrieve the optimal partitions. Note that the delay is constant, but the inter-case time is not since we sum the delay with a random value.

Results. Figure 6 shows the AUC for various delays. As can be seen, GCPAP outperforms the two other approaches, in particular, for low delays. Even though LCPAP loses accuracy compared to GCPAP, this approach considers a limited context (i.e., pairs of events) and is hence very efficient to compute (see the technical report, [7]) and still largely outperforms TAP.

Figure 7 shows the ROC curve for the delays: 0.05, 0.10, 0.30, and 0.50. We observe that TAP curves have an interesting shape: the TPR is saturating before the FPR. For instance, for a delay of 0.5, we can see that the TPR

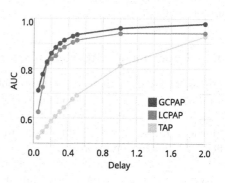

Fig. 6. AUC for various delays.

reaches 100% when the FPR is approximately 60%. We interpret the results as follows: at TPR saturation point, we already retrieved all the partitions and augmenting K is only making the FPR worse, i.e., we are trying to cut the trace at values that are lower than the delay. The LCPAP curves also have an interesting informal characteristic: they show a 'stair-like' shape. We believe that this is due to the lower number of unique values at which we can apply a cut.

In [7], we extended the experiment with 10 new process models and conducted a scalability analysis.

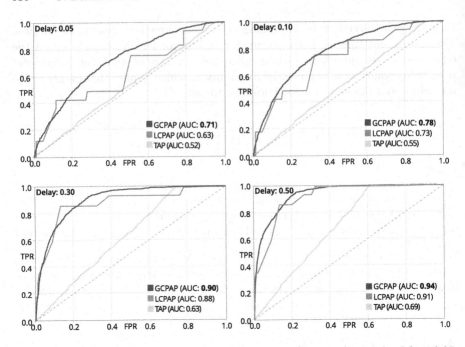

Fig. 7. ROC curves for the experiment with the synthetic datasets for the delays 0.05, 0.10, 0.30 and 0.50.

4.3   Experiment with Real Customer Journey Data

Dataset. We used an event log that contains tickets handled by a service desk of a municipality over a time span of one year. Since tickets have well defined start and end timestamps, it does not meet our definition of long-running customer journeys. However, we use this to our advantage by considering that ticket identifiers are the true cuts that we wish to retrieve using our three techniques. Hence, we keep the ticket identifier for the evaluation as our ground truth and consider customer journeys to be interactions between a customer and the service desk. We only keep the top 1% of customers that generated most of the tickets throughout the year to focus the experiment on difficult cases where many tickets are generated within a short period of time. From this procedure, we obtained a customer journey event log with the following characteristics: 27 customer journeys, 7.9K tickets, and 100.9K 'touchpoints' of 290 types. The median time between events belonging to the same case was 34 s, while the median time between events belonging to distinct cases within a customer journey was 30 min. Despite this massive mean time differences, retrieving the journeys is not straightforward due to the existence of extreme values.

Results. Figure 8 shows the ROC curves and the AUCs of the three CJP methods. Similar to the results for the synthetic experiments, GCPAP outperforms the two other approaches. It is interesting to note that the TPR for the TAP reaches a plateau around 90% and jump to 100% only when $K = |\mathcal{L}_\mathcal{J}|$. In fact, sometimes, two events from two distinct tickets closely follow each other, causing the TAP to wrongfully assign them to the same case. It demonstrates that the extreme values mentioned in Sect. 3 do exist in real customer journey data. We may further observe that GCPAP and LCPAP solve this issue as they can exceed the value of 90% TPR much sooner compared to TAP. Lastly, we note that the LCPAP 'stair-like' shape highlighted with the synthetic dataset is not as strong in Fig. 7 because of the large number of unique events of the real dataset (i.e. 290).

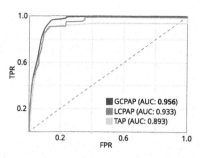

Fig. 8. ROC curves for real customer journey data

5 Discussion and Limitations

In this part, we discuss the limitations of our approach. Our solution for the CJP problem can be easily extended and generalized; furthermore, it does not rely on any knowledge of the underlying process models. However, we make several assumptions about the data that may limit the applicability of our method.

First, we assume that traces within a journey cannot overlap. Specifically, our technique cannot recompose correctly multiple journeys from a single customer that runs simultaneously. Second, we assume that the touchpoints happening along the journey on various channels are available on a uniform granularity level and exhibit reasonable data quality. One may require some preprocessing to level event abstractions, which could be performed using one of the event abstraction techniques studied in [30]. Lastly, being able to extract events logs from heterogeneous information systems is a well-recognized dilemma within the process mining community [1]. We claim that the customer journey's complex nature even exacerbates this challenge. The fact that customer journeys are complex is also what makes it appealing for process mining analysis in the first place.

By offering a flexible framework for partitioning customer journeys into traces, we hope to ease the analysis of customer journeys with process mining. Having said that, we see this work as a stepping stone for improving the proposed methods, which would relax some of the aforementioned assumptions.

6 Related Work

Clickstream analysis requires a preprocessing step similar to the partitioning of customer journeys to extract website usage insights. This step consists of grouping web interactions into user sessions [24]. The predominant technique to partition clickstream data is based on time and is equivalent to TAP, e.g., [2, 18,24]. Other approaches leverage clickstream-specific information not available in a customer journey context, such as the 'referer' [3], or logging events in a service-oriented architecture [14].

In the human-computer interaction community, Leno et al. propose a workers' routines partitioning algorithm of user interaction logs using a graph-based approach [21]. The underlying assumption is that a worker will perform the same task with some variance and noise, and the goal is to partition them. A limitation of this approach is that multiple routines cannot share a single activity label, limiting its applicability to the less-structured customer journey context. Another approach in the same community is presented in [12]. It consists of a custom-made frequent itemset mining that encompasses user behavior-specific metrics. Interestingly, one assumption is that the order of the tasks within a routine is not important. Both these works do not take into consideration the time between events.

Event log abstraction is a recent area of studies within process mining that aims to transform low-level events (e.g., a series of clicks on a website) into meaningful activities to process stakeholders (e.g., canceling an order). One can refer to [30] for an extensive literature review about abstraction techniques. Some of these approaches require business knowledge inputs that can take the form of ontologies [22], annotated event logs [25], interactions with business experts [5], or composition rules [16]. In [23], Mannhardt and Tax propose to rely on local process models (LPMs) introduced in [26] to by-pass the needs to input business knowledge. What makes this approach appealing is that LPMs allows dealing with long and chaotic traces and, hence, with customer journey logs. Most of these abstraction approaches disregard the time and consider only the activity context – the exact opposite of TAP. One interesting exception is the work from [22] where a threshold is required to abstract the activities. Overall, abstracting and partitioning traces fulfill a distinct goal but complement each other to analyze overly complex event logs.

In the process mining community, LSTM based methods have been shown to work well for predictive process monitoring tasks such as predicting the next activity [15,27], timestamp prediction [27], or trace truncation [6]. However, to the best of our knowledge, LSTMs have never been used as a preprocessing step for event logs.

7   Conclusion

In this work, we defined and solved the problem of customer journey partitioning. Our approach generalizes and extends existing process mining methods for finding cuts in traces. We found that the state-of-the-art method for cutting traces, namely TAP, was overrun by our newly proposed process-aware partitioning (PAP) methods that are able to take into account local (LCPAP) and global (GCPAP) contextual information. Both LCPAP and GCPAP outperformed TAP on both synthetic and real customer journey data. Compared to

TAP and using LCPAP and GCPAP, we improved the partitioning of the real customer journey data by 4.0 and 6.3% points, respectively.

In future work, we would like to further employ the flexibility offered by Neural Network architectures, to potentially improve the partitioning of long-running by taking additional contextual information into consideration (e.g., resources, departments, day of the week). In addition, we aim at exploring inter-case dependencies between journeys, since customer interactions are often performed in groups (e.g., family members and co-workers often interact together).

References

1. Aalst, W.: Data science in action. In: Process Mining, pp. 3–23. Springer, Heidelberg (2016). https://doi.org/10.1007/978-3-662-49851-4_1
2. Benevenuto, F., Rodrigues, T., Cha, M., Almeida, V.: Characterizing user behavior in online social networks. In: Proceedings of the 9th ACM SIGCOMM Conference on Internet Measurement, pp. 49–62 (2009)
3. Berendt, B., Mobasher, B., Nakagawa, M., Spiliopoulou, M.: The impact of site structure and user environment on session reconstruction in web usage analysis. In: Zaïane, O.R., Srivastava, J., Spiliopoulou, M., Masand, B. (eds.) WebKDD 2002. LNCS (LNAI), vol. 2703, pp. 159–179. Springer, Heidelberg (2003). https://doi.org/10.1007/978-3-540-39663-5_10
4. Bernard, G., Andritsos, P.: A process mining based model for customer journey mapping. In: Forum and Doctoral Consortium Papers Presented at the 29th International Conference on Advanced Information Systems Engineering (CAiSE Forum), pp. 49-56. CEUR workshop proceedings (2017)
5. Bernard, G., Andritsos, P.: CJM-ab: abstracting customer journey maps using process mining. In: Mendling, J., Mouratidis, H. (eds.) CAiSE 2018. LNBIP, vol. 317, pp. 49–56. Springer, Cham (2018). https://doi.org/10.1007/978-3-319-92901-9_5
6. Bernard, G., Andritsos, P.: Truncated trace classifier. removal of incomplete traces from event logs. In: Nurcan, S., Reinhartz-Berger, I., Soffer, P., Zdravkovic, J. (eds.) BPMDS/EMMSAD -2020. LNBIP, vol. 387, pp. 150–165. Springer, Cham (2020). https://doi.org/10.1007/978-3-030-49418-6_10
7. Bernard, G., Senderovich, A., Andritsos, P.: Cut to the trace: Technical report. Technical report, University of Toronto (Mar 2021). https://github.com/gaelbernard/cjp/raw/master/TechnicalReport/TechnicalReport.pdf
8. Bose, R.P.J.C., van der Aalst, W.M.P.: Analysis of patient treatment procedures. In: Daniel, F., Barkaoui, K., Dustdar, S. (eds.) BPM 2011, Part I. LNBIP, vol. 99, pp. 165–166. Springer, Heidelberg (2012). https://doi.org/10.1007/978-3-642-28108-2_17
9. Bose, R.J.C., Mans, R.S., van der Aalst, W.M.: Wanna improve process mining results? In: IEEE Symposium on Computational Intelligence and Data Mining (CIDM), pp. 127–134. IEEE (2013)
10. Bradley, A.P.: The use of the area under the ROC curve in the evaluation of machine learning algorithms. Pattern Recogn. 30(7), 1145–1159 (1997)
11. Daigler, J., Davies, J., Manusama, B., Bharaj, G.: Market guide for customer journey analytics. Technical report, Gartner (Feb 2019)

12. Dev, H., Liu, Z.: Identifying frequent user tasks from application logs. In: Proceedings of the 22nd International Conference on Intelligent User Interfaces, pp. 263–273 (2017)
13. van Dongen, B., Ferreira, D.R., Weber, B.: Business processing intelligence challenge 2011 (bpic 11). Technical report, IEEE Task Force on Process Mining (2011). https://www.win.tue.nl/bpi/doku.php?id=2011:challenge
14. Dustdar, S., Gombotz, R.: Discovering web service workflows using web services interaction mining. Int. J. Bus. Process Integr. Manag. 1(4), 256–266 (2006)
15. Evermann, J., Rehse, J.-R., Fettke, P.: A deep learning approach for predicting process behaviour at runtime. In: Dumas, M., Fantinato, M. (eds.) BPM 2016. LNBIP, vol. 281, pp. 327–338. Springer, Cham (2017). https://doi.org/10.1007/978-3-319-58457-7_24
16. Fazzinga, B., Flesca, S., Furfaro, F., Masciari, E., Pontieri, L.: Efficiently interpreting traces of low level events in business process logs. Inf. Syst. 73, 1–24 (2018)
17. Hochreiter, S., Schmidhuber, J.: Long short-term memory. Neural Comput. textbf9(8), 1735–1780 (1997). https://doi.org/10.1162/neco.1997.9.8.1735
18. Kumar, A., Salo, J., Li, H.: Stages of user engagement on social commerce platforms: analysis with the navigational clickstream data. Int. J. Electron. Commer. 23(2), 179–211 (2019)
19. Leemans, S.J.J., Fahland, D., van der Aalst, W.M.P.: Discovering block-structured process models from event logs - a constructive approach. In: Colom, J.-M., Desel, J. (eds.) PETRI NETS 2013. LNCS, vol. 7927, pp. 311–329. Springer, Heidelberg (2013). https://doi.org/10.1007/978-3-642-38697-8_17
20. Lemon, K.N., Verhoef, P.C.: Understanding customer experience throughout the customer journey. J. Mark. 80(6), 69–96 (2016)
21. Leno, V., Augusto, A., Dumas, M., La Rosa, M., Maggi, F.M., Polyvyanyy, A.: Identifying candidate routines for robotic process automation from unsegmented ui logs. In: 2020 2nd International Conference on Process Mining (ICPM), pp. 153–160. IEEE (2020)
22. Leonardi, G., Striani, M., Quaglini, S., Cavallini, A., Montani, S.: Towards semantic process mining through knowledge-based trace abstraction. In: Ceravolo, P., van Keulen, M., Stoffel, K. (eds.) SIMPDA 2017. LNBIP, vol. 340, pp. 45–64. Springer, Cham (2019). https://doi.org/10.1007/978-3-030-11638-5_3
23. Mannhardt, F., Tax, N.: Unsupervised event abstraction using pattern abstraction and local process models, pp. 55–63 (2017)
24. Srivastava, J., Cooley, R., Deshpande, M., Tan, P.N.: Web usage mining: discovery and applications of usage patterns from web data. ACM SIGKDD Explor. Newsl. 1(2), 12–23 (2000)
25. Tax, N., Sidorova, N., Haakma, R., van der Aalst, W.: Mining process model descriptions of daily life through event abstraction. In: Bi, Y., Kapoor, S., Bhatia, R. (eds.) IntelliSys 2016. SCI, vol. 751, pp. 83–104. Springer, Cham (2018). https://doi.org/10.1007/978-3-319-69266-1_5
26. Tax, N., Sidorova, N., Haakma, R., van der Aalst, W.M.: Mining local process models. J. Innov. Digit. Ecosyst. 3(2), 183–196 (2016). https://doi.org/10.1016/j.jides.2016.11.001. http://www.sciencedirect.com/science/article/pii/S2352664516300232
27. Tax, N., Verenich, I., La. Rosa, M., Dumas, M.: Predictive business process monitoring with LSTM neural networks. In: Dubois, E., Pohl, K. (eds.) CAiSE 2017. LNCS, vol. 10253, pp. 477–492. Springer, Cham (2017). https://doi.org/10.1007/978-3-319-59536-8_30

28. van der Aalst, W., Weijters, T., Maruster, L.: Workflow mining: discovering process models from event logs. IEEE Trans. Knowl. Data Eng. **16**(9), 1128–1142 (2004)
29. Verenich, I., Dumas, M., Rosa, M.L., Maggi, F.M., Teinemaa, I.: Survey and cross-benchmark comparison of remaining time prediction methods in business process monitoring. ACM Trans. Intell. Syst. Technol. **10**(4) (2019). https://doi.org/10.1145/3331449
30. van Zelst, S.J., Mannhardt, F., de Leoni, M., Koschmider, A.: Event abstraction in process mining: literature review and taxonomy. Granular Comput. 1–18 (2020). https://doi.org/10.1007/s41066-020-00226-2

A Multi Case Study on Legacy System Migration in the Banking Industry

Hasan Emre Hayretci[1,2] and Fatma Başak Aydemir[2(✉)]

[1] DefineX Consulting Technology Labs, Istanbul, Turkey
`emre.hayretci@teamdefinex.com`
[2] Boğaziçi University, Istanbul, Turkey
`{emre.hayretci,basak.aydemir}@boun.edu.tr`

Abstract. Advances in technology, changing customer requirements, and pressure from business goals are the main drivers for innovation in the banking industry. Legacy architectures with monolithic structures prevent banks from implementing new generation banking models. To stay competitive, banks migrate to modular and scalable architectures. This migration has a significant impact on banks' technical and organizational infrastructures, so it is crucial to devise an end-to-end migration strategy and plan the transformation. This paper reports our observations on the legacy system migration of three large retail banks between 2014 and 2020, focusing on the evaluation and prioritization criteria for their application portfolio to be migrated. We compare and contrast the motivations, migration strategies, and migration prioritization methods and discuss key takeaways from these high scale migration projects.

Keywords: Legacy migration · Next-generation architectures · Migration prioritization · Case study

1 Introduction

Rapidly changing customer expectations, advances in technology, and pressure from the business side force banks to constantly assess their current IT infrastructures and innovate. The customers require banking systems to seamlessly integrate into their daily activities as the technology provides tools for multi device, anytime, anywhere access while the business demands lower costs for ever-high quality of service. All these drivers for change demand new models for banking infrastructures, and banks with legacy architecture struggle to implement these new models [21].

Legacy banking platforms are monolithic structures that are complex. Applications for these platforms get complicated over time to maintain. Such applications require development teams to split by functions: user interface, application middleware, database, and others. Another disadvantage of these application is their fragility, for a single bug quickly brings the entire application down

M. La Rosa et al. (Eds.): CAiSE 2021, LNCS 12751, pp. 536–550, 2021.
https://doi.org/10.1007/978-3-030-79382-1_32

To overcome these disadvantages, banks replace their legacy systems with inherently resilient, scalable modular architectures following the modern design principles [27].

The success of the migration from the legacy system directly affects the competitiveness of a bank; therefore it requires careful planning and execution. This paper reports our observations on the legacy system migration of three large retail banks between 2014 and 2020.

In this comparative study, we examine the following research questions:

R1: What are the *key motivations* for banks to start their transforming from legacy systems towards next generation architectures?

R2: What is the *strategy* for application migration?

R3: How are the migrations of individual applications *prioritized*?

This paper is structured as follows. Section 2 provides background information on legacy architectures and migration to modern architectures in the banking industry. Section 3 explains the details on the migration of three retail banks. Section 4 discusses the similarities and differences in these cases. Section 5 presents the related work and Sect. 6 concludes the paper.

2   Background

This section provides background information on the legacy systems in the banking industry and an overview of the legacy migration.

The first core banking system appeared in the 1970s [15,16]. Legacy core banking systems became product–centric structures that have separations for each major product line and developed in silos within a decade. An example of such separation is a product specialization on payment processes for the banking ecosystem.

In 1990s the first internet banking applications appeared along with the evolution of the product–centric paradigm to the customer–centric paradigm with multi-channel integration and service-oriented architecture [10]. Grouping customers into segments led to shared functions across products that create synergies, cost efficiency, and increased sales opportunities.

Figure 1 depicts the legacy information technology (IT) architecture of a typical bank installed after 2000s. It is composed of an online application layer that provides self-servicing functions to its customers running on top of a core banking system that transacts and stores all banking transactions. The core system has a monolithic architecture. While all the online transactions run over the core, separate siloed and mostly batch-based business intelligence (BI) systems are evolved as a side system for serving the reporting and analytic requirements of the bank.

The legacy core banking systems have a monolithic architecture comprised of tightly-coupled components relying on shared resources such as a single code base, databases, and servers. While these systems provide a robust and secure

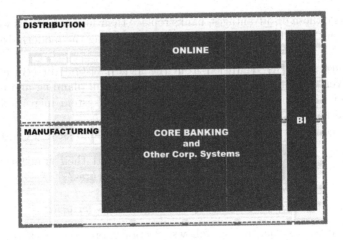

Fig. 1. A typical IT architecture of banks after 2000s

architecture for systems transactions, they hurt modularity, scalability, and flexibility [15]. To meet the increasing and changing needs of the market, monolithic core banking systems have been modified excessively and deviated from the intended architecture over time. Insufficient documentation, risk of a single point of failure, inconvenience of deployment, complexity, and difficulty of scalability have prevented banks from releasing new services and new features in a short time and triggered migration from the legacy systems. More information about the contemporary standards for banking services can be found by the various models by the Banking Industry Architecture Network [1].

3   Three Cases of Legacy System Migration

In this section, we first compare the demographics, motivations, and legacy architectures of each bank. We then discuss the target architecture, migration strategies, migration planning approaches, and prioritization criteria identified and followed by each bank and the reasons leading to these decisions.

Method. Our research has descriptive and exploratory characteristics, as explained by Runeson and Höst [22]. We first portray the situation for each case by collecting information about it. We used questionnaires and surveys for collecting the information. Chief information officers, enterprise architects, solution architects, and application domain leaders of the banks are the key stakeholders of our research. We tried to find out what has happened during these transformation programs, sought insights, and generated ideas and hypotheses for new research. Several one-to-one and group interviews have been conducted with key stakeholders to understand the situation; stakeholders' key decisions and their relationship during the transformation program have been observed and analyzed.

3.1   Description of the Cases

We refer banks in our case study as BankA, BankB, and BankC. Table 1 summarizes the number of ATMs, customers, and total assets of these three banks. Regarding the total assets, each bank is classified in the same category as they rank in the top four private banks in Turkey. In terms of the total customer volume, BankA and BankC are leading, where BankB only has half of their volume. However, the number of digital customers of all three banks, combining active customers that use the web and mobile channels, are comparable. BankA leads in terms of the number of ATMs and branches as they value face-to-face interaction with customers as their tradition.

Table 1. Comparison of cases in terms of the number of ATMS, branches, customers and total assets

	Bank A	Bank B	Bank C
ATMs	6600	4300	5200
Branches	1200	850	900
Customers	19 M	9.5 M	18. 5 M
Digital customers	8.9 M	7.2 M	9.3 M
Total Assets	430B₺	370B₺	385B₺

Legacy Technology Stack. All banks had monolithic architectures prior to their transformation. Table 2 summarizes the context of the banks before the transformation of their legacy technology architectures.

Table 2. Legacy technology stack of banks

Legacy Tech. Stack	BankA	BankB	BankC
Presentation layer	Java (Web& Mobile)	Java (Web& Mobile)	Java (Web& Mobile)
Integration layer	API, BPM, ESB	API	Mainframe, ESB
Backend layer	Custom application with Java/J2EE and .NET Mainframe (IMS) with COBOL	Custom application with Java/J2EE	Mainframe (CICS) with Coolgen and COBOL
Data layer	Mainframe DB2, Oracle	Oracle	Mainframe DB2

Before the migration, BankC was highly dependent on its monolithic mainframe core banking solution. Thanks to the highly modular and parametric mainframe architecture, BankC was still able to deliver business needs conveniently. With the rise of online banking, BankC has adopted service-oriented architecture

(SOA) and developed Java-based web and mobile applications. These custom-developed applications were integrated with the mainframe using an Enterprise Service Bus (ESB) [19]. However, online banking increased the number of transactions on the mainframe and amplified the need for shifting towards open systems due to high operational costs.

BankB had already built its technology architecture on open systems before its migration. Still, BankB's 3-tier open system legacy was architected as a large monolithic core that was modular but not parametric. Core banking modules had very few cross-product service components. The backend of the monolithic core was developed in Java/J2EE, served through four channel applications. Channel applications were also developed in Java, and integration among layers was through API Gateway, and data were stored in Oracle databases.

The legacy technology stack of BankA had the burden of long-term co-existence of both the mainframe architecture and the multi-tier architecture with open systems. Most of the back-end logic was on the mainframe; the multi-tier open system custom back-end applications were developed in Java/J2EE with web and mobile applications developed in Java. The data were stored in mainframe (DB2 database) and open systems (Oracle databases). As a result, the bank spent a significant effort in data synchronization. To utilize SOA, BankA built an Enterprise Service Bus, an API Gateway, and Business Process Management (BPM) [19] layers to address integration requirements. As its legacy was running in product silos, there were a vast number of redundant functionalities. There were very few shared cross-product services such as product engine, pricing engine, fees and commission module used by product silos. New products and services could be developed mostly by new design and development rather than configuration. Besides, the monolithic core was neither modular nor parametric.

Regarding the infrastructure layer, all banks ran their legacy systems on-premises. Due to the strict regulations that restrain banks from moving to the cloud, this typical trait was mainly an obligation.

Although the architectures of the banks were classified as monolithic, the size of their application and service inventory stocks varied. Whether the bank's reliance was on the mainframe or open systems, the technical components like the number of databases, the number of APIs, and the number of applications were different than each other. Table 3 lists the banks' application and interface inventory.

3.2 Key Motivations for Migration

In this section, we discuss R1: Which are the *key motivations* for banks to start their transforming from legacy systems towards next-generation architectures? Three banks have different motivations that lead them to initiate a transformation program.

BankA's pain points were limited multi-channel capabilities, low scalability, and low data quality for regulatory requirements. BankA would like to improve its multi-channel capabilities by introducing omni-channel capabilities to its channel architecture. Several points-to-point integration of product and

Table 3. Application and interface inventory of banks

	BankA	BankB	BankC
Channel applications	15	14	12
External APIs	17	50	70
Internal APIs	1648	125	350
Screens	1645	1250	8800
Domains (service groups)	19	29	200
Backend services	4114	3000	12500
Distinct core databases	305	3	9

architecture components, and redundancy in management of identical products in different silo applications made it difficult for BankA to make new products and features available for its customers through information systems. BankA would like to change its core applications to provide flexible product offering and bundling capabilities through the parametrization of key applications. BankA would like to move to an application and integration architecture that allows higher scalability and performance at a lower cost.

BankB's motivations were improving quality, reducing waste efforts and technical debt, and increasing collaboration, ownership, and scalability. BankB has been introducing hundreds of system or application changes into their information systems yearly. Complexities of making a change have been also increasing exponentially due to the loosely coupled structure of the applications, and configuration and release management processes. To introduce these changes at the required speed, the bank has been duplicating its efforts for designing components. The lack of test automation, large monolithic application packaging, and manual processing of release management processes have created wasted efforts. BankB has been looking for efficient service development and delivery process where they minimize the effort of redundant testing, release, deployment management, and overall quality of the codes being developed. Besides, rapid scalability is required in order to serve high number of digital customers that have higher fluctuating behaviour. Unless hosted on cloud, traditional legacy banking architectures—either in mainframe or open systems— are required to have hardware architectures that support these peak usage behaviour with redundancy which comes with a significant cost. BankB would like to make their applications cloud-enabled to reduce its cost.

BankC's primary concerns were high IT costs and high attrition rates of qualified employees. BankC was having challenges attracting and retaining talent due to the mainframe technology they have been using for many years. Young engineers and software developers were looking for work where they can practice new technologies. After practicing Cobol and understanding the basics of software architectures in the banking industry, these talents were looking for jobs in other banks or different industries to practice new architectures or software programming languages. BankC realized that to sustain their leadership position in banking technologies, they have to upgrade their technology stack to attract the best people and retain them longer. Increased number of customer visits to their bank accounts, execution of payments, and credit card transactions have increased the total number of transactions significantly. The cost of mainframes is typically measured by the amount of money paid per MIPS. As a result, BankC started to have higher costs than its peers for running its core banking applications. Therefore they have a strong business case in migrating their core banking from mainframe-based architecture to open systems. In a very dynamic business environment and highly volatile markets, BankC would like to have an architecture where they could introduce changes more frequently and without sacrificing their systems' quality and robustness.

To compete in the digital era, BankA was the first bank to initiate a transformation program. They have started their program in 2014 and completed by 2019 as a transformed organization that evolved into a customer–centric model. To reflect on technological advances and cost pressures, BankB and BankC aimed to build an IT infrastructure for the next decades and to compete with non-banks; therefore, they targeted to adapt to a digital ecosystem-centric model. BankB's transformation program is planned to be completed by 2023. BankC's plan is in a broader time range, with a target to complete the program by 2025.

Target Technology Architecture. Taking motivations as the driving force and target functional model as the lever, banks have adopted different target technology architectures based on their needs. BankA continues to utilize SOA by using ESB and BPM solutions. They adopted omni-channel architecture with business process-driven logic. BankA's infrastructure remains on-premises.

BankB and BankC adopted similar architectural principles with different solutions. They both follow micro-service architecture [25], where BankB has finer granularity. Their experience on the open platforms was the primary reason for the granularity of their application components. BankB has already running on open platforms and has the necessary tools and infrastructure to monitor and manage high number of independent micro-services components. BankC used to rely on the mainframe's resilient and robust management systems. They prefer to build coarse-grained components, manage them and decided to split them into smaller services at later stages of their transformation. Both banks adopted lightweight front-end architectures, API Gateway as the integration layer, CI/CD pipelines [23] for delivery automation, and container platforms to orchestrate their cloud-ready applications. BankB has built its private cloud infrastructure [7], but the infrastructure of BankC remains on-premises.

3.3   Migration Strategies

In this section, we explore the different strategies for migration to answer R2: What is the *strategy* for application migration?

Every migration journey needs to define a clear migration strategy for every application based on a holistic application analysis. The selected strategy fundamentally affects the expected migration effort, the potential benefits, and possible long term cost savings of the new operations model. Commonly used migration strategies of next-generation architectures are as follows [2,20]:

- *Retain*: Remediation of the application by addressing pain points. Implementing CD/CI capabilities and moving dev/test environments to off-host/cloud infrastructures where possible to reduce costs
- *Replace*: Identification of a managed service/application that can provide the required functionality
- *Re-Host*: Moving application as-is to a cheaper location utilizing the same hardware platform, making no change to the application code
- *Re-Platform*: Move an application without changing the programming language t another platform / Operating system.
- *Re-Factor*: Utilization of a language migration toolkit to transform from legacy to modern programming languages
- *Re-Imagine*: Rewrite the application using cloud-based architectures based on newly developed requirements, domain–driven designs.

After building the target technology architecture, all three banks have identified migration strategies to move their applications and services from legacy to newly built platforms. Re-architecting is the standard strategy for all of them; still, they approach differently while defining the strategy.

BankA already has SOA-based applications; therefore, its primary strategy was to retain the applications with small modifications and remediations. Re-architecting was the second strategy to follow, mainly used for mainframe offloading. As BankB's legacy architecture was on open systems, its primary strategy was to rehost the applications. BankB lifts and shifts the applications from legacy to a newly built cloud platform with minor enhancements. The main driver here is to rapidly migrate applications to the new architecture and to phase-out legacy systems for cost reduction. After re-hosting, BankB starts to re-architect the applications based on the new architectural principles and develops micro-services. BankC was heavily dependent on the mainframe, and application migration means re-architecting for them. Therefore, BankC primarily re-designs and re-implements its applications from scratch, involving business stakeholders in the transformation program. Applications with low criticality and minimal number of transactions are classified to retain. For commodity applications that provide non-differentiating functionality, replacing them with a commercial off-the-shelf product is another strategic decision for BankC.

All three banks have selected different migration planning approaches based on their working cultures and organizational structure. BankA aspired to plan the transformation in a structured way with a focused group leading the program; therefore, BankA followed the centralized approach. The time required to complete the evaluation process was relatively less for BankA compared to other banks, as they executed a series of workshops. Overall program plan and prioritization were prepared much earlier, decided by the architecture team in the initial planning phase. However, BankA struggled during the execution phase due to incorrectly captured domain-specific needs and misidentification of common components. As the prioritization was solely based on expert judgment and previous architecture team experience, the transformation program fell behind in terms of business value realization.

Principles of micro-services architecture and agile delivery led BankB to follow a domain–driven migration planning; thus, domain-specific requirements have been captured by involving domains in an early stage. The know-how is cascaded to the project teams smoothly. As architectural compliance responsibility is on the domain teams, the inconsistency of designed solutions against target technology architecture principles was a significant drawback that BankB has faced. Another pain point was the double effort spent developing common services as every domain developed such services under its responsibility with limited reusability.

BankC has followed a different path by combining two approaches. With a hybrid approach in place, BankC benefits from the advantages of domain-driven execution and centralized planning and control function. Firstly, BankC has defined company-wide common components to reduce replicated functionalities and avoid double effort. Moreover, a central governance body ensures the compliance of solutions to functional and technical design principles. The central body also provided the ability to define priorities and plan in line with transformation goals. Still, BankC could not meet every domain-specific need and spent additional effort to clarify details at the domain level due to limited responsiveness to product level requirements. Establishing a team and organizing workshop execution was a time-consuming activity that BankC had overcome with the central governing body.

3.4 Prioritization

In all our selected cases, banks' overall attitude was to define the prioritization criteria from a technical aspect, with a motivation to overcome the technical obstacles they are facing with the legacy architecture. Besides, the business and delivery objectives of banks also reflected while defining these prioritization criteria. Therefore, the principles of new technology architecture and target banking architecture were two key inputs. The prioritization assessment was commonly conducted as a survey by distributing a set of questions to the organization to understand every domain's needs. The outcome was a list of prioritized applications and a transformation program plan based on the questionnaire results. BankA conducted the prioritization activity by a central authority, mainly a team composed of enterprise and solution architects, at the beginning of the transformation program for each application. The enterprise acknowledged this prioritization assessment as the guideline to initiate the execution stage. However, in the cases of BankB and BankC, the prioritization assessment was executed by each domain per application. The central architecture team only provided a checklist, a content to conduct a survey, to support domains. The main difference between BankB and BankC was on the central governing body, which oversees technical dependencies and schedules the execution plan, did not exist in the former, but it was present in the latter.

During the execution phase of the transformation program, BankA performed the solution development activity during the initial planning for each domain and application. BankB, instead, performed this activity in significantly later stages, mostly during the technical design of the relevant project for the domain and application. The main difference of BankC was centrally governing the domain solution architecture concerning architectural standards and common services, where the domains are the only responsible for the blueprint of the domain–driven migration approach.

3.5   Threats to Validity

The first author actively participated in three of these migration cases, serving as a consultant to the banks. The involvement of the first author in these cases increases the construct validity. To mitigate the impact of this, multiple surveys and interviews with people from various positions are conducted and the data are analyzed with the second author who is not involved in these cases.

The migrations happened in the headquarters of the banks that might raise questions regarding the generality of the results. We emphasize that our cases are specific to the banking industry, so we cannot generalize our findings to other domains. Although there are no extreme differences in the architectures of banks internationally, this external validity remains and more case studies are needed to reach conclusive results.

4   Discussion and Key Takeaways

Industrial Trends. Our interviews with the chief technology officers of the banks reveal that their decisions are affected by the software architecture trends. For the cases of BankB and BankC, the chief technology officers agree that SOA architecture pattern provides a straightforward solution to their problems, yet they opt for the micro-service architecture for it is the trending architecture pattern during their transformation period.

Pattern Selection. The most urging issues of the current operation influence the design pattern chosen for the target architecture. For example, the redundancy requirement of BankA over the application architecture force the bank to simplify the application architecture, eliminate redundant interfaces and components, and increase reusability in the cross-product components. As a result, the bank preferred to apply the SOA pattern over a well-defined functional banking architecture. BankB had problems with high amount of redundant efforts for development, issues during the release of new the versions and difficulties in configuring the management processes. To solve these problems, the bank adopted domain–driven design patterns, the microservice architecture, and the agile development method. BankC suffered from increasing processing costs due to rapidly increasing online transactions from their high number of digital customers, which forced them to move out from the mainframe they were peacefully living in the last 20 years.

Functional Application Models. Historically, the functional application models for banks evolve from product–centric to segment–centric and manufacturing-centric to customer–centric and, recently, to ecosystem-centric functional models. The existing legacy architecture and business requirements of the banks define their target functional application model. BankA has been operating under a manufacturing-centric functional model and strived to apply a more customer–centric banking model. BankB and BankC claimed that they have already been using customer–centric models and aimed for migrating to ecosystem-centric functional models to serve their customers through their ecosystem partners. Therefore, these two banks implemented strong API layers in their integration architectures with lightweight application architectures at the front-end layer.

Multiple Migration Strategies. In all cases multiple migration strategies are followed based on the previous transformation experiences, the existing legacy architectures,the target architectures, and the budget constraints of the banks. BankA, which run on an existing hybrid architecture (mainframe and open system architecture), did not consider a new core banking implementation from scratch due to their past experiences on failed migration to a package core banking software and transformation costs. BankA preferred retaining existing applications by re-engineering them (retain strategy), developing cross-product components that eliminate redundant applications (re-architect strategy), and gradually migrating to a business process based operating model. BankB, which has previously migrated fully from the mainframe environment, preferred to re-platform existing monolithic applications to a different architecture (re-host strategy). BankB also designed and implemented their primary application domains in microservices architecture pattern (re-architect strategy) relying on the domain–driven design and cloud-ready technology stack. On the other hand, BankC which has not conducted a major core banking transformation program in the last decades chose to retain some of the applications, to replace some others and to re-architect their core banking system as a whole through a more extended transformation program.

Governance Organizations and Design Patterns. The culture and availability of strong governance structures such as architecture boards, solution architecture teams, and target architecture patterns play an essential role in how migration planning is conducted. BankA, which has a strong architecture governance organization and a top-down management style, conducted their migration planning exercises relying on central teams. domain–driven design pattern and microservices architecture as target design pattern let the teams conduct planning exercises through domains that maintain an application under a functional domain.

Prioritization. Regardless of the planning approach selected, all banks develop a prioritized list of projects in which they plan to migrate legacy application components to the target architecture. BankA conducted a bottom-up analysis for each project. It identified high-level application inventories to be updated and estimated the effort required. BankB chose to apply a survey and asked the domain architect to evaluate and score the applications they will re-architect under their domain and develop a comprehensive list and application migration prioritization. BankC developed a scoring model based on weights of prioritization criteria and the nature of the applications or domains to be migrated. All these prioritization lists helped them to develop a roadmap that shows them two or three years horizon with more detailed plans for the coming quarters or years. It is essential to prioritize so that program governance over scope, schedule, and budget is managed. On the other than considering the very complex nature of banking application architecture and duration of these programs and continuously changing environment, it was never possible to stick to these plans. The solution seems to develop a more agile program management approach where these prioritize frequently change while still demonstrating that the program delivers the highest possible value. We believe that value-driven program management [4, 18] practice would provide the most optimized prioritization.

Robust Project Management. All three studies confirmed that a robust migration project management is required to ensure the continuity, progress, and quality of the transformation. A robust project management ensures the alignment of business and IT functions. Project management is also crucial for quality assurance throughout the transformation, by providing standard processes, actions to drive consistent reporting of status, risks, issues, and resources. A robust project management enables planning and monitoring the project by centralizing the project level plan, budget, dependencies, and backlog.

Continuous Alignment. As the banks progress through the transformation program and migrate the applications to the new platform, migration evaluation and prioritization criteria are subject to change. Continuous alignment of these criteria with program objectives is essential to succeed in the application migration.

5 Related Work

In this section we overview related work focusing on case study research in software engineering and migration to cloud, microservices, and SOA.

Runeson and Höst provide guidelines for conducting case study research in software engineering [22]. Verner et al. present a framework with finer granularity for industrial case studies [26]. In this work we follow the steps stated by [22] and consult the framework presented in [26] when needed.

Gholami et al. [13] identify the main challenges regarding migrating legacy software to cloud through an online survey conducted with experts from various domains. These challenges include analysing the organisational context, understanding legacy systems, distribution of legacy systems to servers and isolating tenants, among other cloud specific challenges. Jamshidi et al. [17] details a pattern–based approach for multi-cloud architecture migration. In our case studies, the main migration problem is the one from the monolithic legacy system to modular architecture. Migration to cloud is a part of the problem, but not the main focus. Balalaie et al. [5] report on the migration to a cloud-native microservices architecture of a single company. Our work confirms the need for distributed data governance, reusability, and scalability as the drivers for the migration. Bucchiarone et al. presents the changes in the architecture from a monolith microservice architecture in the banking domain [6]. The focus of discussion in [6] is on the changes in the architecture. Dragoni et al. analyse the same case from a mission critical perspective [9]. Fan and Ma comment that two drawback of the migration to microservices are complex structure and increased resource use in their experience report on the migration of a web and mobile application to microservices [11].

Di Francesco et al. survey 17 participants from the industry for their experiences on migration to microservices [8] focusing on the challenges in execution of the migration. Another survey is conducted by Taibi et al. [24] where the participants answer questions on the migration process, cost, and data overhead. We focus on the motivation, strategy, and planning for the migration from legacy systems and our domain is limited to the banking industry.

Gouigoux and Tamzalit share experiences of a single migration from monolith to service–oriented architecture [14]. Main benefits from this transformation are listed as reusability, changability, and efficiency.

Agievich and Skripkin propose using a change matrix to manage enterprise architectures migration [3]. Similar tools are used in all our cases to manage the migration. Furda et al. investigate multitenancy, statefulness, and data consistency for the migration of enterprise architectures [12].

6   Conclusions

This paper presents a multi-case study of legacy system migration from the banking domain. Three cases have a comparable number of digital customers but differ in terms of total number of total customers, and application and interface inventories. Throughout the migration projects, we interviewed the members of projects with different ranks and roles in the projects. We conduct an in-depth analysis of the motivations for the migration, migration strategies, and prioritization for the migration. We discuss the key takeaways and lessons learned for such high-scale migration projects.

We observed similarities in motivations of the banks for the migration even though they had different legacy banking architectures such as reducing costs and improving quality although each bank had its specific triggers for the migration. The most urging issues heavily influenced the target architectures of the bank. The decision makers of the migration projects also admitted that architectural trends were another strong influence for that decision.

All banks applied multiple migration strategies based on their transformation experiences, existing legacy architectures, target architectures driven by technology trends, and cost pressures. Culture and availability of strong governance structures such as architecture boards, solution architecture teams, and target architecture patterns play an essential role in how migration planning is conducted. We observed that as the banks progress through the transformation program and migrate the applications to the new platform, migration evaluation and application prioritization criteria are subject to change.

Finally, continuous alignment of these criteria with program objectives is essential to succeed in the application migration. As applications are migrated, banks evolve to new technology architectures and retire their legacy systems. On top of the technological evolution, our cases aimed to adopt new methodologies like DevOps and agile to maximize the benefits from their new architectures. These changes also drive our cases to shift towards modern IT operating models.

Acknowledgments. The second author has been partially supported by the Scientific and Technological Research Council of Turkey through BIDEB 2232 grant 118C255, Requirements Engineering for Digital Transformation.

References

1. Banking industry architecture network. http://bian.org
2. Migrating applications to the cloud: Rehost, refactor, revise, rebuild, or replace? https://www.gartner.com/en/documents/1485116/migrating-applications-to-the-cloud-rehost-refactor-revi
3. Agievich, V., Skripkin, K.: Enterprise architecture migration planning using the matrix of change. In: ITQM, pp. 231–235. Elsevier (2014)
4. Aitken, I.: Value-driven IT management. Routledge, Milton (2012)
5. Balalaie, A., Heydarnoori, A., Jamshidi, P.: Microservices architecture enables DevOps: migration to a cloud-native architecture. IEEE Softw. **33**(3), 42–52 (2016)
6. Bucchiarone, A., Dragoni, N., Dustdar, S., Larsen, S.T., Mazzara, M.: From monolithic to microservices: an experience report from the banking domain. IEEE Softw. **35**(3), 50–55 (2018)
7. Chilipirea, C., Laurentiu, G., Popescu, M., Radoveneanu, S., Cernov, V., Dobre, C.: A comparison of private cloud systems. In: 2016 30th International Conference on Advanced Information Networking and Applications Workshops (WAINA), pp. 139–143. IEEE (2016)
8. Di Francesco, P., Lago, P., Malavolta, I.: Migrating towards microservice architectures: an industrial survey. In: 2018 IEEE International Conference on Software Architecture (ICSA), pp. 29–2909. IEEE (2018)
9. Dragoni, N., Dustdar, S., Larsen, S.T., Mazzara, M.: Microservices: Migration of a mission critical system. arXiv preprint arXiv:1704.04173 (2017)
10. Erl, T.: Service-Oriented Architecture: Concepts, Technology, and Design. Pearson Education India, Bengaluru (1900)
11. Fan, C.Y., Ma, S.P.: Migrating monolithic mobile application to microservice architecture: an experiment report. In: 2017 IEEE International Conference on AI & Mobile Services (AIMS), pp. 109–112. IEEE (2017)
12. Furda, A., Fidge, C., Zimmermann, O., Kelly, W., Barros, A.: Migrating enterprise legacy source code to microservices: on multitenancy, statefulness, and data consistency. IEEE Softw. **35**(3), 63–72 (2017)
13. Gholami, M.F., Daneshgar, F., Beydoun, G., Rabhi, F.: Challenges in migrating legacy software systems to the cloud – an empirical study. Inf. Syst. **67**, 100–113 (2017). https://doi.org/10.1016/j.is.2017.03.008, https://www.sciencedirect.com/science/article/pii/S0306437917301564

14. Gouigoux, J.P., Tamzalit, D.: From monolith to microservices: lessons learned on an industrial migration to a web oriented architecture. In: 2017 IEEE International Conference on Software Architecture Workshops (ICSAW), pp. 62–65. IEEE (2017)
15. Hariharan, N., Reeshma, K.: Challenges of core banking systems. Mediterr. J. Soci. Sci. **6**(5), 24 (2015)
16. Hu, S.J.: Method and system for integrating core banking business processes, 24 Jan 2006, uS Patent 6,990,466
17. Jamshidi, P., Pahl, C., Mendonça, N.C.: Pattern-based multi-cloud architecture migration. Softw. Pract. Experience **47**(9), 1159–1184 (2017)
18. Kerzner, H., Saladis, F.P., et al.: Value-Driven Project Management, vol. 1. John Wiley & Sons, Hoboken (2011)
19. Liu, Y., Hu, E., Chen, X.: Architecture of information system combining SOA and BPM. In: 2008 International Conference on Information Management, Innovation Management and Industrial Engineering, vol. 1, pp. 42–45. IEEE (2008)
20. Orban, S.: 6 strategies for migrating to the cloud. https://aws.amazon.com/blogs/enterprise-strategy/6-strategies-for-migrating-applications-to-the-cloud/ (2016)
21. Pérez-Castillo, R., Mas, B., Pizka, M.: Understanding legacy architecture patterns. In: 2015 International Conference on Evaluation of Novel Approaches to Software Engineering (ENASE), pp. 282–288. IEEE (2015)
22. Runeson, P., Höst, M.: Guidelines for conducting and reporting case study research in software engineering. Empir. Softw. Eng. **14**(2), 131 (2009)
23. Steffens, A., Lichter, H., Döring, J.S.: Designing a next-generation continuous software delivery system: concepts and architecture. In: 2018 IEEE/ACM 4th International Workshop on Rapid Continuous Software Engineering (RCoSE), pp. 1–7. IEEE (2018)
24. Taibi, D., Lenarduzzi, V., Pahl, C.: Processes, motivations, and issues for migrating to microservices architectures: an empirical investigation. IEEE Cloud Comput. **4**(5), 22–32 (2017)
25. Thönes, J.: Microservices. IEEE Softw. **32**(1), 116 (2015)
26. Verner, J.M., Sampson, J., Tosic, V., Bakar, N.A., Kitchenham, B.A.: Guidelines for industrially-based multiple case studies in software engineering. In: 2009 Third International Conference on Research Challenges in Information Science, pp. 313–324. IEEE (2009)
27. Zimmermann, A., Schmidt, R., Sandkuhl, K., Jugel, D., Bogner, J., Möhring, M.: Evolution of enterprise architecture for digital transformation. In: 2018 IEEE 22nd International Enterprise Distributed Object Computing Workshop (EDOCW), pp. 87–96. IEEE (2018)

A Reference Architecture for IoT-Enabled Dynamic Planning in Smart Logistics

Martijn Koot$^{(\boxtimes)}$ ⓘ, Maria-Eugenia Iacob ⓘ, and Martijn R. K. Mes ⓘ

Department of Industrial Engineering and Business Information Systems (IEBIS),
University of Twente, Enschede, The Netherlands
{m.koot,m.e.iacob,m.r.k.mes}@utwente.nl
https://www.utwente.nl/en/bms/iebis/

Abstract. Increasing customer demands and variability in today's logistics networks force fleet operators to become more reliable and flexible in their operations. As modern-day fleets are well equipped with wireless sensing, processing, and communication devices, fleet operators could proactively respond to dynamic events. However, the use of real-time sensor data to achieve re-optimization is scarce. This observation raises the question of how logistics operators should incorporate the emerging track-and-trace services into their dynamic planning activities. In this paper, we propose a reference architecture that relies on both the Internet of Things and the Smart Logistics paradigms, and aims at enhancing the resilience of logistics networks. Since the decision of when to reschedule the network's configurations remains nontrivial, we propose a hierarchical set of disruption handling systems to facilitate the trade-off between decision quality and response time. In our design, autonomous logistics agents can quickly anticipate on minor changes in their surroundings, while more severe disruptions require both more data and computational power in higher-level processing nodes (e.g., fog/cloud computing, machine learning, optimization algorithms). We illustrate the need of our architecture in the context of the dynamic vehicle routing problem.

Keywords: Internet of Things · IoT · Smart logistics · Enterprise architecture · Disruption handling

1 Introduction

In modern-day supply chains, it is getting more challenging to deliver all goods in the most efficient and reliable way possible. Customer requirements become more variable over time due to the increasing volumes of e-commerce [1], which enables customers to instantaneously demand for more transparency, affordability, and speed in their deliveries [2]. Logistics operators try to gain competitive advantage by including those preferences into their network designs, resulting into an increased individualization of product flows and more direct-to-customer deliveries [3]. The trend towards logistics customization should be performed in

© Springer Nature Switzerland AG 2021
M. La Rosa et al. (Eds.): CAiSE 2021, LNCS 12751, pp. 551–565, 2021.
https://doi.org/10.1007/978-3-030-79382-1_33

an environment characterized by more complex constraints (e.g., just-in-time deliveries, congestion, safety regulations, environmental footprint, etc.). Luckily, logistics planners can rely on multiple decision support tools to create an initial schedule that fulfills both customer requirements and environmental constraints, but it seems almost impossible to fully maintain reliable outcomes during execution due to the dynamic and stochastic nature of real-world logistics networks [4]. Therefore, successful supply chains are characterized by reliable and flexible operations [3,5], which indicates the need for a more active approach towards dynamic events once observed or predicted [6].

Recent IT advancements have enabled logistics companies to manage their fleet in (near) real-time [3,5]. Most vehicles are constantly transmitting a wide variety of data regarding the transportation system's state towards a central planning authority [7]. For example, a modern-day fleet is well-equipped with Geographic Information Systems (GIS), Global Positioning Systems (GPS), Electronic Data Interchanges (EDI), auto-identification technologies and mobile devices [2]. Logistics operators use these sensing devices to monitor their fleet remotely [8], but more advanced data processing is required to learn from the perceived disruptions and re-optimize the supply chain's resource allocations accordingly. The rise of the Internet of Things (IoT) may bridge this gap by empowering physical objects with sensory, communication, and information processing technologies, resulting into an interconnected network of context-aware devices [7,9]. Therefore, the IoT paradigm stimulates logistics operations to progress from remote monitoring towards ambient intelligence and autonomous control [10], a key feature which is also envisioned by the Smart Logistics paradigm [11].

Both logistics researchers and business practitioners are highly interested into IoT and Smart Logistics developments to build a more resilient logistics system. Therefore, a rising number of conceptual models is found in today's scientific literature that define all technological building blocks to anticipate on logistics disturbances (e.g., [12–14]). Other authors focus more on the integration of IoT devices, communication networks, and software required for the detection and/or prediction of dynamic events [9,10,15]. The increasing variety of modelling approaches used in Smart Logistics indicates the need for a uniform IoT-based architecture that explains how real-time data should be processed to proactively respond towards dynamic events. We only found one publication proposing an Enterprise Architecture (EA) for situation-aware Smart Logistics, where the IoT infrastructure facilitates the perception and handling of logistics exceptions [16]. To our knowledge, no other architecture is proposed to align IoT devices, learning mechanisms, and logistics processes together. This is why the main contribution of this paper is the design of a reference architecture that links all necessary components in between the perception layer and final decision making, as reflected by the question we address in the remainder of this study.

> **Research question:** How to design an enterprise system that uses IoT technology for enhancing the resilience of logistics processes in (near) real-time on the basis of dynamic events data?

We will answer the research question by following the design science methodology for information system research [17]. The remainder of this paper is structured as follows. Section 2 includes a literature review. The system's requirements are introduced in Sect. 3, while the IoT-based architecture is proposed in Sect. 4. In Sect. 5, we will elaborate on how the proposed architecture can be improved, while the conclusions and further research directions are given in Sect. 6.

2   Literature Review

The *smartness* in the term "Smart Logistics" refers to the intelligent management of logistics operations by the use of the latest technological advancements [13]. Most logistics operators try to obtain intelligence by the development of a solid IT infrastructure, including recent data-driven processing techniques like the Internet of Things (IoT), Cyber-Physical Systems (CPS), Big Data Analytics (BDA), cloud computing, and Artificial Intelligence (AI) [14]. Real-time access towards the system's conditions enables decision makers to efficiently reallocate resources in case a dynamic event is observed. A more proactive and resilient approach is possible when the real-time data is analyzed to predict disturbances in advance already [18]. Therefore, the main aim of these technological implementations is to obtain a more flexible and scalable system in which the decision making of logistics entities is decentralized [13], a vision that is strongly associated with the Industry 4.0 concept developments of the past decade [11]. The implementation of the six design principles originating from Industry 4. 0 could be helpful to obtain a logistics network that is more intelligent than traditional systems [19]:

1. **Real-time capability:** the ability to collect and analyze data and immediately provide the derived insights.
2. **Interoperability:** the ability of logistics objects to connect and communicate with each other.
3. **Virtualization:** the ability to create a digital/virtual copy of the physical world by linking sensor data with virtual models and simulation techniques.
4. **Decentralization:** the ability of logistics objects to make decisions on their own and to perform their tasks as autonomous as possible, including exceptions, interferences, and/or conflicting goals' handling.
5. **Modularity:** the flexible adoption of logistics networks to the changing requirements by replacing or expanding individual modules.
6. **Service orientation:** the ability to offer the services with other logistics objects or decision entities.

IoT technologies are essential building blocks for many applications related to Industry 4.0 [14]. The IoT network forms a global infrastructure of interconnected physical objects empowered with electronic devices that rely on sensors, communication, and information processing technologies [9]. The dynamic behavior of IoT networks would require a flexible layered architecture, allowing all electronic components to deliver their services [20]. Multiple alternative IoT architectures have been developed over the years [20], but a Service-Oriented Architecture (SOA) is most commonly applied to decompose the IoT network into smaller, re-usable, and well-defined components [8,10]. The number of layers may differ for each application, but all IoT architectures are composed of a perception layer (e.g., identification and sensing devices installed on physical objects), a network layer (e.g., middleware technologies that allow the sensing objects to connect, coordinate, and share information), and an application layer in which the system's functionalities are exposed to the end-users.

The layered configuration of IoT architectures explains how logistics objects can extend their real-time monitoring functionalities with more intelligent and autonomous decision making [10], aiming for a more resilient logistics system [11]. Many IoT-based reference architectures highlight the need to integrate more IoT devices, cloud-based computing, and data-driven processing techniques for better decision making (e.g., [12–14]), while other researchers focus more on the detection and/or prediction of dynamic events [9,10,15]. However, the majority of IoT architectures do not explain how the real-time data should be processed to pro-actively respond towards dynamic events. The reference models proposed by [12] and [16] also highlight the need for new disruption handling systems, but the decision logic encapsulated in those applications remains unknown. Therefore, we need a comprehensive model to better align dynamic planning with the supporting IT infrastructures in logistics domains, allowing decision makers to gain more insights into the added value of their own IoT implementations. We argue that an EA approach enables us to improve the business-IT alignment for logistics execution [21]. We will use the enterprise modelling language "*Archi-Mate*" for the development of an online disruption handling system, inspired by [5], where solutions are computed as soon as a dynamic event occurs during the operational process. All our EA models are based on the ArchiMate 3.1 Specification (https://pubs.opengroup.org/architecture/archimate3-doc/).

3   Requirement Analysis

Today's supply chains are more vulnerable towards both internal and external disruptions due to globalization, lean operations, and customization trends [6]. The presence of dynamic events will cause deviations from the planned operations, which in turn may dissatisfy customers when the Service Level Agreements (SLAs) are not met [16]. A more proactive approach towards dynamic events enables logistics operators to reduce operational risks by re-configuring their resource allocations. However, re-optimization is scarcely done in the logistics domain [12], and if rescheduling happens, than purely reactive by relying on human intuition only. Therefore, the main driver behind this research is to design a logistics disruption handling system with flexible and automated operations to satisfy customer requirements in the most reliable way [3,5].

The next step is to derive the system's stakeholders and their requirements. We base our assessment on the stakeholder analysis made by [12] and [16], both researches derived the requirements from interviews with company representatives of the associated case studies. We limit our design to the most important stakeholders involved in logistics operations only:

1. **Customers:** persons, departments, or organizations who can either send or receive goods. In case a dynamic event disrupts the logistics operations, customers still demand reliable outcomes:
   (a) On-time pick-up and/or delivery of goods according to the SLA;
   (b) Immediate incident notification (including order tracking);
   (c) The ability to alter the decision and/or SLAs in case conflicts among stakeholders emerge.
2. **Logistics operators:** entities who coordinate the physical flow of goods (e.g., order picking, transportation, storage, etc.). Logistics operators are responsible to handle disruptions effectively by re-configuring the network's configurations in a flexible matter:
   (a) Increase responsiveness to disruptions;
   (b) Reduce operational risks;
   (c) Guarantee SLAs to customers.

Our vision is to design a resilient system similar to [6] that incorporates event readiness, autonomous re-optimization procedures, and recovering capabilities. In this system, logistics objects should perform their tasks autonomously under "standard" operational conditions, while decisions are delegated to a central planning authority in case of a severe incident, interference, or conflicting goal is observed [22]. The ability to interchange local and global optimization procedures for different severity levels requires a solid IT foundation, consisting of remote sensing capabilities, wireless communication networks, and distributed processing nodes. Even better performances are expected when the system is able to predict the occurrences of dynamic events by re-examining the decisions previously made, resulting into a positive feedback loop. We will use the six design principles originating from the Industry 4.0 paradigm to define the general properties of our logistics disruption handling system [19].

The *"motivation strategy view"* in Fig. 1 visualizes how the stakeholders, requirements, system outcomes, design principles, and course of actions are interrelated with each other. The implementation of our vision requires three main courses of action:

1. **Logistics IoT architecture:** event readiness is achieved by empowering physical resources with context-aware measuring systems. A regular IoT device extends its sensing function with communication, data (pre-) processing, and remote management capabilities due to the integration of sensors, actuators, micro-controllers, storage devices, data interfaces, and power sources into one device [8,20]. The installation of those IoT devices allows logistics objects to sense and control the physical world [9], while the use of locations receivers and identification tags stimulates accurate monitoring of the objects' business operations in real-time [8,23]. The use of wireless communication networks would improve the system's interoperability (e.g., RFID,

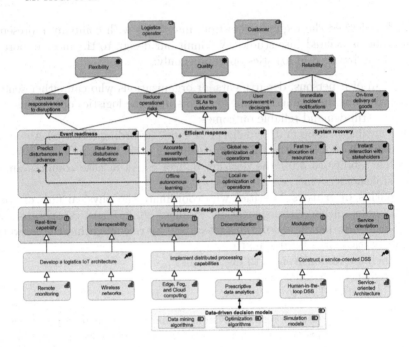

Fig. 1. Motivation strategy view.

NFC, W-LAN, LP-WAN, etc.), because logistics objects are characterized by their dynamic behaviour.

2. **Distributed processing capabilities:** a distributed network of processing nodes has to be equipped with prescriptive data analytical tools to autonomously re-optimize the objects' individual interests. The logistics objects already include some intelligence to handle minor disturbances due to the IoT devices installed, but re-optimization of a large logistics network demands both data and computational time. Therefore, cloud computing is used to create a centralized and powerful pool of computing resources to be shared and accessed when severe incidents emerge [23]. Both data-intensive techniques and centralized data warehouses can run on the core's servers to virtualize logistics networks and accurately assess the severity of incidents without intervening into the actual operations. We make use of IoT gateways to speed up the data interchange and local decision making [20,24]. Therefore, the IoT gateway's purpose is twofold: 1) facilitating the communication of heterogeneous IoT devices over the internet, and; 2) leveraging its network knowledge by executing optimization algorithms for a minor part of the logistics network [9].

3. **Service-oriented Decision support system (DSS):** The IoT's hardware layer will bridge the gap between the physical and virtual world by installing a modular design of interoperable measuring devices [10]. A service-oriented Architecture is required to ensure a fast-reallocation of the heterogeneous

logistics objects once a potential disturbance has emerged [9]. The main aim of our system design is to automate the dynamic planning activities, but dynamic events may also change the stakeholders' preferences during the actual execution of the initial plan. Therefore, our system should include a symbiotic relationship where intelligent agents focus on task execution, while human stakeholders can modify objectives, constraints and decision parameters [25].

4   System Design

In this section, we gradually develop an IoT-based architecture to better coordinate dynamic events in logistics networks. First, we develop a baseline EA that represents how logistics operators embrace IoT techniques nowadays. The baseline EA in Sect. 4.1 is founded on three major sources:

1. a systematic literature review of state-of-the-art IoT developments in today's supply chain and logistics research [26];
2. the business logic modeled by [12] and [16], and;
3. multiple informal interviews with Dutch logistics stakeholders regarding the IT support for their decision making. The results from these interviews coincide with those reported in [27, 28].

Second, we will design our target EA by referring to the *"motivation strategy view"* given earlier in Fig. 1. We explicitly motivate how our reference architecture meets the system requirements in Sect. 3 by *highlighting* the corresponding Industry 4.0 design principles in italic. Finally, we will conduct a gap analysis by evaluating the discrepancies in between the baseline and target EAs in Sect. 4.3, and demonstrate the need for our system design by referring to the Dynamic Vehicle Routing Problem (DVRP) in Sect. 4.4.

4.1   Baseline Architecture

Logistics operators commonly empower their fleet with flexible track-and-trace devices for some decades already to monitor the dynamic behaviour of their logistics networks [8, 9, 23]. Therefore, modern-day fleets are characterized by a sophisticated IT infrastructure that continuously gathers enormous amounts of real-time data regarding the system's state, while wireless communication technologies rapidly transmit those heterogeneous data streams towards a central fleet operator [2, 7, 29]. Human fleet operators can monitor, control, and plan their logistics activities by using the fleet management system's graphical user interface [30], a central application that is fed with data from the vehicles' on-board systems, the organization's legacy systems, and other external applications (e.g., traffic, weather, and news institutions). Cloud computing has become the standard for data processing, mainly due to the internet-based computing platform where configurable resources can be shared and accessed on demand

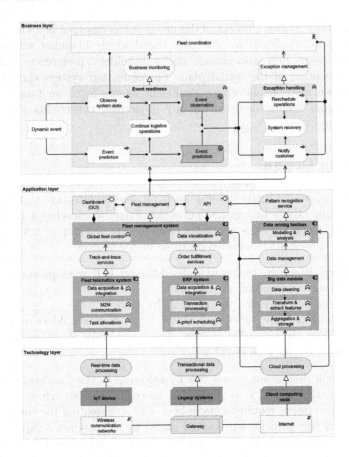

Fig. 2. Baseline EA - layered view

[23]. The predictive power of pattern searching algorithms (e.g., big data analytics, data mining, machine learning, etc.) enables logistics operators to adopt a proactive approach in response to potential disturbances in advance as well [18]. We have summarized the baseline EA in Fig. 2, which indicates that two out of six Industry 4.0 design principles (*real-time capability*, and *interoparability*) are commonly implemented already, mainly to incorporate event readiness into today's logistics networks.

4.2　Target Architecture

As stated earlier in Sect. 3, our vision is to design a resilient system where logistics objects should perform their tasks autonomously under "standard" operational conditions, while decisions are delegated to a central planning authority in case of a severe incident, interference, or conflicting goal is observed [22]. Both the *remote sensing capabilities*, and the *interoperability* offered by IoT devices,

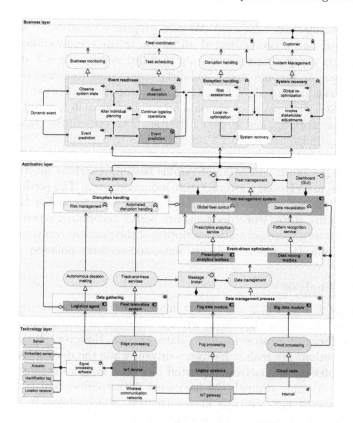

Fig. 3. Target EA - layered view

enables self-operating agents to anticipate on dynamic events in a *decentralized* way. However, more severe incidents require heavier support in terms of data management and computational resources. Therefore, we use self-organizing agents to ensure a *modular*, and *service-oriented* design of the logistics network, while the collaboration with a central fleet management system mitigates the trade-off between decision quality and response time (as visualized in our target EA in Fig. 3). The disruption handling collaboration will automatically *virtualize* the logistics network, and initiate a risk assessment once a dynamic event emerges. The risk management module will decide which logistics activities need to be rescheduled to maintain reliable outcomes, without the intervention of any human operator. Only highly severe incidents require additional input from the fleet coordinator and/or customer, since the stakeholders' preferences may change due to the incident's impact.

The success of our dynamic disruption handling collaboration in Fig. 3 strongly depends on the availability of accurate data sources and fast computational resources. Therefore, we advocate to diversify the logistics objects with a variety of sensors and/or actuator systems (e.g., embedded sensors, location receivers, identification tags, etc.). We also propose a cloud-based architecture for an efficient and process-oriented utilization of the computational resources [31], while fog computing resources are installed nearby the IoT devices in a distributed way to provide "quick-and-dirty" computing responses on sites [24]. The cooperation among edge-, fog-, and cloud computational resources supports both the prescriptive analytics and data mining toolboxes in terms of data (pre-) processing, networking, and storage activities. The prescriptive analytics toolbox will re-optimize the network's configurations by virtualizing the stakeholders' objectives, environmental conditions, and system constraints. We also need a data mining toolbox consisting of various pattern searching algorithms (e.g., classification, association, clustering, rule induction, etc.). The predictive power of classification and regression techniques can be used to predict the system's state at a future state, while decisions are better customized when continuous learning gives us a more accurate description of the problem context (e.g., input parameters, objective functions, constraints, and recovery policies).

4.3   Gap Analysis

The baseline EA in Fig. 2 shows that most logistics operators use their IoT architecture to monitor their fleet, while a cloud-based configuration is implemented to efficiently process incoming data streams. However, all those technological innovations are mainly hardware-driven, while the development of more intelligent software is relatively neglected [2]. Most logistics organizations lack the capacity to mine through the increasing data volumes and transform the observed patterns into valuable knowledge [18], which obstructs fleet operators to efficiently respond towards dynamic events. As a result, data-driven re-optimization is scarcely done in the logistics domain [12]. The central role of the fleet management system enforces fleet coordinators to manually reschedule logistics once disturbances emerge. This means that large volumes of IoT data are still being processed and acted upon by human operators with little decision support [2], a time-consuming operation which reduces the system's responsiveness towards dynamic events. Therefore, techniques for data acquisition, pattern recognition and mathematical optimization have to be merged into the application layer to adequately anticipate on dynamic events as soon as they emerge.

The main aim of our target EA in Fig. 3 is to automate the dynamic planning activities in case a disruption is either observed or predicted. Logistics objects have to quickly reschedule their tasks to become more responsive towards dynamic events, but a (near) optimal reconfiguration of the logistics network requires both data and computational time. Consequently, the dynamic reallocation of resources depends on the disruption's severity, area of impact, and the available planning horizon. We propose an hierarchical disruption handling architecture to compromise the trade-off among the decision's quality and response time, consisting of five main applications (as visualized in Fig. 4):

1. **Logistics agent:** the logistics agent represents the virtual twin of the logistics object on which the corresponding IoT device is installed. The agent's

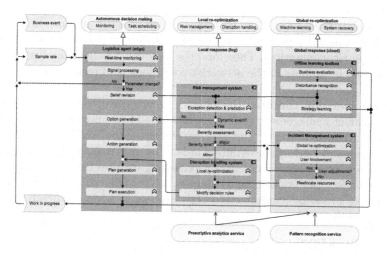

Fig. 4. Application behaviour view - a hierarchical disruption handling architecture

main responsibility is to monitor the object's status and environmental conditions in real-time, while the perceived knowledge can be shared with nearby agents to speed up data acquisition. Logistics agents autonomously act on the gathered data by a fixed set of decision rules stored on the IoT devices' local memory (=edge computing). The agents' behaviour is designed according to the individual Belief-Desire-Intention (BDI) architecture proposed by [32].

2. **Risk management system:** logistics agents can quickly anticipate on minor changes in their surroundings already, but an effective response towards severe disruptions require both more data and computational power in higher-level processing nodes (=fog computing). First, the risk management system aggregates the real-time data gathered by a cluster of IoT devices to detect any harmful exceptions in the network's conditions. Second, the risk management system assigns a severity level to the dynamic events observed, which is used to allocate the recovery tasks more effectively.

3. **Disruption handling system:** less severe incidents (e.g., little impact, minor impact radius, and/or quick resolution) are easily solved by relying on "quick-and-dirty" solution mechanisms. Therefore, the disruption handling system is equipped with optimization heuristics that require limited data and computational time. The disruption handling will anticipate on the network's configurations assessed by the risk management system, and re-optimize the network locally by updating the decisions' rules of all IoT devices affected.

4. **Incident management system:** serious and prolonged events require a more radical re-optimization approach. Therefore, we accept a longer response time to centralize all the network's real-time data gathered (=cloud computing). The incident management system has access to simulation and optimization techniques to automatically reconfigure resource allocations, while data mining tools can either transform dynamic events into parameters for improved decision making, or reduce the available solution space. There is

also a high probability that customer preferences are not met in case the incident causes delays (e.g., delivering in the desired time windows, or delivering the right quantity). Therefore, the incident management system keeps customers up-to-date of the network's conditions, and receives new customer input if preferences change over time.

5. **Offline learning toolbox:** the logistics agents, disruption handling system, and incident management system are developed to immediately anticipate on the disturbances observed. However, an additional toolbox evaluates all online responses and performances afterwards. The risk management system can better recognize severe incidents by extracting features from historical events with a variety of data mining techniques, while offline simulations enable the system to prescribe a suitable recovery strategy in advance already.

4.4   Demonstration

We will demonstrate the need for our target EA (Fig. 3) and the corresponding disruption handling systems (Fig. 4) using the Dynamic Vehicle Routing Problem (DVRP). In the VRP, vehicles are assigned to a sequence of geographically scattered customer locations with the aim to minimize overall routing costs, subject to a set of constraints [4]. In the DVRP, not all information is known in advance, but will be revealed during logistics execution [5]. This implies that all stochastic elements gradually change into static parameters due to the vehicles' remote monitoring capabilities (see technology layer in Fig. 3).We would expect that logistics operators incorporate the fleet's tracking data into their route planning, since there is plenty of evidence supporting the need to reschedule the DVRP when the uncertainty in the network's conditions increases (e.g., [29,33]). However, data-driven re-optimization is often not the case [26–28]. Consequently, the question is not how to detect disturbances, nor to find a suitable recovery strategy, but how to automate rescheduling of the DVRP by assessing the fleet's real-time data. For example, attended home delivery services, such as online grocers and parcel deliveries, can become more flexible if a vehicle autonomously monitors its surroundings, and alters its route to avoid problems beforehand. The deliveries' reliability is likely to be enhanced as well when centralized algorithms search for disruptions that negatively influence customer SLAs, and immediately reallocate the fleet without human delays (e.g., vehicles may interchange orders, dispatch additional vehicles, complete overhaul, etc.).

5   Discussion

The reference architecture in Fig. 3 is designed to obtain more reliable and flexible logistics operations by anticipating on the dynamic events observed in the IoT's perception layer. The hierarchical disruption handling architecture in Fig. 4 autonomously initiates the dynamic planning activities once a severe disturbance emerges, while our edge-, fog- and cloud-based architecture design compromises the trade-off in between response time and decision quality [5]. Therefore, the central role of fleet management systems and human decision making, as depicted in Fig. 2, is replaced by a fully automated collaboration of decentralized logistics agents, "quick-and-dirty" solution heuristics, and data-intensive re-optimization algorithms. However, our initial design is still open for discussion, since other technical approaches may fulfill the stakeholder requirements even better. For example, microprocessors are becoming more powerful, which makes it possible to empower edge devices with deep neural networks [34]. We can also modify the BDI architecture proposed by [32] to alter how logistics agent interact with each other, maybe process mining could be helpful to implement a more context-aware set of agent decision rules [35]. Our claim to speed up dynamic planning with fog computing resources, as inspired by [24], becomes doubtful if we take into account that most logistics operations require minutes, hours, or even days, but not seconds. The decisions when to reschedule, how to classify dynamic events, and how much time to reserve for computations are also far from trivial and require further investigation [1]. The wide variety of design alternatives indicates that validation of our reference architecture should be prioritized before proceeding further. We especially pursue the implementation of real-life demonstrations to evaluate if our reference architecture enhances the reliability and flexibility of logistics networks. Real-life demonstrations also provide the opportunity to reflect on non-technical implementation issues as well (e.g., city regulations, customer habits, and sustainability).

6   Conclusion and Further Research

In this paper, we proposed an IoT-based reference architecture to face the increasing variability of today's digitized logistics networks. Our design improves the system's responsiveness towards dynamic events by replacing the fleet operator's manual rescheduling tasks with a fully automated disruption handling system. The Industry 4.0 design principles inspired us to develop a hierarchical disruption handling architecture that compromises the trade-off among decision quality and response time. Minor events are resolved by logistics agents, while more severe disruptions are processed in higher-level processing nodes (e.g., fog and/or cloud computing). Future research is required to investigate when to initiate the risk assessment module, how to classify dynamic events, and how much time to reserve for dynamic planning. Real-life demonstrations are required to validate the system's benefits as well.

References

1. Speranza, M.G.: Trends in transportation and logistics. Eur. J. Oper. Res. **264**(3), 830–836 (2018)
2. Crainic, T.G., Gendreau, M., Potvin, J.-Y.: Intelligent freight-transportation systems: assessment and the contribution of operations research. Transp. Res. Part C: Emerg. Technol. **17**(6), 541–557 (2009)

3. Dallasega, P., Woschank, M., Zsifkovits, H., Tippayawong, K., Brown, C.A.: Requirement analysis for the design of smart logistics in SMEs, Industry 4.0 for SMEs, p. 147 (2020)
4. Pillac, V., Gendreau, M., Guéret, C., Medaglia, A.L.: A review of dynamic vehicle routing problems. Eur. J. Oper. Res. **225**(1), 1–11 (2013)
5. Ritzinger, U., Puchinger, J., Hartl, R.F.: A survey on dynamic and stochastic vehicle routing problems. Int. J. Prod. Res. **54**(1), 215–231 (2016)
6. Ponomarov, S.Y., Holcomb, M.C.: Understanding the concept of supply chain resilience. Int. J. Logistics Manage. **20**(1), 124–143 (2009)
7. Billhardt, H., et al.: Dynamic coordination in fleet management systems: toward smart cyber fleets. IEEE Intell. Syst. **29**(3), 70–76 (2014)
8. Atzori, L., Iera, A., Morabito, G.: The internet of things: a survey. Comput. Netw. **54**(15), 2787–2805 (2010)
9. Xu, L., He, W., Li, S.: Internet of things in industries: a survey. IEEE Trans. Industr. Inf. **10**(4), 2233–2243 (2014)
10. Li, S., Xu, L.D., Zhao, S.: The internet of things: a survey. Inf. Syst. Front. **17**(2), 243–259 (2014). https://doi.org/10.1007/s10796-014-9492-7
11. Issaoui, Y., Khiat, A., Bahnasse, A., Ouajji, H.: Toward smart logistics: engineering insights and emerging trends. Arch. Comput. Meth. Eng. **28**, 3183–3210 (2020). https://doi.org/10.1007/s11831-020-09494-2
12. Singh, P., van Sinderen, M., Wieringa, R.: Smart logistics: an enterprise architecture perspective. In: CEUR Workshop Proceedings, pp. 9–16 (2017)
13. Ding, Y., Jin, M., Li, S., Feng, D.: Smart logistics based on the internet of things technology: an overview. Int. J. Logistics Res. Appl. 1–23 (2020). https://doi.org/10.1080/13675567.2020.1757053
14. Winkelhaus, S., Grosse, E.H.: Logistics 4.0: a systematic review towards a new logistics system. Int. J. Prod. Res. **58**(1), 18–43 (2020)
15. Bijwaard, D.J., Van Kleunen, W.A., Havinga, P.J., Kleiboer, L., Bijl, M.J.: Industry: Using dynamic WSNs in smart logistics for fruits and pharmacy. In: Proceedings of the 9th ACM Conference on Embedded Networked Sensor Systems, pp. 218–231 (2011)
16. Iacob, M.-E., Charismadiptya, G., van Sinderen, M., Piest, J.P.S.: An architecture for situation-aware smart logistics. In: 2019 IEEE 23rd International Enterprise Distributed Object Computing Workshop (EDOCW). IEEE, pp. 108–117 (2019)
17. Peffers, K., Tuunanen, T., Rothenberger, M.A., Chatterjee, S.: A design science research methodology for information systems research. J. Manag. Inf. Syst. **24**(3), 45–77 (2007)
18. Tiwari, S., Wee, H.-M., Daryanto, Y.: Big data analytics in supply chain management between 2010 and 2016: insights to industries. Comput. Ind. Eng. **115**, 319–330 (2018)
19. Mittal, S., Khan, M.A., Romero, D., Wuest, T.: Smart manufacturing: characteristics, technologies and enabling factors. Proc. Inst. Mech. Eng. Part B: J. Eng. Manuf. **233**(5), 1342–1361 (2019)
20. Al-Fuqaha, A., Guizani, M., Mohammadi, M., Aledhari, M., Ayyash, M.: Internet of things: a survey on enabling technologies, protocols, and applications. IEEE Commun. Surv. Tutorials **17**(4), 2347–2376 (2015)
21. Lankhorst, M., et al.: Enterprise architecture at work, vol. 352. Springer (2009). https://doi.org/10.1007/978-3-662-53933-0.pdf
22. Hermann, M., Pentek, T., Otto, B.: Design principles for industrie 4.0 scenarios. In: 2016 49th Hawaii International Conference on System Sciences (HICSS). IEEE, pp. 3928–3937 (2016)

23. Ben-Daya, M., Hassini, E., Bahroun, Z.: Internet of things and supply chain management: a literature review. Int. J. Prod. Res. **57**(15–16), 4719–4742 (2019)

24. Lin, C.-C., Yang, J.-W.: Cost-efficient deployment of fog computing systems at logistics centers in industry 4.0. IEEE Trans. Industr. Inf. **14**(10), 4603–4611 (2018)

25. Dobrkovic, A., Liu, L., Iacob, M.-E., van Hillegersberg, J.: Intelligence amplification framework for enhancing scheduling processes. In: Ibero-American Conference on Artificial Intelligence, pp. 89–100. Springer (2016). https://doi.org/10.1007/978-3-319-47955-2_8

26. Koot, M., Mes, M., Iacob, M.-E.: A systematic literature review of supply chain decision making supported by the internet of things and big data analytics. Comput. Ind. Eng. **154**, 107076 (2020). https://doi.org/10.1016/j.cie.2020.107076

27. Vermeulen, P.: Internet of things survey: Nederland 2016. https://www.logistiekprofs.nl/uploads/content/logistiekprofs/file/Onderzoek-Hoe-ver-is-Nederland-met-IoT-2016.pdf, Pb7 Research, Technical report (2016)

28. TLN, evofenedex, and Beurtvaartadres: Nationaal onderzoek data en digitalisering in de logistiek. https://www.tln.nl/app/uploads/2019/11/Rapport-data-en-digitalisering.pdf, TLN, Technical report (2019)

29. Zeimpekis, V., Minis, I., Mamassis, K., Giaglis, G.: Dynamic management of a delayed delivery vehicle in a city logistics environment. In: Dynamic Fleet Management, pp. 197–217. Springer (2007). https://doi.org/10.1007/978-0-387-71722-7_9

30. Goel, A.: Fleet telematics: real-time management and planning of commercial vehicle operations, vol. 40. Springer Science and Business Media (2007). https://doi.org/10.1007/978-0-387-75105-4

31. Jede, A., Teuteberg, F.: Towards cloud-based supply chain processes. Int. J. Logistics Manage. **27**(2), 438–462 (2016)

32. Jabeur, N., Al-Belushi, T., Mbarki, M., Gharrad, H.: Toward leveraging smart logistics collaboration with a multi-agent system based solution. Procedia Comput. Sci. **109**, 672–679 (2017)

33. Haghani, A., Jung, S.: A dynamic vehicle routing problem with time-dependent travel times. Comput. Oper. Res. **32**(11), 2959–2986 (2005)

34. Li, H., Ota, K., Dong, M.: Learning IoT in edge: deep learning for the internet of things with edge computing. IEEE Netw. **32**(1), 96–101 (2018)

35. Bemthuis, R.H., Koot, M., Mes, M.R., Bukhsh, F.A., Iacob, M.-E., Meratnia, N.: An agent-based process mining architecture for emergent behavior analysis. In: 2019 IEEE 23rd International Enterprise Distributed Object Computing Workshop (EDOCW). IEEE, pp. 54–64 (2019)

Author Index

Printed in the United States
by Baker & Taylor Publisher Services